MRS. RESTINO'S COUNTRY KITCHEN

MRS. RESTINO'S COUNTRY KITCHEN

THE COMPLETE WOOD STOVE COOKBOOK

BY SUSAN RESTINO

quick fox

NEW YORK   LONDON

International Standard Book Number: 0-8256-3060-6
Library of Congress Catalog Card Number: 74-28704
Printed in the United States of America

In Great Britain: Book Sales Ltd., 78 Newman Street, London W1
In Canada: Gage Trade Publishing, P.O. Box 5000, 164 Commander Blvd.,
Agincourt, Ontario M1S3C7

Book and cover design by Jean Callan King/Visuality
with special thanks to Lily Hou
Cover photographs by Herbert Wise
Illustrations by Susan Restino

This book is dedicated to necessity:
the mother of all our best efforts.

PREFACE

My editors, in New York, have been after me for about a year to provide some sort of introduction to this book, to describe who I am and where I live.

You would think that this sort of thing would be relatively easy to write about. Surely, if I could explain how to curdle cheeses, or brew beer, or smoke a chicken, I ought to be able to explain the way I live, and why I do these things (instead of working at a nine to five job, in a reasonably civilized part of the world, and partaking of the benefits thereof). But here I sit, on a Thursday afternoon in February, facing my Underwood portable at the kitchen table once again, wondering what to say and how to say it, before (1) the baby wakes up from her nap, (2) my husband, who is out there busting his knuckles on the front end of the Volkswagen, comes in for a cup of coffee, or (3) the bread rises beyond redemption.

I could start with where: everybody lives somewhere. We are tucked back here in a steep little valley in the Cape Breton highlands, surrounded by trees and hills and streams. Once there were maybe a dozen little farms out here. Now and again you come across a pile of stones, an ancient, gnarled apple tree. Before we came here, we lived for some four years on a borrowed farm, fifty miles away. It was a nice place, but we were always hunting around for some land we could buy, to get going on our own place. Which is a hard thing to do when you don't have much money. At last we found it, and at the same time I was writing this book. In the

end, the two things came together, which was nice.

The first year, my husband built a little temporary 10- by 20-foot cabin to live in. We cleared a lot of spruce and had a small garden, but in the fall we went back to the farm. Last summer, though, we raised a barn here (with very little cash, and a lot of help from our good neighbors). Now there are goats and chickens and rabbits in the barn and sacks of grains packed in old 50-gallon oil drums. There are apples and cabbages and carrots and beets and potatoes tucked away in a hillside root cellar. There are jars of fruits and jelly packed under the bed. And the cabin has gotten a little bigger this winter, although it's still pretty small for life with two active, growing children (Samantha is 8 now and Carey is 2). Next summer we'll be setting stones for a house foundation and a chimney. In time, we hope, a house will rise around it, big enough for all of us to rattle around in. But, for the time being, we seem to be surviving.

So far, so good. Why? What are we getting out of it, besides a view of the mountains? I wish I could really answer that question; at times I wonder myself. Sometimes (particularly in the fall) it is very hard work. And sometimes there are some really hellish moments, like the time I went out to do the chores and found two baby goats dead, or the time Charley cut his leg with the chain saw. Or even just things like having to dig out the water line to try to find out where it froze up. You know, of course, when you decide to live like this, that things like that are going to happen. But then, it's also true that catastrophes happen to all people, even those who live in the most sheltered environments. Different ones, maybe. It seems like what you have to worry about most, in more densely populated areas, is other people. I guess I'd rather take my chances with the elements.

But it's also a matter of liking to do things for ourselves. Not everything; we're not trying to become hermits, or turn back the clock. There are a great many things about these times we live in for which I'm very grateful. To give you a motley assortment of examples: mail service, rubber boots, snow plows, chain saws, fencing, down parkas, hospitals, tar paper, and modern publishing companies. But that doesn't mean we have to buy the whole package, and pay the price thereof. We find it a lot easier to slow down our consumerism, if I can use that word, out here. We do it in a lot of ways. Our barn is almost completely built of lumber from two other structures which my husband tore down. I keep a complete ongoing set of clothes for kids aged zero through fifteen, in the barn, and the kids just grow up through them; nothing very exotic, but sturdy and warm things.

And we cook with foods which are very near their source. Some we grow and some we buy. But we try to get it down to where we know what we're eating, and know it's not all mishmashed up with insect sprays and defoliants and purifiers and dehydrators and preservatives and artificial God-knows-what-all. That seems important to us, enough so that we have gone to the effort to learn how to cook, all over again, with plain, whole food—mak-

ing use of storable vegetables, all winter, without getting bored and wishing we could afford asparagus (shipped from California, on an airplane); grinding up whole grains and making cookies and breads and cereals and dinner dishes out of them; providing protein without chopping up an endless succession of animals; dealing with two gallons of milk, which suddenly began to arrive in my kitchen every day last spring, when our goats kidded; using what the swamps and hills provide. And it's a good feeling to know, all the time, that we're doing something to slow down our personal consumption of the earth's limited resources.

It's not, however, just that I like the philosophy of our lifestyle; it's also fun. Country cooks do a lot more improvising, experimenting, and inventing in the kitchen than do folks who are handy to the stores. You have to. But after the initial shock wears off (a birthday cake? without eggs?) you really begin to enjoy getting into the essentials of cooking. It becomes less something out of a package or a book and more something you just felt like eating. I've tried to get some of these fundamentals into this book. Maybe when you get through reading it you won't need cookbooks anymore.

It is, by now, Monday afternoon. The VW, with its front end fixed, got spun into a snow bank, and Charley went off on skis to get some chains which our nearest neighbor, two miles down the road, said he had around his barn and would maybe fit our tires. I just cut into the last loaf of that bread I made last Thursday. It's got some very dense patches, here and there.

It did rise too long, after all.

Susan Restino

CONTENTS

INTRODUCTION
THE WOOD STOVE

A wood stove is a great thing. On a winter day, there is nothing like it. There is always a kettle boiling, bread rising, soup simmering, and boots drying around it. You can use the steady warmth to grow sprouts, make cheese and yogurt, dry herbs and fruits, or brew beer and wine. And when you come in from the chores, it's wonderful to stand by the stove and soak up the heat. We have other stoves in the house—principally, a large Ashley chunk stove, which runs twenty-four hours a day, September through May—but it's the kitchen stove that's the heart and soul of our existence, and we love it.

My first wood cook stove was a warped old Kitchen Queen, some seven years ago. When I think back on those days, and my ignorance, it's a wonder I didn't burn the house down. I did in fact burn several large batches of bread, cakes, sauces, stews, and several times, my hands. In time, though, I discovered the oven controls, the drafts, and the ashes in the interior; I learned which woods to burn, and when to cut them. The day came when we could bank the stove (which is very small, as stoves go, and not too tight on top) and find three inches of hot embers there in the morning.

These days, many people are moving out to old farmhouses and rural areas. Many call it a simpler way of living, and there's no question but that its joys are simpler. Long walks, and visits, now and then, replace movies and television. Music is mostly homemade; clothes are individual, so to speak, to the wearer. Seasons change, children grow, and the steady rhythm of chores fills days that were once tense and uncertain. We grow closer to the earth, and life seems good, most days.

However, though our lives are less complicated, our roles in this world are not, necessarily, easier. An outhouse, for example, is a very straightforward sort of thing. But it takes more than the turning of a handle to keep it clean and safe and useful. Kerosene lamps are cheap and lovely things, but they need to be cleaned and trimmed and filled. So with a wood stove; you need to know a little about it, to enjoy living with it. What little I have gleaned from trial and error, I gladly

pass on to you, in the hope that your rice never burn, your bread never fall, and your house be safe and warm.

WORKING PARTS OF THE WOOD STOVE

As far as I know, most wood stoves are constructed inside roughly like this:

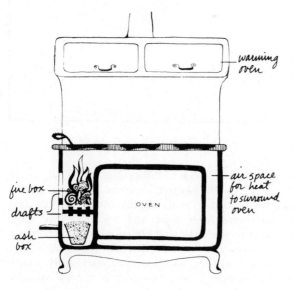

fire box
drafts
ash box
warming oven
air space for heat to surround oven
OVEN

THE FIRE BOX AND THE PLATES

The first consideration, naturally, is the fire box. This is the compartment in which the fire is built. The fire box should be lined with either cast iron or stove brick, cut in special shapes to fit the fire box, so the heat doesn't spread out in all directions.

Stove designs vary. Some load from the side, some from the front, and in some the top of the fire box lifts up in one unit on a hinge.

Under the fire box is a grate for ashes to sift down through. In many stoves this grate can be turned slightly by a removable handle. Turned one way, the grate is suitable for wood; the other, more open, way is for coal. When such a grate is set for coal, it has wider spaces between the cross pieces, because coal tends to build up a very solid bed of clinkers and ash; you always want there to be some draft. The wood grate is tighter, to prevent the embers (which are necessary for a good fire)

from continually falling through. It is impossible to really bank a wood fire over a coal grate. Coal grates and coal/wood grates are more common in coal country. If your stove is in a Vermont farmhouse, it is probably a wood grate. Sometimes grates are built so that they can be turned, slightly, in order to allow you to sift down ashes without getting your wrist black. If the handle is missing, or the grate doesn't turn, use a poker—or, if the stove is cold, a small stiff brush is handy.

The ashes underneath must be removed every few days, for which purpose it is handy to have a removable metal box under the fire box. Deposit these ashes outdoors, far from anything flammable. If your ashes are *all* from hard wood, you may use them to make soap. Ashes are also very useful in the garden mulch pile. If you have an outhouse, you can dump a scoop of ashes down the hole once a day to keep it from getting smelly, but set them aside first for twenty-four hours to make sure they contain no live embers.

On the side (and sometimes the front) of the stove, you will find various sliding or hinged doors, which are called drafts. When opened, they let in a draft of air, making the fire burn hotter. When closed, the fire will be "banked"—it will burn more slowly, and for a longer time.

The equipment for your stove should include a handle for lifting the top pieces out and moving them around. When you use it, hold the circle of cast iron at an angle, so it won't slip off and go clattering on the floor, your foot, or small creatures below.

THE OVEN

So much for the more obvious features. The next thing to consider is the oven. In order to look at the oven closely, change into your least perishable clothes, and arm yourself with a flashlight, a dust pan, brush, and wads of newspaper. Dismantle the top of the stove and take a look inside.

At the center back, where the stove is hooked up to the stove pipe, you will find a small sliding door. This has a control that enables the door to be opened and closed without opening the top of the stove. When the door is open, the oven is OFF. The heat and smoke from the fire will simply go through the open door and up the chimney. Any attempt to bake with the oven off will result in food baked on the top and one side, if at all.

Slide the door shut. The heat and smoke should go across the top of the stove, down the side, along the bottom and up the back—and out the chimney, through a passage up the back. In some models it goes down a divided side, around the bottom in a U-shaped passage, back up the side and out through a passage in the top. The general idea is the same: heat will surround the oven and bake your goodies from all sides. It will, of course, be hottest on the top, since the top is nearest the source of heat. For this reason I like to leave a light layer of ashes on top of the oven when I clean it.

Periodically, the inner workings of the stove become clogged with ashes, and you should clean them out. There is a simple tool designed for this that makes the job very easy; it consists of a length of stiff wire about two feet long with a small square of iron attached to the end at a right angle, like a hoe.

front panel

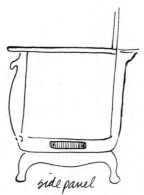

side panel

With it, or some such device, you first sweep the ashes off the top of the oven into the fire box and shake them down into the ash box. Then, under the oven (either on the front or side of the stove) you will find a small removable panel that enables you to get at the ashes under the oven.

Scrape the ashes out carefully onto a newspaper, inspecting from all angles with a flashlight to make sure all the passages are clear. Replace the panel tightly.

You should not have to clean ashes out of the oven liner very often. In the winter, when I run the stove every day, I do it about once a month. In the summer, I do it maybe once. A lot depends on what you burn; the great stove-clogger isn't wood ashes at all but paper ashes. If you dispose of your paper garbage elsewhere your stove will stay clean a lot longer.

While you're at it, you might as well invest in a bottle or can of stove polish and blacken the cast-iron parts of the stove. Stove polishes are mostly combinations of grease and charcoal. You rub them in, wait ten minutes, and polish off the residue. Most of them work a lot better if you let them sink into the cold stove for a few hours before running it again. What brand you use will probably depend on what's available. In a pinch, you can just rub in a little vegetable or mineral oil. The important thing is to keep the pores of the cast-iron oily so that it doesn't soak up moisture and become rusty. I usually polish the stove once a week in winter, and once a month in the summer. Remember to oil or polish the stove thoroughly if you are going off on a long trip, since more moisture will be in the air while you're gone.

STOVEPIPES

The next thing to consider is the stovepipe. Most stoves are hooked up to the chimney with lengths of stovepipe. If you are putting in the connections yourself, keep the system as simple as possible. The more elbows and/or horizontal footage you have, the harder it will be for the smoke to be drawn up the chimney. Also, if you have more than one stove using the same chimney, they shouldn't be connected to the chimney at the same level.

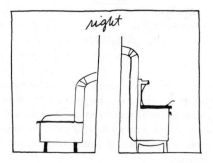

A stovepipe must be fastened together with sheet-metal screws, so it won't fall apart. The vibration of wood stoves is slow but sure, and sooner or later the pipes will fall down. Stovepipes should also be securely cemented into the chimney with stove cement (a special concoction that comes apart easily for stovepipe cleaning). The fine cracks around joints can also be sealed with this stuff, to insure a good tight connection. If you have local natural clay, this will work just as well (in fact, better) on the connection to the chimney, but it won't work between the pipes. Properly fitting pipes will not need cement, anyway.

Periodically (once or twice a year) you ought to pull down the stovepipe and clean it out with a wire brush. Creosote will not collect in it as much

as in stovepipes from heating stoves, but it has been known to accumulate and catch on fire in houses where much soft wood is used. More on creosote under "Chimneys," below.

Your stovepipe should have one or more handles on it. These are the "dampers" and they control the speed at which hot air is sucked up the chimney. Inside the pipe is a flat circle of light metal that can close off, open, or partly open the stovepipe.

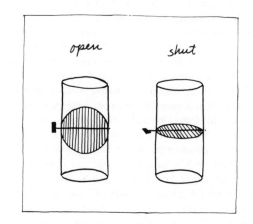

When the damper is all the way open, the fire may burn too fast for your purposes. You will have to experiment with the drafts and dampers to find the combinations that provide the right amounts of heat for your purposes.

If your stovepipe doesn't have any dampers, you certainly ought to get at least one, and install it high on the pipe. Better yet, get two, and set them about 18 inches apart. With one, you will be able to keep a fire going for hours, and since it keeps the heat from shooting up the chimney, the oven will stay hot for much longer. With two dampers, you will probably be able to bank a fire so tightly at night that there will be hot coals in the ashes in the morning to start a new fire with. In any case, the stove will still be warm. Dampers cost less than a dollar, and all you do to install them is drill or punch two small holes in the pipe.

CHIMNEYS

If you are moving into an old house with a wood-burning stove, one of the first things you should do is inspect the chimney. Check it for leaks and loose bricks; a surprising number of old chimneys are in various stages of deterioration. A leaky chimney will draw air through the cracks instead of through the stove, making the stove burn poorly.

Occasionally, after long disuse, chimneys become obstructed by bird or rodent nests. Ashes collect in the bends and in the bottom. The real problem to watch out for, though, is creosote. Creosote is a sticky, black, tarlike substance that collects in chimneys and stovepipes when smoke from creosote-laden wood comes into contact with a cold chimney. It is highly flammable.

The wood with the most creosote in it is pine, but hemlock and other soft woods have plenty of it too, especially if it is "wet" or freshly cut from a living tree. If the chimney is clean to begin with, and you do not burn soft or wet wood, you should not have much problem. In the far north, though, where hard wood is sometimes scarce, people do burn it. They have various ways of cutting down on the danger. One is to have a very thick central chimney, rather than a thin one on the side of the house. A central chimney will stay warmer and hence less creosote will collect. And, of course, if the chimney is thick less heat will be conducted to the wood of the house itself in case a fire occurs in the chimney.

When you first move into a house, and once a year thereafter, you should clean the chimney. One way to do this is to get hold of a nice big bunch of chains, tie them up in a burlap bag, and lower them down the chimney on a clear, still day when the stoves are out. Or you can trim all but the top branches off a soft wood sapling and use it like a giant bottle brush. To clean the ashes out of the bottom there is usually a loose stone or brick at the base of the chimney.

This will generally do the job, but if you really have a big creosote problem, and a nice heavy central chimney, there is another way to deal with it. You can shove a batch of lighted newspaper in the chimney and burn out the creosote yourself. You should, however, choose a very still day for this project, a day with snow on the roof, and collect some friends to help you keep an eye on the fire. This is a very radical measure but infinitely preferable to having an unexpected chimney fire at four a.m. on a windy night.

The sound of a chimney fire is a hollow roaring, but sometimes you can't hear it, especially if it's windy outside. If the creosote is burning near the top, you might see flames shooting out. The one time we had a chimney fire, the only sign was a pervasive stench that came drifting down the stairs

. . . which turned out to be from rodent nests (and worse) packed tightly against the cozy chimney, inside the walls. I shut all the dampers in all the stoves and it went out. There wasn't much creosote, I guess.

If you have a chimney fire, you should really call the fire department, but not everyone has a phone or a nearby fire department. Keep a very close eye on the house, especially the roof. Don't forget, it will take some hours for the heat to work its way through the brick or stone. Keep water handy at all levels until you're sure the fire's spent itself and the chimney has heated up and cooled down.

Another problem people sometimes have with chimneys is that they are not tall enough. They should be higher than the peak of the roof, but sometimes even this is not enough; tall trees (that weren't there when the house was built) or even a strong wind will cause a "down draft" and smoke from the stove will billow out into the room, especially when you first try to light the fire. I have known people to deal with this by shoving a twist of lighted newspaper through the stove into the stovepipe in order to get the draft moving upward. I think this is a dangerous practice, though. If you have to go to such extreme measures, there is something amiss with the system. It may be only a matter of rearranging the stovepipes so there are less bends; but it may also be that your chimney needs to be lengthened. Unless you know a fair amount about masonry, better get somebody who knows how to lay bricks or stones to lengthen it. Nobody wants a loose brick sliding off the roof unexpectedly one day. In any case, don't add stovepipe to make it higher, as creosote will collect in it very quickly. And don't put a stovepipe cap on top of it. Caps slow down the draft and the longer the smoke lingers in there, the more creosote sticks to the inside of the chimney.

STOVEPIPE CHIMNEYS

Stovepipe chimneys are very dangerous. Creosote collects in them very rapidly, especially if they have stovepipe caps on them. When the creosote catches on fire, they transmit a great deal of heat. They fall apart easily, especially when the creosote in them is on fire. I have never heard of anybody who lived with one successfully for any length of time. And I don't see too many hundred-year-old shacks with stovepipe chimneys standing around. I do know of an awful lot of them that did catch on fire, and a lot of hard work and good intentions went up in smoke. It's even traumatic knowing someone who's lost everything in a fire, so I'll say it again: don't mess with stovepipe chimneys.

There is, however, a type of stovepipe, called Selkirk, that is double-thick and lined with asbestos between the layers. If you are unable to build a chimney temporarily, Selkirk pipe might be safe if it's used for a cook stove only, and if you're careful to burn only seasoned hard wood.

In my efforts to cover all the possible difficulties one could have (and the remedies thereof) I have in a sense done the wood stove a grave injustice. For the most part, wood stoves were carefully designed and beautifully made, and they have lasted for hundreds of years. No one wood stove system will ever have all the problems I have described here. If you do have one or more difficulties, they're well worth ironing out, because the result will function so well.

WOOD SUPPLY

Anybody undertaking life with a wood stove should give some thought to the department of wood gathering and splitting. For a wood cooking stove, you will need a readily accessible supply of hard wood with a straight, dense grain. Ash is the very best I know of, a joy to split. Next come maples, yellow birch, poplar, and aspen. Oak makes a terrific fire, but it seems like a waste to use it for firewood. Elm and fruit woods are out of the question: their grain is too curly to split in any quantity. Beech, also, is curly, but it splits readily when frozen solid.

The principle governing firewood is that those trees that grow very slowly have a small cell structure and store the most fuel energy per log. Therefore they burn more slowly, with a hotter fire. Those woods that grow quickly (such as white birch, swamp maple, alder, and the softwoods) have a large cell structure and little stored energy; they burn up fast, giving little heat. And, what's more, large-celled trees absorb and store water; often they will rot before they dry out.

Wood from living trees is best cut in the winter months, November through February, or before the sap starts to flow in the spring. It will be much drier to begin with, and also lighter and easier to truck home. Needless to say, it is also less trouble to get wood out of the woods when the ground is frozen hard.

I've never used a chain saw, so I won't attempt to say much about them. They're noisy, cantankerous, expensive, dangerous, infuriating, and necessary tools. You can resort to hand saws, but it's a little like using a horse and wagon to get to town; it takes at least ten times the time and energy. The best chain saws are the lightest, newest ones. If you're buying one secondhand, make sure it starts easily. Try it out for a week before you make a final decision. Periodically, the bar and chain will need to be replaced, and, more often, the teeth will need to be sharpened. Two things I do know about them: one, never cut alone, and two, never cut when you're tired. If you're going to use one for the first time, get somebody trustworthy and verbose to show you all about working with it.

We usually saw our wood into 4- to 6-foot lengths in the woods, depending on the weight,

ash   yellow birch   red maple   poplar   aspen   beech

and bring it home like that. It's easier to stack that way. We drive some big stakes in the ground and pile the wood outside until we have time to junk it up.

Ideally, wood should dry for about a year before use. You should be cutting every winter for the following year. Sometimes you can find seasoned wood lying unused; look around for a place where roads or power lines have been cleared. The minimum for drying wood, I'd say, is three months if the wood is in a sheltered place. Of course it will dry more quickly if split—and birch wood won't dry at all unless it's split up.

Wood splitting is something of an art in itself. Look at each piece carefully before you hit it. Keep an eye out for knots; it's a waste of energy trying to cut through them.

Large logs are easier to get into if you cut pieces off the sides and gradually work toward the middle. Logs twenty to thirty inches wide often have to be split up first with wedges and a mallet. Make a cut in the wood first with the ax; then insert the wedge and tap it through. If you hit the back of your ax with a mallet, the head will eventually work its way off the handle.

When splitting with an ax, stand back until the head of the ax, at the end of your extended arms, is even with the top of the chunk. Keep your feet apart and even. (Don't get into the habit of working with one foot forward—axes sometimes fly down all the way to the ground when you miss a stroke.) Hold the ax over your head with your right hand low on the handle and your left about three quarters of the way up. As you swing down, slide the left hand down to meet the right.

Once you develop accuracy, work for speed of swing. How fast you can swing will govern your preference for axes. For example, I work comparatively slowly, and I like a heavy ax head. Most people I know use lighter axes and swing faster. As you swing, think of your ax as hitting the splitting block, not the wood. And if your strokes keep hitting the far side of your wood, step back a bit—be nice to your ax handle.

Wood splitting is a real joy when you get into it. It's a nice warm occupation in the dead of winter, especially since wood will split a lot more easily when frozen. And it keeps you from getting soft and prone to wintertime ailments.

Kindling is an important consideration. Unless you can get very dry hard-wood mill ends, cut into very slender pieces, stick with soft wood. Soft-wood mill slabs are usually available at low

cost—or free if you pick them up yourself, since the mills have to get rid of them. If they aren't dry (and they usually aren't) get in the habit of stockpiling them so they have a chance to dry out. Dry kindling isn't a luxury; it's a necessity. In a pinch you can dry it in the oven, every night, for the next day. Be sure that you prop the oven door open, though, or you'll find a very smoky fire in there when the wood dries out. Also, the moisture evaporating from the wood will "rot" the inside of the oven. Be very careful not to let the wood touch the sides of the oven (particularly on the left, where the firebox is).

You will not want to live for long without a woodshed. If you're planning one, it's nice to include enough head room to swing an ax. Nothing is quite as frustrating as trying to split wet wood on a rainy day—and then burn it. Generally we keep some old tarps around, too, for purposes such as covering piles of wood or kindling that haven't made it to the shed yet.

You'll probably need a good supply of newspaper. If you don't buy the things regularly, your neighbors may. Or you can look for them at a reduced price in the local newspaper offices—or free at the dump. Many people prefer to use combinations of dry bark, cones, or softwood twigs; they work just as well.

USING THE STOVE

HOW TO START A FIRE

So it's time to light the fire. Make sure that:
   —the drafts and dampers are open

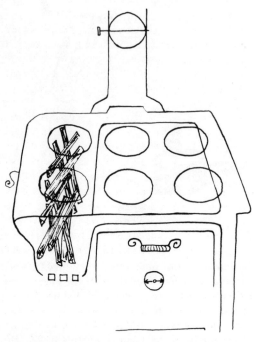

when stove is first lit

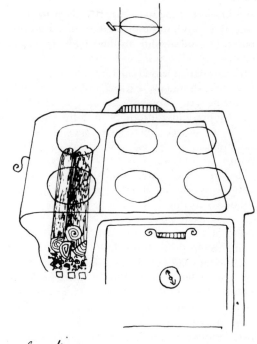

general cooking

—the oven is off (little sliding door open)
—the ash box isn't open
—the grate isn't clogged with ashes.

Crumple into the fire box:

3 or 4 pieces of newspaper

Or distribute loosely, so air can get through:

3 or 4 large handfuls of sticks, dry bark, dry moss, wood shavings, etc.

Add:

a crisscross stack of finger-thick, dry, soft-wood kindling.

Light this as near the bottom of the pile as you can and be sure that the *front* of it is on fire. Then close down the wood feeding door, and hover around collecting or splitting more finger-thick kindling. Don't get distracted. Within 3 minutes the kindling in the fire box should be on fire. Add more, in a crisscross pattern. Don't just throw in handfuls; they will block out the air circulation. When the whole fire box is full of flaming, crackling kindling, add:

2 or 3 2-inch-thick splits

In another 5 minutes add:

2 or 3 2-inch splits
2 4-inch splits

If the fire is going well now you should turn on the oven (close the sliding door) to make the fire burn more evenly, and half close the chimney damper, to keep the heat down.

For the first 8 to 10 minutes, the left rear plate will be the hottest, since the oven is off and thus the heat is going back, over, and up the chimney. By the end of 10 minutes, the hottest plate will be the back middle one. If you want a cup of tea or coffee, that's where to put the kettle.

After you turn on the oven, the emphasis will shift. The two left plates will become much hotter, since all their heat isn't roaring up the chimney; also, the larger pieces of wood will be burning at a higher temperature. By the end of 20 minutes, your kettle of water ought to be boiling, and you can sit down. If you haven't done so already, be sure to turn the damper and draft down, and the oven on. Fill up the fire box and relax. It won't go out.

STARTING A FIRE WITH HOT EMBERS

In the winter, if you also have a wood heating stove, you should certainly start your cooking stove fire with hot coals—it's much easier. When you first get up, *before* you throw a log into the heating stove, open the cooking stove and clear the ashes out of the grate. Open the drafts and dampers. Open the damper on the heating stove as well, so you don't get a face full of smoke, and take out:

2 or 3 shovelfuls of red-hot embers

Ashley stoves come with a shovel that you can easily bend so the scoop is at an angle to the handle—about 60 degrees. This is very useful because it is better not to open the front door of the Ashley too often, or the seal will fall apart. You can scoop coals into the shovel with the ash hoe. Put these coals in the cooking stove, carefully, and follow with a crisscross of:

2-inch splits

You can fill the fire box right up. Close down the wood loading door and go load the heating stove. Then go back and check the cooking stove fire briefly. In 5 minutes, refill the fire box with:

2 or 3 2-inch splits
2 4-inch splits

And turn on the oven. In about 10 minutes you can fill it again with chunks and set the stovepipe damper at half on.

This fire will get going much more quickly than a fire started without hot embers. It will burn much larger pieces of wood earlier, and won't go out if you get involved in something else for 10 minutes.

IF YOUR KINDLING DOESN'T WORK

If you are having a struggle every morning, it is most likely that your kindling is wet, or green, or both. The solution is to split it up very fine the night before and dry it out in the oven—with the door open, so the moisture can evaporate.

If you are sure the kindling is dry enough, but still can't seem to get the fire started quickly, the problem is probably the stovepipe or chimney; read about them on pages xiv-xv.

Whatever you do, don't mess with kerosene or gasoline. It takes eyebrows a long time to grow in again.

GENERAL COOKING

For most cooking, I want part of the stove to be hot enough to sauté things on, and part of it to be slow enough to simmer things on. The combina-

tion that works best on my stove is to have the oven on, the bottom draft open, and the stovepipe damper set at a diagonal, or half on. I use 2-inch to 4-inch splits and check the fire every 15 or 20 minutes. I try to keep the fire box full and a light bed of embers on the bottom—with enough air space for circulation.

If the stove is going well, the most convenient hot plate is the left front one. That's where I sauté and do most of my hot cooking either with the plates on or off. The next best is the one just behind it, the left rear. I usually keep a kettle boiling on it, for two reasons. One, I always have hot water for boiling, steaming, or steeping things in a hurry. Two, I can tell from that steady racket it makes how the fire is doing below. The back middle plate is very hot and good for boiling, but I usually keep it clear—but that's a personal preference, since my stove loads from the top, and I need someplace to put the kettle when I lift the top off the left rear plate.

For simmering, the front middle plate and the right back plate are about the same temperature. The front right gets the lowest heat on the stove—a good place to keep a sauce or a pot of tea warm, or the only place cool enough to simmer something when the stove is running full blast.

Of course, as the wood and weather vary, all of this may change. The only really sure way to find out what temperature a plate is is to toast a piece of bread on it. If it burns before toasting, it's hot enough to sauté, fry, make pancakes, or boil a big pot of water fast. If it toasts nicely, it's about right for cooking eggs, simmering, stewing, and steaming. If it takes forever and dries out, it's right for keeping warm a pot of tea—or time to dry out some wood.

TO RAISE THE TEMPERATURE
OF THE OVEN

Supposing you have had a good fire going all day, and you decide to bake some cornbread. You want to raise the temperature of the oven from its chronic 200° to 450°. Open the draft under the fire box, and poke down any dead ashes. Stir the coals if they have built up in the fire box. Fill the fire box with very dry wood 2 to 4 inches thick. Leave the oven on but adjust the chimney damper to half on. Pay attention to the fire; since it is running hot, you will have to put in a couple of sticks every 15 minutes. When the oven is up to the desired temperature *close the chimney damper and the draft under the fire.* The oven should hold, if you keep the fire box full—though you won't have to fill it often. If the temperature starts to go down quickly, open the chimney draft, the draft under the fire box, and fill up the fire box with 2-inch splits.

A word about birch and rainy days. Birch absorbs moisture like magic. On wet days it won't dry out no matter what. It is a fine wood for slow fires, but if you try to run a fast fire with it on a wet day it will drive you crazy. You may have trouble getting the oven very hot on damp or rainy days anyway; the chimney has a hard time drawing fast. You can usually get it up to 350° without much trouble, but I wouldn't plan anything that requires a really hot oven.

If the stove top is cracked or warped, you may get smoke seeping out through the top as soon as you turn on the oven. In that event, close the draft under the fire and keep the chimney damper open. Some stoves have a draft about the middle of the fire box on the left-hand side; this is handy if the top leaks. You can bake with a leaky stove, and bake successfully, but you really have to watch the fire. Use the smallest and driest pieces of wood you can find, supplement them with soft wood, and experiment with the drafts from time to time. And by all means see if you can find a supplier who can provide you with replacement parts for the faulty pieces. There really is no need to put up with such an inconvenience.

TO LOWER THE TEMPERATURE
OF THE OVEN

First of all, turn off the oven and open the chimney draft all the way, to let your heat go up the chimney. Leave the lower drafts closed around the fire box, though, and throw in a big old piece of damp hard wood, if there's room.

If what's in the oven doesn't mind (like meat) you can always open the oven door. It might take as long as 15 minutes to bring the temperature really down, though; cast iron-lined ovens really hold their heat.

TO BANK THE FIRE

A good deal of the time, you will simply want to keep the wood stove running banked—in other words, as slowly as possible. You will need, first of all, a good bed of embers in there. So run the fire hot, with the draft open, the oven on, and the damper half on, and check it every fifteen minutes. In an hour or less there will be a 2- to 4-inch layer of embers. Don't stir them down. Simply fill the fire box with large pieces—4- to 6-inch splits and limbwood. It needn't be dry. Shut down everything as much as you can: close the chimney damper, close the drafts, and leave the oven on. With luck and a tight stove the fire won't go out for 3 hours. It will burn down considerably, though, so if you're going to be around, refuel it every hour or so. If your fire box is really tight and you're burning wood with a dense grain (like beech), there will be a good bed of hot embers left from a banked fire 7 or 8 hours later.

IF YOUR FIRES KEEP GOING OUT

If you have a terrible time keeping a fire going, there are two possible causes of this. One is that your wood is too heavy and wet. The big chunks will just sit there, steaming and smoking. If you have a wood heating stove running, you can keep them going with shovelfuls of hot embers from the other stove. If not—well, maybe some kindling can be stuffed under the wet wood, although that's a pretty smoky situation, and one to be avoided. If it happens more than once you had better get into splitting the wood finer and drying it out in the oven.

More commonly, fires go out because they are burning too fast. Typically, it happens when company arrives. Suddenly you remember the stove, and too late—there's a handful of tiny embers winking at you. If the stove is running hot, you *have* to refuel it every 15 minutes. So if you want to do anything that is going to take longer than that, you had better bank the fire. If you haven't got a stovepipe damper, install one, and use it. Check the fire box for leaks and patch them with stovepipe cement. And remember to close the drafts and dampers when you aren't going to be near the stove.

COAL

Coal has its good points and its bad points. It burns much hotter and more slowly than wood. A fire banked with coal is much more efficient. There are different kinds of coal; the cheapest, and softest, leaves great big clinkers that won't sift down through the grates and have to be picked out by hand when the stove is cold. The intense heat of coal warps the tops of many wood cooking stoves. I don't like to use coal because it also costs money, smells dreary, and makes the snow around the house sort of gray.

TOOLS AND ACCESSORIES

WARMING OVENS: Personally, I happen to be very fond of those old cast-iron stoves with nothing but a curlicued shelf above the cooking surface. But I have to admit that the warming oven is an incredibly useful invention. Not only can it be used to keep food warm (without cooking it further) but it is also invaluable as a place to make yogurt, raise bread dough, grow sprouts, warm plates, and dry socks. It maintains a constant, draft-free temperature of 90° to 120° F.

A note of warning: whether your stove has a warming oven or a shelf, the bottom surface of it probably gets much too hot for living organisms (such as yeasts and bacteria). Unless the container you're using is very thick ceramic or wood, it's best to slip a heavy tile or a bit of board end under the container to insure the safety of the contents.

(particularly when hot air is circulating around the oven) makes the water heat up. It holds around 5 gallons. You fill it with cold water and in a few hours it is too hot to stick your hand in. It's good for washing dishes, etc. It has no drain, so it is difficult to clean out; most people don't use the water in it for cooking.

In addition to this attachment providing hot water, its top surface is an excellent place to put hot pans, casseroles, pots of tea, or a bowl of something you want near the stove but not cooking (such as pancake batter).

The second type of hot water heater that runs off a wood stove is considerably more efficient, and the hot water comes out of a tap at the sink. It's a tall tank, and it sits close to the stove, just behind the fire box. Cold water runs into the bottom, and is circulated through a pipe on the side of the fire box. The line to the tap comes out of the top. The fire in your stove will both heat the water and cause it to circulate, since the water in the pipe will continue to rise as long as it is being heated.

To install this type of hot water heater you must have room in the stove for the heating pipe. This pipe runs behind the cast-iron liner on the left side of the fire box. You must have two holes in the

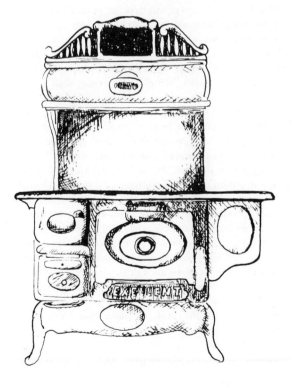

HOT WATER HEATERS: There are actually two types of hot water heaters that run off a wood stove. The first of these, the older design, is a large metal box that hangs off the right-hand side of the stove. The top, made of cast iron, has a hinged lid, and lifts up so you can get at the water. The lower part of the box is made of sheet metal and lined, usually with copper. There are no fancy parts to it. It just hangs there, and the heat of the stove

back of the stove for the pipe to pass through. Many of the newer models of stoves (the kinds with enameled doors and backs) are set up for this. The pipe is set into a piece of cast iron called a hot water "front." The front may crack if the stove is run with no water in the pipe. Some fronts are lined with copper, which, of course, will melt if the stove is run with no water in the pipe. The fronts are fortunately replaceable, but expensive.

The best of these heaters have glass liners. They also come in cast iron, but cast iron corrodes when old, turns your water reddish, and doesn't heat up as much or as fast. Periodic draining will relieve this problem somewhat, although it may not totally eliminate the pinkish cast. You should drain a hot water heater twice a year anyway, just to keep it clean; nobody's water is perfectly pure.

A good glass tank will heat about 20 gallons to almost boiling in 2 hours. They don't usually come equipped with pressure-release valves, but it's a good idea to put one in. They show the temperature and, when the water boils, let off steam rather than allowing the tank to blow up. They cost a few dollars and are easy to install.

OVEN THERMOMETERS: Most wood stoves were built with an oven thermometer on the door, and a good many of these thermometers are broken. If yours isn't working, it's worth every penny to go downtown and buy one to set inside. It's very difficult to bake without one. Bread, for example, comes out dense and soggy at 200°; and at 450° it burns on the top long before it cooks on the bottom.

You might be able to fix the old thermometer, although I can't tell you how. I do know that they operate on a bimetallic strip.

POTS AND PANS AND SUCH ITEMS: If you expose pans to direct heat (with the plates off) the fire will blacken the bottoms. For this reason, many people never do that. Some do it only occasionally, and so that the soot will be easier to wash off, they keep the bottoms of the pans coated with soap. I belong to the lowest order of pan keepers. I don't bother with any of this, but simply keep the pans out of the dishwater altogether, washing only the insides. I have a nice collection of blackened board ends that I use when I want to put a pan on the table or counter.

Cast-iron pans are the thing for a wood stove, of course. Often the old black kind can be picked up cheap (or free) from a secondhand store or from people who don't want them because they're so heavy. Rusty iron can be rescued with a wire brushing, steel wool scouring, and "seasoning." To season a piece of cast iron you brush on cooking oil (thinly) and leave it in a slow oven for about a week (off and on). Don't cook water base foods in it for a few months, but use it for sautéing with oil or for baking as often as you can. To clean seasoned cast iron, you may wash it as you would any other pan (except not with steel wool); but don't leave it soaking too long; usually I just wipe them with a soapy rag and rinse briefly. Always dry cast-iron pans quickly by setting them on the stove for 5 minutes.

It's not a good idea to expose light metal or enamel cookware to direct fire. Eventually they will scorch through. Plastic handled pans and utensils won't last long; trade them with somebody or give them away.

MISCELLANEOUS: Keep a good supply of pot holders. They will get unspeakably filthy in about six months. When they do, you can cover them with a nice dark wool material.

If you don't have a side shelf or hot water heater on the side, it's handy to invert a seldom used baking or frying pan on the right front plate. This is a useful place to put pots full of cooked grain, a sauce, or a bowl of pancake batter that you need close at hand but don't want to cook.

If you spill something like milk or oil on the stove while it's going, sprinkle the surface thoroughly with salt or baking soda. This will eliminate the smell and the fire hazard. I always keep a big box of baking soda on top of the stove anyway, just in case of grease fire. But I've never had to use it.

1

GROWING YOUR OWN VEGETABLES

Gardening is one of the great joys of living in the country. No matter how much, or how little you have done it, it is always something of a success, and there is always more to learn. Through the garden, you become much more aware of the soil beneath your feet, the climate you live in, and the weather. The seasons pass; you turn the earth, plant seeds, mulch, weed, prune, and harvest. I always kind of like the finality of winter snow—covering it all for a few months; it's like wiping clean the slate. Next spring you can start another, new, and different garden.

If you haven't gardened before, you ought to go at it gradually. Seeds are so inexpensive, and the catalogs have such marvelous promises of what will come of them—but they aren't you. They don't have your soil, your weather, your schedule, and your back. A few reliable vegetables will do to start: lettuce, chard or spinach, radishes, peas, beans, and summer squash. Talk to your neighbors about what they grow; gardeners are always happy to give advice.

For several years now, in Cape Breton, we've been trying to grow all the vegetables that our family (of four) will need for the year. This means that we not only think about what can be grown, but what will keep best over the winter. Our gardens, therefore, tend heavily toward root crops, carrots and potatoes and beets and such. But we've also been fortunate in having the use of a freezer, which we keep on a neighbor's porch; so we also grow a lot of things like peas and beans.

Even if you don't have a garden at all, though, it makes sense to eat vegetables in season. Eggplant in April means that somebody had to drive a truck or fly a plane, consuming gasoline and spewing fumes all the way. The seasons of this chapter are New England and Maritime seasons. Vegetables that grow in this climate will be found under the following categories:

SPRING

Asparagus
Cattail Hearts
Greens
Japanese Knotweed
Jerusalem Artichokes
Parsnips
Peas
Snow Peas
Salsify

SUMMER

Beans
Cattail Cobs
Corn
Cucumbers
Day Lilies
Wild Mushrooms
Purslane
Summer Squash and Zucchini
Green Tomatoes

FALL

Broccoli
Brussels Sprouts
Summer and Savoy Cabbages
Cauliflower
Celery
Kohlrabi
Green Peppers
Tomatoes

WINTER

Beets
Cabbage
Carrots
Onions
Potatoes
Sprouted Seeds
Turnips
Winter Squash

SPRING VEGETABLES

Although a tremendous amount of work goes into a garden in the spring, most of the vegetables planted from seed don't ripen until summer. There are a few early ones, though, and the earliest are greens: lettuce and spinach, soon followed by chard, mustard greens, and beet greens. Radishes, too, grow very quickly. Early peas may come by late spring if you put them in soon enough.

PERENNIALS: These are vegetables you plant once (in a warm spot) and then harvest every spring. The earliest is the Jerusalem artichoke, soon followed by asparagus. These come along very early in the spring, as soon as the snow melts, and well before the peas and greens.

FORAGEABLES: Forageable foods grow much faster in the spring than garden foods; they're in their natural habitat, with the right soil conditions, and thus have a head start. Some of the best foraged foods will grow right in the garden. I'm always out there one day before the plow, cutting all the tender young dandelions that have migrated from the pasture. Pigweed shoots up faster than any spinach, especially if you use pig manure; and it tastes just as good when young. Cattail hearts are easy to find in the swamps. Mustard greens and chicory add to salads and other greens a flavor you seem to crave in the spring.

WINTERING-OVER VEGETABLES: Some vegetables can be wintered over, or held in the ground until spring. The commonest and most successful are roots, such as carrots, parsnips, and salsify (oyster plant). Parsnips and salsify actually taste better in the spring than in the fall, and the carrots left in the ground certainly have more crisp tenderness than those tough old remains in the root cellar. Sometimes a row of spinach or chard will make it through, if planted in September. Heap dirt over the rows of roots, leaves and hay over the greens.

ASPARAGUS

An asparagus bed is a worthwhile investment of energy and initial cost; the first year you dig in the roots, and thereafter all you do is mulch it every year and reap the benefits. Besides tasting great, asparagus has the advantage of being a very early crop.

Generally, I cut up asparagus stalks before cooking and divide them up into two or three categories, since the tougher white bottoms require more cooking time than the tender green tips. The really woody bits I set aside for soup. The rest I cook as follows:

STEAMED ASPARAGUS

In a deep saucepan with a tight lid, bring to a boil:

1 cup water

Place in the pan a vegetable steamer or rack, and put in:

the bottom halves of asparagus stalks

Steam these 7 to 10 minutes, then add:

asparagus tips

Steam 5 to 7 minutes longer. Test them with a fork from time to time to get an idea of what's happening; within minutes of being done, the tips will turn to mush, so watch it. If you have to hold them, let them cool. Cold asparagus is no failure. Serve with:

Hollandaise Alvino (page 177)

Or you can use melted butter with a squeeze of lemon.

CATTAIL HEARTS

Cattails (their hearts) are the most widespread, easily identified and gathered, substantial, and universally well liked wild vegetable I know of. They taste a little like cucumbers, raw, and like a cross between grass stems and asparagus, cooked. The only tricky thing is that you should try and get the hearts when they are young. This time varies—from May in Connecticut to July in Newfoundland; wherever you live, try to gather them before the grasslike blades separate and spread out, or you will find them a little tough.

To gather cattails, wear boots and carry a knife along. Grasp the stalk inside the outer leaves—just like pulling out a stalk of grass to chew. The tender bottom 6 inches is what you eat, so you can whack off the top if you have a knife. Gather around 7 cattails per serving. When you get home, go through them. The white ones are tenderest; if any are green at the base, peel off layers until you get to the white. Check for tenderness with your fingernail. Chop off tough tops.

Cattail hearts may be eaten raw, chopped into salad, or cooked, simply, as follows:
Steam, over hot water:

5 to 10 cattail hearts per serving

for about 10 minutes. Serve with:

lemon and butter or Hollandaise Alvino (page 177).

It's better not to mix them with other vegetables, or sauces, since you may find it better to eat them with your hands, perhaps peeling back a few tough layers you missed here and there.

GREENS

The young and tender leaves of greens are the very first of the vegetables to appear in the spring. Greens are easy to grow and will continue to produce new leaves all summer.

One pound of uncooked greens equals one cup of cooked greens. You should allow ½ cup of cooked greens per serving. Greens should never be cooked in aluminum pans; they pick up a metallic taste, not to mention some questionable qualities. Among the many greens are:

DANDELION: Some do and some don't mind the slightly bitter flavor of wild dandelion greens. The younger you pick them, the milder they are. You can greatly reduce the edge by cooking them

together with a complete protein, such as milk, or salt pork. There is a cultivated, broad-leafed variety that produces a larger plant and is less bitter.

LETTUCE: There are many different kinds of lettuce and they all come up fast in the early spring. Lettuce can be cooked as well as used in salad; because of its delicacy, it is ready to eat in minutes.

MUSTARD GREENS: As you might expect, mustard greens are a little peppery; they are best cooked with milk or salt pork, or mixed in with other cooked greens. Wild mustard is a little stronger than the cultivated variety.

RADISH AND TURNIP GREENS: These are strong, as greens go, and should be picked when very young. They're a little tough for salad but very tasty when cooked with complete protein, such as milk, or with salt pork. They may be used in dishes calling for curds and greens as well.

BEET TOPS: If planted from seed, it will be a month or more before you can find enough greens in the beet patch to make a meal. One spring, however, I noticed a whole crop of them growing out of the compost heap where we had thrown a mess of half-rotten beets over the winter. Since beets are biennials, they had promptly taken root and sent up a leafy flower stalk. This year we simply left some beets, well mulched, in the garden. Beet tops are cooked like spinach or chard if young, a little longer when full grown.

chard

SPINACH, NEW ZEALAND SPINACH, AND CHARD: As a gardener, I prefer chard; it's hardier and doesn't go to seed. As a cook, spinach has the advantage of keeping longer in the fridge; it's also a little more tender and doesn't have the heavy central stalk when full grown. All three are fine salad material as well as good to cook and easy to freeze.

YOUNG BROCCOLI, CAULIFLOWER, BRUS-SELS SPROUTS, AND CABBAGE LEAVES: As these grow, they produce many extra lower leaves, which will eventually wilt and fall off; might as well pick them and make some early slaw or add them to sautéed vegetables. Or use them as creamed greens.

PIGWEED, LAMB'S QUARTERS: These are real spring crops. Use just as you would spinach; they are very mild and tender.

Washing and Preparing Greens: It's very important to wash greens enough. If they're not very sandy, put them in a wire basket and submerge in cold water. Then whirl the basket (outdoors) to remove the moisture. If they're definitely gritty, wash each leaf separately—then whirl in the basket. In either case, the only way to be sure they're clean is to taste a few. No amount of fancy cooking later will make anybody want to eat sand.

After you wash them, consider the stems. If you can nip them off with your fingernail, they're tender; if not, they will take much longer than the greens to cook. Fold the leaf lengthwise, underside out, and tear out the stems and any tendrils that come with it. If the leaves are very large, you may want to tear them into smaller pieces.

Steaming Greens: Once upon a time, the universal Western method of cooking greens was to sub-merge them in a huge pot of boiling water. This effectively cooks out all the vitamin C in them, so it makes more sense to steam them.

There are two ways to steam greens. One, put the wet greens in a lidded pan, either with or without oil, and cook until the greens are wilted and tender. Two, use a vegetable steamer. This device has adjustable leaved sides to allow it to fit into almost any size pan and it can be lifted out easily, enabling one to remove all the contents at once as soon as they are done.

GREENS WITH ONIONS

Use a mild-flavored green, such as spinach, chard, lettuce, or pigweed. Wash carefully:

1 lb. greens

Heat in a heavy frying pan:

2 Tb. light oil or butter or drippings

Slice or chop and add:

1 or 2 onions
1 or 2 cloves crushed garlic (optional)

Sauté the onions and garlic until transparent. Add the greens and cover the pan closely; simmer about 5 minutes, until wilted and tender.

Variations
Cook as above, but add one cup milk when you put in the greens. This is especially good for pep-pery greens such as mustard, dandelion, turnip tops, and radish greens. Cover and simmer over low heat so that the milk does not boil.

AEMONO

This is an authentic Japanese dish, except that they serve it cold, and I like it better hot. Use a tender green, such as spinach, young chard, lamb's quarters, or lettuce. Wash carefully:

1 lb. greens

In a heavy frying pan, heat:

2 Tb. dark sesame oil

Add the greens, cover, and simmer over low heat until the leaves wilt—about 5 minutes. Meanwhile, in another pan, roast until brown:

¼ cup sesame seeds

When the greens are cooked, add the seeds and:

¼ cup Tamari soy sauce

CREAMED GREENS

As far as I'm concerned, greens are fine without sauce. But suppose you are serving a dry meal: say, fish, rice, and greens. It might be nice to serve the greens creamed. There are two ways, the first for tender greens, the second for the toughies.

For Tender Greens
Wash carefully:

1 lb. greens: spinach, chard, pigweed, or beet greens

Melt in a heavy frying pan:

4 Tb. butter or oil

Add the greens, toss lightly, cover closely, and steam over low heat until thoroughly wilted. Sift over them:

2 Tb. hard-wheat flour or white flour

Stir and cook a couple of minutes. Add:

1 cup cream, milk, canned milk, or stock
a pinch nutmeg or coriander

Cook very slowly, on the right front plate, for about 15 minutes.

For Tougher Greens
Wash carefully:

1 lb. greens: turnip, mustard, kale, dandelion

Put them in a heavy frying pan, along with:

1 cup milk

Simmer over low heat (don't let the milk boil) until the greens are tender—about 15 minutes. About 5 minutes before done, in a separate pan, melt:

3 Tb. oil or butter

Stir in:

2 Tb. flour

Cook over gentle heat for about 3 minutes, butter foaming; then, off the heat, beat in all at once:

¼ cup hot milk or stock

Add this to the milk and cooked greens. Stir and cook for 5 minutes, as the milk thickens. If the stems look tough, chop them up a bit with a paring knife. Creamed greens may be garnished with:

1 chopped hard-boiled egg

JAPANESE KNOTWEED

Once you learn to identify Japanese knotweed, you see it everywhere—by roadsides, barns, houses, in back of supermarkets, by railways, schools, etc. I don't know if our forefathers thought of it as food or decoration, but they certainly must have liked it.

Knotweed usually grows in patches, and once you've identified a bushy spot, you can return in the early spring and harvest what a friend of mine calls "wild bamboo." The shoots are very tender when up to a foot high, and may be used as a vegetable. Longer shoots tend to be tougher, but you may still use them, like rhubarb. To transplant, dig whole small plants and set them someplace where you won't mind if they spread into a 10-foot thicket, which they probably will in a few years.

WILD BAMBOO

Select:

Japanese knotweed shoots under 1 foot long

Steam over, not in, boiling water, 3 to 5 minutes or until tender. Serve with:

butter
Plain Sweet-Sour Sauce (page 178)

Or serve cold, with yogurt or mayonnaise dressing.

SWEET KNOTWEED

If using knotweed shoots over 1 foot long, judge their tenderness by first peeling off the thin outer layer of purplish skin; taste. Chop into 2-inch pieces:

2 cups knotweed

Mix in:

½ cup sugar

Let the sugar draw out juice for 5 minutes, then cook, covered, until soft. You may or may not want to flavor this with:

3 Tb. lemon juice

JERUSALEM ARTICHOKES

Many an old house has by it a big patch of stalky-looking plants. They bloom yellow in June-July, nothing special, but they look as if somebody planted them once long ago. Unless they are Golden Glow (a much prettier, chrysanthemum-like yellow flower that blooms in August) they are probably Jerusalem artichokes. At their base they have a tangle of tiny tubers, thin and wasted in the

Jerusalem artichoke

summer, but fat in the winter and delicious in the early spring, before they start to grow again. Go after them at midday, when the ground has thawed, and you will find them 2 to 4 inches below ground, scattered within a foot of each stalk. Eat them soon after you dig them, since they won't keep but a week or two. Old, withered roots may be planted someplace new, such as your own backyard, where you will soon have a crop of your own.

Jerusalem artichokes taste a little like parsnips, only they're more delicate and tender, and less sweet. They shouldn't be cooked very long.

SAUTÉED JERUSALEM ARTICHOKES

Scrub well:

a handful of Jerusalem artichokes

Heat in a heavy skillet:

3 Tb. clarified butter or ghee (page 120)

Add:

1 chopped onion
Jerusalem artichokes, sliced

When they have browned a bit, add:

½ cup water

Cover tightly and steam 5 to 10 minutes (check with a fork after 5).

RAW JERUSALEM ARTICHOKES

Scrub well:

a handful of Jerusalem artichokes

Trim off tops and rootlets. Slice and serve as hors d'oeuvres or in a salad.

PARSNIPS

Parsnips are technically a fall or winter vegetable, since they take a whole summer to mature—at least 4 months. However, since they're so soft, they don't really keep very well in a root cellar. You will find after a month or so that the flesh begins to shrink and get tough. Parsnips are better kept in the garden until spring, well mulched with wood chips, sawdust, or lots of hay. As soon as the ground thaws enough to get at them, start digging them up. Use them within a week of harvest for maximum freshness. If you have more than you can use before they send up seed stalks (or before spring plowing) make a batch of parsnip wine.

BAKED PARSNIPS

Wash and quarter or slice about ½ inch thick:

about ¾ cup parsnips per serving or
about ⅓ cup parsnips and ⅓ cup carrots, turnips, or winter squash per serving

Arrange them in an oiled casserole or frying pan. You may also put in with them, for every serving:

2 Tb. chopped walnuts or Brazil nuts
2 Tb. breadcrumbs
1 Tb. brown sugar

2 Tb. thinly sliced or chopped sautéed onion

Add:

½ cup water or stock

Cover the pan and bake at around 350° for 45 minutes. You may add or serve them with:

Plain Sweet-Sour Sauce (page 178)

SAUTÉED PARSNIPS

Wash and slice ¼ inch thick on a diagonal:

5 or 6 parsnips

Heat in a heavy frying pan over the left side of the stove:

2 Tb. oil

Sauté the parsnips, stirring every few minutes to brown as many surfaces as you can—about 10 minutes. Then add:

½ cup water or stock

You may add at this point:

½ to 1 cup frozen or raw peas

Steam for about 5 minutes (or until the peas are done). You may add at the end:

a sprinkling of brown sugar
2 Tb. chopped parsley
2 Tb. butter

PEAS

You can never plant enough peas—they're too good. Like sweet corn, they should be picked just before cooking. If this isn't possible, at least keep them cool; their sweetness will quickly turn to starch at room temperature. You can add ½ tsp. sugar to old peas to improve them, but nothing will recapture the indescribable flavor of the fresh young ones.

STEAMED PEAS

Peas take about 5 minutes to steam in a tightly lidded pot. You may also try simmering them in ¼ to ½ cup milk or cream sauce from 10 to 15 minutes. I wouldn't use any seasoning at all on fresh peas, but old or frozen ones are nice with a little fresh basil, mint, or parsley chopped into the pot.

If you never have enough for a serving all round, combine them with other vegetables, such as:
parsnips, carrots, celery, leeks, summer squash.

Cook the vegetables separately and mix before serving. Or serve the peas raw in salad. Or just put a bowl of peas (pods and all) on the kitchen table and watch them disappear.

Pea pods contain too much cellulose to be completely edible, unless you grow snow peas, but their sweetness can be used in stocks.

SNOW PEAS

Snow peas are a special variety of peas that, very early, develop tender, flat, edible pods. Later they will fill up with peas, like an ordinary pod; they'll still be edible, pod and all, but you'll have to peel off two tough strings from the sides. The trick is to keep stripping the vines of pods before they fill out. If you can't eat them all, freeze them (see page 248).

SWEET GLOSSY SNOW PEAS

Bring to a boil: ½ cup water

Add: 2 or 3 cups fresh or frozen snow peas

Steam until tender: fresh ones take 5 minutes, frozen ones maybe 15 (taste them to see how they're coming along). Mix in a small cup:

¼ cup water
2 Tb. wine vinegar or 1 Tb. white vinegar
3 Tb. brown sugar
1 Tb. cornstarch

Stir into the cooked snow peas. Simmer for a few minutes.

SALSIFY

Often called oyster plant, salsify does in fact resemble oysters in both texture and flavor. Salsify is greatly improved by freezing, and though you may harvest them, if you wish, in the fall, they will be much better if mulched over and dug in the first spring thaw. Roots come black or white; black has more flavor.

SAUTÉED SALSIFY (MOCK OYSTERS)

Scrub well and slice or leave whole:
salsify roots
Dip quickly in:
milk

Then roll in:
flour seasoned with a pinch of salt and pepper
Sauté slowly 5 to 10 minutes in:
butter or light vegetable oil

SALSIFY STEW

Tomatoes change the flavor completely. In 2 Tb. olive oil, sauté:

1 chopped onion
2 stalks chopped celery

Add and simmer 20 minutes:

1 cup canned or stewed tomatoes
a pinch pepper
1 tsp. dried basil
1 cup water

Bring heat up to boiling and mix in:

6 to 8 chilled coarsely grated salsify roots

Cover, move to a middle plate, and steam 20 minutes, until the roots are tender.

SUMMER VEGETABLES

Summer is outdoors. Everything is so different, in smells, in looks, in sounds, and in the way you think, and eat, and work, that it might as well be a different place, altogether, than it was in the winter. The green, everywhere, splashed with color; the slamming of the screen doors, the pounding of bare feet through the house, the flapping of sheets on the line. And, most of all, the garden, the endless overlapping flow of vegetables and fruits—so many, so wonderful, so delicious.

It isn't all free, of course, and much of the quality of summer living has to do with the long hours spent over the rows, amid the black flies and mosquitoes, weeding and pruning and gathering. Even when people visit, they tend to gather in the garden, talking of success and failure, of mulches and insect problems and the effect of the weather this year. It is always the rainiest, or the driest, or the least or most buggy summer. (Bugs, as you might gather, are a considerable factor in Nova Scotia; we have them from June through September.)

Meals are in large part shaped by vegetables in season. And, too, by the fact that nobody wants to stand around the stove, cooking, for any longer than absolutely necessary. It's too hot inside, and too glorious outside. Fortunately, vegetables cook quickly, and you don't have to run the oven if you don't want to. Kindle a quick fire, simmer a pot of grain while you chop and stir-fry some vegetables. Add eggs, or fresh-caught fish, or a mound of cottage cheese curds. Once a week, or so, when it rains, bake bread, cook beans, simmer a soup. Otherwise, let the garden cook for you.

BEANS

Snap beans, string beans, pole beans, bush beans, green beans, yellow beans: dozens of names, endless varieties. They vary in texture, but mostly taste about the same. The real division is between slender, young fresh beans and large, old, or wilted beans. The only way to get them young and tender is fresh from the garden, and, fortunately, they grow very easily in almost any soil or climate. Young beans are so delicate and delicious that I can never bring myself to do anything fancy to them. Sometimes we even eat them raw. But there are lots of things that can be done with older, larger, tougher, or frozen beans.

YOUNG FRESH BEANS

Nip off the ends; rinse quickly under cold water if dirty. A handful will do for a serving; you may chop them or not, as you please. Steam over:

boiling water

for about 10 minutes, or until tender. If you must hold them before serving, remove the water and keep them barely warm in the warming oven.

LARGE BEANS

Chop or nip off the ends; if necessary, string them. Slice them into 2-inch pieces, straight or diagonally; or, if you have time, they may be "Frenched" into long thin strips. Do your cutting just before cooking to preserve the vitamins. Steam over:

boiling water

tightly lidded, for 10 to 15 minutes, or until tender. Before serving, you may season them with:

1 chopped leek or a few chopped chives
and/or 2 Tb. chopped parsley
and/or freshly grated pepper
and/or a pinch of celery seeds or thyme

FANCY BEANS

1. Sauté in a heavy skillet till browned:

   2 strips bacon

   Then remove bacon and sauté about 5 minutes in the rendered fat:

   1 chopped onion

   Return crumbled bacon to the pan along with a pot of cooked beans, toss lightly, and serve hot or cold.

2. Heat in a heavy skillet:

   2 Tb. butter or corn oil

   Add and sauté until golden:

   ½ cup sliced mushrooms
   and/or ½ cup sliced almonds or shelled sunflower seeds

   Add a pot of cooked beans, toss lightly, and serve hot.

3. Add to a pot of steamed beans any of the following:

   2 Tb olive oil and 1 Tb. vinegar; serve hot or cold
   ½ cup mayonnaise; serve hot or cold
   ½ to 1 cup sour cream (page 122); serve hot or cold
   ½ cup Hollandaise Alvino (page 177); serve hot
   ½ to 1 cup white sauce (page 174); serve hot
   ½ cup breadcrumbs that have been fried in bacon fat or ham fat
   ½ cup grated Cheddar or Parmesan or Romano cheese; serve hot

BEANS AND TOMATOES

A light and easy dish.
In a heavy skillet, heat:
2 Tb. light oil (olive oil, if you have it)
Add:
1 chopped onion
1 chopped green pepper (optional)
When the onions are limp, add:
1 clove crushed garlic
Sauté a minute; then add:
2 cups fresh or canned chopped tomatoes, drained
1 tsp. oregano
½ tsp. salt
½ tsp. freshly ground pepper
Simmer gently for 10 minutes, then add:
1 or 2 qts. fresh or frozen beans

Cover tightly and cook gently for around 10 minutes, or until beans are tender.

CATTAIL ON THE COB

Cattails on the cob are so good that they just about take the edge off one's desire—and endless wait—for fresh ears of corn. Soon after the hearts

cattail
on the cob

become too tough to deal with, the slender heads appear, encased in pale green wrapping, not unlike the inner husks of corn. Just break off as many as you need—5 per serving is about right—and as soon as possible, boil or steam them, 7 to 10 minutes. Remove wrappers, dip in melted butter, and eat as you would corn on the cob.

CORN

CORN ON THE COB

In my father's house, one first brought to a boil:

a large pot of water

When the water was boiling, the table set, the meal cooked, we then (and only then) went down to pick the corn. For corn on the cob we only picked the most perfect ears, pale yellow, the tops not yet ripened. Within minutes (in the corn patch) they were stripped and cleaned of silk. Then we sprinted back and plunged them in the boiling water. They were cooked about 5 minutes, then lifted out and served forth, with plenty of butter and salt.

After that we had dinner.

The reason for all this bother is that as soon as corn is picked, the sugar in it begins to convert to starch. The process is gradual; it doesn't happen all at once. Corn picked a few hours before cooking will still be sweet, although not quite as sweet as by the above method. In a day or two, however, it is pretty boring; and after a week it will be as tough as old leather.

Corn is one of the very few vegetables I ever cook in large amounts of water; that is because there are very few vitamins to be lost. However, if you prefer, there is another way to cook corn, though I recommend you only do a few ears at a time this way.

Heat in a cast-iron kettle or large pot:

½ cup water
½ cup milk

Steam fresh ears of corn 5 to 10 minutes, until tender. Serve at once.

CHOCLOS

In Peru, where corn on the cob is plentiful, it is cooked in the husk over charcoal braziers (a familiar street sight) and they spread it with things like:

garlic butter
butter mixed with a bit of tomato sauce
butter with lemon rind grated into it

And I haven't tried it yet, but I bet it would be good with a mild **Pesto (pages 181-182)** or a good hot **Barbecue Sauce (page 181)**.

CORN CUT FROM THE COB

There are two ways to cut corn from the cob. In the first, one cuts off the whole kernels; corn cut this way is good by itself but also very good mixed in with other vegetables, whether raw, steamed, or sautéed.

With a sharp knife, cut whole kernels from fresh ears of corn. Simmer 3 to 5 minutes in:

½ cup milk

If the corn is old you may cook it longer and also add:

1 tsp. sugar

Corn cut from the cob is excellent in combination with green peppers, steamed with the corn or sautéed separately. Or you may add to 2 or 3 cups of cut corn:

1 chopped sautéed onion
1 minced sautéed garlic
½ cup sausage or other ground, cooked meat
1 or 2 cups canned tomatoes, with liquid

CREAMED CORN

There isn't any cream in this; it's just a different way of cutting it off the cob. There are actually two ways. One is to grate it coarsely, raw. In the other, you first cook it on the cob and then cut corn from the cobs about halfway through their kernels. Then, using the back of the knife, scrape the cobs over a bowl and out comes the "cream."

CORN PUDD'N

Grate into a bowl:

2 cups fresh corn

Add:

½ to 1 cup cream (until the corn mixture is as thick as half-melted ice cream)

Bake in a slow oven, about 300°, for an hour, in a greased shallow baking dish. Serve hot.

CORN FRITTERS

These definitely fall into the category of treats—something to be made for three disappointed children (who were going on a picnic) on a rainy afternoon. Serve hot from the pan with molasses. The children, of course, do most of it!

Grate:

a dozen ears of corn

Separate:

3 eggs

Beat the egg whites until you can turn the bowl upside down. Mix the egg yolks into the corn, along with:

1 Tb. flour
1 tsp. salt

Gently, with your hands, mix together the egg whites and corn. Heat up a knob of butter as big as your thumb (or some corn oil) in the frying pan and fry the batter in pancakes, until light brown. Serve hot and eat them right away!

CUCUMBERS

There are three kinds of cucumbers. One is very small and has a tough, knobby skin. This is for making pickles; its dense flesh will not fall apart as it soaks in brine. It is a little tough in a salad, however; you might want to peel it (alas for vitamins).

The second is fat and very watery, with a thinner skin. It is terrible for pickles (falls apart) but great in salad, the smaller the better.

The third is a hybrid called (by most seed catalogues) "Burpless." It is longer than the others and, in fact, doesn't look at all like a cucumber; nonetheless it's very good and sweet and keeps very well.

Cucumbers are what I crave in the summer—delicious raw crunch. They are good with other things (lettuce, tomatoes, onions) or by themselves. Sometimes I marinate them in olive oil and vinegar for a couple of days, along with tarragon or dill. Sometimes we have them with dill and sour cream. Sometimes people just eat them plain.

DAY LILIES

If you are lucky enough to have day lilies around, you probably know that they can be eaten; and if you have tried them, you know that they are exquisitely tender and sweet. So tender, in fact, that they need no cooking; we used to chop the buds and flowers, alike, into salads (see Endless Summer Salad, page 13). However, they may also be cooked, in a variety of ways:

STEAMED DAY LILY BUDS

Steam over ½ cup water:

2 cups unopened day lily buds

Serve with butter, or butter and grated lemon rind.

DAY LILY SOUP

Heat:

3 cups water
2 Tb. Tamari soy sauce
4 Tb. miso, mashed together with ¼ cup cold water

When hot, add:

1 cup withered or dried day lily blooms
Simmer 3 minutes. Serve immediately.

Other Uses for Day Lilies (buds or blossoms)
Tempura (pages 14–15)
Mixed Vegetable Stew (page 14)
Stir-Fried Vegetables (page 15)

Day lily buds and blossoms are easily dried on racks over the wood stove, or on newspaper spread in a warm room. They should be dried separately and stored in screw top jars.

WILD MUSHROOMS

Some people are crazy about wild mushrooms. Some people just like them, now and again. I fall into the latter class, for which reason I haven't taken the time to really learn how to identify them. However, many of my friends have, very successfully; they all know at least a few reliable specimens that grow near where they live and that can't be confused with anything similar and disastrous.

If you are hungering for mushrooms and eying those succulent-looking fungi behind the barn, I suggest that you first buy or borrow a couple of good mushroom books and spend a summer gathering and identifying everything you can find. Mushrooms are not at all a cut-and-dried subject, as you will soon find out. They can cross-breed with one another, so any close relative of a baddy is a potential baddy. Sometimes they look very different in their early stages from what they will later. All of this is taken into consideration when you take the time to really learn about them.

Here are two good mushroom books to consult:
Alexander H. Smith: *The Mushroom Hunter's Field Guide* (Ann Arbor: Univ. of Michigan Press; 1958)
Orson K. Miller, Jr.: *Mushrooms of North America* (New York: E.P. Dutton; 1972)

PURSLANE

Purslane is a spreading, ground-cover plant with tiny, thick-fleshed, darkish-green leaves, which are very good to eat. In India they are domestically grown as a vegetable (the leaves being somewhat larger); here they are classed as a "weed." If you are so fortunate as to have your garden overrun

with them, leave them there; they don't choke anything out, they look rather nice, and they make good eating.

purslane

STEAMED PURSLANE

Pick off the small sprigs and wash very well:
about 1 lb. purslane
Steam over ½ cup boiling water for about 5 minutes. Serve with:
melted butter and lemon juice

SUMMER SQUASH AND ZUCCHINI

Ah, zucchini! most abundant and versatile of summer vegetables, filling the garden with broad leaves, the larder with heavy fruits. Zucchini plants always seem to provide twice as many squash as any other type of plant, but there are many other squashes to choose from: summer, yellow, crookneck, cocozelle, and vegetable marrow. All have about the same texture and flavor and may be cooked in the same ways.

Summer squash is a short-lived delight; we have tried various methods of canning and freezing them with little success. It is my belief that anything that is mostly composed of water, with very light and tender fibers holding it in place, is at best a tenuous affair and will not keep well, by any method. Even under refrigeration, the smallest and best will shrivel in a few weeks, although larger ones will keep a little longer—but they won't taste any better for it.

Generally, the best squash is about 12 inches long, although we pick them all sizes, for various purposes. Some people steam or boil them; I sauté them, see below, or serve in a casserole, or stir-fried. They are very absorbent and will pick up almost any flavor or spice you cook them with.

SAUTÉED SUMMER SQUASH

This is a very easy, simple dish. It may be made with any summer squash (such as crookneck, yellow, zucchini) so long as it is under a foot long.

First, chop the squash. You could slice it into ½-inch-thick rounds, or diagonals, or cut it lengthwise into finger-sized slivers, or just chop it into small bits.

Figure on:

1½ cups per person (it shrinks in the pan)

While you're at it, chop up:

1 onion

Heat in a large, heavy frying pan:

3 Tb. vegetable or olive oil

Arrange as many slices of squash as you can fit in the pan and sauté them until browned on one side, about 5 minutes. Turn and cook 1 minute or so on the other side; remove them to a warm dish and do more until they are all cooked. Finally, sauté the onions and scatter them over the squash.

TAMARI SQUASH

These taste amazingly like mushrooms, without the sort of musty flavor. Follow the recipe above, but return the squash and onions to the pan and toss with:

1 to 2 Tb. Tamari soy sauce per squash

Put a lid on and simmer 5 minutes.

ZUCCHINI À LA RESTINO

One of these halves of stuffed squash will suffice for two ordinary appetites, or one big eater . . .

Slice 12-inch **squash** in half and scoop out all but a ½ inch of shell of each. Oil the shells lightly and put them on an oiled baking sheet.

For every whole squash, sauté in 2 Tb. olive oil:

1 finely chopped onion
the well-chopped insides of the squash
½ cup sunflower seeds (shelled)

Cook gently about 5 minutes. Then add:

½ cup chicken broth or liquid from canned tomatoes
1½ cups breadcrumbs and cubes (stale or fresh)
a generous pinch of basil

Stew gently, with the lid on, for 5 to 10 minutes. Remove and stuff the squash, packing them lightly.

When you are ready to cook, have the oven very hot, about 400°. Cover the squash halves lightly with a piece of aluminum foil or a lid that doesn't quite fit the pan. Bake about 30 minutes until a fork will go into the flesh easily.

Very good with spaghetti, or a roast, or steaks.

zucchini à la restino

Another Way to Stuff Summer Squash

You may stuff very large squash; the flesh will not be as tender or fresh-tasting, but they will still be delicious. Several large stuffed squash halves make a festive, easy dish for feeding a lot of people. Since the servings will be in the form of slices through the boatlike shell, the stuffing should be firm, with a couple of eggs in it to hold it together. I use rice instead of breadcrumbs because I just never have that much bread to spare.

Slice 1 18-inch **squash** in half and scoop out all but 1 inch of the shell. Oil the shells lightly and put them in an oiled baking pan which has a lid.

Sauté in 3 Tb. vegetable oil:

1 large or 2 small well-chopped onions
1 clove crushed or minced garlic
1 cup shelled sunflower seeds
2 stalks chopped celery
the well-chopped insides of the squash

Cook gently 5 to 10 minutes. Then add:

1 cup drained canned tomatoes or 3 fresh chopped tomatoes (optional)
1½ to 2 cups cooked rice
1 tsp. basil or oregano (optional)

Simmer gently, lid on, for 15 minutes. Remove the lid and, watching closely, simmer until the liquid is almost dried away. Remove from heat and cool for about 10 minutes. Then beat and stir in:

2 eggs

Stuff the squash, packing them lightly.

When you are ready to cook, have the oven at 350° or so. Set a lid on the pan, or cover well with aluminum foil. Bake ½ to 1 hour, until a fork will go into the flesh easily.

For a mob, I would serve this with summer beans, cornbread, and fruit salad for dessert.

GREEN TOMATOES

GREEN TOMATOES FRIED

Choose, if you can, firm-fleshed light-green tomatoes. Slice them, not too thin—about 3/8 inch.
Mix, in a small, shallow bowl:

1 beaten egg
half an eggshell of water

In a cake pan, mix:

½ cup wheat germ
½ cup whole-wheat flour
1 tsp. salt

Dip tomato slices in the egg, then the flour; set on a rack to dry for 30 minutes.
Heat in a heavy skillet:

¼ cup olive oil
2 cloves crushed garlic

The garlic is very important—you must not omit it or substitute "garlic powder." Fry the sliced tomatoes until golden brown on each side. Remove, drain, and serve hot (they may be kept warm in a low oven for half an hour).

GREEN TOMATO CASSEROLE

Rather like Eggplant Parmesan, but with a bittersweet tang instead of the peppery solidarity of eggplant. Assemble:

24 dredged, fried green tomato slices (see preceding recipe)
1 cup grated Mozzarella or other soft cheese
2 cups spicy tomato sauce (page 180)
an oiled casserole or 8-inch frying pan

Arrange half the tomatoes in the dish or pan; follow with half the cheese and half the tomato sauce.

Arrange the rest of the tomatoes, following with the tomato sauce first this time, and then the cheese. Bake at 350° for 30 minutes.

VEGETABLE COMBINATIONS

ENDLESS SUMMER SALAD

Dog days, summer months: Who wants to run the stove in the heat of the day? Yet we all get hungry, so here's what you can make: an endlessly changing salad, full of everything fresh from the garden.

For something to sink your teeth into and to contrast with leaves and crunchies, keep a few stashes of cooked things in the fridge:

potatoes
green or yellow beans
cauliflower
grain, such as rice or bulgar
cooked dried beans

Better yet, you can keep these marinated in:

3 parts light oil
1 part vinegar or 2 parts lemon juice

Add to the marinade (but be careful to keep out of the salad):

1 clove raw garlic
1 sliced onion

When you're ready to eat, wander through the garden and woods for the rest of it. Depending on your plantings, findings, and the season, you may use:

Any Handy Greens: **lettuce, small leaves of cabbage, broccoli, or cauliflower; small greens from spinach, chard, beets, or pigweed;**

For Spice And Tang: **mustard greens, sorrel, nasturtium leaves, watercress, cowslips, chopped or sliced radishes, green onions, peppers, raw peeled broccoli stems and the flowerets;**

For Sweet, Tender Munching: **raw peas, snow pea pods, tiny green beans, sprouts, chopped cucumbers, raw summer squash, celery, corn sliced off the cob;**

For Color: **day lily blossoms, nasturtium blossoms, and the lovely blue flowers of borage;**

For Unexpected Flavors: **fennel, thyme, savory, basil, parsley;**

For Added Richness: **things fresh and marinated, such as tomatoes, cucumbers, mushrooms, and summer squash chunks.**

You May Also Add: **sunflower seeds, sesame seeds, and/or buckwheat groats that have been soaked in water for 24 hours.**

Toss all of this in just enough oil to lightly coat all the tender green leaves; then add vinegar to taste. The usual proportions given are:

3 parts oil

to:

1 part vinegar or 2 parts lemon juice

but I find it safer to add things like that in bits and then taste as you go. You may also add, by the same system:

salt, pepper, herbs
gomasio (roasted ground sesame seeds)
Tamari soy sauce
grated Cheddar or Parmesan cheese
yogurt
bits of chopped ham, hard-boiled eggs, cheeses

VEGETABLE STEW

There are as many versions of this as there are kitchens, gardens, seasons, and cooks. Some call for the vegetables to be sautéed first; some steam in water, broth, tomatoes; some add sour cream or yogurt at the last minute. Be free.
In a deep pot, sauté in 2 Tb. oil:

2 sliced or chopped onions
1 chopped green pepper
2 cloves chopped garlic
chopped celery, or celeriac, parsley root, parsnip
You may also sauté, as the spirit and larder move you:

chopped carrots
chopped summer squash
chopped eggplant
chopped potatoes
shredded cabbage
After 10 or 15 minutes, add some liquid, such as:

2 cups stewed tomatoes
1 cup broth or water
and any vegetables that you didn't sauté but that need 30 minutes of steaming/stewing, such as:
cauliflower
okra
lima beans
After 15 or 20 minutes, finish the stew with:

green beans
peas
parsley
bean sprouts
leeks
1 tsp. salt
herbs, such as rosemary, thyme, caraway, or fennel
Steam and stew all of this until everything is tender—about 10 minutes longer. If you are going to add yogurt or sour cream, do so just before serving and don't allow it to boil, as it will separate; it'll be just as tasty, but not as pretty.

TEMPURA

A summer favorite with gardeners, tempura is nevertheless something not to be tackled on a hot day, with a wood stove, and a lot of people to feed; you'll pass out from the heat.

Tempura, basically, is tiny tender vegetables dipped in egg-and-flour batter and deep-fried in vegetable oil. There are various recipes for the batter. Here are two:

1. Break an egg into a bowl, with one swift stroke, so the shell is neatly broken. Using half an egg-shell as a measuring cup, add to the beaten egg 2 half-shells of white flour and 3 half-shells of water.

2. Mix together: 1 egg, 1 cup water, ½ cup white flour, ½ cup whole wheat flour (very well ground and sifted) and ½ tsp. salt.

Of course, one expands the recipe as needed. Slice or trim your vegetables. Heat a heavy, deep pan half full of light vegetable oil (I don't recommend unrefined soy oil; it makes fine tempura but smells terrible in cooking). Heat the oil slowly to 375°; when it is ready you can drop into it a cube of bread and count slowly to 60; it should be brown. *Don't let the oil smoke!*

Have ready before you start: a slotted spoon, brown paper on a tray to drain the finished vegetables, plenty of potholders, and, just in case of fire, a lid for the pan and a big box of baking soda.

Vegetables will cook best if chilled. Some people like to dip them in batter, chill for 30 minutes, then fry; it makes a neater job.

Fry pieces a few at a time; how many depends on your pot, but too many will lower the temperature of the oil. From time to time skim the batter bits out of your pot.

Here is a list of some of the vegetables one may use:

Raw Unchopped
asparagus tips
green beans
mushrooms
watercress
small spinach leaves
day lily flowers and buds
bamboo shoots
Japanese knotweed shoots
tiny onions
Jerusalem artichokes

Raw, Cut in Small Pieces or Sliced 3/8 Inch Thick
broccoli flowerets
cauliflower flowerets
eggplant

summer squash
sweet potatoes
cucumbers
onions
green peppers
celery
winter squash

Half Cooked
winter squash, cut in chunks
sliced carrots

Shredded or Chopped Fine
To cook these, add more flour to the batter so they will hang together in small fritters, alone or in combination:

corn cut from the cob
onions
carrots
cabbages

STIR-FRIED VEGETABLES

This dish is really a method of cooking rather than a set "dish." It's the backbone of summer garden meals around our house, and many others. It involves, mostly, imagination, freshly gathered vegetables of any sort, a lot of chopping and slicing, and very brief cooking.

Basically, you divide your chopped and sliced goodies into categories, depending on how long they take to cook: carrots take longest, sprouts take the least time, and other things fall in between, depending on your idea of whether they should be crunchy or soft.

Heat **2 or 3 Tb. oil** in a wok or cast-iron skillet. Toss in carrots and other roots; stir to coat with oil, and cook rapidly 5 minutes. Add medium-cooking things, such as celery, onions, cabbage, and cook 5 minutes; then add sprouts and leafy things, **2 Tb. Tamari, ¼ cup water.** Clap a lid over all and steam 5 minutes. Serve with rice.

Almost any vegetables may be used. Here are some suggestions:

carrots	parsnips	Jerusalem artichokes	small
beets	turnips	winter squash	salsify celery
celeriac	onions	broccoli cauliflower	cabbage
kohlrabi	kale	sprouts chopped greens	day
lilies	loose corn	beans peas	green peppers
eggplant	buckwheat leaves	bamboo shoots	

The only vegetables I never add are potatoes and tomatoes, which are somehow a different thing, and cattail hearts, which might have tough outer sleeves and have to be peeled by hand.

If you wish this dish to be a meal in itself, complement the grain protein of the rice by adding a handful of cooked beans, cooked meat chopped in small pieces, or fish or poultry bits. Or you might use nuts. Add these just before steaming.

If you'd like a slightly sticky consistency, mix **1 to 2 Tb. cornstarch, arrowroot, or kuzu** in with the water and Tamari.

FALL VEGETABLES

Bonanza . . . the larders overflow. The kitchen is cluttered with box after box of harvest coming in—crates of tomatoes, piles of peppers, sacks of potatoes, every kind of apple, great bundles of herbs drying over the stove, and, surrounding everything, the steady rattle of the canning kettle. A yeasty scent of brewing wines hovers behind the stove; the windows cloud with steam as vegetables are blanched for freezing.

In the midst of all this, almost every kind of vegetable is available to cook with. The few I've listed are really only those you have in such profusion that you hardly know where to put them all—especially those that have to come in just before the frost.

And it's a kind of justice, and certainly helpful, that just when you have the least time for preparing meals, the most food is available. You certainly don't have to think too hard to figure out what to eat; it's all around you. In general, use up what you can't keep and save the rest for winter. But there's so much.

Gradually, though, you make some headway through it all, and eventually get it all packed away, in one form or another—just about Thanksgiving time. So we gather, with our neighbors, bringing pots of this and dishes of that, pies and stories to share. Push benches along the table until there's hardly room to walk in the kitchen, and all hold hands for a moment in greatful silence, in the din. Grateful to what? God, the earth, the summer sun? Or just glad to be alive, and done with harvest for another year?

POTLUCK SUPPER: 11/24/73, BOULARDARIE ISLAND

Dry Sherry	Marinated Sprouted Lentils
Celery Soup	Curried Butternut Squash

Curried Meat Pastries	Sautéed Cabbage, Sliced
Venison Stew	Carrot Pudding
Brown Rice	Home-brewed Blueberry Wine
Sesame Cookies	Squash Pie
Sweet Muffins	Blueberry Pie
Coffee	

BROCCOLI

Like all members of the cabbage family, broccoli is high in vitamin C. It's easy to grow, can be started either indoors or out, for early and late crops. The late crop will ripen to a fuller head; broccoli likes cool nights. You must be careful to harvest it as soon as it's ready—a few days later, and the tightly curled buds will flower. Cut heads with the stalks as short as possible, and the plant left behind will go on producing small flowerets until it snows.

STEAMED BROCCOLI HEADS

Wash, trim, and split vertically, if very large:

broccoli

Steam over, not in, boiling water, for about 10 minutes. Serve at once with:

Hollandaise Alvino (page 177)

Or: lemon and butter

BROCCOLI IN BROTH

After the heads have been cut, miniature heads keep appearing along the sides of the stalks. There never seem to be enough to make a complete vegetable serving, but you can serve them, or slices of peeled broccoli stalk, this way:

Cut into rough chunks:

1 cup broccoli stems
½ onion
½ tsp. salt

Simmer for 1 hour in:

2 cups water or chicken broth

Strain broth. Add to it:

1 cup broccoli flowerets

Or:

1 cup peeled sliced broccoli stems

Simmer 5 minutes. Just before serving, add:

½ cup Tamari soy sauce

Do not allow broth to boil. Serve hot, in soup bowls.

BRUSSELS SPROUTS

Brussels sprouts take a long time to mature but will grow well after the frost, so they make good late vegetables. In places where the frost doesn't strike hard, they will send out more new buds in the spring as well. The plants have a sort of Gargantuan beauty.

Brussels sprouts will keep for about 2 weeks, but after storage you may have to pull off the tough outer, yellowed leaves.

To make sure they cook in the middle at the same rate as the outside, cut a cross in the bottom of each sprout.

Brussels sprouts

STEAMED BRUSSELS SPROUTS

Cook over, not in, rapidly boiling water for 10 to 15 minutes:

¾ cup Brussels sprouts per person

Serve with:

butter
Parmesan cheese
lemon juice
Hollandaise Alvino (page 177)
Cream Sauce (page 174)
Sautéed mushrooms

SUMMER AND SAVOY CABBAGES

These cabbages ripen in the fall and don't have firm enough heads to be suitable for winter storage. They are very high in vitamin C and tenderer than winter cabbages. They do not need as much cooking, and, when made into coleslaw, they may be chopped rather than grated. They will keep for a month or two, becoming gradually less tender and nutritious.

For cabbage recipes, see pages 22-23 under "Winter Vegetables."

CAULIFLOWER

Cauliflower, a member of the cabbage family, grows well in cool climates, although, if you have a cabbage worm problem, they will make life in the cauliflower patch difficult, since the worms get into the heads and are impossible to pick out. The solution seems to be sometimes rich soil and sometimes luck; anyway, for better or worse, we usually grow quite a bit of it.

Cauliflower all by itself you may find a bit of a bore, as vegetables go. They have an elegant shape, but not much taste or color. They are good mixed with other vegetables, good raw, good stir-fried, and they hold their shape well in a casserole dish.

STIR-FRIED CAULIFLOWER

Cut cauliflower into very small flowerets. Cut stems left over into ½-inch slices. Fry in light oil for 5 minutes, turning once or twice to coat pieces evenly in oil. Add:

½ cup chicken broth or
½ cup water and 2 Tb. tamari soy sauce

Cover and steam 5 minutes. Serve immediately.

Needless to say this recipe lends itself to many other vegetables; you could cook along with it:

wedge-cut onions
shredded or wedge-cut cabbage, green or red
summer squash
mushrooms or puffballs
green tomatoes
carrots, cut ½ inch thick
parsnips, cut ½ inch thick
celery, cut in 1-inch chunks

Or you might add after cooking:

½ cup grated Cheddar
½ cup walnuts or roasted chopped peanuts

STEAMED CAULIFLOWER

Steamed cauliflower is rather tasteless, and lends itself to sauces or mixing with other vegetables. I include it because it is the first step in cooking cauliflower from the freezer. Be careful: like cabbage, it becomes mushy and smelly when overcooked.

cauliflower

Steam over ½ inch boiling water in a tightly lidded pot:

moderate-sized cauliflower pieces

Check stems with a fork after 8 minutes, and every 2 minutes until done. Serve with:

Tomato Sauce (pages 179–180)
White Sauce (page 174)
Hollandaise Alvino (page 177)

CAULIFLOWER WITH A LITTLE BUTTERY CRUNCH

Steam cauliflower as above. Meanwhile, melt in a small frying pan:

3 Tb. butter

Add and sauté 5 minutes:

½ cup very fine breadcrumbs

Toss with the hot cauliflower. You may also add:

2 Tb. chopped parsley
2 chopped hard-boiled eggs

CELERY

Mostly celery is used to cook with, rather than made as a main dish. A great many recipes start out with the sautéing of a chopped onion and two stalks of chopped celery; somehow the combination is greater than the sum of its parts. Celery is also very nice raw, plain, salted, or stuffed with anything from cheesy dips to peanut butter.

Celery can be grown in the north, but it keeps only a few months even in the best of root cellars. However you can, after your homegrown is exhausted, buy it by the crate, fresh from someplace sunny, and store it up to 2 months.

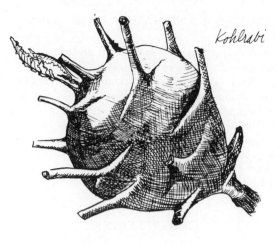

Kohlrabi

KOHLRABI

Nongardeners may not be familiar with kohlrabi, a member of the cabbage family; the part you eat is the stem, which swells out into a round, pale-green vegetable, about as big around as an apple. Kohlrabi must be picked and eaten before it reaches its maximum girth, or the center will become tough and woody with little white fibers that cannot be softened or removed by any process whatsoever. Tender kohlrabi has a texture rather like the inner flesh of a broccoli stem, but it is somehow crisper, sweeter, and finer.

KOHLRABI RAW

I first had kohlrabi as a raw vegetable, sliced into pieces about the size of a 3-inch-long pencil, along with other cut vegetables—carrots, beets, squash, cucumbers, tomatoes, and a big dish of Liptauer cheese (page 129). It was a very elegant and delicious dish of hors d'oeuvres.

KOHLRABI COOKED

Peel and slice ½ inch thick:

1 to 2 small kohlrabis per serving

Simmer them gently in a pan with:

½ to 1 cup milk

They should be tender in about 15 minutes; pierce with a fork to be sure. You may, if you wish, make a roux (in a separate pan) of:

3 Tb. melted butter
3 Tb. flour

Let the roux foam for about 2 minutes on low heat. Add the milk from the kohlrabis, and beat rapidly until the sauce thickens. Season with salt, maybe a little parsley, add the cooked kohlrabi and serve as Creamed Kohlrabi.

KOHLRABI IN STIR-FRIED VEGETABLES

Simmer the kohlrabis as above and drain before adding them to the cooked vegetables. You may add to the milk:

a bit of ginger root

GREEN PEPPERS

Peppers have a very long growing season, but since they spend the first three months growing the first 6 or 8 inches, you can start them inside and harvest a bonanza just before frost—even in Nova Scotia. Raw, peppers have an almost legendary quantity of vitamin C, and they also have some cooked.

Uses for Raw Pepper
Raw pepper may be sliced or chopped into almost any type of salad, being tender and sweet.

You may serve raw slices, plain or with creamy mayonnaise or yogurt dips, as a dish in itself.

Slices of raw pepper are almost never refused by children in lunches.

Uses for Cooked Peppers
Peppers are often cleaned and stuffed, with mixtures ranging from rice-and-onion to breadcrumb-and-hamburger, then covered with a variety of sauces, usually of the tomato family.

I can hardly bear to cook a pepper, but when I do, it is usually in a grain dish. One very small chopped pepper has the ability to transform a whole pot of wheat or rice into something very special and exotic; see page 44, under Steamed Cracked Wheat.

TOMATOES

Tomatoes, the pride and delight of any gourmet gardener, are also among the most nutritious vegetables around, being so high in vitamin C. They are also a very useful staple to have on hand, since they make so many bland, dry, or boring foods taste delicious and interesting. You can combine tomatoes, cooked or raw, with potatoes, legumes, all grains, all meats, and most vegetables, and these instantly take on a new flavor, texture, and look.

Most recipes having to do with tomatoes you will find under recipes for other foods, such as Beans and Tomatoes (page 8), or Moussaka (page 170). There are also recipes for various sauces, pages 179–181, that are tomato based.

TO RIPEN GREEN TOMATOES

At the first warning of a frost (whether by radio or sixth sense) you should instantly bring in every last tomato. Green tomatoes that have been "burned" by frost (have brownish spots) will rot instead of ripen.

Sort your tomatoes. Those that are almost ripe may be set on a windowsill. Those that are dark green and hard will probably not ripen, so use them in a relish or a mixed vegetable dish. Those that are pale green and unblemished should be set in a cool dark place to ripen, perhaps two layers deep—but not more—if you have a lot of tomatoes. There are various methods.

1. Pull the tomato plants, roots and all. Inspect fruit carefully and remove those that are discolored or almost ripe or too small and green to ripen. Hang the plant upside down in the cellar and check it every few days for ripe fruit. The advantage of this method is that it is easy to do. The disadvantage is that ripe fruit may fall off onto the cellar floor.

2. Wrap the "ripeners" separately in newspaper; set them in the pantry in shallow boxes, one or two layers deep. Try to put tomatoes of approximating size and color in each box so they will all ripen at the same time. This method requires no special equipment, but wrapping and unwrapping so many tomatoes can be tedious, and some may go ripe and rot before you find them.

3. See if you can get a fruit-and-vegetable man at a nearby store to save you some fruit dividers, shaped to hold each fruit separately, to hold

your tomatoes. Lay slabs of cardboard between layers to support them. This method is best, no sorting or wrapping is necessary.

4. Set tomatoes on the windowsill to ripen, unwrapped. They will ripen more quickly but will taste a little more acid in the middle than cellar-ripened fruit.

TOMATO SALAD

Chop, slice, or cut in wedges:

3 ripe tomatoes

Cut in similar style:

1 ripe cucumber

Soak them overnight in a mixture of:

3 Tb. olive oil

1 Tb. wine vinegar

1 tsp. tarragon or chervil (fresh or dried)

1 Tb. chopped fresh chives

1 tsp. salt

½ tsp. pepper

Just before serving, add:

2 Tb. chopped parsley

TOMATOES IN SOUR CREAM

Follow the above recipe, but instead of oil and vinegar, use:

1 cup thick plain yogurt; or 1 cup buttermilk and ½ cup dried milk; or 1 cup sour cream and ¼ cup fresh milk or yogurt.

COLD STUFFED TOMATOES

To stuff tomatoes, cut the caps off large, regularly shaped tomatoes, and scoop out their innards with a small sharp spoon.

Chop the tomato pulp and add to it:

1. an equal amount of cottage cheese, chives, parsley, Tamari soy sauce to taste.

2. fish salad made with mayonnaise or yogurt and almost any cooked fish; flavor with lemon and tarragon.

3. chopped cucumbers or parboiled summer squash and yogurt or sour cream.

BAKED STUFFED TOMATOES

You can also bake a stuffed tomato, for about 15 minutes at 350°. Fillings for baked tomatoes should be precooked. You could stuff four medium-sized tomatoes with a mixture of:

½ cup dry breadcrumbs

1 cup grated cheese (a mixture of hard and melty is best)

3 Tb. chopped green onions

3 Tb. melted butter

chopped tomato innards

Mix all the ingredients and stuff the tomatoes.

STEWED TOMATOES

Sauté together in 3 Tb. vegetable oil for 5 minutes:

1 chopped onion

3 stalks chopped celery

Add and simmer 20 minutes:

8 to 10 chopped tomatoes

Just before serving, add:

1 cup cubed dried bread or toast

WINTER VEGETABLES

The vegetables you can eat in the winter (in a snow-bound farmhouse) depend mostly on your method of storage. For the most part, we have relied on the root cellar; and, if you don't have electricity this will probably be your main source of vegetables when the snows are deep and the nights are long.

Our root cellar, the past four years, has been an enclosed wooden room, set on stones on the dirt floor of the cellar. To discourage rodents, it's lined, around the floor and corners, with old sheet metal from the dump. It has one vent near the bottom on the right, and one near the top on the left.

The bin itself has worked very well, but, unfortunately, the cellar floor beneath is far from dry; whenever we get a thaw, the field above the house drains into the cellar. That's how I happen to know that it's absolutely necessary to keep cabbages dry, as well as cool. Our cabbages always rot as soon as the cellar floods. Everything else is pretty much okay, but next year, when we build our new house, over our new root cellar, it's going to be on top of a slope, not at the bottom, and we'll have cabbages all winter long.

BEETS

Beets are very hardy, and will keep well, right up to warm weather. The larger ones will keep best, so eat up the small ones in the early winter months. Beets aren't particularly strong in any one nutrient, but they have traces of almost every vitamin.

beets

Since beets take a long time to cook, you should either start them cooking well ahead of dinner or cut them up very small. Beets should be cooked separately from other vegetables for this reason, and also because the red juices color everything else pink. (Hash with beets in it is called Red Flannel Hash; if you've ever thrown a red flannel shirt in a white wash you'll know why!)

Unlike most roots, beets can be cooked ahead of time, cooled, and reheated without getting mushy. But they should be cooked as fast as possible, with their skins on, to retain the most possible vitamins.

STEAMED BEETS

In a heavy, lidded pot, boil:

1 cup water

Meanwhile, scrub well and trim off tops and roots of beets. Figure on a couple of small beets, or one large one, per serving, plus one or two extra. Dice, slice, or cut in chunks around 2 inches in diameter:

beets

Put them in the pot, in a steamer or on a rack; cover tightly and steam for ¾ to 1½ hours, depending on their size. They are done when they taste tender. Serve with butter, or:

1. **¼ cup sour cream** (per serving)
   a pinch of dill, basil, chervil, or rosemary
   2 Tb. chopped parsley
2. **1 chopped, sautéed onion**
   a couple of chopped apples, raw or sautéed with the onion
   a pinch of cinnamon
   1 Tb. brown sugar or honey

HARVARD BEETS

A fancy name for an old favorite in many an old farmhouse. Wash, dice, and steam for about 1 hour:

½ cup beets per person (plus ½ cup beets for the pot)

Meanwhile, mix together in a small pan:

½ cup vinegar (cider vinegar is best)
¼ cup brown sugar
½ tsp. salt
2 whole cloves or a pinch of dried cloves
1 Tb. cornstarch, arrowroot, or kuzu

Heat slowly, stirring, as sauce thickens; if you have used cornstarch, set it on the right front plate of the stove (low heat) to simmer for 10 minutes. When the beets are tender transfer them to a serving dish and add the sauce. Mix and serve.

SAUTÉED BEETS AND CARROTS

A colorful dish; serves three or four.
Wash, slice, and steam for 15 minutes:

1½ cups beets

Heat in a heavy frying pan:

2 Tb. light oil

Add:

1½ cups carrots, cut in finger-sized pieces

Sauté for 5 or 10 minutes; then add the beets and:

½ cup water

Cover the pot and steam for 15 minutes.

BEET SALAD

Steam for ¾ to 1½ hours:

4 to 8 beets

When they are tender through, take them out and chop them up fine. Mix and add to the beets:

3 Tb. oil
1 Tb. vinegar
1 pinch salt

Let the beets sit in the refrigerator for a few hours before serving. You may add at the last minute, for color and flavor:

2 Tb. chopped parsley

CABBAGE

The commonest cabbages are summer, winter, and red cabbages. Summer cabbage is tender and does not keep well. It can be shredded into coleslaw or cooked, but it doesn't hold together well in a whole stuffed-cabbage dish. Red cabbage has a slightly sweet flavor, and keeps fairly well, for a few months, in a cool, dry root cellar. Winter cabbage is the toughest and keeps the longest. How your cabbages keep will depend on how cold your root cellar is; a mid-winter thaw may rot every one of them. If you see that happening, quickly put up a huge mess of sauerkraut (page 236).

Cabbages have an extraordinary amount of vitamin C, most of it stored in the outer green leaves. These leaves are somewhat tougher than the inner leaves, however, so you may find it better to steam them separately, and longer, or chop them finer than the heart of the cabbage. Vitamin C is water soluble, so if you boil the cabbage you should use the water somehow. Also, cabbage has a fair amount of calcium, but this is only available to your body if you have something like milk or eggs at the same time. It also has a bit of iron. All these things are twice as concentrated in the outer leaves, so, whatever you do, don't throw them away, even if they aren't as tender or easy to chop.

Prepared properly, cabbage is a crisp leafy contrast to other winter vegetables. But, as almost everyone discovers sooner or later, overcooked cabbage is absolutely tasteless and fills the house with a reek like old socks from the bottom of a damp laundry hamper. So learn to cook it carefully, no longer than 10 minutes; in soup, add it at the very end.

Basically, there are three ways to deal with a cabbage:

1. Serve it raw (as in coleslaw or salad)
2. Steam it (as in steamed, baked, or stuffed cabbage [pages 170–172])
3. Sauté it and then steam it (as in Stir-Fried Vegetables [page 15], etc.)

slicing cabbage

PLAIN SAUTÉED CABBAGE

Shred:

1½ cups cabbage per serving (it cooks down a lot)

Heat in a heavy skillet:

2 Tb. light vegetable oil or bacon or ham fat

Sauté the cabbage over the left front plate, stirring once or twice, for 5 minutes, or until it begins to go limp. Add:

2 to 4 Tb. water or milk

Cover tightly and steam for 5 minutes over middle front plate (medium heat). Serve while cabbage is still somewhat crisp.

CABBAGE TAMARI

This is a very sophisticated and flavorful version of cabbage, which, if you weren't the cook, you probably wouldn't believe was cabbage.
Shred:

1½ cups cabbage per serving (it cooks down a lot)

Heat in a heavy skillet:

2 Tb. vegetable oil; the best is dark sesame oil

Sauté the cabbage over the left front plate (high heat), stirring once or twice, for 5 minutes, or until it begins to go limp. Add:

a generous shot of Tamari

This varies; I never measure it but I figure about a tablespoon for two servings. You can make a milder version by adding half Tamari and half water. Cover tightly; steam over medium heat for 5 minutes. Serve while cabbage is still somewhat crisp.

TART RED CABBAGE

A very good accompaniment to a big pot of stewed meat and root vegetables, and cornbread or corn pudding; a meal as colorful as fall.
Cut in half:

a red cabbage

Slice off pie-shaped wedges, one or two per person, with a bit of the core in the center of each slice to hold it together. Steam them in, not over, an inch or so of water for about 15 minutes, until almost soft.

Meanwhile, heat a little fat or oil in a large, heavy frying pan and sauté:

a sliced onion

When the cabbage is soft, fork in the pieces, being careful not to break them up. Sauté them for a minute or so on each side over low heat.

Stir into the remaining cabbage water in the pot:

enough liquid to bring it to about 1 cup (water, cider, fruit juice)
2 Tb. cider or wine vinegar
3 Tb. brown sugar
½ tsp. salt
2 Tb. cornstarch

Heat this, stirring with a spring stirrer or whisk, until it is clear and thick. Pour it over the cabbage, cover, and simmer 5 minutes.

SWEET CABBAGE

You can use red or green cabbage for this. It will serve three or four people.

Shred:

3 to 4 cups cabbage

Chop coarsely:

2 or 3 apples
1 large onion

Heat in a heavy frying pan:

3 Tb. bacon or ham fat or oil

Toss in all the vegetables and cook over lively heat for 5 to 10 minutes, until they begin to brown. Then add:

2 tsp. Tamari soy sauce
1 Tb. malt or cider vinegar
1 Tb. catsup
2 Tb. brown sugar

Cook and stir a couple of minutes more before serving.

COLESLAW

Coleslaw is a very versatile dish; there are lots of possible ingredients and dressings. Mainly, what you put in depends on what you have around. For every:

2 cups grated winter cabbage

or

2 cups shredded summer or red cabbage

you may add:

1 small (tender) grated carrot
½ grated onion (Bermuda, if you have it)
¼ cup grated radishes
1 cup chopped or grated apples
3 stalks chopped celery
½ cup grated kohlrabi or parsnip
½ cup tiny flowerets of raw or steamed broccoli or cauliflower
½ cup raisins
1 cup cooked bulgur
1 cup raw chopped tomatoes
1 cup chopped cucumber
1 cup shredded lettuce

And so it goes. Some people add a dash of sesame or sunflower seeds, chopped cooked potatoes, sprouts, and so forth. You may add, for flavor:

fresh dill, chervil, parsley, tarragon, chives

COLESLAW DRESSING

Every time I do it differently; here's the way I did it last night:

½ cup yogurt
¼ cup mayonnaise
4 tsp. tomato paste
1 tsp. lemon juice
2 tsp. olive oil
2 pinches salt
1 tsp. tarragon vinegar

But you can substitute all mayonnaise, sour cream, or all yogurt, or invent your own combination of wet and spicy ingredients: use your imagination.

CARROTS

Carrots keep quite well most of the winter, in a cool, damp root cellar. As with beets, the larger ones keep longer, so use up the small ones first. When the weather begins to warm up they will start to sprout and become tough and withered or rotten. However, if you've given the matter some forethought the previous fall, you should have a nice crop of wintered-over carrots out in the garden, ready to dig just as the ones in the cellar go bad.

Carrots have a phenomenal amount of vitamin A. Half a cup of cooked carrots supplies the normal daily need for A (though not much of anything else).

I find plain steamed carrots boring, so before or after steaming them I usually sauté or bake them with a little oil, maybe a pinch of herbs, seeds, or brown sugar and vinegar. Carrots are very good combined with other vegetables (as in stews, tzimmes, stir-fried vegetables, etc.). Grated carrots also combine well with grains, in making muffins, cakes, and puddings.

CARROT SALAD

Use only very tender carrots for carrot salad. Grate:

2 carrots per serving

Add:

lemon juice and peanut oil to taste

You may add:

¼ cup peanuts per serving, ground into small chunks
¼ cup raisins per serving, whole or chopped
¼ cup mayonnaise

You may season the salad with:

dill, rosemary, chives, tarragon
cardamom, nutmeg, cumin, coriander

SAUTÉED CARROTS

Slice into rounds or ovals, about 1/8 inch thick:

about ¾ cup carrots per serving (they'll cook down a bit)

Heat in a heavy frying pan on the left side of the stove (over high heat):

2 Tb. oil

Sauté the carrots for about 10 minutes, stirring once or twice. When they begin to look cooked, but still taste crunchy, add:

¼ to ½ cup water

Lid closely and steam for 5 minutes or so, turning them maybe once. A larger quantity will take longer. Serve plain or add any one of the following:

a sprinkling of poppyseeds, sesame seeds, sunflower seeds, or nuts
wheat germ
2 Tb. brown sugar and 1 tsp. cinnamon per serving
¼ tsp. curry and 2 Tb. raisins per serving
Plain Sweet and Sour Sauce (page 178)
a squeeze of lemon juice, to taste

ONIONS

Onions can be kept all winter and into the late spring if you have been careful about drying them to begin with and keeping them dry. They are not kept in a root cellar, but in a dark, dry, cool room of the house or barn.

Onions aren't particularly strong in any nutrient, but they're indispensable in making other, more nutritious foods tasty. It's a rare person who enjoys raw onions, but they change character when cooked, becoming sweet and gently flavorful.

ONIONS WITH CHEESE

The sort of thing to serve at a robust meal with lots of gaiety and schnapps. Peel and slice into slabs about half an inch thick:

1 large onion per person

Lay them on an oiled baking dish; rub them around a bit and turn them over. Bake in a 300° oven until soft, about 15 minutes. Meanwhile, mix, for every onion:

2 Tb. grated sharp Cheddar
1 Tb. beer or wine
1 tsp. mustard

Mash these up with a fork into a thick paste. Take out the onions, spread on the cheese, and, if you have them:

slices of tomato to cover

Bake on the top shelf of the oven 5 to 10 minutes. Let them cool a bit before serving.

cut cross-shaped gash in onion, top and bottom ...

or this will happen

baked onions

BAKED ONIONS

Leave the onions in their jackets, but cut shallow crosses in both ends to keep the insides from popping out. Bake at 300° to 350° for about 1 hour.

STEAMED ONIONS

Leave the onions in their jackets, but cut shallow crosses in both ends to keep the insides from popping out. Steam medium-sized onions 15 to 20 minutes, white pearl onions 10 minutes.

CREAMED ONIONS

Steam and then sauté for 5 to 10 minutes in butter or oil **whole onions**; remove them from the pan and melt:

2 Tb. butter or oil

Add:

3 Tb. wheat flour

Let it foam for a few minutes; then add, beating briskly:

⅓ cup hot juice from steaming onions

Keep stirring as you add:

⅔ cup hot milk

When the sauce is thick, return the onions to the pan and cook gently for a few minutes before serving. You may also put it in the oven and top it with:

grated cheese and/or fried breadcrumbs

Heat for 10 minutes in the top of the oven, or until browned.

CHOPPING ONIONS: I use onions a lot; their sweet and pungent flavor makes almost any meat or vegetable taste better, and it adds a lot to grains. Standing around dicing onions for a long time can make life in the kitchen a real ordeal, though, unless you learn to chop them quickly. So here's how you do it:

1. Slice off the top and bottom. Cut a shallow slit from top to bottom and slip off the skin with a fingernail or the edge of your knife.

2. Slice the peeled onion through the "equator." Turn the halves so the centers face down. Holding the onion half firmly, cut it into vertical slices, turn, and cut again at right angles to your first slices, so your cuts form a rough grid. Don't be too slow and fussy. Close cuts yield a

fine dice; wide cuts a "roughly chopped" onion.

3. If yours is a very large onion, you may wish to give it another horizontal slice. Hold the onion half closely and saw through slowly, so as to be careful of your fingers. When you are almost through to the other side, let the last segments fall back and chop through to the cutting board.

slicing onions, fast

POTATOES

Potatoes keep very well, often into the spring. They should be stored in a cool, moderately moist root cellar. In cooking, cut out any green spots that result from exposure to light; they are somewhat toxic (give you a stomachache). Also cut off sprouts, in the spring, using only clean flesh.

If you haven't already done so, you should discard any previous notions about cooking potatoes in great vats of boiling water or peeling them beforehand. Potatoes have little food value, and what they do have is completely lost by these traditional cooking methods. Even roasting them with meat, though delicious, is wasteful of their value. They need to be cooked with skins on, and without water.

The goodies in potato skins are mostly iron and vitamin C. One potato skin has all the iron you need in a day, and about a third of the vitamin C. Both of these are water soluble; they are also destroyed by enzymes that go to work as soon as you cut into a room temperature potato. So you should keep the potatotes very cool right up to the moment you cut into them, and if you aren't going to cook them immediately, refrigerate them.

If you have to eat commercially grown potatoes, you might object to all the chemicals that are sprayed on before, during, and after harvest, and wish to peel your potatoes anyway. In that case you may peel them after steaming them, slipping off the outer brown husk easily with your hands. The vitamin C and iron are actually in a waxy greenish layer just under this husk, so nothing will be lost.

BAKED POTATOES

For a real baked potato—flaky and light, with a thick crunchy crust—there are two requirements: one, you must have real baking potatoes, a special variety grown mostly in Idaho; two, you must have a very hot oven. Most baked potatoes do not taste very different from steamed potatoes, so they are hardly worth the bother of getting the oven up to 425° for an hour just before dinner. For that rare occasion, however, choose:

2 baking potatoes per person, all the same size (cut large ones in half)

Scrub them well; you may dry them and coat lightly with:

oil, butter, or bacon fat

if you don't want a crisp crust. Put them in the oven on a rack, not touching each other, and low enough so you can reach in with a fork to pierce the skins when they are half done, in 20 minutes. (To make this job easier you can impale them on skewers, if you have them.) If they are not punctured they will fill up with steam and may explode unexpectedly—it's happened to me, I must admit,

and it made an awful mess of the oven.

The potatoes will be done in about 45 minutes; when a fork slides easily through the center, put them in the warming oven in an open pan or dish. Serve with all the below:

butter

sour cream or yogurt mixed with fresh chopped chives, parsley

a few drops of onion juice

BAKED STUFFED POTATOES

These are incredibly good, well worth the extra effort. Start them well before dinner: about three hours before serving, or make them up to 24 hours ahead and refrigerate until the final baking. You need not use real baking potatoes, but choose perfect potatoes, evenly shaped and all the same size: about 2½ inches in diameter and 3 to 4 inches long. Bake, as in **Baked Potatoes**, at 425° for 45 minutes:

1 potato per person

When they can be easily pierced with a fork, take them out and cut each one in half crosswise. Scoop out the middles, turning each shell upside down on the counter as you do so. Mash the potatoes with a ricer, food mill, or masher (or a fork). Add, for every 3 potatoes:

½ cup milk mixed with ¼ cup dried milk

or

1 beaten egg and ½ cup milk

1½ Tb. butter

½ tsp. salt

1 Tb. chopped parsley and/or chives

a little onion juice

Refill the potato skins, heaping the mashed potatoes up on top somewhat, and put the stuffed potatoes in the wells of a cupcake tin.

To reheat and finish, bake at around 350° for 15 to 20 minutes in the top of the oven until browned.

SCALLOPED POTATOES

The faster you cook potatoes, the better; since the traditional method takes hours, this way seems better. Recipe serves three or four. Wash well and slice about ⅛ inch thin:

3 to 4 cups potatoes

Arrange them in three layers in a large greased casserole. Over each layer put:

sliced onion, cut thin and separated into rings
1 to 2 Tb. whole-wheat flour, sprinkled
¼ to ½ tsp. salt, sprinkled
1 to 2 Tb. bacon or ham fat or butter, in dabs or chunks
a grating of fresh pepper or a pinch of paprika
1 to 2 Tb. chopped fresh parsley (optional)

Over the top of the dish pour:

1 cup top milk, evaporated milk, or milk with ½ cup dried milk mixed in it
a sprinkle of paprika

Cover this pan and heat rapidly over high heat, one of the left plates; then simmer over low heat, the front middle plate, for 20 minutes. When the potatoes can almost be pierced with a fork, uncover the pan and put it in the top half of a 350° oven for 15 minutes. If you want it to look fancy, sprinkle on:

grated cheese

or

breadcrumbs fried in bacon fat or sesame oil

NOTE: If you wish to double the quantity, cook and bake the potatoes in a large flat pan or two pans rather than a deep dish, so the heat can penetrate.

POTATO CHIPS

A nice snack on a snowy day, these really do taste like potato chips, as long as you eat them while they are still warm. Children can make them if they are old enough to watch out for the hot pan; but it's better to get a grownup to do the slicing.

Scrub a potato or two, and slice them as thin as you can. Meanwhile, heat in a cast-iron frying pan, over a hot fire:

2 Tb. vegetable oil

Put a few slices of potato in the pan. Don't overlap them. Fry until golden; turn them with a spatula and cook the other side until golden. Put them on a folded paper bag and salt them a little. Eat as soon as you can. Make more.

"BOILED" POTATOES

By this method, the potatoes are actually steamed, thus retaining all the water-soluble vitamins which boiled potatoes lose in cooking. Small potatoes steam best; save large ones for other dishes, or cut them up. Figure one to three medium-sized potatoes per person, depending on whether people are dieting or have just spent the afternoon digging a truck out of the mud.

Scrub potatoes well. Cut into pieces the size of the smallest potato. Put them in a pot with a wire rack over a cup or so of boiling water. Cover tightly and steam 20 to 35 minutes, until a fork pierces them easily. Remove lid and set the pan in the warming oven, if you have to hold them for a while. Serve with butter or Gomasio (page 55).

Variations

Home-Fried Potatoes: Steam potatoes, as above, until barely done—not soft. Cool for 15 minutes; meanwhile, heat in a heavy frying pan:

5 Tb. bacon or ham fat, or vegetable oil

Chop the potatoes into the hot fat in pieces the size of walnuts. Add:

1 chopped onion

Flatten the potatoes with the back of a spatula and cook in an open pan over a middle plate (moderate heat) until golden on the bottom. Slide the spatula under them and turn in batches, as if they were pancakes, to cook on the other side. Do not cover pan at any time or they will become soggy. Serve with ketchup or fresh tomato sauce, or sprinkle with Gomasio (page 55).

Mashed Potatoes: Steam potatoes as above, until well-cooked, even falling apart. Put them through a food mill, or mash with whatever contrivance you have. Add:

milk, reconstituted dried milk, or canned milk

gradually, until the consistency is the way you like it. You may add **1 tsp. butter** per potato, if you like, but it isn't necessary. Most people like to add **½ tsp. salt** per potato, but maybe you like less; stir in some, taste, and decide. Mashed potatoes take very well to seasoning; you might add:

a pinch or two of curry, paprika, or ground pepper;
1 chopped, sautéed onion and/or 2 cloves crushed, sautéed garlic;
summer savory (makes it taste a little like sausage);
chopped fresh chives and/or parsley;

onion juice (slice an onion in half through its equator; cut slashes ½ inch deep in a grid pattern, and scrape a knife across the cut surfaces, over the potatoes).

Mashed potatoes may be returned to near the top of the oven, in a greased casserole dish. They will brown on top, in 15 or 20 minutes, since the heat in a wood stove oven comes from the top. In a modern stove, brown them under the broiler.

SPROUTED SEEDS

Sprouted seeds, of course, may be grown at any time of year; I grow them more in the winter, though, because we feel the lack of crisp, fresh vegetables most then—not to mention the vitamins. Sprouted seeds have a high ratio of protein, as well, if combined with a grain dish. Because of the actions of the enzymes released by the sprouting process, this ratio of protein is actually higher than that of the dried and dormant seeds; and the seeds are more digestible.

There are lots of different kinds of seeds you can sprout. The easiest and cheapest is the mung bean. Mung beans are so easy to sprout that they say in Vietnam that the Viet Cong survived their meager diet largely by supplementing it with mung bean sprouts, which they grew by keeping the beans in their pockets (which were always damp from wading through rice paddies and swamps).

Two other popular sprouts are soybeans, which are not quite so tasty but are very high in protein; and alfalfa, which has such a tiny seed and a long, lacy tangle of sprouts that it makes really wonderful salad. Then there is fenugreek, a funny little square seed with an odd, friendly flavor; lentils, or any small peas or beans, and grains: wheat, oats, and rye. Grain seeds soften as they soak, and have a chewy rather than crisp texture.

You can also grow the seeds of mustard, watercress, buckwheat, and radishes, for instance—which take a little longer than sprouts—until they form the first two leaves; at this point eat them as salads. Since leaves form, though, you grow them by a different process.

SPROUTING JARS: To grow sprouts you will need one piece of equipment: a sprouting jar. Here are different ways to make them:

1. Take any wide-mouthed jar with a good screw lid and punch small holes in the lid with an ice pick. This is very easy to do but in time the holes become rusty and the lid needs replacing. Punch the holes very small if you plan to grow alfalfa.

2. Take any wide-mouthed jar and cut a piece of loosely woven cloth (muslin or cheesecloth) to a circle about one inch larger in circumference than the mouth of the jar. Buy a packet of strong brown rubber bands to hold on the cloth (they disintegrate).

3. Take a wide-mouthed canning jar or one that has threads a screw-top mason jar ring will fit on (such as a mayonnaise jar). Cut a piece of nonrustable screen to fit below the jar ring and glue it in place with two or three applications of white glue.

TO SPROUT BEANS: Fill the jar ⅓ full of beans. Add warm water to the top of the jar and set in a warm spot (say, over the warming oven) for 4 to 8 hours, until you see they have swollen. Empty out the water and rinse them with more warm water by refilling it, then letting the water drain out. Wrap the jar in a damp towel and lay it on its side in a dish on the warming oven.

Every 4 to 6 hours, you should refill the jar and drain out the water, partly to warm the beans and partly to keep them clean of bacteria or mold. If you skip a damping, however, it won't matter. The more often they're rinsed, though, the more quickly and evenly they will grow.

Mung bean sprouts will sprout 2 inches in 3 days, sometimes 3 inches in 5 days.

Lentils will sprout 2 inches in 4 or 5 days.

Soybeans will sprout 2 to 4 inches in 5 days. You should be a little more careful about rinsing them frequently than is necessary with mung beans and lentils. After sprouting you may have to pick them over and throw out the ones that didn't sprout. Some soybeans rot instead.

Dried unsprouted mung beans will keep up to 3 years; soybeans and lentils 1 year.

TO SPROUT GRAINS: Fill the jar ¼ full of seeds (wheat, oats, rye). Add warm water to the top and set them in a warm place (such as over the warming oven) to soak for 4 to 8 hours, until you see that they've swollen and softened. Empty out the water and rinse them twice with warm water by refilling it, then letting the water drain out. Wrap the jar in a damp towel and lay it on its side in a dish on the warming oven.

Every 4 hours you should refill the jar and drain out the water; you can leave them overnight, but in the morning rinse them first thing. They usually sprout in about 5 days. You should look closely after 4 days, because they are best when the sprouts are very small, only about ⅛ inch long, the length of the seed.

TO SPROUT ALFALFA SEEDS: Proceed as in sprouting beans, but only fill the jar ¼ inch full; sprouted alfalfa occupies a lot of space. Alfalfa sprouts are best eaten when the sprouts are about 1 inch long, but they will grow several inches and even will grow leaves if you set them in a sunny window for a day or two to finish them as "green salad"; be sure to keep them damp, though.

TO SPROUT MUSTARD, WATERCRESS, RADISH GREENS: These are sprouted, like beans and grains, in a warm, damp dark place; but since they are grown into leaves, in a sunny window, it is easier to keep them damp if you grow them on a tray. Lay a closely woven cloth (muslin or cheesecloth) or Handi-wipe layer over 3 or 4 layers of any cloth in a rustproof tray and add enough warm water to just reach the top cloth, but not cover it. Sprinkle seeds on thickly and cover with a damp towel. Keep the tray in a warm, dark place for 3 to 5 days, or until you see the seeds sprouting; be sure to keep it watered with warm water. Then remove the top cloth and move it to a window. Water every 4 hours except overnight. Within 10 days the watercress will be a tiny forest. Eat plants, seeds, and all. Mustard and radish take longer, about 15 days; the taste is also more peppery.

SPROUT SALADS: If you want to supplement your rather limited supply of salad materials in the winter with sprouts, regularly, you would do well to have a variety of sprouting seeds and beans and several bottles and trays on hand so that different batches can be grown at the same time. The essence of salad is variety and contrast. Moreover, mung beans on Monday and soybeans on Wednesday still require that you have two sprouting jars going on Sunday.

All sprouts are highest in vitamins when raw. Those that may be grown until leaves appear are highest in vitamin C after they turn green. Some are better than others raw. Mung beans are crisp; alfalfa is a tender tangle; mustard, watercress, and radish are fresh and biting.

Sprouts may be dressed with light vegetable oil and a very little light-flavored vinegar or lemon juice. Mung beans in particular are so delicious that they really shouldn't have much dressing.

SAUTÉED SPROUTS AND SEEDS: Sprouts may be sautéed by themselves or in combination with other sprouts, for 2 to 3 minutes in very hot light vegetable oil. If they are to be added to nituke (stir-fried vegetables) they should be added at the very end, just tossed in lightly with the cooked vegetables and cooked the last 2 minutes.

Mung beans are traditional in nituke, but other sprouts may be used as well. I would go easy on the quantity of grain sprouts, so as not to overpower the vegetable mixture with coatings of chewy little seeds; a few tablespoons are fine. You could add a whole handful of mung beans, lentils, or fenugreek; you could add alfalfa sprouts in little clumps.

OTHER USES OF SPROUTS: Grain sprouts are very nice in bread, about ½ cup per loaf. Sprouts are good in (and good for) soups and stews of all kinds. Sprouts are great (especially alfalfa) in sandwiches.

WINTER SALADS

One year I tried to grow lettuce and chard indoors for salads. It didn't work; leafy things really live on sunshine. The best way to get green crunch in the snowbound months is with sprouts, but you can add other things as well.

Potatoes: Steam them (page 27), chill and dice. Marinate overnight, or longer, in a mixture of 3 **Tb. oil, 1 Tb. vinegar, 1 tsp. salt** for every cupful.

Beets: Cook them (page 21), chill, dice, and marinate in 2 **Tb. oil, 2 Tb. vinegar** for every cupful.

Sunflower Seeds: Dry-roast in a hot pan, stirring constantly, for 10 minutes. Add them to the dressed salad just before serving.

Celery: Chop tender center stalks, add to salad.

Carrots: Carrots are best in a special carrot salad, see page 24.

Dressings: To a salad which is mostly potatoes, you can add, if you like, some **mayonnaise, yogurt, or sour cream**. A sprout salad is better tossed with:

3 Tb. vegetable oil

1 Tb. vinegar or lemon juice
1 tsp. salt

To my mind, any salad is better with a dash of **onion juice**, but that's up to you.

FROZEN MUNG SALAD

This is really a recipe for half frozen, marinated mung beans. You may use them in salads together with other ingredients or serve the salad plain, as is. Toss:

2 cups sprouted mung beans

with:

3 Tb. light oil (olive, sesame, or peanut)
1 Tb. light vinegar (wine vinegar is the nicest)
1 tsp. salt
1 tsp. onion juice

Put them in the shelf just below the freezer, and chill for at least 3 hours. Or leave them 24 hours, or 48; they will keep up to 3 days just as they are. Serve half frozen.

TURNIPS

Turnips keep well all winter in a cool, damp root cellar. They have some vitamin C; half a cup, cooked, has about a third of what most people need in a day. Turnips may be steamed, baked, sautéed, or cooked with other vegetables. They have a sweet strong flavor that people either like or don't; best to find out before serving a big potful to guests. In any case be careful not to overcook them; take them off the heat as soon as they are soft through.

You may plant your old leftover turnips in the spring for a quick crop of fresh greens; turnip greens have a great deal of vitamin A and C, plus calcium.

STEAMED TURNIPS

Wash and slice about ½ inch thick:

about ¾ cup turnips per serving

Put in a heavy pot with a good lid, in a steamer or on a rack, over:

1 cup boiling water

Steam about 20 minutes, turning once or twice. When a fork goes through them easily, they are done. Serve plain or mashed.

MASHED TURNIPS

Put through a food mill:

steamed turnips

You may add:

½ tsp. salt per serving
¼ cup dried milk, dissolved in a little water, per serving
1 Tb. brown sugar and a pinch of cinnamon per serving

HIMMEL UND ERDE

Steam together:

any amounts of apple, turnips, potatoes, parsnips

Put them all through a food mill and season with:

cinnamon
salt
brown sugar

SAUTÉED TURNIPS

Slice:

¾ cup turnips per serving

Heat in a heavy frying pan:

3 Tb. oil or ham or bacon fat

Add the turnips and sauté until golden. Add:

½ cup water

Cover closely, move to moderate heat, and steam for 10 minutes or until soft.

WINTER SQUASH

There are many types of winter squash, with various qualities, and I count pumpkin as one of them. Squash can be kept in a very dry root cellar or in a cool room of the house; it is much more important to keep them dry than it is to keep them cool. The ones with tougher skins keep longer. However, you should check all of them every week or two and use the ones with soft spots right away. You may also freeze squash (cooked and mashed) in plastic containers, for spring and summer use.

Half a cup of squash has enough vitamin A to meet the average daily requirement; pumpkin, being more watery, has about half enough. The other nutrients are sort of minimal.

Squash is an incredibly versatile food. You can bake or steam them in whole pieces; mix them with

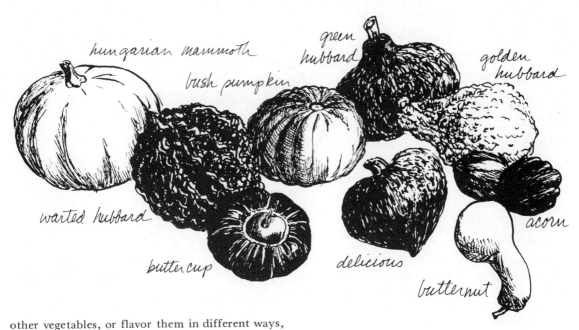

hungarian mammoth
bush pumpkin
green hubbard
golden hubbard
warted hubbard
buttercup
delicious
butternut
acorn

other vegetables, or flavor them in different ways, since their taste is very bland to begin with. (For this reason they make fine baby food.) You can make a very mellow soup with winter squash, or a variety of cakes, pies, and muffins; and there is even one old Vermont recipe for Pumpkin Beer!

STEAMED SQUASH

Plain steamed squash doesn't have a very interesting texture or flavor, but steaming is a first step in other cooking processes.

Halve and clean your **squash.** You will need a large and very sharp knife to cut into raw squash; I sometimes butcher them with an ax, especially the large hubbards. If you want it to cook very quickly, chop it up into 2-inch chunks or ½-inch slices. Add the **squash** to **½ cup boiling water,** lid the pot tightly, and steam until done (20 minutes for **pumpkin,** 30 minutes for **acorns and butternuts,** 45 minutes for **hubbards and buttercups**). When a fork will pierce the squash easily it is done.

"BAKED" SQUASH

Unless your oven happens to be very hot—around 400°—you do better to steam squash first and then finish it as "baked" squash in the oven. The reasons are: first, squash dries out at low temperatures; second, the vitamins are less damaged with faster cooking.

Halve, clean, and steam until almost done:

about 1 cup squash per person

Remove them from the pot carefully and put them skin side down on an oiled pan. Paint on top:

oil or melted butter

And sprinkle on, if you like:

a little brown sugar or honey

a squeeze of orange or lemon juice

cinnamon, ginger, nutmeg, or allspice

Place them in a moderately hot oven or one on its way up—as close to the top of the oven as you can get them. Bake 10 minutes.

MASHED SQUASH

Halve and chop into 2-inch chunks:

about 1 cup squash per person

Steam until very tender. Put through a food mill hot. Add:

¼ cup canned milk per serving, or "double milk" (milk to which dried milk has been added so it is very thick)

a big hunk of butter or 2 Tb. oil

salt to taste

cinnamon, ginger, nutmeg or allspice to taste

Leftover mashed squash is sort of heavy; to reheat it, add some water, milk, or a beaten egg, and reheat slowly in the oven in a tightly lidded casserole.

slicing squash

STUFFED SQUASH

Halve and clean:

½ **medium squash per person: acorn or butternut**

Steam the squash in ½ inch of boiling water in a lidded casserole in the oven at 400°. The squash should be face down. Remove them before they are done all the way, in about 20 minutes; invert them, and fill with stuffing you have made in the meantime as follows:

Heat in a heavy frying pan:

2 Tb. oil or bacon fat

Add, for every squash you want to stuff:

½ finely chopped onion
1 Tb. finely chopped celery

Sauté until limp, then add:

½ cup breadcrumbs
½ cup stock
2 Tb. wheat germ
2 Tb. chopped parsley

Season with:

a pinch of thyme, basil, marjoram, or savory
a pinch of salt
a grating of pepper

Mix well and stuff the squash, packing the stuffing in small mounds. Place as close to the top of the oven as possible and run a hot fire for about 10 minutes.

WINTER STIR-FRY

Or, mixed sautéed winter vegetables. Traditionally, the Chinese cook this in a wok, a great rounded pan used mainly for stir-frying and steaming. Intense heat is directed to the center; the vegetables are "surprised" by fast cooking at first, and then pushed up around the sides as more are added. The longest-cooking roots and stems are cooked first, then the lighter vegetables, and finally the greens are added. Then a small amount of liquid is added, the pan is lidded, and the vegetables are steamed for a few minutes.

A wood stove is especially well suited to wok cooking; remove the hottest plate and the wok sits easily in it with no other device needed. You may also cook stir-fried vegetables in a regular cast-iron frying pan, though. Just be careful to time your vegetables. This is a flexible dish, and what you use depends on what you have; below are some winter vegetables and the amounts of time they should be sautéed in a little hot oil before steaming so that they will all be done at the same time.

The wok or frying pan should be hot before you put in the oil.

carrots	slice diagonally, thinly	10 minutes
gomo (burdock root)	slice diagonally, thinly	10 minutes
winter squash	chop & slice thinly	8 minutes
turnips	chop & slice thinly	8 minutes
parsnips	slice diagonally, thinly	5 minutes
onions	slice as you would a pie, thinly	5 minutes
cabbage	shred	5 minutes
sprouts	add loose	2 minutes

When all the vegetables are sautéed, add:

tamari soy sauce or **water**

Or you may add a mixture of:

komo miso and water, mixed into a liquid paste

Add about 1 Tb. liquid for every serving of vegetables. Cover tightly and steam for 5 minutes. Serve hot with rice and tamari soy sauce and Sesame Salt (**Gomasio**, page 55).

TZIMMES

Slice into flat pieces and steam:

1 decent-sized squash

Slice into thin rounds and steam in another pan:

4 carrots (about 1 cup)

Oil a 2-quart casserole or frying pan and make layers of cooked squash,

sliced tart apples,

and cooked carrots, in that order, ending with carrots. Mix together in one of the steaming pans (so as not to have to wash extra pans):

¼ cup oil
½ cup honey
grated rind of 1 lemon
¼ tsp. salt
¼ tsp. coriander or a grating of nutmeg
a squeeze of lemon juice

Pour this over the casserole and cover tightly. Bake at 300°-350° for about 30 minutes. You may remove the lid for the last 10 minutes; it makes the dish prettier.

2
ON FRUITS AND FORAGING

When you live in the country, there are a great many fruits that can be gathered with no other resources than a bucket and some spare time. There's enough, in fact, so that it really isn't necessary to buy fruits in the supermarket, which are shipped from Florida, Israel, or California. So I've limited my recipes to the fruits we forage in New England and the Maritimes. They include:

rhubarb
wild strawberries
raspberries
blueberries
blackberries
apples

Of course, there are others, like plums, or pears, or pie cherries; if you happen on some, or grow them, you know what a luxury they are. You may can them, or make jam out of them; or you can give them away (spread the wealth around).

There are also odd fruits and berries such as seckle pears, elderberries, sumac, and rose hips. For the most part people don't eat such fruits as they are, but find them very good in juices, jellies, and preserves; and they are often high in vitamins (mostly C).

RHUBARB

First among fruits comes spring rhubarb. Around here, and almost everywhere I've lived in the East,

you can get your hands on astonishing quantities of it if you look hard, and ask questions. Usually the rhubarb patch will be close by an old house or cellarhole, if the place is not too overgrown. It will be some place where the livestock can't get at it, because its leaves are poisonous.

Rhubarb stalks are what you use, and they come in many varieties; the best and sweetest are bright pink and slender. (The redder the better.) Don't bother with the thick greenish stalks, or the heavy central flower stalks; they're sour and stringy. To pick it, break back the stalk. Collect an armload, and then sit down under a tree and whack off leaves with a knife. Fill a couple of cardboard boxes if you are serious about canning or freezing for the whole year. Rhubarb keeps equally well both ways.

To cook rhubarb, wash it, pick off the papery brown flaps at the bottoms, and make sure there are no bits of leaves attached; then chop them up roughly into 3- to 5-inch pieces (kids can do that). Use an enameled pot to cook them in, and put a little water in the bottom—about half a cup. In about half an hour the pot full of stalks will suddenly be transformed into half a pot of frothing, bubbling cooked rhubarb.

Depending on how sour it is, add sugar. It usually takes from half a cup to a cup per quart of rhubarb to sweeten it satisfactorily. That's all there is to cooking rhubarb, which is one of the main reasons I like to do up a lot of it. It's plentiful, easy, and the tart flavor seems to be just what we feel most like eating in the early summer. When the stalks are in full bloom, the rhubarb season is over; the stalks become woody, hollow, stringy and tastelessly sour. It's time for strawberries.

WILD STRAWBERRIES

When spring is beginning to turn into summer, it's time to think about strawberries. If you live where you've always lived, you probably know where they are; but if not, have an eye, first, to the blossoming patches—they will tell you where the fruit will be. Where the grass is thin, they will be plentiful but small; by the sides of sandy roads they grow, but they get covered with grit. The best I've found grow in the deep grass mowings up on top of hills.

Keep an eye on them; when they're ripe, then, take the first good windy morning and go after them early, before the sun brings out the black flies. Don't wait and wait . . . they won't be like that next week!

There are two schools of thought regarding wild strawberry hulls. I belong to the leave-them-on-who-cares side of the fence; but if you prefer your strawberries pure, hull them as you pick, thus avoiding a tiresome chore later (and an opportunity for nonpickers, in passing, to make off with free handfuls of what you thought was going to be dessert and two pots of jam).

Wild strawberries are denser, sweeter, and tastier than commercial ones; so they require, in cooking, less sugar, no lemon juice, and quite a lot less time on the stove. There's also, of course, quite a lot less of them, so don't get dreams of rows of jars in the pantry unless you have pretty small jars.

Fresh Strawberries go well on the milk-and-egg abundance the cows and goats and hens thoughtfully provide in early summer—yogurt, pancakes, cottage cheese, puddings, custards, and so forth. They are good too with Familia or oatmeal, but tend to get lost in the strong flavor of granola.

Frozen Strawberries aren't like fresh, and no use pretending they might be. They're good in sauces, though, or ice cream, or punch; they have lots of flavor, just no texture worth speaking of—unless you eat them still frozen.

Canned Strawberries are very nice; use hot pack (with cold pack you wind up with half a jar of red juice and half a jar of deflated strawberries). Or make preserves (see pages 232-233). Be sure and seal the strawberries with Mason jar lids; paraffin is not enough.

STRAWBERRY PANCAKES

In Cape Breton, one picks blueberries by the pail, raspberries by the jar, and strawberries by the glass. Here's what I did with them yesterday when three very hungry children, with stars in their eyes and about a cup of tiny strawberries, appeared in my kitchen and demanded that I "make something yummy."

Mix up a batch of:

French pancake batter (page 81)

This will make a thinner and more eggy pancake than usual; very easy to roll. Heat up a couple of cast-iron skillets on the left-hand plates; put a few drops of oil in each. Make the pancakes about 6 inches in diameter, either with small pans, or by careful tilting and spreading of the batter. Cook both sides, remove the pancake, setting it aside, and pour in more batter. While the cooked pancake is still hot, put about a tablespoon of:

fresh wild strawberries

in a rough line, and roll it up. Eat it hot. Make more.

RASPBERRIES

Raspberry season is plain wonderful. It's not just that I like raspberries. It's not only the plenitude of a good thing; nor is it the ease with which one can pick and fill a bucket, although I'm sure those factors have something to do with it. What it is, most of all, is the meandering nature of raspberry picking. There is always, it seems, a better patch: just over that hill, or up the road, or down by that fallen-in barn. There are patches you remember and new ones you discover; but more important (although you don't think of it, at the time) are the wanders in between.

The best raspberries grow where homesteads were, though. The reason being that raspberries, left to themselves, grow up so thickly that they choke each other out and have less fruit. But in and around an old barn or house foundation, the fallen timbers and stone walls separate the plants somewhat. Then too, the soil is richer . . . so I stand, and pick, and think idly about the old place, in the late afternoon sunlight; perhaps finding a sign, or message, the way those stones were set: somebody, once, spent a whole summer (or maybe two) building that retaining wall there by the orchard, to keep the hill back. I have a look to see how the apples are shaping up and whether there are any keeping apples this year on that big tree by the shed. Apples come and go by the years . . .

But not raspberries, not unless it rains a lot. Then the fruits go big and wet and the berries have no taste and fall off before you get to them, wading through the tangle. After it rains I let them go, a day or two, before I slip my 2-quart bucket around my neck on its long strap (I like both hands free to work, berrying) and slip out "just for a look, up the hill—I won't be long" (I promise, faithlessly). After all, coming home with my bucket full, nobody could ever say I wasn't doing something worth the while; not while they're reaching for a handful of those lovely berries . . .

BLUEBERRIES

A good blueberry patch is worth a long travel. Other wild fruits (except apples) are treats, to be used sparingly; blueberries are a staple. They're pretty reliable, too. They don't often have an off-year; one patch might be better one year than another, but in general you can always go someplace and get gallons of them, if you pick in a serious sort of way. Blueberries may be kept fresh, for up to two weeks in the fridge; they may be dried, canned, and frozen, made into jelly, jam, and wine. In the north, we use them just as Southerners use grapes and raisins—in everything.

Blueberries come ripe in the middle of the summer, and continue to ripen for about a month. I like to wait until about mid-season, and then go at it full tilt. I take a lunch in a big bucket, and whatever kids I can find, and a 2-quart container that ties either to my belt or hangs around my neck. I never bother much with bushes that have a few berries, no matter how fat they are. I like to pick in bunches, the berries rolling lightly through my fingers; when there are no more handfuls, I move on quickly.

A little kid can pick a quart; a big kid, maybe more, depending. But a real serious adult berry picker in a good berry patch can pick a gallon in an hour, or 6 gallons in a day. It's sort of exciting, in a way, like indulging a fathomless greed; and you know they're going to last you all winter, which makes it even better.

Fresh Blueberries: On cereal, cooked or uncooked; in muffins, cakes, pies, tarts, pancakes, baked apples, puddings, fruit salad, etc.

Frozen Blueberries: Just plain frozen is fine; on yogurt, in pie, cake, etc. as above. Frozen blueberries are maybe even better than fresh.

Canned Blueberries: No sugar necessary—blueberries are sweet already. Hot pack (see pages 226–227) in water and blueberry juice, serve as pancake syrup or separate out the berries to cook with, the sauce to make juice with.

Dried Blueberries: It takes several days, and sometimes a week of drying on a rack over the stove; a gallon of fresh blueberries shrivels down to a quart, maybe, dried. Use in muffins, pancakes, etc., or soak overnight in water to make sauce with.

Blueberry Wine: Thick and tart, if you use lemons too. I have yet to devise the perfect recipe, but I'm working on it.

BLACKBERRIES

Blackberries don't grow everywhere, so count yourself lucky if you find a good patch, and don't tell every single person you know. They come in the fall, and if there's an early frost, all those green and red ones you've been eyeing expectantly won't happen. Pick your blackberries while you may, is the sad truth; for tomorrow, who knows what may come.

Blackberries are seedy, in the East; they make better fresh than frozen fruit, better jelly than they do jam. Best of all, though, are the jars of thick purple juice that I brew and can. Mixed with a little water, they're like grape juice; or steaming hot, a cordial to cup in curved hands as you sit as close as you can to the stove, fighting off a chill that almost got you. For blackberries are very high vitamin C sources; none better, not even rose hips. They make those "organic vitamin C" tablets, often, out of blackberry juice. Blackberry juice as it is is pretty fine syrup on a pudding or a custard, too. Or pancakes . . .

BLACKBERRY JUICE OR CORDIAL

Put your blackberries in an enameled pan and crush some with a clean bottle to bring out a little juice. Simmer them slowly on the side of the stove until soft, 2 to 4 hours. Then hang them overnight in a bag or several bags to strain out the juice. Next morning knead out any remaining juice before discarding the berries. Heat the juice and stir in honey or sugar until sweet enough to drink; simmer until thick. Pour boiling hot into a clean jar or jars and store in a cool place; will keep several months. To keep longer, seal in canning jars: see page 229. To make jelly of this juice, see page 231.

APPLES

Of all the fruits on the farm, apples come last, and best, and most. You can pick a box or two of early yellows, maybe, in August; or have a pie or two of green drops in September. But the real apple season is after the frost, when other fruit and garden work is done. And thank goodness, because there is an awful lot to be done with the apples.

To begin with, there is gathering. Apples come and go, in the old orchards; a tree untended might yield heavily only once in five years. So no matter how many trees of our own we have, it seems I'm always on the lookout for a bonanza yield, by some deserted farmhouse, cellar hole, or even just a clearing.

There are hundreds, maybe even thousands of varieties of apples, and although it might be fun to try to identify them, it's really not important unless you're into botany. I sometimes wonder if the folks who planted them knew their names, though. I think more likely they thought of them, as I do, by their functions, which are:

Pie Apples: Large, tart, green apples, these are nevertheless soft and watery when they ripen, and bruise easily. They are the best apples for pie and applesauce. A good pie-apple tree is hard to find, and yields rarely. Perhaps they need a lot of tending.

Keeping Apples: Firm, often small, and very dense, with a thick, leathery skin. Keeping apples aren't hard to find; they survive well. Usually they're too sour to eat until they've been stored a few months in a cool place; then they become suddenly crisp and sweet. However, keeping-apple trees frequently bear few apples, even in their best years. They should be picked before they drop, so they ripen without bruises.

Eating Apples: Sweet apples, whether crisp or grainy, aren't meant for long keeping, although they will keep for a month or two. They tend to make mushy pies, too. If you have a surplus, use them for applesauce, which will require very little sugar or sweetening; but you should throw a few tart apples in that sauce to pick up the flavor.

Red Crabs: Almost every old orchard has a tree of tiny red crabs. You can make apple jelly or syrup out of almost any kind of apple, but there's more pectin in the crabs, and red-skinned crabs make a special tart, red jelly or syrup that literally glows on the pantry shelf.

Hawg Apples: If you've ever wondered what the use is of all those trees that bear bushels and bushels of small, green, sour apples, they are for feeding up pigs before slaughter. These trees bear every year and are very sturdy, being more than half wild. The apples can be used in cooking but are greatly inferior to those bred for specific purposes.

When possible, I pick apples into separate crates and boxes for the above purposes. I stack the boxes in the pantry, or any cool place (the barn might do) until I'm ready to deal with each box. Pie and eating apples will keep a couple of months, during which time we eat them, or can them as applesauce or slice apples. Crabs are made into jelly, and hawg apples fed to the animals.

Keeping apples should be stored outside (frost or no frost) in a cool place for about 2 weeks, in shallow boxes, no more than 2 or 3 apples deep. Then you should bring them in and sort through them carefully, weeding out all those with bruises, splits, or wormy spots. Only the most perfect apples really keep. Wrap each in newspaper or stack in those pressed paper racks you can get free from the supermarket (especially in the fall). They ought to be good until mid-February. When you notice one in five is going bad, bring them all up and use whatever you have within a week.

BAKED APPLES

Whoever heard of baking apples without stuffing them? We did! What a joy! Have them for tea! Serve a mob without any fuss! Wash, if dirty, and stick in the oven in a greased pan:

as many ripe, sweet apples as you want to eat

Bake at 350° for 30 minutes. Serve as they are or with unshelled, hot nuts that you just put in there along with the apples.

BAKED STUFFED APPLES

Well, if you want to get fancy. Carve shallow circles in the top of each large, perfect, sweet apple.

Scoop out the core with a small sharp spoon. For four apples, mix together:

1 Tb. brown sugar
1 Tb. butter
1 Tb. raisins or currants
  or blueberries
3 Tb. flour or breadcrumbs
1 pinch cinnamon
1 pinch allspice or a grating of nutmeg
1 Tb. chopped nuts (optional)

Stuff the apples, place on a greased pan, and bake at 350° for 30 minutes. Baked apples are lovely cold, too. Sometimes people pour cream over them, or serve them with lots of chilled yogurt.

APPLESAUCE

Applesauce is about the easiest thing on earth to make in large quantity, if you have a food mill. No peeling or coring is necessary; just chop, cook, and run it through, maybe add a little sweet or spice.

The best apples are large, ripe, tart apples. You can use sweet apples if you like (they will require little or no sweetening) but they have no flavor, so throw in a few tart ones along with them.

Always use enameled, pyrex, or stainless-steel pots, bowls, and containers when working with fruit; iron and aluminum are affected by fruit acids and darken the fruit.

This applesauce will be brown, not pale blond. If you desire light-colored applesauce, add a teaspoon of ascorbic or citric acid, or 3 Tb. lemon juice to the water you chop apples into. Be sure water coats every apple by tossing them as you pile them in.

Put in a large pot:

1 cup water

Fill the pot with:

halved apples

Put on a lid and bring the water to a boil. Stew and simmer until they burst with softness; mash them down and simmer 30 minutes more. Run through the largest plate of a food mill. Return to the pot, and add water as needed. Sweeten to taste with:

sugar, honey, or molasses

If you are not going to can this applesauce, you may flavor it with ground spices. For every quart of applesauce, add up to:

½ tsp. cinnamon
a good grating of nutmeg
1 pinch allspice

1 pinch cloves
1 tsp. vanilla

Another way to flavor applesauce is to put whole spices in a little cloth bag and cook them along with the pot of apples. You might use:

2 sticks cinnamon
3 cloves
half a nutmeg
a small piece of ginger root   •

Take out the bag and wash it, and the spices; dry them in the warming oven. You can use them again once or twice before they lose all their flavor.

ROSE HIP APPLESAUCE

If you have some handy, throw a couple of handfuls of rose hips in with the apples as they stew. The applesauce will be much higher in vitamin C and will also need less sweetening; it might even need some lemon juice.

APPLESAUCE SUNDAES

There is no applesauce on earth quite like those first fragrant kettles full in late September; that stuff needs nothing but a spoon to be enjoyed. Later, though, our jaded palates seem to take more pleasure in mixtures. For example:

1. Heap applesauce in a dish; follow with a liberal scoop of yogurt, a sprinkling of brown sugar or a dash of honey, and a few broken walnuts or pecans.

2. Heap applesauce in a dish; pour over some apple or raspberry syrup; top with frozen raspberries or strawberries.

3. Beat until stiff:

1 cup thick cream or chilled evaporated milk

Mix with:

1 cup applesauce
½ cup broken walnuts or pecans

Spread in a loaf pan and freeze for 1 hour. Take it out and whip with a wire whisk; refreeze for 15 to 30 minutes and serve with:

hot blackberry cordial

4. Heat up some applesauce, adding water until it is thin enough to pour. Ladle it over:

hot gingerbread cake

If you like, you can top this with:

whipped cream or yogurt

There are so many ways to serve applesauce. It's an elegant side dish with pork or beans (or both!) and cornbread. We often have it on pancakes (who can afford maple syrup these days—and we can't *all* make it). It's the best baby food on earth, and since it's easy to can or freeze, you can have it all year round.

OTHER FRUIT IDEAS

FROZEN FRUIT

Everybody knows you can cook with frozen fruit, but did it ever occur to you that it's perfectly delicious plain? You can try:

blueberries
raspberries
strawberries
chopped or sliced apples
chopped or sliced peaches
chopped or sliced melons
cherries
chopped or sliced pineapple
grapes
plums

Plain or in combination, they are very good on yogurt, ice cream, custard, cereal, or just served in a bowl in the middle of the table to munch on. The main thing is to eat them all up before they defrost.

FRESH FRUIT COCKTAIL

Any fruits can be chopped, mixed, and served together. There are really no rules for fruit cocktail. However, some fruits are a little better if they are mixed with each other and some juice (or you can extract juice from them by mashing them a bit, or sprinkling them with sugar) for a few hours prior to serving.
These include:

chopped peeled oranges, grapefruit
raspberries, blueberries, strawberries, blackberries

Other fruits discolor and lose shape and flavor if sliced too soon. They should be added at the last minute, such as:

apples, peaches, pears, bananas

For additional flavor, you can add some dried coconut, or a little white wine (May wine is nice) or some kind of fruit juice: orange, apple, or cranberry. Or you might give it a shot of some special liquor, if you have such a thing around; or a sweet white brew such as that sticky sweet ginger-flavored dandelion wine that nobody wanted to drink because it made you thirsty.

FRUIT LEATHER

Fruit leather can be made with the pulp of any fruit, but those that are slightly tart are best. You can use:

tart apples
peaches
raspberries
strawberries
dried apricots or prunes
blackberries

Cook the fruit over low heat with a little water in the bottom of the pot to keep it from scorching at first.

When it is soft, run it through a food mill, and set it in a very heavy pot, to cook down. Add honey to taste, if you think it is needed.

When it becomes too thick to cook without scorching, spread it lightly on oiled cooky sheets, ¼ inch thick or less. Cover with light cloth and set it in the sun to dry every day for 1 to 2 weeks. If by that time it is still not really dry, set it in a 100° oven until it is. Dust the top with cornstarch, very lightly; turn, and dust the other side. Lay a piece of waxed paper or cellophane over the top and roll it up to keep for winter treats, in a jar, in a cool dark place.

3

GRAINS, NUTS, AND SEEDS

GRAINS

A field of ripe grain is very impressive; to the eye, it almost sings as the wind moves across it. It holds the seed of promise, of fulfillment and harvest, of survival and rebirth. An Austrian friend described, one night, the process of mowing and harvesting and threshing the grain by hand at times in his youth when the machines (like all machines) broke down, and they all pitched in to get it done.

"It was awful hard work," he said. "At the end of the day, you had chaff in your hair and dust in every pore of your body; our faces were black with it, our arms ached, we longed only for bed. But I tell you, when you look at a big pile of grain on the threshing floor, you really feel rich; and there is nothing like it, no money or anything money can buy can compare with it."

And I can see how that is, though I have yet to grow and thresh and winnow grain myself. For grain is at the very base of our food chain, the broad bottom of the pyramid. Most of what you eat in a day comes from grain. Well, cereal, you say. That's grain. Sure, and so is bread, and muffins, pie, and cake; so are noodles, and so is beer and even crackers. Neither dairy, poultry, nor meat products would be possible without grain. In fact, grain is at the source of almost everything you eat, except fruits and vegetables.

One afternoon, not long ago, a friend of ours was standing by her field, a field of wheat newly ripe and being cut, and she said to my husband:

"When we first came to the farm, we used to buy whole-wheat flour. Then we began to get our grains whole, and grind them up; wheat was brown kernels, it came in a sack. Now—" She paused, fingering the ripe sheaves in her arms. "Now we grow it ourselves; and wheat is wheat."

FOOD VALUE IN GRAINS

What's in grains for you? What nutrition do they offer? As far as we know, grains have three general categories of important food value: protein, vitamins, and roughage. The values in whole grains are not highly concentrated, as they are in some special foods such as liver or brewer's yeast. On the other hand, most people don't want to eat liver every day, or make up special concoctions of brewer's yeast and wheat germ. Most people don't even need to do that, anyway, unless they have a particular vitamin deficiency. It is easy enough to keep a steady flow of the nutrients you normally need by cooking and eating with whole grains every day.

THE PROTEIN IN GRAINS: All grains have a certain amount of protein; it varies a little with the type of grain and the richness of the soil it grew in, but in general it is about 3 to 5 grams per cup of cooked grain. (Or, about 2 grams to a cup of whole-grain flour; that is because flour incorporates more air than unground grain, not because it has less protein.)

Proteins are made up of amino acids, and the human body can only absorb protein when it has these amino acids in a certain, specific pattern. Since all grains are low in at least one necessary amino acid, we say that grain is not a "complete" protein, by which we mean that is lower in protein than it would be if the missing amino acids were supplied. However, the foods we ordinarily eat with grains supply those missing amino acids. These "companion foods" include meat, fish, poultry, dairy products, eggs, and beans or soybean products (such as soy sauce). When the missing amino acids are supplied, you can count on getting half again as much protein out of the grain—not to mention what you get from the companion food.

To learn more about your specific need for protein and how much you can get from whole grains, turn to Family Dishes, page 146.

THE VITAMINS IN GRAINS: All whole grains provide well-rounded amounts of vitamins A, E, and the dozen or so substances spoken of as the B-vitamin complex. They also contain the oils and minerals needed by your body for various purposes, including that of absorbing the vitamins they have. These vitamins, minerals, and so forth are subtle things. You would not notice the lack of them overnight; rather, you would "wonder where some people get all the energy" or feel tired and stiff after an ordinary day's work; you take naps, don't think too hard, aren't much interested in sex, and feel in general as though you're getting old. Many people do lack these nutrients, because they are mostly concentrated in the germ of the grain, which is sifted out of refined grain products. "Enriched" cereals and flours only replace tiny amounts of some of the vitamins, which is of little use; the reason they are called the "B complex" is that they operate together. If you lack one, you lack all the others; if you're low in one, you're low in all.

Other than grains, there are very few sources of this B-vitamin complex in the average human diet. You can get them from pills, or shots, but you might not be able to absorb them unless you balance them with other B vitamins, and have some oil at the same time, and so forth; body chemistry is a complicated business, and I think it is better not to spend your time worrying about levels of this and that, as if your body were a test tube. If you stick with whole grains, you don't have to.

ROUGHAGE IN GRAINS: In every kernel of whole wheat, there are three parts: the germ, the starch, the bran. The germ, the innermost part, we know to be full of vitamins and oils; the starch around it contains much protein. The outer bran, however, has little nutrition. It is mostly used as "roughage"; it goes right through the system and, together with other solids, passes out.

For a long time, nobody thought this was very important. Now, however, it appears that people who lack roughage because of eating refined-grain products instead of whole-grain products have a much higher incidence of bowel troubles. The solids from other foods, such as meat, or milk products, or even vegetables and fruits, don't form as substantial a bulk in the intestines. Sometimes they linger there, too hard or too pasty a substance to be passed. After a day or two this becomes very uncomfortable. The repeated strain of trying to eliminate them, however, will eventually lead you to hemorrhoids. Sometimes infections occur from these problems; and continual intestinal difficulties often lead to more serious illness, even cancer of the bowel, which is virtually unknown in parts of the world where grains are eaten whole and roughage from the bran is a part of the daily diet.

So bran, and other grain "roughage," is not really unimportant at all. They have always been a part of man's diet, and should be still.

GRINDING AND MILLING

A grain mill is a tremendously useful piece of equipment. Not only can it be used for making fresh, whole-grain flour on the spot, but you can also grind a wide variety of other products, from cereals to coffee, breadcrumbs to nuts.

WHOLE GRAINS:

1 cup barley	= 1½ cups barley flour (in several moderate grindings)
1 cup coffee beans	= 1 cup ground coffee (in one easy grinding)
1 cup whole corn	= 1½ cups cornmeal (in several hard grindings)
1 cup millet	= 1 cup millet meal (in one easy grinding)
1 cup rolled oats	= 1 cup oat flour (in one very easy grinding)

1 cup brown rice	=	1¼ cups rice flour (in several moderate grindings)
1 cup rye	=	1¾ cups rye flour (in several hard grindings)
1 cup soybeans	=	1¼ cups soy grits (in one hard grinding)
1 cup soybeans	=	1½ cups soy flour (in several hard grindings)
1 cup whole wheat	=	1¾ cups cereal (in one or two moderate grindings)
1 cup whole wheat	=	1¾ cups flour (in several moderate grindings)
1 cup steamed dried whole wheat	=	1 cup bulgur (in one easy grinding)

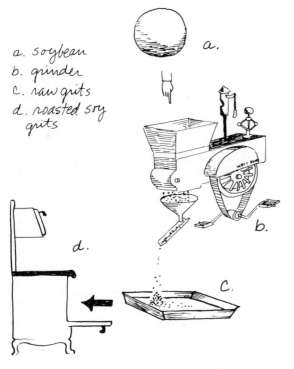

a. soybean
b. grinder
c. raw grits
d. roasted soy grits

BREADCRUMBS: When you see that nobody is going to eat that old end of the loaf, don't let it mold away in a plastic bag. Break into 1 inch pieces and store in an open-topped container until dry and hard. Grind at very loose setting for breadcrumbs. Endlessly useful.

NUTS AND SEEDS: For extra flavor, roast them first; set grinder very loose to make chunks, or fine to make nut butters. Add oil to smooth out nut

butters, as you like. Seal and store in a cool dark place so the oil doesn't become rancid.

ROSE HIPS: Picked in the late fall and dried on racks over the stove, rose hips are easy to grind and store for winter vitamin C drinks, hot or cold.

EGG SHELLS: If you have chickens, and want strong shells (less breakage), dry shells in the warming oven, grind, and add back into their feed.

WHEAT

The grain we eat most often in America is wheat. Wheat has the highest level of protein of any grain, and it grows well in a cool climate. There are (in general) five categories of wheat grown commercially.

Hard Winter Wheat: Grown where the winter is not too harsh, this wheat is seeded in the fall and harvested the next spring or early summer. It is good for bread and cereals, having high gluten and 12 to 14 percent protein.

Hard Spring Wheat: This wheat is grown in the summer where the winters are too cold to grow winter wheat, and used for bread; depending on the season, the protein and gluten may be slightly higher.

Soft Winter Wheat: Soft wheat is grown for pastry flours or "cake flour." The seed is fatter, with a soft husk that doesn't grind up. Soft wheat is used because it is light and has little gluten, comparatively; but it also has less protein (10-12 percent).

White Wheat: Specially developed for pastry, this is a very light spring wheat grown in the West having the lowest protein level of all, 7 to 9 percent.

Durum Wheat: Durum wheat is a northern wheat, seeded in the spring. It has the highest level of protein, some 15 to 17 percent. This is a little hard for bread; it makes a rather rubbery loaf, but is just what's needed for noodles and pasta.

ABOUT WHEAT: Long ago, people mostly harvested their own wheat, and took it, every so often, to the miller, who ground it up for them, with two huge millstones driven by water or other power. Time went by, technology proliferated, and people gravitated to the cities. Flour had to be ground on a more massive scale, so the roller mills, which were developed during the first part of the nineteenth century, came into wide use. When wheat is ground by this process, the germ and bran are flattened rather than chopped into particles, thus making it easy to sift them out. As wheat germ spoils rapidly, due to its oil content, it was to the advantage of the milling companies to sift it out, along with the bran, and market only the fine white starch, which, having all the gluten necessary for making breads or thickening sauces, was acceptable to most people. Moreover, it resembled the fine white flours that had heretofore been available only to the very wealthy. White flour became a status symbol and, finally, a common commodity. Wheat germ and bran were fed to pigs and other animals.

Eventually, however, it began to be evident that people who ate white flour products, exclusively, lacked the elements in their diets once supplied by the germ of the wheat. During World War II widespread vitamin deficiencies caused the British government to enforce "enrichment" of flours by adding synthetic vitamins. The development of "Hovis" bread, with wheat germ added, or put back in, was due to this recognition of the need for vitamins in the daily diet. Eventually American flour producers followed suit and advertised "enriched flour." They also put on the market "bran" or "graham" flour, with the bran put back in; but no commercial American flour is sold with wheat germ put back in, because it will spoil easily unless kept refrigerated or frozen.

What, exactly, are the beneficial results of wheat germ? And is there anything for you in the bran? These questions are easy to evade because the results of vitamin deficiencies aren't rapidly evident or uniform; that is, you don't feel them overnight, or in a week, and not everybody feels them the same way. It has been shown over the years, however, that people who eat whole grains and whole-grain products do not contract the same illnesses in their later years as people who eat white-flour products. Heart disease, for one, is almost unknown in cultures where vitamins B and E are present in large quantities in the daily diet. The oil that spoils so rapidly in wheat germ also contains some lecithin, thought to be the element needed to break down cholesterol in the bloodstream. And good old bran is now coming into the forefront as supplying the crude fiber needed to keep the bowels healthy and functioning regularly.

So, while it is true that white flour isn't, really, in itself "bad for you," it's like giving children water instead of milk. Some children would do all right; others would gradually fall behind those who did drink milk. You can't see it in a meal, a day, perhaps a year; but nobody would willingly risk depriving their kids of milk for all their growing years. It is the same way with wheat. You need what it has, so why bother with the other stuff? It is true that white flour does make some foods (to which we have become accustomed) easier to make and to store. Bread made with white flour and chemical preservatives keeps practically forever. Bread made with whole wheat only keeps for a week; therefore you must make it yourself or pay a high price for it. Piecrust and some sauces and cakes are hard to make with hard whole-wheat flour; we could make them with soft flours, but it is hard to find soft whole-wheat flour, and we have to pay more, in any case, because it has to be kept refrigerated.

What it comes right down to is your own personal choice: whether or not you believe that vitamin deficiencies and the need for roughage really cause all these weakened, pale, malfunctioning bodies, or whether you can change your diet (as it is changed) radically from the diets of the generations that came before us. We pay a lot for schools and roads and hospitals; but they don't do us much good in the end if we wake up every morning feeling half dead. We pay a lot for meat, too, yet we hesitate at the thought of paying more for whole-wheat flour.

wheat

Of course, in the end, whole-wheat costs less, when you consider the cost of hospital bills, vitamin pills, and so forth. Besides, the more people demand whole-grain flours and products, the more facilities will be built to handle them. Whole-wheat flour will never be as cheap as white flour, it is true. But neither will milk ever be as cheap as water.

STEAMED WHOLE WHEAT

Cooked whole-wheat berries are very chewy; that can get to be a bore if you serve too big a plateful at once. Stick to small quantities and serve with a good sauce—say, cheese or miso.

Soak overnight in 3 cups water:

1 cup whole-wheat berries

The next day add twice as much water as the quantity of berries and:

1 tsp. salt

Bring to a boil; then simmer, covered, for 3 hours. If the water is not all taken up cook it a while longer with the lid off.

Variations

1. Add **1 Tb. tamari soy sauce** along with the salt.

2. Use leftover whole-wheat berries in bread (¼ to ½ cup per loaf)—especially a dense loaf with rye or barley flour in it.

3. Add whole-wheat berries to meatloaf. Some people like them in egg dishes, soufflés—things like that.

My kids like them for breakfast, with milk and blueberries.

STEAMED CRACKED WHEAT

To grind for steaming, put the wheat twice through a Corona hand grinder or once through a Quaker Mills grinder at loose setting, so that it is cracked evenly. Wheat cooked this way will be thick, like cereal or cornmeal grits; it is very good with tamari soy sauce and/or butter, or cooked with vegetables (especially green peppers).

To Steam
In a deep, heavy pot, bring to a boil:

2 cups water

Add slowly, stirring:

1 cup cracked wheat
½ tsp. salt

Cover closely, move to lower heat, and simmer 20 minutes. Remove from heat. You may stir cracked wheat during cooking to be sure the bottom is not too hot and getting scorched.

To Sauté and Steam
In a deep, heavy pot, heat:

2 Tb. light oil

Add and cook over moderate heat, stirring, for about 5 minutes:

1 cup cracked wheat

Let the pan cool for a minute, then add:

2 cups boiling water
½ tsp. salt

Cover closely, move to low heat, and simmer 15 to 20 minutes.

Variation

Sauté in 2 Tb. oil in the pot:

1 minced onion
1 slice green pepper

Add and sauté the cracked wheat (1 cup) for a minute, let the pan cool, then add:

2 cups beef broth or water
½ tsp. salt (if the broth isn't salted)

Cover closely and simmer 20 minutes. Remove from heat.

BULGUR: The great advantage of bulgur (as compared to whole wheat) is that it can be cooked more rapidly. A little of it goes a long way. It is very loose and dry, so it combines well with rice. Put in a colander, and submerge in a large bowl of water:

2 to 4 cups whole-wheat berries

Rub the wheat between your hands until the water is cloudy. Discard the water and fill the bowl again; wash 3 or 4 times. Then put the wheat in a pot with water to cover. Bring to a boil; then simmer for about 30 minutes, or until the water is absorbed and the wheat is soft.

Spread the wheat by handfuls on a cookie sheet, one kernel deep, and roast it in a very slow oven (150° to 200°) for about an hour. Sometimes it takes an hour and a half. I test it by taste; when it's no longer the slightest bit squishy, it's done.

Put it through a grain grinder, adjusting so it comes out in chunks too small to be recognizable as wheat berries and too large to be flour.

Store bulgur in a closed jar, in a cool, dark place.

STEAMED BULGUR

To Steam
In a deep, heavy pot, bring to a boil:

2 cups water

Add:

1 cup bulgur
½ tsp. salt

Cover closely, move to lower heat, and simmer 20 minutes. Remove from heat.

To Sauté and Steam
In a deep, heavy pot, heat:

2 Tb. light oil

Add and cook over high heat, stirring, for about 5 minutes:

1 cup bulgur

Let the pan cool for a minute, then add:

2 cups boiling water
½ tsp. salt

Cover closely, move to low heat, and simmer 15 to 20 minutes. Remove from heat.

Variations

1. Sauté some vegetables in 2 Tb. oil in the pan before adding bulgur; you may use:

   ½ cup chopped onion
   2 stalks chopped celery
   1 green pepper

   Then add the bulgur and sauté and steam, or steam as is. You may use water or clear broth as liquid.

2. Add to the liquid:

   2 Tb. tamari soy sauce

3. Cooked bulgur is very good mixed with ground or minced meat, as a dish, in meatballs and meatloaf, or as stuffing for scooped out vegetables. Bulgur used this way is traditional in Syrian cooking.

RICE

Rice is the staple food for nearly three fourths of the world. One reason for this is that rice grows easily in so many places, and is easy to store and ship. It is also easy to prepare, for people who have limited tools and fuel supply. Rice is easy to digest and in its natural form has an abundance of B vitamins.

In the nineteenth century, it became the vogue to "polish" the outer bran off rice kernels. Whether it was done in order to make the rice less sticky, or to cut down the cooking time from 45 minutes to 12 minutes, one result was massive, grim epidemics of beri-beri, all over the Far East.

Nothing then was known about vitamins, and it was not until 1911 that a Polish scientist named Kasimir Funk discovered that there are, after all, substances that the human body cannot do without; he named them "vitamines," and advised against polishing rice. Beri-beri subsided. Not all the effects of B vitamin deficiency are as dramatic as beri-beri, however, and today many Americans suffer from ailments directly traceable to their B vitamin shortage: difficulty in digesting food, short tempers, and general fatigue.

rice

TYPES OF BROWN RICE

Short-Grain Brown Rice: A good deal of this (including "Chico-San") is grown in Sacramento, California; some is grown in Arkansas. This rice is full and fat and noticeably browner than other types of rice. When steamed, it has the most flavor and nutrition of any type of rice, and is also slightly sticky.

Medium- and Long-Grain Brown Rice: These are grown in California, Louisiana, and Texas. Long-grain rice is lighter colored, ranging from pale tan to off-white; the grains are thinner and, when cooked, less sticky than short-grain rice.

Sweet Rice: This is grown in California, or, more often, imported from Japan, where it is popular. It is a tan or greenish round grain, and when cooked, is very sticky and glutinous. Used for breakfast cereal, desserts, such as rice pudding, or pounded to make rice cakes.

ABOUT STEAMING BROWN RICE: From the thousand cultures in which rice is prepared and eaten, daily, there are at least a thousand methods of cooking it. In all, however, one principle remains constant: it is necessary to surround each grain of rice in the pot with water or steam, for at least half an hour.

In order to do this, you must use a pot that holds steam. That means a tight lid, as, for example, a pressure cooker (you don't have to use the pressure). My Dutch oven isn't tight enough; steam leaks out, and the top grains stay dry. Your pot must also be heavy, so the rice doesn't scorch on the bottom. Some people say that it should stick a little on the bottom, but I think that just makes an awful lot of work for the dishwasher. I even oil the bottom of the pot a little to help keep that from happening.

The outer layers of rice grains are very starchy. If you stir the rice while it is cooking, you will loosen the starch and make the rice gummy. Some cooking methods call for washing the rice first; you can do this, but it will cost you some vitamins in the outer layers. In any case, it should not be stirred after water is added. If you want to peek at the bottom and see whether all the water has been absorbed, a quick poke with a small spoon will suffice. Another way to see if the rice is done is to taste a few grains on top.

After the rice is cooked, it is best to let it rest for 15 minutes, in the pot, with the lid on, but off the heat. This will help finish the rice and let each grain "set" before you serve it.

Brown rice takes about 45 minutes to steam. However, if you roast or fry the grains first, they will take slightly less time to cook.

Salting the Rice: Some people cook rice without salt, but they serve it with soy sauce, which is very salty. Others use as little as possible; about ¼ teaspoon per cup of dry uncooked rice. Americans, accustomed to much salt in their cooking, tend more toward 1 teaspoon per cup. I like it in the middle; ½ teaspoon per cup. You should not take salt for granted; find your own level.

Proportions of Water and Rice: Each crop of rice is a little different. Some brown rice takes 2 cups of water per cup of rice; others 2½ cups water.

STEAMED BROWN RICE

This method of cooking rice is the heaviest, and brings out the most natural flavor of the rice. It is a very good way to cook short-grain brown rice, or sweet rice, very chewy and delicious.
Bring to a boil, in a deep, heavy pot:

2½ cups water
½ tsp. salt

Add gradually:

1 cup rice

Boil one minute. Cover the pan closely and move to a simmering spot. In five minutes, check to make sure it's not boiling furiously. Cover again; cook 40 minutes. To see whether it is done, taste a top grain, then poke lightly at the bottom with a spoon. When the water is absorbed, remove rice from heat; let it sit 15 minutes, with the lid on.

Flavoring Rice (Variations)

1. If you wish to add herbs, fresh or dried, chop or crumble them into the water before cooking the rice. Use **parsley, thyme, tarragon, chervil, chives, saffron.**

2. On the other hand, if adding spices, such as **curry, cumin, coriander, tumeric,** they will have more flavor if you toss them in after cooking and let the pot sit for 15 minutes.

3. **Tamari soy sauce** is a favorite Japanese flavoring; add 1 tsp. to 1 Tb. before or after cooking.

SPANISH RICE

Spanish rice is made by flavoring steamed rice with tomatoes and bacon or ham fat.
While the rice is cooking, heat:

2 to 3 Tb. bacon or ham fat

Sauté in it:

1 chopped onion
1 chopped green pepper
3 chopped stalks celery

After 5 minutes, add:

1 cup tomato sauce

or

½ cup stewed tomatoes and ½ cup tomato paste
1 tsp. basil

Simmer this until the rice is done; you may add to it bits of seafood, or ham. Mix rice and sauce lightly. Some people think you should crumble bacon in (in memory of days when bacon was thicker), but thinly sliced bacon just gets lost; serve it separately, crisp.

ROASTED OR FRIED STEAMED BROWN RICE

If the kernels of rice are roasted or fried before steaming, the texture and flavor is completely changed. The grains will be both fluffier and firmer; the taste will be nutty.

To Roast

Put in a deep, heavy pot:

1 cup brown rice

Place over high heat, shaking the pan lightly now and then to keep the rice from burning. A pleasant nutty smell floats up, full of promises; the rice turns yellowish-brown. Let the pan cool, so there won't be a volcano, and add:

2 cups water
½ tsp. salt
1 Tb. tamari soy sauce (optional)

Cover closely and simmer gently 35 to 40 minutes.

To Fry

Heat in a deep, heavy pot:

2 Tb. vegetable oil

Add and stir:

1 cup brown rice

After 5 or 10 minutes of cooking and stirring, let the pot cool, then add:

2 cups boiling water
½ tsp. salt

You may also add:

1 Tb. tamari soy sauce
1 cup chopped sautéed vegetables (onions, celery, greens, etc.)

Cover tightly, simmer gently for 35 to 40 minutes.

Variations on Fried Steamed Rice

Indian rice: Use ghee (page 120) as the oil and add **1 chopped sautéed onion.**

Italian rice: Use **olive oil** and substitute **2 cups broth** for water. Risotto sometimes has sautéed vegetables in it, sometimes not.

FLUFFY STEAMED BROWN RICE

There are various ways to make brown rice light and fluffy. You can use long-grain rice, for one; it is naturally less sticky. You can also wash off some of the starch (and vitamins); and you can start it in cold water, which, for some inscrutable reason, makes it stick together less.

Wash in 2 to 4 changes of cold water, rubbing grains between your palms, until the water stays clear:

1 cup long-grain brown rice

Place it in a deep, heavy pot, with:

2 cups cold water
½ tsp. salt

Seal the pot with a tight lid, and bring rapidly to the boil. Move to lower heat and cook 35 to 40 minutes. To see whether it is done, taste a top grain, then poke lightly at the bottom with a spoon. When all the water is absorbed, remove the rice from the heat; shake the pot a few times and let it sit 5 to 10 minutes.

Additions to Rice

1. Before cooking the rice, you may heat 2 **Tb. light oil or clarified butter** (page 120) in the rice pot and sauté any of the following:

   1 chopped onion
   1 chopped green pepper
   ½ cup chopped celery

   When the vegetables are translucent, let the pot cool, and add the rice and hot or cold water. Cook as above.

2. Before cooking the rice you may add to the pot:

   ½ cup raisins or currants or other chopped dried fruits
   ½ to 1 cup chopped walnuts

   Cook as above; you might want to spice this with tumeric, curry, etc. Add spice by pinches, tossing and tasting.

CORN

Corn was the staple grain of the American Indians, and was passed on to the first white settlers. It was a long time before these settlers branched out and began growing other kinds of grains, so it's small wonder they had so many recipes for corn, or that many of them are so simple, involving little more than grain, salt, and water.

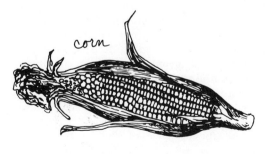

Fresh corn was then (as it is now) eagerly awaited each year; it was called "green corn" while it was still sweet and tender. But piled in open slatted corncribs, it soon became as hard as nails. It was easy enough to get off the cob, but pretty tough eating. Once it dried hard, it could be ground up, as any hard working Indian woman could have testified, between two rocks; but it was a slow process, so other means were found to make it palatable. One was by soaking it in a rough lye made from water and hard wood ashes. After the lye softened the skins, the corn was washed before pounding it into "hominy." This was done by the bucketful in the top of a burned and hollowed-out stump, with a smaller log as the pounder; the heavy pestle would be suspended from a bent, limber sapling, so even a child could operate it. And children did; usually there would be one hominy block in a neighborhood, and the kids were sent around to pound a bucketful for the week's use. After pounding, the hominy was washed again, and boiled up into a soft white pudding.

Once mills appeared, corn could be ground into coarse meal, or twice ground into a fine powder. Cornmeal could be boiled, with water, to make "grits" or "mush." The mush would firm as it cooled; it could be refried for another meal. Uncooked ground corn could be mixed with salt and water and a little rendered fat from a bear or pig, and fried or baked (in a three-legged kettle— who had ovens?) as Corn Dodgers. If you were rich, or lucky, and had a cow or a hen, milk and eggs were added; then you could make cornpone, batter cakes, hush puppies, and Indian pudding. A Southern favorite was spoonbread, an egg-rich corn pudding, served hot and puffy; in the North they liked to make what they called Johnny bread, or Journey cake, crisp and thin, for carrying on a day's march.

Eventually, fields got stumped, the woods (and Indians) pushed back, and other grains were grown, particularly the protein-rich wheat that the newer immigrants remembered from the Old Country. But corn had gotten to be so much a part of life that many people just went on cooking with it, mixing it in with the wheat. So you find recipes for samp cereal (a mixture of corn and cracked wheat), and corn-wheat breads, cakes, brown breads, gingerbread, and so forth.

Despite the evidence of the hardy folk who made so much use of it, corn is the least nutritious of all grains, having only slightly more than half the amount of protein in wheat, rye, oats, or rice. It also has fewer minerals and B vitamins, although

it does have a substantial amount of vitamin A. Indians and settlers alike depended much more on meat and fish for their protein. Perhaps one reason for our national habit of high meat consumption (compared to other cultures) has its roots in the settlers' dependence on a grain that didn't have much protein. Interesting to think about, anyway.

Because corn does not have as high a level of protein as most other grains, you should be careful when serving it to include other protein foods such as milk and eggs, to make up for its deficiency.

CORN MUSH, POLENTA, OR GRITS

Boil in a deep, heavy pot:

4 cups water

1 cup dried skim milk

1 tsp. salt

Sprinkle in slowly, stirring as it thickens:

1 cup coarse cornmeal

When it is thick, set on a lid and move to low heat. Simmer 20 minutes.

If you add the cornmeal too quickly, it will become lumpy. Put it through a food mill to make it smooth again.

Variations

1. *Polenta*: After cooking, before serving, add:
   1 cup grated hard cheese, like Parmesan.

2. Substitute **2 cups milk** for 2 cups water; do not allow it to boil, but heat to just under boiling and add cornmeal. Leave out dried milk.

3. Cool and then refrigerate the mush in a greased loaf pan. Slice into thick slabs and fry in olive oil, butter, or bacon fat.

4. Serve corn mush with **poached eggs** on top, ham on the side, or sausages.

5. Cool the cooked corn to a temperature your hand is comfortable in; mix it with **2 or 3 beaten eggs.** Bake at 400° 30 minutes, until crisp. Serve, if you like, with thick tomato sauce.

OATS

Oats are a plump, pale, delicious, high-protein grain, and they are easy to grow in any northern climate. The only real practical drawback to home-grown oats is that whole oats have a tough husk that doesn't really grind up very well, either in the hand-operated mills or in one's mouth. It sort of flattens, like wheat chaff, and then sticks in the throat.

oats

This husk softens easily in water, however, and by a simple method of steaming and flattening we have rolled oats, which are not only palatable and nutritious, but also partly precooked, so that they can be eaten without cooking. Rolled oats can be bought in 50- or 100-pound sacks from bulk health food distributors for very little (around 10 cents a pound now, in 1975) and are a good deal no matter how you look at it. You can add milk and a handful of raisins and have very good instant food; or cook them briefly for a quick hot bowl of oatmeal. You can mix rolled oats with a little oil and honey, and toast them in the oven to make your own granola. Or you can bake them into all sorts of oatcakes, bars, cookies, cakes, and breads. The Scots traditionally mixed oats and water with ground or diced meats for a kind of cereal-based sausage; they stuff all sorts of things with this mixture, including their famous Haggis (sheep's stomach). Rolled oats are very, very easy to grind into a very fine, heavy flour, which has many uses. It is much better for dredging meats or vegetables than is home-ground whole-wheat flour (which tends to be on the gritty side). This flour is good to bake with too. Being very high in fat it is terrific for cookies and pie crusts, especially mixed with wheat germ or bran.

Hulled whole oats also have their uses. You may steam them overnight for a really chewy full-flavored oatmeal. Or you can soak the raw grains and serve them in a salad; or sprout the seeds for salads, stir-fried vegetables, or as an ingredient in bread.

FAMILIA

If you don't have a grinder, you can leave the rolled oats whole, and bash up the nuts with a mortar and pestle of some sort.

Set a grain grinder very loose and put through it:

3 cups rolled oats
1 cup whole unroasted almonds

Put these in a big wide bowl and add:

1 cup rolled oats, unground
½ cup raw sugar
1 cup currants
1 cup chopped dried apples
1 cup roasted wheat germ

Mix very well with your hands and store in a glass jar.

ROASTED OAT CEREAL

Spread on cookie sheets and roast at 150° to 200° for 30 minutes:

2 cups rolled oats
1 cup wheat germ
1 cup chopped walnuts
1 cup coconut

Put through a grain grinder, set very loosely:

2 cups rolled oats, unroasted

Mix everything together in a big wide bowl and add:

1 cup chopped dried apples
1 cup chopped dried dates
2 Tb. nutritional brewer's yeast (optional)

Mix by hand; store in a glass jar.

LIGHT GRANOLA

This is a very light, dry version of granola, and it isn't very sweet. It is very good with fresh or frozen fruit.

In a small saucepan, mix:

⅓ cup light vegetable oil
⅓ cup honey
⅓ cup water
1 pinch salt

Heat gently (so that the honey and oil will mix). Meanwhile, mix together in a big wide bowl with your hands:

6 cups rolled oats
1 cup coconut
1 cup sunflower seeds
½ cup ground hazelnuts

Give the liquid mixture a last stir before you pour it over the dry ingredients. Mix everything together with your hands and strew the uncooked granola over cookie sheets or baking pans, thinly, so there are no lumps or deep spots. Do it in batches if your oven can't take it all at once.

Bake at 150° to 200° for 30 minutes.

Cool and store it in glass jars.

OATMEAL

Oatmeal should be firm, not soupy. If you are cooking it quickly, for less than half an hour, use less water than if cooking for a long time. For getting started in the morning, always have something else with oatmeal; milk is easy, but it could be eggs, or cheese, or meat, or even tamari soy sauce and roasted sunflower seeds; any of those will bring the level of protein in a cup of oatmeal up, from 3 grams to 5 grams, as well as adding to it.

To Cook Quick Oatmeal
Bring to a boil:

3 cups water

½ tsp. salt

Add:

2 cups rolled oats

Move to moderate heat, cover, and cook 10 minutes.

To Cook Slow Oatmeal
Bring to a boil:

4 cups water

½ tsp. salt

Add:

2 cups rolled oats

Move to low heat, cover, and simmer 1 hour or longer. If it gets too thick, add more water so it won't scorch on the bottom.

Variation: Roasted Oatmeal
Before steaming, put:

2 cups rolled oats

in a heavy iron skillet over good steady heat and roast them, stirring constantly, for about 5 minutes, until they begin to smell nutty. Then add:

3½ cups water

and steam 10 minutes. Serve with tamari soy sauce, gomasio, roasted sunflower seeds, and/or butter.

MILLET

Millet is widely grown in Africa, and in other areas where the climate is too warm for wheat or rye and too dry for rice. A lot of people depend on it for daily grain; but to those who have the choice, rice is more popular. Nevertheless, millet is more nutritious, having more amino acids; it's closer to being perfect protein for human consumption than any other grain.

millet

Steamed whole, millet makes a dense, bland grain with a curious crunch. It has more flavor if it is first roasted, dry or in oil. Like buckwheat, it is best when combined with other grains or vegetables. It cooks quickly, in 10 to 15 minutes.

Ground millet is almost exactly like cornmeal and may be used too instead of cornmeal; unlike corn, it is very easy to grind.

STEAMED MILLET

Heat a deep, heavy pot, and put in:

1 cup millet

Shake the pan a little to roast it evenly for 5 to 10 minutes. Let the pan cool and add:

2 cups water

½ to 1 tsp. salt

Cover closely, bring to the boil, and simmer for 10 to 15 minutes, until the water is taken up. Shake the pan and let it sit, covered, for 10 minutes.

Variations

1. Use half buckwheat, half millet; roast and cook as above.

2. Add sautéed vegetables; toss in with cooked millet, or steam them in the pot along with it.

3. Add ground sautéed meat to the millet before steaming.

RYE

My relationship with rye is ambivalent. Sometimes I go on long binges (usually in the winter) having to do with pickles and herring, sour cream and borscht, or black bean soup, slabs of funky cheese, and great crusty loaves of solid, chewy, sour rye bread. Rye speaks to me: of troikas, and potato moonshine, and endless snow, the vast steppes shining under the fierce cold stars. Rye tells of a sustenance that goes beyond the moment.

rye

Rye is the wheat of the north, and is in fact very like wheat, both in the way it's used and the nourishment it gives. As a flour, it grinds up finer than wheat, though, and thus makes a very much denser bread. Rye is harder than wheat: difficult to grind, heavy to knead, and slow to chew. Rye breads are often made with some sourness in them, such as whey, or sourdough yeast, to liven the mouth, set juices flowing. But rye itself has a special flavor, a tasty tang that curls around the tongue and stays with you. And a loaf of rye bread, being less airy than a loaf of wheat, doesn't dry out as fast. It's better bread for traveling, for keeping.

Rye has other uses: it can be used whole, as cereal; steamed and rolled rye is eaten like rolled oats, or added to them; rye crackers are terrific. But bread remains the most common use of rye grain, at least around my house . . . See **Breads, pages 59, 62, and 64.**

BARLEY

Barley was once a staple in the English, Scottish, and northern European diet; those old cookbooks are full of recipes for barley stews and puddings and breads. It was easier for the small farmer to grow than wheat. Nowadays, with wheat readily available, few people realize how versatile and useful it can be in the kitchen.

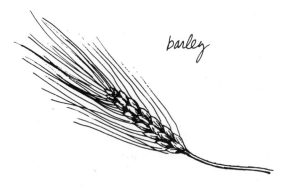

barley

Barley is "pearled," the inedible outer husk being partly or wholly removed. As with most grains, many vitamins are on the outside, so barley that is less rigorously pearled is more nutritious. (You can tell; good barley is brownish.) Barley is almost as high in protein as wheat, especially if it is grown in rich soil (the best comes from Minnesota and South Dakota).

The two best uses of barley I have found are in breads (ground) and in soups (whole). It makes the bread chewier, denser; it is particularly good in unyeasted breads, which tend to be heavy and dry if all whole-wheat flour is used. In soups, it should be cooked at least 6 hours; it is edible in 2, but not nearly so good as after hours and hours of simmering.

SOAKED GRAINS

Grains soaked in water until they soften are delicious, and very high in vitamins. They become slightly sweet, and chewy. You can eat them as they are (instant food, good on trips) or add them to salads.

Soaking grains is a lot like sprouting them, except it doesn't take as long. Put a cup of grain in a wide-mouth quart jar and fill with water. Different types of grain take different amounts of time to soften:

wheat: 2 days
oats: 6 hours
buckwheat: 3 hours
barley: 4 hours

If you decide, after all, to cook them, soaked grains cook very much faster than raw grains.

OVERNIGHT CEREALS

Whole oats, cracked wheat, cracked rye, ground corn, and samp (a traditional New England mixture of cracked wheat and ground corn) are at their best if simmered at very low heat for 6 to 8 hours, or overnight. You could do this on the right front plate of a wood stove, or on a heat stove. If you are not sure the heat will be slow the whole time, you should do it in the top of a double boiler, over simmering water. The hot cereal will be ready for eating just as you stumble down the stairs or ladder buttoning your shirt and on your way out to milk the cow; it's much better than a dry hunk of cold bread, or breakfast after milking.

SIMMERED GRAINS

Bring to a boil in a deep, heavy pot:

3 cups water
1 tsp. salt

Add and stir in:

1 cup whole oats, ground corn, cracked wheat, or samp

Cook rapidly for 15 minutes; then move to a slow spot and let it simmer. If the heat is not very slow, cook in the top half of a double boiler. Simmer 6 to 8 hours, or overnight.

LEFTOVER SIMMERED CEREAL

Refrigerate, then slice and fry in hot butter, ham fat, or oil.

Put through a food mill to get out the lumps; add to muffins or bread.

CREAMED CEREALS

Good breakfast cereals, or baby food; have it with tamari soy sauce and butter instead of milk and sugar. Little kids love soy sauce. You can make up

cereal creams every 3 days and store them, refrigerated, for easy instant infant food.

RICE CREAM

Roast lightly in a dry skillet:

1 cup brown rice or sweet brown rice

When golden brown, take off the heat and grind two or three times, to a sort of gritty flour. Put in a deep, heavy pot:

2 tsp. light vegetable oil

When hot, add the ground rice and cook until a lovely smell comes up. Very gradually (watch your hands) add:

1 cup hot water

stirring as it thickens. Then add:

3 cups hot water
½ tsp. salt

Bring to a boil, stirring from time to time, then cover tightly and simmer 45 to 60 minutes.

OAT CREAM

Bring to a boil:

3 cups water
1 tsp. salt

Add and boil 5 minutes:

1 cup rolled oats

Cover tightly and simmer 30 minutes. Put through a food mill.

GRAINS AND SUMMER VEGETABLES

Rice and ground wheat, together, make a very solid and substantial dish. They are best complemented, therefore, by the lightness of sautéed summer vegetables. Served with a bean dish, this is not only delicious but also provides plenty of protein.

Sauté together in 2 Tb. oil:

1 to 2 cups zucchini (or half an eggplant), chopped the size of walnuts
1 chopped onion (or ½ cup chopped scallion tops)
½ cup sunflower seeds
1 chopped green pepper (optional)
½ cup chopped mushrooms or puffballs (optional)

Add:

2 cups cooked ground wheat or bulgur

1 cup cooked rice
¼ cup water
2 Tb. tamari soy sauce
½ tsp. curry powder

Cover and cook over low heat or in a casserole in the oven for 30 minutes. Serve with a wet dish such as:

French or Italian-Style Beans (page 157)
Lentil Stew (page 159)

BUCKWHEAT (A SMARTWEED)

Buckwheat is not a grain nor, as some people suppose, a legume. It's a member of the smartweed family, which includes, of all things, burdock, and rhubarb. However, it is high in protein, minerals, and B vitamins, like the true whole grains, and it is cooked (more or less) like them, so we think of it as grain, mostly.

buckwheat

As a plain steamed "grain dish," buckwheat is seldom a popular item. It is better roasted first, either dry or in oil, and better yet combined with yogurt, which somehow changes the dry texture into something quite a lot tastier.

Buckwheat is easy to grind, and makes a very delicious nutty-flavored flour. This flour is a little heavy to use alone but is good combined with wheat in breads, muffins, and especially pancakes.

Buckwheat is also good combined with ground or minced meat, in meatballs, meatloaf, and in stuffings for poultry or game.

Soaked uncooked buckwheat is delicious in salads.

STEAMED BUCKWHEAT, OR KASHA

Most people prefer buckwheat (also called kasha, or groats) roasted before it is steamed. Roasting firms the texture, which is otherwise mushy and dry, and brings out the strong nutty flavor.

In a deep, heavy pot, heat 3 Tb. oil and add:

1 diced onion
1 cup buckwheat

Cook rapidly 5 to 10 minutes, stirring. Cool the pan a bit and add:

2 cups water
½ to 1 tsp. salt

Simmer 15 minutes, until dry. Toss in:

½ to 1 cup yogurt

The yogurt disappears; the grain becomes tender and delicious. Serve at once.

Variations

1. Use clear broth (any kind except fish) instead of water.

2. Mix with cooked millet, or cook millet and buckwheat together.

3. Mix with cooked rice.

4. Sauté **green pepper, celery, or ground meat** along with the onions. After cooking, substitute **tomato juice** for yogurt.

5. Other uses: See **Soaked Grains** (page 52), **Stuffings** (page 189), **Meatballs and Meatloaf** (page 165).

SEEDS AND NUTS

Seeds and nuts are similar to grains in their nutritional value, but their goodness is more concentrated. They're rich food, and we eat them in small amounts.

You can buy nuts and seeds shelled, or unshelled. Unshelled they will keep practically forever. With the shells off, however, the high oil content soon causes them to go rancid, unless you keep them (along with your wheat germ) in the freezer.

Different kinds of nuts and seeds have different uses (and prices). Buy a variety and learn to use them in your cooking.

Sesame Seeds: These are expensive, but a few go a long way. Sprinkle them on bread, rolls, or mix in toppings for casseroles. Roasted and coarsely ground with a little salt, you can make gomasio, a delicious garnish for rice, fish, and any grain dish (see next page).

Sunflower Seeds: These are very high in protein and very inexpensive compared to other seeds and nuts. Dry-roasted or sautéed in oil, they make good nibbling in the afternoon or evening. Add them to granola, or roast them and add to familia. Or roast and mix them with dried fruits and other nuts for a hiking mix or traveling food; they supply the oil that any survival expert will tell you is hard to forage in the wilds. Raw or roasted, they may also be ground, added to breads, cookies, and cakes, or used as part of the "flour" for whole-grain pie crust. Roasted and coarsely ground, they may be used as a variation on gomasio.

Pumpkin or Squash Seeds: When you whack open a squash, take out the seeds and separate them from the stringy flesh; toss them in a little oil or oil plus tamari soy sauce. Roast 20 minutes in a hot oven.

Almonds: Almonds are hard nuts, with a very special flavor that fades soon after shelling. You may slice or grind almonds and use them on cookies, or in familia; or you can chop and sauté them in a little butter and mix them with green beans or on top of fish.

Brazil Nuts: Large, soft nuts, Brazils are very good in cookies or as topping for yeasted rolls and pastry.

Cashew Nuts: Cashews are a soft, sweet nut, very good raw in a hiker's mix, or roasted as a snack. Sometimes used on yeast rolls.

Filberts or Hazelnuts: Fresh filberts have a wonderful flavor, brought out even more by roasting. Use like almonds: in familia, granola, or baking.

Pecans: Pecans are ridiculously expensive. Softer than walnuts, with a gentle flavor, they are good raw or baked. Very good in custards, pies, or ice cream.

Walnuts: Walnuts are an old standby in baking, but they aren't as good raw; they have a funny bite unless they are very freshly shelled. Use them in cookies, nut breads, nut loafs, in cakes or on

breads. Deep-fried in hot oil for a minute or so, they are terrific.

Peanuts: Peanuts are a great buy, raw and shelled. Roast them for snacks or "pocket food"; make tamari peanuts or even fancy beer nuts. To make peanut butter, roast them 1 hour at 150°, then grind them and add a little oil. Or you can roast and grind them coarsely, for dessert toppings or as a condiment traditionally served with an Indian curry.

ROASTING SEEDS AND NUTS: Seeds and nuts aren't quite so nutritious roasted, but they sure are tasty. There are two basic ways you can roast them: in the oven, or in a pan on top of the stove. In the oven is a bit better, from the point of view of even roasting. In the pan is safer, however, if you are (as I am) forgetful. Five minutes after they're done they begin to burn; instead of lovely toasted seeds, you have a smoky kitchen and a whole tray of chicken feed.

OVEN ROASTING (DRY)

Scatter the seeds lightly over a baking sheet. Put them in the oven, and don't forget them.

SEED	TEMP.	TIME
Sunflower seeds, hulled	150°–200°	20 min.
Pumpkin or squash seeds, unhulled	400°	20 min.
Sesame seeds, hulled	150°–200°	5-10 min.
Peanuts	150°	1½–2 hours

TAMARI NUTS AND SEEDS

In a small bowl, mix:

1 tsp. to 1 Tb. tamari soy sauce

1 tsp. light oil

½ cup sunflower seeds, peanuts, or other nuts

Roast as above.

BEER NUTS

Roast 1 hour at 150° in an oiled pan:

1½ cups peanuts

Mix in a bowl:

2 Tb. honey

1 tsp. tamari soy sauce

1 tsp. light oil

1 pinch salt

Take out the peanuts and toss them in the mixture. Roast for ½ to 1 hour longer at 150°. Roll them around in the pan as they cool to pick up the honey.

GOMASIO

Gomasio, goma shio, or sesame salt, is a garnish of ground sesame seeds and salt, commonly found on the Japanese table; it is served with rice or other bland foods. It tastes a little like peanut butter. Kids love it.

Sesame seeds must be imported and, to us, are expensive—but they're well worth it for gomasio. Since only a few tablespoons are used in a meal, a pound or two of sesame seeds will do my family for a year.

The main thing about gomasio is roasting the seeds without burning them. You can do this in the oven, for 20 to 30 minutes at 275°. In 45 minutes they will burn, however, so if you are forgetful, perhaps it would be better to do it in a frying pan, stirring constantly for 10 or 15 minutes over low heat.

In any case, roast:

1½ cups black, brown, or white sesame seeds

Add:

1 tsp. salt (macrobiotic cooks favor sea salt)

Grind loosely in a blender, grain mill, or with a suribachi (a Japanese mortar with a scored surface) and pestle until the seeds are mostly pulverized— leave about a fourth of them whole, so the gomasio is crunchy rather than pasty.

Gomasio loses much of its flavor within a few days, so you shouldn't try to make too much at one time. Store in a tightly lidded jar in a cool place.

4
BREAD MAKING

Some of my earliest memories are of my father or mother making bread. Homemade bread leans more to ritual than recipe: first of all, there is the moment when you realize you're almost out, and plan a day to make the next batch. Then there's the mixing, deciding which goodies go in this time: Shall we make raisin bread? Is there a little wheat germ around? How about one loaf mixed with thyme and garlic? Then the kneading; my mother used to put the big enameled baby bathtub with dough in it on the kitchen floor and let us pound and fold it as long as we liked (with clean hands). Finally, the whole house is transformed by the smell of baking bread, and anyone in it suddenly finds some good excuse to hang around the kitchen, waiting for a "test" slice. The big loaves cooling on clean cloths, a lovely sight, and when a neighbor stops by, you give one loaf away because how can you not. It's such a luxury to have fresh bread—you feel so rich, and yet have spent so little.

Equipment for making bread varies from house to house. You need a very large container. I recommend:

A heavy ceramic bowl: It should be large enough for the dough to double in, and thick enough so that in rising the heat is distributed evenly. The sides should not slope out too much. Metal bowls conduct too much heat to the bottom and not enough to the top. You will also need:

A clean cloth: Wrung out with warm water, this is used to cover the bowl during rising so that the dough doesn't get cold and crusty on top from evaporation. Better not use terrycloth; if the dough rises up to touch it and sticks, you will have a time washing it off.

Kneading surface: It should be dusted lightly with flour, and low enough to work on without getting tired shoulders. The more you enjoy your work the more you will knead, and well-kneaded bread is the best, no matter what recipe.

Wooden spoon: Some people like a rubber spatula for stirring up the first mixture of liquid and special ingredients, because it's very good for scraping down the sides. I like a wooden spoon though, because I can measure some ingredients with it (yeast, salt) and because it's nicer to look at.

Baking pans: As long as they're smooth inside and aren't smaller on top than on bottom, you can use about anything. Bread pans, cookie sheets, casseroles, frying pans, muffin tins, cake pans, pie plates, flower pots—to name a few.

HOW LONG WILL IT TAKE TO MAKE BREAD?

In general, you start making bread from 4 to 6 hours before it comes out of the oven. You don't spend all that time working on bread; most of it is rising time.

Before you decide to make bread, you should

read the recipe and figure out how long it will take and whether you are going to be free to work on it at the right times. It is (for example) best not to be baking bread in a wood stove at dinner time. Besides being distracted by other cooking, you will have to have the oven at just the right temperature for an hour or so; and, moreover, it will be full of bread (no room for a casserole).

There are two other considerations in the business of baking bread. One is flour and the other is fuel. If you buy flour preground, all you have to do is check the supply against the recipe (bread takes a lot of flour, about 5 pounds for 4 loaves).

If you grind it yourself, in a small hand grinder, it takes a lot of time and energy. You might consider doing it the day before you bake bread, and thus spread the work out a bit.

The other thing you should do, if you have a wood stove, is slip on your boots and go have a look at the wood pile, preferably the day before. You need dry wood; there is nothing like 4 lovely puffed up pans of dough ready to go in and a slow, hissing fire that won't budge the oven one hair over 200°. If your wood is green, it should be split up good and small and brought in to dry overnight.

KNEADING

The purpose of kneading bread is twofold: (1) to mix in more flour than is humanly possible with a spoon; (2) to stretch the gluten in the flour so that when the yeast releases carbon dioxide into the dough, tiny bubbles will form, with the softened gluten around them like little balloons.

At least 15 minutes of kneading the finished dough will always give you a better bread. You may find it easier to knead bread dough in divided batches. I find 4 loaves at once hard work, and any more seems impossible.

You should knead on a smooth, lightly floured surface. From time to time wipe the surface with more flour. Keep a pile of it handy in one corner to keep your hands dry too.

When you first turn the dough out, it will be very sticky. Keep the surface lightly floured; pat and fold, rather than digging in. Gradually, it will become more workable, and you can become more vigorous. The idea is to keep stretching it, so work it out into a flattened round, using the heels of your hands. As you do so, you may find the mid-dle is still a little sticky, so powder it evenly with a little flour, spread it around, and then fold the dough. Give it a half turn on the board and begin again. Continue around and around for about 15 minutes. Take your time, and when the dough doesn't seem sticky, don't add any more flour, but keep kneading for a while. You can't knead bread too much, or too vigorously. (Kids love kneading—they can punch it, slap it, pound it.)

White bread recipes say to stop when the dough is smooth and glossy. But whole-wheat bread, or other whole-grain breads, will not have a "glossy" dough, especially if the flour is home ground in a small mill. Well kneaded whole-grain dough will hold its shape in a rounded mound, and should be evenly textured throughout. Dough with a large proportion of rye should still be slightly sticky when done; too much rye flour will make the bread heavy.

LETTING THE DOUGH RISE

A steep-sided ceramic bowl is best for rising dough. It distributes heat evenly and keeps warmth in too. Whole-grain dough needs the sides of the bowl to "climb" on, so don't grease the bowl. Sometimes people grease the top of the dough lightly, to keep it from drying out and forming a crust, but I find that if you cover the bowl with a damp tea towel, large enough to fold the edges under the bowl, it isn't necessary to do anything else. The tea towel helps keep warmth in, too.

The temperature in a wood stove warming oven (90° to 100°) is too hot for rising whole-grain bread dough. It is better to raise it more slowly and evenly, at 70° to 80°. Over the warming oven is fine. If you don't have a wood stove, use a thermometer to find a spot in the kitchen (or elsewhere) that will stay at 70° to 80°, out of drafts. Usually these places are high up in the room—on a shelf, or fridge. Also, it'll be out of the way of marauding pets and kiddies.

Let the dough rise until it just doubles in size—an hour, usually, unless otherwise indicated in the recipe.

"KNOCKING DOWN" RISING DOUGH

Dough can rise to triple its original size, but it's best to knock it down before that, when it's about doubled. You can just punch it down, if you're in a terrific hurry; but it's better to do it with a little care. Take it out, scraping down the sides of the bowl. Knead it for a minute, carefully flattening all air bubbles, and finally tucking the sides in to the center. Put the dough into the bowl again, tucked side down. Wet the towel and replace it tightly.

SHAPING LOAVES

To shape any kind of loaf—whether it is to be baked in a pan with high sides or on a flat sheet—don't roll it into a shape. Flatten it slightly, and bring the edges together. Pinch them firmly, without leaving any air holes underneath. Place it on the pan tucked side down (except in the case of **French Bread**, page 65). This stretches the gluten on top of the loaf to form an even crust.

Generally I weigh out dough, to divide it evenly between pans, in my weekly "ordinary baking." I find 2 pounds of dough is the right amount. Unevenly divided, some loaves will be smaller, rise faster, bake quicker—no end of bother.

To form buns and rolls, you may use the same method with smaller pieces. To make bread sticks or fancy rolls, chop pieces of dough the size of your fist and roll them out, slowly, into ropes. These can be baked straight, or wrapped into fancy shapes for supper rolls.

GREASING THE PANS

You can use oil to grease the pans, but sometimes dough will stick to the supposedly oiled surface. I find it much better to grease them with lard. Use a light film. If using oil, flour the pan lightly with fine cornmeal.

INGREDIENTS

Most of what you do or don't do, and how long it takes, depends on the ingredients of the bread you're making. It is good to understand how they work. The two most essential ingredients are:

Flour and Water: For one loaf of bread you use 1½ cups of water and about 4 cups of flour, give or take a cup. One reason this varies so much is the weather: on damp days, flour will absorb water from the air. Another reason is that the same amount of flour will measure out to more cupfuls if it is freshly ground or sifted than if it is scooped out of a sack, where it has gotten packed down. So you add flour until the texture is right, rather than depending on measurements.

Gluten in Flour: Mature wheat contains a great deal of a substance called gluten. If you put an equal amount of wheat flour and water together and stir, it will look and feel like cereal: grainy and easy to stir. But if you let it soak some hours at 70°, it begins to soften and turn gluey. You can easily feel the difference. Lift up the spoon in the mixture; great strings of it will trail after. If you leave it to soak overnight at 70°, even more gluten will be softened, and you will find it hard to lift the spoon at all without bringing the whole mixture along.

Immature or soft wheat has somewhat less gluten. Durum wheat has the most gluten—in fact, it tends to make a tough loaf. Rye and oat flours have some, though not nearly as much as wheat.

Yeast: Farmer's, or baking yeast, and sourdough starter yeast are used in making bread because they make the bread rise to a light, even, pleasant texture. Yeast is a living organism, and when you buy it in either dry or block form it is dormant. It stays alive, but "asleep," until mixed with liquid, given sugar to eat, oxygen to breathe, and kept at 70° to 105°. Under those conditions it begins to divide and multiply and will continue to do so until it runs out of food or air, gets too cold, or is killed by too much heat. As it grows it turns sugar and oxygen into alcohol and carbon dioxide. The alcohol is what smells so divine; the carbon dioxide is what makes the bread rise.

When this carbon dioxide is released into a

dough of nonglutenous flour, it doesn't rise much and it makes a dense, crumbly sort of bread—very tasty, but heavy. When it is released into a gluten-ous dough, however, the gluten stretches around the bubbles of gas like little balloons. A lighter, higher bread, not so likely to fall apart, results. This sort of bread is best for making sandwiches.

However, there are many other uses for bread besides sandwiches, and many other sorts of good bread than yeasted or glutenous bread. You can also make breads by combining different flours with wheat. The wheat will provide the gluten, and the other flours will give your breads texture, vari-ety, and flavor.

Rye Flour: Rye makes a very fine, dense flour. It's hard to grind, and makes the dough harder to knead. I therefore use a little more yeast in a dough with rye in it, and let it rise longer. The flavor is finer and a little sour or dry compared to wheat flour. Rye goes well with sourdough starter yeast, molasses, and sour milk products such as yogurt or whey. Or you may head in a different direction—with honey, eggs, cardamom, and lemon or orange rind. Rye makes a firmer, denser-tex-tured bread; ¼ to ½ cup per loaf, added to whole-wheat bread, makes better sandwich bread than wheat or rye flour alone.

Buckwheat Flour: Buckwheat is a heavy, dense flour, although it's easy to grind. It has a strong nutty flavor, which is even more pronounced when the buckwheat is roasted. A little of it will go a long way; ½ cup per loaf makes fine "buckwheat" bread.

Oats: Oats are dense and chewy when ground. (You can grind rolled oats, too, just as well as whole oats.) Oats have a mild nutty flavor.

Cornmeal: The addition of cornmeal makes bread crunchier on the outside, crumbly on the inside. It's excellent for rolls or gravy-sopping bread.

Soy Flour: Since soybeans aren't grain, soy flour isn't really flour. However, it's a wonderful addi-tion to bread, since soybeans are rich in the amino acids that grains are low in. One cup of soy flour to every 8 cups wheat is enough to increase the protein level of your bread by about a third. Soy flour won't add any noticeable taste to your bread, but it does make it somewhat heavier; I usually add an egg and increase the yeast to balance this.

Beans: In the absence of soybeans, you can add almost any kind of ground beans to bread. They will also bring up the protein level, although not as much as soybeans do.

Ground Seeds: Ground seeds, such as pumpkin, sunflower, and sesame, add delicious flavor to bread. They are even tastier if roasted. They con-tain quite a lot of natural oil, so you should de-crease the oil a little in the recipe. You need not add much; a few tablespoons per loaf are suffi-cient.

Wheat Germ: Wheat germ, like soy flour, supplies the amino acids missing in wheat flour. Half a cup for every 10 cups of flour will bring up the protein level tremendously. Wheat germ is sweet and light, and does not "weigh down" a loaf. The only thing to watch out for is that it goes rancid easily—so keep it refrigerated or, over longer periods, frozen.

Dried Milk: Dried milk adds crunch to the crust and makes the inner bread lighter and tenderer. It's also good for you, cheap, and easy to keep. Half a cup per loaf, added to the water in the beginning, is a good addition to bread. If you are using noninstant dried milk, though, mix it with an equal amount of flour for easier mixing.

Eggs: Eggs do amazing things to bread; they make the loaves both lighter and stronger. They are very good to add to sandwich breads for this reason. You can use up to 3 eggs per loaf, if you have a surplus. Eggs are traditional in holiday loaves—that sweet, luxurious touch to the ordinary.

Sweetening: All sweeteners make the yeasts grow faster, since yeast feeds on sugar. Bread can be made without them, however, since grains have natural sugars in them.

My preference in all breads is molasses, because it has so many minerals and B vitamins, both of which are lacking in white sugar and are much less concentrated in honey and maple syrup. Besides, we like molasses—it tastes good.

Brewer's Yeast: I have never been a big Brewer's Yeast user, but I know it's full of good things, and has the missing amino acids as well. It is not a live yeast and will not leaven the bread. It doesn't have a particularly appealing flavor (to many people) but a couple of tablespoons per loaf will not be noticeable.

Spices: One day last year Tom and Tully Fels served me some bread with sage and thyme in it, and it really opened my mind about what you can put in bread for variety and flavor. I can't think of a spice I haven't tried since then, and they were all good. Spiced breads are specially good with homemade cheeses and home-brewed beer.

Whole-Wheat Berries: Soaked overnight and cooked in 4 cups water, 1 cup of whole-wheat berries add a chewy texture and are particularly good in a dense bread such as rye.

Raisins, Currants, Dried Fruits: Raisin bread is an old favorite, but there are lots of other fruits you can add: chopped figs, prunes, dried apples, apricots, pears, peaches, blueberries, and so forth. Usually I add an egg to these breads to help them hold together. Remember to mix the fruit with flour before adding it or, better yet, a mixture of flour and 1 tablespoon cinnamon, or 1 teaspoon ginger, allspice, nutmeg, or a pinch of cloves.

Onions: A very good addition to bread is half a cup of chopped sautéed onions. You can knead in the onions or flatten the dough with a rolling pin and make Herb Bread (page 63).

Cheese: 1½ cups Cheddar per loaf makes a very crisp, tasty change. Grate the Cheddar in after the sponge has risen. You should decrease the salt by ½ teaspoon per loaf (unless your Cheddar is homemade and unsalted) and use 1 egg per loaf to make the bread stronger and lighter.

IF YOUR BREAD ISN'T ALL YOU EXPECTED

Everybody has different taste in bread, and everybody likes to experiment with it. Sometimes you get bogged down, can't ever seem to get that dream loaf, no matter what you do. Here are a few observations; maybe they will help:

IF YOUR BREAD IS TOO HEAVY, DENSE, SOLID: Most likely the yeast didn't work enough. You need not add more yeast but you should read about yeast and gluten, see pages 58-59, and be sure you're kneading it enough, letting it rise at the right temperature, and punching it down before it drowns in carbon dioxide. The yeast might be getting killed from too much heat in the rising stages. If you're using sourdough yeast or dense flours such as rye or buckwheat, allow a couple of hours of rising time in the pan.

Some people remedy dense bread by substituting white flour; if you substitute up to ¼ white, your bread will be lighter and nobody will really tell the difference. But there are other remedies:

Substituting eggs for part of the liquid makes bread lighter.

Grinding fine flour makes bread lighter.

Careful attention to kneading, rising, and punching down makes bread lighter.

A 350° oven (or 400°, falling to 350° during baking) works wonders, as compared to a 300° oven.

IF YOUR CRUST ISN'T CRISP ENOUGH: You could substitute milk for part of the liquid, or dried milk for part of the flour. You might cut down on the oil or shortening, or substitute sugar for molasses. The way to get that really thick crunchy layered crust, though, is to permeate the crust with water and then bake the water out. There are several ways to do this. The old kiln bread was made crisp because the old kiln ovens, in which the baking fires were built, had to be scrubbed out before the bread went in; hence the dough was hit with a cloud of steam first thing. You wouldn't want to do that to the inside of a stove, but you could preheat a brick in the oven and just before baking, fill a baking pan with boiling water and stick the brick in it, in the bottom of the oven.

Another route to crisp crusts is brushing water on the crust in the last 15 minutes of baking.

IF YOUR BREAD SAGS IN THE MIDDLE: You could be letting it rise in the pan too long.

You could be adding too little flour.

IF YOUR BREAD IS TOO DRY AND CRUMBLY: Mostly this is a problem with white flour; try all whole grains.

Sometimes this is from using white sugar; try molasses or honey.

Leave out eggs or milk; substitute oil for shortening.

Try substituting ¼ rye or oat flour for added weight and chew.

IF YOUR BREAD TASTES YEASTY: Your oven is baking at too low a temperature.

IF YOUR BREAD IS BURNING BEFORE IT BAKES THROUGHOUT: Most likely, your oven is at fault, not the bread. If the oven temperature is rising as the bread bakes, it will burn the bread on the bottom (if it's a modern stove). If you're baking in a wood stove, make sure that it's preheated; otherwise bread will burn on top. If your oven is beyond reproach, though, it might be that you are adding too many strange ingredients for the amount of wheat flour and yeast.

IF YOUR BREAD IS BORING: Try sourdough, see pages 69-70.

Add ground nuts or seeds, see page 59.

Try adding new flours, such as rice, barley, rye, etc. by substituting ¼ of the usual whole wheat with new flour.

Experiment with herb breads.

WHOLE-WHEAT BREAD

This is the standard recipe around our house for just plain bread. It makes 4 loaves (the most that will fit into an average oven). We always grind flour freshly for it; about 5 pounds, or 4 loaf pans filled about ¾ full. That is a lot of grinding and you might want to do it one day, then bake bread the next.

Mixing the "Sponge"
Measure into a very large ceramic bowl, in this order:

2 cups dried milk
7 cups warm water
½ cup vegetable oil
½ cup molasses
2 Tb. (or 2 pkgs.) dried baking yeast

Mix and let rest; mix again, to stir in dissolved yeast. Then add:

1½ Tb. salt
7 cups whole-wheat flour

Beat this "sponge" until your arm gets tired. Cover it with a damp rag and put it over (not in) the warming oven to rise slowly until doubled, about 1 hour.

The Dough: Kneading and Risings
Beat it down and add, cup by cup:

4 cups whole-wheat flour

Beat in each addition until well mixed. When you can't stir any more, spread a cup of flour on the counter and scrape out the dough in a pile. Cover the dough with a handful of flour, pat and fold to mix it in (trying not to get glued in) until you can begin kneading. Gradually knead in:

4 cups whole-wheat flour

Stop adding flour when the dough is firm but not dry; however, keep your hands lightly floured as you continue kneading for 15 minutes (see page 57).

Return the dough to the bowl, cover with a damp towel, and place over the warming oven or at 70°, no drafts, to rise until doubled, about 1 hour.

Sometimes I let this finished dough rise once or twice before forming into loaves, and sometimes I allow as much as 4 risings. The important thing is to "knock it down" (deflate the yeast bubbles) every hour or so. To make the best bread, you should form the loaves when you notice that the dough has become very light and springy to the touch. But when you make this bread regularly sometimes it has to be worked into other schedules; you form loaves when you have time.

When you "knock down" the dough empty it out on the counter and re-form it.

Shaping the Loaves
To shape loaves, turn out the dough and cut into four equal pieces, each about 2 pounds. With lightly floured hands, turn under the sides, seal, turn again, seal. Place each loaf in an oiled or greased bread pan. Decorate and slash tops if you like. Let rise about ¾ hour in the warming oven on pieces of wood, or in a warm place (70°–90°). Meanwhile, raise oven temperature to 400° and bank.

Baking the Loaves
To bake loaves, slide the pans carefully into the 400° oven. In a wood stove, the temperature will probably drop to 350°; that's fine.

After 20 minutes have a look at your bread. If the oven is small (as mine is) the loaf on the firebox side is probably getting pretty brown on one side; you should rearrange it so it doesn't get scorched.

Keep an eye on your fire box when you put bread in the oven. Don't let the wood run out. That sounds absurd, but I make that mistake about once a month, so probably other people do too.

This bread takes about 40 minutes to bake. To be sure it's done, take out a loaf and gently shake it out of the pan onto its side. The bottom should be light brown. If not, return to oven and bake some more.

Cooling the Loaves
When loaves are done, take them out, shake loose from pans, and let them cool on their sides on a very clean dishtowel. Hot bread is hard to slice—except the heel, of course, which is best hot.

SANDWICH BREAD

Of course, any bread will do for sandwiches; but my favorite is one of these: mostly wheat, with half a cup of rye, soy, or buckwheat per loaf. Since these are dense flours, they tend to make the bread a little more compact than all-wheat bread. This recipe is for 2 loaves, and takes about 5 hours to make.

Beat in a large ceramic bowl:

2 eggs

Add:

2 cups warm water
½ cup honey or molasses
1 Tb. dried yeast
1 cup dried milk
5 cups whole-wheat flour

Beat this well and allow to rise for ½ hour, covered with a damp cloth. Beat again and allow to rise another ½ hour, or until doubled, covered with a damp cloth. Then beat in:

1 Tb. salt
2 Tb. heavy oil or 4 Tb. light oil
1 cup soy, rye, or buckwheat flour
¼ to ½ cup roasted ground sesame or sunflower seeds

Beat well, and add, cup by cup, mixing well after each addition:

5 cups whole-wheat flour

After the first 2 or 3 cups you will have to turn the dough out on a floured work surface and knead in the rest. Stop adding flour as soon as the dough is compact enough to work with; keep the surface of the dough lightly floured to avoid it sticking to your hands.

Return to the mixing bowl. Cover with a damp cloth and allow to rise 1 hour, or until doubled in size, in or above the warming oven.

Turn the dough out again and knead it for 15 minutes or so. Be very careful about the gluten; this dough will be heavier and less elastic than whole-wheat bread dough. You must flatten, push it out, and fold it much more slowly and firmly. Keep the bowl warm while you do this.

Return the dough to the bowl and cover with a damp cloth. Allow it to rise again, 1 hour, or until doubled in size, in or above the warming oven.

Take out the dough and flatten it; cover with a damp cloth while you grease the pans. You may make two loaves or make one loaf and a pan of hard rolls and bread sticks (it makes very good bread sticks). Whatever you decide, form your shapes more slowly and carefully than you would with all whole-wheat bread.

Put the bread in pans; slice the tops and decorate if you wish.

Place the loaves, covered with a damp cloth, in the warming oven, and raise the temperature of the oven. Wait until the loaves are really doubled before baking. It may take as long as 2 hours if the weather is damp.

Bake bread sticks at 400° to 450° for 15 minutes;

Bake rolls at 350° to 400° for 20 minutes;

Bake whole loaves at 350° for 45 minutes. If

you would like a very crisp crust bake loaves at 400° to 450° for the first 10 minutes, then let the temperature drop to 350° for the rest of the baking.

ANADAMA BREAD

As the story goes, this feller had a wife named Anna who used to bake his bread; and one time she up and left him, so he had to bake his own. Anna, damn her, he said bitterly, as he threw everything in his dough except the kitchen sink. This will make 3 loaves; or you might try making rolls with it. It takes 4 to 5 hours.

In a heavy pan, bring to a boil:

3 cups water
2 tsp. salt

Sprinkle in slowly, stirring constantly:

1 cup cornmeal

Continue to stir and cook over moderate heat as the cornmeal thickens. Remove from heat and add:

⅓ cup lard or oil
⅔ cup molasses

Stir these in and let the mixture cool to lukewarm. Then add:

2 Tb. yeast that has been dissolved in ½ cup warm
   water
2 eggs
½ cup wheat germ
½ cup dried milk
2 Tb. brewer's yeast
2 cups whole-wheat flour

Beat well and allow to rise in the warming oven, covered with a damp cloth, for 1 hour or until doubled in size. Then add:

1 cup soy flour
1 cup whole-wheat flour

Spread whole-wheat flour on the work surface; turn out the dough and work in:

3 cups whole-wheat flour

cup by cup, slowly, stopping when the dough holds its shape. Knead gently for 5 to 10 minutes. Put the dough in a large warm ceramic bowl and let it rise for 1 hour or until doubled, covered with a damp cloth, in the warming oven.

Turn out; reshape, return to bowl, and recover; allow to rise a second time.

Turn out; shape into 3 loaves or into rolls. Place loaves in well greased or oiled pans and allow to rise for 1 hour while you bring the oven temperature up to 375° and bank it.

Bake at 375° for 40 to 45 minutes or until crusty all over.

HERB BREAD

This recipe makes 2 loaves, or 3 pans of rolls. The aroma while it is baking (from the bread, onions, and garlic) is incredible; and it tastes pretty good, too. This bread makes a good holiday gift. It takes around 5 hours.

In a heavy ceramic bowl, mix:

3 cups water
2 tsp. thyme
1 Tb. dried yeast
1 egg
½ cup dried milk
2 Tb. dark sesame oil
1 Tb. salt
¼ cup molasses
½ cup soy flour
3 cups whole-wheat flour

Beat this well and set it to rise for 1 hour, covered with a damp cloth, in the warming oven. When this sponge has doubled, take it down, and add, by cupfuls:

3 to 5 cups whole-wheat flour

kneading in the last two or three cupfuls on a floured working surface. When the dough is firm, knead for around 10 minutes. Return to the bowl, cover, and let it rise another hour.

Meanwhile, heat in a heavy frying pan:

2 Tb. oil

Add and sauté until limp:

1 chopped onion
2 cloves crushed garlic

Cool these and add:

2 Tb. chopped fresh parsley
1 Tb. chopped fresh chives

When the dough has doubled, take it down and roll it out about half an inch thick and spread it with the onions and herbs. Roll it up like a jelly roll and then mash it around so the goodies are mixed in. Set it to rise, covered, another hour in the bowl.

When the dough has doubled, take it down and shape it into loaves or rolls. Grease your pans and put the dough to rise in them. Raise the oven to 350° while the bread is rising, and bank it. When the oven is hot and the dough well risen, bake it for about 35 to 45 minutes (for bread) or 20 minutes (for rolls). Remove the bread from the pans to cool it.

DENSE PUMPERNICKEL

What they call in the old country black bread. Since it is all rye flour it has a very dense, chewy texture, a crunchy crust and a flavor like rye crisps. It's not sour, but if you like you can make it sour, either by substituting very funky old yogurt for some of the milk, or by substituting sourdough for yeast. You may also add half a cup of steamed whole-wheat berries to the dough for a true Westphalian pumpernickel. This recipe takes 3 hours and makes 1 loaf.

In a large heavy ceramic bowl, mix:

2 cups warm milk (it may be soured)
2 Tb. dried yeast
½ tsp. caraway seeds (optional)
2 Tb. black molasses or treacle
2 or 3 cups rye flour

Cover the bowl with a warm damp cloth and let this "sponge" rise for about 1 hour in the warming oven. Then add:

2 tsp. salt
3 to 4 more cups rye flour

Add this flour by half cupfuls, beating or kneading in each addition as the dough thickens. Stop when the dough is still sticky to touch (working with floured hands) but holds together in a rounded lump. You don't have to knead this bread after adding the flour, but it is important not to let the dough get cold; if you have to go off and leave it in the middle of adding flour, put it back in the bowl and stash it in the warming oven.

When the flour's all in, cover again with a damp cloth and set it to rise 1 hour, in the warming oven. You may let it rise a second and even a third hour if you don't have the oven ready, but punch it down every hour and keep the cloth damp.

You may shape this bread either into one loaf for a loaf pan, or into a round loaf or two long loaves on a cookie sheet. Grease the pan well and shape the loaf or loaves. It is nice to paint the top with:

egg yolk, egg white, or beaten egg

and sprinkle it with:

caraway seeds

Set the bread to rise while you bring the oven up to 350°.

Bake at 350° for about 1 hour, or until the bread is browned and crisp on the bottom. Remove from the pan to cool.

WHEY-SOURED RYE BREAD

While I'm not knocking sourdough, there's more than one way to make bread sour. You can use sour whey for your liquid—either from making curds (pages 127-129), or from dripping a batch of overdone yogurt through a bag. This recipe makes 1 loaf of pumpernickel and takes 4 to 5 hours.

In a large ceramic bowl, mix:

1 cup warm sour whey
2 tsp. dried yeast
½ cup molasses
2 tsp. salt
1 tsp. to 1 Tb. caraway seeds
½ cup dried milk
2 cups whole-wheat flour

Beat well and cover with a damp cloth; let rise 1 hour in the warming oven or until doubled in size. Then beat in:

½ cup oat or soy flour

Turn the dough out on a surface well dusted with rye flour and work in by hand:

1 to 1½ cups rye flour

When the dough is firm enough to hold its shape, stop adding flour; use only enough to keep the surface from sticking to your hands. Knead lightly for about 10 minutes. Return it to the bowl and cover.

sour rye bread

Let it rise for 1 hour, or until doubled, in or over the warming oven. Take out; knead, and return to the bowl.

Let it rise for another hour, or until doubled, in or over the warming oven. Take it out and shape it into a loaf. Cut the top surface and coat with egg white; sprinkle with caraway seeds. Place in a greased pan. Set to rise, from half an hour to 1 hour, or until doubled.

Meanwhile, raise the temperature of the oven to 350°, and bank. The bread will take about 1 hour to bake, so don't put it too close to the top of the oven. You may allow the oven temperature to sink to 300° as it bakes. Take it out when the bottom is crisp and firm. Remove from pan to cool.

FRENCH BREAD

If you make French bread with all white (unbleached) flour, it's indistinguishable from a Paris original. Or you can make it with half whole-wheat flour; it will be just as crisp and delicate, but a little harder to handle and a little smaller. I've tried to make it with all whole wheat; that came out very small and hard as rock. But perhaps you could do it with very finely ground whole-wheat durum flour.

The important thing about French bread is the method—how you handle it. The first time it seems awfully complicated, like cheese. Then you get used to the steps and it seems quite easy.

Mixing
In a small warm bowl, mix:

1½ cups warm water
1½ Tb. dried yeast

While that brews, measure into a large, warm ceramic bowl:

1½ cups white or whole-wheat flour
1½ cups unbleached white flour
2 tsp. salt

When the yeast is dissolved, mix it up. Make a well in the flour and pour in the liquid, stirring in circles around the pool with a wooden spoon, until it is all one gooey mass. Spread:

½ cup white flour

on your counter; turn out the dough, cover with a little of the flour, and roll it around. Set the bowl in the warming oven meanwhile. Knead gently, not tearing the dough, 5 minutes or so.

Rising
Return the dough to the bowl; cover with a damp cloth. Using a thermometer, find a draft-free spot in the room which is 70°. Take a last look at where the dough is in the bowl; you will want it to triple in size. It should take about 2 hours. In any case punch it down when it starts to level off.

Rising Again
When it is risen, punch it down and re-form it into a large bun. Let it rise again at 70°, this time only to double its size.

Shaping the Loaves
Punch down the dough and turn out on the lightly floured counter. Shape into an oblong and divide into 3 equal pieces. Flatten each piece and fold it over. Let them rest five minutes this way.

Meanwhile, get out a cookie tin, and a piece of cardboard the same size; cut the cardboard in 3 pieces, the long way. Sprinkle them thoroughly with fine cornmeal.

Take a piece of dough and very gently and smoothly flatten it into an oval about the size of your hand. Press the side of your hand along the middle and fold it over; seal the edges by pressing. Turn so the seal is on top, and flatten again as before; fold and seal again.

Now roll the loaf out as long as your cookie sheet. To do this, place your hands lightly in the middle of the loaf and roll back and forth, moving your hands out toward the end. Work slowly, repeating two or three times until it is long enough.

Put the loaf on the first piece of cardboard, seal side UP. Now shape the other two loaves and lay them on the other pieces of cardboard. Cover with a dry cloth that has a little flour rubbed into it.

Raising the Loaves
Let the loaves rise 1 to 1½ hours (at 70°) or until about 4 inches in diameter (for white) or 3 inches (whole wheat). Meanwhile, fire up your oven to 450° and heat up a brick in the oven. Also, boil a kettle of water.

Turning the Loaves
Now you want to turn the loaves upside down, to expose the bottom, slightly sticky side, which will rise higher than the top would. Lift each cardboard and gently roll the loaves onto the cookie sheet. If one sticks to the board, invert it (cardboard and all) then slash it loose with a sharp knife.

Slashing and Decorating

That done, you may (if you have a razor or very sharp knife) slash the loaves. This requires a light touch, the blade held almost horizontally. If your knives are all blunt and you can't find any razors, forget it. You may also paint the loaves with egg white and sprinkle them with poppy seeds or sesame seeds.

Steaming the Oven

The crisp layer of outer crust on French bread is made by steam in the oven at the beginning of the cooking time. To duplicate it, half fill a large baking pan with boiling water, put it on the floor of the oven, submerge the hot brick that's been heating up, and very quickly close the door. Get your bread and slide it in on the rack, also as quickly as possible.

Baking

French bread doesn't take long. In 15 minutes you can check it and take the steam bath arrangement out. In another 15 minutes lift out one loaf and tap it sharply on the bottom. It should be light and crisp, and sound hollow.

SUMMER BREAD

The great virtue of this bread is that it can be cooked very quickly in a reasonable oven (300°-350°) and therefore you need not bake everybody out of house and home just to get bread.

Start the bread about 1 hour before lighting the stove.

Mix:

2 eggs
2 cups warm water
1½ Tb. yeast
3 Tb. molasses
3 cups whole-wheat flour

Beat this mixture with a wooden spoon about 100 times and put it in a warm spot to rise for about 1 hour. It should double in size and the gluten should make the dough sort of stringy by the end of the rising time. Now it's time to start up the stove, and add to the dough:

1 Tb. salt
¼ cup any oil or butter or lard

You may add:

¼ cup wheat germ, ¼ cup soy flour, and ½ cup dried milk

Beat in, by cupfuls:

2 to 4 cups white flour, whole-wheat flour, or half and half

When the dough becomes too thick to beat, mix and knead in the flour by hand. When it no longer sticks to your hands stop adding flour. Roll the dough out about ½ to 1 inch thick and place it on a greased cookie sheet. If you want, you can make it look extra fancy by brushing the top with:

1 egg yolk

And sprinkling on:

sesame seeds

Let it rise until double its height, then bake about 30 minutes.

HOLIDAY BREAD

To get a dry, light, tender texture (such as you find in Danish pastry, or European holiday breads) you need plenty of eggs—from 1 to 3 per loaf. The following, for 2 loaves, has 4 eggs, but you may try it with only 2 if that's all you can spare. Start 5 hours before serving, or 4½ hours before baking (at 400°).

Beat briefly in a 1-pint measuring cup:

4 eggs

Add warm (not hot) water to bring the level up to 2 cups of liquid. Empty this into a large ceramic bowl and add:

1 Tb. dried yeast
1 cup sugar or ⅔ cup honey

Allow this to soften for 5 minutes; beat with a fork, then add:

1 cup dried milk
½ tsp. cardamom or 3 husked, ground pods of white cardamom
2 cups whole-wheat flour

Beat well until your arm is tired, and allow the sponge to rise, covered, in or over the warming oven for about 1 hour, until doubled. Then beat again until your arm is tired and add:

¼ cup light oil (corn, safflower, sunflower, or peanut)
2 tsp. salt

Beat these in thoroughly before adding:

2 to 3 cups more flour (white, whole wheat, or half and half)

Add the flour by half cupfuls until you can no longer mix the dough with a spoon. Then turn out on a floured surface and knead it in. Stop adding

holiday bread

flour when the unfloured surface of the dough is still slightly sticky, and knead 5 minutes longer.

In a heavy ceramic bowl, in or over the warming oven, allow it to rise twice for about 1 hour each time, or until it doubles, punching down between risings.

When the dough has risen a second time, decide what you want to do with it. You may bake it in any sized pans, filling each one ⅔ full, or divide it into many small rolls and bake them on a cookie sheet or in muffin tins. Or you may braid the dough into one gigantic or two medium-sized rings or loaves.

To Braid Bread

Divide the dough with a sharp knife into 3 or 6 equal portions; cover all but one with a damp cloth. Roll the first portion between your palm and the kneading surface lightly. The kneading surface should be slightly damp, not floury. Then roll with both hands, moving them very slowly as you roll back and forth, out to the ends. Repeat this over and over, being careful not to let the roll break or stretch too quickly in any one spot. Roll it out to about 2 feet long and set it aside; on to the next.

When all the dough is rolled out in long thin ropes, grease a cookie sheet and place three of these rolls on it with their ends crossed in one corner; the one in the middle should be on the bottom of the pile.

Now simply braid the three together, crossing the middle strands alternately over right and left strands. When you get to the end, either tuck the ends under (for a straight loaf) or join them with a bit of water to make the ends stick together (for a circle).

To Decorate Bread

Beat an egg, or either the white or the yolk, in a cup, and paint it on top of the bread. You may sprinkle on:

ground nuts

and then:

cinnamon sugar

or some other topping, such as poppy, sunflower, or sesame seeds—whatever. Don't put on raisins, though, they will burn black.

The Final Rising

This will take about 1 hour; you need not cover the loaves, but keep them over the warming oven. Meanwhile, pay close attention to the temperature of the oven. Have plenty of well split dry wood, both hard and soft, handy, and keep the oven rising until the temperature is up to 400°.

Baking

Bake at 400° for 30 to 45 minutes, depending on the size of your loaves; bake rolls 20 minutes.

ROLLS

Rolls are creatures of the imagination: you can make them small and crisp, flat and tender, tall and puffy. You can also coat the tops with nuts, seeds, and other things.

You can make rolls with any sort of bread dough, although I like to add an egg and half a cup of dried milk for every two pounds (equivalent of one loaf) of dough, to insure a crisper crust and lighter insides. Rolls are smaller, so they rise faster, are baked at a higher temperature, and take less time in the oven. You might serve rolls for dinner on bread-baking day, since you don't have to wait for them to cool.

ROLL RECIPE

This recipe takes about 3 hours and makes 1 pan of rolls.
Mix:

1½ cups warm water
½ Tb. dried yeast

Let the yeast dissolve; stir it in, then pour into a mixing bowl and add:

1 egg
½ cup dried skim milk
1 Tb. honey or molasses
2 Tb. melted butter or oil
1½ tsp. salt
2 cups whole-wheat flour

Beat 100 times and cover with a damp cloth; let it rise until doubled, about 45 minutes, over the warming oven. Then beat it again and add:

2 to 3 cups whole-wheat flour

Add the flour gradually, turning out to knead when no longer mixable. Knead 10 minutes. Return to bowl, cover, and set to rise until doubled, about 30 minutes. Take out and slice into roll pieces with a sharp knife. Shape, decorate, and place in greased pans to rise 30 minutes. Bake at 400° for 20 to 30 minutes, until brown.

Toppings

Egg Wash: Toppings won't stick by themselves; you glue them on by brushing with either:

1 egg yolk and 1 tsp. water (dark yellow)
1 egg white (clear)
1 beaten egg (pale yellow)

Seeds: Sprinkle on lightly or coat heavily with:

poppy seeds, sesame seeds, or coarsely ground sunflower seeds

Nuts: Any coarsely ground or pounded nuts are fine; my favorites are:

Brazil nuts
walnuts mixed with white sugar

Sweet: Or you could just coat with a bit of sugar and cinnamon. Fancy toppings include bits of candied lemon peel, etc., but I like them better in, not on, the rolls.

Onions: Chop very fine and sauté in butter:

1 small onion

Cool and add:

2 Tb. chopped fresh or dried parsley
herbs: sage, thyme, oregano, basil—a pinch of each or any

Be forewarned: Anything you bake in the oven along with onion rolls tastes like onion rolls—like, for example, sweet rolls.

To Soften Roll Tops
While the rolls are still hot from the oven, rub them with butter or paint with melted butter.

To Crisp Roll Tops
Remove rolls from the oven after the first 10 minutes of baking and brush each top quickly with a little water. Return and bake 5 to 10 minutes longer, until brown.

If you have too many rolls to do that, use the brick-in-pan-of-boiling-water method described in **French Bread**, page 65.

STICKY ROLLS

Take:

1½ lbs. bread dough (Holiday bread [pages 66–67] is best)

Roll it out on a floured surface to about 10 by 10 inches. Melt and pour over it:

½ cup butter (you can use oil if you are out of butter)
3 Tb. chopped nuts
½ cup brown sugar or honey (if you use honey, melt it with the butter)
¼ cup currants or raisins or other fruit

Sprinkle over with:

1 tsp. cinnamon
½ tsp. allspice
1 Tb. candied lemon or orange rind, chopped well (optional)

Roll up tightly as you would a jelly roll. Cut into slices about 1½ inches thick and place them on end in a 7 by 7-inch greased baking pan. Let them rise about 30 minutes, until doubled; bake at 400° for 20 minutes. Brush with butter as they come out of the oven.

These may be reheated (in their pan) for a late Royal Breakfast.

PIZZA DOUGH

Choose a cool, windy day to make pizza with a wood stove, since you will be getting the oven pretty hot; on a hot day a 500° oven is unbearable, and on a rainy day it is difficult to get the oven that hot. Start the sauce (page 181) in the morning, and let it simmer all day. About two hours before pizza time, start the dough.
In a large warm bowl, mix:

2 Tb. dried yeast
2 cups warm water
2 tsp. sugar
2 cups whole-wheat flour
½ cup dried skim milk

Let this sit about 10 minutes; then beat 100 times with a wooden spoon. Set it to rise to double its size in the warming oven, covered, with a bit of wood under the bowl to keep the bottom from cooking. After about 30 minutes, beat it down and add:

½ cup light vegetable oil
1½ tsp. salt
1½ cups unbleached white flour (sometimes I use
    1 cup white and ½ cup corn or millet flour for
    more crunch)

Add the flour ½ cup at a time, and when you can't mix with a spoon any more, flour the counter well and knead it in. Knead well; you want a very smooth, elastic dough, light and warm. Return to bowl, covered with damp cloth, and let rise one-half to 1 hour.

While it is rising, bring your oven up to 500° and bank it. Gather pizza toppings such as:

1 lb. soft fresh cheese
sautéed onions
sautéed celery
half-cooked chopped bacon
sharp hard (aged) cheese
sauce
sliced fried sausage
sliced green peppers
sliced mushrooms or puffballs
oregano

When the oven is 500° and the dough doubled, take out the dough and slice in half; cover half with damp cloth, and knead the other half 5 minutes. Roll out the dough on floured counter with a floured rolling pin, quite thin (½ to ⅓ of an inch) except around the edge, where you leave a slight raised border.

Slide onto an oiled cookie sheet.

Paint the dough lightly with oil. Spread on half the sauce and top with whatever you are putting on your pizza. Then sprinkle on:

½ lb. grated soft cheese
2 Tb. dried oregano

Put the pizza in the oven for 10 to 15 minutes. Meanwhile construct the other pizza and have it ready to go in when the first one comes out.

Serve with salad and cold beer.

SOURDOUGH STARTER BREADS

To begin with, sourdough is really the same yeast we buy, dried or in cake form, to make bread with. The difference is that when sourdough is made, the yeast is allowed to remain in the flour and water mixture at the right temperature for growth for a much longer time. It eats up not just some, but all, of the sugar in the flour. It creates a great deal of carbon dioxide, and, finally, running out of air and food, it dies—not, however, without leaving some seeds behind, dormant, just in case conditions should ever happen to improve.

The reason it is called sourdough is that in eating up every last iota of sweetness, it makes the flour sour-tasting.

Sourdough is, according to most cookbooks, supposed to be kept in a sealed, sterile container, in a cool, dark place, and renewed once a week or so. However, I have heard stories of trappers who came upon deserted cabins and scraped the crud off the inside of the old sourdough crock back of the rusty stove and used it to get bread going. So I think maybe sourdough is a little more durable than they say in the books.

The sourdough I have is purported to be 22 years old (going on 23). I keep it in a jar in the pantry. Sometimes it gets warm; sometimes it freezes. I use it around once a month. It always works.

SOURDOUGH STARTER

Soak together in a clean jar:
½ Tb. dried yeast
½ cup water
When the yeast dissolves, add:

1 cup water
⅔ cup flour (rye or whole wheat)

Set over the warming oven (around 75°) to rise and fall (24 hours) and when it stops working, store in a cool place.

SOURDOUGH BREAD

Sourdough bread is very simple compared to yeasted bread; though it takes much less effort, however, you do have to start it the night before. This is for 2 loaves, and it takes 3 or 4 hours (not counting the overnight).

The night before you make sourdough bread, the

culture must be renewed—that is, warmed up and fed something to wake up the yeast.

Mix in a ceramic bowl:

1 cup sourdough starter
3¾ cups warm water
4½ cups whole-wheat or rye flour

This mixture must only half fill a bowl. Cover with a damp towel and leave over the warming oven to rise overnight.

In the morning, take out 1 cupful of the batter and refrigerate it in a clean jar—this is starter for another batch if you've used up all the other. To the remainder, add:

½ cup oil
1 Tb. salt
5 to 6 cups whole-wheat flour

Add flour gradually, by half cups, beating after each addition. When the dough comes easily away from the bowl, but is still sticky, knead for 5 minutes, adding flour as necessary. Sourdough should not be mixed as dry as ordinary yeasted bread—it should remain on the sticky side.

Shape into 2 loaves and place in very well oiled and floured pans. Do not fill pans above half full; sourdough will not support itself much above the level of the pan. Slit the tops, sprinkle with seeds if you like (caraway is nice).

Sourdoughs take a long time to rise and are unpredictable; I've had some rise in 2 hours; others went all night and were just right by morning. Usually it just sits doing nothing for a long time and then within 30 minutes rises all it's going to. Keep an eye on it; when you see it increasing its girth, see to the fire. Bring the oven to 375°-400° and bank it.

Bake from 1 to 1½ hours at 375°. For a crisp crust, remove loaves in the last 15 minutes of baking and brush on water—with a duck's tail feather, says Bobby Dann, who gave us the culture.

LIQUID YEAST STARTER

Boy, when I first heard about this stuff, I really thought I had it: a self-perpetuating nonsour yeast starter. I mixed up a batch and brewed it into bread, saving some in the fridge. Next week I added it to more potatoes and made more bread. Fine, a little mealy, as bread goes, but O.K. The fourth week I noticed it smelled a little like a brewery, but I went ahead and made bread with it anyway. It worked fine but smelled funny. I don't know to this day if it just got too yeasty or if some wild yeast got in there, but nobody ate the bread. So I recommend this to you if you're snowed in and running out of yeast; but I won't stand behind it as a way of life. This recipe is for two loaves.

Peel, cube, and boil together:

1½ cups water
3 potatoes

When they begin to fall apart, cool and mash the potatoes in the water. Add:

¼ cup sugar
1½ Tb. salt
1 Tb. dried yeast
enough water to make 3 cups of the mixture, altogether

Leave it in a warm place overnight to brew and froth. Take out one cup in the morning and store in a clean jar in the fridge—your reserve. Use the remainder to make bread.

LIQUID YEAST STARTER BREAD

To 2 cups starter add:

3 Tb. oil or bacon fat
¼ cup sugar or molasses
1 tsp. salt
5 cups whole-wheat flour

Beat well and cover with a warm, damp cloth; let rise and double 1 hour. Then add:

4 to 6 cups whole-wheat flour

cup by cup. When you can no longer beat in flour, knead until firm. Let it rise to double, punch down, let rise again to double, punch down and shape into 2 loaves. Let them rise 30 minutes. Bake in a very hot oven, 450° or so, for 25 to 35 minutes.

SALT-RISING BREAD

A moist, tangy sourdough, with a slightly different flavor, reminiscent of corn on the cob. Salt-rising bread is leavened by a ferment you brew yourself. It takes days to make—not a hurry-up bread. This is for 1 loaf.

Mix in a clean jar:

1 cup lukewarm scalded whole milk
1 Tb. molasses
½ cup cornmeal
1 tsp. salt

Set this to brew in a warm place like the warming oven on a bit of wood, with a lid on the jar. In a couple of days it will begin to bubble and smell like fresh corn (check it every so often). When it does, pour it into a large ceramic bowl, and add:

1 tsp. salt
3 Tb. melted shortening or oil
2 cups lukewarm water
2 cups whole-wheat or rye flour

Beat 100 strokes and cover with a damp cloth; leave in the warming oven 8 to 12 hours, until it bubbles and smells fermenty.

Beat in, cup by cup:

4 cups whole-wheat flour

Turn out on a floured counter and gradually knead in about:

2 cups whole-wheat or unbleached white flour

When the dough is stiff, but stickier than is usual with ordinary yeast breads, shape into a loaf and place in a well-oiled and floured bread pan, or make into a long or round loaf and place on a flat pan. Let it rise 4 to 6 hours, or longer; as with sourdough, it just sits there for a long time mulling things over, and then takes off. When you notice some action, bring the oven up to 375° and bank it. Or you can leave it to rise overnight, and bake in that hot morning fire.

Put the loaf in a hot oven, then let the temperature drop to 325°, and bake for about 1 hour. Take it out, brush with water, and return for 15 minutes, for a crisp crust. Remove it before it burns on top and cool it before slicing.

UNLEAVENED BREAD

Unleavened bread is made with no yeast. It often incorporates different flours, such as barley, rye, and buckwheat; sometimes it is made with ground dried beans or soybeans as well. The only commercial bread that resembles it is Westphalian pumpernickel, sold in delicatessens and specialty stores.

Unleavened bread is very dense and nourishing. In the seventeenth and eighteenth centuries, European farm wives learned to make lighter breads, using wheat and yeast; but they would still make unleavened bread at harvest time, when the work load was heaviest and the need for protein was greatest. Soldiers, laborers, and servants were also given "black bread," not as a sign of their lower class (as was thought by many) nor out of any lack of materials to make lighter, risen breads, but simply because it packed the most grain into the least space, while still being portable. In times of famine or hardship it was made with a cup of "pease" or ground dried beans for every three loaves or so. This was a custom, but like most customs, it had its roots in reason, for the added legumes would increase the protein in the bread by about 50 percent.

Most of my friends, around New England and the Maritimes, make unleavened breads regularly, and none of them use recipes—the delight of creation being partly invention and partly a matter of what grains, sweeteners, and farm products they have in stock. See **Ingredients** (page 58) to get an idea of what will happen with various different grains and other ingredients.

I find unleavened breads keep better than light bread, if wrapped in cloth and kept cool. My taste for it increases as my workload becomes greater in the fall, and then it drops off as winter drives us, finally, indoors, to knit and read and whittle away the idle hours.

DUTCH OVEN BREAD

This was invented by Judy Barns when she was living with a kerosene space heater while she and Sam built their house. She thinks the heat was about 212°, which would make it about right for

baking on top of an Ashley, Warm Morning, or a pot-bellied stove as well.

You will notice this bread has no oil added; the sesame seeds provide the oil. It also has no yeast, so it is rather dense, but good and heartening in the way of dense breads. It is started the night before, when you put in a bowl on top of the stove or heater:

2 cups whole-wheat flour
2 cups water

The next day beat this well and add:

2 tsp. salt
1½ to 2 cups ground sesame seeds
2 cups oat flour

Knead in more oat flour as needed to make it workable, and continue kneading for 10 minutes.

Shape into a round, flat loaf, and dust this well with oat flour. Dust the Dutch oven inside with oat flour. Bake for 1 hour on top of the stove or heater, opening the lid occasionally to let steam out. Turn the loaf over and bake another 30 minutes or so, until crusty on the bottom.

TIBETAN BARLEY BREAD

Very dense, dark, and somewhat sour, this unleavened bread does rise somewhat if left in the warming oven overnight before baking.
Roast in a frying pan:

1½ cups barley
1 cup sunflower seeds

Grind very fine together. Pour over them:

3 cups boiling water

Stir well; then add:

⅓ cup vegetable oil
2 tsp. salt
½ cup dried milk

Add, by cupfuls, stirring after each addition:

4 to 5 cups whole-wheat flour

The dough should be quite sticky but workable if you keep the outer surface continually floured. Knead for 10 minutes and return to the bowl, covered with a damp cloth; put it in the warming oven on a bit of wood for 3 to 6 hours.

Take it out and knead it well, using flour to keep the surface from sticking to your hands. Shape into a rough round loaf and score the surface with a knife in a tic-tac-toe pattern. Let it rise in the warming oven overnight.

Next morning, preheat oven to 400° and bake

for 20 minutes. Paint the top with water, return to the oven, and bake at 350° to 400° for another 45 minutes.

Excellent with homemade farmer cheese, green onions, pickles, and home brewed beer.

PASTA

THIN WHITE NOODLES

Noodles aren't really hard, although they do require time and patience and a flat, smooth surface to roll them out on. For this, marble is the absolute best. You will also find it much easier to use one of those big French rolling pins with no handles.

In a shallow mixing bowl, make a mound of:

2⅓ cups white unbleached flour

Mix together well and add:

2 large eggs
2 Tb. water
1 tsp. salt
2 tsp. light oil

Stir these into the flour, lightly, with your fingertips, trying not to get glued in there. Add a little more flour as needed to form the dough into a firm sticky ball.

Clear off the counter top and put a handful of flour in one corner; wipe this across the surface so it is lightly dusted and knead the ball of tough dough until it is no longer too sticky to handle. Push and slap at it with your palms; lift it up and pound it against the edge of the counter. Be loud and ungentle. In 5 to 10 minutes it will become smooth and glossy. Place it in a covered container in the warming oven for 1 hour.

Take out the dough and work it some more. Now divide it with a sharp knife into 4 parts; put 3 of them back in the container and cover. Roll out the first fourth on a flour-dusted counter. It isn't easy to roll out. Try holding one edge with your stomach pressed against the counter edge while you roll away from the edge. Turn the dough often. When it is thin enough to read through, set it aside and start on the next one.

Let the rolled-out dough rest 20 minutes before cutting. To make thin noodles, roll the sheet of dough up in a loose spiral, as if it were a jellyroll, and cut the roll into fine slices. For other shapes, see **Manicotti** (page 168), etc. Use the scraps for soup noodles.

You may dry the noodles on a rack and store

them in a cool, dry place in a paper bag, or cook them immediately for 5 to 7 minutes in lots of rapidly boiling, salted water.

Variations

Whole Wheat: Use half white and half hard whole-wheat flour, which has been sifted 3 times in a fine sieve. This is a little more difficult to manage than all-white flour; you might want to try white noodles first.

Buckwheat: Use one third buckwheat flour, two thirds white flour.

Green Noodles: Before mixing up the noodle dough, steam for half an hour:

½ cup spinach or fine tender greens

Put them in a sieve and press down hard to squeeze out any moisture. Then dump on a board and chop very fine. Add to the noodle dough along with the eggs:

⅓ cup greens

Durum Whole Wheat: Noodles from the stores are made with very high protein durum wheat, rich in gluten. If you can get your hands on some of that stuff I presume it would be possible to make whole-wheat noodles without any white flour.

5
QUICKBREADS

Quickbreads serve an end similar to yeasted/unyeasted breads, in providing a form of ground, cooked grain, which is easy to keep, and is good to eat cold. Slice for slice, though, quickbreads actually contain less grain than bread, and more of other stuff (eggs, milk, etc.). The texture's different, too; rather than "bringing out" the gluten (as in a yeasted bread) the aim in quickbread is a "light crumb," meaning as little gluten as possible. The other stuff (particularly the eggs) are responsible for holding it together.

INGREDIENTS

Baking Soda and Powder: Most quickbreads are leavened by baking soda or powder, and here's how they work: when bicarbonate of soda is combined with something acid, it gets all fizzy, letting off little bubbles of carbon dioxide; if this happens in the batter, it fills the bread or cake with nice little holes. But, to have it work, you have to use it with something acid: buttermilk, sour milk, yogurt, sour cream, whey, molasses or honey, even tea or coffee. Baking powder, on the other hand, doesn't need something acid, because what's in it is baking soda combined with something acid (in dried form): namely, cream of tartar. So, all you have to do to activate the baking powder is to dampen it.

As soon as you start the reaction, either with soda or powder, the fizzing starts, and all the bubble making that's going to occur happens within a few minutes. That's why many recipes say to mix up wet and dry ingredients separately, and all recipes say to stir the final batter quickly and pop it in the oven.

Many people are beginning to wonder if these leaveners are really good for you. Baking soda, of course, neutralizes acids: not only in foods, but also in your stomach. Without stomach acids, your body cannot digest B vitamins (which you went to such work to get, if you grind your own flour!). It seems to me that if you use very little soda or powder, only using soda in combination with acid foods, that the alkaline substance will be all used up by the time you eat it; but of course, it's up to you. Baking powder and soda are not included in the macrobiotic diet, incidentally; they are considered too yang.

If you prefer not to use these leaveners, you can substitute beaten egg whites in many recipes (muffins, pancakes, loaves) and leave them out altogether in thin pancakes or biscuits.

Flour: If you grind your own, do it well, or sift out the rough stuff when making quickbreads. That's because the flour is only dampened for a brief period between mixing and baking; there'll be no soaking to soften the grit. An even lighter version of many of these recipes can be made by using half hard whole-wheat flour and half soft.

Eggs: Eggs hold quickbreads together, so they're pretty important; but if you don't mind the crumble, you can leave them out.

Milk: You can use whole milk, or skim, or reconstituted powder; it doesn't make any difference.

Sweets: This is one place where you can use honey and molasses instead of sugars. Very little sweetening is usually called for.

BISCUITS, MUFFINS, AND ALL

BISCUITS

These are fine and light, but tastier than white-flour biscuits. Don't crumble the shortening too fine; roll the dough out thick, and bake at a high temperature. This recipe makes 15 biscuits.

Sift together:

1½ cups hard whole-wheat flour
1½ cups soft whole-wheat flour (or unbleached white)
1 tsp. baking powder
½ tsp. salt

Add and mash in with a fork until well mixed, but still lumpy:

½ cup lard or butter or vegetable shortening (don't use oil)

Beat together:

¾ cup liquid (can include up to 2 eggs; may be milk, buttermilk, sour milk, whey, or water)

Stir liquid into the dough swiftly and knead it for a couple of minutes with swift hands. Form into a ball and refrigerate if necessary until oven is up to 400° to 450°.

Roll out dough ½-inch or slightly thicker. Cut into shapes with a small glass or biscuit cutter. Set on an ungreased sheet; bake 10 minutes.

WHOLE-WHEAT MUFFINS

Preheat oven to 400° to 450°; put muffin tins on the stove and paint them with oil or lard. This recipe will make 15 or 20 muffins.

In a bowl, beat briefly:

1 egg

Add and beat in:

1½ cups milk
¼ cup oil
¼ cup molasses

Dump on top, without mixing:

2 cups whole-wheat flour, freshly ground or sifted
2 tsp. baking powder
½ tsp. salt

Mix in the dry ingredients swiftly and, using the measuring cup, fill the muffin tins ⅔ full with batter. Bake for about 20 minutes.

Variations

You can put all sorts of things in muffins. Add to the flour, before mixing it in with the wet ingredients, any of these:

½ to 1 cup fresh or frozen blueberries, raspberries, blackberries, well chopped apples, or fresh chopped banana; currants, raisins, chopped dates or figs, nuts, seeds, coconut; well chopped, sautéed onion, 2 Tb. chopped parsley; 3 or 4 pieces of fried, crumbled bacon, or cooked ham.

You may substitute any of these for ½ cup of the whole-wheat flour:

½ cup corn, buckwheat, rye, or barley flour
½ cup dried milk (add to the fresh milk before mixing)
½ cup soy flour
½ cup roasted ground sesame or sunflower seeds

BRAN MUFFINS

Bran muffins are traditional as a way of serving up roughage, a commodity notably lacking in the American diet, if one can believe the subway signs advertising relief for hemorrhoid sufferers. Bran is good, as somebody's granny said, for what ails you.

Fire the oven up to around 400°, and bank it. Set a muffin tin to heat on top of the stove; paint the insides of the cups with oil. In a large bowl, beat briefly:

1 egg
1½ cups milk
½ cup molasses

Add quickly, without stirring, in a heap on top:

1 cup wheat flour
1 tsp. salt
1 tsp. baking powder
2 cups bran

With a fork or your fingers, sort of mix the dry stuff together a bit, so as to spread out the salt and the baking powder before dipping low in the bowl to bring up the wet ingredients. As soon as they are all mixed together spoon into the muffin tin cups about ⅔ full and pop them right in the oven. Bake for about 20 minutes. You can bake these plain or you can add, after you put in everything else, ½ cup or so of dried fruit, any kind.

BUCKWHEAT BREAD OR MUFFINS

Before starting, bring oven up to 350° (for bread) or 400° (for muffins). Grease your pan or tins, and if you are using cast iron, set them on top of the stove to heat up.

In a bowl, mix:

1 egg
1 cup soured milk or buttermilk
½ cup dried milk
¼ cup molasses

Dump in without mixing first:

1 cup buckwheat flour
½ cup whole-wheat flour
½ tsp. salt
2 tsp. baking powder

Beat in the dry ingredients quickly, pour the mixture into the pan or muffin tins ⅔ full. Bake bread 20 minutes, muffins 15 minutes. Be careful—they burn easily.

JOHNNY CAKE

Also known as Corn Pone or Journey Bread, this is a dry, firm cake. It should be baked in a 9-inch pan. It also makes a dozen nice muffins. Preheat oven to 350° for bread or 400° for muffins and bank it. If you are baking in cast iron, put the pan on the stove first and grease it with a brush and oil or lard.

In a bowl, mix up:

1 cup milk (or better yet, sour milk, or half milk and half yogurt)
3 Tb. oil, lard, or bacon or ham fat
3 Tb. molasses
2 eggs

Dump in without mixing first:

1 cup cornmeal
1 cup whole-wheat flour
1 tsp. salt
2 tsp. baking powder

Beat in the dry ingredients quickly, pour the mixture into the pan or muffin tins ⅔ full. Bake cornbread at 350° for 45 minutes, muffins at 400° for 20 minutes.

SOUTHERN SPOONBREAD

This is almost a pudding, and it ought to be timed carefully so you're ready to serve dinner the moment it's done.

In a heavy pan, heat:

2 cups milk
½ cup dried milk

When the milk is almost boiling, but not quite, add slowly, mixing as you do:

1 cup cornmeal

Stir as the cornmeal thickens, and remove from heat. Add:

3 Tb. lard or bacon or ham drippings (or oil)

Allow this to cool for 15 or 20 minutes. Meanwhile, raise the temperature of the oven to 400° or so and bank it there. If you are going to use a cast-iron pan, put it on top of the stove to heat up. Paint the inside with grease or oil. When the mixture is room temperature, add to it:

2 eggs
1 tsp. salt
1 tsp. baking powder
3 Tb. molasses

Beat briefly and pour into the pan (9 inches in diameter). Bake for 30 to 40 minutes. Serve immediately; it will puff up in the oven and fall as you cut it, but that's all right as long as you don't let it sit around too long before eating it.

STEAMED BROWN BREAD

Steamed bread isn't difficult to make, but it does take a long time: 3 hours, or 45 minutes in a pressure cooker. It's a very useful thing to know how to make; for example, on rainy days when you just don't feel like battling the oven up to 350°, or for campfire cookery.

Brown bread is tenderer and more delicious if you use soured milk. You may sour it by adding ½ teaspoon of vinegar or 1 teaspoon of lemon juice to 2 cups milk an hour before you start mixing the bread.

Just before you mix up the bread, scout up two 14-ounce cans and grease them inside. You will also need a couple of squares of brown paper (from paper bags) and some string or 2 strong rubber bands.

In a bowl, mix up:

2 cups buttermilk, soured milk, or half yogurt and half milk
½ cup dried milk
⅔ cup molasses

Dump on top, without mixing first:

1 cup cornmeal

1 cup whole-wheat flour
½ cup rye flour
½ cup soy flour
1 tsp. salt
2 tsp. baking powder
2 Tb. brewer's yeast
½ cup raisins or currants; but mine always sink to the bottom no matter what I do (optional)

Mix together dry and wet ingredients swiftly and pour the tins ¾ full. Tie paper over the tops; punch a few holes in each paper. Put the tins in a deep pot or Dutch oven (preferably on a rack) with a couple of inches of boiling water; or put them in a pressure cooker, with 2 cups boiling water. Steam 3 hours on very low heat, on the middle back plate; with a pressure cooker, steam over low heat for 15 minutes, with the valve open; then put on the rocker thingy and bring it up to 15 pounds (light rocking) and rock it for 30 minutes.

You need not remove the bottoms of the cans to get the bread out; just cool it somewhat and it comes right out. Slice carefully; it's crumbly.

POPOVERS

What an easy way to impress people! Only two important rules: use a preheated, cast-iron popover pan, and have your oven up to 450°. (Makes 9 popovers.)

Melt in one cup of a cast-iron popover pan:

3 Tb. butter

Dip out:

1 Tb. melted butter

into a bowl; use the rest to paint the insides of the pan just before you fill the cups. Add to the butter in the bowl:

1 cup milk
2 eggs

Beat them together a bit, then add:

½ cup whole-wheat flour
½ cup whole-wheat pastry flour or white flour
2 pinches salt

Beat just enough to mix. Paint the insides of the cups. Pour each cup ¾ full and set in a 450° oven. Don't add wood to the fire so that it will go down a bit as it bakes, to 350° or so. In all, they will bake for a little over 30 minutes. Don't take them out until they are brown on all sides.

DUMPLINGS

Dumplings are a kind of quickbread—but simmered or poached in liquid instead of baked in the oven or in a frying pan. They are sticky on the outside, soft and tender within. They are good in almost any soup, particularly well loved with chicken soup or stew.

CORNMEAL DUMPLINGS

In a wide bowl, mix:

1 cup cornmeal
¼ cup whole-wheat flour
1 tsp. baking powder
½ tsp. salt

In a smaller bowl, beat together:

2 eggs
½ cup milk
1 Tb. corn oil

Add liquid gradually to cornmeal mixture and, when sticky, drop by spoonfuls into a wide soup pot that is simmering slowly; cover and simmer for 15 minutes without removing the lid.

CRACKERS

The hardest thing about making crackers (I find) is remembering to take them out of the oven before they burn. At 450°, they take 10 minutes; at 600°, only 5. The hotter you bake them, the better they are. When you first light up a stove, on a good clear day, it has a tendency to climb to high temperatures; that's a good moment to quickly make up and bake some crackers.

WHEAT OR RYE THINS

In a mixing bowl, mash together:

1 Tb. honey
2 Tb. lard or oil
½ cup yogurt
¼ tsp. salt
1½ cups whole-wheat or rye flour

Turn out on a floured counter and work in:

½ cup whole-wheat or rye flour

Roll out quite thin, ⅛ inch or less. Stamp out shapes; bake on an ungreased cookie sheet at 400° to 650°, 5 to 15 minutes, checking every 5 minutes or less.

SUNFLOWER SEED CRACKERS

A good crisp cracker; together with cold home brew and a dish of sliced raw vegetables, the finest sit-around-the-table-and-rap-food:
Roast at 200° for 20 minutes on a large cookie sheet or toast in a dry frying pan about 10 minutes:

1 cup sunflower seeds

Grind these coarsely, so that some seeds are still half intact. Mix them in a shallow bowl with:

1 cup rye flour
½ cup soybean flour or powder
½ tsp. salt

Then mix in with your hands, until all the flour is sort of oily:

2 Tb. oil

Sprinkle in, by teaspoons, mixing lightly with a fork until a stiff dough is formed:

3 to 4 tsp. cold water

You may refrigerate this, in a covered bowl, up to 30 minutes; any more will make the dough too stiff to roll out. Preheat oven to 350° or 400°.
Sprinkle on your work surface:

rye flour

Coat a rolling pin with rye flour as well, and roll out the dough as thin as you can without breaking it. Cut into clean shapes. (You will need to add a few drops of water to leftover dough before rolling it out again.)
Bake at 350° to 400° for 7 to 12 minutes. Cool for at least 30 minutes before you serve them.

FRITOS

Sift together:

1 cup corn flour
½ cup whole-wheat flour
¼ tsp. salt
⅓ cup dried milk
a pinch of paprika

Mix and add:

2 tsp. oil
1 tsp. tamari soy sauce
⅓ cup water

Mix this stuff up with your fingers until it is all stuck together. Flour a working surface and roll it out as thin as you can; cut into pieces. You may sprinkle the tops lightly with:

salt

Bake at 350° for 15 minutes.

GRIDDLE COOKING

Top of the stove baking is something you never hear much about anymore. Modern ovens heat up so quickly that no one hesitates to bake a cake in the middle of July; and most gas or electric burners don't adjust low enough, anyway, to bake on top of the stove. So the gentle art of English muffinery, of hoecakes and oatcakes and brown breads has gone the way of soups and cheeses and syrups—people get them from the store.

If you cook on a wood stove, however, you will soon discover that there are plenty of times when you can't or don't want to run the stove for several hours at high speed. For example, in the heat of the summer. Or when you're in a hurry, or in the morning, or just after a trip to town. On the other hand, we all depend on grain-based portable munchies. If you don't want to buy your summer breads, you can bake them quickly—on top of a wood stove, early in the morning.

Few modern stoves are adaptable to slow baking on top of the stove. When gas or electric burners are turned very low, their heat doesn't spread out evenly. It can be managed, though, if you can hunt up an old cast iron plate from a wood stove, and place it over the burner, under a cast iron frying pan. I baked all summer, that way, on a Coleman stove.

Here are a few basic principles of top of the stove baking:

1. Bake thin and small. If you are working with a liquid, such as pancake batter, pour it out into cakes your flipper can handle. If you're making a dough, such as oatcakes, roll it out no thicker than half an inch and cut them into wedge-shaped slices before putting them in the pan (the Scots refer to these pieces as "farls").

2. Prick the dough of scones and oatcakes before placing them in the pan; this allows the steam to escape.

3. Bake dough-type breads slowly. A copper-bottomed pan transmits too much heat. The best is a good old cast-iron skillet with a lid. When making pancakes, however, you need fast heat. Often it is necessary to remove the cast-iron wood stove plates from under the pan, thus exposing it to direct flame—but after a while, if it gets *too* hot, you should replace the plates.

4. Avoid sugar; it heats up too much and burns

the flours. A few recipes call for a tablespoon or two of sweetening, but more than that can be a disaster.

5. When baking quickbreads, especially pancakes, preheat the pan rather than greasing it, for light, dry, cakelike results. For thicker doughs you may oil or butter the pan a little—or dust the dough with oat flour or cornmeal. For yeasted cakes (English muffins) it is better to use cornmeal than grease the pan.

ENGLISH MUFFINS

For years I tried to duplicate commercial English muffins, thinking nothing else would do. Then one summer during a heat wave I was mixing up a batch of bread dough, and I thought, why not? So I rolled it out, cut out a few circles, let them rise, and baked them in a pan on top of the stove—which is, no doubt, how English muffins first got their start in the world. Any bread recipe will do, although I find it works best if you double the yeast and keep the flour very light. This is the one we use now:

Break into a 2-cup measure and beat slightly:

2 to 4 eggs

Fill the rest of the measure with:

warm water

Place this in a large ceramic mixing bowl and add:

1 cup dried milk
1 Tb. dried yeast
⅓ cup sugar or honey
1½ tsp. salt
2 Tb. oil
2 cups whole-wheat flour

Allow this sponge to rise for an hour. Then beat in:

½ cup whole wheat or soy flour

Dump around half a cup of:

white unbleached flour

on a smooth work surface. Turn the dough out on it and sprinkle some more white flour on top. Knead in white flour as needed (in all, about a cup) until the dough is smooth and elastic.

Let the dough rise in a warm place, covered, for 1 hour; or, if you're in a hurry, you may make up the muffins at once. To make muffins, roll out the dough ½ inch thick. Cut into circles with a round cookie cutter or an old tuna fish can.

Sprinkle a cast-iron frying pan lightly with:

cornmeal

and place the muffins in it. (They won't all fit; you will wind up doing it in 2 or 3 batches, or in several pans.) Let them rise until doubled (30 minutes to 1 hour, depending on the heat wave). When they're ready, put a lid on the frying pan and put it over medium heat. Bake about 10 to 15 minutes on each side, checking the middle muffin now and then to make sure it isn't burning. The main thing is to have medium heat evenly distributed over the entire pan. Cool the pan (in cold water) before placing the second batch of dough in it—or use 2 pans, and have one batch baking while the next is rising.

HONEY SCONES

Summer bread for sure—a scone is just a top of the stove muffin.

Sift together:

1 cup whole-wheat flour
¼ cup soy flour
¾ cup ground rolled oats (fine oat flour)
1 tsp. baking powder
¼ tsp. salt

Mix into the flour with your fingers until lumpy:

2 Tb. butter, lard, or corn oil

Mix together separately and add:

½ cup water
¼ cup dried milk
2 Tb. honey (or maple syrup, if you're rich in it)

Mix until damp. Divide the dough into 2 parts and roll each one out ½ inch thick; trim off the rough edges and cut into four wedges. Prick the dough and heat up your pan. You may grease the pan with a few drops of butter or oil, or flour the dough. Bake the scones slowly over moderate heat with a lid on for about 5 minutes; turn them, and bake on the other side 5 minutes. They keep well for about 12 hours.

OATCAKES

Thin and crisp, with a delicious nutlike flavor; everybody around our house eats these up as fast as they get made. Thankfully, they don't take long to make.

Grind up rolled oats coarsely to make:

2 cups oat flour

Add and mix in with your fingers:

½ tsp. salt

oatcake farls

And then:

2 Tb. butter or corn oil

And:

2 cups rolled oats

Mix in with a fork:

½ cup hot water

Turn the dough onto a board sprinkled with oat flour, and press into 2 tight balls. Flatten and then roll out each ball to around ¼-inch thickness, trimming the edges if you like; cut into four wedges, and prick each wedge with a fork.

Preheat a cast-iron frying pan and sprinkle lightly with oat flour. Bake the "farls" about 5 minutes on each side over medium heat with a lid on the pan (you can tell when the first side is done because the edges will curl up slightly).

HOE CAKES

We call them hoe cakes to differentiate them from pancakes, which they are, but don't taste like. However, there's no way our forefathers, in their primitive days, ever had these ingredients, so I don't imagine they were ever really made on a hoe like this. At any rate, they are terrific bits of bread to make hastily on top of the stove and serve with soup or beans.

Stirring rapidly, pour:

2 cups boiling water

into:

2 cups cornmeal

Add:

1 to 3 Tb. finely chopped onion
1 tsp. salt
½ cup dried milk

When it has cooled, mix in:

1 or 2 eggs

They are very good fried in bacon or ham fat, but if the pan is preheated, you may also cook them in a dry pan. The results are different but equally delicious. This recipe serves 3 people.

WHOLE-WHEAT PANCAKES

Enough for 4 *moderately* hungry people. In a big bowl, mix:

1½ cups whole-wheat flour
½ cup wheat germ (if you don't have it, use more flour)
2 tsp. baking powder
½ cup dried milk
1 tsp. salt

In another bowl, beat together:

2 eggs
½ cup light oil
1½ cups milk or ½ cup dried milk plus 1½ cups water

Combine the mixtures, and bake on very hot griddles until browned on both sides.

To make them thicker, add:

¼ cup whole-wheat flour

To make them lighter, add:

¼ cup white flour

To make them thinner, add:

¼ cup milk

BUCKWHEAT PANCAKES

Makes enough tender cakes for 3 people. In a big bowl, mix:

1 cup whole-wheat flour
½ cup buckwheat flour
½ cup well ground sunflower seeds
2 or 3 tsp. baking powder
1 tsp. salt

In another bowl, beat together:

3 eggs
1½ cups milk or ½ cup dried milk plus 1½ cups water
¼ cup oil or melted shortening

Combine the mixtures and bake on a moderately hot griddle until browned on both sides. Serve hot off the griddle.

PANCAKE MIX

In the absence of good old prepackaged pancake mix, you may find it convenient to make up a mix of your own, either for speed in the morning, camping, or so that noncooks in the house can put their hands on something easy to make without spending half an hour searching through jars of flours. I keep mix in a special jar with instructions for pancake making right on the lid, and I try to keep it full.

You can make lots of different kinds of mixes, with different flours. The main thing is to keep to these proportions:

½ cup whole-wheat flour (spring or hard wheat)
½ cup whole-wheat flour or other stuff—such as dried milk, soy flour, buckwheat flour, rye flour, cornmeal, wheat germ)
1 tsp. baking powder
½ tsp. salt

Here are two versions of pancake mix using these proportions:

Whole-Wheat Pancake Mix
3 cups whole-wheat flour, well ground
1 cup soy flour
1 cup powdered milk
1 cup wheat germ
2 Tb. baking powder
1 Tb. salt
2 Tb. brewer's yeast (optional)

Buckwheat Pancake Mix
3 cups whole-wheat flour, well ground
2 cups buckwheat flour
½ cup dried milk
½ cup soy flour
2 Tb. baking powder
1 Tb. salt
2 Tb. brewer's yeast (optional)

Pancakes Using Mix
Tape to the jar of pancake mix the following instructions:
To 1½ cups mix add:

1 or 2 eggs
2 or 3 Tb. oil
1 cup milk
or,
to 3 cups mix add:

2 or 3 eggs
¼ to ⅓ cup oil
2 cups milk

FRENCH PANCAKES

French pancakes are very thin and delicate, not at all like our lumberjack behemoths of the Western hemisphere. They are the basis of **Blintzes** (page 153). This recipe is enough for 3 people, or 17 blintzes.

In a shallow ceramic bowl, beat:

3 eggs

Add:

2 cups water mixed with 1 cup dried milk
½ tsp. vanilla or grated lemon rind
1 cup whole-wheat flour
½ tsp. salt

Beat briefly with a whisk. Heat a frying pan—any kind will do as long as it is good and hot. Test with a few drops of batter; if it sticks, it's not hot enough. If it separates into hopping spatters, it's too hot.

Put about ¼ cup (or less) batter at a time in the pan and tilt to spread it around. When the top looks dry and the edges have curled up a little, turn them over and cook a minute or so longer. Stack in warming oven or serve immediately.

CORNMEAL PANCAKES

Tender, crisp, and lighter than a whole-wheat pancake, these are our particular family morning favorites. You shouldn't try to make them too big; 3 or 4 inches is about the maximum possible turnable size. This recipe is enough for 2 hungry people.

In a heavy ceramic bowl, put:

1 cup cornmeal
2 Tb. molasses
1 tsp. salt

Stir as you pour in:

1 cup boiling water

Cover the bowl and let it sit for a few minutes (while you make coffee, scout up the maple syrup, and feed the cat); then add:

2 eggs
½ cup dried milk
¼ cup wheat germ
2 Tb. oil or bacon or ham drippings
2 tsp. baking powder
2 Tb. brewer's yeast (optional)
¼ cup whole-wheat flour

Mix it all up; put the bowl on an inverted frying pan on the side of the stove; heat up a couple of skillets and make the pancakes.

TORTILLAS

I'm not making any Real Authentic Claims here. Mexican tortillas are made with cornmeal ground by a limestone mortar and pestle, and the limestone helps glue things together. You must, however, grind your own corn or get a very fine-grade cornmeal, since most commercial cornmeal is too coarse for them.

Sift together:

1½ cups very fine cornmeal
½ cup unbleached white flour
a pinch of salt

Make a well in the middle and drop in:

1 beaten egg

Mix this up as best you can and add:

water

until it sticks together in a firm, damp ball. Sprinkle a very smooth work surface or waxed paper with cornmeal and roll out the dough as thin as you can. Find something to cut 6-inch rounds with—an old can, soup bowl, or wide-mouthed jar. Cut out as many tortillas as you can and stack them with cornmeal dusted in between on a plate. You may have to add a little water to the dough to ball it up and roll out a second and third time.

In a heavy frying pan or two, heat until sizzling:

2 Tb. oil

Fry the tortillas one by one, 1 minute on each side. Remove and put on brown paper to dry; if you are going to roll them up with filling inside, do so immediately, before they get hard. If they won't roll, you're cooking them too long. You may have to add more oil as you go along, and remove and put plates back on the stove to keep the pans at the right temperature.

6
DESSERTS

Sweetening, in any form, is sort of addictive: the more you eat of it, the more you want, and the less of other things you eat.

Large amounts of sugary foods are definitely not good for people. When you eat something very sweet, your system digests it immediately and the blood gets a kind of jolt, like overloading an electrical wire with too much voltage. To compensate for that, your body quickly releases insulin, to balance it. So the blood sugar level rockets up, and then drops, rapidly, as the insulin tries to straighten things out. It's hard for your system to be exact in such a hurry; often your body releases too little, or too much insulin, or keeps feeding it in long after the need is gone. High blood-sugar superenergy is followed by depression and weariness.

So, cook with less sugar. Make your cakes, cookies, pies, and custard desserts flavorful instead of just sweet. Use fresh fruit, or freeze and can your own with little sugar; avoid canned fruit, which is ridiculously sweet.

SOURCES OF SWEETENINGS

There are three common sources of sweetenings available on the market today (not counting chemicals). They are: sugar cane products, honey, and maple sugar. Sugar cane products include white and brown sugars, and molasses.

MAPLE SYRUP: Forty gallons of sap boils down to one gallon of syrup, and to do it in any quantity, it also takes a fair amount of equipment. If you want to get into it, there's a good book by Noel Perrin called *Amateur Sugar Maker*, put out by the University Press of New England, Hanover, N.H., $4.50.

If you want to make just a little syrup, you can do that on the stove. Nothing more is involved than tapping trees, gathering sap, and boiling it down until you like the taste. Seal it in a screw-type jar, or can it, to keep mold out; store in a cool place. Use it about the same way you would use honey: see below.

HONEY: Honey is the answer for many people who want to produce their own sugar. I wouldn't say it's less work than maple sugaring, but the labor is spread out over the year, and you don't have to have sugar maples. You do have to have a fair bit of equipment, however, and read up on bees, which, like all livestock, have their needs and quirks. The definitive work on bees is a packed volume called *The Hive and the Honey Bee*, ed. Roy A. Grout, put out by Dadant & Sons, Hambilton, Ill.

Honey is about twice as sweet as sugar, and comes in all colors and flavors, from pale, mild clover honey to dark, thick buckwheat. Some commercial honeys (not all) have little taste or food value: the bees are confined and fed sugar syrup.

You can use honey (or maple syrup) in any kind of baking and for sweetening fruits; it makes things darker, and adds to the flavor in subtle ways. I find that using some yogurt or cultured buttermilk instead of milk is very tasty in honey, molasses, and maple syrup baked goods.

SUGAR CANE PRODUCTS: When cane is processed, it is first crushed, and the juice that comes out is then boiled down, until it begins to crystallize. Then it may be spun in cylinders, and the liquid thrown out is sold as unsulphured molasses. Or it may be boiled and treated with sulphur to separate sugar crystals and sulphur molasses. After three boilings, and removal of more sugar crystals, the stuff left in the pot is called Blackstrap Molasses. The sugar crystals are either sold as "raw" sugar, or further refined by straining through charred cattle bones to make white sugar. Brown sugar is either white or raw sugar with a little molasses put back in.

Whole Molasses: Refined or unrefined, this contains a lot of sugar and cup for cup is as sweet as brown, raw, or white sugar. It has a lot of minerals, some vitamins, and a very distinctive flavor when used in quantity. For example, you cannot really taste the small amounts used in breads; but it is very noticeable in cakes and cookies; they will be browner, chewier, and molasses-flavored. It is best to go along with this, using spices that taste good with it, like cinnamon, ginger, nutmeg, allspice, and cloves.

Blackstrap Molasses: has very little sweetening and a *very* strong taste; some like it, and some don't. You will notice the flavor in anything you add it to. You can cook with it but should not consider it a sweetening but rather a food additive, like brewer's yeast; it is very high in minerals. You can add a few tablespoons to bread, cornbread, or grain dishes. The American Indians used it the way soy sauce is used in the East.

Raw and White Sugars: Both are crystals of almost pure sugar; neither has any food value. There is very little taste difference. The main advantage to refining sugar is that it will not cake in storage. Use in sweetening fruits, brewing beer or wines.

Brown Sugars: As some molasses is returned to the sugar crystals, it gives it some minerals—about as much as maple syrup or honey. The only place it is really worth the extra price is in crumble toppings on fruits, or on oatmeal or yogurt.

SUBSTITUTIONS

1 cup brown sugar
1 cup raw sugar
1 cup molasses*
¾ cup maple syrup*   = 1 cup white sugar
½ cup honey*

CAKES

The art of baking cakes is not nearly as exacting as many cookbooks would have you believe. Some recipes tell you to sift even the sugar. But generations of perfectly good cooks have slapped together trillions of cakes, and seen them all disappear before they even had a chance to cool.

It's true that not everything can go into a cake; there are some ground rules. But once you get a basic sense of ingredients and proportion, you can vary and invent, put things in or leave them out. The best way to go at it is to pick a recipe you like, and make it often for a couple of months, varying ingredients as you go. Eventually you won't have to look at the recipe, or measure things; you'll know by the consistency and taste of the batter what the cake is going to do.

INGREDIENTS IN CAKES

Flours: Flour is pretty important in a cake. Most recipes are for wheat; it can be hard, soft, or white, but it should be pretty fine, or you'll have something more like cornbread than cake. Other flours (rye, oat) are sometimes added, but sparingly, since they are heavy and make a dense texture.

Oils and Shortenings: The lightest cakes are made with solid shortening, such as lard, butter, or vegetable shortenings. Cakes made with oils aren't really denser—they're damper, chewier. Oils are better for you . . .

Sweetenings: Sugars (white and brown) make a drier, lighter cake than do molasses and honey. Molasses has a particular flavor, which will dominate a cake; honey is less noticeable. To substitute liquid sweets for dry ones, either add more flour or less of another liquid (such as milk).

---

*For every cup of these sweeteners used in place of crystallized sugars subtract ½ cup of liquid from the recipe.

Eggs: Eggs make cakes hold together, make them fine-textured, and if separated and beaten, can be used to leaven the batter. You can add more eggs than a recipe calls for or, sometimes, you can leave them out.

Milk and Milk Products: Milk makes cakes tender inside, and crumbly brown on the outside. You can substitute reconstituted dried milk for whole milk in any cake; in a pinch, you can use water or fruit juice. Buttermilk, yogurt, and sour cream will make a cake both lighter and tenderer.

Baking Soda, Baking Powder: Baking soda works by reacting with an acid food (honey, molasses, buttermilk, whey, yogurt) to produce carbon dioxide, thus leavening the batter. Baking powder is a combination of soda and cream of tartar, an acid powder; when moistened, they react with each other.

Cakes must have some leavening. You can use beaten egg whites, whipped cream, or yeast if you prefer not to use baking soda or powder.

PANS

All cakes, and particularly those without baking powder or soda, rise much better if they are baked in a ring or tube pan, or in muffin tins.

Some tube pans separate into an outer ring and a bottom-with-middle. These are used for very fluffy batters with lots of beaten egg whites, such as sponge or angel food cakes. The pan is built this way because no matter how well the pan is greased, these cakes will stick to them. In fact, since there's no point in trying, the pan shouldn't be greased at all; the cake will cling to the sides and middle and rise that much better. Afterward, the outer ring is cut loose and taken off, and the bottom can be cut free.

Cakes with a runny batter can't be baked in two-part pans, because batter will leak out. They will do better, though, in a loaf pan or in a single-piece tube-shaped pan than in an ordinary cake pan.

ICING

If your cake was good to begin with, it doesn't need an icing. Most icings are 90 percent sugar, and using honey instead doesn't make it any better for you. If you want to dress it up, serve with a thick fruit sauce, a custard sauce, or applesauce; or

bake in raisins, blueberries, or other fruits and nuts.

COFFEECAKE

I've been making this cake for 10 years. I've made it with every conceivable lack, substitution, and variation, and in a chancy oven; I've made it with oil, lard, butter, and no shortening; with sugar, molasses, honey, and no sweetening; with no egg, 1 egg, 3 eggs; with the egg whites beaten and no rising powder; with milk, yogurt, buttermilk, sour milk, sour cream, dried milk, whey, and no milk at all. I've also made it with white flour, whole-wheat flour, half whole wheat and half anything from rye to soyflour. I've used it as the basis for upside down cake, banana bread, raisin cake, muffins, coffeecake; flavored with cinnamon, almond, coriander, nutmeg, berries, apple juice, oranges, lemons, coconut. It stands. Preheat oven to 350°.
Mix:

⅓ cup oil, or ¼ lb. softened butter or shortening
½ cup sugar, molasses, honey, or a mixture

Add:

1 to 3 eggs, whole or separated and whites beaten till stiff
¾ cup milk, buttermilk, sour milk, or water or whey with ½ cup dried milk added

Beat; then add:

1½ cups whole-wheat flour, or half whole wheat and half any other flour
2 tsp. baking powder, which may be omitted if egg whites were beaten
½ tsp. salt

Flavor with:

1 tsp. almond, vanilla, grated lemon rind, or ¼ cup orange, lemon, or apple juice

Upside Down Cake
Grease the pan well with butter, and sprinkle with

flour before lining it with:

a layer of overlapping sliced fruit, such as apples, berries, peaches, pineapple, and ½ cup of nuts, if you like

You may sprinkle over the fruit, if tart:

½ cup brown sugar

¼ cup whole-wheat flour

Pour on the batter, and bake for about 30 minutes. If the temperature is lower it will be denser but still good.

APPLE CAKE

No eggs! Also, no butter and no sugar—a bottom-of-the-barrel special.

Preheat oven to 350° and grease a 9-inch pan. In a mixing bowl, combine and beat:

⅓ cup oil

⅔ cup water

½ cup powdered milk

2 Tb. nutritious yeast

½ cup honey

1 tsp. vanilla

Add all at once, then beat with a few swift, masterful strokes:

2 cups whole-wheat flour

or

1 cup whole-wheat flour

¼ cup soy flour

¾ cup rolled oats or oat flour

and

2 tsp. baking powder

1 tsp. salt

½ tsp. cinnamon

1 pinch cloves (optional)

Then add:

3 chopped apples

¼ cup chopped currants (optional)

½ cup chopped walnuts (optional)

Mix it up, pop it in the oven, bake about an hour at 350° or so.

BANANA BREAD

I hardly ever make this anymore, because bananas have become a rare treat in our household and get all eaten up the minute they are discovered. To make a really good banana bread you must have an overripe old banana all covered with brown spots.

Preheat oven to 350° and bank it.

Sift together:

2 cups whole-wheat flour (or 1½ cups plus ½ cup soy flour)

1 tsp. salt

2 tsp. baking powder

Add and mix:

1 cup chopped walnuts

3 Tb. soy or other oil

⅓ cup honey

1¼ cups skim or whole milk

Mash and add:

1 banana

Spoon the batter into a greased loaf pan and bake for about 45 minutes, until the middle bounces back to touch. Cool before taking out of the pan.

FRUIT ROLY POLY

Some people make this like a giant sandwich, others roll it up like a jelly roll. Use blueberries, raspberries, strawberries, or chopped apples.

Cut:

¼ cup butter

into a mixture of:

2 cups soft-wheat flour or 1 cup whole-wheat and 1 cup white flour

1 tsp. baking powder

½ tsp. salt

Mix and add:

2 eggs

½ cup milk or buttermilk or yogurt

2 Tb. honey or sugar (optional)

Roll out the dough and cover with:

2 to 4 cups fruit (if apples are tart, sprinkle with sugar, honey, and cinnamon)

Roll up or cover with more dough. Bake on a cookie sheet in a very hot oven, 400°, for a little over 30 minutes.

DATE NUT BREAD

You can always bake it as date bread, without the nuts, or substitute another dried fruit, such as figs, raisins, currants, dried apricots or apples . . .

Fruity breads make very good hiking and camping food since they are moist and keep well for a week or so.

Before you mix the batter, preheat the oven to

350° and chop up your fruit and nuts.
In a mixing bowl, beat:

2 eggs

Add and beat some more:

½ cup brown sugar
3 Tb. oil
juice of 1 small orange
½ cup milk (or water, with ¼ cup dried milk in it)

Sift together on top of the liquid, without mixing it in:

2 cups whole-wheat flour
2 Tb. brewer's yeast (optional)
2 tsp. cinnamon
2 tsp. baking powder
½ tsp. salt
½ tsp. coriander

Dump on top of the sifted things:

1 cup chopped dates (or other dried fruits)
½ cup Brazil nuts, walnuts, or sunflower seeds

Lightly, with your fingers, mix the flour around with the nuts and fruits. Then take your spoon and mix it all up with a few swift strokes. Pour into a well greased loaf pan and bake at 350° for an hour or until bouncy in the middle. Cool before removing from the pan.

CHRISTMAS PUDDING

This can be made up several days before the eating, and left in the mold until it is to be served.
Mix up:

1 cup whole wheat flour
½ cup brown sugar
2 tsp. baking powder
½ cup dried milk
½ tsp. salt
1 tsp. cinnamon
1 tsp. allspice

Add and mix in by hand (it's really the only good way):

1½ cups raw grated carrots
½ cup ground walnuts
1 cup dried currants (or raisins)

Pour into a measuring cup:

½ cup whole or skim milk

Add to it:

1 egg
2 Tb. molasses
2 Tb. light oil

Beat this, in the cup, with a fork, and add to the other ingredients. Mix well. Pack into 2 or 3 greased and floured cans or pudding molds, filling them ⅔ full. Tie pieces of oiled or greased brown paper (from bags) over the tops, with stout string, and set them on a rack in a tight pan or pressure cooker. Fill up the pan with 3 inches of boiling water, and cover tightly. Bring the water just to a boil, and steam for 2 hours. In a pressure cooker, steam at 15 lbs. for 45 minutes. Cool before removing from cans; it may be necessary to pierce the bottom of the can to take out the pudding.

GINGERBREAD CAKE

Preheat oven to 350° and bank it. This cake rises best in a tube-type baking pan.
In a mixing bowl, combine:

1 egg
¼ cup oil
1 cup molasses
1 cup water, milk, or whey
½ cup dried milk

Beat well; then dump on top without mixing:

2½ cups whole-wheat flour
½ tsp. salt
1½ tsp. baking powder
1 tsp. powdered ginger
1 tsp. cinnamon or allspice

If you like gingerbread with more bite, add an extra teaspoon of ginger. Pour in a greased pan and bake at 350° for about 45 minutes, or until a knife slipped in the middle comes out clean. Cool before unmolding.

Serve with applesauce, yogurt, or whipped cream.

THE MOST INCREDIBLE CHOCOLATE CAKE

From a nutritional standpoint there is just no excuse for this cake. It is absolute sheer total sin. And worth every bite.
Preheat the oven to 375° and bank it.
In a small pan, mix and melt over low heat:

½ cup water
3 oz. baking chocolate or 7½ Tb. unsweetened cocoa

Meanwhile, mix together in this order, beating well after each addition:

2 beaten eggs
1½ cups brown sugar

½ cup softened butter

1 pinch salt

Then add and beat in:

the chocolate

1 tsp. vanilla

In the chocolate pan, mix together:

¾ cup cultured buttermilk or yogurt or soured cream

1 tsp. baking soda

Add to the batter, by half cups:

1½ cups white unbleached flour

alternately with the buttermilk and soda mix, beating well after each addition. Pour the batter into a well greased cake or tube cake pan and bake at 375° for about 30 minutes. Cool before unmolding. This creature has the tenderness of cake, the richness of candy, the slight crunch of brownies, and is very very good with a generous dab of whipped cream.

CHOCOLATE STEAMED PUDDING

This is more like cake than pudding, except that it tastes so much better fresh out of the oven than it does later on.

Beat together:

1 cup sugar or brown sugar

1 egg

1 cup milk or coffee with ½ cup dried milk in it

3 Tb. melted butter

1 tsp. vanilla

Add all at once and beat well:

1½ cups well sifted flour (¾ cup whole-wheat, ¾ cup white)

3 Tb. unsweetened cocoa

¼ tsp. salt

1½ tsp. baking powder

Grease 5 or 6 custard cups, or a tube-shaped pan (not the kind that comes apart) and fill with batter about two-thirds full. Place in a pan of hot water, and bake at 350° for 30 minutes. To steam on top of the stove, cover the batter container(s) with aluminum foil and steam over gentle heat for 30 minutes. Test with a bit of straw to make sure batter is cooked in the middle.

Serve with whipped cream, if you can get it, or with a sauce made out of:

¼ cup honey

1 Tb. cornstarch

1 cup water

Cook and stir these together over low heat until clear and thick.

Add:

3 Tb. butter

Cool and add:

1 tsp. vanilla

Needless to say, this pudding is pretty good without toppings, too.

RHUM BABA

When at last my parents decided to make the long (and sometimes perilous) journey to visit our northern home, I was determined to show them we didn't lack for any of the finer delicacies of city life. As a child, I remembered the most gala occasions were marked with trips to Sutter's, and so I duplicated their most glorious treat as follows:

The Cake

Mix together in a large warm ceramic bowl:

1 cup warm water

1 Tb. dried yeast

½ cup sugar

1 cup whole-wheat flour

½ cup dried milk

Let this rest 5 minutes; beat well and put in the warming oven for 30 minutes. Then beat in:

4 eggs

½ tsp. salt

⅔ cup oil or melted butter

2½ cups whole-wheat flour

You may add, if the spirit moves you:

1 cup raisins

Beat, knead, and work this dough until it is glutinous. Cover with a cloth and set to rise in the warming oven for about 1 hour, until it doubles in size.

Butter and flour well a deep mold or two, or cupcake tins. An 11-inch tube pan will do all of it, but if your pan is smaller, use two, or put the extra in muffin tins. Fill whatever you are using only half full, and let it rise 1 hour, until doubled. Meanwhile, get your oven up to 350° and keep it there. When the dough is ready, bake it for about 30 minutes (20 minutes for small cupcake-sized cakes). Cool before unmolding.

The Syrup

As children, we delightedly imagined rum cakes to be soaked in straight rum, and lurched around accordingly. Actually, it's mostly sugar syrup, flavored with a little liquor. You may substitute honey and use as little or much as you like; you may also make it as mild or strong as your taste dictates. What I do is this:

Boil together for 10 minutes:

2 cups water
1 cup sugar (or ¾ cup honey)
juice of ½ lemon
1 grated lemon rind

Cool and add:

⅓ to 1 cup rum or strong gingery wine, such as parsnip

Put the cakes in a large pan, up sides down, and poke them all over with a fork or skewer as you pour on the syrup. Let them sit 15 minutes; then maneuver the excess syrup out and dose them again. Continue doing so until all the syrup is used up.

These cakes will keep pretty well. I mailed one to Florida once and it was said to have arrived intact.

YEASTED COFFEE CAKE

Both as batter and as cake, this looks and tastes like a quickbread. It's as easy as quickbread, too— but the rising agent is yeast.

Mix in a large ceramic bowl:

1 cup warm water
½ cup dried skim milk
¼ cup brown sugar or molasses
1 Tb. dried baking yeast

Let this sit for 5 minutes, or until the yeast dissolves. Beat well.

Then add:

¼ cup oil
2 or 3 eggs
3 cups whole-wheat flour
1 tsp. salt
1 tsp. vanilla or almond extract

Beat very thoroughly, with a wooden spoon, 100 strokes or more. Grease two cake tins or a 9- by 13-inch baking pan and pour in the batter. Let it rise in the warming oven while you stoke up the fire to 375° oven and crumble together:

½ cup cold butter
⅓ cup brown sugar
1 tsp. cinnamon
½ cup wheat germ or chopped nuts
½ cup whole-wheat flour

Sprinkle this mixture on top of the rising dough (or risen dough). In all it should rise 45 minutes.

Bake 30 minutes in a 375° oven with a banked fire in the stove. Cool before slicing into squares.

ANGEL FOOD SPONGE CAKE

Incredibly light. This cake often sticks to the pan; you should use a separating type of tube pan. After baking, let the cake cool for 1 hour before cutting it loose.

Fresh eggs do not beat well; use eggs at least 3 days old, and have them at room temperature. Separate them.

In a wide bowl, beat 100 strokes with a whisk:

4 egg yolks

When they are pale and very thick, slowly add, as you beat:

¼ cup sugar

Then add, in a thin stream:

¼ cup boiling water

Mix this well; then add and beat in:

1 Tb. lemon juice
grating of ½ lemon rind
1 cup whole-wheat flour
¼ tsp. salt

Have the oven ready at 350° and banked before you beat until stiff and dry:

4 egg whites

Scoop the whites over the batter and fold in gently with your flat hand. Be sure to mix in the batter at the bottom. Bake at 350° for 30 minutes. Remove from oven; cool 1 hour, cut sides free with knife, and remove the ring. Then cut the bottom and center free and serve.

Unimaginably good with heaps of raspberries.

NORTH BRANCH BIRTHDAY CAKE

Leavened by nothing more than beaten egg whites, this is a very light, moist cake.

Beat together:

3 egg yolks
1½ cups milk
½ cup honey

Mix in a separate bowl:

1 cup whole-wheat flour
½ cup oat flour
½ cup rice flour

1 Tb. cinnamon
1½ tsp. coriander
½ tsp. salt

Preheat oven to 375° and bank well; then sift dry ingredients into wet ones and beat until almost dry:

3 egg whites

Empty these onto the batter and fold together with your hand. Pour into an oiled cake pan or ring mold and bake at 375° for 45 minutes. Serve with:

whipped cream and raspberries

COOKIES

Cookies can be flat and crunchy, fat and soft, plain and satisfying, or full of surprises. They don't have to be very sweet; they can have interesting flavors or textures instead.

The great virtue of a cookie is its portability. You can always stuff a handful in your pocket, your knapsack, your saddlebag, or your lunchpail.

WHAT'S IN COOKIES

Fats and Oils: The reason cookies are so crunchy and keepable is that, generally, they have a high measure of oils or fats. Solid fats make cookies lighter; oils make them denser, and, after a day or two, not so crunchy. But oils are better for you.

Flours: If you're used to white-flour cookies, you can switch to whole-wheat pastry flour for more nutrition; nobody will know the difference. Hard wheat is better, but it must be very finely ground to be really good in cookies (because they bake so fast and hot). Oat flour is nice—sort of dense, but tasty. A little millet or cornmeal thrown in adds crunch.

Milk and Milk Products: Milk makes the insides of cookies tender, and the outsides crisp. Cultured buttermilk or yogurt does it even better.

Sweetenings: These affect the texture as well as the flavor. Sugar and brown sugar make a light, dry cookie. Molasses or honey makes them chewy; molasses has a distinct flavor.

Eggs: Watch out for eggs and oats. The high temperatures used in baking often make eggs tough, especially when mixed with oat flour. When I first began inventing cookies I used to use lots of eggs;

all my cookies were soft and tender for about one hour, after which they became so hard that the only way you could eat them was to put them in a tin for a month with a slice of apple. Eggs do hold cookies together; but use other liquids, too.

Ground Nuts, Seeds, and Wheat Germ: These all have a lot of oil, so they're very good cookie materials. You may roast and grind them for more flavor, or leave them raw for more nutrition. Brazil nuts, walnuts, and pecans are the softest; they can be added in big chunks, but hard nuts, such as almonds and filberts, should be sliced or ground.

Baking Soda, Baking Powder: See Cakes (page 85).

CAPE BRETON OAT CAKES

Thin, light, crisp, and sweet. Cape Bretoners today don't use whole wheat and oat flour, but their grandmothers did.

Mix:

¾ cup solid shortening (lard, butter, whatever)
¾ cup white or brown sugar

Mix together and add by cups:

1½ cups whole-wheat flour
1½ cups oat flour
½ tsp. salt
1 tsp. baking powder

Then add and mix in alternately:

3 cups rolled oats
enough water to soften so it can be rolled out (¾ to 1 cup)

Chill dough 1 hour, and roll out ¼ inch thick. Bake at 350° for about 10 minutes.

ALMOND COOKIES

Sift together:

1½ cups whole-wheat flour
1 cup whole-wheat pastry flour
1½ tsp. baking powder
½ cup sugar

Mix in by hand, very thoroughly:

½ cup light oil

Mix in a measuring cup and add:

¼ cup cold water
2 tsp. almond extract

Mix well and shape into balls the size of large walnuts. Set on a cookie sheet and press to flatten slightly, ½ inch thick.

Mix in the measuring cup:

1 egg yolk
1 Tb. water
Paint tops of each cookie. Set on each:
1 slice of almond
Bake at 350° to 400° for 10 to 15 minutes.

HARD GINGERBREAD

This is a very strong, firm dough, and it makes a very hard cookie. Its virtue is that it holds its shape very well in the oven and keeps practically forever. We use it to make Christmas gingerbread every year, to decorate the tree and the house. You can also use it to take the imprint of a Springerle stamp or rolling pin, or to make a gingerbread house.

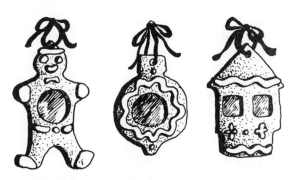

stained glass gingerbread

It is good dough for children to work with, but a little hard for them to mix up. However, you can make up a giant batch of dough and keep it in the fridge or pantry for a week or two, breaking off hunks for them to roll out and cut up or shape in their own ways.

In a large bowl, mash up:

½ cup solid shortening
½ cup sugar
½ cup molasses

Sift together into another bowl:

4 cups whole-wheat flour
1 tsp. baking powder
½ tsp. ground cloves or allspice
2 tsp. ginger
½ tsp. salt

Add the flour mixture to the other stuff slowly, by half cups, mixing thoroughly after each addi-

tion. When it gets too stiff to mix anymore add 1 Tb. water. Continue mixing in flour; add water up to 4 Tb. in all. Most likely, you will have to knead in the last cup of flour. Flatten the dough on a plate and cover with a cake tin; put in the fridge to cool 30 minutes, before rolling out.

If you refrigerate it for longer you should take it out 15 minutes before rolling and let it warm up some; you may have to knead it to unstiffen it enough to roll.

To Roll Out
Gingerbread is best rolled out ¼ inch thick. More important, however, is that you get all the dough on one sheet of the same thickness, or some will burn before the other cooks. Scraps may be re-rolled or shaped into balls and "snakes." Pieces may be stuck together with water.

Decorating
Use nuts, seeds, bits of candied fruit rind, coconut, sugar; for children, you may put each kind of decoration in the cups of a muffin tin, so they won't spill. Avoid raisins or currants, though, because they just swell up and blacken. Remember you can use dough for decoration, too, if stuck on with water. Patterns can be made with blunt knives, chopsticks, forks, etc.

Springerle
Roll out dough ½ inch thick; then press on mold or roll with a special patterned rolling pin to print on the design. Cut out the cookies and transfer carefully to greased cookie sheet. Let rest, uncooked, overnight, in a cool place. Next day bake as below.

Stained Glass Gingerbread
To make this you need a very smooth lightweight cookie sheet, a good sharp spatula, an eye on the clock, and a bag of hard candies. Cut out large cookie shapes, such as gingerbread men or houses. Cut holes in them about ¾ inch square (as for houses) or 1 inch diameter (the size of doughnut holes). Place the cookies on the sheet and put a hard candy or life saver in the middles of the holes. Bake as below. When the cookies are ready and the candy melted, take them out but *don't touch them* for 5 minutes and then quickly slide your spatula under each one. Not necessary to move them elsewhere, just get that spatula under each one at the 5-minute mark. (If you do it sooner, they glom up and stick to the spatula; if

you do it later, they're stuck to the sheet. No use greasing the sheet. This is a single-method operation, no alternatives.) Don't forget to punch holes in the tops of each cookie before baking so you can hang them up on the tree or at a window, with a bit of ribbon or bright yarn.

SOFT GINGERBREAD

This is Peggy Ryan's recipe. She never measures the flour, and neither do I, and you don't have to if you don't want to.

Beat together until creamy:

¾ cup lard
1 cup brown sugar

Beat in:

2 eggs
1 cup molasses
1 tsp. salt
1 tsp. cloves
1 tsp. allspice
2 tsp. ginger

Mix together and add:

½ cup black tea (you can use coffee, too)
1 tsp. baking soda

Peggy adds flour until you can roll it out; she uses white.

If you'd rather use whole-grain flours, I'd suggest you use less, and make drop cookies. You could use:

3½ cups whole-wheat flour
3 cups pastry flour, oat flour, or white flour

Beat well and chill 2 hours before baking. Scrape large spoonfuls onto a cookie sheet. Bake at 350° for 10 to 15 minutes.

Excellent with butter and applesauce.

PEANUT BUTTER COOKIES

Rich, delicious, and addictive, these can be made with either smooth or crunchy peanut butter.

Mash together in a shallow bowl:

½ cup brown sugar
½ cup butter or ¼ cup vegetable oil
1 cup peanut butter

Add and mix in:

1 egg
½ tsp. salt
½ tsp. vanilla
1½ cups whole-wheat flour (or slightly more, as needed)

Roll the dough into small balls; place on cookie sheet and flatten with a fork. Or press flat with your thumb and top each mound with:

an unroasted peanut

Bake 15 minutes at 375°. Keep a very close eye on them after 10 minutes. When they are lightly browned on top, take them out and let them cool for 10 minutes before attempting to remove them (with a spatula) from the cookie sheet. If you have children in the house, and are planning to serve these cookies as dessert or in lunches, hide them carefully.

COCONUT MACAROONS

You want to be sure and bake these on greased brown paper. There isn't any way to keep them from sticking to the pan.

Mix:

⅓ cup milk
1 cup powdered milk
⅓ cup honey
2 tsp. almond extract
a pinch salt
2 cups dried unsweetened coconut
¼ cup wheat germ

Beat until stiff and fold in:

3 egg whites

Drop by teaspoonfuls, from a wet spoon, onto greased brown paper, on a cookie sheet. Round the cookies nicely. Bake at 350° until lightly browned, about 15 minutes. Cool and scrape free with a spatula.

OATMEAL DATE BALLS

Nothing in here except healthy stuff. Stuff your pockets with them on your way out to work in the woods.

Grind to flour and mix:

1 cup sunflower seeds (1 cup sunflower meal)
1 cup rolled oats (1 cup oat flour)
1 cup whole wheat (1¾ cups whole-wheat flour)
½ cup soybeans (⅔ cup soy flour)

Add and mix in:

1 cup rolled oats
1 cup chopped nuts or sunflower seeds
1 tsp. salt
¼ cup brewer's yeast
1 cup currants
1 cup chopped dates

When this is well mixed, moisten with about 2 cups warm water, or as needed, to make a dough you can form into firm balls. The nuts and ground seeds have much oil in them but you may add along with the water, if you like: 2 Tb. light oil. Bake the balls at 300° to 375° (doesn't much matter) 10 to 20 minutes, or until light brown.

CHEESECAKE BARS

This is a two-part recipe: crunchy stuff underneath, and cheesecake stuff on top. You can split up the crunch and put half underneath and half on top; or you can put the crunchy all on the bottom and top it with fresh or frozen blueberries.

Crunch
Mash together:

½ cup cold butter or corn oil
⅓ cup brown sugar or maple sugar
½ cup whole-wheat flour
½ cup rolled oats
½ cup roasted ground nuts: walnuts, sunflower seeds, Brazil nuts, pecans, cashews, or a mixture

Press this, or half of this, into an 8-inch baking pan or cake pan and bake for 15 minutes at 350°. Take it out and add a mixture of:

Cheesecake Part
1 cup dry curds, cottage cheese, sour cream, or cream cheese
1 egg yolk
2 Tb. melted butter or corn oil
¼ cup honey (or brown sugar)

Top with remainder of crust or with:

1 cup fresh or frozen blueberries

Bake at 350° for a little less than 30 minutes. Cool, cut into squares.

FIG OR DATE BARS

For these you use very sweet, sticky dates or figs that come packed tightly together. Chop up into a small saucepan:

1 cup dates

and add:

½ cup boiling water

Simmer until dates are soft, about 1 hour. Cool and add:

grated rind of ½ lemon

Meanwhile, mix up:

½ cup cold butter, chopped in small pieces
1 cup whole-wheat flour
½ cup rolled oats
½ cup coconut (if you like coconut)

Mash half the dry mixture into a greased 7-inch by 7-inch pan. Spread carefully with date mixture and top with dry mixture. Bake at 350° for 30 minutes. Cool and cut into squares.

BERRY BARS

One summer we missed out on blueberries altogether and then wound up with a super haul of blackberries. Whereupon I discovered that blackberries are great in muffins, cakes, and pancakes, or in this mixture:
Beat together:

1 or 2 eggs
¼ cup oil or lard
½ cup molasses

Add:

½ cup sugar (if you are into sweets)
½ cup soy flour
½ cup wheat flour
1 cup ground rolled oats
1 cup rolled oats
1 tsp. salt
2 tsp. baking powder (optional)
1 cup blackberries, raspberries, blueberries, or wild strawberries

Spread this batter thin and bake very fast at 450°, for a bar. If you put it in a smaller pan and bake it slower, it's a good tea cake. I reckon it could be a cookie, too . . .

HALVAH

Very rich, very small, very special.
Toast for 15 minutes at 200° in separate pans:

1 cup sunflower seeds
1 cup sesame seeds

When the seeds become golden (not brown) take them out and drop a few sunflower seeds in the grinder, and put them through (if there was any old buckwheat or coffee lingering in there, it will come out; throw it out). Then set the grinder pretty tight and put the sesame seeds through. Follow with the sunflower seeds, which will clean the last of the sesame out of the crevices, where sesame seeds tend to linger. Mix the seeds with:

½ cup honey
¼ cup light oil or dark sesame oil
¼ tsp. salt

Press into muffin tins, about ½ inch high. Scatter sesame seeds over the tops and press them in with the bottom of a glass or something flat. Unmold, store in refrigerator.

PIES

Pie crusts have two basic purposes. One, they provide a crisp contrast to the contents of the pie. Two, some pie crusts (not all) enclose the pie, thus enabling the contents to be steamed rather than baked.

There are several different kinds of pie crusts, with various aims in mind. Some people are after perfect appearance. Some want that flaky, melt-in-your-mouth texture. Some wish to use only whole grains and unrefined vegetable oils. Well, you can't have everything at once; you have to choose a priority. (But you can choose a different one for each pie, if you like.)

FLAKY PIE CRUSTS

A flaky pie crust is a little complicated; it takes some practice. The process is every bit as important as the ingredients. It is made with cold hard shortening, soft flour, salt, and cold water, as follows:

Shortening: You may use butter, home-rendered animal fat, or any of those hydrogenated lards, margarines, or vegetable shortenings. Myself, I stick to animal fat and butter; I have a basic mistrust of hydrogenation. The idea is to chop up cold, hard little bits of fat into the flour so that the mixture resembles coarse uncooked cereal. You cannot make flaky pie crust with warm fat or with oil; it will just soak into the flour, making a crisp rather than a flaky crust.

Flour: The ideal flour is soft-wheat flour, also called whole-wheat pastry flour. If you grind soft wheat yourself, you should sift out the husky bits, which are not really very tasty in pie crust.

If you cannot get soft-wheat flour, you have to resort to white flour, or half white and half hard whole wheat. Or you can add wheat germ or bran to white flour; since they are rolled flat by the mills, they are already headed in the direction you want them to go. Use only fresh products; supermarket "whole-wheat flour" makes cardboard crust, no matter how carefully handled.

I have spent a lot of time fruitlessly trying to make and roll out pie crust with all hard whole-wheat flour. It is very difficult to work with and never makes a flaky crust.

Salt: Salt is mixed in with the flour, ¼ to ½ teaspoon per cup.

Water: The water should be very cold, and added a little at a time, after the grease and flour are mixed. The idea is to glue the mass into a firm, but not sticky ball, with as little water as possible. Sprinkle in a few tablespoons, stir with a fork, and sprinkle more water in the driest places. Eventually you can lift out the parts that are stuck together, and, adding a touch more water, clean the bowl.

KNEADING AND REFRIGERATING: Very lightly work the dough so that it forms a firm, compact ball, and flatten it. Wrap in plastic or set in a covered bowl, and refrigerate for 30 minutes; this will rechill the fat, and also make the dough a little more pliable.

ROLLING OUT: Have the oven up to the right temperature before you roll out the dough. Use a very smooth surface lightly floured, a little heap of flour in one corner to work from, and flour your rolling pin. If the dough is hard from long chilling, beat it 3 or 4 times with the pin. Then commence rolling out from the middle, gently. Turn the dough often, sliding your hand under to make sure the counter stays floured. Try to roll out even-shaped pieces of dough, both top and bottom. Don't roll too thin; ⅛ of an inch is thin enough. Lift the dough in the pie dish and press it down around the bottom.

Sometimes, rolling pie crust can be really exasperating, especially with whole-wheat flours. If you just can't get it into the pan, try rolling it out on a piece of lightly floured waxed paper. Or, better yet, keep a piece of floured canvas handy for the purpose. When it's rolled out, invert the pie dish on the crust, and gently turn them both over. With any luck, the crust will slide into the dish without too much damage.

TRIMMING AND SEALING: If holes appear, patch them swiftly with a little water (for glue) and a bit of dough; don't be overly fussy. Trim with a knife, not too close to the edge; it will shrink a little in baking. Fill the pie and just before laying on the top crust, paint the rim lightly with a little water. Then seal with a fork or your fingers. Prick the top to allow steam to escape.

You may, if you like a brown crust, paint the top with a little milk or egg yolk. It doesn't do anything for the taste, but it sure makes a jazzy looking pie.

BAKING: For a flaky crust, you must have a very hot oven, 400° to 450°, or even a little more. The fire must be banked and steady, or the excessive heat across the top will burn the crust. In a wood stove, you must also turn the pie after 20 or 30 minutes, so that one side is not burned before the other cooks.

PASTRY FLOUR AND BUTTER

Mix:

2 cups whole-wheat pastry flour
⅔ cup butter
½ tsp. salt

Add:

¼ to ⅓ cup cold water

Mix well, ball, and chill 30 minutes or longer. Bake at 400° to 450°.

Variations
Substitute ½ cup wheat germ for ½ cup of the flour.
Use lard, animal fat, or solid vegetable shortening for butter.

Note: You may have to roll this crust out on waxed paper or a floured canvas, then invert into the pan —unless you're a really expert hand with whole wheat crusts.

WHITE FLOUR, WHEAT GERM, AND BUTTER

Mix:

1½ cups unbleached white flour
½ cup wheat germ
½ tsp. salt
⅔ cup butter

Add:

¼ to ⅓ cup cold water

Mix well, ball, chill 30 minutes or more. Bake at 400° to 450°.

Variations
Substitute **bran** for wheat germ.
Use **lard, animal fat, or solid vegetable shortening** for butter.

QUICHE OR TART SHELL

This one holds its shape really well, yet is very light and puffy.
Mix:

1½ cups unbleached white flour
½ cup wheat germ
½ tsp. salt
¼ cup lard
¼ cup butter

Mix and add:

1 egg
⅓ cup cold water

Mix well, kneading vigorously. Shape into a ball and chill in a covered dish or plastic bag 2 hours or longer. Roll out quite thick, ⅛ of an inch. Line pie dish; bake at 400°. To make a free-standing quiche or tart shell, or a crust for topping with creamed stuff, shape the dough carefully over an upside down cake pan or muffin tin cup or on flat surface. Prick it very well every ½ inch all over, with a fork, so it won't swell up with steam and get soggy underneath. Bake at 400° for 7 to 10 minutes.

WHITE FLOUR, WHOLE-WHEAT FLOUR, ETC.

Mix:

1 cup unbleached white flour
1 cup sifted whole-wheat flour
½ tsp. salt
⅓ cup butter
⅓ cup lard

Add:

¼ to ⅓ cup cold water

Mix well, ball, and chill 30 minutes or more. Bake at 400°.

CRUMB CRUSTS

Crumb crusts are traditionally used for surrounding fillings that hold their shape—such as cheesecake, chiffon pies, custard, pumpkin, and so forth. You can use them for fruit pies, too, if you don't mind the pieces falling apart as you serve them.

Crumb crusts include those made of cake, cookie, or cracker crumbs, and those made of hard whole-wheat flour. Melted butter or light oil is mixed in, and sometimes other things: cinnamon, nuts, sugar, and milk.

Crumb crusts aren't rolled out; they are pressed into the pie dish. You can use your fingers; but an easier way to do this is to distribute the mixture evenly in the pie dish, and firmly press another pie dish down over it.

If crumbs are used, the pie crust need not be baked. It should, however, be thoroughly chilled (in the dish) before pouring in the filling.

If you wish to bake the crust, empty, put it in a very slow oven (200° to 300°) for 10 to 15 minutes, being careful not to burn it. Cool before filling.

If you are baking a filled crust, it must be done in a slow oven, and turned around once or twice to prevent the heat of the fire from burning it on one side. If the filling is not yet done and the crust begins to burn on top, cover with greased brown paper.

CRUMBS AND BUTTER

Mix:

1½ cups ground crumbs: gingerbread, oatmeal cookies, or graham crackers
⅓ cup melted butter or oil
1 tsp. cinnamon

Press into pie dish; chill 30 minutes. Fill and bake or rechill filling.

Variations

1. *For a firmer crust,* add ¼ cup cream or canned milk.
2. *For a nutty crust,* add ½ cup ground nuts or seeds. These are even better if roasted (roast before grinding: see page 54).
3. *For a sweet crust,* add 2 Tb. brown sugar or white sugar.

WHOLE WHEAT AND OIL

Mix:

1½ cups hard whole-wheat flour
½ cup light oil: peanut, corn, sunflower, safflower, sesame
½ tsp. salt

Add:

¼ cup cold water

Press into pie dish; chill 30 minutes or more. Fill and bake with filling. Without filling, bake 15 minutes at 300°.

Variations

1. *For a nutty crust,* add ½ cup ground nuts or seeds, plain or roasted.
2. *Soy crust:* Substitute ½ cup soy flour for ½ cup wheat flour.
3. *Cornmeal crust:* Substitute ½ cup corn meal for ½ cup wheat flour.

JUDY'S NO-OIL PIE CRUST

Mix:

½ cup ground sunflower seeds
½ cup ground rolled oats or wheat flour (hard or soft)
½ cup wheat germ

Add: **enough water** to loosely mix it. Press into pie dish, chill 30 minutes or more. Fill and bake; without filling bake 10 minutes at 300°.

Variations

1. Chop 2 Tb. butter in with the flours.
2. With the addition of slightly more water, this crust becomes rollable, though not without difficulty. You may find it easier to roll it out and place it into the pie dish if you use a floured piece of canvas.

APPLE PIE

If the reputation of American Motherhood is based on the gooey messes that pass for apple pie these days, no wonder so many women are heading for other roles. The first problem is the apples; it's hard to buy in a supermarket a good tart apple that will hold its shape and lend some flavor. If you're not a forager and never will be, take a ride out to the hills and buy some good pie apples.

This recipe is for tart but ripe apples; if using unripe apples, increase the sugar by ½ cup. Also: you can put butter in the pie if you like; I don't, anymore, because it's so expensive.

Make the pie dough (see pages 95–96) and chill it for 30 minutes.

Chop into a pie dish the same size, cutting

around the core but leaving the skins on:

enough apples to fill the pie dish heaping full

Empty the apples into a bowl and sprinkle over them:

½ cup brown sugar (or more, if the apples are unripe)

½ cup whole-wheat flour

½ tsp. cinnamon and ½ tsp. allspice

Mix this in with your hands, coating all the slices. Then sprinkle over it:

¼ cup milk or top milk or sour cream

Preheat the oven to 400° and bank it. Roll out two-thirds of the crust (see page 94) and line the pie dish. Fill with the apple mixture; roll out the other third of the dough carefully, in an even piece if you can. Paint the rim of the bottom crust with a little water. Lay the top crust over it and press around the edge with a fork or crimp with your fingers to seal the crust. Trim the edges. Poke a few holes in the top to vent it and then pop it in the oven.

After 30 minutes have a look; perhaps turn the pie, so it doesn't burn on one side. Bake 45 minutes in all. Cool 15 minutes before serving.

BLUEBERRY PIE

One of the nicest things about blueberries is that they need very little or nothing to sweeten them.

Make a pie crust (see pages 95-96) and chill 30 minutes. Roll out two-thirds of it and line the bottom of a pie dish.

Pour a cup or so of blueberries into the lined dish, and sprinkle about a tablespoon of cornstarch over them. Mix them around a little, a quick stir. Then pour in another cup of berries and scatter on more cornstarch. Repeat this process 3 times, using in all:

4 cups blueberries

4 Tb. cornstarch

You may sprinkle the top, if you like, with:

2 to 4 Tb. honey

Stir the top layer until no cornstarch shows.

Roll out the other third of the pie dough. Brush the rim of the bottom crust with a little water; cover the pie, and flute the edges by pressing them together with a fork or your fingers. Trim the edges and cut holes in the top to let out steam as it bakes. Bake at 400° or so for about 30 minutes, or until blueberry juice bubbles out the top holes.

Cool 30 minutes before serving.

RHUBARB PIE

Chop into 1- to 2-inch lengths:

enough fresh rhubarb to fill a pie dish (about 15 stalks)

Dump the rhubarb in a mixing bowl and toss with:

1¼ cups sugar or brown sugar

⅓ cup sifted whole-wheat flour or unbleached white flour

a good pinch salt

Empty this into an unbaked pie shell (page 95); cover with pastry and bake at 375° for 15 minutes; then let the oven go down to around 325° and bake 45 minutes longer. Rhubarb pie is very runny when hot. It also sometimes bubbles out of the crust as it bakes, so keep an eye on it; you may have to put a pan under it to catch the drips.

PUMPKIN OR SQUASH PIE

Chop up the pumpkin or squash (reserve seeds if you wish to toast them) and steam with ½ cup water in a tightly lidded pan for about 1 hour, until soft through. (You should have about 2 cups.) Put it through a food mill.

This will be a single-crust pie, so only use ⅔ of a flaky pie dough recipe (page 95); mix dough and chill 30 minutes.

In a mixing bowl, mix up:

1 cup pumpkin or squash, steamed and strained

⅓ cup brown sugar or molasses

1 tsp. cinnamon

½ tsp. ginger

¼ tsp. salt

1 or 2 eggs

1 cup milk

½ cup dried skim milk

Preheat oven to 400°. Roll out pie dough, and line pie dish; prick with a fork, and weight it down with smooth stones or dried beans. Bake 10 minutes; take it out and cool it, and leave the oven door open for 5 to 10 minutes to cool it down to 325°.

Fill the half-baked pie shell with pumpkin or squash filling; bake at 325° for 30 minutes. (You can bake it in a 200° oven; leave it in 2 to 3 hours.)

MOCK PUMPKIN PIE

1. Substitute for pumpkin:

1 cup cooked unflavored mashed soybeans (page 157)

This sounds unlikely, I know, but it's hard to tell the difference.

2. This is really a dense Indian Pudding in a pie shell. Make, roll out, and half bake a pie shell, as above. Meanwhile bring almost to the boil:

2 cups whole milk

Sprinkle in a little at a time, stirring constantly:

½ cup cornmeal

When it is thick, take it off the heat and add:

½ cup brown sugar
½ tsp. salt
½ tsp. each cinnamon, ginger, freshly grated nutmeg

Pour in the pie shell. Bake at 300° for 1 hour or until solid. Cool before serving.

3. Use cooked mashed carrots instead of pumpkin or squash. Or leftover Tzimmes (page 33) . . .

MINCE MEAT PIES

Mince meats are an old traditional English way of preserving meat along with fruits, spices, sugar, and a good measure of brandy, from butchering time until Christmas. It was kept in a crock, sometimes with a lard coating on the top; in this brew, anything would keep. This is a small recipe; expand, if you will.

Simmer 1 hour and mince (do not grind):

1 cup lean beef (½ lb.)

Put it in a soup pot and add:

½ cup chopped beef suet
1½ cups chopped tart apples
¼ cup chopped raisins
2 Tb. minced candied lemon rind
½ cup whole raisins or currants
¼ tsp. mace
1 tsp. each cinnamon, cloves, and allspice
½ nutmeg, grated
1 cup broth from simmering the beef
¾ cup cider
1½ Tb. vinegar
3 Tb. molasses
1 cup sugar
juice of ½ orange
juice of ½ lemon

Simmer all this for an hour or two; then add:

½ cup brandy
½ cup chopped almonds (optional)

To keep this any length of time, instead of simmering it in a pot on the stove put it in a ceramic crock and bake at 300° for 1 hour or so, letting the fat rise to the top; then let the oven cool with the mince meat in it, fat on top, so that it is more or less sealed underneath against air. The old recipes say to add brandy at the last, just before serving, but I would think the brandy would help to preserve it and help the flavor too. In any case, to bake it, just make a flaky crust (page 95), pile it full of mince meat, cover with a good tight top, and bake for 45 minutes at 350°.

CUSTARD PIE

Make pie dough; since this is only a single crust pie, you only need ⅔ of a double crust recipe (pages 95–96). Refrigerate 30 minutes.

Preheat oven to 400° and bank it; roll out dough and line a pie dish, being generous around the rim. Prick with a fork here and there and weight with dried beans or smooth stones. Bake 5 to 10 minutes, until lightly crisp; take out and cool. (Remove rocks!) Leave the oven door open 10 minutes or so to cool it down to 325°.

Beat in a bowl:

3 eggs
⅓ cup honey or sugar
1 cup milk and 1 cup cream (or evaporated milk)
or
2 cups milk and 1 cup dried skim milk
1 tsp. vanilla
¼ tsp. salt

Pour this into the half-cooked pie shell. Bake at 325° for 30 minutes.

Variations

Applesauce Custard Pie: Substitute **1 cup applesauce** for 1 cup milk. Substitute **1 grated lemon rind** for vanilla.

Coconut Custard Pie: Sprinkle top with **1 cup unsweetened coconut**.

Date or Raisin Custard Pie: Add **½ cup dates or raisins**, sprinkling the fruit in the bottom of the shell before pouring over the egg mixture. Decrease honey to **3 Tb. honey**.

Orange or Lemon Custard Pie: Substitute **½ cup undiluted frozen orange juice** or **juice of 1 lemon (¼ cup)** for equivalent amount of milk; grate in **1 lemon rind** or **1 orange rind**.

BLUEBERRY TARTS

A very fancy dessert, made ahead of time and

chilled for at least 3 hours. You may make it in one dish or in four individual tart shells.

Make up flaky pie dough (page 95). Chill 30 minutes; then roll it out and line the dish or tart shells, making sure there is a good thick rim around the edge of each one. Prick the shell(s) and weight them with small rocks or dried beans. Bake at 400° for 5 to 10 minutes, until flaky but not brown. Meanwhile, pour into a bowl:

1 qt. (4 cups) blueberries

Sprinkle over them:

2 Tb. cornstarch
¼ cup honey
2 Tb. lemon juice

Take out the half-baked shells, fill with blueberries, and return to the oven for 15 minutes or so (it's okay if the oven goes down a little) until the shell rims brown slightly and the blueberries get hot and red and a little soft. Take out the tarts or pie and cool.

Mix in a small bowl or the top of a double boiler:

1 egg
1 or 2 egg yolks
½ cup cream or evaporated milk
¼ cup honey
a pinch salt

Cook and stir until thick, over boiling water. Be careful not to let it lump; this is a delicate mixture, easily spoiled by too rapid cooking. When it is thick, take it off the heat and cool it for 15 minutes; pour over the cooled blueberry tarts or pie. Place in the fridge or a cold pantry and chill for at least 3 hours.

REASONABLE STRUDEL

This really isn't strudel; but it's easy enough so you can make it any old time, in 30 minutes or so.

Make up a batch of *butter, white flour, and wheat germ* pie crust (page 95). Chill ½ hour.
Chop very fine:

3 tart apples

Heat:

2 Tb. butter

in a frying pan and sauté the apples for 5 to 7 minutes. Remove them from the heat and sprinkle over them:

1 tsp. cinnamon

Cool and add:

2 Tb. honey

On a lightly floured surface, roll out the dough as thin as you can in a long oblong shape. Trim the edges so they are even.

Distribute filling everywhere on it except near the edges. Brush the edges with a little water. Roll it up, like jelly roll. Refrigerate 30 minutes.

Preheat oven to 400° to 450° degrees. Bake 20 minutes.

Variations

1. You may add a few raisins or currants and/or nuts to the cooled apple mixture—say, ½ cup in all.

2. You could use only raisins and nuts—¾ cup in all. No need to sauté them or add honey. Instead, melt ¼ cup butter and brush in on the inside, shake over a little cinnamon, and scatter on nuts and currants/raisins.

3. Instead of one big strudel, you can make little tarts; cut out rounds of dough with a small bowl and fill with a few tablespoons of filling; paint and seal edges, and vent tops. Very tasty travel food, that is.

RHUBARB CRUMBLE

This is a very rich dessert by itself. With yogurt it is better—and the rhubarb makes it taste like whipped cream.
Mix:

2 cups diced fresh or frozen rhubarb stalks
1 cup brown sugar

Deposit this in a greased baking dish (8 inches or so). Now mix in the same bowl:

1 cup whole-wheat flour
½ cup wheat germ
½ cup brown sugar
⅓ cup oil

Crumble together with your fingers. Spread this mixture all over the rhubarb. Bake at 350° for 40 minutes.

APPLE CRUMBLE

It is very important that the crumble be spread *over* the apples, forming a kind of crust, so that the apples below will steam and cook.
Mix:

2 to 3 cups chopped fresh or frozen tart apples
¼ cup water

Deposit this in a greased baking dish (8 inches or so). Now mix in the same bowl:

1 cup whole-wheat flour
½ cup wheat germ
½ cup brown sugar
⅓ cup oil
1 tsp. cinnamon

Spread the topping over the apples; bake at 375° for 30 to 40 minutes. Serve hot or cold; plain or with yogurt.

Variations on Crumbles

1. Mix in with the fruit ½ cup raisins or berries
2. Substitute for wheat germ in topping ½ cup chopped walnut meats

A VERY EXCELLENT CHEESECAKE

Line a pie shell with a crumb crust (pages 95-96) and chill for 2 hours.
Beat together:

½ cup sugar
¾ lb. cream cheese

Then beat in:

2 beaten eggs
1 tsp. lemon juice
½ tsp. salt

Or beat together:

2 egg yolks
2 cups sour cream
½ cup sugar
1 tsp. lemon juice
½ tsp. salt

Pour the mixture into the pie shell and bake at 300° for about 35 minutes or until the top puffs up a bit. Take it out and cool it until the top falls. Then mix together and spoon on:

1½ cups sour cream
2 Tb. honey
a pinch salt
½ tsp. vanilla
grated rind of 1 lemon

Bake at 400° for about 5 to 10 minutes, until the top just begins to brown. Take it out and cool well. Top with:

2 cups fruit thickened with cornstarch and sweetened to taste

After adding fruit let it chill at least 3 hours.

PUDDINGS

Desserts such as these are easy to make, and there are so many ways to make them. The Commercial Ice Cream generations are getting robbed; strawberry, chocolate, and vanilla all taste the same, and so handy in their plastic containers; nobody knows anything about the astonishing variety of textures and flavors that used to grace our tables. Branch out; learn about egg custards, gelatins, and yogurt cream whips. Serve up your precious home-canned or frozen treasures in a dozen different forms. Save sugar; strawberries taste more like strawberries when they're a little sour. Think about your meal: Does it need a light ending, or a generous scoop of rice pudding? Could it use eggs or milk for protein, or some fruit to balance a lack of vegetables? If you have kids, turn them loose at a quiet hour (you can make rhubarb sherbert if you wash up after yourself!). Invest in a few fake cut-glass dessert dishes to make gels and whips in. Or some nice brown custard cups. Remember, too, you don't have to serve desserts for only dessert. The English serve them for tea, after sandwiches; they're known as a "trifle." And many a wise mother has discovered that children who normally despise breakfast willingly devour a trim egg custard, or a raisined rice pudding.

INDIAN PUDDING

Most likely the American Indians originally made this with water, corn, and maple, perhaps a little piece of bear fat thrown in to render as the grain cooked. It was quickly adapted by settlers to include more ingredients; it is the sort of food that takes well to adaptation. You put in what you think right.
Scald:

1 qt. milk

Sprinkle in and stir:

½ cup cornmeal, cracked wheat, or samp (a mixture of the two)

When thick, remove from heat and add:

⅓ cup molasses
⅓ cup maple sugar or brown sugar
½ tsp. salt
½ tsp. cinnamon, ½ tsp. allspice, ½ tsp. nutmeg
½ cup raisins, ½ cup chopped nuts (optional)
1 Tb. butter (optional)

Mix well, pour into a greased or buttered baking dish, and bake at 250° to 300° for about 3 hours.

BAKED CUSTARD

Delicious in its utter simplicity, a custard is anybody's favorite. Be sure to bake it in a slow oven, though, or it will toughen and separate.

Beat together:

3 eggs
2 cups whole milk
⅓ cup honey
1 tsp. vanilla
1 pinch of salt

Pour into a greased casserole or ovenproof custard cups (teacups work nicely) and set them in a cake tin of hot water (to keep the bottom from toughening). Bake at 300° to 325° for about 1 hour. When a knife inserted in the center comes out clean, it's done.

ORANGE OR LEMON SPONGE CUSTARD

Custardlike on the bottom, frothy on top, and fruit-flavored, these elegant desserts must, like all egg custards, be baked in a slow oven or they will toughen and shrink. Bake them in 4 custard cups or in a small, deep casserole, for best results.

Beat together:

3 egg yolks
5 Tb. sugar or 3 Tb. honey
2 Tb. melted butter
1 cup whole or skim milk
grated rind of 1 lemon or 1 orange
3 Tb. unbleached white flour
juice of 1 lemon or 1 orange

Beat until stiff and fold in just before baking:

3 egg whites

Bake in a greased casserole or custard cups, set in a pan of hot water, for about 1 hour at 300° to 325°.

RASPBERRY OR STRAWBERRY SPONGE CUSTARD

Substitute for juice and rind of fruits above:

⅓ cup raspberry or strawberry juice
2 Tb. lemon juice

After folding in beaten egg whites, fold in:

1 cup fresh or frozen berries

Bake as above.

BAKED RICE PUDDING

Mix together:

2 beaten eggs
2 cups cooked rice
¼ tsp. salt
¼ cup honey
2 cups milk
½ cup dried milk
½ tsp. vanilla
½ cup raisins

Pour into a greased baking dish or casserole; bake ½ hour at 300°.

Variations

Substitute **chopped dates, currants, nuts** for raisins.
Substitute ⅓ cup molasses for honey.
Add **fresh chopped fruits or berries**, up to 1 cup.

CREAMY RICE PUDDING

This is another kind of thing altogether; the rice cooked with milk makes it really soft and sweet.

Mix together:

1 cup uncooked rice
¼ tsp. salt
¼ cup honey
1 qt. milk
½ cup dried milk
½ tsp. vanilla

Pour in a greased baking dish or casserole and bake at 300° for 3 hours; or cook in a greased heavy pan on the side of a wood stove, milk barely simmering, for 3 hours. You may stir it, if you like, and mix in ½ cup raisins, nuts, or fresh fruits and berries in the last 30 minutes of cooking.

BREAD PUDDING

Mix together:

½ cup molasses
2 eggs
2 cups milk
½ cup powdered milk
1 pinch salt
½ tsp. cinnamon

When smooth, add:

3 to 4 cups whole-wheat bread, broken into pieces as big as hazelnuts, more or less

Empty into a greased ovenproof container; bake at 300° for about 1 hour, or until a knife inserted in the middle comes out clean.

FRUIT PUDDING

Raspberry, strawberry, blueberry, blackberry, apple, etc.

In a pan, cook:

1 qt. berries or sliced fruit
with a little butter

until soft. Meanwhile, beat:

4 eggs

until frothy; add:

1½ cups breadcrumbs

and blend into the berries. Add:

honey

as needed, to taste; cook and stir over very low heat on the right of a banked stove or over boiling water until it thickens. Serve hot or chill to set.

CHOCOLATE SOUFFLÉ

One does not produce such a dish on the spur of the moment, or on the off-chance that somebody might like it. A chocolate soufflé is made with great love and considerable effort, for 5 or 6 guaranteed-hungry chocolate lovers to eat at once.

Melt together over low heat or in the top of a double boiler:

¼ cup butter
2 oz. chocolate or 5 Tb. cocoa (unsweetened)
½ cup sugar

Stir in:

2 Tb. unbleached white flour

When it is thick, add:

2 cups whole milk

Keep this warm but do not boil. Beat together in a bowl:

6 egg yolks

Add a little of the hot mixture to them, and beat well; then gradually pour it back into the pot on the stove and cook, stirring with a whisk, until it thickens slightly. Don't let it boil or cook too long. Let it cool and then add:

2 tsp. vanilla

Preheat oven to 350° and lightly butter a large, straight-sided ovenproof pot. Beat until peaks can be formed:

6 egg whites

Scoop them on top of the cooled custard mixture and fold everything together with your flat hand,

being sure to scoop up all the chocolate from the bottom. Set the soufflé pot in a cake pan with a little hot water in it. Bake for 20 minutes. Serve at once.

Serve with whipped cream or plain thick cream.

GELATIN DESSERTS

Gelatin, according to *The Columbia Encyclopedia*, is a "glutinous material or animal jelly obtained from the supporting structures of vertebrate animals by the action of boiling water ..." In other words, it's the same stuff that makes boiled bone stock jell. "The final product in its purest form is brittle, transparent, colorless, tasteless, and odorless, and has the distinguishing property of dissolving in hot water and congealing when cold." The Columbia goes on to itemize an astonishing list of foodstuffs in which gelatin is used (would you believe powdered milk? coffee?) and to point out that it is very easy to digest, therefore making good baby food or invalid fare.

Gelatin is mostly thought of, these days, in terms of Jello-type desserts, which combine gelatin, sugar, and artificial flavoring and colorings. Fortunately, it's still available in plain form; and it's not hard to make your own gelatin desserts, with real fruit flavor and color, and lots less sugar.

To mix up plain gelatin, you first soak it in a little cold water; then add hot water or juice to dissolve it, and sugar, if needed. After that you can add more juice, water, fruits, whatever.

One package or tablespoon of gelatin will jell two cups of liquid.

You can use any fruit in it except for fresh pineapple, which has an enzyme that dissolves gelatin. If you want to use pineapple, cook it, first. (You can use canned pineapple—it's cooked.)

If you wait until gelatin is half chilled and jelled but not solidly, you can whip it, to double its volume and have a very fancy texture.

Gelatin desserts must be chilled in a refrigerator or cool pantry, not the freezer or subzero arctic winter. They cannot be frozen and rethawed; but gelatin is added to frozen sherbert-type desserts to "stabilize" them, or keep them from forming ice crystals as they freeze.

LEMON JELLO

Rather a bore by itself, but good over berries or chopped fruit.

Soak:

1 pkg. (1 Tb.) plain gelatin
¼ cup cold water

Add:

1½ cups boiling water
½ cup sugar
3 Tb. lemon juice (squeeze half a lemon)

Stir well. Pour over 1 cup strawberries, raspberries, blueberries, or sliced fruit—or a mixture, in a cake tin or dishes. Chill 2 hours.

Orange Jello: add only:

½ cup boiling water

Mix thoroughly, then add:

1 cup fresh or frozen orange juice

Pour over sliced oranges, bananas.

FRUIT JUICE JELLO

Soak:

1 pkg. (1 Tb.) plain gelatin
¼ cup cold water

Add and stir well:

1¾ cup hot juice: raspberry, blackberry, cranberry, elderberry, apple

Add to taste:

sugar

Pour over fruit, as in Lemon Jello, if you like. Chill 2 hours.

Wine Jello: Substitute fruit wine for 1 cup of fruit juice.

WHIPPED FRUIT PUDDING

Thick, smooth, and delicious. It's hard to believe it's just gelatin and mashed fruit:

Soak:

1 pkg. (1 Tb.) plain gelatin

in

¼ cup cold water

for 3 minutes. Mix in:

1½ cups hot sweet applesauce, or puréed pears, plums, or peaches

Cool for 30 minutes, then refrigerate for an hour or so, until it begins to thicken.

Beat with an eggbeater or whisk for 5 minutes. You can fold in, if you like:

1 cup whipped cream or whipped evaporated milk

Chill for 3 hours, or until set. If you didn't add whipped cream, you can serve it with a generous dollop of:

plain yogurt

YOGURT BAVARIAN CREAM

An endlessly variable dessert; if your yogurt is very sour, add a little more honey; but it need not be a stiff yogurt.

Mix:

1 pkg. (1 Tb.) plain gelatin
¼ cup cold water

Let them sit. In another bowl, mix:

1 cup hot water or fruit juice
½ cup fresh or frozen fruit (anything except fresh pineapple)
¼ cup honey

Mix the gelatin again and stir it into the fruit. Add:

1 cup yogurt

Pour in a serving container and chill 2 hours.

Variations

Rhubarb: Mix **½ cup hot water** and **honey**; add **1 cup rhubarb**

Apple: Mix **½ cup hot water** and **2 Tb. honey**; add **1 cup applesauce**; Or mix **1 cup hot cider** and **2 Tb. honey**; add **½ cup sliced apples**

Blueberry: Mix **1 cup hot grape juice** and **2 Tb. honey**; add **1 cup blueberries**

Raspberry, Strawberry: Mix **½ cup hot water** and **honey**; add **½ cup cranberry juice** and add **½ to 1 cup berries**

Blackberry: Mix **1 cup hot water** and **⅓ cup honey**; add **1 cup blackberry juice**

Vanilla: Mix **1 cup hot milk** and **¼ cup honey**; add **2 tsp. vanilla**

Orange: Mix **½ cup hot water** and **¼ cup honey**; add **½ cup fresh or frozen orange juice (undiluted)** and, if you like, **1 chopped orange**, and **the grated rind**

Lemon: Mix **1 cup hot milk** and **⅓ cup honey**; add **2 Tb. lemon juice** and **1 tsp. vanilla** or **1 grated lemon rind**

STRAWBERRY FOAM

Soak:

1 pkg. (1 Tb.) plain gelatin in ¼ cup cold water

Add:

2 cups hot milk in which **1 vanilla bean** has cooked
¼ cup sugar
½ cup wild strawberries (fresh, frozen, or canned)
1 Tb. lemon juice

Chill until almost set, about 2 hours. Whip until frothy. Chill again 30 minutes or so. Meanwhile whip:

½ cup thick cream

Fold whipped cream into fruit gelatin and add:

1 cup wild strawberries (fresh, frozen, or canned)

Chill 2 to 4 hours until set. Garnish the top with a few berries and serve.

YOGURT AND FRESH CHEESE DESSERTS

It is easy to make plain homemade yogurt (see pages 120-122) into yogurt desserts. All you need is a little sweetening and maybe something else—some nuts or fruit. The fruit can be fresh, or dried, or canned, or frozen. If the fruit has been sweetened first, you don't even have to add the sweetening. (See also **Yogurt Bavarian Cream**, page 103).

FRUIT YOGURT

Mix together:

½ cup unsweetened yogurt
1 Tb. brown sugar or runny honey
2 Tb. unsweetened canned fruit (raspberries, blueberries, blackberries, apples, strawberries, peaches, pears—whatever you have around)

Or:

¼ cup fresh fruit, chopped if necessary

Or:

2 Tb. dried fruit, chopped if necessary

Let the mixture sit for about 3 minutes until the brown sugar or honey melts into the yogurt.

NUT YOGURT

If you have a special stash of pecans, save it for yogurt.

Mix together:

½ cup unsweetened yogurt
1 Tb. brown sugar
2 Tb. chopped pecans or walnuts or Brazil nuts

If you like you can also add:

1 Tb. dried currants or blueberries or other dried fruit

PASHKA

Probably you have had pashka, although you might not have known it had such a fancy name. In Russia it is served at Easter.

Put through a sieve or the fine grate of a food mill:

1 cup cottage cheese

Mix it very well with:

¼ cup sour cream
¼ cup honey or brown sugar

Then mix in:

¼ cup currants or raisins
¼ cup chopped pecans or toasted walnuts
grated rind of about half a lemon

In Russia they also add:

2 Tb. candied fruit rind (lemon or orange)

Press this into a bowl and chill it for a couple of hours. Turn out and serve.

YOGURT CHEESECAKE

Thick, tangy, rich tasting but relatively low in calories:* from the kitchens of Moma Restino we bring you a cheesecake that entered our back door as milk and eggs.

You will need:

1 qt. yogurt

It need not be fresh or mild yogurt, but it should be fairly thick; use yogurt that has been made with 1 cup dried skim milk added to the fresh skim milk. Line a bowl with 4 or 5 layers of cheesecloth; dump in the yogurt, and tie up the cheesecloth. Hang the bag to drip over the bowl for a couple of hours, but don't squeeze it; the yogurt will come through. The stuff that drips out is whey and may be used for making Sour Rye Bread (see page 64).

Meanwhile, make and bake at 350° for 15 minutes:

---

*68 calories per 2-inch slice (dividing cake into 16 slices), as compared to cream-based cheesecake, which is 250 calories per 2-inch slice.

a crumb crust (see pages 95–96)

When the yogurt is thick enough (down to about 2 cups) scrape it out into a bowl and add:

2 egg yolks
1 whole egg, beaten in
1 grated lemon rind
1 to 2 cups sugar or ¾ to 1¼ cup honey (or a mixture)

Since every batch of yogurt is different, I sweeten to taste rather than by recipe. I used some really strong stuff that had been forgotten in back of the warming oven for 24 hours one time; that took 1 cup sugar and half a cup of honey. If you want this to be a Neapolitan Cheesecake, you can add:

½ cup whole pignola nuts (pine nuts)
¼ cup chopped candied lemon or orange rind

Pour the yogurt mixture into your half-baked crumb crust and bake at 300° for about 30 minutes, or until the top begins to swell and crack. Cool before serving.

FRUIT TOPPING FOR YOGURT CHEESECAKE

A plain cheesecake is very nice covered with:

1 to 2 cups fruit: blueberries, apples, peaches, cherries, strawberries, raspberries

Heat the fruit in a sauce pan; pour off a few tablespoons of liquid and mix with:

4 Tb. cornstarch

Return the liquid to the fruit and stir as the sauce becomes thick and clear. Pour over the cheesecake and allow the fruit to "set" on top of the cake for a couple of hours in a cool place before serving.

Despite the low calorie count, this is rich stuff. Don't eat more than a slice or two at a time unless you have a cast-iron stomach.

SNOWS AND ICES

RASPBERRY FOOL

So named because even a fool could make it, they say.
Whip until stiff:

1 cup whipping cream
Add:
1 cup fresh raspberries (or any berries)
Set to chill 1 hour or more. There is some talk in a few old recipes of sugar, but I think that is clearly unnecessary.

FRUIT SHERBERT

Soak together 5 minutes:

2 pkgs. (2 Tb.) plain gelatin and ½ cup cold water
Add:
1½ to 2 cups hot, sweetened fruit juice
Freeze to a soft mush, about 2 hours. Whip, fold in:
1 cup whipped cream or whipped evaporated milk
Add a tablespoon or two of lemon juice if necessary to pick up the flavor. Freeze about 30 minutes, or until just firm.

RASPBERRY RHUBARB ICE CREAM

Technically this isn't really ice cream. But it's hard to tell the difference; and you don't need to haul out the ice cream freezer. You do, however, need to freeze it. This is a good dessert to make in the winter, using frozen fruits.
Mix together:

1 pkg. (1 Tb.) plain gelatin
¼ cup cold milk
Let that soften while you heat:
¾ cup milk
⅓ cup honey
Pour that over the gelatin mixture and stir, then add and mix in:
1 pt. rhubarb
Put the bowl into the fridge or outside in the cold to jell for 1½ to 2 hours. Then whip into it:
1 cup frozen raspberries
Place that in the freezer or pack in snow for 30 minutes to 1 hour, until just slushy (if you set it to half freeze, just before dinner, it's generally right to serve at dessert time).

SNOW ICE CREAM

A favorite with children: you cook up a bunch of syrups, they provide snow and mix it up, with as much or as little snow as they like. The syrups must be cooked to dissolve the sugar, but you need not make a great deal of it. Half a cup of the stuff goes a long way.

Vanilla: Simmer together until honey dissolves:

½ cup cream or milk

½ cup honey

Cool and add:

2 tsp. vanilla

a pinch salt

Chocolate: Mash together:

3 Tb. cocoa

3 Tb. milk

Add:

½ cup milk

½ cup sugar

a dash of salt

Simmer until sugar dissolves. Cool and add:

1 tsp. vanilla

Bug Juice: Simmer together any fruit juice and enough sugar to make it ridiculously sweet. Cool and add vanilla or a drop of lemon if you like.

ICE CREAM

There's one ice cream freezer in our neighborhood. Whenever anybody has a birthday, it duly arrives, and is assembled, filled with sloshing syrup, and packed round with layers of crushed ice and rock salt (1 cup salt in all). Then, while one person holds it, somebody else starts the first stage of slow, uneven cranking. For a while it's turned at 40 revolutions per minute (Sarah's timing revolutions; Duncan says, "I can do it by feel"). It begins to feel heavy, and turns more evenly, but takes more effort. That's the signal to speed it up to as-fast-as-you-can-go; the bucket is passed around as people's arms fall off and finally everybody wants to have a look: is it ice cream? So off with the lid, and it is, only kinda slushy. The lid is readjusted, new ice and salt packed round, and you crank it for another 5 minutes at 80 revs.

If you want hard ice cream, you then stick the inner container (lid, dasher, and all) out in the snow, or in the freezer, for 30 minutes.

RECIPES

Unlike store-bought ice cream, which contains an amazing assortment of chemical flavorings, colorings, and preservatives, homemade ice cream is really very simple stuff—basically it's just cream, beaten as it's frozen. Sugar or honey sweetens it; fruits, vanilla, or chocolate flavor it. In strongly flavored ice creams you can use canned evaporated milk instead, but you must disguise the taste; canned milk is no good for plain vanilla, but is fine for chocolate and passable for fruit flavors *only* if you add the juice of a lemon. For a really smooth texture, mix up the syrup the day before and keep it refrigerated.

VANILLA

Heat together until sugar dissolves, being careful not to boil:

1 cup cream

½ cup sugar or ⅓ cup honey

a generous pinch salt

Cool and add:

3 cups cream

Just before churning, add:

2 tsp. vanilla

RASPBERRY, STRAWBERRY, BLACKBERRY, PEACH, CHERRY

Mix together and let stand overnight:

2 to 4 cups berries or crushed fruit

¾ cup sugar

juice of 1 lemon if you're using evaporated milk

Before churning, mix in:

1 qt. cream or evaporated milk

ORANGE

Heat together, being careful not to boil:

1 cup cream or evaporated milk

1 cup sugar

Chill; just before churning, add:

1½ cups orange juice

¼ cup lemon juice

2 cups cream or evaporated milk

BUTTERSCOTCH NUT

Heat together, being careful not to boil:

1 cup cream

½ cup brown sugar

¼ tsp. salt

Cool and add:

3 cups cream

When ice cream is half churned, remove lid and add:

1 cup chopped walnuts or pecans

CHOCOLATE

Heat together, being careful not to boil:

2 cups cream or evaporated milk
2 oz. unsweetened chocolate or 5 Tb. unsweetened cocoa

(If using cocoa, mash it with a bit of the milk before adding.)

1 cup sugar
a generous pinch salt

Cool and add:

2 cups cream or evaporated milk
1 tsp. vanilla

DESSERT SAUCES

Since these are very sweet, and a bit of an extra bother, I don't make them often. But supposing it is someone's birthday, and a horrible blizzard is raging outside, and there's nothing to do . . .

FRUIT SAUCE

Usually I make these out of a jar of canned fruit (blueberries, apples, cherries, or peaches). I drain off the syrup and mash a bit of it with:

2 Tb. cornstarch

The rest of the syrup is heated, then the cornstarch is stirred in until it thickens. Then I add, by tablespoons, until it is just right:

sugar or honey

Sometimes I add:

2 Tb. butter

Finally I add the fruit, and stir, and serve. If I had some, I'd add:

2 Tb. brandy or sweet wine

RASPBERRY MELBA SAUCE

The absolute epitome of elegance.
Heat together slowly:

½ cup currant or apple jelly
1 cup raspberry juice

Dip out a bit of juice and mix with:

1 Tb. cornstarch

Return to the mixture and stir until it clarifies and thickens a little. Cool and store. Use on ice cream, cake, or custards.

VANILLA SAUCE

Heat very slowly, stirring constantly with a small whisk:

1 cup milk
¼ cup sugar or honey
1 Tb. cornstarch

When clear and slightly thick, cool, and add:

1 tsp. vanilla

If you have a vanilla bean, you can cook it in with the milk and leave out the last step.

LEMON CUSTARD SAUCE

Heat together slowly:

2 cups milk
½ cup sugar
1 pinch salt
grated rind of 1 lemon

Separate into a small bowl and beat:

2 egg yolks

Pour a little hot milk into the egg yolks and beat; then return them to the pot, stirring continually and simmering for 2 or 3 minutes as the mixture thickens slightly. Don't overcook it; it's not going to turn into heavy custard, or anything like that. Moreover, it will go on cooking off the heat.
Stir in:

the juice of ½ lemon

Cool. Add, if you like:

½ tsp. vanilla

CHOCOLATE FUDGE SAUCE

Dreadful stuff. Guaranteed to rot the insides and curl your hair. You keep it in a small pot in the fridge and heat it up to go on ice cream. Melt together over low heat:

3 Tb. butter
5 Tb. unsweetened cocoa

Stir this well, and then add:

½ cup boiling water
1 cup sugar

Bring to a full rolling boil and cook for 5 or 10 minutes. The longer you boil it, the thicker it will get; after 10 minutes it will be the kind of stuff that hardens on ice cream.

SYRUP

Maple sugar is great, if you have it; if you don't, here's how to fake it:

Heat together:

1 cup water

4 cups brown sugar

When sugar dissolves, cool and bottle the syrup. You can make it a whole lot tastier if you add:

1 cup real maple syrup

YOGURT OR SOUR CREAM SAUCE

Mix:

1 cup thick yogurt or sour cream

½ cup brown sugar or maple syrup

If you have it, you can even add:

2 Tb. heavy rum or brandy

7
HOMEGROWN EGGS

Anybody who has ever broken into an egg from a down home barnyard chicken can see, even before it's cooked or eaten, that there's quite a difference there between it and a commercially produced egg. The yolk is dark yellow, or orange; the white, even after a week, is thick and gelatinous. Appearances are not deceiving: the egg has more food value, is easier to cook with, and tastes better. Partly, of course, this is because a chicken who forages on greens, grains, bugs, and assorted "organic garbage" gets more nutrition than one who lives in a cage on a steady diet of 15 percent this and 12 percent that. It is also a matter of how often the hen lays, though. Commercial hens lay more eggs because they are fed minute quantities of an arsenic compound that speeds up their metabolism and production tremendously. If store-bought eggs taste watery to you, it's not because they're old; it's because they *are* watery. We sometimes buy absolutely fresh eggs from a commercial farmer up the road and the whites are just as runny as those of any eggs you buy in a store.

RAISING CHICKENS

Chickens are about the easiest farm animals there are to keep. As long as they have a marauder-proof place to go at night, they virtually take care of themselves. All they have to be fed is cracked grain, water, and some source of calcium—either cracked oyster shells, or their own shells, dried and ground, mixed in with the grain. They will forage the rest, either from the yard and barn, or from your organic garbage. Wherever you dump that garbage (whether in their house or in their yard) it will be turned into the best garden fertilizer known to man. One friend suggests moving the chicken yard fence every year and planting the

hungrier vegetables—cabbages, tomatoes, squashes, and cucumbers—right where the hen yard was last year. Certainly it is easier to move the fence than to move the earth.

If your chickens are to wander, unfenced, they will return to the house each night, once they get used to it (keep them locked in the first few days after you get them). After that, as long as they are laying, don't let them out until ten or eleven a.m., by which time they will probably have laid, if they're going to. Shut them up every night; don't depend on a dog. Any fox worth his salt can easily decoy a dog away and clean your henhouse out completely in one night.

A hen still on the nest by mid-afternoon, especially in the spring, should be suspected of having gone "broody." This means she has a mind to accumulate 8 to 12 eggs (her own or any others that come along) and sit on them for 21 days and see what comes out. It does not matter whether they are fertile or not, whether you have a rooster or not. She will only leave that nest at dawn for a quick drink and a bit of food; and she will peck at anyone who comes near. With a quick hand, you can remove all but one egg every day; she'll go on laying. Or you can stop her from going broody: put her in a burlap sack and hang it up for 24 hours. If she has fertile eggs, or you can get fertile eggs, though, and want her to hatch chicks, you had better move her into hatching quarters. Set a crate on its side, inside a separate pen in the chicken house or barn; arrange things so you can stick food and water in without descending over her head or going near her. Move her and her nest of eggs into hatching quarters, at night as quietly as possible. The reason for all this bother is that other hens will peck new chicks to death if they get separated from their mother, by chance. Sad, but true.

All this sounds like trouble, but it is amazing what good care hens take of their chicks, and how easy it is to raise chicks with a mother, compared to without a mother. New chicks don't eat for the first 24 hours, so they can be ordered and shipped from a hatchery, arriving (mostly) alive and well; from then on for a month or so they need constant warmth and require quite a lot of cleaning, feeding, and watering; plus they make a terrific din 24 hours a day. Incidentally, while I don't put any stock in laying mash, I should say that chicks fed "growing mash" grow twice as fast, become twice as big, and lay better, in general, than those fed homeground grain mixtures. Maybe if you were to grind it really fine, to flour? And add soybeans?

Chicks born in April will start laying in August or September, and lay all winter; they will lay less when it is cold, but will pick up production in a thaw. After the first year, they generally molt, or lose feathers and grow new ones, from December through February, every winter. Molting chickens seldom lay, so don't be surprised. About three weeks before Easter, you are suddenly flooded with all shapes and sizes of eggs, as their hormones adjust; your rooster will become active and start crowing a lot; if you have more than one rooster, they will get into fights. The sudden egg bonanza is the first sign of spring, and explains why Easter and Passover cakes and breads have so many eggs in them; and also why colored eggs are traditional at Easter.

Once in a long while, chickens get colds or other infections. There isn't much you can do: in my experience a chicken gets sick only once. Always separate a droopy chicken from the flock, in the hope that the others won't get it too. It might recover, if kept warm; but if it's a chick, it will be small and prone to get other diseases. Best to do it in.

If your hens went broody and you got chicks hatched and they grew up, chances are you now have a major problem with cock fights. Not to mention the poor hens, who begin to look browbeaten. One cock is plenty; into the pot with the others—see page 207. Many people prefer to keep cross-bred chickens, which, like hybrid vegetables, don't reproduce. The eggs will be fertile, but the hens seldom go broody. You should check into this before you buy or order chick or chickens.

ABOUT EGGS

Eggs are extraordinarily versatile. They're easy to cook, making quick, high-protein snacks, or super-elegant quiches, soufflés, and desserts. They provide a perfect vehicle for milk and cheeses; thicken sauces; leaven and increase the protein of grains, and combine well with fish, poultry, and all sorts of vegetables.

Any person of normal health who has been warned to avoid eggs is being hoodwinked. For although they do contain cholesterol, they also provide the lecithin necessary to break down not only the cholesterol they have but also some of that which your own body manufactures.* They also contain tremendous amounts of vitamins A

_____

*If you do have a cholesterol problem, you may eat eggs boiled, or poached; or gently sautéed in unrefined vegetable oil rather than solid fats such as butter, bacon fat, .etc.

and B_{12}, calcium, iron, and other minerals; many of the substances in eggs are found in very few foods, and are needed in order for the body to digest and utilize other vitamins and minerals. These nutritional values are naturally much higher, egg for egg, in fertile products of home-fed chickens, who forage a wide variety of foods and lay at a normal pace.

COOK EGGS GENTLY

Rule one about cooking eggs is *always use low heat*. Too hot a pan or oven makes the protein shrink and toughen, rapidly; there is nothing you can do to recover their lost volume and tenderness. In a 450° oven, a soufflé will deflate; a quiche or custard will separate. When adding eggs to sauces, the liquid must be at a low simmer, and stay that way. Often it is wise to beat the egg in a shallow bowl, add a little hot liquid, and beat well before returning the mixture to the sauce on the stove. As soon as an egg-thickened sauce, soup, or custard thickens (usually in no more than 5 minutes) you must take it off the heat. Let it cool; these things are better cold than curdled. Watch out, too, when you mix eggs into hot batter (such as in Cornmeal Pancakes); the eggs will cook, just as if they were on the stove.

BEATEN EGG WHITES

To get the most volume out of an egg white, choose eggs at least three days old, at room temperature. To be absolutely sure no yolk gets into the whites, separate each white first into a small cup—then, if you break a yolk, it'll only be in with the one white. (If yolk, or any greasy substance is in with the whites, they won't rise as well.) Beat the whites in an absolutely clean bowl, preferably copper and never aluminum, with an egg beater until they will stand up in peaks when you lift the beater out; but stop before they stick in an upside-down bowl. If you expand them too much they will collapse when mixed with batter.

To fold in beaten eggs whites, empty them on top of the batter. With your flattened hand, lift batter up and through the whites, gradually mixing in the heavier ingredients; be sure to get to the bottom of the bowl. Scrape the mixture into the cooking pan with your hand, too, before you go wash up.

There are any number of recipes using beaten but uncooked egg whites, such as mousse, fruit whips, and so forth; but I hesitate to serve them, for two reasons. One is that uncooked whites contain a substance called avidin that combines with a B vitamin, biotin, and prevents it from reaching your system. The other is that many children and even some adults are allergic to raw egg whites, when for some reason their bodies don't produce enough cortisone. It all sounds a little too complex to be true, but any pediatrician or child care manual will tell you that egg whites should be introduced last in a baby's diet, and with caution; and that they should always be thoroughly cooked.

Beaten egg whites may be cooked in grain dishes, such as cornbreads and other quickbreads and cakes; or they may be mixed with cream sauce and yolks, to make soufflés of many kinds. Cakes baked with a lot of egg whites will almost always stick in the pan; you should use a separating type tube pan so you can cut the cake loose.

HARD-BOILED EGGS

Very fresh eggs will stick in their shells. For best results use eggs that are two or three days old.

To prevent the eggs from cracking, make sure first that you have eggs with sound shells: hold them up to the light and look for flaws. Then set them in cold water to cover, bring to a boil, and simmer 10 minutes. If you really want to be sure they don't crack, prick the large end with a pin first.

After they are done, set them in a pan of cold water for 5 to 10 minutes. This also helps the shells separate more easily.

FLAVORED AND COLORED
HARD-BOILED EGGS

After hard-boiling and shelling eggs, you may simmer them for 30 minutes in any of these mixtures:

Brown: Mix:

3 Tb. strong black tea
3 Tb. tamari soy sauce
2 Tb. salt
½ tsp. powdered anise seed (optional)
1 Tb. ground pepper (optional)
3 cups water

Pink:

1 panful of water in which beets have been cooked
½ cup vinegar or lemon juice
2 Tb. salt
1 Tb. dill

Yellow:

3 cups water
2 Tb. tumeric

CHINESE TEA EGGS

Do not shell the eggs after boiling, but crack the shell all over very well with the back of a spoon and place them in the tamari-tea mixture (**Brown**) above. Simmer 30 minutes. Wash, cool, and shell; the eggs will be laced with a delicate brown tracing.

STUFFED HARD-BOILED EGGS

Boil and cool the eggs; shell them and cut in half with a very sharp knife. Slice off a little of each end so they will sit upright. Take out the yolks and mash them up.

1. 4 mashed yolks
   3 Tb. mayonnaise
   ½ tsp. mustard
   ½ tsp. tamari soy sauce
   pinch of paprika, pepper
   ½ tsp. salt

2. 4 mashed yolks
   2 Tb. yogurt
   1 Tb. grated onion
   1 Tb. chopped parsley
   ½ tsp. salt

SCRAMBLED EGGS

Fond as I am of scrambled eggs, I have a deep-seated dislike of the watery texture of this dish when milk is added. If you do too, use cream or evaporated milk when you need to dilute them. Mix:

For 1 Person:

2 eggs
(2 Tb. cream)
pinch salt

For 2 or 3 People:

4 eggs
(¼ cup cream)
2 pinches salt

For 4 or 5 People:

6 eggs
(⅓ cup cream)
3 pinches salt
(grating of pepper, dash of paprika, chopped fresh herbs, etc.)

Heat gently:

2 or 3 Tb. butter

or

unrefined oil

in a heavy frying pan until it bubbles but does not smoke. Add eggs; tilt the pan around and then cover it and let the eggs cook for 30 seconds. Off with the lid and give it a stir or two; cover and cook 1 minute, scramble again, cover and remove from heat. Leave the lid on until they are ready to be eaten.

Variations
Scramble the eggs in a pan in which you have just cooked up:

½ cup sliced mushrooms
1 small chopped onion or 3 to 4 chopped green onions
½ chopped bell pepper

Or add to the eggs before cooking any of the following:

½ cup grated cheese: Cheddar, American, Swiss, Jack
½ cup cottage cheese or sour cream (instead of cream, above)
2 Tb. chives, parsley, chervil, etc.
2 egg yolks
2 Tb. dry white wine
½ cup cooked sausage meat

SOFT-BOILED EGGS

Bring a pot of water to a full, rolling boil. Slip in one to five uncracked fresh eggs; cover and boil:

banty eggs	—	2½ minutes
small eggs	—	3 minutes
medium, large	—	3½ minutes
jumbo, duck	—	5 minutes

Remove from water; serve immediately on toast. To serve children, break toast into small pieces in a bowl, breaking the egg over it. Chop up the white and serve hot, with a little salt.

CODDLED EGGS

This is an English refinement; eggs to be used should not be absolutely fresh, or the white will harden before the yolk thickens. The aim is a soft-cooked white, and thick yolk.

Set the eggs in simmering, not boiling water; leave the lid off, to keep an eye on them, and cook:

banty eggs	—	3½ minutes
small eggs	—	4 minutes
medium, large	—	5 to 6 minutes
jumbo, duck	—	10 minutes

A coddled egg, properly, is served in an egg cup, with a small silver spoon.

FRIED EGGS

Use very fresh eggs, when possible. Heat a little butter (1 to 2 tsp.) in a heavy frying pan; watch carefully and break in the eggs just as the butter begins to bubble, but before it sizzles. Cover the pan immediately and cook for 3 minutes. If you wish to turn them, turn and cook for 30 seconds. Serve and eat at once.

WOOD STOVE TOAST

Lay the sliced bread directly on the front middle plate and cook 1 minute on each side. If the bread begins to burn before it toasts, move to a cooler plate. Butter and keep warm in the oven, if necessary, but not for longer than 5 minutes, as it will dry out.

OMELETS

Nothing is simpler than the making of a good quick omelet; and nothing so defies description. Like the making of bread or cheese, it is just something you learn how to do and do it.

For 1 person allow **2 eggs**
For 2 people allow **3 eggs**
For 4 people allow **5 to 6 eggs**
For 6 people allow **8 eggs** and use a very large pan; for larger groups, make more than one omelet,

since more than 8 eggs will not set, and more than 6 is difficult. No omelet should take more than 5 minutes to cook.

If it is to be filled, prepare the filling first and set it in a small dish in the warming oven, ready to hand. Fillings include:

½ cup sautéed mushrooms
½ cup cooked crab, lobster, or flaked haddock
½ cup tomato sauce with lots of chopped vegetables in it
½ cup cheese, any kind except Mozzarella

Now beat up the eggs, until frothy, in a bowl; you may use just plain eggs, or the following rich and delicious mixture:

4 whole eggs
2 egg yolks
¼ cup cream or canned milk
½ tsp. salt
freshly ground pepper
2 Tb. each fresh chopped chives and parsley

Heat gently in a cast-iron skillet or cast-iron omelet pan:

3 Tb. butter

Watch the pan closely; when the butter begins to froth a bit, but hasn't yet sizzled, pour in the eggs (they should go *swish* as they hit the hot pan) and let them set for 1 minute. Then cautiously give the pan a shake or two to make sure they're loose on the bottom. Cover and cook 3 minutes. Remove lid, tilt, fold, and cook 1 minute more. Serve immediately.

POACHED EGGS

Poached eggs are cooked directly in boiling water. (Eggs cooked over boiling water in little patty pans are steamed, not poached.) To poach eggs, heat water to boiling in a wide-mouthed pot (such as a Dutch oven) and break no more than 3 eggs into the water, widely separated. The water should be gently, not furiously boiling; if the eggs are fresh, they will hold together. Cook, uncovered, 2 minutes. Spoon a little water over each yolk; cook 30 seconds more and remove with a slotted spoon immediately.

Poached eggs may be served on toast, as a breakfast, tea, or part of dinner.

Variations

Eggs Florentine: Cover **toast** with **chopped creamed greens** and top with **a poached egg**. Egg may be poached in water or clear broth.

Eggs Benedict: Fry slices of **ham** and make up a **Hollandaise Sauce** (page 177); as eggs are poaching, make a slice of **toasted English muffin** for each egg. Cover muffin with a slice of ham, an egg, and top with Hollandaise.

Tarragon Eggs (a very elegant dish): Sauté in the poaching pot, in **2 Tb. butter: 3 Tb. chopped scallions**. When soft, add:

2 Tb. dried or 2 tsp. fresh chopped tarragon
¼ cup dried or fresh parsley
2 cups white wine

Simmer this in an open pot until the liquid is down to 1 cup. Then break in the eggs and poach them. Serve over rice, using the liquid as sauce.

FRENCH TOAST

French toast is bread, soaked in eggs, and fried in fat.
Break into a very wide bowl or a cake pan:

4 eggs

Beat them up with a fork and then add:

¼ cup milk or cream

Now slice:

6 pieces of bread

If the bread is a very large loaf you might cut each piece in half. Put each piece in the egg mixture and turn it over so both sides are eggy. Pile the eggy pieces together in the bowl and leave them to soak.

Now you should go set the table and have everything ready; get out butter or maple syrup or apple jelly or whatever you want to serve with French toast. Yogurt and jam are nice too, and applesauce is great.

Get out a very heavy frying pan and put it over a good hot part of the stove.

Put in it:

2 or 3 spoonfuls fat or oil (any kind except butter)

After a little while, shake a drop of water into the pan. If the water "spits" then the pan is ready. Lay in the French toast so the pieces don't touch one another. They will start to bubble and sizzle right away. Look at the clock; in 2 minutes, take a fork or spatula and peek under one to see if it's done. Turn them when they brown and cook on the other side just as long.

When the French toast is cooked, you should take it out and lay each slice on a piece of brown paper from a paper bag, to soak out some of the fat, for 1 minute. Then put it on a plate and serve it.

KEEPING EGGS

Although the egg surplus comes in the early spring, the best time to put them up in storage is in the fall, during the last few months before the hens stop laying altogether (from December to March, when they molt). Separate rooster from the flock for a couple of weeks before you start collecting eggs to store. Make sure all eggs have sound shells. You may "candle" them to weed out flawed eggs, by placing a light in a cardboard box with only one small hole to let light out; in a dark or dim room, hold eggs up to the hole, and any flaws can easily be seen.

WATERGLASSING EGGS: You can buy waterglass (sodium silicate) from building supply or hardware stores. Dissolve:

⅓ cup waterglass

in

1 quart water

in a glass jar or crock. Wipe eggs if necessary but do not wash them. Pack 12 eggs to a jar, leaving a couple of inches of solution on top of the eggs. Set in a cool place.

Use within 6 months. Wash eggs before using them. They are fine for cooking many things, but the shells are too thin for boiling, and the whites too runny for fried eggs or for beating stiff.

SALTING EGGS DOWN: Use coarse pickling salt; you will need at least 10 pounds to put up a few dozen eggs. Put in a crock an inch or so of salt, and set unwashed eggs, small end down, in the salt, and pack it around the eggs until they are half covered. Then set another layer of eggs in between but not touching those in the first layer. Cover eggs completely. They will keep for 2 or 3 months in a cool place but the eggs will be quite salty and the whites will not whip.

WAXING EGGS: Dip eggs briefly in melted beeswax; allow wax to cool slightly, then take up each egg between your palms and rock it around until the shell is sealed, smooth and waxy, but not so thickly waxed that it will peel off. Pack waxed eggs in straw, and keep in a cool place, up to 2 or 3 months. A variation of this method is packing eggs in a crock of melted, but not hot, lard.

All eggs kept longer than a month should be broken separately into a bowl and sniffed suspiciously before being used.

8
MILK, BUTTER, YOGURT, AND CHEESE

There are many different sorts of animals that have been used as milk producers, their various types of milk being preferred for different products. Mozzarella was traditionally made of the milk of water buffalo. Blue cheeses are at their best when made from ewe's milk. Yogurt and brine cheeses began, at least, as goat's milk products; and hard, aged cheeses were made with the milk from mountain cows.

Today, most American milk products are made with the milk from a Holstein cow, an animal bred to give gallons upon gallons of low butterfat milk. While the Holstein is a wonderful producer of quantity, she is hardly the right choice for quality milk products. So if you can afford and support a milk animal of your own, and decide to get goats, or a smaller sort of cow (such as Guernsey, Brown Swiss, Ayrshire, or Jersey) you will be able to make dairy products of a quality unavailable on the mass market today.

COWS

Before you think about getting a cow, think about your facilities. A cow needs a warm, dry stable, and well fenced pasture of at least two acres, with shade and a water supply. You also need hay and storage space for it (around 80 bales for the winter, if it's really good hay). A cow also needs quite a lot of grain when she's milking: 1 pound

for 2 to 4 pounds of milk she gives. If your cow gives 3 gallons a day, that's around 100 pounds a month, or more. Clearly, a cow is only an economical investment if you can use the milk—and all the milk.

To buy a cow, be patient. Pass the word around, talk to people, and wait for the right cow to come along. Cows from large herds frequently have not been handled much, and are not used to personal human contact, or life without 50 other cows. You are looking for a gentle cow, who will not kick you or the bucket, who will not balk at being led around, or jump the fence while you're in town. In short, you want a family cow, and probably one that has been raised as a family cow is the

best bet. Make sure she's been tested, and has no history of difficulties, such as being hard to breed. If possible, buy her from a local farmer, a friend of a friend, so that if she's awful, you can take her back.

GOATS

Goats, naturally, give less milk than cows; but they are better producers for their weight and the amount they eat. Goats are also hardier than most cows; they can eat rougher pasture, and are more likely to breed and deliver easily. On the other hand, they're better at getting over, under, around, and through fences. You will have to fence them well, or fence in your garden, hay field, barns, and pastures (not to mention house, flower garden, apple trees, and the car). Some people use stakes and tethers, but that only works for some goats, and usually only if they're brought up to graze on tethers. To keep a goat you will need a small, but tight stable and a milking stand; you will also need storage space for 25 bales of hay. A goat in milk will eat about a pound of grain a day; if dry, about half a pound.

Cows, generally, are bred by artificial insemination, but to breed a goat you will probably have to find a neighbor with a buck. It isn't hard to transport goats—just load her in the car.

To buy a goat, look for one who has a record as a good milker and a steady disposition. Never mind papers; pay more attention to her barrel (which should be round), her teats (which should be long) and her general state of vigor. Ask a lot of questions: has she had kids before? How many? How much milk did she give at first? How long did her milk hold out? And so forth. Ask about her disposition and habits as well. Make sure you are getting an animal you can handle.

Now and then, a goat will give odd-flavored milk. In some cases, it is the fault of her diet (goats are notorious browsers). More often, though, it's a result of improper handling of the milk. The composition of goat's milk causes it to sour or become "goaty" if it isn't treated with great care. It is important to wash the udder well, to strain the milk immediately after milking, and, most of all, to chill the milk as soon as possible.

Goat's milk does differ from cow's milk in two important respects, however. One is that the fat globules are very much smaller. So although it has just as much fat as cow's milk, the cream will not rise to the top as well. To separate the cream you need to use a centrifugal separator—see page 119. The other big difference is that goat's milk contains twice as much caprylic acid as cow's milk. This is not noticeable in the milk, but gives the cheese a peppery tang—sometimes only noticeable after aging.

MILK

All dairy animals respond well to gentle, firm handling. They can't be punished, or neglected. They must be protected from dogs; goats, in particular, will often attack dogs, with the goat the loser. When you have a milking animal, somebody has to be there twice a day to feed, water, and milk it.

Milking is a habit of rhythm; at first it seems a little weird, and gradually it becomes part of life. First you wash your hands with hot water and soap, then the teats and udder with an iodine-based substance bought in feed stores. Milk out the bag, then "strip the teats" (the last milk is the richest, and insures that the milk supply will not decrease).

The milk should be strained immediately through a piece of clean cloth or paper filter, into jars, and cooled rapidly, unless you are going to culture it right away into cheese or yogurt, or pasteurize it. (See **Pasteurization**, next page.)

All milk from your animals should be tested every six months for tuberculosis and Bang's disease; and if you suspect mastitis (infection of the milk bag), have it checked out right away, both for the sake of your health and the animal's. Like most disease, these problems can be remedied easily if they're caught early, but can really mess life up if you let them go too long.

MILKING EQUIPMENT

For a start, you'll need a milking bucket, which should be stainless steel, enamel, or plastic. You'll also need milk filters (try the grain store) and plenty of wide-mouth glass jars—and a clean bottle brush!

As long as your animal is healthy, you don't have to sterilize everything every day. But you must get into a habit of cleaning all the milk containers as soon as they are emptied. Because milk is high in protein, heat will make it tough and sticky; so, first, you rinse and scrub each container out with cold, not hot water. Then you scrub it with hot water and a disinfectant. Dairies generally use Javex, or some sort of bleach-based stuff; soap tends to leave a film of greasy, soap-flavored residue. Finally, you rinse it out, again with hot water.

BACTERIA

All fresh raw milk contains some level of bacteria in it; usually about 2 percent. These are what we call "healthy" or "friendly" bacteria, if the milk comes from a healthy animal. They are what sours the milk if you leave it at room temperature for 24 hours or longer. Their presence is the reason that it is so important to chill the milk quickly, if you don't want it to sour. On the other hand, their presence is helpful, in a way: as long as they are present, and active, you can be fairly sure that no other bacteria is active in the milk, because they will kill off any other organisms that come around looking for a free meal.

How can you be sure they're there, and doing their thing? Well, you can't, without a microscope, really. But you can be fairly sure things are working right if (1) your milk animal is tested for disease, (2) your animal acts vigorous and milks well, (3) you are very careful to keep your containers clean and your milk strained and covered, and (4) you use your milk up within a few days. The last is because the bacteria can only remain active for a limited period of time. After a week, refrigerated, or a few days at 55° or 60°, they will become dormant. Even if they are busy souring the milk, they

will eventually use up all the available sugar in the milk and go into hibernation. Then the coast is clear for all sorts of things—yeasts, molds, and other bacteria. Yeasts can generally be smelled; a sort of brewery or fruity odor. Yeasts often turn milk pinkish, or make pink spots on it. Molds take longer to form, into gray patches, and they smell musty. Other bacteria are harder to spot unless they've been at work a good long time.

Another organism that shows up once in a long while in dairies is a virus called bacteriophage. It isn't poison or anything, but it sure is a hassle; it kills bacteria. Its weakness is that it chooses only one bacteria to work on, like your yogurt culture, or buttermilk culture. The symptom of phage is that suddenly you can't get your culture to work at all, ever. The solution is to change cultures. And, of course, sterilize everything that comes into contact with the milk, as best as you can.

PASTEURIZATION

Should you pasteurize your milk, or not? There is much to be said for both sides of the question. There is no question that the advent of pasteurization has effectively controlled transmission, through milk, of a great many common and fatal diseases, including tuberculosis, typhoid, scarlet fever, undulant fever, and infectious abortion. However, people and dairy cows are nowadays inoculated against many of these killers; and dairies that sell milk are required by law to have their cows or goats tested every six months for TB and undulant fever (also called Bang's disease). If you have a dairy animal you should have it tested, too, or pasteurize every drop of milk.

On the other hand, raw milk is certainly a better food than pasteurized milk. It contains vitamins, minerals, enzymes, and bacteria that are helpful to digestion and that are in part destroyed by the heat. These "good" bacteria may also be used in making cheese. If you are absolutely sure of your milk, the source being not only tested for dread diseases, but also obviously healthy and robust, then there is no cause to pasteurize; but it is a decision that should be made carefully, not lightly.

There are two methods of pasteurization; one is more trouble than the other, but it makes the milk tastier (if it is to be drunk, rather than used in cooking or for cheese or yogurt). If the pasteurized milk is to be kept for any length of time over 24 hours it should really go into sterile bottles.

That is because killing off all the "friendly" bacteria (which normally sour milk in a harmless way) leaves the milk defenseless; any bacteria in an unclean bottle will quickly go to work in the warm milk.

TO STERILIZE BOTTLES: Use canning jars, if possible; their wide mouth makes them easy to clean and the glass is stronger than that of ordinary bottles, so they are less likely to break at high temperatures or with a rapid heat change. Place them upside down on a rack in a pot with a couple of inches of water; put a tight lid on top. Boil the water rapidly for 15 minutes. Leave the bottles there until you use them.

The bottle lids should be boiled along with the bottles, of course.

Method 1: Set the milk in a clean, heavy stainless-steel or enameled pot and gradually (over the course of 10 to 15 minutes) bring the temperature up to 143°, using a dairy thermometer, or 145° to 150°, using a household thermometer. Keep it steady at that temperature for half an hour, stirring from time to time with a sterile spoon to make sure all the milk is evenly heated.

Pour the milk into sterile bottles, cap, and submerge them immediately in cold water (35° to 40°), changing the water as needed to cool the milk rapidly. Or you may set them in a refrigerator or freezer or in snow; the idea is that the rapid cooling keeps the milk from developing a boiled flavor. It also helps to preserve nutritional value, although some will be lost.

Method 2: Pour raw milk into sterile bottles and cap. Set in a pan on a rack, separated from one another, and fill the pan with water at 160°, up to the level of the milk. Keep the temperature of the water at 160° for 15 minutes, if the milk was warm to begin with, or 30 minutes, if it was cold. Take the milk out, cap, and chill rapidly, as above.

PASTEURIZING BY SCALDING MILK: This is an easier way to kill any bacteria in the milk, but it leaves it with a funny flat taste, no matter how rapidly chilled. Set the milk in a stainless-steel or enameled container and bring to a rapid boil, stirring constantly. Just as it foams up, take it off the heat. This milk is suitable for using with cheese or yogurt or any other sorts of cultures; but you must be sure to cool it first, or your culture will be done in by the heat.

SEPARATING MILK AND CREAM

The cream in cow's milk rises readily to the top of the milk container within 12 to 24 hours, unless it is homogenized; but the cream from goat's milk may take longer to rise, and all of it usually does not come to the top. Although there is just as much cream (or butterfat) in goat's milk—sometimes more—the fat is enclosed in smaller sacs or globules, and stays mixed in with the milk. If you wish to separate cow's milk, you may do a fair job by skimming, although you won't get all the cream out of the milk. But to separate goat's milk and cream you really do need a cream separator.

OLD-FASHIONED SEPARATING: Set a wide, shallow pan of fresh whole milk covered by clean muslin on a stone pantry floor (at about 50°) overnight. In the morning remove the cream with a skimmer, a sort of flat wide ladle with holes in it.

This method is only really successful with Jersey cream, which is very thick, almost solid. It is certainly an invitation to all sorts of bacteria and also exposes milk to light, thus destroying the vitamin D.

OLD-FASHIONED SEPARATING, REVISED: Store whole milk in a wide-mouthed jar in your refrigerator or at 40° in a dark place overnight. The top of the jar must be wide enough to admit a gravy ladle, with which you remove as much cream as you can in the morning.

This method, while more sanitary, doesn't get all the cream, but it works well enough for lots of people who just want to skim off ½ pint of cream every day and make butter at the end of the week. Some say it works better if the milk is pasteurized.

SEPARATING IN A SHOTGUN CAN: In some old dairies or milk-producing farms you can find a special tall can with a spigot at the bottom and a glass tube running up the side. The whole milk was poured in after milking and left to separate; the amount of milk in the can and the proportion of cream could be seen in the glass tube. When they had separated, you let the milk out the bottom and left in the cream until needed. The shotgun can was kept submerged in cold water to chill the milk. This method is pretty good, if you can find such a container. It isn't perfect, but it beats skimming with a ladle and doesn't have the mechanical complexities of a centrifugal separator.

USING A CENTRIFUGAL SEPARATOR: This is a very Victorian hand-crank machine that has a wide bowl on top for the milk and two spigots—for the skim milk and the cream—at the bottom. Once it is properly adjusted you crank it gradually up to the right speed and the spinning milk separates readily and thoroughly. Less than 2 percent milk fat is left in the skim milk. The machine takes some adjusting, however, and some practice to learn how to use it.

MAKING BUTTER

There are various kinds of churns; two are pictured here. Whatever you use, however, you will find that it takes twice as long for the butter to come if the weather is bad (also, the stove won't draw and the bread won't rise—better stick to making quilts or cleaning out the pantry!). Probably something to do with low-pressure centers. Butter takes a long time to churn even on a bright windy day. People used to sing songs as they churned:

Come butter come
Come butter come
Peter standing at the gate
Waiting for a butter cake
Come butter come

The cream and the churn should both be warm—60° to 70° is usual. If it is too cold, the butter won't stick together.

Cow's milk butter is naturally pale yellow (Jersey butter is a little darker than other butters) and

butter churn

goat's milk butter is pure white. If you wish to color it, there is a variety of yellow coloring available from Chr. Hansen's Laboratories (see page 135). Coloring is added to the cream before churning. The thick sour substance left in the churn is real buttermilk. There is nothing like it on a hot day, after haying.

FRESH BUTTER

This makes 1 pound of butter and 1 quart of buttermilk. Place in a churn:

1½ qts. heavy cream, 2–3 days old, at 60° to 70°

Churn steadily for about 30 minutes. When fat lumps stick to the churn, remove the lid and stir around for a few minutes to gather the butter on the paddles. Or you may strain the buttermilk, to get all the butter. Set the butter on a plate and, using a flat paddle, press and work to expel all the buttermilk—rinse with cold water halfway through job. Work in, if you like:

¼ to ½ tsp. salt

Chill the butter overnight, sealed in a good tight jar or container.

COUNTRY BUTTER

This method is recommended only for cow's milk; goat's milk will develop an off-flavor. Cow's milk

butter churn

119

will develop a kind of tang that is hard to describe: it sort of tickles your palate. It is also called Tub Butter or Ripe Butter. It makes 1 lb. butter and 1 qt. buttermilk.

Set to ripen at 50° for 3 to 5 days:

1½ qts. heavy cream

When it smells nutty, but not yet sour, place it in the churn and work it for about half an hour. When fat lumps stick to the churn, remove the lid and stir around for a few minutes to gather the butter, or strain the buttermilk. Set the butter on a plate and work out the buttermilk but do not rinse or salt it until after it is chilled 12 hours.

Chilled butter may be molded with little old-fashioned butter molds. The mold, as well as the butter, should be quite cold.

BUTTER WITHOUT A CHURN

Buttermaking is a tedious job without a churn. If you are determined to give it a try anyway I suggest you shake no more than:

1 pt. heavy cream at 60° to 70°

in a wide-mouth quart jar. Take turns with somebody else. It will make about a third of a cup of butter.

I am told an easier way to do this is to wrap the jar in a bit of towel and lash it to the back of the tractor during spring plowing.

CLARIFIED BUTTER

When butter is heated, the sacks that hold the globules of fat in suspension are destroyed, and the texture and flavor are radically altered. If a lot of butter is heated in a small pot, the solid material will sink to the bottom, and a clear yellow oil will float on top. This oil is called clarified butter. It has two great virtues: one, it keeps better than ordinary butter. Two, when used as a cooking oil, it doesn't burn or sputter, as butter does. Clarified butter is commonly used in French cooking.

GHEE

Indian ghee is just clarified butter; but since the common dairy animal in India is not a cow but a water buffalo, the flavor of their ghee is quite different—less buttery, so to speak. To make an approximate equivalent, melt together:

⅔ cup clarified butter
⅓ cup lard

Cool and store in a closed jar in a cool place.

YOGURT

Yogurt is a traditional form of food in many parts of the world, particularly in the Mediterranean and Middle East. Without refrigeration, the daily milk quickly sours in the heat; so people eventually hit on a souring bacteria that makes milk thick and delicious. This type of bacteria also rendered the milk safe to drink, because (for various reasons) it kills off any other bacteria that might get into the milk, including those that are harmful to man.

The process of making this soured milk is as simple as its history implies. A little of the live culture from a previous batch is added to fresh milk, and kept between 90° and 118°. (In the Mediterranean summer, it makes itself; on cooler days, it was set over the stove.) It takes about 10 to 14 hours—the amount of time from morning milking to supper, or from evening milking to the following day. If left unjiggled, it becomes the delicate, firm, custard-like product we call yogurt. If shaken, it's about as thick as milkshake; we call that "cultured buttermilk." And when it's made with cream, it's called "sour cream."

Yogurt, or any type of cultured milk or cream, is an amazing food. It has all the value of the milk it was made of, but is much more digestible, since it has already in part been broken down by the bacteria. When you eat fresh, uncooked yogurt, moreover, you are also eating the minute bacteria that yogged it. These bacteria stay alive inside, as they are able to withstand both our body temperature and our stomach acids; so they travel along, killing off any other bacteria that might be around. You might say that yogurt is a kind of mild antibiotic; at any rate, it does the same sort of work as an antibiotic. But while antibiotics (particularly orally taken ones) destroy B vitamins, the bacteria you eat in yogurt actually goes to work in the intestine manufacturing B vitamins for you.

The process of making yogurt is very simple, but it is not, alas, very flexible. You can't vary the procedure much; for example, you can't add culture to scalding milk; you can't leave culture for a month in the fridge without renewing it; you can't incubate it for two days. If you stick to the hard and fast rules, though, you will find it easy to keep stocked up with as much yogurt as your household will eat.

THE CULTURE

There are two sources for yogurt culture. One is packets of dried yogurt culture, either from a dairy supply place, such as Hansen's (see page 135), or from a health food store. These are good strong cultures and can be renewed every week for about 3 to 6 months. They cost about three dollars a packet, but you can share fresh culture with a friend; then she can buy one and share with you.

The other source is a container of fresh, unsweetened, unpasteurized yogurt that has no additives or preservatives in it. (Preserved or pasteurized yogurt is quite dead.) I know of two brands in the United States you can count on: Dannon and Colombo. Probably there are others; look around. These cultures can be renewed every week for about 2 or 3 months.

When a culture begins to get old, it is really just getting adulterated by other bacteria, from the jars, the milk, the air, etc. Gradually your culture starts to taste sour, or the yogurt takes longer to yogg, or doesn't yogg any more at all. The more careful you are to keep things clean, the longer this takes; but even laboratories aren't perfect.

One way to extend the life of your culture greatly is to make some of your yogurt, each time, in a special small jar which you have carefully sterilized. Fill this jar with the milk and culture mixture, screw on a good lid, and check it sooner than the others—say, in 6 hours. As soon as it begins to thicken, pop it straight in the fridge.

People will always dip spoons into the yogurt jars, leave lids off, leave the yogurt out; but let nobody mess with your mother culture. That is the stuff you use to make your next batch of yogurt. Always renew that culture in one week, even if the other yogurt isn't used up yet.

CONTAINERS: The best containers I've come up with are brown glass pint-size containers with wide-mouth tops and screw lids. (The brown glass keeps light out—light destroys vitamin B_2.) In any case, glass is better than plastic, and easier to clean. As soon as a yogurt container is empty, soak it with cold water; then scrub with hot water and soak 15 minutes. Rinse with hot and let it drain; store the jars upside down. Just before you fill them with fresh yogurt, rinse them out again with hot water. Sterilize the jar used for the mother culture.

THE MILK: If you have really healthy dairy animals, and can use fresh milk, that's the best. Don't even chill it. Just milk the cow or goat (or sheep, even!) and make yogurt with the milk, right away. If your milk is pasteurized, you don't have to do it again; but it should be fresh, and you should leave the milk container unopened until you make yogurt. And if you use dried skim or whole milk, you don't need to pasteurize it, either; but if your water supply is, say, a stream, and it's July, maybe boil the water first.

If you're not sure how old the milk is, especially if it's raw milk, then you ought to pasteurize it. The reason is that it may contain lactic bacteria already, which will weaken your culture.

ADDING DRIED MILK: People are always complaining about their yogurt being runny. Natural yogurt is runny. To make it stiff, like the lovely texture of commercial brands, you have to add some dried milk—from 2 Tb. to 1 cup per quart. (You can experiment toward the amount you like best.) Even if you make the milk with dried milk first, you have to add some extra to make the yogurt thick.

KEEPING A CONSTANT TEMPERATURE: Since cultured milk must be kept at a fairly even temperature for such a long time, it's a good idea to find a spot where it will stay warm *and* out of your way until it yoggs. This spot will be personal to you, your house, and the season. I can give you some ideas, but you will have to check them out yourself. Set a regular household thermometer in a jar of 100° water and see if it will stay between 90° and 110° in any warm spot, such as:

1. In the warming oven of a warm wood stove (with the doors closed, a piece of wood or tile under the jar just in case it's too hot).

2. On a high shelf in a room that has a heater or wood stove in it.

3. Within 2 or 3 feet of a banked heat stove (such as an Ashley).

Or you can set the jar in a pan of 90° to 110° water and place it:

1. Over the pilot light of a gas stove.

2. Next to the hot air vent of a refrigerator,

freezer, heater, or second floor heat register.

3. On a shelf over the hot water heater; or on a wood stove box-type hot water heater.

In the summer, it is harder to find heat sources. You might try a sunny windowsill, or an insulated container such as a thermos, a picnic cooler, or a fairly tight wooden box, lined with hay or newspaper.

When you actually make the yogurt, it may take as long as 14 hours, so don't have those jars in your way as you try to cook dinner or raise bread or dry boots. Also remember that light destroys certain B vitamins; unless your jars are brown glass, keep them wrapped in a dish towel.

RECIPES FOR MAKING YOGURT

USING A CULTURE FROM STORE-BOUGHT YOGURT

Use only pure, unpasteurized yogurt, with no preservatives. There are two methods: the first is quicker, but the second is better if you are trying to keep the same culture going for a long time (say, if you live at the end of three miles of unplowed road, and it's early, early March!).

1. Mix together with a whisk or egg beater:

   1 qt. whole or skim milk at 90° to 100°
   ½ to 1 cup dried milk
   ½ cup yogurt

   Pour into clean, freshly rinsed jars. Incubate at 90° to 100° for 4 to 5 hours.

2. As above, but use only:

   ¼ cup yogurt

   Incubate for 10 to 12 hours.

USING HANSEN'S CULTURES
(Yogurt, Acidophilus Milk, or Acidophilus Yogurt)

Mix together with a whisk or egg beater:

1 qt. whole or skim milk at 98° to 110°
½ to 1 cup dried milk
1 package starter or 2 Tb. previously made yogurt or cultured milk

Pour into clean, freshly rinsed jars. Incubate at 98° to 110° for 6 to 10 hours (starter sometimes takes longer—up to 14 hours).

Chilling Yogurt
It takes 2 to 3 hours to thoroughly chill fresh yogurt. You will find it much denser and creamier after chilling. It will keep safely, chilled, for two weeks, or slightly longer; but to renew the culture you should make a fresh batch every week, replacing the old mother culture with a new one.

CULTURED BUTTERMILK AND SOUR CREAM

Cultured buttermilk is not the same product as real buttermilk, although they taste similar. It is made by the same process as making yogurt, but you use a milder-tasting culture and incubate it at a lower temperature. Sour cream is made in the same way, except that you use cream instead of milk.

CULTURED BUTTERMILK

Mix together with a whisk or egg beater:

1 qt. whole or skim milk
½ cup dried milk
1 package starter or ½ cup previously made buttermilk or store-bought cultured buttermilk

Pour into clean, freshly rinsed jars. Incubate at 86° to 95° for 5 to 7 hours. When the culture becomes thick, shake and refrigerate.

SOUR CREAM

Mix together with a whisk or egg beater:

2 cups whole cream
2 Tb. dried milk
2 Tb. previously made or store-bought buttermilk

Pour into a clean, freshly rinsed jar, and incubate at 86° to 95° for 7 to 10 hours.

CHEESE MAKING

The first time I made cheese, surrounded by kids, confusion, and various other kitchen projects, it seemed like a very odd, complicated process. As it turned out, however, the only real difficulty was dealing with the unfamiliar. Since that day it has gotten easier and easier, to the point where I would say it is less bother to make cheese than bread, or beer, or butter. Anybody with a good milk supply shouldn't hesitate to give it a try; after the first few attempts, the end product will suffice to spur you on.

I must say, though, that I envy the cheese making system traditionally practiced in mountain villages of Europe. As spring arrived, and the upper pastures became green, the young people gathered all the cattle, goats, and sheep together and took them up into the hills; they gave over all their attention to the animals—to birthing and milking, and milk-product-making. For these purposes, they kept a rough dairy/bunkhouse by a fresh flowing stream; and they stayed there for some months, herding the animals to new pastures every day, while the fields in the village below ripened into hay for the next winter. There the baby animals were born, and pan fed (a demanding chore: babies must be babied). Butter was churned, the milk soured and thickened for curds and cheeses, both fresh and aged. Once a week the packhorse would descend, carrying cheeses and returning with supplies from the main village below.

Not only was the task of milking and the production of cheeses on a large scale thus simplified, but the cheese itself was different stuff from "lowland cheese," which was thought to be rubbery and tasteless by comparison. The milk of an animal that forages spring pasture, wandering and choosing from a variety of herbs, shrubs, leaves, and grasses is thicker, less watery, and more flavorful than that of animals that stand around munch-

ing plain grass all day.* There will be less milk; but it will make better cheese.

Nor is it only a matter of milk, though the milk is the most important factor in making any kind of cheese. In the warmth and dampness of spring and early summer, the bacteria and molds that we introduce to produce certain flavors are most likely to grow and work well in the milk.

All cheese is made by the firming of casein, a substance in the milk. As this casein becomes firm, it gathers together the milk solids in its elastic webs; this is called the curd. The pale, yellowish liquid left over is called the whey.

There are two ways to firm casein. One is by bacterial action; the other is by rennet action. "Fresh" cheeses, such as cottage cheese, cream cheese, pot, farmer, and Ricotta, are made by firming casein with bacterial action alone. They are to be eaten fresh, within a week or two. "Hard" cheeses are made by combining the bacterial action with the added firming enzyme action of rennet, and then pressed, to expel whey and make a firm shape, which can be eaten within a few months, or sealed and aged, or, finally, inoculated with mold to make blue or Stilton-type cheeses. The aging of hard cheese takes months, sometimes years, depending on what you want.

EQUIPMENT: It is always easier to do anything with the right tools, but you really do not need very much in the way of tools to make cheese. The most important thing, I think, is a source of very low, steady, diffused heat, such as a banked wood stove. The other tools include:

A Pot: For making a 1-pound cheese, a 6-quart enamel or stainless-steel pot—or a crock, if you have one. Aluminum and iron will not do, and glass can crack.

A Wash Boiler: or a great big canning kettle, which will hold the pot in it. This is optional, but helpful.

A Thermometer: Cheese books recommend dairy thermometers, which are very accurate and float. Any old thermometer will do, though, as long as it is marked off in degrees, rather than fives. At first you will need the thermometer continually, but after you get a bit of practice, you probably won't use it.

---

*Although modern commercial cheese makers duplicate the processes by which fine cheeses are made, they can't duplicate the flavor and texture without "upland milk" —compare real Swiss and supermarket Swiss sometime, if you can get a real Swiss.

Cloth: Some people use cheesecloth, a very loosely woven muslin. I find it disintegrates rather too quickly and prefer very soft thin material such as is used in making Curity diapers. Another possibility is Handi-Wipes, a porous paper material that will last 3 or 4 rounds of cheesemaking. You will need some cloth cut to the size of your mold, so it overlaps the top of the cheese, and another piece cut smaller to wrap around the side during the final pressing. For making cream cheese you need several larger pieces, about 12 inches by 18 inches, and some soft cord.

A Sieve: To drain curds, you need a large, fine sieve and a container to set it over as the curds drain. A small, very fine tea strainer is best for scooping out Ricotta.

Miscellaneous: A small metal spoon, a large, sharp knife, a paddle or wooden spoon, and a measuring cup.

Cheese Press: In the old days every household had a variety of cheese hoops, made of thin hardwood, bent in a circle, and followers, or circles of wood that just fit in the hoops. The hoop was lined with muslin, filled with curds, the cloth folded over the top, and topped with the follower and a convenient-sized rock for weight. You can improvise a similar press by using a coffee can and cutting a piece of wood to fit in it; or you can punch holes in the bottom of a plastic or waxed cardboard container such as they sell cottage cheese in. This last device has the advantage of not needing a fitted follower; just cut the rim down to about ¾ inch below the level of the fresh, unpressed curds, and follow with a board and a small weight. This only works for 1-pound cheeses; for larger ones, use larger containers. Cheeses will pack down more firmly if the container is large enough so that the

old-fashioned hoop press

finished cheese is wider than it is tall. These flat, firm cheeses will keep better than soft, tall ones. The fitted press is needed only for the first 2 hours of pressing; after that the cheese will retain its shape and you can press it with a simple board and weight, or a homemade press with dowels to hold the follower in place, as pictured below:

If you make a press at home, use seasoned hard wood and put it together without glue, nails, or screws; remember, it is going to see a lot of soap and hot water in its day. Every so often, give it a rub with a little light vegetable oil.

CULTURES: Chr. Hansen's Laboratory sells several dozen different kinds of cultures variously recommended for making different kinds of cheeses, from cottage to blue cheese; the prices range from 2 to 4 dollars. You can write and specify the type of cheese you wish to make, and they will send you a recommendation of the culture they currently have that is best for that cheese. Surpris-

square cheese press

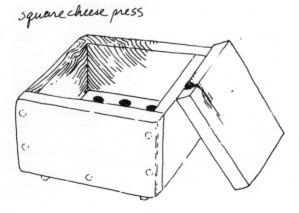

ingly enough, many cheeses with very different textures and flavors are made with the same cultures. Most can be made with the Buttermilk Culture.

And so, of course, you can make most types of cheese with plain old store-bought cultured buttermilk. Chances are it is the same strain Hansen's sells, although it will never be as fresh as a new culture would be.

For making Mozzarella, Hansen's recommends that you use Yogurt Culture; for making Swiss, use Yogurt Culture plus a special culture called Propioni shermanii, which they also sell, for around 5 dollars. For address, see page 135.

RENNET: All hard cheeses are firmed up by the addition of rennet. Rennet is an enzyme taken from the fourth stomach (the abomasum) of a very young, unweaned calf. Our homesteading predecessors had therefore to slaughter one calf each spring; the stomach was soaked overnight in salt water, and the water used to make the cheeses. The stomach itself was then cut up and dried with salt; small pieces could be kept for later use or sent to neighbors.

Rennet is available today in tablet form, combined with salt and about 4 percent boric acid or sodium benzoate. It can be bought from Chr. Hansen's Laboratory by mail for about 3 dollars per dozen tablets, or from many supermarkets and drugstores in a package labeled plain Junket tablets, marketed by Salada, for about 50 cents. While Junket seems very much cheaper, it isn't; it takes 2½ Junket tablets to do what ¼ of a Hansen's tablet will do. I find the Junket-made cheeses a little tougher and more rubbery than those made with Hansen's rennet.

Hansen's now also markets a "Vegetable Rennet Tablet" for making cheese, at the same price as regular rennet. It's not really rennet, but a microbial coagulant. It's said to work just as well as rennet. (See page 135 for the addresses of Hansen's and of Horan-Lally, which sells Hansen's products in Canada.)

CHEESE COLORINGS: Most commercially made American and Cheddar cheeses are colored yellow or orange nowadays. The original practice of coloring cheeses began, I believe, in Wales; they tinted their cheeses with marigold or annatto to distinguish it from English cheese. There is no real reason for using cheese (or butter) coloring; it doesn't change the taste, or texture, or keepability. The natural color of most cheeses is beige, or off white. Some aged cheddars made with Jersey milk are darker, and goat cheeses are bone-white. It seems to me a little like tinting your mashed potatoes blue, but to some people I guess it looks more attractive.

Marigold: Bruise the heads of fresh, open marigold blossoms in cream or butter, and add boiling water. Strain off the liquid when it is cool. Add this liquid to the milk that is to be made into cheese, while the milk is still fresh. (If added to sour milk it will not "take.") Marigold adds not only color but also a slightly bitter flavor.

Annatto: Annatto is an orange coloring that comes from the pulp around the seeds of a West Indian tropical tree. As far as I know it has no unhealthy properties (but who knows if it is what cheese makers use today?). Annatto is available from Hansen's and Horan-Lally, a few bucks for a dozen tablets. A little goes a long way (see page 135).

MAKING FRESH CHEESES

To make fresh cheeses, you may use the bacteria present in fresh milk from a healthy, tested animal; or you may add a culture (such as cultured buttermilk) to pasteurized milk or reconstituted dried milk.

INCUBATING: To get a firm curd from plain bacterial action, you incubate the milk at 86° to 95° for about 24 hours. The firming of the curd is actually a byproduct of the bacterial action; the bacteria change the milk sugar (lactose) to milk acid (lactic acid), and it is the acid that activates the casein webs. After 10 to 14 hours you will notice that it has become thick and sour, like yogurt or buttermilk; that, in fact, is what it is. But you leave it longer, until there is a firm curd separated from the whey. Be careful not to stir or jiggle it, or the milk solids will escape the frail bonds of casein.

CUTTING THE CURD: The purpose of cutting up the solid mass of curd is to allow the whey to circulate freely into the central part of the curd. It is the whey that contains the acid, as the bacteria change it. So after you cut the curd up into cubes you let it rest a while longer.

To cut curd, take a long, sharp knife, and cut through the curd all the way to the bottom of the

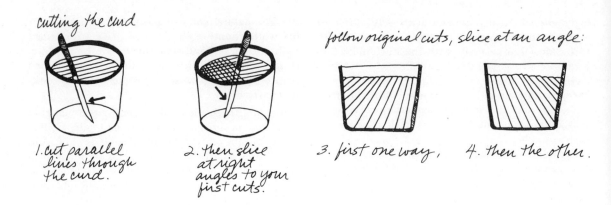

cutting the curd

1. cut parallel lines through the curd.

2. then slice at right angles to your first cuts.

follow original cuts, slice at an angle:

3. first one way,

4. then the other.

pot in parallel lines. Then cut them in the other direction. This gives you a pretty but deceptive pattern of cuts; the cubes are all as deep as the curd. So you cut them again, this time at slanted angles, all around the pot, until they seem pretty well chopped up to you. Take your time. Curd made by lactic acid alone is weak and delicate, yet oddly elastic; it should be cut slowly.

HEATING THE CURD: For all this, curd formed by lactic acid alone is too fragile to hold its shape when you try to separate it from the whey. It must be heated, and heated gently. Heat will cause the webs of casein to shrink, expelling whey and making the curds small and firm. But if you heat it too fast, the casein will shrink so quickly that they dump the milk solids back into the whey.

There are three ways to raise the temperature of the curds and whey gradually enough so that milk solids are retained by the casein:

1. Set your pot on a rack on the right hand side of a well-banked wood stove, or over a slow heating stove. This method is safe only with heavy pots. You should keep a close eye on the temperature with a thermometer and a clock.

2. Set the pot on a rack in a larger kettle of water (almost level with milk) that is at the temperature of the milk; gradually raise the temperature of the water, either by direct slow heat or by dipping out water and adding warmer water.

3. Ladle out a few cups of whey; heat it to around 100°, and return it to the pot gradually.

All these methods should be accompanied by a little gentle stirring of the curds, as soon as they are firm enough to be moved without falling apart. The best way to do it is by hand; you can also keep a closer watch on temperature by hand. After

you have made curds a number of times, you will come to know the temperature by touch. Also, you can tell a lot by feel. At first the curds will be pretty soft. Gradually they come to have more shape and the outer skin shrinks a little.

If you have been making hard cheeses and are accustomed to the kind of curd you get by using a lot of rennet, let me caution you: fresh cheese curd isn't like that. It's delicate, and it stays delicate. It won't look like anything recognizable until after it's drained.

Whatever you do, don't heat it up suddenly in a fit of be-done-with-this. The casein will shrink like a snapped elastic, and you'll be stuck with a handful of rubbery "cheese" (95 percent casein) and a large pot of slightly sour, extremely nutritious whey.

DRAINING, RINSING, AND SALTING: The whey from making fresh cheeses is usually quite sour. It is useful in making Ricotta and Sour Bread. If you want to keep it, set a 6-quart pot under your sieve.

Line the sieve with cheesecloth, or a Handi-Wipe (my next-door neighbor doesn't, but she makes better curds than I do, by some mysterious process I have never been able to duplicate). Gently ladle curd into the sieve. Generally I hang the bag up to drip overnight. But if you happen to be a really ace curd maker (like Peggy) you can rinse them, in the sieve, with cold water. After that you salt them, sprinkling on 1 to 2 tsp. salt to a batch of curds. It's surprising how much salt curds will absorb, and the salt helps keep them from souring.

At this point, you can add herbs: good ones are chives, parsley, chervil, sage, and thyme, or caraway seeds.

If you're making lightly pressed cheeses, such as

pot and farmer, or want to expel more whey from a cream cheese, pack in a small press and weight with 2 or 3 pounds for a few hours.

Fresh cheeses will keep, unrefrigerated, in a cool place, for 1 week; refrigerated *and* salted, they keep for 2 weeks.

CREAM CHEESE

The cream cheese you buy in a supermarket is very bland, rich, and almost pasty compared to home-made cream cheese. One suspects them of harboring Secret Ingredients. In any case, be prepared for a difference when you make it at home; it will be looser, lighter, and have more flavor or sourness (depending on the culture you use).

Cream cheese isn't really a cheese; it's just a cultured milk that's been allowed to go a little longer than yogurt, and is then drained. You can make it of skim, whole milk, milk enriched with cream, or all cream. It will be correspondingly light, medium, or dense. I use a bland-flavored culture with the denser versions, and sharp cultures (such as natural milk souring, or yogurt culture) when making it of skim milk. The milk is incubated for 10 to 24 hours, depending on how long it takes the culture to form a firm curd that has separated from the whey. Then the curd is ladled into several pots, each lined with cheesecloth, muslin, or a Handi-Wipe, and hung for several hours, until it has stopped dripping. After that it should be packed into a clean jar and stored at 40° (as in a fridge). It can also be frozen for future use in cooking things like cheesecake.

This version most closely resembles "store-bought" cream cheese. Mix together very well:

1 gallon whole milk at 86°
1 cup dried milk or 1 cup cream
1 cup cultured buttermilk
or
½ cup buttermilk from Hansen's culture

Incubate at 85° to 95° for 8 to 14 hours, until firm. Ladle into 2 or 3 bowls lined with cloth; hang the bags for 2 hours or until dripping stops. Empty out the bags and work in salt to taste (about 1 to 2 tsp.).

Add herbs if desired. Pack in jars, screw on lids, and store in a cool place. Will keep up to 2 weeks.

LIGHT, DRY CREAM CHEESE

This one is very good for making cheesecakes and other cookery.
Mix together very well:

1 gallon skim milk at 85° to 90°
1 cup dried skim milk
1 cup cultured buttermilk (for a bland cheese)
or
½ cup yogurt (for a tangy, sour cheese)

Incubate at 85° to 90° if using buttermilk, or 90° to 100°, if using yogurt, until firm. Ladle into 2 or 3 bowls lined with cloth; hang the bags for 2 hours or until they stop dripping.
Empty out the bags and work in:

1 to 2 tsp. salt

Pack in jars, screw on lids, and store at 50°. Will keep up to 2 weeks.

A RIGHT SOUR CREAM CHEESE

This can be used as the base for cheesecake, if you add enough honey; but it is best mixed with herbs and spread on pumpernickel.
Mix:

1 gallon whole raw milk
1 cup cream or 1 cup dried milk

Let it sit at 75° to 85° until it thickens (24 to 36 hours). Ladle it into 2 or 3 bowls lined with cloth; hang the bags for 4 hours or until they stop dripping. Empty out the bags and work in:

1 to 2 tsp. salt

Pack in jars, screw on lids, and store at 50°. Will keep up to 2 weeks.

CLOTTED CREAM

This is an old recipe for a very heavy cream, such as you get from Jersey cows.
Mix together:

1 pt. heavy cream
2 Tb. cultured buttermilk

Line a colander with muslin or a Handi-Wipe and spread the cream thickly over it. Cover the top lightly with another cloth. Every 2 hours check it and spoon cream up the sides. In 10 or 12 hours it will be thick; scrape it off into a jar, and screw on the top. It will keep for 1 week.

CURDS

This is small-curd, country style cottage cheese. To make cottage cheese of any kind you must have skim milk; to make curds, this way, you must have raw skim milk.

Mix:

1 gallon fresh raw skim milk at around 75° to 85°
1 cup dried milk

Set a lid on it and let it sour for 24 to 36 hours. In the summer it will sour practically anywhere; in the winter, best set it over the warming oven or on a shelf above the stove. It is a good idea to set it to curdle in the morning, so that if it isn't ready by the same time the following morning, you have all day to keep checking it and can catch it at the right moment.

The right moment is when there is a firm-looking, jelly-like cake of curd floating in the whey. It is actually not very firm, so don't fool with it or shake it up too much. You can cut it into ½-inch cubes if you like but it isn't really necessary. Set the pot of curd in a larger pan and fill the larger pan up to the level of the milk with water at 100°.

Let it sit (with a lid on) for 30 minutes to 1 hour, or until the curd feels warm and firms a bit.

Set the whole business on the stove and bring the temperature of the water in the outer pot to 105°. Or ladle out some water and replace it with hotter water; or ladle out some whey and heat it up. Whatever the method, bring the temperature of the whey gradually up to 105°. Hold it there for about 30 minutes.

The curd will still be quite tender and must be drained gently. Lift cupfuls of curd out and empty them gently into a bowl lined with clean muslin. Hang the muslin up as a bag to drain the curds for 4 hours or so.

If you wish very dry curds, wring and squeeze the bag gently.

If you do not wish sour curds, salt them well. You may add cream if you like your curds bland but not dry.

RENNET CURDS

For some inscrutable reason known only to bacteria, it is difficult to curdle milk properly in the winter, so folks generally add just a touch of rennet after the milk has soured a bit. It makes larger, blander curds (some people do it in the summer too, just because they like the rennet curd better).

The milk should be soured first—either 24 hours for raw milk, or 4 to 8 hours if you are adding buttermilk culture. Either way, it should be kept at around 75° to 85°, or on top of the warming oven.

Mix very well:

1 gallon "ripe" skim milk at 85°
1 cup dried milk
1 crumb of Hansen's or ¼ Junket rennet tablet dissolved in ¼ cup cold water

Depending on how sour the milk was, it'll take from 1 to 3 hours to firm up. When a crooked finger makes a clean break, cut into rough ½-inch cubes. Let it sit for another half an hour as the curd separates from the whey.

Some recipes say to gradually heat it up to 100°, but it never seems to work for me. I've made the best curds just hanging it in a bag to drain overnight. Next day, I worked in:

1 tsp. salt (or more, to taste)

If you like a softer curd, you can add some cream; it'll soak up quite a bit in a few hours.

POT OR FARMER'S CHEESE

Pot and Farmer's Cheese are pretty much the same thing, except that Pot Cheese is made with skim milk and Farmer's is made with whole milk.

Just make curds by the above recipe; salt them, but don't add cream, and press lightly with about 3 pounds weight for a few hours.

GOAT'S MILK CURDS

If you have goats that give rich milk, and you don't have a centrifugal separator, you may find it difficult to make curds by either of the preceding recipes. One afternoon, quite by accident, I happened on a method for making the most delicious curds, using whole goat's milk. It doesn't make any sense; you should be able to make the same product with a smaller amount of rennet, at the peak of its firmness; but no amount of experimentation has come up with curds quite like these:

Mix very well:

1 gal. warm whole milk, at 85°
1 cup buttermilk culture

Let it sit for 2 hours at 85°. Then add:

¼ tablet Hansen's rennet (or 2½ tablets Junket rennet)

Let it sit at 85° for 3 hours more. The curd will firm, sink, and become soft and flaky. Cut it into ½-inch cubes. Set the pot in a larger pot of water at 100° and heat the curd over 30 minutes to 100°. Dip out whey and heat it to 150°. Return to the pot and heat the curds to 120°. They will not shrink as they would in making hard cheese; but they will firm up somewhat.

Drain the whey out by dipping cups of curds and whey into a cloth-lined sieve. Stir and salt with:

1 tsp. salt

Turn the drained curds into bottles or plastic containers and chill.

FIRSTLING PUDDING

The first milk of a dairy animal after she gives birth is not ordinary milk, but a special stuff called colostrum, very high in protein and other food values. Even the most efficient dairies make sure their new calves get it; but there is more than is needed, so you may use the excess to thicken milk, just as eggs do:
Mix:

1 cup firstlings
4 cups ordinary milk
1 tsp. vanilla
½ cup honey

Bake at 300° for 1 hour or until a knife inserted in the center comes out clean. Cool and serve.

BUTTERMILK CHEESE

A tart, tangy curd cheese, made of real (not cultured) buttermilk.

Pour the contents of your churn into a pot and heat it gently, to around 100°, until the curd sinks. Let it cool overnight and the next day pour off the whey and drain the curd in a muslin bag. Work in a little butter and some salt, to taste; pack in a bag and hang it for a week, or press lightly in a cheese press for a day and a night. It is good to keep for 2 or 3 months.

CROUDIE

A sour, firm pudding, traditional in Scotland.
Mix:

2 cups scalding hot new milk
4 cups ice-cold fresh buttermilk

Let it stand until it is firm and cold. Remove the skin on top; drain in a cloth bag, and press in a mold, lightly, for 4 hours or until it comes dry. Turn it out and serve with cream and sugar.

LIPTAUER CHEESE

This is a soft, delicious spread that is good on dark bread, with soup or salad. Or you might just keep a pot of it for snacks. Some people like to flavor it with onion juice or chopped herbs, but it is also good just plain.
Measure out:

3 Tb. butter

Let this sit in a dish until it becomes soft, for about 1 hour. Mash it up with a fork. Then mash in:

1½ cups cottage cheese

You can use dry curds instead if you have them, or you can let the cottage cheese sit in a sieve for a while before adding it, to drain out the cream; but it is good made with cottage cheese just as it is.
To flavor it, you can add:

2 Tb. chopped parsley
1 Tb. chopped chives
1 Tb. onion juice

LIPTAUER CHEESE FOR DESSERT

Mash together:

2 cups cream cheese
1 cup sour cream
1 tsp. vanilla
2 Tb. honey or brown sugar

Lay a piece of damp, wrung-out cheesecloth in a bowl. Press in the cheese and let it sit and chill in the refrigerator for 2 hours. To serve, turn a plate upside down over it and then turn the whole business right side up so the plate is on the bottom. Remove bowl and cloth. Decorate with fresh berries or sliced fruit.

Variations
Instead of cream cheese, use cottage cheese; first drain it for 15 minutes through a sieve, then put it through a food mill (or use plain curds, put through the mill).

THE STEPS INVOLVED IN MAKING HARD CHEESE

Please read first the general information about cheesemaking and the section on fresh cheeses.

Hard cheese is made by a combination of bacteria-acid action and rennet action. Since rennet works much more quickly than bacteria, it is not added until the bacteria has had a few hours to get moving.

MIXING: Bring the milk up to the right temperature for incubation, if you are adding culture. If you are depending on the bacteria in your own fresh, raw milk, you should use a cup of previously soured milk in place of the cultured buttermilk.

I find cheese has a firmer curd and in general is easier to deal with if a half cup to a cup of dried skim milk, per gallon, is added. In effect you are increasing the casein, protein, and other solids considerably, without adding more liquid or fat.

INCUBATING: The rennet and the culture will work not only on the milk but on each other as well. The rennet will speed up the bacterial action when it is added. So you don't have to incubate bacteria alone for very long; two or three hours is usual. There will not be any noticeable change in the milk when you go to add the rennet.

ADDING RENNET: Rennet comes in very hard tablets, which only dissolve with much mashing in a little cold water. When you can't see any grains floating in the water, stir it into the milk. Stir with a whisk for a whole minute.

SETTING THE CURD: The more bacterial action has taken place, the faster this will happen. Set curd looks like milky Jello. It has a texture more like that of chilled egg custard, though. If you tilt the pot a little, it will come away from the side in a clean mass. If you dip your finger in a little way and crook it up, the curd should break smoothly; that's called "clean break." Finally, if you're still in doubt, take a metal spoon and cut a heaping spoonful from the edge. If the curd stands up sharply, and doesn't droop or settle in the spoon, that's it. Time to cut the curd. It is important to cut curd as soon as it reaches this point. Afterwards, it will start to get droopy again rather rapidly.

CUTTING THE CURD: As with fresh cheeses, this is done with a big sharp knife, and the curds cut in a grid, and then at an angle (see page 126). You will find it easy to cut rennet-formed curd, and rather fun. The smaller you cut the cubes, the firmer the cheese will become. Try to cut even-sized cubes, so they will all shrink at the same rate of speed and all be ready to drain together. Let them sit and rest for half an hour, at 86°.

HEATING AND STIRRING: Although rennet-formed curds are firmer, you must still be careful not to heat them too fast, or the casein will shrink and dump the milk solids back into the whey. Heat either by very slow, indirect heat (as on the side or back of a banked wood stove); by placing cheese pot in a larger pot of warm water, and gradually heating the water; or heating the whey. The curds will gradually become firm and bouncy, like little marshmallows, and then start to shrink. When they start to shrink, that's it. Take them off and drain them.

DRAINING AND RINSING AND SALTING: Hard cheese curds are pressed, and they should be emptied into the press still warm, or they will not hold together as cheese. Therefore you should assemble all the things you will need before you drain them. Get out the press, and cloth to line it with. Dampen the cloth so it fits in the press. Locate the salt, and a sieve. If you want to keep the whey, find a 6-quart container for it.

Rennet-formed curds are hardy enough to rinse under running water, but be sure it's warm, not cold. Salt the curds in pinches, tossing the curds around to mix it in. Add herbs or caraway if you wish.

PACKING AND FIRST PRESSING: Generally I stuff handfuls of curds into the press and pack them down with my knuckles. Then fold the cloth over the top and add the follower and 2 or 3 pounds of weight. In this first pressing the cheese will expel quite a lot of whey and reduce in size considerably, in a couple of hours.

TWENTY-FOUR-HOUR PRESSING: This is a very nice moment. Take off the weight and unwrap the cheese. Pare off a bit to taste it. (It'll taste—slippery, but nice.)

If the sides are really out of shape, pare them a little, but don't be too fussy. The only thing to look out for is deep crevices where mold might later get in.

Take a piece of cloth, as wide as the cheese is high, and long enough to wrap around the side once or twice. Pin it tightly into place. Lay a clean cloth on the press; set the cheese on it and fold the top over the cheese. Add a wooden follower and weight, of 3 pounds or so. Press the cheese for 24 hours.

If you want to press it more firmly, add more weight after a few hours, and even more after a few days. Cheddars are sometimes pressed with up to 20 pounds.

FORMING A RIND: To make the rind, you rub salt on the cheese. The salt draws moisture out of the outer layer of cheese, turning it into a rind. While this is going on, the cheese should be on a rack, or something that will let whey drain off. Some moisture will accumulate and make the bottom wet if you don't. It takes 2 or 3 days to make a good rind. When the salt stays dry for 24 hours, your cheese is done.

SEALING AND AGING: Most cheeses taste better after aging for at least 6 weeks, at around 50°. If you leave them in the refrigerator, they will be too cold to age. If you leave them at room temperature, in the kitchen, they will dry out; my neighbors once made 20 pounds of grating cheese this way, not on purpose. But, if you set them in a suitably humid, cool place, they will certainly begin growing mold before 6 weeks are up. This problem discourages more cheesemakers than any other single step: how do you keep it? The answer is to wax them, but just any wax won't do. Paraffin will chip off, especially around the sides. My best solution so far has been to sew a single-layer strip of Curity diaper material around the side of the cheese, and then dip it in a mixture of two thirds paraffin and one third beeswax. I choose only my most perfect cheeses, those that seem firm and have no cracks or holes in the surface, for dipping and keeping. To dip them, melt at least 6 inches of wax in a small pan over low heat. Dip one side in for three seconds, then hold it until the wax hardens, about 30 seconds. Let it cool for a

couple of minutes on the counter. Then dip the cheese so the new coating overlaps about half of the first coat; cool it the same way. Continue around again, so the whole cheese is double or triple coated.

STORING CHEESES: Tie your cheeses up securely with soft cotton cord. Suspend them with wire from nails in the beams of your root cellar or cool pantry. If you're not sure about the wax coating, check them every couple of weeks. Sometimes mold will grow in a wax crack or bubble. It isn't hard to chip the wax off and recoat it—nor is it hard to peel off the mold and have cheese for lunch.

Cheeses may also be frozen (see page 250).

SMOKING CHEESES: A dense, young cheese of 1 pound or less may be smoked. It should have neither rind nor seal; if it does, pare them off. If it's larger than a pound, cut it up into 1-inch slabs.

Hang the cheese in a string bag or in cheesecloth. Use a light smoke—heavy smoking will give the cheese a sooty flavor. Smoke at 65° to 80°, no higher, for about 2 hours. See pages 259–262 about smoking and smokehouses.

The cheese will lose some moisture in smoking, becoming denser, lighter, and smaller. It has a strong flavor and if kept in the refrigerator should be well wrapped in freezer plastic or two layers of ordinary plastic. It will keep for a longer time than ordinary cheese.

Bring it up to room temperature before serving—for best flavor.

AMERICAN CHEESE

Usually this is sold as Colby, Monterey Jack, or Cheddar cheese (mild, medium, or sharp, depending on how long it's incubated and aged). It isn't really Cheddar, though, as you know if you've compared real Cheddar with the supermarket version. This tastes better than supermarket cheese, in any case; a nice, tasty, all-purpose cheese.

Mixing
With a whisk or egg beater, mix very well:
1 gallon whole milk at 86°
½ cup dried milk
1 cup store-bought cultured buttermilk
or
½ cup buttermilk made with Hansen's culture

sealing in paraffin and beeswax

Incubating

Find a place where it will stay at 86°.
For mild cheese, let it sit 2 hours.
For medium cheese, let it sit 3 hours.
For sharp cheese, let it sit 4 hours.

Adding Rennet

Crush the rennet very well in:

¼ cup cold water

Use:

¼ tablet Hansen's rennet

Or:

2½ tablets Junket rennet

When the rennet is dissolved in the water, stir it into the milk for 1 minute.

Setting the Curd

Return the milk to the 86° spot and let it sit for half an hour or 45 minutes, or until the curd is firm (like custard; page 130).

Cutting the Curd

When the curd is quite firm, cut into ¼-inch to ½-inch cubes (see page 126 about cutting curd). Return the cut curd to the 86° spot and let it sit for 30 minutes.

Heating and Stirring

Gradually, over the course of 30 minutes, heat the curd to 100°. Dip into the pot with your hand and lift curds around to heat them evenly; cut any large curds into small cubes *with a knife*, not your fingers. Over the next 30 minutes, heat it up to 104°; stir with your hand every 10 or 15 minutes to heat evenly and prevent curds from sticking together. Then hold it for 30 minutes to 1 hour at 104°, stirring every 10 or 15 minutes. When the curds have visibly shrunk and are firm, prepare to rinse and press, getting out your strainer, cloth, salt, press, and hoop.

Straining and Rinsing

If you wish to use the whey, strain the cheese over a 6-quart container, through a fine sieve. Rinse the curds, in warm (not cold) water, stirring with your hand.
Sprinkle over them:

½ tsp. salt

Stir them and turn them over; then sprinkle on:

½ tsp. salt

At this point you may add herbs or caraway seeds if you like.

Packing and First Pressing

Pack the still warm curds into a press lined with cloth (see page 130) and cover with cloth and follower. Weight with: **3 lb. weight.** Let it sit and pack for 2 hours or more.

24-Hour Pressing

Take out the packed curds and carefully unwrap. If the shape is distorted on the sides, trim it a little. Wrap around the side with a "bandage cloth" (see page 130) and cover under and over with clean cloth. Weight with: **3 lb. weight** and let sit overnight at 50°.

Longer Pressing

If you are making a sharp cheese and wish it to be quite firm, take it out after 24 hours, rewrap in clean cloth, and press with: **5 lb. weight** for 24 hours longer.

Forming a Rind

Take out the cheese, wash it in cold water, and dry it. Sprinkle over with salt and set on a rack overnight.

The next day, wash and dry it again. Rub in salt and set it on the rack again, bottom side up.

If you wish to age it for a long time, repeat this process until the cheese is dry after 24 hours; but continue, in any case, to turn it every 24 hours for 2 weeks, or until you eat it.

To Wax or Age It

See page 131. This cheese is ready to eat in 1 week. It's better after 3 weeks. Sharper versions should be aged longer.

Variations

Muenster or Brick Cheese: Cut the curd into ¾-inch cubes rather than ¼- to ½-inch cubes. Treat as for American. It will be ripe in 2 weeks.

CHEDDAR CHEESE

Cheddar is quite a lot denser than most cheeses. From a gallon of milk you get ½ to ¾ pounds cheese, rather than a whole pound. It is meant to be aged at least 4 months. It is best made with Jersey, Guernsey or Toggenburg milk.

Mixing

With a whisk or egg beater, mix very well:

1 gallon whole milk at 86°

½ cup dried milk

1 cup store-bought cultured buttermilk

or

½ cup buttermilk made with Hansen's culture

Incubating

Find a place where it will stay at 86°. Let it sit for 3½ to 4 hours.

Adding Rennet

Crush the rennet very well in:

¼ cup cold water

Use:

¼ tablet Hansen's rennet

Or:

2½ tablets Junket rennet

When the rennet is dissolved in the water, stir it into the milk for 1 minute.

Setting the Curd

Return the milk to the 86° spot and let it sit for 30 minutes to 45 minutes or so until it is quite firm (like custard, see page 130).

Cutting the Curd

When the curd is quite firm, cut it into ¼-inch cubes (see page 126 about cutting curd). Return the cut curd to the 86° spot and let it sit for 30 minutes.

Heating and Stirring

Gradually, over the course of 30 minutes, bring the temperature up to 100°. Dip into the pot with your hand and lift curds around gently to heat them evenly; cut any large curds up with a knife. Over the next 30 minutes, heat it up to 104°, stirring by hand every 10 minutes or so. Hold it at 104° until the curds are really firm and have shrunk quite small, as long as an hour. There should be no marshmallow-like curds at all.

Cheddaring

Put the pot in a larger pot that is half full of water at 105°. Ladle the whey out of the curd kettle. Add to the cheese:

1 tsp. salt

Continue to cook the curds, without whey, until they form a mass in the bottom of the pot. Cut this mass into 1-inch cubes (being careful not to let it cool) and drain off any remaining whey.

Straining and Rinsing

Dump the curds into a strainer and rinse them in warm water. Shake the strainer a couple of times to remove water.

Packing and First Pressing

Jam the warm curds into a press lined with cloth (see page 130) and cover with cloth and follower. Weight with a 3-pound weight and let it sit and pack for 2 hours or more. If it is not down to the level of the press (if you're using a cottage cheese container press) add a few more pounds and press until it's down as far as it will go.

24-Hour Pressing

Take out the packed curds and carefully unwrap. Wrap around the sides with a tight bandage cloth and cover under and over with clean cloth. Weight with 5 pounds and press overnight.

Second 24-Hour Pressing

Remove cheese and cloth; turn cheese and replace cloth with a clean one. Return follower and press with 10 pounds for another 24 hours.

Third 24-Hour Pressing

If you have a screw-type press, or a cider press, or some kind of leverage arrangement, turn, rewrap, and give it another 24 hours at 20 pounds. This is for a very dense, firm, Cheddar that will keep very well and age without getting moldy.

Forming a Rind

See American Cheese (pages 131–132).

To Wax or Age It

See page 131.

SOUR CHEESE

This cheese may be made with any milk, either fresh cow's, or goat's, whole or skim. If it is made with skim cow's milk or whole goat's milk, it tends to have a dry, crumbly texture that goes well with the sour flavor.

Incubating

Set:

1 gallon unpasteurized milk

in a 1½-gallon pot to sour slightly at 75° to 85° for 12 hours.

Adding Rennet
Crush the rennet very well in:

¼ cup cold water

Use:

¼ tablet Hansen's rennet

Or:

2½ tablets Junket rennet

When the rennet is dissolved in the water, stir it into the milk for 1 minute.

Setting the Curd
Let the milk sit at 85° for 15 to 30 minutes, or until the curd is firm (like custard, see page 130).

Cutting the Curd
When the curd is quite firm, cut into ½-inch cubes (see page 126) and keep it at 85°, more or less, for 1 hour. Dip your hand in from time to time and make sure the curds are cut into small enough cubes, but be careful not to mash them; cut finer, if necessary, with a knife.

Heating and Stirring
Over the course of 1 hour, raise the temperature gradually to 100°, stirring gently by hand to distribute the heat evenly and make sure the curds don't mat. Keep the temperature at 100° or so until the curds visibly shrink and feel firm (see page 130).

Straining and Rinsing
If you wish to use the whey, strain the cheese over a 6-quart container. Use a fine sieve to hold the curds, and rinse them gently with warm (not cold) water, stirring them as they are rinsed. Sprinkle over the curds:

½ tsp. salt

Stir them about and sprinkle another:

½ tsp. salt

Stir again. You may add herbs or caraway seeds, if you wish, at this point.

To Pack, Press, Form Rind, and Keep
See American Cheese (pages 131–132).

BRINE OR GRATING CHEESE

This makes a very bland, hard cheese, which may be stored in brine for use within 2 or 3 months, or may be kept longer until it is as hard as any Parmesan or other grating cheese.

Mixing
Crush very well in ½ cup cold water:

1 tablet Hansen's rennet

When it is dissolved, add it to:

1 gallon skim milk or goat's milk, at 90°

Setting the Curd
Set the milk where it will stay at 90° for 1 hour or more, until the curd is firm (like custard, see page 130).

Cutting the Curd
When the curd is quite firm, cut into ¼-inch cubes, or as small as you can (see page 126). Let the cut curd sit for about 30 minutes at 90°.

Heating and Stirring
Gradually, over the course of 1 hour, heat the curd to 104°, stirring gently with your hand to distribute the heat evenly and keep the curd from matting. Hold at 104° for 30 minutes. Then gradually raise it to 110° or higher, stirring now with a paddle or with your hand in a plastic glove. The curds will begin to hang together in a mass.

Straining
Set the curds to strain in a strainer or a bag, but do not wash them or salt them. Let them drip for 1 hour.

First Pressing
Take out the curds, being careful not to disturb the mass, and pack into the hoop press, lined with cloth; cover and top with the follower and a **3-pound weight**.

24-Hour Pressing
Remove the cheese and bandage it (see page 130) and press with **5-pound weight** for 24 hours.

To Brine
Add:

2 Tb. salt

to

1 qt. cold water

and stir thoroughly until it dissolves. Lay the cheese in it and cover it; leave it to sit in a cool place for 2 to 4 days, or keep in brine until a day or two before you plan to use it.

To Age as Grating Cheese
Soak in brine for 4 days; then take it out and rub

well with salty butter. Turn every day for a month and wipe off butter from time to time and butter it freshly. Pare off any mold that appears. Keep at 40° to 50° in a relatively dry place.

RICOTTA

Ricotta, a very fine-curd cottage type cheese, is easy enough to make if you save your whey, if the whey is good and sour. The cheese is not actually made out of whey; it is just milk that is quickly curdled by the souring action of the whey. Traditionally it was made by pouring milk into whey and heating it, but I find it much easier to use dried milk powder.
Heat:

1 gallon whey (more or less)

to a good simmer. Pour in:

3 cups dried milk

and stir well. As the tiny Ricotta curds appear on the top, ladle them out with a tea strainer into a cloth-lined sieve. Let them drain for about 30 minutes.

You can use more dried milk, but I presume the action of the whey is not infinite, as the acid in it gradually becomes neutralized by working on the milk.

SOURCES OF CHEESE AND YOGURT SUPPLIES

Chr. Hansen's Laboratory, Inc., is an international mail-order supplier for all types of cheese-making cultures, rennets, and miscellaneous things that cheese makers use. They are really geared to dealing with cheese manufacturing companies, not amateur cheese makers, and would rather you tried to get your druggist to order what you need, by the boxful; but they've never failed to send what a customer orders, and promptly.

Horan-Lally Company, Ltd., handles most of the Hansen products in Canada, as well as some of their own. They are also very prompt, as they are accustomed to dealing with customers by mail.

Chr. Hansen's Laboratory, Inc.
9015 West Maple Street
Milwaukee, Wisconsin 53214

Horan-Lally Company Limited
26 Kelfield Street
Rexdale, Ontario M9W 5A2

Here is a listing of some of the products they offer, which they recommend as useful to people making cheeses at home. At their suggestion I haven't included prices; but they're not expensive. At this writing, in 1975, their rennets and cultures are available for less than $3, and colorings less than $2. Write for an Order Blank to find out current prices and what's available.

CULTURES

1. Yogurt Culture: used for making Yogurt, Swiss Cheese, and Mozzarella

2. Acidophilus-Yogurt Culture: used for making Yogurt

3. Acidophilus Culture: used for making Acidophilus Milk

4. Buttermilk Culture: used for making Cottage, Cream, Baker's, Cheddar, Monterey Jack, Edam, Gouda, Blue, and Brick Cheeses, as well as Buttermilk.

RENNETS

1. Hansen's Cheese Rennet Tablets, available in vials of 12 and 25.

2. "Hannilase" Vegetable Rennet Tablets for making Cheeses. This is a microbial coagulant, non-animal in origin, and works like rennet. Available in vials of 12.

COLORINGS

1. Cheese Color Tablets: a water-based coloring made from annatto seed pulp, used for coloring cheese and ice cream.

2. "Dandelion" Butter Coloring: an oil-based liquid used for coloring butter, nut butters; also made from annatto.

MISCELLANEOUS: Hansen's and Horan-Lally also carry a number of other products you might write and ask about. There is a special culture called Propioni shermanii, which is used for making the holes in Swiss cheese. There is a Yogurt Tablet, which you can dissolve in milk and drink, so as to get the benefit of yogurt without having to taste the yogurt flavor or sourness. They also carry cultures for making Kefir, a Middle Eastern fermented milk. And of course they carry many many strains of cultures that cheese makers use in rotation, so as to prevent the possibility of phage, which is not ordinarily a problem in a cheesemaking household, but can be a devastation in a cheese factory.

Both Hansen's and Horan-Lally were exceedingly helpful and kind, answering all sorts of questions very promptly and thoroughly. They seem like very good people to do business with.

9
SOUPS

There are, in general, three types of soups. The first is clear soups; they may or may not have things floating around in them. The second is thickened soups, such as pea or bean soups, or soups made thick by mashed up vegetables (like potatoes, squash, or beets). The third is cream soups, which are clear or thickened soups with milk or eggs added to them, to make them thick and creamy.

Home-made soups are really an important part of my kitchen. They make good lunches and snacks, and keep people from eating up all the bread in the house as they come foraging through the kitchen. You can also run a bowl full of soup through the food mill and have an instant supply of baby food. And when unexpected guests arrive at dinnertime, you can stretch a meal by tacking a soup course on at the beginning.

Although it is possible to make some soups without stock, most soups are better if the liquid is stock. Stock is just water in which bones and/or vegetables have been boiled for a long time to extract the flavor and nutrition. It's easy to make, particularly if you have a wood stove running all day.

MEAT AND BONE STOCK

Bones are a great source of calcium, minerals, and flavor, if you know how to get those things out of them. You can usually get plenty of free bones—

often the best source is the fanciest, most expensive butcher in town. You can also use leftover bones from people's plates—they'll be sterilized by the cooking. To get the most out of them, whack them up with an ax or saw them into manageable hunks, and cover with water. To extract the flavor, add:

1 Tb. salt per gallon, or 1 tsp. salt per 2 cups water

To get the calcium into the water, add:

¼ cup vinegar per gallon

or

1 Tb. vinegar per 2 cups water

If you have a pressure cooker, cook the bones at 15 pounds pressure for around 1 hour; if not, boil

them rapidly, covered, for 4 to 6 hours. The pot won't smell good, I should warn you, but I think the odor must be a byproduct of the extraction of calcium, since the soups themselves smell and taste fine.

After boiling out all the goodies, you will find the meat on the bones tough and flavorless; and of course it has no nutrition worth speaking about. So if you want meat in your soup, add it later in the cooking process.

Next, you should strain your bone stock and get the fat out of it. Just run it through any old strainer or colander into a tall container with a wide mouth, and stick it in a cool place for a few hours. The fat will rise to the top and solidify; remove it. If you use venison in your household, you should save this fat to mix with the ground venison.

So now you have a pot of bone stock. To make this into soup stock, you cook in some vegetable flavors: see below, under Vegetable Stock.

CHICKEN STOCK

I make chicken stock several ways: most commonly I simmer an old hen all day in water and the water from that is my chicken stock. Another time I might use bones, backs, and necks after a feed of roast chicken, and since there is very little meat I would boil it rapidly, as above, with a little salt and vinegar. If you are using commercial chicken meat, throw the neck away, alas: although it's full of good meat, it's also full of drugs, since they are injected in the neck. Finally, you can make chicken stock out of chicken feet. All of these stocks take less time than meat stock; 30 minutes in the pressure cooker at 15 pounds, or 2 to 3 hours boiling or simmering will extract most of what you want.

BEEF TEA

Place in a pressure cooker on a rack or birch twigs:

2 lbs. beef or venison, flank or shank
1 minced or grated onion
¼ tsp. cloves
2 tsp. salt

Cover with water and seal on the lid. Cook at 15 pounds pressure for 2 hours or simmer all day over low heat. Remove beef and boil down the broth. Strain, boiling hot, into a canning jar and store in a cool place up to 3 weeks. Dilute to serve, to taste: for an invalid, or to use as broth for making sauce, gravy, and soup. This can be done with mutton or chicken as well but you must skim off the fat after it is chilled.

FISH STOCK

Fish makes the most delicate of all stocks. I use heads, tails, skins, and bones; add to them:

water to cover

And for every quart of water:

1 whole onion with a clove stuck in it
1 bay leaf
⅓ cup white wine (optional)
1 stalk celery
3 white peppercorns
1 tsp. coriander seeds
1 tsp. salt

Bring this to a boil and simmer it gently over very low heat, the right front plate; don't let it boil at any point if you can help it, since it will stink up the house and discourage you from making it again. Simmer, covered, about 3 hours. Strain, being careful to get the peppercorns and corianders out. This is a finished stock, for fish soups or sauces, and needs no additional cooking. If you are not going to use it within a couple of days, freeze it.

VEGETABLE STOCK

If you make this with water, it is plain vegetable broth; if you make it with beef or chicken stock, it finishes them into soup stocks.

In a deep, heavy Dutch oven or pressure cooker, heat:

2 Tb. oil or fat

Add, for every quart of soup stock you want to make:

2 thinly sliced carrots
2 whole onions with 2 cloves stuck in each one
1 stalk whole celery or about ¼ cup celery tops
2 or 3 sprigs parsley
1 bay leaf
1 tsp. salt
a couple of peppercorns

Sauté all of this lightly for a few minutes, not long enough to brown anything; then pour in:

1 qt. liquid: this can be bone stock, water, or a combination of both

Simmer this, covered, for about 2 hours. Strain it through a sieve (be sure to get those peppercorns out). This is now soup stock, to be used in gravy, sauce, or soup.

CLEAR SOUPS

CLEAR ONION SOUP

This is the quickest, easiest, most rewarding soup on earth.
Heat in a heavy soup pot:

2 or 3 Tb. corn oil or butter

Slice very thin and add:

2 or 3 onions

Sauté these carefully, so they don't burn, until they are good and brown. Then add:

3 Tb. whole wheat flour

Stir and cook gently for a couple of minutes. Then add:

1 qt. soup stock (pages 137-138)

Cover the pot and let it simmer for around 30 minutes over the front middle plate, medium heat. Serve with croutons or you may slice and toast:

1 piece of bread per serving

Sprinkle the bread with:

grated Parmesan, Swiss, or Cheddar cheese

Float the bread in the soup pot and put the pot in the top half of a medium oven for 10 minutes, or until the cheese melts.

CLEAR MUSHROOM SOUP

Heat in a heavy soup pot:

2 or 3 Tb. corn oil or butter

Slice some, chop some, leave some whole, and add to the pot:

1 to 3 cups mushrooms

Sauté gently until they begin to brown; then add:

1 qt. soup stock (chicken broth is best [page 138])

Simmer, uncovered, for about 15 minutes over the front middle plate, medium heat.

CLEAR GREEN SOUP

Bring to a boil:

1 qt. soup stock

Add:

1 cup chopped fresh or frozen greens

Simmer around 15 minutes, covered, until greens are tender.

CLEAR MIXED VEGETABLE SOUP

What goes in this one is mostly a matter of your imagination and what you have. In a heavy soup pot, heat:

2 or 3 Tb. oil or butter

Add any or all of the following:

1 chopped onion
2 stalks chopped celery
2 chopped carrots
1 chopped parsnip or ½ cup chopped turnip
1 or 2 chopped potatoes
½ cup chopped summer or winter squash or pumpkin
½ cup whole mushrooms

Sauté these over high heat until they begin to go limp, but not brown. Then add:

2 qts. soup stock (pages 137-138) or water

And any of the following, alone or in combination:

1 cup diced cooked meat, chicken, or fish
1 or 2 chopped fresh or canned tomatoes
½ cup chopped beans, peas, corn, greens
½ cup cauliflower or broccoli flowerets, fresh or frozen
½ cup tiny Brussels sprouts
½ cup well-shredded cabbage, red or green

Simmer the pot gently for about 30 minutes, or until the roots are tender.
About 10 minutes before serving you may add:

½ cup dried or fresh small noodles

CHICKEN OR BEEF NOODLE OR RICE SOUP

I use the word beef loosely. You can use any meat you want.
Bring to a boil:

1 qt. soup stock (for chicken noodle, use chicken stock, see page 138)

Add:

1 cup dried or fresh noodles

or:

½ cup uncooked brown rice
1 tsp. salt

Boil, covered, until noodles are al dente—about 10 minutes, or rice is done—about 45 minutes. Then add:

1 cup diced cooked meat or chicken
2 Tb. chopped parsley
1 tsp. chopped chives (optional)

½ cup chopped celery or ½ cup fresh or frozen peas (optional)

Simmer 5 minutes more or so to soften vegetables if you use them.

CLEAR CABBAGE SOUP

Heat in a heavy soup pot:

1 or 2 Tb. oil or butter or bacon or ham fat

Add:

1 large chopped onion

2 cups well-shredded green cabbage

Sauté these until they are limp and beginning to brown. Then add:

1 qt. soup stock (see pages 137–138)

Simmer about 10 minutes, uncovered; don't let this soup boil or overcook, since the sulfur compounds in the cabbage will break down and release very unpleasant-smelling and indigestible gases. If you must hold the soup for a while, let it cool and reheat it.

TAMARI SOUP

You may, if you prefer, sauté your vegetables first and use an onion or grain in this soup. I have offered this version because it is very easy on the digestive tract and makes a good soup for recovery of an upset stomach or fever. It's very easy to make and good for small children or old people, too; a sort of vegetarian's version of good ole chicken soup.

Boil:

1 qt. water

1 tsp. salt

Add:

1 cup chopped vegetables, such as: carrots, cauliflower, kohlrabi, celery

Simmer for 30 minutes, covered. Then add:

1 Tb. chopped parsley

1 Tb. chopped chives

¼ cup tamari soy sauce

1 cup green vegetables, such as greens, broccoli flowerets, summer squash, green beans

1 cup dried noodles

Simmer about 15 minutes, uncovered, being careful not to let it boil. Serve as soon as the noodles are al dente.

BORSCHT

"Borscht!" sounds more like something you're supposed to yell to lagging sled dogs rather than the name of an exotic red sweet-and-sour soup. Borscht is, basically, beet soup; tomatoes and perhaps a dash of lemon or vinegar are added to cut the sweetness. It's a good fall soup, best served with its traditional accompaniments (see below). Combine:

3 cups clear bone or vegetable broth (page 138)

1 qt. stewed fresh or canned tomatoes

½ cup chopped leeks, scallions, or onion tops

Bring to a simmering point; add:

2 cups grated raw beets

Simmer, covered, 30 minutes to 1 hour, until beets are tender. Meanwhile set out:

Thick Yogurt (page 122) or Soured Cream (page 122) garnished with chopped dill and/or chives

Whey-soured Rye Bread (page 64) or Rye Crackers (page 77)

Dill Pickles (page 234)

Pickled Herring (pages 212–213)

lemon wedges

MISO SOUPS

Miso, like soy sauce, is a product of fermented soybeans. It comes in a thick black paste and smells a little like cheese. It is very high in protein, keeps well without refrigeration, and it makes delicious instant soups.

There are three kinds of miso:

1. *Hacho Miso*: Made from fermented soybeans. A very dark, firm miso with a strong, almost musky Cheddar-like flavor from long aging.

   Use 1 heaping tsp. hacho miso to 1 cup water

2. *Kome Miso*: Made from fermented soybeans and rice, kome miso is lighter in color and texture. The flavor is more acidic, less heavy.

   Use 1 heaping Tb. kome miso to 1 cup water

3. *Mugi Miso*: Made from fermented soybeans and barley, mugi miso is very thick and pasty.

   Use 1 heaping Tb. mugi miso to 1 cup water

Of course these are general guides; you may increase or decrease as you see fit. There are, however, several things to remember about miso. It is very salty, so do not add salt until after you have the soup all made; then do so only with great care and restraint. Miso (like soy sauce and yogurt) contains enzymes that are helpful to digestion but that are destroyed by too much heat. Therefore the method of cooking for miso soups is to add the miso at the end, and do not boil it, ever, at all. Finally, all miso, and hacho miso in particular, is hard to mix directly with hot water. Measure your miso into a cup and work a little warm water into it with a spoon; then add more liquid, and finally empty it all into the simmering soup.

Miso soups are traditionally composed of sliced simmered root vegetables, nuts, and seafoods that float around in the clear dark broth.

CARROT–ONION MISO SOUP

In a soup pot, heat **2 tsp. light oil** and sauté lightly:

1 sliced onion (cut like thin wedges of a pie)
2 sliced carrots (cut in thick diagonals)

After 5 minutes add **3 cups water** and simmer, lid on, 15 minutes. Mash **miso** in a cup with a little water; add to soup and serve.

TAI MISO SOUP

Traditional is the use of fresh water fish: bream, carp, or perch; but I use any fish with a mild flavor and firm flesh. Bake the fish until just done (or cook it in any way; use leftovers) and take it apart in generous flakes.
Place in each bowl:

½ cup fish
1 Tb. fresh chopped parsley

Mix in a small pan:

1 cup hot water for each serving
miso to taste
a grating of ginger

Heat and simmer the miso, and pour it over the fish.

MUGI MISO SOUP

The Japanese harvest, salt, and dry thousands of little fish, shrimp, and shellfish, and later use them in soups such as this.
Sauté in **1 tsp. oil**:

1 cup whole green onions, chopped
½ cup thinly sliced burdock root* or radishes
½ cup minced salted dried fish or dried shrimp

After 7 minutes of cooking and stirring, add:

3 cups water

Simmer for 30 minutes, until all ingredients are tender.
Mash with a bit of water and add:

3 Tb. mugi miso

Stir, cook briefly, and serve hot.

CREAM SOUPS

Cream soups can be made very quickly and are always impressive, warming, and nutritious. They are not necessarily made with cream. Their thick, smooth texture may come from canned milk, dried skim milk, flour, or mashed potatoes. Their delicate flavors are mostly onions and some carefully hoarded water from cooking a strong vegetable (such as broccoli or asparagus) or steaming seafood. It's a nice touch to garnish the soup with a little chopped cooked food—whatever flavor is in the broth. For example, you might have a feed of steamed lobster or asparagus once in a blue moon. Keep the cooking water (put it away as soon as you finish cooking, so nobody throws it out) and save out a little lobster meat or some asparagus tips. Make the soup a day or two later, and garnish with the bits you saved.

CREAM OF SOMETHING SOUP

In a heavy cooking pot, heat:

2 Tb. butter or light cooking oil

Add:

1 chopped onion or ½ cup chopped scallions

Sauté 3 to 5 minutes, until limp, over medium heat. Add:

1 to 3 chopped potatoes
4 cups liquid (see stocks, pages 137–138)

This is where providence and brainstorms come in: You may use, in part or in full, bone, chicken, fish, or vegetable broth; water from steaming seafood or vegetables; or plain water. If you wish to make, say, cream of broccoli soup, but have no

---

*Burdock root is a favorite Japanese root, very firm, with an odd flavor. If you have burdocks around you may dig the roots, but only use those from first-year plants. Burdock is a biennial, taking two years to mature. The first year it has low, spreading leaves and mild roots; the second year it puts up a seed stalk and the roots become too tough to eat.

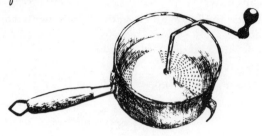

food mill

broccoli-flavored cooking water, you could throw in a half cup to a cup of tough old broccoli stems and leaves, along with 4 cups of water. If it is to be clam chowder, you add the skins of necks and rubbery parts only, and the clam juice, at this point. You also add:

1 tsp. salt
1 bay leaf
3 peppercorns

Put a good tight lid on it; bring it to a rapid boil, and move to a slow plate, low heat, and simmer for 30 minutes to an hour, until the potatoes are soft. Put everything through a food mill, being sure to get out the peppercorns. Then add:

1 cup canned milk; or 1 cup cream; or 1 cup milk plus ½ cup dried milk; or 1 cup water plus 1 cup dried milk

If you have used only one potato your soup may be on the thin side; you may wish to thicken it with a roux. Roux-thickened soup is smoother and creamier than potato-thickened soup. Heat in a separate small pan:

3 Tb. butter or oil

Add and stir with a spring stirrer:

3 Tb. flour (white or whole wheat)

Let this foam over moderate heat for about 2 minutes. Meanwhile, heat:

your cup of milk or cream (see above)

Then off heat, add this all at once to the roux, beating briskly. When thick, add to the soup, stirring constantly.

Add to the soup:

any small bits of tender seafood or vegetable (or chicken) you may have, up to 2 cups

Or garnish with:

chopped parsley, chives, sautéed scallions, or paprika

GOLDEN SOUP

Orange-gold and creamy, this soup can be made either with carrots or squash. The procedures are a little different, but the end results are pretty much the same.

SQUASH (OR PUMPKIN) SOUP

Chop into 2-inch chunks:

1 large or several small winter squash or pumpkins

Put them in a large pot with:

2 cups boiling water

Cover closely and cook until very tender. Meanwhile, in a heavy frying pan, heat:

2 Tb. oil

Add:

1 chopped onion

Sauté until limp, then add to the squash. When the squash has cooked, put it through a food mill, and back in the pot. Then add:

2 cups dried milk

If it is too thick, thin it with:

whole milk

Season with:

1 tsp. coriander
2 tsp. or more salt (to taste)
a generous grating of fresh pepper

Simmer till hot, and serve.

CARROT SOUP

Heat in a heavy skillet:

2 Tb. oil

Add:

1 chopped onion
½ cup uncooked brown rice or barley

Cook over high heat for 5 minutes; then add:

2 or 3 cups grated carrots
1 cup stock
3 cups water

Cover and cook for about 1 hour, over medium heat. Then put the vegetables through a food mill back into the pot and add:

a pinch of sugar
1 cup dried milk
2 tsp. salt and more salt to taste if needed
a generous grating of black pepper
1 tsp. coriander

If it seems too thick you may add:

more milk

Golden soup is very good served with croutons (fried bread cubes); it is also very good baby food.

EGG LEMON SOUP

Thick, warm, and lemony, a very good thing for a cold that's getting better, or a hasty meal after a long hike.
Heat:

6 cups chicken stock (page 138)

Add:

½ cup brown rice

Bring to a boil, then cover and simmer until rice is soft (45 minutes). Meanwhile separate 4 eggs and beat until frothy:

4 egg yolks

Squeeze and grate into them:

juice of ½ lemon (3 Tb.)
grating of one lemon rind

When the rice is done, pour a little soup into the eggs. Beat well. Add more soup and mix again; then pour all back into the pot. Simmer about 5 minutes, stirring constantly, and being careful it doesn't boil, until it thickens slightly. Serve at once with:

hot toast

THICK SOUPS

Thick and hearty soups are a mainstay in any working farmhouse. One kind of thick soup is made with mostly dried beans, peas, or lentils. The other is a sort of everything-but-the-kitchen-sink mixture that's a meal in itself. Both are very high protein foods, and both are best if simmered for 4 to 8 hours. Thick soups are very filling and satisfying; but they're at their most delicious when served with something a little sour—cheese and crackers, pickles, sourdough rye bread.

To cook dried beans, peas, or lentils more quickly, you may soak them overnight (if you don't, they'll cook anyway, eventually). Then sprinkle them slowly into a pot of boiling, salted water and cook rapidly, covered, for half an hour. Add whatever else and simmer, covered, until they're tender; the amount of time depends on how big the beans are, mostly. The flavor of dried legumes is greatly improved by a few chopped tomatoes, or a couple of spoonfuls of tomato paste. If you are a meat-eating family, you will also find that a little pork fat, added one way or another, will make the legume flavor richer.

Whole grains also take a long time to cook to a consistency that is really good in a soup. The grains should soften completely and swell up; their starch thickens the soup after long cooking. Barley is wonderful, but you can use about any whole grain, as long as you cook it sufficiently. Noodles, another grain product, are very high in protein since they're made of durum wheat. You could try making your own noodles—nobody minds if they're a little too thick, in soups.

You can add vegetables in two different ways. One is to add them at the beginning and cook their flavor completely into the soup. You can do that with carrots, onions, potatoes, and some green things; but don't ever do it with members of the cabbage clan. Later, you mash these up, or take them out; they won't have much flavor by then; it will all be in the soup.

Then you can add vegetables in the last 30 minutes of cooking. Chop the roots small, and give them about 15 or 20 minutes. Peas, chopped green beans, cauliflower, broccoli, sprouts, cabbage, and greens should be added no more than 10 minutes before serving. They will just cook, but not go soft. Meat should be cooked slowly so that it doesn't become tough.

The essence of these soups is flexibility—using what you have, and blending flavors in one direction or another. Do a lot of tasting and think ahead; don't just throw in half a cup of anything without due consideration. Go easy on the herbs, too. If the soup is any good it will speak for itself.

143

BEAN SOUP

You can make bean soup out of any kind of dried beans or peas, keeping in mind that some varieties take longer to cook than others. In general, the larger, the longer, ranging from 2 to 6 hours. All legumes cook faster if soaked overnight.

Sort through and pick over:

1 cup dried legumes

Soak overnight in:

2 cups cold water

In the morning, empty them (and their water) into a heavy cooking pot and add:

6 cups boiling water
1 large onion stuck with 3 cloves
1 clove garlic
3 stalks celery, with leaves, or 2 Tb. dried celery leaves
1 carrot
1 ham bone, or piece of bacon or ham fat
1 bay leaf
3 peppercorns
½ tsp. salt

Boil rapidly, covered, for 30 minutes, then simmer, covered, until the beans soften, from 2 to 4 hours. Take out ½ cup of cooked beans and put the rest of them, plus anything else that will go, through a food mill. Return the whole beans to the pot and adjust the salt.

Variations

U.S. Senate Bean Soup: Use marrow beans; add a potato and mash it along with the beans.

Tomato–Bean Soup: Add 1 cup stewed canned tomatoes and their water in place of 1 cup water.

Whole-Bean Soup: Chop the vegetables and sauté them in bacon or ham fat before adding the beans and water. Use ground pepper; mince the garlic and omit the cloves. Do not put through a food mill but mash some of the beans with a potato masher or spoon against the side of the pot.

Black Bean Soup: Omit carrots; use black beans. Serve with wedges of lemon and hard-boiled eggs.

SPLIT PEA SOUP

There are various ways to get a rich ham flavor into split pea soup. One is to sauté the onions in bacon fat. Another is to float a hunk of bacon or ham fat in the pot. Or you can simmer a ham bone

(shin, hock, or other cuts with little meat can often be bought for less than 50¢). The main thing is that rich, smoky flavor.

In a deep, heavy soup pot, heat:

3 Tb. bacon or ham fat

Add and sauté until golden:

1 sliced onion

Add and bring to a boil:

4 cups water
1 ham bone if you've got it
3 chopped carrots
1 cup split peas, green or yellow
½ tsp. salt
1 bay leaf

Cover and cook over moderate heat for 2 to 3 hours. Serve with cornbread or hoe cakes, or croutons fried in bacon fat. Some people slice hard-boiled eggs on top, or crumble them on as a garnish.

SCOTCH BROTH

This is a very, very good soup, if you cook it long enough. You should start by making a bone stock (pages 137–138) at least one day before.

In a heavy Dutch oven or soup pot, heat:

2 Tb. bacon or ham fat, or oil

Add and sauté 5 minutes:

2 thinly sliced carrots
1 chopped onion
1 stalk celery

When these are limp, add:

1 cup bone stock
3 cups water
¼ cup tomato paste
a grating of pepper
1 tsp. salt
a pinch of thyme
a bay leaf

Bring this to a rapid boil, covered, and pour in:

1 cup pot barley
⅓ cup white or pea beans

Keep the soup boiling, covered, for half an hour; then move the pot to low heat, the middle or right of the stove, and simmer, covered, for 4 to 6 hours. An hour before serving, add:

1 cup diced raw meat (lamb is traditional, but anything is fine)

Or wait until the last 10 minutes and add:

1 cup diced cooked meat

And, if you have them:

1 cup fresh peas or beans or both

One bowl of Scotch broth has about 12 grams of protein, which means that two bowls, plus a glass of milk and a peanut butter sandwich provide about a third of the daily protein needs of a hard-working farm hand—not to mention calcium, iron, and all kinds of vitamins.

MINESTRONE SOUP

Definitely our favorite soup, this one combines beans and grain to complete the missing amino acids in both and thus makes a bowl or two fulfill a third of your daily need for protein without meat or dairy products. A flexible soup—I've never made it quite the same way twice.

In a deep, heavy pot, heat:

1 Tb. oil or pork fat

Add:

1 chopped onion
2 stalks chopped celery (with leaves)

When the onions are limp, you may add, if you like:

1 clove crushed garlic

Sauté 1 minute longer; then add:

2 quarts hot water or bone broth (pages 137–138)
1 tsp. salt

Bring to a rapid boil over high heat; add slowly, so it keeps boiling:

½ to 1 cup navy, white, or speckled beans
1 cup barley

Boil for 30 minutes, covered. Then add:

1 to 2 cups cooked or canned tomatoes (with liquid)
a couple of pinches of oregano
a grating of pepper
2 fresh basil leaves or ½ tsp. dry basil

Move the pot to a simmering plate and cook slowly, covered, for 30 minutes or longer. In the last 15 minutes you should add some fresh vegetables, such as:

½ cup fresh or frozen corn, green peas or beans, mushrooms, chopped summer squash, chopped greens

You may also add:

½ cup uncooked egg noodles (any shape, as long as they're small)
½ cup cooked meat (the leftovers!)

This soup is even better the second day, with last night's vegetable leftovers added.

LENTIL–BARLEY SOUP

Lentils are far and away the quickest soup bean around; they can be eaten in an hour and fall apart in two. Barley cooks in about two hours. Together, lentils and barley have about 50 percent more protein than they do separately.

In a heavy soup kettle, boil:

8 cups water

Add gradually, so it keeps boiling:

2 cups barley
1 cup lentils
2 tsp. salt

Cover; boil rapidly for 30 minutes. Cool to simmering, remove lid, and add:

1 whole onion, stuck with 3 cloves
2 whole carrots
2 stalks of celery, with leaves on (optional)
¼ cup tomato paste
2 bay leaves
1 ham bone, with a little meat on, if you have it
1 clove peeled garlic

Simmer, covered, for 2 hours. Remove the vegetables and ham bone; pick out any meat, chop it up, and return it to the pot.

I like this best with black rye bread, pickled herring, funky cheese, and beer.

10
FAMILY DISHES

ABOUT PROTEIN

The first thing to think about, when you fix a meal, is protein. Lack of it is what made you hungry in the first place. Protein is what your body converts into energy every day, to work and think, to digest food, to grow, or heal and mend any part of you that has gotten hurt or sick.

Different people need different amounts of protein at various times. In general, though, you can begin learning how much of it you (and the people you cook for) need, by consulting the following chart:

DAILY PROTEIN NEEDS

Infant	— age 0 to 1	1 gram per pound
Child	— age 1 to 5	30 grams
	— age 5 to 10	40 grams
	— age 10 to 12	50 grams
Boys	— age 12 to 18	50 to 60 grams
Girls	— age 12 to 18	50 to 55 grams
Average woman		55 grams
Average man		65 grams
Pregnant or nursing woman		75 grams

Of course, this varies. Generally, you can tell how much you need by your appetite; if you're still hungry at midnight, eat more protein.

WHICH FOODS HAVE PROTEIN?

In general, the highest protein foods are animal products, such as eggs, milk, milk products, meats, fish, and poultry. Protein is also stored by plants in their seeds. So beans, peas, seeds, nuts, and grains also have varying degrees of protein. In most cases, though, the amount of protein in the vegetable foods is lower than the amount in animal foods. That is, partly, because the protein in all vegetable sources is lacking in one or more of the nutrients necessary to make all of its protein available. But, if you complement the food with other foods that contain these nutrients, the level of protein will be increased. For example, a bowl of oatmeal has about 3 grams of protein. A glass of milk has about 7. But if you have both, at the same time, you will be getting about 12 grams of protein, instead of 10, because the milk contains amino acids that oatmeal lacks. Another example: a cup of cooked rice has around 3 grams; ⅓ cup cooked kidney beans has 2. But together they provide almost 10 grams of usable protein, the equivalent of an average-sized hamburger.

WHY NOT STICK TO
HIGH-PROTEIN FOODS?

Traditionally, Americans have depended on mostly animal-product foods, which do not have to be complemented to yield high amounts of protein. It's hard to change, but it looks as though we're going to.

In the first place, these foods are becoming much more expensive than they were a few years back. If you grow your own, you have a very much clearer idea of the expense, and it isn't only money. A quart of milk, an egg, a pound of cheese, a roast—these are crowning achievements, not to be taken lightly. Vegetable protein is cheaper, both in terms of money and in terms of your own work.

In the second place, high-protein foods are an extravagant use of the resources of the earth. As Frances Moore Lappé has pointed out so clearly in *Diet for a Small Planet*, livestock must be fed enormous amounts of vegetable protein in order to produce, for our pampered palates, one pound of meat protein. Beef is the worst—21 pounds of usable protein (not just measuring grain, or feed, but protein itself) for our pound of usable protein on the chuck wagon. Pigs, sheep, venison, and goats are somewhat better, using about 7 to 10 pounds protein for a pound of meat protein. Chickens and fish use about 5. A pint of milk protein represents about 4 pounds vegetable protein, and so do 9 large eggs.

In the third place (and after this, I'll stop, I promise) it actually turns out to be much healthier not to eat so much meat or other high-protein foods as Americans have been eating. In parts of the world where people eat less meat, and more grains, legumes, etc., they live longer and more physically rewarding lives. There are other factors, of course, which contribute to their health: lack of psychological stress, hard physical work, and various things that they do eat, such as yogurt and whole grains. All these things work together, in a way. The earth that produced us supports us best when we keep an ear tuned to its rhythm.

WHAT IS PROTEIN: HOW DOES IT WORK?

The proteins that people can use are made up of 22 amino acids, in a particular proportion to one another. Think of it as a sort of irregularly shaped, 22-pointed star. The more usable protein a food has, the bigger the star would be.

However, if you were to measure the exact amounts of amino acids in each kind of protein food you eat, you would quickly find that the stars you drew would be all different shapes. The only food that is proportioned absolutely correctly (for us) is human milk. The next closest is an egg. Others have varying shapes, and many are even lacking in a few amino acids. In some cases that doesn't matter, because the human body can manufacture some of the amino acids needed for itself. But there are 8 amino acids that the body can't manufacture. They have to be present in order for your body to get any protein at all out of a meal. What's more, they have to be there in a particular proportion. Think of the star again, paying particular attention now to the 8 essential points on it. If one of them is smaller than it should be, it doesn't matter how much bigger the others are. The 8 essential amino acids have to be present, simultaneously (like in the same meal) in the right proportion, in order for you to absorb all of the available protein in the food.

COMPLEMENTARY PROTEIN

This sort of chemical attitude toward food can get to be rather a bore, and most people would rather not think about it at every meal. But you can form habits, as people have, all over the world, of serving certain foods together with other foods to get the most out of both. In most cultures there are traditional dishes that incorporate two or three foods that complement each other, or supply the missing amino acids to make the level of protein in the whole meal greater than the sum of its parts. Such dishes are legume–grain combinations, such as beans and corn in Mexico; rice and soybeans or azuki beans in the East; bread or noodles and white beans in western Europe; kasha and lentils in eastern Europe; barley and split peas in Scotland; millet and chickpeas in Africa; rice and black beans in South America; bulgur and chickpeas in the Middle East. Another common combination translated into many cultures is milk products and grains and eggs, which make a good pudding, served hot and cold, sweet and nonsweet. And there are lots of ways to make high-protein snacks out of nuts or seeds and grains and dairy products. All these dishes are the result of thousands of generations of cooking by trial and error, and a tribute to the people who invented them not knowing how or why such foods fed them better together than apart.

We are, by comparison, in a somewhat privileged position, in that we have some idea why such

	TRY	ISO	LYS	SU-C	USABLE PROTEIN* (grams)
SEAFOOD: *about ½ cup*					
tuna; mackerel	B	B	A+	B	18–19
halibut	B	B	A+	C	17
salmon	B	B	A+	B	16
bass; shad; sardines; cod; haddock; herring; crab; lobster	B	A–	A+	A–	14–15
flounder; sole	B	B	A+	C	12
scallops	A	B	A+	B	12
oysters	A	B	A+	B	9
EGGS AND DAIRY					
1 medium egg	A	A	A+	A	6
1 cup milk or yogurt, whole or skim	A	A	A+	B	7
5½ Tb. instant skim milk	A	B	A+	B	8
½ cup cottage cheese (creamed)	B	A	A+	B	11
½ cup plain curds	B	A	A+	B	13
½ cup ricotta	B	A	A+	B	10
1 oz. American; Gouda; Edam cheeses	B	A	A+	B	6
1 oz. Cheddar cheese	B	A	A+	B	5
1 oz. mold-ripened cheeses	B	A	A+	B	4
LEGUMES: *⅓ cup uncooked, 1 cup cooked (more or less)*					
soybeans; soy grits	A	B	A	C	10
mung beans	C	C	A+	D	7
broad beans; peas	C	B	A	D	6
black beans	B	A+	A	C	5
black-eyed peas	B	C	A+	C	5
kidney beans	C	B	A+	D	5
lima beans; chickpeas (garbanzos)	C	B	A+	C	5
lentils; navy, pea, and white beans	C	B	A+	D	4
soy flour, 1 cup, full fat	A	B	A	C	3
soy milk					
tofu, 2″ x 2″ x 2½″	A	B	A	C	5
Tamari soy sauce					
Miso					
GRAINS: *⅓ cup uncooked, 1 cup cooked (more or less)*					
whole wheat, bulgur	B	C	C	B	4–5
rye	C	C	C	B	4
barley	A	C	C	B	4
oatmeal	B	C	C	B	3
millet	A+	B	C	A	3
brown rice	B	C	C	B	3
1 cup cooked noodles	B	B	C	C	3–4
1 cup cracked wheat, whole wheat flour	B	C	D	B	2
1 cup dark rye flour	C	C	C	B	2

	TRY	ISO	LYS	SU-C	USABLE PROTEIN* (grams)
1 cup dark buckwheat flour	B	C	C	B	2
1 cup cornmeal (uncooked)	C·	C	C	B	2
2 Tb. wheat germ	C	B	A+	B	2
SEEDS AND NUTS: *3 Tb.*					
sesame seeds	A	C	C	A	3
sunflower seeds	A	B	C	B	4
peanuts or peanut butter	B	C	C	C	3
walnuts	B	C	D	B	3
Brazil nuts	A+	C	C	A+	2
VEGETABLES: *½ cup cooked*					
lima beans	A	A	A	D	4
green peas	B	B	A+	D	3
Brussels sprouts	B	B	A	D	3
corn	D	C	C	B	3

*Not total protein

foods combine well to make whole protein out of half proteins. Protein can be measured; amino acids can be counted. You can refer to the accompanying list, or copy parts of it and make a chart to hang on the kitchen wall.

KEY TO THE CHART: Of the 8 essential amino acids, 4 are usually found in most protein foods in sufficient quantity to make them adequate to the human diet. But four others vary. They are:

Tryptophan and sulphur-containing amino acid: These are pretty low in most of the legumes, but high in the nuts, and fairly well supplied by most of the grains.

Isoleucine and lysine: These are lacking in grains and nuts, but very high in the legumes.

The "usable protein" is the amount of protein available if you eat the food alone, without any accompanying dishes. If complemented with a food high in amino acids which the first food lacks, the amount of usable protein will increase from ⅓ to ½. For more about this read *Diet for a Small Planet*.

PART I: HASTY SUPPERS

Hasty Suppers are not necessarily less elegant or tasty than Works of Art (see Part III). They differ only in that they take less time to prepare. If you have a wood stove, it's best to do your hasty cooking on top of the stove, since it would take quite a while for the oven to heat up. And, if you're starting a meal and kindling a fire at the same time, keep an eye on that fire. It's all too easy to get distracted and let it go out.

There are other tricks to serving meals in a hurry. It's a good idea to get into the habit of thinking ahead about meals, especially if your schedule is going to be hectic (as during haying, or harvest seasons). At least half the energy of cooking is in decisions and preparations, such as soaking beans or simmering bones. You can bake stews, beans, and many casseroles ahead of time and then reheat them in a short time. Soups are mostly better if made a day in advance. And in a pinch you can chop vegetables ahead, if you're careful to seal them tightly in plastic and refrigerate them.

While you hastily assemble meals in a hurry, keep food on hand for munching. Nothing's more demoralizing than a peanut butter fiend in your way as you try to produce a balanced meal—or a brigade of hungry kiddies yammering for "Something—anything!" Set them out a plate of sliced vegetables to dip in yogurt or cottage cheese; serve salad first, or a dish of roasted sunflower seeds. Relax, and don't do more than you have to.

Some of the quickest and easiest foods to cook are in other parts of the book. Search around; check "Homegrown Eggs" and "Cooking Meats, Poultry, and Seafood."

SLOPPY JOES

A Sloppy Joe is a sandwich made with ground meat and toasted buns. If you like, you can cook some vegetables along with the meat. This is a meal a kid can make.

Get out all the things you will need:

about ¼ cup ground meat for each person

one bun each

a little fat or butter (about 1 Tb.)

a few chopped vegetables, if you like them: use half an onion, very finely chopped up, and a piece of green pepper, also well chopped, or a couple of fresh or canned chopped tomatoes

Set the pan on the stove and melt the butter or fat. When the pan sizzles a little, put in the onions and pepper, if you have them, and cook them for about 1 minute. Then put the meat in. Stir it while you cook it. If any fat sputters on your wrist the pan is too hot; move it over. Add tomatoes if you have them.

When the meat is all gray, put a lid on the pan and move it over to a part of the stove where it won't cook but will stay warm.

Cut your buns in half and put them on the stove. Toast them for 1 minute on each side, then turn them with the fork.

When they are toasted on both sides, lay them on a plate and cover half of each with a pile of meat (and vegetables). Cover with the other half of the bun.

CHEESE FONDUE

A cheese fondue supper is a classic work of art, the ultimate in intimate dinners. The fondue is a hot mixture of cheese and wine (served in a chafing dish at the table) into which each person dips crusty cubes of toasted bread (with a long fork) and is accompanied by wine, salad, and maybe some onion soup, perhaps a good dessert—no more. It requires almost no preparation and very little cleaning up; the only requisites are the ingredients:

A Chafing Dish

You have to have something in which to keep the cheese and wine hot; as soon as they cool, they separate or become gummy. You need a heat source at the table, with a pan to go over it. Usually you acquire along with it some long-handled, two- or three-tined forks with heatproof handles for dipping bread.

Cheese

Swiss fondue is supposed to be made with Emmenthaler or Gruyère cheese, both of which are almost impossible to get in most country places. Settle for anything marked Swiss, as long as it's fresh, not processed (those little foil-wrapped Gruyère-flavored things are no good for fondue). Or use, if you have any, your own homemade American cheese.

Wine

A dry white wine, but it doesn't have to be grape, as long as it isn't sweet. I hear potato wine is good in fondue . . .

Kirsch

Kirsch is a distilled cherry wine, used to flavor fondue. It's phenomenally expensive. I just leave it out; but I reckon you could substitute a little Corn Likker, if you had it, or something . . .

Bread

French bread is usual, but any good homemade bread will do, as long as it's not too fresh. Break it up into bite-sized hunks and set it to toast in the oven as you make the sauce.

Salad and Extra Bread

Make a really good salad, something with things to find in the bottom: cucumbers, or tomatoes, or sprouts, or beans, sliced onion rings, marinated this-and-that, a nice tart oil-and-vinegar dressing. As for the extra bread, slice two or three pieces per person, and coat each with garlicky butter; wrap in foil and set in the oven.

Fondue

Have everything else ready first, even to setting the table and making sure the heat source at the table is going to work.

Grate:

1 lb. Swiss cheese

Toss with:

2 Tb. cornstarch or ¼ cup unbleached white flour

Rub the fondue pot with:

a clove of garlic

Pour into the pot:

2 cups dry white wine

Heat until it bubbles, on the stove, over moderate heat. Throw in the cheese, by handfuls, stirring as it melts. Add:

3 Tb. Kirsch or other dry liquor

As the fondue thickens, taste it; maybe add:

a pinch of salt, a grating of pepper

Set it on the table and keep it warm. Serve cubes of bread in a basket, garlic bread on the side. Eat at once.

WELSH RAREBIT

They've come and they've gone, and what's left in your refrigerator? A bottle of flat beer, half a loaf of stale bread, and a hunk of cheese as dry as a rock. So—grate, grind, pound, or dice:

about 1 lb. sharp Cheddar cheese

Heat:

a cup or so of beer

Stir in cheese by handfuls. When it melts, go **beat an egg** and pour it in, stirring constantly until it thickens; don't let it boil, or heat too fast. Add for seasoning:

½ tsp. salt

1 tsp. dried or prepared Dijon mustard

Some people like to add a pinch of **curry**. Pour the rarebit at once over toast.

MILK RAREBIT

Somebody invented this, certainly not a Welshman.

Grate, grind, pound, or dice:

about 1 lb. fairly sharp cheese

In a small, heavy saucepan, heat up:

3 Tb. butter

Add:

1 cup milk
½ tsp. salt
1 tsp. tamari soy sauce
a grating of pepper

When the milk is hot, stir in the cheese, by handfuls. When it is all melted, beat in a bowl, and add:

1 egg

Stir until thick and serve on toast.

POTATO PANCAKES

Potato pancakes aren't at all like flour-based pancakes; they're crunchy on the outside, mushy in the middle, and very quick and easy to make. Together with a jar of applesauce and some sour cream or yogurt, maybe jam or maple syrup, they're a meal that anybody can whip up in half an hour (and they taste like "city food," say my kids).

Grate:

about 1 small potato per serving
½ onion per serving

(Do the potatoes first because the onions make your eyes weep.)

Add:

2 Tb. white or whole-wheat flour per serving
1 beaten egg for every 2 servings

This makes a rather runny gray mixture. Never mind. Heat in a large skillet:

4 Tb. corn or safflower or peanut oil

Spoon about 3 tablespoons of the potato mixture on the hot skillet and spread it out thin to about 4 inches in diameter. Repeat until skillet is full (you can use two skillets at a time); cook on each side until the cakes are a rich brown. Stash finished cakes in a 200° oven or warming oven until they are all done.

Serve good and hot.

HASH

Hash is made out of 5 or 6 cold cooked potatoes and some cooked meat. You could use 1 cup of any of these:

turkey, ham, beef, lamb, chicken, pork

Or you could open a tin of **corned beef,** or use some **ground raw meat.** Some people also like to add vegetables and spices to hash, to make it tastier.

You could use:

1 onion
1 green pepper
2 stalks celery

Chopping

The first thing to do is to chop everything up into

bite-sized hunks. Chop the meat and vegetables rather smaller than the potatoes.

Cooking the Vegetables

Heat up some fat in a big heavy frying pan, over very high heat. Add the chopped onion and stir it while it cooks. If you are going to cook some green pepper or celery or use ground raw meat, add it to the onions as they cook and cook them all together, stirring as they cook, for about 3 minutes, or until the onions get soft and the meat turns gray.

Meat and Potatoes

Then stir in the cup of meat and the chopped potatoes. If you like, you can stir in some seasoning:

about ½ tsp. thyme or basil

Also add:

1 tsp. salt

Press down the mixture firmly with a spatula and cover the pan. Cook over *medium* heat for about 5 minutes.

Turning

Take off the lid and turn the hash over with the spatula in big flat scoops. Cover again and cook 5 minutes to brown the other side. Serve it and eat.

Variations

Egg on the Hash: Just after you turn the hash over, break an **egg** for each serving on top of the hash. Cover and cook until the eggs are done, from 3 to 5 minutes.

Red Flannel Hash: Use half **potatoes** and half **beets**. Cook as above.

Gravy in Hash: Some folks say it ain't hash if it don't have gravy. Add about ½ **cup gravy** just after you add the potatoes.

NOODLES

Noodles are one of the quickest-cooking and most popular forms of grain around. Store-bought noodles are made with semolina, a very high-protein durum wheat that holds together well. Homemade noodles (pages 72-73) are tenderer, and because of the fresh eggs, have almost as much protein. Dried noodles cook in 10 or 15 minutes,

if the water is boiling well and there is lots of it. If your stove is going too slowly to keep a rolling boil with the lid off, invert the lid over the pot to hold some heat down; but you can't leave the lid on tight or it will boil over.

MACARONI AND CHEESE

Grease or oil a casserole and fill it with:

3 cups cooked macaroni

Toss in evenly:

½ cup to 1 cup grated Cheddar or American cheese

Pour over it:

1 cup cream, sour cream, or evaporated milk

or

1 cup milk mixed with 1 cup dried skim milk

Grate a little more **cheese** over the top. Bake at 350° about 20 minutes, near the top of the oven, until it browns.

Variations

Use Cream Sauce, page 174, instead of milk or cream or sour cream.

Add ½ to 1 cup sliced mushrooms, or cooked shrimp, or cooked chopped lobster, or cooked chopped poultry meat.

Instead of hard cheese, use **1 cup cottage cheese.** Grate hard cheese over the top.

Instead of milk or cream, use ½ **cup milk or cream** beaten with **1 or 2 eggs**. This will make a rather solid loaf that you can bake for a longer time and then unmold; it looks really incredible if it's done in a ring mold. Bake about 1 hour at 350°.

NOODLES NONNIOFF

Boy, I remember Nonny used to cook this stuff up by the gallon, to feed to the starving thousands. It was sublime. This recipe is for four.

Boil a large pot of:

1 lb. or so of noodles

Heat a heavy skillet and sauté, until soft:

1 large chopped onion

Crumble in and stir until gray:

1 lb. ground hamburger

Add:

2 cups or more sour cream

Keep just warm but don't let it boil, for about 10

minutes, or until noodles are done.
Add:

¼ cup wine or sherry

(any kind—the better it is, the better it will taste). Drain noodles. Serve meat over noodles, immediately.

BLINTZES

Traditionally, these are served with applesauce and sour cream; a glorious late Sunday morning brunch, or special supper. You can also serve them with Cream Sauce (page 174). This recipe serves three people.

The Pancake
In a shallow ceramic bowl, beat:

3 eggs
2 cups water
⅔ cup dried milk

Then beat in:

1 cup whole-wheat flour
½ tsp. salt
1 tsp. baking powder (optional)

Heat a couple of frying pans over direct flame. It's nice if they're 6-inch pans, but anything will do, as long as they're heavy and don't develop hot spots. When the pans are hot, pour in:

2 Tb. batter

and tilt it so it makes a thin, evenly shaped pancake, about 6 inches in diameter. Let them cook about 2 minutes, then turn them out, on a smooth counter, *uncooked side down*. Continue cooking until all batter is used up.

The Filling
Meanwhile mix up:

1½ cups dry curds or drained cottage cheese
1 egg or 2 egg yolks
1 Tb. soft butter
1 tsp. lemon juice

Put 1 heaping tablespoon of the cottage cheese mixture on each pancake, spread out in a line, and roll it up tightly. (You can tuck in the edges if you like as you roll it up.)

Heat a large iron skillet over direct flame, with **¼ cup oil** in it. When the oil begins to crackle, fill it with blintzes, but don't let them touch one another. Cook until brown on each side. (You may have to move the pan around to keep just the right

heat under it.) Drain on newspaper and keep in the warming oven until they are all done. Serve at once, with applesauce spooned on top.

Filling Variations

1. **½ cup chopped greens**
    1 cup dry curds
    1 egg or 2 egg yolks

2. **2 cups mashed potatoes**
    ¾ cup grated Cheddar cheese
    1 egg
    salt and pepper to taste

3. **7 scrambled eggs, made with ½ cup canned milk or cream**

Serve these variation mixtures with cream sauce over the blintzes rather than applesauce.

COTTAGE CHEESE CAKES

Mix:

1 cup very dry curds or well-drained cottage cheese, or pot cheese
1 cup breadcrumbs, soaked in 1 egg
2 Tb. flour
1 tsp. salt
2 Tb. finely chopped parsley
2 Tb. grated onion (optional)
a pinch of nutmeg (optional)

Shape into patties; coat with flour. Sauté in oil, 2 to 4 minutes on each side. These patties may be immersed in Mama Restino's True Spaghetti Sauce, where they will be mistaken for eggplant, or veal scallops, or something equally exotic (see page 180).

Variations

1. Substitute **1 cup cooked, chopped, drained spinach** for the curds, or use half curds and half spinach (or other greens).

2. Serve with a generous dab of homemade Catsup (page 228) or White Sauce (page 174) and toast or noodles.

SPANISH RICE

This is a really fast meal only if your rice is already cooked. But since Spanish Rice is really much better with leftover rice (fresh rice tends to get gummy when served this way) we will assume it is cooked already.
In a heavy skillet heat:

3 Tb. bacon fat

Sauté in it:

1 onion, cut in thin pie wedges
1 green or red sweet pepper
2 or 3 stalks chopped celery
1 chopped chili pepper (optional)
1 clove crushed garlic (optional)

After a few minutes, add:

½ lb. ground meat

Toss and cook until meat turns gray.
Add:

3 cups cooked rice
1½ cups canned tomatoes or tomato sauce (pages 179–180)
1 tsp. oregano
½ tsp. basil

Cover and simmer for 15 minutes, or place in the oven. As long as the heat is not too high and the pot is covered, you can keep this dish for hours. Serve with a garnish of:

crumbled bacon
grated cheese

Variations

Meat, Seafood, or Chicken: Instead of ground meat, sauté a cup of either:

shrimps
cooked lobster, chopped
cooked halibut or haddock
chopped cooked poultry
chopped cooked meat: beef, venison, rabbit, pork, ham, lamb, goat, etc.

Do not cook these meats very long—just toss them in the oil and add the rice and sauce.

Cheese: Sauté vegetables in olive oil instead of bacon fat. Leave out meats; garnish servings with ¼ to ½ cup grated cheese on each plate.

SPAGHETTI

Spaghetti can be an all-day thing if you make a real sauce (page 180) or a quick hearty dinner if you make it with just a can of tomatoes, lightly seasoned (page 180). Unaccompanied, it doesn't have much protein, so serve it with lots of cheese, or meatballs, or a bean dish.

Bring a large pot of water to a rolling boil and add:

⅓ lb. uncooked spaghetti noodles per large serving

Heat the sauce.

Cook store-bought noodles 15 minutes, homemade noodles (pages 72-73) 10 minutes. Taste a noodle to see if it's done; or throw one on the ceiling. If it's done, it'll stick.

Serve sauce on noodles.

CLAM SPAGHETTI

Cook noodles as above. Meanwhile, heat:

¼ cup olive oil

in a small pan and add:

1 pt. canned clams
¼ cup chopped parsley

Do not cook them longer than is needed to just heat them up. Serve with plenty of:

grated Parmesan cheese

SPAGHETTI CARBONI

Said to be a favorite with Italian coal miners, although where in Italy they mine coal I'm not sure. Cook noodles as above. Meanwhile break into a bowl and beat:

1 egg per serving
¼ cup grated hard cheese per serving

Drain spaghetti well. Grease the pot with olive oil and return the spaghetti. Pour in eggs and mix everything together; stir as the eggs cook so that the noodles are covered with crumble.
Add:

¼ cup diced ham or crumbled cooked bacon per serving
1 Tb. chopped parsley per serving

Serve immediately.

CODFISH CAKES

In a heavy deep pot, heat:

¼ cup bacon fat, butter, or oil

Add and sauté until golden:

2 chopped onions

Then add:

1 cup water
6 sliced potatoes
½ cup dried milk
3 parsnips (optional)

Cover and cook the potatoes until soft, about 20 minutes, over moderate heat. If the lid doesn't fit tightly, keep an eye on it so the milk doesn't boil away. Remove and mash the vegetables together in a food mill or with a potato masher.
Add:

1 cup flaked cooked codfish
1 tsp. salt if you have used fresh or frozen cod
(not salted)
½ Tb. sugar if you have not used parsnips

Thicken with flour or thin with milk as needed to make firm cakes. Fry in bacon fat, or other fat.

Variations

1. Use a turnip instead of parsnips.
2. Add a couple of tablespoons of chopped parsley.
3. Cool the potatoes a little and add an egg.
4. Thicken with breadcrumbs instead of flour.

LEFTOVERS À LA KING

Cooked chopped meats, poultry, fish, shellfish, and vegetables can all be reheated with a cup or so of cream sauce and thus converted to a rich and glamorous dish.

CHICKEN OR OTHER POULTRY À LA KING

Combine:

1 cup cooked diced chicken (or other poultry meat)
1 cup cream or white sauce (page 174)
½ cup chopped, sautéed green peppers (optional)
¼ cup chopped pimentos (optional)
½ cup sliced mushrooms (optional)
2 Tb. sherry or white wine (optional)

Simmer these together for a few minutes, and serve on:

toast, noodles, or crackers

Or you can turn the dish into a baked pie shell or a greased casserole and bake for 20 minutes at 375° to 400°.

SEAFOOD À LA KING

The best seafood to serve this way is firm-fleshed fish or shellfish, so it doesn't fall apart. Some good choices are:

lobster
shrimp
clams, oysters, mussels
haddock
crab
salmon

Combine a cup of seafood with a cup of cream or white sauce (page 174).
Jazz it up with:

a little lemon juice
or
white wine
some parsley
maybe a pinch of dill

You can also add, if you like:

3 chopped hard-boiled eggs
½ cup sautéed mushrooms

Serve on toast, noodles, or crackers. Or you can bake it in a baked pie crust or greased casserole. It is best to serve salmon baked in the sauce; and be careful not to break up the meat too much as you stir it in.

VEGETABLES À LA KING

Vegetables that hold their shape well can be combined with an egg-enriched white or cream sauce and perhaps ½ cup of diced ham or other cooked meat to make a dish with enough protein to keep the troops content.
Combine:

1 cup cream or white sauce (page 174)
1 or 2 egg yolks

and beat it until it thickens slightly.
Pour over any of these:

1 cup cooked asparagus stalks and ½ cup diced ham
1 cup cooked peas and ½ cup diced ham or chicken
3 heads broccoli
1½ cups cauliflower and ½ cup diced ham or hard-boiled eggs
2 cups sautéed mushrooms and ½ cup grated cheese
1 cup spinach or other cooked, chopped greens, and a poached egg on top
1 cup spinach or other cooked, chopped greens, and ½ cup shellfish (clams, oysters, etc.)

Clearly, the variables are infinite; I leave it to you to improvise from your garden and larder.

POTATO HAMBURGERS

There isn't enough meat in one of these to fill the protein needs of an alley cat, so you had better serve a grain with them in some form. They are an excellent way to stretch hamburger meat, however; nobody will even notice. Use very lean meat or venison.

Grate in a shallow bowl:

1 cup potatoes, skin and all

Add and mix well with your hands:

½ lb. (1 cup) lean hamburger meat

1 egg

⅓ cup whole-wheat breadcrumbs or whole-wheat flour

1 Tb. tomato paste or catsup

a little onion juice or grated onion

1 Tb. parsley

Shape into patties or meatballs; dust with white flour. Remove the front left plate and heat a heavy frying pan to smoking. Add:

2 Tb. light oil

Immediately, add the meat and brown on both sides over high heat, quickly. Replace the plate and move the pan to lower heat; cover and simmer for 10 to 20 minutes (depending on the size of the meat shapes).

PLAIN HAMBURGERS

A kid can make these. Take out a handful of ground beef for each serving:

about ½ cup hamburger meat

Pack it into a very firm hamburger. Heat up a frying pan over high heat. Add:

1 Tb. fat or oil or butter

When the pan sizzles, put in the hamburgers. Cover the pan if it spatters on the stove, so it won't make the stove all greasy. Cook it for a minute on one side. Take off the lid and turn it over; cook it on the other side (covered) for another minute. Then move the pan to a spot in the middle or on the side of the stove where it is not quite so hot and let the meat cook for 5 minutes. Meanwhile, slice a bun or piece of toast for each hamburger. Toast it 1 minute on each side, turning it with a fork. Take off the bread and set it on a plate. Put on the hamburger.

PART II: DRIED BEAN DISHES

Dried beans are God's gift to the thrifty household, as they provide an inexpensive and nonperishable source of protein. They aren't as cheap as they used to be, but they're still a whole lot cheaper than meat, eggs, and milk products; and some beans (kidneys, pintos, lentils, white, and pea beans) are easy to grow, even in a northern climate. You can buy beans wholesale, too. Figure out how many pounds you use in a year, and order bulk from a health-food outlet; or split a sack of beans with a friend. They'll keep, as long as you store them in jars.

The protein in all beans is low in at least one amino acid (the sulphur-containing one) and most beans are also low in tryptophan. That means that the amount of protein you get from them is lower than what you could get if you supplied the missing amino acids, by eating a food such as a grain (rice, or bulgur, corn, or even bread); or you could include a dish with sunflower or sesame seeds or nuts in the same meal; or, of course, eggs or milk products, or meats. See pages 146–149 for more about complementary protein.

Many people complain that beans, to put it bluntly, make them fart. There's no question but that beans do give rise to a certain amount of gas. It shouldn't, however, turn you into a writhing emergency case, or drive your friends away. To avoid problems:

In the first place, if you have a problem with beans, it's because your diet is deficient in B vitamins and roughage. Eliminate refined food and start eating whole-grain bread and a serving of cooked whole grain (cereal or brown rice) every day; spike your baked foods with wheat germ or brewer's yeast, and eat liver often.

When you eat beans, don't eat too many. Half a cup is plenty for one serving; if you're a big eater, one cup of beans is enough. Always eat whole grains *with* dried beans.

Don't eat a lot of eggs in the same meal or the same day (one is enough), since they also give rise to gas. And be sure to cook your beans thoroughly. Meatless dishes are marked with an ornament ♦.

COOKING WITH DRIED BEANS

There are lots of different kinds of beans, and the amount of protein in them varies, as does the flavor, texture, and the time they take to cook. They all cook much faster if soaked in water overnight, or even less if first brought to a boil, then soaked in water overnight. Subtract about a third of the cooking time below if you soak them overnight.

Small beans, such as lentils and split peas, cook quickly and disintegrate entirely if cooked for hours and hours. If you wish to keep beans from popping apart, soak them first and cook them slowly until almost done; then let them sit overnight. They will then absorb more liquid.

Some people pressure-cook beans to shorten the cooking time. This can be dangerous, since the valve may become clogged with foam and fail to operate properly. I think simmered beans taste better anyway, but if you use a pressure cooker, just be sure not to fill it more than halfway with water and beans.

(UNSOAKED) BEANS	COOKING TIME	PROTEIN IN 1 CUP COOKED
soybeans	6 hrs.	10 mg.
garbanzos (chickpeas)	6 hrs.	5 mg.
kidney, pintos	4-5 hrs.	5 mg.
black beans	2-3 hrs.	5 mg.
blackeye peas	3 hrs.	5 mg.
lima beans	2-3 hrs.	5 mg.
navy, pea beans	2-3 hrs.	4 mg.
lentils	2 hrs.	4 mg.
split peas	2 hrs.	6 mg.
mung beans, sprouted, raw or sautéed		7 mg.

If you eat another food that has a lot of the amino acids beans are low in, increase the protein level by about 40 percent. For every ½ cup of cooked beans, you could use one of these:

1½ cups cooked grain
⅓ cup cheese
2 Tb. cottage cheese
2 Tb. dried milk
1 oz. meat or fish or poultry
1 egg
¼ cup seeds or nuts

FRENCH STYLE BEAN DISH

Soak overnight to soften:

1 cup white or navy beans (or lima beans)
3 cups cold water

Next day add to the water:

1 onion stuck with 2 cloves
1 minced or crushed garlic
1 carrot cut in quarters
1 piece ham fat or bacon
½ tsp. pepper
1 tsp. salt
2 celery tops

Bring all this to a boil and simmer (covered) until the beans are tender, adding water as needed to keep the sauce liquid—about 2 hours. Chop into 1-inch pieces and add:

3 medium-sized potatoes
2 stalks fresh celery
½ cup ham or 1-2 cups cooked sausage (optional)
¼ tsp. thyme
½ tsp. basil
½ cup tomato juice

Remove ham fat, celery tops, and carrots. Chop carrots small and return to the pot. Serve hot. (These beans can be kept over and reheated very well.) Serves 4.

ITALIAN STYLE BEANS

Soak overnight to soften:

1 cup dried lima beans (or navy beans)
3 cups cold water

Next day, sauté in 3 Tb. olive oil:

1 chopped onion
1 minced or crushed garlic
2 stalks celery

Add to the beans and bring to a boil in a heavy pot. Add, also:

1 tsp. salt
½ tsp. ground pepper
1 tsp. oregano
1 cup canned tomatoes
1 piece ham fat
½ tsp. basil

Cook, covered, for 1½ hours. You may add:

1 cup Italian sausage, sliced ½ inch thick

Simmer 30 minutes longer. Just before serving, add another:

pinch of oregano

Serves 4.

CUMIN-FLAVORED BEANS

Soak overnight in 3 cups water:

1 cup pinto or kidney beans

Next day, bring to a boil, along with:

1 onion
2 celery tops
½ tsp. ground pepper
1 piece of pork
1 tsp. salt
1 sliced carrot

Cook 4 to 5 hours; if possible, cool and let sit 24 hours. Half an hour before serving, add:

1 tsp. cumin

A favorite Mexican and South American dish consists of these beans, cooked until almost dry, then mashed and refried in corn oil.

◆ GINGER-FLAVORED CHINESE STYLE AZUKI BEANS

Azuki beans are a very small, dry, red Oriental bean with a little white stripe. Sometimes they are mixed with rice, sometimes served plain. It is good to serve something else with a cornstarch sauce to balance the dryness—such as stir-fried vegetables with a sweet-sour sauce. And, of course, brown rice. Bring to a boil:

3 cups water
1 cup azuki beans

Tie in a cloth bag:

1 clove garlic
5 or 6 peppercorns
1 inch fresh ginger root
¼ cinnamon stick
10 coriander seeds
2 whole cloves
a pinch of star anise (optional)

Put that into the pot, along with:

1 tsp. salt
1 cup azuki beans
1 whole onion

Bring to the boil again, then cover and simmer for about 2 hours. Remove onion and spice bag. Add:

¼ cup molasses or plum jelly
1 to 2 Tb. sweet sherry
1 Tb. tamari soy sauce

Serves 4.

NEW ENGLAND BAKED BEANS

Traditional are white pea beans, but any bean will do—my favorites are great big kidney beans or speckled trout beans. Pick over, then soak overnight in 1 qt. water:

2½ cups beans

Next day add:

1 tsp. salt
2 celery tops
1 onion stuck with 2 cloves
1 piece fat pork (fresh or smoked)

Cover and simmer until beans are soft: 2 to 6 hours (page 157).

Remove onion, celery, and let the beans sit overnight. Next day heat in a deep pan:

3 Tb. bacon or ham fat

Sauté:

1 chopped onion

Cool the pan and add the cooked beans, along with:

3 Tb. molasses
1 Tb. tamari soy sauce or blackstrap molasses
2 Tb. tomato paste
2 tsp. mustard
1 tsp. cider vinegar

Cover and set in a slow oven (200° to 300°) all day (6 to 8 hours) adding water if needed. Stir now and then. The last hour, leave the top off to brown the crust. Serve with plenty of cornbread, coleslaw or sauerkraut, and a slice of ham or pork. Serves 6.

REAL FANCY BEANS

Soak overnight in 4 cups water:

2 cups lima or white beans

Next day, set them in a pot with:

½ tsp. salt
½ tsp. dried thyme
2 bay leaves
2 tops celery
1 2-inch square of salt pork
½ tsp. ground pepper

Bring to a boil and simmer, covered, until beans are soft—2 hours. In another pan, heat:

3 Tb. butter

Sauté until soft:

1 chopped onion
2 stalks chopped celery

Remove the piece of salt pork and celery tops; add the vegetables and simmer, uncovered, about 20 minutes. About 5 minutes before serving, add:

1 cup any wine
2 Tb. fresh chopped parsley

The beans should be fairly dry when you add the wine. Serves 5 or 6.

◆ BRAZILIAN BLACK BEANS

Sauté in a deep pot, in 3 Tb. oil or bacon fat:

1 chopped onion
2 cloves crushed garlic

Add and bring to a boil:

1 cup black beans
½ tsp. salt
2 bay leaves
3 cups water (or wine and water)

Simmer for an hour or two. Then add:

2 stalks chopped celery
2 to 3 canned tomatoes
1 chopped orange
½ tsp. ground pepper

Simmer until beans are soft, an hour or two more. With a potato masher or pestle, mash up some (not all) of the beans. Let sit overnight. Serve the next day with rice pilaf and salad or greens.

◆ LENTIL STEW

In the summer, when you want to run the stove as little as possible, lentils are a good choice; they take only an hour to soften, 2 hours to disintegrate entirely. Cook up a pot of them; use for sauces, soups, and stew. They go well with tomatoes and vegetables:

In a heavy frying pan, heat:

2 Tb. light oil (olive oil, if you have it)

Chop into big pieces and add:

1 onion
1 tsp. basil or oregano
1 green pepper
3 stalks celery
1 zucchini squash or eggplant
1 cup chopped tomatoes

When soft, cover and simmer. Add:

3 cups cooked lentils

Serve with rice or bulgur.

◆ CURRIED BEANS

Soak overnight and cook until tender (see p. 157):

1 cup beans (soybeans, garbanzos, white beans, or part beans and part raw peanuts)

In a heavy frying pan, heat **2 Tb. oil**. Sauté in it:

1 chopped onion
2 chopped apples
1 Tb. curry

Add the beans and:

½ tsp. ginger
½ tsp. paprika
1 Tb. tamari soy sauce

Cook and stir 5 minutes; take the pan off the heat for a few minutes and when it is cooled a bit, add:

2 cups yogurt

Serve with rice or bulgur or a mixture of the two.

◆ MIXING BEANS AND RICE

Beans and grains can be mixed together too. Particularly good with rice or bulgur (or both) are:

Brazilian Black Beans
Cumin-Flavored Beans
Ginger-Flavored Chinese Style Azuki Beans

Cook the beans and rice separately, or add cooked beans in with the uncooked grain (and the usual amounts of water) and steam. Season the beans and rice with lots of fresh chopped parsley if you have it.

CHILI CON CARNE

Chop well: **1 whole onion, 2 stalks celery**, and crush **1 clove garlic**.

Heat in a heavy skillet: **3 Tb. bacon fat or ham fat**. Sauté the vegetables 3 minutes, then add:

½ lb. ground meat

Toss and cook the meat until it is gray. Then dump it in a pot along with:

2 quarts water
2 cups kidney or pinto or chili beans
1 tsp. salt
1 bay leaf
1 tsp. chili powder (or 2, if you're brave)
1½ cups canned tomatoes and juice

Bring to a boil, then simmer all day, covered. Add water if needed.

If you have leftover beans, you can add the meat and chili and vegetables and make them into chili.

Traditionally served with tortillas, you can also try cornbread.

◆ CORNMEAL-BEAN PIE

A cornbread crust, surrounding leftover beans (or beans and rice)—use any kind of beans (see recipes above).

Gradually pour **2 cups boiling water** over **1 cup cornmeal**. Stir constantly as you pour and afterwards, as it thickens, so it doesn't lump. (If it does, put it through a mill or sieve quick.) Add:

2 cups rolled wheat or oats
1 Tb. light oil
1 tsp. salt
1 tsp. baking powder

Spread this mixture in the bottom of an oiled pie dish, then push some up around the edges to form a side crust. Before the sides collapse, fill with: **4 cups cooked beans, or mixed beans and rice; a few tomatoes or slices of apple** thrown in are nice too.

Bake at 350° for 20 to 30 minutes or until sides brown on top.

MASHED BEAN RECIPES

Traditional in many of these recipes are garbanzo beans, or, as some call them, chick peas. They are round and sort of wrinkled and take at least 6 hours to cook until soft. You can substitute, if you like, soybeans; they don't take any less time to cook, but they are cheaper and do have more protein.

◆HUMMUS

A pungent, eye-watering spread used often in the Middle East and adored by passionate garlic lovers everywhere.
Cook for a day and mash through a food mill:

¾ cup garbanzo beans
3 cups water
1 onion

To 1 cup mashed garbanzos, add:

2 to 4 cloves crushed or smashed garlic
¼ cup olive oil
½ cup tahini*
juice of 1 good-sized lemon
salt to taste (about 2 pinches)
1 to 2 Tb. fresh chopped parsley

◆REFRIED BEANS

Soak overnight:

1 cup kidney or soybeans and 3 cups water

Next day, put them in a pot, along with:

1 onion stuck with 3 cloves
a couple of celery tops
1 tsp. salt
1 clove garlic

*Tahini is sesame paste; you can buy it in health stores, Middle Eastern stores, or make it out of sesame seeds.

Let it simmer 5 hours (for kidney beans, if soaked) or all day, for soybeans; at any rate, until the beans are soft. Then remove the vegetables.

Mash up some of the beans with a pestle or potato masher. Add to them:

1 tsp. cumin
chili powder to taste
2 to 4 Tb. flour, as needed, to thicken

Shape into rough patties and fry in plenty of oil. Serve in tortillas (see pages 81–82) with rice.

◆EGYPTIAN BEAN CAKES

Rumor has it that the pyramids were built on the strength of people who ate nothing but onions. More likely, they lived on Tamia, as they call these patties:
Soak overnight:

1 cup pea beans or lentils
3 cups water

Next day, add **1 tsp. salt** and bring to a boil; cover and simmer 1 to 1½ hours, until beans are soft but still hold their shape. Let them sit overnight in a cool place (for best results). Next day, mix the beans with:

1 grated or minced small onion
2 Tb. flour
3 Tb. minced parsley
1 beaten egg
1 clove crushed garlic

Shape into cakes, adding more flour if needed. Let them sit and dry in the warming oven for 1 to 2 hours. Fry in oil until crusty and golden on each side. Drain on newsprint; keep warm until you serve them.

◆FALAFEL

Falafels are small, fried, meatball-like bean cakes. They are served along with a mess of chopped lettuce, tomatoes, and cucumbers, in half a pita, or Syrian bread, topped with a fiery yogurt sauce, on every street corner in Israel. There is no question but that that is the best way to eat them; however, you can also serve them in a light tomato sauce, or with rice or stir-fried vegetables. Israeli falafels are made with garbanzos and sesame seeds, which are presumably less expensive there than here. Mix:

1 cup cooked puréed soybeans (or garbanzos—chickpeas)
½ cup roasted ground sesame seeds

¾ cup roasted ground sunflower seeds
1 Tb. lemon juice
1 egg yolk
1 Tb. onion juice

Mix well; add more sunflower meal as needed to make the mixture thick enough to shape into small balls. Fry in ½ inch oil. Drain on newsprint; serve as suggested above.

PART III: WORKS OF ART

These are dishes that take a little while to fix, and provide a focal point around which you build the rest of the meal. Most of them have a substantial amount of protein, but not all contain meat. The meatless dishes are marked with ornaments ♦.

A work of art should be considered beforehand. If guests are coming, you might find something that can be prepared before they arrive, and stuck in the oven at the last minute. If you're not sure when somebody will arrive, it's best not to get involved with a dish that has to be eaten the moment it's ready (like a soufflé). Most of all, a work of art should be something you enjoy making.

QUICHES

A quiche is a simple, elegant egg custard pie, endlessly variable by slipping in a few scraps of ham, bacon, cheese, or vegetable leftovers.

In a quiche, the crust is half the dish; you should take care to make a good one, chill it well, and half bake it in a hot oven so that it doesn't become soggy underneath when the filling is poured in. And although some cookbooks call for milk, I find it better to use evaporated milk or cream; milk soaks into the crust too easily.

Finally, bake the filled pie at a low temperature: 300° to 325°, or the eggs will toughen and the custard may even separate.

Quiche may be served hot or cold. It is very good with potatoes, salad, and, or course, a bottle of light dry white wine. . .

♦ BASIC QUICHE

Make, chill, and roll out:

quiche crust (page 95)

Shape the crust in a pie dish, shallow casserole, or over a cake pan, for a free-standing quiche crust.

Prick at ½-inch intervals all over with a fork; weight with dried beans or small smooth stones and bake at 400° for 10 minutes, until crisp and just beginning to turn color. Take out the crust and cool for 10 minutes.

Mix in a bowl:

For 2 to 3 people:

2 eggs
1 cup cream or evaporated milk
½ tsp. salt

For 4 to 5 people:

3 eggs
1½ cups cream or evaporated milk
¾ tsp. salt

Pour mixture into the shell; bake at 300° to 325° for 30 minutes, until brown and puffy.

Variations

Cheese: Grate 1 cup Cheddar, Swiss or fresh homemade American cheese into the shell before adding egg mixture.

Bacon (Quiche Lorraine): Sauté and crumble 6 strips thick Canadian bacon or 3 slices chopped ham into shell before adding egg mixture.

Onions: Sauté 1 chopped onion and spread in shell before adding egg mixture.

♦ ONION TART

This is a lot like a quiche, but has a thicker crust on bottom. It is rather dry and should be served with something damp—say, zucchini in tomato sauce, or sweet-sour cabbage.

Make and cool slightly:

1 cup white sauce (see page 174)

When it has cooled, beat into it:

1 egg

Mix well, in a mixing bowl:

1⅓ cups whole-wheat pastry flour
½ tsp. salt
1 tsp. baking powder

Cut in:

⅓ cup butter or other solid shortening

Soften with:

½ cup milk

Spread this mixture in a greased pan, about 9 by 9 inches, and cover with:

2 thinly sliced, sautéed onions

Cover onions with cream sauce and bake in a very hot oven, about 425°, for 20 minutes.

Cover onions with cream sauce and bake in a very hot oven, about 425°, for 20 minutes.

Variation
Omit onions; grate ¼ cup Swiss cheese into cream sauce and cook as above.

SOUFFLÉS

Soufflés do fine in a wood stove oven, provided your oven is preheated to 350° and your fire banked and steady with good dry hard wood. Too much heat from the top will burn the upper crust; you can peek at a soufflé as it bakes, and if you think the top is getting too hot, lay aluminum foil over it, quickly.

Soufflés start to deflate a little as they cool, so have the table set and everything else hot and ready to eat the moment they're done. They deflate more as you cut into them, but don't worry—it'll be delicious.

◆CHEESE SOUFFLÉ

In a small pan, melt ¼ **cup butter**, and add ¼ **cup fine wheat flour** or **unbleached white flour**. Stir well and let the roux bubble for 2 or 3 minutes. Meanwhile, heat **1 cup whole milk**. Take the roux off the heat, add the milk all at once, stirring vigorously with a wire whisk, and then put sauce back over low heat.

Add to the sauce and simmer until it melts:

¼ **lb. (1¼ cups) grated cheese: Cheddar, Swiss, or half Swiss and half aged cheese**

Cool until you can comfortably stick your finger in the sauce.

Meanwhile beat until frothy:

4 egg yolks

When the cheese sauce is cool enough, add the yolks and stir for 30 seconds.

You may set this mixture aside until 30 minutes before dinner time, or until the oven is at 350° and well banked.

Beat until almost stiff but still moist:

4 egg whites

Deposit the whites over the yolk mixture and stir in by hand.

Scoop the entire mixture into a well-greased casserole and bake for 30 minutes, or until brown and puffy. Serve at once. Makes 6 servings.

◆FISH SOUFFLÉ

An elegant way to serve leftover fish; this is good with any fairly dry fish that holds its shape in flakes.

Flake into small pieces:

2 cups cooked fish

Mix it with:

2 tsp. lemon juice
a grating of fresh (white) pepper
¼ tsp. salt

Make a roux in a small pan by melting **2 Tb. butter** and stirring in **2 Tb. unbleached white flour**. Cook, stirring often, for 2 or 3 minutes over low heat, then add off the heat: **¼ cup warm milk**. Stir well and let cool.

Separate **3 eggs**; beat the yolks until frothy and stir them into the cool roux. Add the fish and **fresh chopped parsley**.

Beat the egg whites until they reach full volume.

Dump the beaten whites over the other ingredients and mix by hand. Scoop into a greased, ovenproof casserole. Bake at 350° for about 30 minutes, until brown and puffy.

Variations

Fish Mousse: Add ½ **cup beaten whipping cream**; or use **2 eggs** and **1 cup whipping cream**. Fold whipped cream in along with egg whites.

◆VEGETABLE SOUFFLÉS

Make a roux of: **3 Tb. melted butter** and **3 Tb. fine flour**. Let it bubble 3 minutes; take it off the heat and add **1 cup whole milk**, all at once, stirring vigorously. Cool; add **3 to 4 beaten egg yolks**.

Add to this one of the following:

1 cup grated carrots and ½ cup minced onion
1 cup creamed or whole corn and ½ cup minced onions
2 cups fresh or frozen peas
2 cups cooked finely chopped greens and ¼ cup minced onions
1 finely chopped broccoli head

Beat until stiff, but not dry:

3 to 4 egg whites

Fold whites into the vegetable mixture and bake in a greased casserole at 300° for 30 minutes.

OTHER WORKS OF ART

◆ EGGS, POTATOES, AND CHEESE

Into a broad, greased casserole or heavy frying pan, slice 1 at a time:

4 large potatoes, barely boiled

Slice or grate between the potato layers:

¾ lb. soft cheese
sprinklings of pepper, scatterings of salt
½ cup hard cheese
chopped parsley

Brush the top with:

½ cup melted butter

Bake, covered, at about 350° for 30 minutes. Break on top:

4 to 6 fresh eggs

Bake 15 minutes longer, or until eggs are set but not hard. Serves 4.

◆ RICE PIE

Rice pie is a perfect example of pie crust adding glamour to a dish. It is simply amazing. You surround all the old ho hum leftovers with pie crust and, zam, people get all enthusiastic. (Oh, wow, what's that? Yum!)

Make and refrigerate a pie crust that can be rolled out (see page 95). In a heavy skillet, heat **2 Tb. oil** and sauté:

1 chopped onion
2 chopped carrots
2 stalks chopped celery

Add any vegetables you have around (a few chopped greens, peas, beans, maybe even potatoes or parsnips) and:

2 Tb. fresh chopped parsley
2 Tb. tamari soy sauce
2–4 Tb. water

Cover and simmer over low heat until vegetables are soft, about 10 minutes. Then take the pan from the heat and stir in:

3–4 cups cooked rice and any other leftover whole grain, such as whole-wheat berries, kasha, bulgur, millet, rye berries

If you would like the pie to be a complementary protein dish, also add:

1 cup cooked beans (kidney beans, azuki beans, black beans, soy beans, navy beans, etc.)

Let the mixture cool; then beat and add:

2 eggs

Stoke up the fire and have the oven banked at 350° to 400° before rolling out pie crust. Fill the pie and cover with a tight crust. Bake 30 minutes. Serve hot or cold. Or make into tarts; splendid on-the-road food.

Variations

Vegetable Pie: Instead of 4 cups rice, sauté in butter and fill pie with:

3 cups chopped vegetables:
cauliflower
carrots
broccoli
eggplant
greens
parsnips
cabbage
summer or winter squash

You may use beans or grate into the vegetables:

1 cup sharp cheese (any kind, as long as it is aged hard cheese)

RICE–CHICKEN PILAF

Or, how to stretch a cup of chicken to feed four without complaints.

Heat in a deep heavy pan:

4 Tb. oil, butter, or bacon fat

Add:

1 medium-sized chopped onion
2 cups brown rice
2 cloves crushed or minced garlic
1 to 2 tsp. curry powder

Cook and stir over high heat until the rice is turning light brown and the onions are limp. Then add:

4 cups water or chicken stock
2 chopped tomatoes or canned tomatoes
1 pinch thyme
1 tsp. salt

Cover and cook 30 minutes; uncover and cook 15 minutes or until all liquid is either absorbed or evaporated. Toss in:

1 cup cooked chicken, cut in 1 inch chunks

CHINESE CHICKEN-PEANUT

This is a special dish, and involves lots of preparation but a short cooking time.

Preparations

1. Skin, bone, and chop **a young chicken** into bite-

sized hunks (not too tiny). Toss in **sesame or peanut oil.**

2. In a mortar, smash up:

    a 1 inch piece of fresh ginger root, peeled
    2 cloves garlic

3. Grind or pound into coarse meal:

    1 cup raw, blanched peanuts

4. Chop up fine:

    2 onions or a bunch of green onions

Cooking

Heat up a Chinese wok over direct heat until very hot. Spill in **4 Tb. sesame or peanut oil;** tilt wok to coat it evenly.

Frazzle the garlic and ginger for about 30 seconds.

Add the chicken and toss it around a bit; then add:

3 Tb. sherry or white wine
peanuts and onions

Let this cook for a minute, stirring occasionally, while you mix up:

2 tsp. cornstarch
2 Tb. tamari soy sauce
¼ cup water
1 tsp. molasses (preferably blackstrap)

Cover and let it steam until chicken is cooked—about 4 minutes.

Serve with:

brown rice
fresh or fried sprouts or aemono
soy sauce

Or cooked chicken may be mixed with stir-fried vegetables.

EGG ROLL CASES

You can put all kinds of things in egg rolls—cooked cabbage, chopped celery, onions, ground or chopped pork, fish or chicken; bean sprouts, or other kinds of sprouts, nuts, seeds, chopped cooked roots—in fact anything that goes in stir-fried vegetables. This recipe will make 15 to 20 egg rolls, depending on how thin you make them.

In a bowl, mix:

2 eggs
2 cups water
½ tsp. salt
1 cup white unbleached flour

Heat up a frying pan. It is easier—but not absolutely necessary—to have a 6-inch frying pan. Grease it with a few drops of oil; you will have to add a few drops every 3 egg rolls or so, when the pan begins to look dry.

Give the batter a stir and pour about 2 tablespoons into the pan. Quickly tilt the pan so the batter spreads around. Fry over medium heat about 2 minutes on one side, 1 minute on the other. Don't let them get hard and crisp.

As you take out each pancake, let it cool; then you can stack it on top of the others without having them stick. Make all the pancakes before you start stuffing.

To stuff them, put about 2 tablespoons of filling in the middle of each egg roll. Fold the sides over and paint them with a glue made of:

2 Tb. water
1 Tb. white unbleached flour

Roll them up and seal the flap with some more glue. They will seal better if you let them sit for at least 30 minutes before frying.

Fry egg rolls about 5 minutes on each side, until they become golden brown, in:

5 Tb. oil

Serve hot, with rice and Sweet-Sour Sauce (page 178).

EGG ROLL FILLINGS

Egg roll fillings are really creative ventures. I like to put in a lot of mung bean sprouts because they make egg rolls and rice have enough protein so that you don't get hungry after dinner. For this you must grow your own sprouts; canned ones have the beans removed, and so have no nutrition worth considering. See about growing sprouts, pages 28-29.

In general, to make 15 to 20 egg rolls you will need:

3 cups of something green and crunchy
1 cup of something firm-fleshed and very tasty (chopped fine)
1 diced sautéed onion or ½ cup chopped green onions
¼ cup tamari soy sauce

Here are two possible recipes:

2 cups sautéed mung bean sprouts
1 cup chopped sautéed cabbage
1 chopped sautéed onion
½ cup roasted sesame seeds
½ cup finely chopped cooked pork
¼ cup chopped cooked water chestnuts
¼ cup tamari soy sauce

1 cup sautéed mung bean sprouts
½ cup alfalfa sprouts
1 cup sautéed Chinese cabbage
1 cup chopped cooked chicken
½ cup chopped sautéed green onions
2 cloves crushed sautéed garlic
½ cup tiny dried, soaked shrimp
¼ cup tamari soy sauce

HAMBURGERS, MEATBALLS, MEATLOAF, AND OTHER MEAT DISHES

Ground meat is very flexible; so many things can be mixed in with it (breadcrumbs, grains, potatoes, cheese, spices, eggs, etc.). The additions are made partly with the aim of stretching the meat, and partly to loosen the texture and add to the flavor. Stretched meat is usually bound with egg, so it won't fall apart.

If you use 2 parts meat to 1 part other stuff, the addition won't even be noticeable. You can use up to 1 part meat to 2 parts filler, and still have a strong meat flavor, but the texture won't be very meatlike.

Plain beef meatballs and meatloaf are traditional only in America. In other parts of the world, venison, goat, lamb, pork, and horse meat are commonly used to make ground meat dishes of all kinds and flavors.

BREADED MEATBALLS OR MEATLOAF

Beat:
1 egg
Add and soak for 15 minutes:
½ cup dry breadcrumbs
Meanwhile, mash up in your hands together:
1 cup (½ lb.) ground beef, lamb, or venison ground with fat
3 Tb. chopped parsley
2 pinches dried thyme
½ tsp. salt
¼ tsp. pepper
optional:
2 Tb. catsup or tomato paste
1 Tb. tamari soy sauce
1 clove crushed garlic
Add to breadcrumb mixture and mix well.

Meatballs: Roll tightly into small balls and dredge in white or whole-wheat pastry flour. Sauté in 2 Tb. hot fat for 1 minute on each side; reduce heat, add gravy (see Koenigsburger Klops, below), and simmer, covered, for 10 minutes.

Meatloaf: Shape into a firm loaf on a greased baking dish. Bake at 300° for 45 minutes. Cool 10 minutes before slicing.

Variations
1. Use 2 eggs, 1 cup breadcrumbs, 1 cup ground beef.
2. Add 1 tsp. or more caraway seeds; serve with sour cream gravy (see Koenigsburger Klops, below).

BUCKWHEAT MEATBALLS OR MEATLOAF

In a small, heavy pan, heat 3 Tb. vegetable oil and sauté 1 clove minced or crushed garlic and 1 small minced onion. When they are transparent, add and brown ½ cup buckwheat flour. Cool. Add 1 cup water, ½ tsp. salt. Cover and simmer 10 minutes or until buckwheat is soft. Meanwhile mix together by hand:
1 pound (2 cups) ground meat (beef, venison, lamb, goat, etc.)
1 egg
½ tsp. paprika
3 Tb. chopped parsley
whole-wheat flour as needed
Mix in buckwheat and add whole-wheat flour until you can shape it into balls or a loaf.

Meatballs: Shape into firm balls and fry in bacon fat 1 minute on each side; add gravy, cover, simmer 10 minutes. Add ½ cup sour cream and 2 Tb. wine; serve.

Meatloaf: Shape into a firm loaf on a greased baking dish. Bake at 300° for 45 minutes. Cool 10 minutes and slice.

KOENIGSBURGER KLOPS

Soak together:
1 egg
½ cup breadcrumbs
Meanwhile, mash together by hand:
½ cup ground beef or venison
½ cup ground calf or beef liver
½ cup pork bacon
½ small sautéed onion

2 Tb. chopped parsley
½ tsp. salt
½ tsp. ground pepper
a squeeze of lemon juice, a grating of lemon rind

Shape into large firm balls and chill for 1 hour. Drop them into 3 cups boiling beef or other meat stock and simmer, covered, for 15 minutes.

Gravies for Meatballs

Plain Quick Gravy: In a small, heavy pot, heat 3 Tb. butter or animal fat. Sauté in it: 1 small minced onion. When onion becomes transparent, sprinkle over with 3 Tb. whole-wheat pastry flour or unbleached white flour. Cook and stir for 3 minutes; then add: 1 cup beef stock. If you have no beef stock, add 1 cup water and ¼ cup ground meat; add a pinch of salt, a pinch of dried thyme. If you like you can toss in a carrot and a celery-stalk top; fish them out later. Simmer gravy ½ to 3 hours, as long as you can.

Sour Cream Gravy: Just before serving, stir in ½ cup sour cream. You can also add 2 Tb. wine or sherry, or a dash of wine vinegar; ½ tsp. dill, or a generous pinch of thyme. Do not allow sour cream gravy to boil or it will separate.

HAMBURGER COTTAGE CHEESE PIE

A very high-protein dish, very elegant and delicious. Make up and bake at 400° for 10 minutes:

a bottom-crust pie shell (use ⅔ of a flaky pie crust recipe, page 95)

In a heavy frying pan, sauté in 2 Tb. oil or butter:
1 finely chopped onion
½ chopped green pepper

When soft, add:
1 cup ground meat (½ lb.)

Brown the meat; sprinkle over it:
2 Tb. whole wheat flour

Simmer for 5 minutes and cool. Meanwhile, mix up:
1 cup dry curds or drained cottage cheese
2 beaten eggs
1 tsp. salt
a grating of fresh pepper
a pinch or two of paprika

When hamburger mixture cools, spread it in the pie shell and top with the cheese mixture; sprinkle with paprika.

Bake at 350° for 20 minutes or until brown on top. Serves six.

SOYBEAN–HAMBURGER PIE

Simmer all day (6 to 8 hours):
1 cup soybeans
4 cups water
1 tsp. salt
1 tsp. tamari soy sauce

Mash them through a food mill. Mix with:
1 tsp. curry
1 egg

Make up and bake at 400° for 10 minutes:
a bottom crust pie shell (use ⅔ of a flaky pie crust recipe, page 95)

In a heavy skillet, in 2 Tb. butter or fat, sauté:
1 chopped onion
a clove minced garlic and/or 1 chopped green pepper

When soft, add:
1 cup ground meat (½ pound)

Sauté until meat is brown; sprinkle over:
2 Tb. whole-wheat flour
½ cup canned tomatoes

and simmer 5 minutes. Cool and season with 1 tsp. basil or thyme.

Fill pie crust with soybean mixture and top with meat. Sprinkle over hamburger: 1 cup grated cheese (American, Cheddar, or Swiss). If you don't use cheese on top, cover the pie with a crust. Bake at 350° for 30 minutes. Serve with rice or some other grain and vegetables.

SHEPHERD'S PIE

When the hot lunch program was instituted in our school, this was our favorite dinner. They used to issue a sheet once a month planning all the meals; and even children who failed to memorize a single multiplication table were never absent on Shepherd's Pie Day.

Make up a bunch of mashed potatoes, see page 27. Let them cool; beat in 1 egg and some grated onion (for flavor).

In a heavy skillet, heat 2 Tb. beef fat or butter and sauté:
1 sliced onion
1 cup hamburger meat

When the hamburger is gray, sprinkle over it 3 Tb. wheat flour and stir and cook for 5 minutes. Then add, a little at a time, stirring:
1½ cups beef broth

Set it to simmer for 15 minutes (without a lid)

until it is cooked down to a thick gravy.

Meanwhile, bring the oven up to around 400° and make up a batch of biscuit dough (page 75). Roll out the dough and cut out biscuits.

Grease or butter a large, shallow casserole. Spread the bottom with mashed potatoes, and smear over with hamburger and gravy. Pack biscuits tightly on top, covering the whole surface, with only small holes for gravy to bubble up. Bake for 15 to 20 minutes, or until biscuits brown.

Allow to cool before serving. This is the easiest dish in the world to burn your mouth on. Good with cabbage or cauliflower.

PIROG

An ancient and still popular Russian meat pastry, pirog can be made as one large pastry or many small ones (the latter are good travel food). There is also a cabbage-and-egg-stuffed version.

Make a batch of roll-out pie dough (page 95).

Meat Filling
In a heavy skillet, melt 3 Tb. beef fat or butter. Add and sauté:

2 chopped onions

Then add:

1 lb. ground meat

Stir and cook until meat becomes just gray. Toss over it: **2 Tb flour** and stir; cook 3 minutes, then remove from heat. Cool, then add:

1 beaten egg
¼ cup chopped dill
½ cup sour cream (optional; do not substitute yogurt)

Assembly
Roll out pie dough into a long oblong, 10 by 16 inches. Lay filling in a line along the middle, leaving a generous margin, particularly on the ends. Paint edges with water and seal, folding ends up first, then the two long sides. Prick with a fork. Paint top with: **melted butter.** Sprinkle over with: **breadcrumbs.**

Bake at 400° for about 30 minutes, until golden.

Variations

Pirozki: Cut dough into 4-inch squares, heap 1 to 2 Tb. filling in each, paint edges, and fold into a triangle. Prick, bake only 20 minutes.

◆ *Cabbage Filling*: Shred **1 head cabbage** and sprin-

kle it over with **1 Tb. salt.** After 15 minutes, pile the cabbage in a dishcloth and wring out the moisture. In a heavy skillet, heat: **¼ cup butter.** Sauté in it the cabbage and also: **1 large diced onion.** Cool and add:

½ tsp. salt
¼ tsp. pepper
¼ cup fresh chopped dill
1 Tb. caraway seeds

Shell and chop fine: **4 hard-boiled eggs.** Roll out pie dough, heap on cabbage, and sprinkle eggs over it. Seal and bake as above.

Cabbage and Meat: Make meat filling as above but use:

½ lb. ground meat
2 cups shredded cabbage

Add cabbage to meat and sauté 3 minutes. Cover and simmer over low heat 5 minutes. Then cool and proceed as above.

◆ LASAGNE

Lasagne is fast becoming an American favorite. It's a good thing to serve to a lot of people; thus it appears at all sorts of occasions. It is, however, markedly better hot than cold, as the Mozzarella cheese in it becomes quite rubbery when it cools (as, at a picnic or cookout).

Be very sure when making lasagne to take your time, and to use a thick well-cooked tomato sauce, as a thin sauce will get mixed in with the cottage cheese and carry off curds.

1. Make up a potful of **Mama Restino's True Manicotti, Lasagne, and Pizza Sauce** (page 181).

2. Make **Noodles** (pages 72–73). Cut them into strips 2 inches wide. Make half of them twice as long as your lasagne pan, and half twice as wide. Hang them over a dowel or cord line, to dry, until you're ready to cook them.

   Bring a large pot of water to a good rolling boil; add to it: **2 tsp. salt** and **2 Tb. oil.**

   Drop five noodles into it, one at a time, and cook until al dente (just done): about 7 minutes. Fish them out (not easy: try using a bottle grabber in one hand and a slotted spoon in the other) onto a clean dishtowel.

3. *Filling*
   Mix:
   1 beaten egg or 2 egg yolks
   2 cups dry curds or 1½ cups ricotta cheese

½ cup grated hard cheese (Parmesan, Romano, or homemade)

½ tsp. salt

2 Tb. fresh chopped parsley

4. Grate ½ pound of **Mozzarella cheese** or very fresh **American cheese** and set aside.

Assembly

In a greased baking pan, spread a very thin layer of tomato sauce. Follow with layers, being careful to keep sauce and curd separated in cooking. I do it this way, starting with the bottom layer:

thin layer of tomato sauce

noodles going North-South

curd mixture

noodles going East-West

sauce

Mozzarella

Bake in a 400° oven for about 30 minutes, until sauce "sets" and cheese browns. Cool 15 minutes and serve at once.

Lasagne is a substantial protein dish in itself and needs no other accompaniment than bread and salad—and a good bottle of red vino.

◆ MANICOTTI

Manicotti, or Canneloni, as it's sometimes called, is a glorious Italian dish along the lines of Lasagne; the main difference is that the cottage cheese filling is enclosed in rolls of noodles, instead of lying in flat layers. They sell Manicotti shells, and Canneloni shells, but it's actually easier to deal with squares of noodle—although whichever you decide to do, you should be prepared for a slippery job, requiring much patience.

Sauce

Make up a nice big batch of **Mama Restino's True Manicotti, Lasagne, and Pizza Sauce** (page 181) and let it simmer all day.

Noodles

Make **Noodles** (pages 72-73) and cut them into 3-by 4-inch squares. Let them dry an hour or so, on the cutting board, while you bring to a boil a huge pot of water.

Add to the water:

1 tsp. salt

2 Tb. oil

Cook 5 noodles at a time in rapidly boiling water for 7 minutes, or until al dente (just cooked); be careful not to overcook them. Remove with a skimmer and set them on a damp cloth, on a tray or bread board; as you make more, add more damp cloths. (Sorry to make such a production out of it, but there really is no other way to keep them from sticking to each other—or the world.)

Filling

Mix:

1 beaten egg or 2 egg yolks

2 cups dry curds or 1½ cups ricotta cheese

½ cup grated Mozzarella cheese (or other soft, melty cheese)

1 cup grated hard cheese (Parmesan, Romano, or home)

2 Tb. flour

2 Tb. minced parsley

Assembly

Oil a shallow, ovenproof casserole or pan and smear a little tomato sauce on the bottom. Put a few spoons of filling into the middle of each noodle and roll it up (sort of) and set it, seam side down, in the pan. If you have more than one layer of rolls, spread a little sauce between. Cover with sauce and some more grated cheese if you have it. Bake in a hot oven for 30 minutes or until it looks "set" (which entirely depends on how thick your sauce was) and serve with garlic bread and greens or salad.

EGGPLANT

Eggplant, really, is not indigenous to our northern climate. From time to time it appears on the Superama vegetable counter, costing, per pound, about twice the price of a T-bone steak. However, once in a long while (about once a year) I find one that's in the last stage of ripeness: slightly wrinkled, with a few brown spots. Triumphant, I bear it to the vegetable clerk: surely, you can't charge full price for this? Sometimes it's a dime, sometimes a quarter. Frankly, those brown spots only indicate a shallow decay, easily cut out. And so we have eggplant.

There are two general directions you can take eggplant in. One is a water-based stew, such as a vegetable stew. The other is an oily, spicy sort of dish; eggplant will absorb endless quantities of oil. Keep in mind that eggplant has a peppery flavor, and that children who are unused to it may find it a little weird.

EGGPLANT STEW

This is a very quick but exotic dish, good with noodles; sometimes I make it on return from a long hard day in town.

Sauté in a heavy frying pan, in 3 Tb. or more olive oil, for 5 minutes:

1 chopped onion
1 clove minced or sliced garlic
2 stalks chopped celery

Add and sauté 5 to 10 minutes, until meat is cooked:

1 small eggplant, whacked into ½-inch cubes
½ cup ground meat

Then add and simmer 20 minutes, with a good lid over it:

1 18-ounce can or 1 quart canned tomatoes
1 tsp. dried basil or 5 fresh chopped basil leaves
½ tsp. salt
½ tsp. pepper

Serve on noodles or with rice.

◆ EGGPLANT PARMIGIANA

This dish is an all-day affair with the stove and eggplant. Fortunately you can assemble it on one day and bake it the next.

Sauce
Turn to page 181 and start a batch of Mama Restino's True Manicotti and Lasagne Sauce.

Cheese
You will need two kinds—a hard, aged cheese, such as Parmesan, or Grating Cheese; and a soft, melting cheese, such as Mozzarella, or fresh American Cheese.

Eggplant
To prepare the eggplant, slice into ¼-inch slabs:

2 small eggplants

Set them to dry on a rack or paper towels for about an hour. Mix:

2 eggs
½ cup milk

Dip the slices in the egg–milk mixture, then in:

flour (maybe a little wheat germ thrown in for flavor, etc.)

Let them sit again for an hour in a cool place, to dry a bit. Then fry them until golden, turning once in:

½ cup olive or vegetable oil

Drain on brown paper.

While you are waiting around for the sauce to get mellow, grate:

1 cup hard cheese
2 cups soft cheese

Assembly
Place in layers in an oiled baking dish: eggplant, sauce, cheese; eggplant, sauce, cheese; eggplant, sauce, cheese.

Set aside until the next day in a cool place or bake at 350° for ½ to 1 hour, until the cheese browns on top.

Serve with lots of something bland: Noodles Alfredo, French Bread or Risotta à la Pesto and Pita, or Polenta and big, bready, bland meatballs.

◆ IMAM BAYALDI

"The priest has fainted," the Turkish title proclaims, although the explanations are conflicting. For this dish one needs small, whole, unblemished eggplants, one half for each serving. This recipe is for four people.

Cut in half, lengthwise:

2 small eggplants

Scoop out the insides, leaving ½ to ¼ inch of the shells. Chop the innards. Heat in a heavy iron skillet:

¼ cup olive oil

Add and sauté until translucent:

1 large finely chopped onion
1 clove garlic, minced or crushed

Add and simmer 20 minutes, then allow to cool:

2 large chopped tomatoes (fresh or canned)
1 Tb. tomato paste
the chopped eggplant
a pinch of sugar, a pinch of pepper
½ tsp. salt

Oil the eggplant shells with olive oil. Place in a baking dish. Add to the cooled mixture in the pan:

2 Tb. chopped parsley
½ cup stale breadcrumbs
3 Tb. roasted pine nuts (10 minutes at 300°)

Fill the eggplant shells, packing the mixture down in a firm mound. Bake in a 350° oven for 20 minutes. Remove from the oven as soon as the eggplant shells are cooked; keep warm in the warming oven if necessary. Serve with lots of bulgur or brown rice, beans, meatballs, or sausage, and a lightly dressed salad.

MOUSSAKA

A Moussaka is simply a vegetable stew, made with a light sauce, perhaps a little ground meat.
Break into flowerets and steam:

1 large cauliflower

Meanwhile, chop fine and sauté:

3 to 5 strips bacon

Add:

2 chopped onions

Sauté until onions are limp. Add to this and sauté until gray:

½ lb. ground meat

When the cauliflower is tender, take it out and arrange it in an oiled casserole in two layers, each topped with meat and onions. You may pour over it:

1 cup béchamel or velouté (page 174) or 1 cup light tomato sauce (pages 179–180)

Bake at 350° for 45 minutes to 1 hour.

Variations
Instead of cauliflower, use **a large head of cabbage,** cut in pie-shaped wedges (including some core to hold them together), or **2 small eggplants,** or **1 lb. green beans.**

moussaka

♦ GREEN BEAN AND CHEESE CASSEROLE

This is a main dish, with enough protein for four reasonably hungry people.
Nip off ends and chop:

2 lbs. fresh green beans

Steam over boiling water until tender; about 10 minutes. Cool. Place half of them in an oiled casserole. In a separate container, beat:

3 or 4 eggs

Add to the eggs:

1 tsp. salt

1 well chopped onion, or ¼ cup chopped green onions (greens included)
½ to 1 cup grated cheese (something with flavor)
1 cup dry cottage cheese
1 clove crushed garlic (optional)
½ tsp. dry mustard or coriander

Spread half this mixture over the beans. Add the rest of the beans and top with the remainder of the egg-cheese mixture. Top with:

½ cup dry breadcrumbs which have been fried in butter and garlic

Oh boy. Bake in a 350° oven for about 30 minutes, until it browns on top. Serve with something light —perhaps bulgur with a little kasha and a few noodles or mushrooms mixed in, or plain noodles, or noodles with a light tomato sauce.

BEANS WITH TOMATO SAUCE

This is the sort of thing I might concoct on a cold winter's afternoon, since the sauce is best if simmered for hours on the back of the stove.
Concoct:

1 or 2 cups good strong tomato sauce (page 181)

You might add:

½ lb. sautéed sausage meat

Steam:

1 to 2 lbs. fresh or frozen beans

until almost done—barely tender. Arrange beans and sauce in layers in an oiled casserole; maybe add a layer of Mozzarella cheese or a sprinkling of Parmesan. Bake 45 minutes in a 300° oven. Very good with noodles and salad.

STUFFED CABBAGE

Stuffed cabbage is a special favorite of mine. It takes some work, but it's well worth the preparation. You'll need a winter cabbage, a cup or two of cooked grain, and maybe some sauce. Together with a root vegetable, it makes a satisfying winter meal.

There are two ways to make stuffed cabbage. In the first, you slice off top, scoop out middle, steam, and stuff a whole cabbage. In the second, cabbage leaves are cut off, steamed, wrapped around stuffing, and tucked in a pan covered with sauce. The whole stuffed cabbage trip takes less than an hour (most of the time it's cooking). The individually wrapped leaves take longer to prepare, but are more fun eating.

stuffed cabbage leaves

There are endless ways to make stuffing; I've suggested five possibilities and a basic rule of thumb for making up your own.

To Stuff a Whole Cabbage

Choose (to serve 3 or 4 people):

a small, compact winter cabbage

Remove (and save for other purposes) any loose leaves. Slice a couple of inches off the top. With a sharp spoon and a small knife, scoop out the middle as best you can. Put the cabbage upside down in a heavy pan with an inch or two of boiling water and steam it for 10 minutes. Take it out; you should be able to scoop out more.

Stuff with any of the suggestions below, or your own brainstorm. Return to the pan, right side up, and steam 15 to 20 minutes. It doesn't matter if you do this in the oven or on top of the stove; the lid should be on, and steaming is steaming.

To serve, slice the whole cabbage as you would a pie. You may serve it plain or with a light tomato sauce (pages 179–180) or with a roux-based sauce (pages 173-174).

Cabbage Stuffing

What you use in your cabbage stuffing is definitely a personal matter. Basically you need:

1 to 2 cups grain
1 chopped sautéed onion
½ cup sautéed vegetables, nuts, ground meat, etc.
1 beaten egg
spices

Here are some possibilities:

◆ 1

1 to 2 cups cooked rice
1 chopped sautéed onion
1 chopped sautéed celery stalk
2 to 3 chopped canned tomatoes
1 beaten egg
1 tsp. curry powder

◆ 2

1 cup cooked rice
½ cup softened soygrits
1 chopped sautéed onion
¼ cup tomato paste
1 beaten egg
2 Tb. chopped parsley
1 Tb. caraway seeds

◆ 3

½ cup cooked kasha
½ cup cooked rice
½ cup roughly chopped walnuts
1 chopped sautéed onion
2 Tb. brown sugar
¼ cup yogurt or sour cream
1 beaten egg
½ cup raisins

4

1 cup cooked bulgur
½ cup sautéed ground meat
1 chopped sautéed onion
1 clove crushed sautéed garlic
3 chopped canned tomatoes
2 leaves fresh basil
1 beaten egg

◆ 5

1 cup crumbled breadcrumbs
1 cup finely chopped sautéed cabbage

171

1 chopped sautéed onion
1 clove crushed sautéed garlic
1 beaten egg

To Stuff Cabbage Leaves

The inner leaves of a large cabbage are best for this; choose those that don't have heavy ribs in the centers. Figure out how many rolls you'll need (2 to 4 per person) and tear off enough leaves (plus some extra ones in case any rip). Steam them, 4 or 5 at a time, for about 5 minutes. Pile the steamed leaves on a plate when done.

Meanwhile, mix your stuffing and oil a baking pan. To fill the leaves, lay each one out on the counter, and put a couple of tablespoons of stuffing on it, packed in a long mound along the width of the leaf.

Fold both sides up over the ends of the stuffing mound.

Now just roll it up toward the stem. Place it seam side down in the pan.

When they are all done, cover them with a cup or two of: **light tomato or fresh tomato sauce** (pages 179-180) or a **roux-based sauce** (173-174). If you really want to dress the dish up, you can top it with grated cheese, breadcrumbs fried in oil, or both. In any case, put it in a 300° to 400° oven (it doesn't much matter) and cook it for about 30 minutes; if the sauce is skimpy, use a lid on the pan.

◆SPINACH PIE

This has so many variations. Make up and refrigerate:

1 double-crust pie dough mixture (see page 95)

Meanwhile steam or cook as in any of the preceding recipes:

1 lb. greens

Cool the greans and chop them well. You may add to them any or all of the following:

1 to 3 beaten eggs
2 to 5 strips cooked crumbled bacon
1 cup dry cottage cheese
a squeeze of lemon
a dash of rosemary
another chopped cooked vegetable

Heat the oven to 400-450°. Roll out the crust and put it in its pan. Prick it and weight it with stones or beans; half bake it, for about 7 minutes, until it begins to dry and flake. This is to keep the bottom crust from getting soggy. Take it out; remove the weights, and fill with greens; top with another crust and bake at 350-400° for about 30 minutes, until the shell browns.

Very good served with brown rice.

◆SPINACH PANCAKES

These are really patties, but I hate the word. They are good lunch quickies, with a little leftover white sauce on top.

Soak:

1 slice whole-wheat bread, crumbled

in:

1 beaten egg

Meanwhile wash and steam:

½ lb. spinach

Chop the spinach, and mix with the egg and bread. Add:

2 Tb. oil or melted butter
a pinch of nutmeg
2 Tb. grated onion
2 crumbled hard-boiled eggs (optional)

With wet hands, shape into fat patties. Sauté in hot oil over medium heat for 5 minutes on each side.

Serve hot with: **Cream Sauce** (page 174) or **Tomato Sauce** (pages 179–180).

11

SAUCES

A good sauce is a worthy thing, and is often the touch that turns an ordinary meal into something special. Let's face it—some foods are kind of boring. Others are on the dry side. A good sauce can save the day, if you know how to make it.

It's easy to be intimidated by sauces—there are so many of them, they have such fancy names, and it is not immediately evident what went into them. Actually, there are usually three basic ingredients in a sauce—something liquid, something tasty, and a thickener of some sort to keep the tasty liquid from running all over the plate. The reason there are so many sauces is that there are so many possible combinations of these three things. The reason they have such fancy names is that they taste so good. Most of them are really very uncomplicated, once you understand the thickening process.

If you feel uncertain about trying out a new sauce, save it until you have a quiet, boring dinner to cook and nothing to distract you. You don't need a lot of tools—a heavy iron skillet, a small deep pan and lid (I like a cast-iron enameled pot with a wooden handle), a rotary beater or small whisk, and a spring-type stirring device.

Here are the main sauce categories described in the chapter.

Roux-based Sauces: The thickener is flour, mixed with oil or butter. The liquid can be either broth or milk. Since the basic sauce is very bland, many different flavors can be added.

Brown Sauces: The thickener is browned flour, mixed with oil or butter. The liquid is broth, tomatoes. The sauce is almost like gravy, strongly flavored. You can't change it much.

Egg Sauces: The liquid varies from melted butter to cream, thickened with egg yolk. The flavors added are usually acidic: lemon juice, white wine, or vinegar.

Cornstarch, Arrowroot, or Kuzu Sauces: These fine powders all thicken a sauce quickly and become translucent and tasteless as they do. Usually they are added to broths; they lend themselves to piquant flavorings (ginger, etc.).

Tomato Sauces: Tomatoes provide the liquid, thickener, and most of the flavor. Usually onions are added for sweetness, and various other ingredients to round out the flavor.

Pestos and Flavored Butters: Herbs and spices, pounded fine, are mixed with oil or butter. These are so strong that one spoonful is usually enough for a whole dish of food.

Marinades and Gravies: You will also find some on pp. 189-94.

ROUX-BASED SAUCES

A roux is an equal amount of oil or butter and flour cooked over very low heat for about 5 minutes. It is used to thicken liquid without having the flat taste of uncooked flour dominating everything. It should be cooked over very low heat, for about three minutes. If you have a wood stove, this is easy; but if your more modern stove does not adjust very low, you may have to use a double boiler.

Roux can be used to thicken milk, in which case the sauce is known as béchamel (or white sauce, or cream sauce). Roux may also be used to thicken fish, meat, or vegetable stock or broth; this is called velouté. I have even used it to thicken water; this has no name, but makes a perfectly acceptable base for a cheese sauce. In any case keep in mind this rule of thumb:

3 Tb. roux thickens 1 cup liquid

Which flour is best? That's up to you. What you are really after in the flour is the gluten, which will "glue" your sauce together. So a hard-wheat flour is the most effective. Unbleached white flour will make a very fine, bland, almost pasty sauce—the traditional cream or white sauce. Whole-wheat flour will make a browner sauce with a whole-wheaty flavor. If you are grinding your own flour, do a very fine grinding and sieve it well. You may use soft wheat, but in that case use 5 tablespoons per cup of liquid, since it has less gluten. And if you are grinding your own soft wheat, sieve it to remove the husks.

You may use oil instead of butter. I would stick to the light oils: unrefined peanut, safflower, or sunflower.

VELOUTÉ AND BÉCHAMEL (CREAM SAUCE)

Heat in a small heavy pan over moderate heat:

3 Tb. butter or light oil

When this is hot and bubbly, add and stir in:

3 Tb. hard whole-wheat or white, or 5 Tb. soft-wheat flour

Move the roux to very low heat or the top of a double boiler and cook gently 5 minutes. Don't let it burn. Measure out, and heat:

1 cup milk (for béchamel) or 1 cup stock (for velouté)

When roux has foamed enough, take it off the heat and add the hot liquid all at once, stirring very briskly with a spring stirrer or whisk, until it thickens. Then move it back to low heat and let it simmer 5 minutes, stirring often. If it is to be served as is, add:

½ to 1 tsp. salt

This sauce may be cooled and reheated without ill effects if it's reheated slowly, with occasional stirring. It will be a thick sauce; if you want it thinner, add:

½ cup milk or stock

Additions:

You can put lots of different things, alone or in combination, into these two sauce bases. Some, like curry or tomato paste, make a very specific flavor. Some, like hard-boiled eggs, change the texture. And a lot of them, like mustard or chives, sort of add to their deliciousness without being recognizable. Here are some things you can add:

½ cup sautéed celery, mushrooms, onions, or scallions
1 crushed sautéed or raw garlic
1 tsp. curry or mustard
1 Tb. caraway seeds (good on cabbage or sauerkraut)
2 to 4 Tb. dill or dill seeds (for fish, lamb, baked tomatoes)
1 Tb. tomato paste (together with the onions, very nice)
¼ to ½ cup good white wine or sherry or port

If you add cheese and/or dried milk, the sauce will become very nutritious and will complete the partial protein of grains or legumes. You may add:

up to ½ cup cheese: Cheddar, Swiss, Parmesan, or a combination
up to ½ cup dried milk

Toward this end you may also add:

2 to 4 sliced or crumbled hard-boiled eggs

I prefer to slice these over the dish (such as grains or potatoes) and pour the sauce over that; it has more aesthetic appeal.

FLAVORED WHITE SAUCE

When I flavor a cup of béchamel or velouté without any particular recipe in mind, this is what usually ends up in it:

1 or 2 pinches of curry powder
1 tsp. tamari soy sauce
2 Tb. dandelion wine (or any white wine, even Vermouth)
2 pinches salt and a grating of fresh pepper
a little onion juice

tools needed for making sauces

HORSERADISH SAUCE

Very nice with boiled beef, corned beef, or meat fondue. Heat, in a saucepan:

1 cup velouté

Add:

1 tsp. dried mustard
3 tsp. grated or prepared horseradish (or just radishes)
1 tsp. sugar
1 Tb. vinegar
½ cup chopped scallions or onions

Simmer over low heat for 5 to 10 minutes.

MACROBIOTIC WHITE SAUCE

This might also be good to make for somebody who has been having stomach troubles and should be on a light diet, since it is a very mild sauce.
Heat, in a small, heavy pan:

1 Tb. light vegetable oil

Add:

1 Tb. hard-wheat flour

Stir with a spring stirrer and place over right front plate, for five minutes. Add, in thirds:

1 cup warm water

stirring after each addition until sauce thickens. It does not make a very thick sauce by usual standards. Season with:

1 pinch sea salt
1 pinch ginger (for fish)
½ tsp. nutmeg or coriander (for vegetables)

BROWN SAUCES

Brown sauce is a rich, thick gravylike mixture. Generally, brown sauces are used for meat dishes. They are particularly useful for meats that don't exude the drippings necessary for pan gravy, such as:

liver   game   steak
heart   venison   chops
kidney   veal   cold cuts

The thickening agent of brown sauce is flour (as in roux-based sauces). However, because the flour is browned or roasted first, it comes out dark in color and nutty in flavor. Brown sauce is made over a long period of time, simmered slowly all day, and is something I would never attempt without a wood stove.

BROWN SAUCE

To begin with, brown the flour. I prefer hard-wheat

flour, ground very fine and sifted well (coarse flour will give your sauce the texture of cereal). I usually roast a whole cup and make a lot of brown sauce; no point in simmering one cup of sauce all day. Place in a heavy dry skillet:

1 cup whole-wheat flour

Place this over the left front plate, very low heat, on the stove. Don't take the plate off; the pan will develop hot spots and burn the flour. Stir and shake the pan from time to time as the flour browns. It will take from 20 to 30 minutes. You may also brown flour in a 350° oven for 30 minutes or so. Meanwhile, in a second skillet, heat:

½ cup oil

If you want to use butter, fine, but the flavor will never be noticed over all the other things in this sauce. Beef drippings or pork fat are possible. Chop very fine and sauté in this:

1 carrot

1 onion

3 stalks celery (optional)

When the vegetables are limp, add the browned flour to them and stir thoroughly.

At this point you add:

tomatoes

beef broth

The proportions are flexible. If your beef broth is nice, strong stuff, 4 cups is plenty. If it's sort of watery, better use 6. If you have fresh tomatoes to use up, chop in 6 large or 12 small ones. Or you may use a quart of home-canned tomatoes, or a large can of commercial tomatoes. If you use tomato paste, the end product will taste rather like the sauce in baked beans.

Also add some herbs:

1 bay leaf

6 basil leaves or 1 tsp. basil

½ tsp. marjoram

¼ tsp. thyme

5 peppercorns

Don't add salt, though; the sauce is going to cook down, quite a lot, and the right amount for a quart of liquid is too much for a cup or two.

Let the concoction simmer slowly, on the front middle or right plate. Don't let it boil, and don't cover it. Keep an eye on it after a few hours, when it begins to get thick. When it has the consistency of heavy cream (about 4 hours), take it off the stove. Purée it through a sieve or food mill to mash up any bits of vegetable and remove the peppercorns. This is now basic Brown Sauce. If it is to be used as is, season to taste with:

1 tsp. salt (per finished cup)

A use of leftover brown sauce I've found shouldn't be overlooked; it makes terrific soup. Just thin it down with water and add a few chopped vegetables (carrots, etc.) and some leftover grains or noodles.

Brown Sauce Variations

Brown sauce is really very strong thick stuff, and there isn't much you can do to alter its basic taste. Most of the "variations" merely compliment what's already there. There are a whole raft of fancy names for these supposedly different sauces, but what it all cooks down to is this:

Wines: you can add from 2 tablespoons to ½ cup of any acidic liquid, such as red, white, or rosé wine, port, sherry, or beer. Since brown sauce has a hearty flavor, the wine or beer sort of lightens it up. Other things that have a similar effect are up to 2 tablespoons of lemon juice or light vinegar. To get just the right amount for your particular dish, add a tablespoon or so at a time and taste it. If you are adding a really fine wine, do so at the last minute so the full aroma won't be cooked away.

Other Things You May Add:

2 Tb. to ½ cup finely chopped sautéed scallions

2 Tb. to ½ cup finely chopped sautéed onions

¼ to ½ cup sliced sautéed mushrooms

3 large sprigs chopped parsley

1 tsp. powdered mustard and 1 pinch sugar

1 to 3 cloves crushed or minced sautéed garlic

2 tsp. tomato paste

A Piquant Version for Pork:

2 Tb. chopped sautéed onions or scallions

½ cup white wine

½ tsp. chopped chervil or tarragon

2 Tb. chopped sour pickles

An Herby Version for Lamb:

In a small pan, bring to a boil:

½ cup good white wine

a pinch each of marjoram, rosemary, sage, basil, thyme, and 1 bay leaf

Boil 1 minute and remove from heat. Let stand 10 minutes. Strain wine into 1 cup brown sauce. Simmer sauce 5 minutes and serve.

EGG SAUCES

A sauce thickened with eggs is one of the most

delicious, nutritious, and perishable things in the kitchen. Egg-based sauces have the reputation of being "difficult." This is too bad, and untrue. Once you understand what's going on in an egg sauce, everything follows.

Egg yolks thicken when cooked. (For this reason many egg sauces call for yolks only.) Think of the yolk of a perfectly soft-boiled egg: that's the thickness you want in your sauce. Now consider what happens to an egg yolk when the egg is boiled too long. That's what you don't want to happen. No matter how well mixed into the sauce, the tiny particles of yolk will harden, the sauce will turn thin and grainy. The great secret is therefore very simple. *Take the sauce off the heat as soon as it thickens—never let it sit on stove more than 15 minutes.* Nor can you reheat it. Chefs in restaurants, with six pots of sauces brewing, add a spoonful of béchamel or velouté to make it more keepable, but I seldom have any around at that moment. Fortunately, egg-thickened sauces are perfectly good at room temperature or even cold the next day, if you should have to hold them for any length of time.

I have a personal prejudice against using yolks only, and in many cases have found it unnecessary. Using the whole egg makes egg-thickened sauces so simple that you tend to have them more often.

HOLLANDAISE ALVINO

So named in honor of my father, who, in the early years of his marriage, came up with this simple and delicious version of hollandaise sauce. Traditionally, he used to make it in a water dipper that he balanced on top of the vegetables as they cooked. You can make it in any small pan, as long as the bottom is rounded and just slightly larger than your rotary beater. With a wood stove, there is no need to make it over hot water; place the pan on the front middle plate. Put in it:

a lump of butter the size of an egg
the juice from 1 small thin-skinned lemon
   or ½ the juice from 1 large thick-skinned lemon

Taste the mixture with your finger. It should be lemony, but not *too* sour (if it is, add more butter). Let this simmer gently until serving time, 15 minutes at the most. If it crackles alarmingly move it to the front right plate; you don't want the butter to brown or get too hot. Break into a small bowl and beat briefly:

1 egg

Now, stand over the pan with the bowl in one hand and the rotary beater in the other. Slip the egg in the pan and give the sauce a quick stir as you put the bowl down. Then beat until the sauce thickens. It will take about 2 minutes; the hotter the butter and lemon, the less time it takes. As soon as it thickens (and there is no mistaking it) take it off the heat (put it in the warming oven if you have to wait). Immerse the beater in cold water (I'll leave the reason for that up to your imagination).

This is good with almost any vegetable, hot or cold, and lovely with fish or chicken. You can double or triple the ingredients; beyond that I haven't tried.

SAUCE BÉARNAISE

Cook over lively heat:

½ cup red or white wine
2 Tb. tarragon vinegar
1 Tb. finely sliced green onions
a grating of pepper
½ tsp. dried tarragon or chervil

Simmer until it cooks down to half its original volume, about 15 minutes. Add:

½ cup butter

Move the pan to the middle plate, medium heat, and cook until butter melts. Beat briefly in a small bowl:

1 or 2 eggs

Now, stand over the pan with the bowl in one hand and the beater in the other. Slip in the egg and give the sauce a quick stir as you put the bowl down. Then beat until the sauce thickens. The hotter the sauce is, the faster it will thicken. Remove from heat when thick and place in the warming oven. Serve quickly.

This sauce is traditionally served on Chateaubriand or Filet Mignon. It's pretty good on fish, too.

HOLLANDAISE À LA CRÈME

In a small, round-bottomed pan, heat gently until just simmering:

¼ cup heavy cream or sour cream
juice of ½ small, thin-skinned lemon
   or juice of ¼ large, thick-skinned lemon
a dash of salt, a grating of nutmeg

Taste this mixture with your finger; it should be lemony but not unbearably sour. Then beat briefly in a small bowl:

2 eggs

Now stand over the pan with the bowl in one hand and the rotary beater in the other. Slip in the egg and give the sauce a quick stir as you put the bowl down. Then beat until the sauce thickens. Remove from the heat immediately and serve or allow to cool.

FIGARO SAUCE

Add to the finished Hollandaise à la Crème:

2 Tb. tomato sauce

2 Tb. chopped parsley

GREEK EGG LEMON SAUCE

This is traditionally served with lamb or dolmas, but it's good with lots of other things—particularly cabbage family vegetables. It makes a great deal of rather rich sauce—about a cup, or enough for 4 people.

Beat in a medium-sized bowl:

3 eggs

Squeeze in as you beat:

the juice of 1 lemon

Pour in slowly, beating constantly:

1 cup hot stock, from lamb, veal, chicken, or vegetables

Put this in a medium-sized saucepan and place it over medium heat, on the front middle plate. Stir with a whisk or spring stirrer as it thickens (you need not stir continually until it heats up and begins to thicken on the bottom).

Season with:

a pinch of salt, a grating of pepper

a generous pinch of rosemary

CORNSTARCH, ARROWROOT, AND KUZU-THICKENED SAUCES

These sauces become translucent as they thicken. They are also almost tasteless, and are most often used to make sauces that contrast with the foods they accompany. They include sweet-and-sour sauces, soy-flavored vegetable sauce, and piquant sauces flavored with wine, mint, ginger and so forth.

As a general rule of thumb, it takes:

1 Tb. cornstarch to thicken 1 cup liquid

2 Tb. arrowroot or kuzu to thicken 1 cup liquid

but this varies considerably from sauce to sauce as different thicknesses are desired.

These thickeners are in the form of very fine powders, and will lump if added directly to hot liquid. They must be mixed first with an equal amount of cold liquid and carefully mashed into a paste. Then more liquid may be added and the sauce heated and stirred as it thickens. Or a little liquid may be added to the paste, and the mixture stirred into the hot sauce.

Sauces made with arrowroot and kuzu (which is a Japanese version of arrowroot) are ready to serve as soon as they thicken, and should not be kept hot any longer than 10 minutes. Cornstarch is stronger, and should be simmered gently on the right side of the stove (or over hot water) for 10 minutes to cook out the starchy flavor.

PLAIN SWEET-SOUR SAUCE

Something to mix with cooked beets or carrots, onions, parsnips, turnips, or fried apples.

Mix in a small, heavy saucepan:

½ cup brown sugar

1 Tb. cornstarch

½ tsp. salt

a pinch of dried cloves

Add slowly, stirring:

½ cup cider vinegar, white wine, or cider

Make sure the cornstarch is well mixed in before setting it over the heat. Stir and cook on the front middle plate, medium heat, until very thick (you may thin it further with water if you prefer). Simmer on the front right plate, low heat, for 10 minutes or mix with cooked vegetables and allow to cook 10 minutes.

STIR-FRIED VEGETABLE SAUCE

A soy sauce-flavored condiment for stir-fried vegetables. It is also very nice with meatballs, particularly if they're on the dry side.

Heat in a small saucepan:

2 Tb. oil

Add and sauté for five minutes over lively heat, the left front plate:

3 chopped scallions

Add:

¾ cup vegetable or chicken stock

a grating of dried or fresh ginger

Move this over to the front middle plate, medium heat, and let simmer. Meanwhile, mix in a small container:

1 Tb. cornstarch
2 Tb. tamari soy sauce

When this is pasty, add:

¼ cup cold vegetable or chicken stock

Pour this into the simmering stock in the saucepan and stir gently with a whisk or spring stirrer as it thickens.

You may serve this separately or mix it with cooked vegetables.

HOT CUMBERLAND SAUCE

Something to serve on cold cuts the day after Christmas—if you have any leftover wine to make it with. You need not have *all* the ingredients listed here.

Heat, in a small, heavy saucepan:

1 cup red wine
1 tsp. dried mustard
a pinch of salt
a grating or pinch of ginger
a pinch of cloves

Let this simmer while you mix in a small container:

2 Tb. cornstarch
2 Tb. red wine

Pour a little of the hot sauce into the cornstarch paste; then return all to the pot, stirring continually as the sauce thickens. Add:

½ cup currant or tart apple jelly
juice of 1 orange and of ½ lemon
gratings of orange and lemon peel
1 Tb. brown sugar

Let the sauce simmer for 10 minutes over low heat, the right side of the stove, before serving.

THICKENED MINT SAUCE

I can't imagine why people like mint sauce runny, but if you do, leave out the cornstarch.
Mix together in a small saucepan:

¼ cup cold water
2 tsp. cornstarch or 1 Tb. arrowroot
2 tsp. granulated sugar or 2 Tb. powdered sugar

Heat gently, stirring as it thickens, about 5 minutes. Allow to simmer 10 minutes over low heat, on the front right plate. Remove and cool. Add:

½ cup fresh shredded mint leaves or 3 Tb. dried mint
½ cup vinegar

Allow this to sit for half an hour, cool. Reheat briefly before serving.

TOMATO SAUCES

Most Americans are on more or less familiar grounds when it comes to tomato sauce. There are more variations than you might guess, though; they range from the light stewed tomato through the pasta sauces, all the way to thick spicy barbecue sauce. Their thickness depends largely on the evaporation of liquid, which means long and slow cooking to avoid burning. A tremendous shortcut is the use of tomato paste, available in any supermarket. You can make your own tomato paste, if you have the tomatoes and the patience.

Different thicknesses and flavors of tomato sauces depend on the dish being served. With plain noodles, for example, you will want a somewhat thinner sauce than with lasagne or pizza. Barbecue and antipasto sauces are very strong and meant to be used in small quantities. Almost all tomato sauces are greatly improved by cooking from 2 to 6 hours, adding a little water or stock from time to time. That is because it takes hours for the flavors of the onions, celery, garlic, and tomatoes to completely marry.

One final word about tomato sauces; forget about commercially prepared, elaborately presented "spaghetti sauces." I don't know what it is that makes them so utterly tasteless and boring, but I suspect the use of a lot of sugar and monosodium glutamate. Whatever it is, the addition of one small jar of that stuff to a whole pan full of good tomato sauce will overpower it all with the unmistakable flavor of cafeterias, institutions, and suburban sameness. If you are in a hurry, there's nothing wrong with a nice light sauce of canned tomatoes, onions, and oregano, cooked for 10 minutes.

FRESH TOMATO SAUCE

Tomato sauce made with fresh tomatoes tastes quite different from sauce made of canned or stewed tomatoes. It's sort of light and sweet. It's good on noodles, rice, mashed potatoes, meat, fish, poultry, or by itself.
Heat in a heavy frying pan:

2 Tb. olive or other light oil

Chop or slice and add:

1 large onion

When limp, crush in:

1 clove garlic

Sauté 1 minute longer. You may add:

½ lb. ground meat

Cook the meat gently until it turns gray. Chop and add:

3 large or 6 small tomatoes
2 Tb. fresh or dried basil
2 Tb. parsley

Cover and cook over medium heat for 10 minutes.

STEWED TOMATO SAUCE

Follow the recipe above for Fresh Tomato Sauce, but instead of fresh tomatoes use:

1 qt. home-canned tomatoes and the juice
   or 1 28-oz. can store-bought tomatoes

TOMATO PASTE

Chop into quarters:

30 to 40 ripe red tomatoes

Heat in a heavy, deep pot:

¼ cup olive oil

Add and sauté for 10 minutes:

5 large chopped onions
1 chopped celery plant

Add tomatoes and:

1 Tb. dried or 1 stalk fresh oregano
1 Tb. dried or 10 leaves fresh basil
1 tsp. dried marjoram
10 whole peppercorns
10 whole cloves
2 sticks cinnamon

Simmer all this very slowly for about 4 hours, stirring from time to time to make sure nothing sticks to the bottom. If the bottom should burn, don't scrape it; instead, transfer the paste into another pan and discard the burned part. After 4 hours you may put it through a sieve or food mill, discarding the whole spices. Put it back on the stove and keep simmering it until the pulp becomes too thick to cook safely on top of the stove. Spread it out about ½ inch thick on pyrex, enamel, or china plates or trays, and cut grooves through it with a knife to help it dry through. Set it in the sun (covered with cheesecloth to keep off flies) or cook 2 to 3 hours in a 200° oven. When the paste is dry enough, rub your hands in:

olive or other light oil

Shape into 3-inch patties and submerge them in oil, to keep them from becoming moldy. They will keep up to 3 months in a cool place, in a covered container.

MAMA RESTINO'S TRUE SPAGHETTI SAUCE

This is a sauce for noodles, gnocchi, ravioli, or anything that doesn't fall apart. It's good stuff. Don't put any prepackaged bottles of "sauce" in it.

Every time you make spaghetti sauce you have different possibilities. On the left are necessary ingredients; on the right, options.

In a heavy frying pan, heat:

2 to 4 Tb. olive or other light oil	2 Tb. bacon, ham, or pork fat

Add:

2 coarsely chopped onions	1 chopped pepper
2 cloves crushed garlic	1 sliced carrot
	1 sliced stalk celery
	¼ lb. ground meat (any kind)

Cook for 5 minutes, stirring, until vegetables are limp. Add:

either:	12 small ripe tomatoes 6 large ripe tomatoes 1 qt. canned tomatoes	either:	1 5½-oz. can tomato paste 2 patties homemade tomato paste

2 chopped fresh basil leaves or 1 tsp. dried basil
2 Tb. chopped parsley
1 Tb. red wine
2 Tb. Parmesan or Romano cheese
a pinch of thyme
¼ tsp. marjoram
2 Tb. dried or fresh oregano
1 cup water

Cook for 2 hours, tightly lidded, over medium heat. Give it a stir every half hour or so, adding water as needed to keep the original consistency. When you are ready to serve, finish the sauce with:

1 Tb. fresh or dried oregano	2 tsp. tamari soy sauce
1 tsp. salt	1 clove crushed garlic
½ tsp. grated pepper	½ cup sautéed sliced mushrooms

½ lb. ground sautéed meat
   or meatballs
2 Tb. chopped parsley
Simmer a few minutes.

MAMA RESTINO'S TRUE MANICOTTI, LASAGNE, AND PIZZA SAUCE

Sauce for elaborate dishes such as manicotti, lasagne, eggplant parmigiana, and so forth must be made thicker than Spaghetti Sauce, so that it does not disturb the layers of curds tucked in between the noodles. You may make and refrigerate this sauce for one of these dishes up to a week ahead of time, if you can keep it safely hidden from the Snack Fiends.

Follow the recipe for Spaghetti Sauce, but instead of a 5½-ounce can of tomato paste, use:

1 11-oz. can tomato paste
   or 4 patties of homemade tomato paste

Add water as needed, but you should finish with a thick sauce, watching it closely in the last stages of cooking.

BARBECUE SAUCE

Barbecues are lovely, outdoors and in, but this sauce is also useful to coat on baked meats, such as chicken, pork, spareribs, and chops.

Brush the meats with oil or lard before cooking them. Ten minutes before they are done, coat on the barbecue sauce; 5 minutes before they are done, turn them and coat again.

In a heavy frying pan, heat:

3 Tb. meat drippings, lard, or oil

Add:

1 finely chopped onion

Sauté until limp; add:

2 cloves crushed garlic

Cook 1 minute longer. Add and simmer for 30 minutes:

either 1 5½-oz. can tomato paste
   or 2 patties homemade tomato paste
1 cup water
3 Tb. cider vinegar or 2 Tb. wine vinegar
2 Tb. tamari soy sauce
3 Tb. brown sugar
½ tsp. salt
1 tsp. freshly grated black pepper
1 tsp. mustard
¼ cup lemon juice (juice of ½ lemon)

PESTOS

Pesto, or paste, is simply a number of herbs pounded together with a mortar and pestle and thickened with oil. Traditionally olive oil was used, but any good light oil will do; the difference is pretty much drowned out by the other ingredients. Pestos are really so strong that you might not want to use them straight, but they are great to add to sour cream, bland sauce, or gravy. They can be mixed in with a big dish of starchy food, such as rice or noodles. Or spread, very lightly, on bread, and toast it in the oven for a midnight snack that will wake the whole house up.

Flavored butters are a little less wild. You can serve them with fish, fowl, or vegetables, as you see fit.

Refrigerated and tightly lidded, these spicy little mixtures will keep for a long time (two weeks to two months) so you can make up a batch and try it out on different things when you get the notion.

A mortar and pestle are hard to do without. In a pinch, use a wine bottle and the deepest bowl you have around.

GARLIC PESTOS

There are about a million ways to make garlic pestos, all varying in proportions, which goes to show that Middle Eastern cooks probably never

garlic

measure at all, but just pound up whatever's handy. Here is one possible recipe, in three quantities: Pound together in a mortar:

basil leaves:	½ cup	1 cup	2 cups
garlic:	2 cloves	4 cloves	8 cloves
parsley:	¼ cup	½ cup	1 cup

You may also add, and pound:

pinenuts or pistachios:	1 cup	2 cups	4 cups

When these are thick and pasty, add, in a thin stream, as you stir and pound:

olive or light oil:	1 cup	2 cups	4 cups

Mix well and store, tightly lidded, in the refrigerator or at around 37°. Pesto will keep up to 2 months.

BASIL OR PARSLEY PESTO

Pound together in a mortar until very thick and pasty:

¾ cup fresh basil leaves or parsley
¼ cup pinenuts or pistachio nuts

Add:

½ cup grated Romano or Parmesan cheese

Add, in a thin stream, stirring and pounding:

½ cup olive oil or other light oil

You may omit the cheese but in that case you will need to add:

½ tsp. salt

Mix and store, tightly lidded, in the refrigerator or at around 37°. It will keep up to 2 months.

FLAVORED BUTTERS

All of these call for lots of butter, around ½ cup or ¼ pound; if you have a cow, you're all set! Flavored butters are very delicate and subtle, and most often used as complements to mild flavored fish, fowl, shellfish, vegetables, or very fine steak. They are also fantastic on toast.

BERCY BUTTER

Two hours before starting, take out ¼ **pound butter** and let it soften.

Simmer together in a small, heavy pan until reduced by half:

2 thinly chopped scallions
¼ cup dry white wine

Allow this to cool completely. Then cream in the butter. Add:

1½ tsp. lemon juice
1 tsp. chopped parsley
a dash of salt if butter is unsalted

Chill before serving.

Creamed Flavored Butters
For each of the following, you will need:

½ cup room-temperature butter

Paprika (*good on baked potatoes*): To the butter, add and cream: **1 Tb. paprika** and **2 tsp. chopped chives.**

Gomasio (*good on rice, potatoes, fish*): To the butter, add and cream: **2 Tb. roasted ground sesame seeds.**

Tarragon or Chervil (*very good with fish*): Mash well with a mortar and pestle: **2 Tb. fresh chervil, 1 tsp. fresh tarragon, 1 tsp. chopped chives** and **2 minced scallions.** Add the butter, in gobs, to the pounded herbs. Chill before serving.

Garlic (*on rice, in mashed potatoes, noodles*): Mash well with a mortar and pestle: **4 minced scallions, 2 cloves garlic** and **2 Tb. chopped parsley.** Add butter in gobs. Season with: **a grating of pepper and a pinch of dried thyme.**

Cinnamon (*for pancakes or as icing*): To the butter, add and cream: **1 Tb. cinnamon** and **2 Tb. honey.**

BLACK BUTTER

A simple, elegant sauce for vegetables, fish, or shellfish. Heat and stir in a small, heavy pan, over moderately rapid heat:

½ cup butter

When it is dark brown and nutty-smelling, pour it off into a small pitcher. Rinse out the pan with:

2 Tb. red or white wine or lemon juice

Add the wine to the butter, along with:

1 Tb. chopped parsley

MARINADES

Marinades, I suspect, were first invented to help preserve meats in the prerefrigeration days. They also provide variety of flavor. (If you butcher your own you sure can get tired of one kind of meat!) They are, in addition, great tenderizers for tough meats from old animals, and cuts from the neck and front legs.

Marinades are also used for some vegetables. Cooked green beans, potatoes, Jerusalem artichokes, cauliflower, broccoli, and Brussels sprouts may be marinated, as can cooked or raw mushrooms; and raw cucumbers, tomatoes, and summer squashes.

Basically, marinades are a mixture of oils, herbs, vegetables, and something acid such as wine, beer, vinegar, or lemon juice. The proportions given in this and other cookbooks are merely recommendations. You shouldn't feel limited by them; use what you have around.

Stew meats and cuts 2 inches thick (or less) are marinated for 3 to 6 hours. In these you may use uncooked vegetables to flavor the marinade. A small roast of 2 to 3 pounds is marinated for from 1 to 3 days; a larger roast, 3 to 5 days. In these, the vegetables must be sautéed first; otherwise they will spoil.

Remember that marinades are acid, and use only ceramic, Pyrex, enameled, or porcelain containers.

Don't forget to dry your meat with a towel after you take it out of the marinade, if you are planning to brown it.

You can use marinades to flavor gravies and sauces, provided they are balanced with other ingredients (such as stock). Add marinade to the finished sauce a little at a time, testing as you go.

RED OR WHITE WINE MARINADE

Whether you use red or white wine—or vermouth— is up to the meat you are marinating and the flavor you want. Strong red meats such as venison and beef are usually combined with red wines; chicken and veal with white. With others you have the choice.

If the meat is to be marinated for more than 24 hours, sauté the vegetables. Turn the meat every few hours and keep it refrigerated while marinating. For marinade, see chart on page 184.

LEMON JUICE MARINADE

A good one to use on lamb or chicken, for those tasty morsels in shish kebab or vegetable stew. For every pound of meat, mix together:

juice of ½ lemon
½ cup olive or other light oil

INGREDIENTS	FOR LARGE ROASTS	SMALL ROASTS	PIECES
Sliced onions	1 cup	½ cup	¼ cup
Sliced carrots	1 cup	½ cup	¼ cup
Sliced celery	3 stalks	2 stalks	1 stalk
Crushed garlic	3 cloves	2 cloves	1 clove
Red or white wine	5 cups	2 cups	1 cup
Wine vinegar	1 cup	½ cup	¼ cup
Salt	1 Tb.	2 tsp.	1 tsp.
Cloves	2	2	2
Parsley	5 sprigs	2 sprigs	1 sprig
Bay leaves	2	1	1
Rosemary	1 Tb.	2 tsp.	½ tsp.
Juniper berries	1 Tb.	1 tsp.	3 or 4

See Red or White Wine Marinade, preceding page.

½ tsp. salt
a grating of black pepper
1 Tb. tamari soy sauce
1 crushed garlic
a little grated fresh ginger, or a pinch of dried ginger
¼ cup apple or other juice

If you want to make the meat bright yellow, add:

½ tsp. tumeric

Marinate for 3 hours, turning every half hour or so.

YOGURT MARINADE

A good use for yogurt that has gotten too sour to eat. Good for bits of pork or lamb to be served in a Middle Eastern concoction. For every pound of meat, combine:

1 cup yogurt
1 tsp. dill or rosemary
1 clove crushed garlic

If the yogurt is not good and sour, add:

1 to 2 Tb. lemon juice

Marinate for 3 hours, turning every half hour or so.

BEER MARINADE

Very good and funky; it definitely adds a different taste to venison, beef, pork, or mutton. For every pound of meat mix:

1 cup beer (this can be flat, too sweet, etc.)
1 Tb. tamari soy sauce
2 Tb. marmalade or jelly
½ tsp. ground ginger
1 clove crushed garlic
1 Tb. sugar or brown sugar
1 Tb. dried or prepared mustard
¼ tsp. salt
a grating of black pepper or a pinch of chili pepper

Marinate 3 to 6 hours, refrigerated, turning every half hour or so.

SPICY MARINADE

Especially recommended for pork. For every pound of meat, mix:

1 Tb. tomato paste
1 Tb. lemon juice or wine vinegar
1 Tb. chili powder
¼ tsp. mustard
1 Tb. tamari soy sauce

Coat the meat and marinate, refrigerated, for 3 hours, tossing every half hour or so.

12

COOKING MEATS, POULTRY, AND SEAFOOD

American meat is famous the world over; we're fortunate in living on a continent able to support so many meat animals. Perhaps because it's so plentiful, we don't tend to pay as much attention to meat cookery. As a result, much of our meat arrives at the table tough, nutritionless, and indigestible. If you're a new cook, utterly lacking in experience and understanding of the hows and whys of meat cookery, I suggest you read the section on meats in *Let's Cook It Right*, by Adelle Davis. I still like to read it, once or twice a year, just to remind myself of things it's easy to forget if you don't cook meat often.

Meat, as we all know, is high in protein. And protein, as you may have discovered, becomes tough when it's cooked at high temperatures. The fibers in the meat shrink, squeezing out the juices, and the protein itself becomes so rubbery and tough that even if you're willing to chew it up, you can't digest it. The aim in meat cooking, therefore, is to cook it as slowly as possible.

In general, there are three methods of cooking meat.

1. Dry-roasting: used for large, tender pieces of meat. This method requires that the surface of the meat be coated with fat, either naturally or by brushing oil or fat on it.

2. Stewing and braising: I use the terms loosely, to include all kinds of meat cookery making use of liquids, from Veal Scallopini to Pot Roast,

Stroganoff to Boiled Ham, etc. Often these meats are browned first, to firm the shape of each piece of meat by slightly searing the outer layer of meat, but it should never be for long, and the meat must simmer, not boil. Tender, thin-cut meats are simmered for short periods; tougher meats take a longer time.

3. Broiling, pan-broiling, frying, and cooking over coals: used for tender meats cut fairly thin, usually 1 to 1½ inches. The business of cooking meat slowly by this method is tricky, and requires concentration; fortunately, not for too long.

ROASTING MEATS

Provided your stove is reliable, and your oven will stay at a steady, low temperature, roasting is about the easiest (if not the most economical) kind of cooking there is. The only problem, really, is in estimating how long it will take for a particular roast to cook. The chart on page 186 may help, but remember as you read it that the times given are only approximate. Thin pieces (such as rib roasts) will cook faster than fat, solid ones (like legs). Fat doesn't heat up as much as meat; but bones heat faster. So a well-marbled boneless rolled roast will cook very slowly compared to a bone-in shoulder roast.

If you're really unsure, plan to have it come out

early, rather than late; you can always take it out, a little underdone, and keep it cooking very slowly in the warming oven. It'll also slice more easily that way. And plan the rest of your dinner around your uncertainty: serve foods that can be kept warm indefinitely, or cooked in a moment.

PREPARATIONS: Your aim in roasting is to produce a piece of tender, flavorful cooked meat. You don't want it to dry out. There are three ways you can mess up a roast and make it dry out and become tough: by salting it, searing it, and basting it. So don't do any of that, even if your mother did, or your favorite old cookbook says to. Sometimes people do those things, and get away with them, but it's only because it was a very tender piece of meat to begin with; if they hadn't done those things, it would have arrived at the table so tender and perfectly cooked that you could have cut it with a fork, as they say.

A roast of meat should not be covered, or cooked in a plastic bag. You can do those things, but then it won't be a roast; it'll be steamed, which is a different story, more akin to stewing.

Your roast should, however, be covered with fat. In the case of a leg of lamb or a ham, this is no problem. Many cuts, however, have a good deal of exposed meat on them; and meats such as rabbit, chevon, veal, and venison have no fat at all. So you should brush the meat with oil, or rub it with lard, or toothpick thin slabs of pork or other fat over the top before you put it in the oven. Or you may skewer holes at 2-inch intervals and insert lardoons, strips of pork fat.

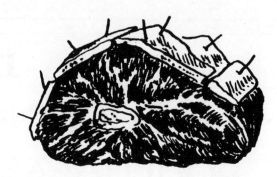

If the meat is to be in the oven for a very long time, I usually recoat it every hour or so; or make a paste of flour and lard for it.

A roast should also be set on a rack in its pan. Otherwise the bottom part will fry in hot fat as it drips down.

If you like, you can coat your meat with spices before roasting it. But don't use salt: it draws out the juices, leaving the meat dry. You can head in one direction, with pepper, thyme, and marjoram, or rub it with crushed garlic or onions, or use a little of one particular flavor, like sage (with chicken) or tarragon (with lamb) or mustard (with pork). Sometimes meat to be roasted is soaked first in marinades (pages 183–184) but I usually prefer to stew meats that have been treated in this way.

HOW DO YOU KNOW WHEN A ROAST IS DONE? Using the chart below, you can go at it in a sort of hit-and-miss way until you get the hang of it. But the best way to be sure what has happened inside your meat is to use a meat thermom-

MEAT	MINUTES PER POUND	OVEN TEMP.	TEMP. OF MEAT THERMOMETER WHEN DONE
Beef, rare	30	200-250° F.	135° F.
Beef, medium	35	200-250	150
Beef, well done	35-40	200-225	160
Ham, home-cured	30	300	170
Leg of lamb or chevon	30	300	160
Shoulder of lamb or chevon	45	275	160
Mutton or old chevon, any cut	60	225	180
Pork, any cut	40	300	170
Rabbit, domestic	30	300	180
Rabbit, wild	35	275	180
Spareribs	30	300	185
Veal, any cut	45	275	185
Venison, rare	35	250	145

eter and cook it until it registers the right temperature. Insert the thermometer into the thickest part of the meat (not next to bone or into fat) and keep an eye on it. If you plan to take it out early and keep it warm for a while, until-they-arrive, take it out when it registers 5 degrees below the desired temperature.

USING A ROAST: Nowadays, with the rising cost of meat and the recognition that it isn't healthy to eat a lot of it, every day, people don't cook big roasts as often. However, they can still have a place in your cookery, if you use them economically. Just because you cooked a great whack of meat doesn't mean you have to stuff yourselves on it. Serve a variety of foods along with your roast, the first night, and keep it, chilled, for use in other dishes, cold cuts, sandwiches. I'm reminded of an old ditty called "Vicarage Mutton":

Hot on Sunday, Cold on Monday, Hashed on Tuesday
Minced on Wednesday, Curried on Thursday, Broth on Friday, Cottage pie on Saturday.

ROASTING CHART FOR MEATS (opposite page): Set all meats on a rack over a pan. Coat any exposed meat surfaces with oil or lard. Follow information in chart.

ROASTING BIRDS

Any type of bird may be roasted, but the best are those that are young and clean-plucked with the skin intact. The skin has a layer of tasty fat under it that automatically keeps it from drying out. Any spots that are torn should be kept well greased, especially with chicken.

Ducks and geese have so much fat that it's best if you poke holes in the skin as they cook just where the fat is thickest (on either side of the tail, for one) to let some fat out.

Birds are often stuffed (pages 188-189) fore and aft; you can lightly salt the body cavity, first, if you like, to draw some juices down into the stuffing. Sew or skewer the cavities shut until serving time.

SMOKE ROASTING OR HOT-SMOKING

If you have a smokehouse or can easily devise one (see page 258) you can cook and smoke meats at the same time by smoking them at temperatures around 200° to 250°. Tongue, beef or venison, and pork are particularly good this way, and birds are terrific. Smoked meat makes wonderful cold cuts and will keep a little longer than ordinary roast meat.

The meat can be cured, in ordinary brine mixture (page 256) for 2 days to the pound, if desired. That will change the flavor, but because it will be cooked meat after hot-smoking, it won't keep for months on end—a few weeks, refrigerated, at the most.

Birds, generally, are split and placed on racks; or they can be disjointed. Care must be taken to coat young broilers and turkey with plenty of fat or oil, else they will dry out. With a very large bird, use a meat thermometer to gauge when it is done; if it's smoked all day and you're tired of waiting around, you can always pull it out and finish roasting at 300° in the kitchen stove oven.

If a very strong smoke flavor is what you want, smoke the meats first at low temperatures (75° to 85°) for 2 hours or more. Then raise the temperature and roast them.

SMOKING: Hang meat by strong cord, threading under skin or tying securely around it with half-hitches; or place it on racks, covered with perfo-

BIRD	MINUTES PER POUND	OVEN TEMP.	TEMP. OF MEAT THERMOMETER WHEN DONE
Chicken, young	35	300°F.	185°F.
Chicken, old	60	225–250	185
Duck	30	300	185
Goose	30	300	185
Turkey, small	25	300	185
Turkey, large	15	300	185

MEAT	COOK UNTIL
Beef roast	Meat thermometer registers 135° to 150°
Pork roast	Meat thermometer registers 170
Spareribs	Until crisp
Venison	Meat thermometer registers 145-150
Chicken, small birds	Meat thermometer registers 185
Turkey	Meat thermometer registers 180
Tongue	Meat thermometer registers 150
Sausages, hamburgers	Until browned, about 30 to 45 minutes

Smoking

rated aluminum foil. Set dripping trays under meat. Coat with herbs and spices if desired. Preheat smoke oven 200° to 225°, and follow information in chart above.

ROAST TURKEY

If your bird is frozen, please read about defrosting poultry, page 243; even a six-pounder will take over 24 hours to defrost properly. Hastily thawed turkey will be dry, no matter how you cook it. Stuff with Thanksgiving Stuffing, or any other stuffing. Set the giblets and neck to simmer for gravy (see pages 192–193).

Place your bird on a rack in a large roasting pan and contemplate it. First off, check for pin-feathers, and pull them out or burn them off with a quick match. Grease or oil the bird all over; my method is to use ¼ cup of garlicky butter. Now truss the bird; this means, tie it up with soft, strong cord, so the legs and wings don't flop all over and dry out. Finally, find some sort of suitable covering to keep down a little of the moisture. A loose piece of aluminum foil will do; so will a piece of greased brown wrapping paper.

For the first half hour leave the covering off, while the top browns, at 350°. Then let the oven sink to 300°. Meanwhile take out the turkey, baste it, and arrange its cover. (If there isn't enough juice in the pan to baste with, add some grease or other.) Continue to roast at 300°, taking it out every hour or so to baste it and see what's going on. You can baste with a baster, spoon, or pastry brush.

You should allow about 25 minutes per pound if it's a small bird, or 15 minutes, if it's very large. That means that to serve a 7-pound turkey by 4:00 you should take it out of the fridge, defrosted, by 12:00, and get it into the oven by 1:00; if it's a 17-pound bird, get it in by 11:45. Clearly, turkey cooking is an all-day project, so if you are using one

small oven, you had better plan your other dishes to be top-of-the-stove cooking, and bake your pies the day before.

Remove the truss and unlace the stitching before presenting the finished bird at the table. Serve with an extra plate on which to put sliced meat as you carve it up.

STUFFINGS

I always used to love stuffing best, until everybody started using those prepackaged breadcrumbs flavored with a few dried onions and a heavy dose of sickeningly stale sage.

When I started making it myself, I soon discovered why. Crumbs become soggy, especially if they're from white bread. Save all the dried heels and stale whole-wheat bread around the house, tearing them into small pieces and letting them dry out in open containers (bread wrapped in plastic goes moldy). If you have to use fresh bread, cut into cubes and toast in the oven first until dry. Add lots of fresh vegetables, sautéed in a little butter, and go light on seasonings. And, if you can help it, never serve the same stuffing twice. Invent and vary ("Hey! This stuffing has cherries in it!").

THANKSGIVING TURKEY STUFFING

A turkey has considerable space in it, both fore and aft. If you're serving 20 guests, however, you may wish to double this recipe and then bake some of the stuffing in a covered casserole, dampened with turkey broth.

Sauté for 5 minutes in 3 Tb. butter:

1 chopped onion
2 cloves crushed garlic (optional)
3 stalks chopped celery
½ cup roasted sunflower seeds
2 cups cubed dry whole-wheat bread

Add and mix in well:

2 Tb. fresh chopped parsley
1 Tb. brewer's yeast
1 tsp. salt
½ tsp. dried sage
¼ tsp. dried thyme
¼ tsp. freshly ground pepper
¼ tsp. dried marjoram
½ to 1 cup assorted chopped fresh vegetables or fruit: apples, orange slices, cherries, carrots, parsnips, cauliflower or broccoli

Mix well. Salt inside of turkey lightly. Stuff bird, not too tightly, and sew up all the holes, or skewer them shut.

BREAD STUFFING

Sauté in 3 Tb. butter:

1 chopped onion
1 stalk finely chopped celery
1 to 2 cups cubed whole-wheat bread

Add and mix well:

½ tsp. salt
¼ tsp. white pepper
2 Tb. fresh chopped parsley

You may also add:

1 Tb. fresh chopped chervil or Florence fennel
¼ cup roasted sunflower seeds or walnuts

GRAIN STUFFING

Roast and steam:

2 cups buckwheat, millet, or brown rice

Sauté in 2 Tb. butter or sesame oil:

1 minced onion
1 stalk chopped celery
1 clove minced garlic (optional)
⅓ cup sliced mushrooms
1 chopped green pepper

Season with:

3 Tb. chopped parsley and 1 tsp. summer savory

Add grain.

Moisten as necessary with broth or water to stuff into cavity. If you like a really compact stuffing, moisten with:

½ cup broth or water
½ beaten egg

APPLE STUFFING

Slice without peeling:

3 tart pie apples

Sauté in:

hot butter or other fat

until slightly browned on both sides (more or less). Add:

¼ cup roasted sunflower seeds or walnuts

And: **1 cup whole-grain bread cubes**

Very good stuffing for duck, pork, or rolled flank.

POTATO AND SAUSAGE STUFFING

Grate **2 large potatoes** and dry them by wrapping in a dish towel and squeezing out moisture. Slice an onion. Rub a heavy skillet with a little oil and crumble into it:

¾ cup pork sausage

As soon as some fat is rendered, add the onion and potatoes. Brown them well over moderate heat; set on a lid and steam for an additional 4 or 5 minutes. Use as stuffing for pork, duck, game birds, or rabbit.

GRAVY

Gravies are based on the meat drippings that escape from meats as they are roasted. If you are planning to make gravy, oil your roasting pan lightly so that the drippings won't stick and burn.

Liquid
If you are hoping for a full, meaty flavor, you will want to use meat stock as the liquid in the gravy (see pages 137–138). If you have no stock around, slice a little meat from the roast before you cook it, and make some. Add to the meat:

2 cups water
½ tsp. salt
1 sliced onion
a bay leaf
1 sliced carrot
1 sliced celery stalk (optional)
a few peppercorns
whole herbs & spices as you see fit for this sauce

Bring this to a boil and let it simmer while the roast cooks. It should cook down some as the liquid evaporates, so that you end up with 1 cup of stock, roughly.

You may also use the liquid of the marinade, if you have marinated your roast. Consider it flavoring and add it a little at a time, testing as you do so.

Extra Grease
Some meats, such as pork, lamb, goose, duck, and

sometimes chicken or beef, have a good deal of grease in them. Few people enjoy greasy gravy. So remember to allow time *before* you make the gravy to pour off the drippings into a tall glass (so you can see what's happening) and skim off the extra grease as it rises to the top. Leave 2 or 3 Tb. of grease per cup of sauce. Keep your roast warm in the warming oven as you do this and make the sauce.

Deglazing

Often, the tastiest drippings stick in the pan, although they will seldom burn if you oil the pan first. They should be removed and added to the gravy by "deglazing" the pan. This is done by adding ½ cup of stock, wine, or beer, and putting the pan over the front left plate; scrape and stir with a spatula to loosen the drippings as they cook, and then pour them off into the small heavy pan you are going to make gravy in.

Thickeners

You may serve your gravy unthickened, or use flour, cornstarch, or arrowroot to thicken it. Unthickened gravy may be made thicker if you slice into the roasting pan, prior to putting it in the oven:

1 carrot
1 onion
1 stalk celery (optional)
1 parsnip (optional)
½ cup diced turnip (optional)
1 cup diced potato (optional)

When you deglaze the pan, mash the vegetables up with a fork or put them through a food mill. They will add flavor. The texture of a sauce thickened with vegetables will not be as smooth, however.

Flavors

Various flavors can be added to gravy. Generally, people prefer gravies in which the meat flavor is complemented rather than drowned out. With this in mind, I recommend that you go lightly with the strong wines and sherries. A pinch of this, a dash of that, and a lot of tasting in between. Watch out for sage, rosemary, and lousy sherry; they can mess things up pretty badly.

Coloring

Commercial gravies are a nice dark brown; homemade gravies are usually sort of gray. They sell stuff to make gravy brown, but I really wouldn't want to eat it. Other things which help to brown gravy include:

Coffee: 1 to 2 Tb. per cup.

Cocoa: 1 to 2 Tb. per cup. Use the unsweetened kind, of course, and mix it first with an equal amount of water.

Tamari Soy Sauce: 1 to 2 Tb. per cup. Remember tamari is very salty, so you won't need to add salt as well.

Browned Flour: 2 Tb. per cup. This will also thicken the sauce, although less so than unbrowned flour. Brown the flour in a heavy dry skillet over moderate heat, stirring it with a spatula, or in a 350° oven until it turns dark brown—about 15 minutes.

Salt

Don't add salt to gravy (or any sauce) until the very end, when you're ready to serve. Gravy cooks down as it simmers; the less liquid in the final sauce, the less salt is needed.

If you have a disaster and it's too salty, quickly slice a potato into the sauce and simmer 15 minutes. The potato will absorb the salt.

BEEF GRAVY

Before starting the roast, oil the roasting pan. You may slice some vegetables into it, as described in the gravy section. Start a beef stock as well, on top of the stove (see above or pages 137–138).

1. About 15 minutes before serving (or when roast is within 5° of being done) take out the meat and transfer it to a serving platter; put it in the warming oven. Pour the loose drippings into a small gravy pan (if they look greasy, skim some fat off).

2. If you wish to thicken the gravy with flour, add to the gravy pan: **2 Tb. flour** for every cup of gravy you plan to make. Stir this with a spring stirrer and cook over low heat, on the right side of the stove, for 5-10 minutes.

3. Meanwhile, deglaze the pan with beef stock. If you have cooked vegetables along with the roast, mash them up and add to the stuff in the gravy pan.

4. Move the gravy pan over to the left front plate where it will bubble as it cooks. Add the rest of the stock in two parts, stirring after each addition until it thickens. When it's all together, move it to the middle or right plate and let it simmer. You can go off and leave it at this stage; it won't lump or burn.

5. Seasoning beef gravy is mostly a matter of options. I wouldn't add *all* of these things; they would drown out the beef flavor. Taste after each addition and remember that it will take a few minutes for the herbs to wake up.

For Flavor
2 Tb. red wine (for a full, spicy taste)
or 3 Tb. beer (it may be flat; for a rich, funky taste)

To Lighten a Heavy Sauce
a pinch of thyme
½ tsp. basil, or 3 fresh leaves
½ tsp. marjoram, or 3 fresh leaves
2 Tb. fresh parsley
a few drops of red wine vinegar

To Sweeten It
1 tsp. currant or apple jelly
2 or 3 sliced green onions

To Make It Stronger, Muskier
2 Tb. tamari soy sauce
½ cup sliced sautéed mushrooms

To Make It More Mellow
2 Tb. butter, swirled in at the last minute
¼ cup cream, sour cream, or dried milk

To Color It
Tamari soy sauce, coffee, or browned flour

Salt
½ tsp. per cup, to start with. Add more, by pinches, to taste *after* all other ingredients are in.

VENISON GRAVY

Before starting the roast, oil the roasting pan. You may slice some vegetables into it, as described in the gravy section. Start a venison stock on top of the stove (see above or pages 137–138).

Venison fat (not venison meat) has a gamey flavor; most people don't like it. So cut off all the fat on the roast and either rub it well with lard or butter or skewer thin slices of pork fat to the roast. You may also want to rub the roast with sliced garlic.

About 15 minutes before serving (or when roast is within 5° of being done) take the roast out and transfer it to a serving platter; put it in the warming oven. Taste the drippings. If they are too gamey, pour them into a tall glass and let the fat rise to the top. Spoon it all off and use for grease:
3 Tb. butter
If it tastes fine, pour the drippings into a small gravy pan and follow the recipe for beef gravy.

Special Venison Seasoning
You can experiment with any of the ideas outlined in the Beef Gravy recipe, or try this:
Melt:
1 tsp. oil or butter
in a small frying pan, and add:
2 cloves crushed or minced garlic
Sauté until the garlic browns, about 1 minute. Add:
¼ cup beer
Stir well and add to the gravy.

VEAL GRAVY

Before starting the roast, oil the roasting pan. You may slice some vegetables into it, as described in the gravy section. Start a veal stock on top of the stove (see above or pages 137–138).

Veal has very little fat, and therefore tends to dry out unless fat is added. Rub it well with lard or butter, or skewer thin slices of pork fat to the roast with toothpicks. You may also want to rub the roast with sliced garlic.

About 15 minutes before serving (or when roast is within 5° of being done) take it out and transfer it to a serving plate. Put it in the warming oven. Pour the loose drippings into a gravy pan. Deglaze the pan with veal stock.

Thickening
At this point decide whether you want to make flour-thickened or cornstarch-thickened gravy. Since veal has a very delicate taste you might prefer a lighter gravy.

Flour: Probably there is not enough grease in the pan to make a roux, so make one of:
2 Tb. oil or butter
2 Tb. white flour

Cook and stir these together and simmer them 5 minutes before adding to the drippings. Add the rest of the veal stock in two parts, stirring after each addition until the sauce thickens.

Cornstarch: Mix together:

1 Tb. cornstarch
2 Tb. cooled veal stock or white wine

Pour a little hot stock into this to thin it; then add the cornstarch paste and the rest of the veal stock to the drippings. Cook and stir over the middle plate, medium heat, until thick.

Special Veal Seasoning

Veal has a finer, more delicate flavor than most meats, and its gravy should be seasoned lightly. Use white rather than red wine; dandelion wine is very nice. If there is almost no meat flavor to begin with, add a little sautéed garlic and a teaspoon of tamari soy sauce. A nice fancy flourish is:

1 cup sour cream

Colorings

Rather than mess with trying to color veal gravy, add a couple of tablespoons of:

fresh chopped parsley

PORK GRAVY

Before starting the roast, oil the roasting pan. You may slice some vegetables into it, as described in the gravy section. Start a pork stock on top of the stove (see above or pages 137–138).

About 20 minutes before serving (or when roast is within 7 to 10° of being done) take the roast out and transfer it into another pan. Put it back in the oven. Pour the drippings into a tall glass and let the grease (which is probably considerable) rise to the top. Spoon out all but 2 to 3 Tb. Pour the drippings into a small gravy pan and follow the recipe for beef gravy.

Special Pork Seasoning

Pork Gravy is strong, tasty stuff, and no matter how well skimmed, it always seems to have a thick, heavy flavor. To balance this you can experiment with almost anything sweet or acid, such as:

2 to 4 Tb. currant or apple jelly
2 Tb. grated horseradish or prepared horseradish
either:
{ shot of vinegar or squeeze of lemon juice
2 Tb. white wine
1 Tb. sherry
3 Tb. beer

Fruits are nice in pork gravy; I wouldn't hesitate to toss in some orange juice, pineapple chunks, apple brandy, or ginger-flavored parsnip wine, to cite a few possibilities. This sort of thing really depends on what you have around.

LAMB OR MUTTON GRAVY

Before starting the roast, oil the roasting pan. You may slice some vegetables into it, as described in the gravy section. Start a lamb or mutton stock on top of the stove (see above or pages 137–138). You may want to rub the roast with sliced garlic.

About 20 minutes before serving (or when roast is within 7 to 10° of being done) take the roast out and transfer it into another pan. Put it back in the oven. Pour the drippings into a tall glass and let the grease rise to the top. Skim off all but 2 or 3 Tb.

Thickening

At this point decide whether you want to make flour-thickened or cornstarch-thickened gravy.

Flour: Put the drippings into a small gravy pan and add:

2 Tb. whole-wheat flour

Cook and stir these together and simmer them 5 minutes. Meanwhile, deglaze the pan with stock. Add that to the dripping-roux in two parts, stirring after each addition until the sauce thickens.

Cornstarch: Mix together:

1 Tb. cornstarch
2 Tb. cooled stock

Pour a little hot stock into this to thin it, and put it in a gravy pan, stirring over the middle plate until it thickens. Let it simmer while you deglaze the pan with the rest of the stock. Add this as well.

Special Lamb or Mutton Seasonings

Lamb (or mutton, which is often sold as lamb) has a thick, rich flavor. I like it that way, myself, but if you want to lighten it up, use:

½ cup white wine
a pinch of rosemary

A little sautéed garlic is a nice touch; 2 or 3 cloves per cup. You might try throwing in a couple of mint leaves, or some fresh basil, which is very much like mint when fresh. Chopped parsley is nice; you could add up to ¼ cup, if you have it.

Coloring

I wouldn't put any cocoa in this one. Stick to coffee, tamari, or caramel coloring.

POULTRY GRAVY

Duck, goose, chicken, and game birds are very different, but their gravies are made in more or less the same way. With duck and goose you will want to be sure to leave enough time to let their excessive amounts of fat rise to the top so you can skim it off.

Before starting, oil the roasting pan. You may slice a few vegetables, such as carrots and onions and celery, into the pan with the bird.

Start a stock on top of the stove. I usually leave out the liver until later, as too much cooking makes it dry. In a small lidded pot, put:

2 cups water
1 stalk celery
½ tsp. salt
3 whole white peppercorns
neck, heart, giblets and wingtips of the bird
1 whole onion, stuck with 3 whole cloves

When the bird is done, transfer it to a serving platter and put it in the warming oven. Pour the loose drippings into a tall glass; skim off all but 2 or 3 Tb. Put the drippings in a small gravy pan and add:

1 Tb. flour

Mix this roux with a spring stirrer and allow it to cook over the middle or front right plate for a few minutes. Meanwhile, deglaze the drippings from the roasting pan with chicken stock. Add this, in thirds, to the roux base; stir after each addition until the gravy thickens. If you have cooked vegetables along with the bird, you may mash them and add them as well.

Seasonings and Additions
You may add:

chopped sautéed chicken liver
½ cup sautéed mushrooms
3 or 4 sliced green onions, sautéed or raw
either: { ½ tsp. tarragon
¼ tsp. rosemary and a few drops lemon juice
a pinch of thyme
a few gratings of white pepper
a crushed clove of garlic
a pinch of sage
¼ cup white wine

Or you may add, instead:

¼ cup fruity wine or brandy, and/or
the juice of 1 orange and a little grated lemon rind

Or you may add:

½ cup fresh or sour cream or yogurt and/or
¼ cup dried milk

After everything else is in, add:

½ tsp. salt

Add additional salt in pinches until it tastes just right.

AIOLI

This is a very thick, garlicky sauce for chicken. You will not need stock for it.

Before starting the roast, oil the roasting pan. At the same time, set:

½ cup dry breadcrumbs

to soak in:

¼ cup light (wine) vinegar

At least 15 minutes before roast is done, mash in a mortar or crush:

6 cloves garlic

Add and beat well:

6 egg yolks

Add, in a thin stream:

1 cup oil (olive oil is traditional but light oil will do)

When roast is done, remove bird onto a serving plate and put it in the warming oven. Mash up the breadcrumbs, add them to the sauce, and deglaze the roasting pan with:

a little water

Pour this, hot, into the garlic-egg sauce, beating with a whisk. Place this over low heat, on the right or middle front plate, and continue beating until it becomes thick and glistens slightly. Take it off the heat right away and serve immediately as it will not hold well.

DUCK SAUCE FOR DUCK À L'ORANGE

The traditional way of making this is rather complicated and if you would prefer not to take all that time you may try this. It tastes very good on chicken, incidentally.

Before starting, oil the roasting pan. Start a duck stock on top of the stove, using:

2 cups water
1 stalk celery
½ tsp. salt
3 whole peppercorns
1 whole onion, stuck with 3 whole cloves
neck, wing tips, heart, liver, and giblets of duck

When the duck is done, put it on a serving platter and place it in the warming oven. Pour the drippings into a tall glass and skim off the grease as it rises. Put the drippings into a small gravy pan.
Combine in a glass:

2 Tb. arrowroot or 1 Tb. cornstarch
2 tsp. unsweetened cocoa
3 Tb. fruity wine or port

Mash this into a smooth paste, then add:

½ cup duck stock (strained)

Add this to the drippings in the gravy pan; cook and stir until it thickens over medium heat, front middle plate. Meanwhile deglaze the roasting pan with:

½ cup duck stock (strained)

and add that to the gravy. Then add:

the juice of 3 or 4 oranges
2 Tb. red wine vinegar
2 Tb. brown sugar
grating from 1 orange and 1 lemon rind

Simmer sauce 5 to 10 minutes before serving.

POT ROASTING AND STEWING

Meats cooked this way are kept damp as they cook —either by steam or liquid. This is a better method than dry heat for the "tougher" cuts of meat. Muscles that are more frequently used (such as neck, shoulder, etc.) are also tastier, and make better gravy; also, the liquid used in cooking helps break down the tough connective tissue.

Meat cooked this way is frequently browned (unless it is very lean) but care must be taken in both browning and simmering to keep the heat very low, or the protein in the meat will become tough. If, by accident, you let the heat get too high, you can cook the pot longer, and eventually, the meat will soften again. In fact, it will fall apart completely, and you wind up with one of those mushy stews, the kind that gets between your teeth. So cook slow, so slowly that the liquid barely bubbles. This is one of the things that's a lot easier to do on a wood stove, as many modern stoves don't adjust low enough.

MEAT TO USE

Beef: Brisket, neck, shanks, rump, chuck, oxtail, flank.
Lamb: Shoulder, shanks, breast, neck, riblets.
Pork: Pork is ordinarily cooked by dry heat, except chops; see page 199.
Rabbit, chicken, and small game: If they are over 6 months, the entire animal, disjointed; do not brown rabbit.
Veal: Breast, neck, riblets, shanks; do not brown.
Venison: Any cut except loin and sirloin.
Other: This is an excellent way to cook tough organ meats such as heart and beef kidney, chicken giblets, in combination with other meat. Do not brown them.

MARINADES: Meats to be stewed or pot roasted may first be soaked in a marinade (see pages 183-184). Marinades include some acid, such as wine, beer, vinegar, or lemon juice, which helps to tenderize the meat as well as flavor it. They are particularly good with game; some affinity between alcohol and wild blood.

BROWNING THE MEAT: To help keep meat from losing its juice, and to hold it together a bit, you can brown it first. Before doing this, though, you should always toss or rub the meat with fine flour. This will also protect the meat from too much heat, and make the gravy thick and brown. If you like, you can add ground pepper or other spices to the flour, but never salt—it draws out moisture. There's no need to grease the pan, either, especially if you're using a heavy pan and moderate heat. Fat in the pan will become fat in the gravy, and you'll have to skim it off later—a dreary job. Also, fat cooks the meat too fast, and hardens it.

Never brown rabbit or veal. Never brown heart or kidney meat. All it will do is make them tough, because they're so lean.

FLAVORING THE POT LIKKER: Ah, now we come to the part that's up to you. The fine art of stewing is all in the pot likker. For a start, I always chop fine and sauté 5 minutes:

1 onion
1 carrot
1 stalk celery

and maybe:

½ turnip or 1 clove crushed garlic (but, generally, not both)

Now then, if you want a real down home country stew, nothing fancy, just use broth or water for liquid. But if you want something with a little extra zip, add **½ cup red or white wine or sherry.** If you like a little Mediterranean flavor, add **½ cup canned tomatoes and ½ tsp. basil or oregano.** Sometimes people add milk, especially with pork gravy. And if you really want to try something new, add **½ cup beer** (it can be flat); that's very good with venison, beef, and rabbit.

Herbs vary according to the meat and vegetables and other ingredients. Thyme is always good. Rosemary is nice with lamb, but just a touch (one time a friend used 2 tablespoons of rosemary; he still can't stand the smell of it). Bay leaf is nice—subtle; basil is a little more minty. Sometimes a pinch of curry or a dash of tamari soy sauce is a good thing, but, again, not too much. Or, if you're making a rolled flank roast, add a tablespoon of molasses or Blackstrap molasses to go with a fruit stuffing.

BONES AND ACID: Since acid draws the calcium out of bones, it's always good to include both bones and acid in your pot likker. If you're making pot roast (which is steamed on a rack, over, not in, the liquid) add a cracked rib or two to the liquid; if you're making boneless stew, add a few bones, and remove them before serving. The acid can be wine, beer, tomatoes; or you can add:

2 Tb. lemon juice or vinegar

Wine vinegar, of course, is better than plain vinegar. The acid also helps cut the fatty taste of thick gravy.

ADDING VEGETABLES: In the bad old days of overcooked vegetables, folks loaded the stew pot and set it to cook until the meat was just done the rest was mush. Vegetables are much better if you add them toward the end, so they're just at the firm, sweet moment of perfection.

TIME BEFORE SERVING TO ADD	VEGETABLE
30	carrots (quartered)
30	halved large potatoes
20	new potatoes
20	chunks of turnip
15	quartered parsnips
15	sliced kohlrabi
15	tiny white onions
10	Jerusalem artichokes
10	green beans
10	cabbage in wedges
5	green peas or snow peas

Add five minutes or so if the vegetables are frozen. You can also add, just before serving: **mushrooms.**

POT ROASTING

First off, you need a good tight heavy pot. I favor a pressure cooker, because the lid really seals on well, and holds the moisture in best. However, I don't use pressure heat for pot roasting—it's too hot.

MEAT: The meat for a pot roast should be a solid 2- or 3-pound piece (see introduction for a list of good cuts). To use a piece of flank, which is dense and thin, make a stuffing of:

1. 2 cups whole-wheat bread cubes
   1 cup sautéed onions
   ½ tsp. each thyme, pepper, marjoram

2. 1 cup breadcrumbs
   1 cup diced apples
   ½ cup chopped prunes

Wrap the flank around the stuffing and tie every inch or so with cotton cord.

A boneless piece of rump, chuck, or shoulder should be stabbed all over with a good sharp knife—cut through at right angles to the grain of the meat, here and there, except near the edges.

BROWNING: To brown beef, lamb or venison, dredge or rub it with fine flour; herbs may be added. Brown in a dry pan over moderate heat 10 minutes on each side. Remove the meat.

POT LIKKER: Liquid in the pot should be about an inch deep.
For beef or venison:

1 cup broth or water
½ cup red wine or beer
½ cup chopped vegetables
1 sprig parsley
1 bay leaf
¼ tsp. thyme
a couple of bones

For lamb, veal, rabbit:

1 cup broth or water
½ cup white wine or 2 Tb. lemon juice
½ cup chopped onion, celery
1 sprig parsley
1 bay leaf
1 pinch rosemary or thyme
a couple of bones

MEAT	NOTES	TIME
Beef: brisket or rump	flour and brown; stab	3 hours
short ribs	cook as is	2 hours
oxtail	flour and brown; pick out bones before serving	2 hours
flank	stuff; flour and brown	3 hours
Lamb: breast, shank	flour and brown; stab	2 hours
riblets	cook as is	1½ hours
Venison: any cut	flour and brown; stab	3 hours
Veal: breast, shank	cook as is	1½ to 2 hours
Rabbit, small game	cook as is or rub with fat	3 hours

Pot roasting

Set the mixture in the pot over moderate heat and bring just to a boil; then move it to a spot where it barely bubbles. Put a rack over the liquid and place the meat on it, fat side up (if it has fat). Close the pot tightly, and simmer until done. If you feel that a lot of liquid is escaping your pot, more water may have to be added; and, in the last 45 minutes of cooking, you may wish to add vegetables; to see how long they'll take to be done to perfection, look in the introduction to this section.

Using a 3-pound piece, see chart above for a rough estimate of how long each meat will take.

GRAVY: To skim excess fat out of pot likker, or spruce it up a little, see **Gravy, pages 189-193.**

SERVING COLD: If the roast is to be served cold, leave it to cool in the gravy or pot likker, so it won't dry out.

STEWING

MEAT: One reason I'm so fond of stews is that you can really stretch a little meat a long way. One way to get extra gravy is to buy or ask for (free!) what they call "dog" bones, at the butcher shop—especially a high class, fancy place, where you can be sure nobody wants the bony bits in their sirloin round. Often those bones will have enough meat for a small family stew. Or, if they don't, buy half a pound or so of stewing meat, as well. (Of course, if you're stretching a little meat a long way, you should serve other protein foods: green peas, muffins with soy flour, or custard for dessert.) You can also stretch stew meat along with inexpensive but flavorful and nutritious meats like heart, or kidney.

BROWNING: To brown beef, lamb, or venison, dredge or rub it with fine flour and herbs if you like. Brown pieces in a dry pan over moderate heat, 5 to 7 minutes on each side, or until brown. Don't brown heart or kidney meat. Take meat out of the pot.

POT LIKKER: Liquid in the pot should cover the meat. Chop any vegetables fine, and sauté them in a teaspoon of fat if you like; they'll disintegrate into the gravy.

For beef or venison:

2 cups broth or water
½ cup red wine or beer
2 sliced carrots
1 large diced onion
2 or 3 sprigs parsley
1 tsp. thyme
1 bay leaf

For lamb, rabbit:

2 cups broth or water
½ cup white wine, or 2 Tb. lemon juice
1 clove crushed garlic
1 large diced onion
2 stalks chopped celery
1 tsp. thyme, a pinch of rosemary
1 bay leaf

Set the liquid (without meat) over moderate heat until it just boils; then move to a spot where it barely simmers, and add the meat. Add more water if needed to cover meat (and bones). Simmer beef, venison 3 hours; lamb, rabbit 2 hours; heart 2 hours; kidney 1 hour. Add vegetables as desired, using chart on page 195 to cook them each the proper length of time.

Just before serving, pull out the bones, cool them, and pick off the meat. To adjust and season or otherwise fool with the gravy, see pages 189-193.

MUTTON HOTPOT

With the meat of an older animal, whether sheep or venison or beef or rabbit, it is best to stew even the more tender cuts. Here is a recipe that doesn't require much watching—you can make it up and go off to do the chores.

Flour and pepper **mutton or other chops**, and sauté 5 minutes on each side in **drippings** in a heavy iron skillet. When they are browned, pack them in a Dutch oven, tails up. For every 3 chops, dice and sauté in the skillet: **1 onion, 1 carrot, and ½ cup turnip**. Pack them in among the chops. For every chop, slice thickly: **1 potato**. Lay them over the tops of the chops, and sprinkle among the potatoes some **chopped fresh parsley and ½ tsp. thyme**.

Take up the fat in the skillet with **3 or 4 Tb. flour** and brown it well for 5 minutes; then add broth or water and thin it out to make a gravy. Season gravy with:

1 tsp. tamari soy sauce
1 tsp. sugar
1 tsp. cider or wine vinegar or 2 Tb. beer

Pour in the gravy up to the level of the potatoes but not covering them. Cover closely and bake at 300° for 2 hours. In the last 10 minutes of cooking, remove the lid and brown the potatoes.

BROILING

Broiling, ultimately, is just like roasting, except that the cuts of meat are smaller. Therefore, you can expose the meat to rather fast heat, and take it off just as the middle warms up. Because the outer surface will be toughened by such treatment, however, it is best to use only very tender meats, such as fish, liver, and the loin or tenderloin cuts of larger animals (this includes rib chops, T bone and sirloin steaks, and the like).

WOOD STOVE BROILING: If you use a wood stove, and don't have a broiler, try one of these:

1. Pan-broiling: This works very well for liver and fish, and pretty well with chops, if they're tender. Dry the meat, and dredge it in a mixture of: **whole-wheat pastry flour or white flour, wheat germ** and **freshly ground pepper or other herbs**. *Never* add salt. Let the meat rest on a rack for 30 minutes. Build up a pretty good fire in the stove. Remove the rear plate over the firebox, and set a cast iron skillet on it; grease it very lightly with oil or a bit of suet wrapped in muslin, for chops; or with about 2 tablespoons oil for fish and liver. When it just begins to smoke, toss in the meat, brown on one side, turn, and brown on the other. Small chicken livers, brook trout, and fish fillets will be cooked through, but larger meat will take a little longer; take it off the direct flame, moving the pan to a cooler plate (covered) and cook more slowly until, by testing with a knife, you see that the middle is done. If cooking pork chops, cook until the middle is gray. Serve at once.

2. For very thin, tender cuts and shish kebabs, oil them lightly. Build up a good *hardwood* fire and let it die down to 2 or 3 inches of hot embers. If the stove opens from the front, prop a rack or skewers over (not on) the coals; cook until brown, turn, cook another minute or two, and serve. If it opens only from the top, this is difficult, but if the draft is good, it can be done.

3. For very thick, but guaranteed-tender steaks: clean the top of the stove well and open enough windows so you have a decent draft in the room. Slap the steak down on top of the stove and cook 1 minute. Turn, cook 1 minute. Transfer at once to a rack over a baking pan and stick it in a moderate (300°) oven and roast for 30 minutes. If you like, you may coat the top with butter, or garlic butter, or some other herb plus fat combination. This doesn't work too well with 1-inch steaks but it can be done if they're tender; it's an unmitigated disaster, however, with chuck steaks.

SWISS STEAK

A Swiss steak is any cut of beef or venison that isn't too tender and isn't too tough—such as shoulder, chuck, rump, or flank. Generally it is cut 1- to 1½-inches thick and pounded with a mallet that has a rough surface—to tenderize it.

Dredge the meat in flour, and sauté in **3 Tb. vegetable oil or lard**. Then move the pan to a simmering spot or a 300° oven and cook slowly, uncovered, for half an hour, until meat thermometer registers 140° to 150°. Be careful not to cook it fast, or it will just get tough.

When steak is done, move it to a warm serving plate and make gravy in the pan, using browned flour, onions, and, as liquid, canned tomatoes. Season with basil, savory.

Swiss steak is also sometimes cooked as for pot roasts: see pages 195–196.

COOKING TENDER CUTS OF MEAT

The tenderest cuts from all animals are those along the back, since these muscles do the least moving and working. They can be roasted as large pieces, but more often they are cut into 1- to 2-inch slices, and called, variously, chops, scallops, and steaks. Because they are the tenderest and choicest pieces, thousands of recipes for them have been dreamed up by gourmet cooks the world over. Fortunately, most of them follow the same basic pattern: sear the meat on both sides, then simmer it for 15 minutes to an hour in some sauce or other.

Many recipes call for first coating the meat with flour or breadcrumbs. I think this is a much better practice than searing meat ungarnished, which toughens it, especially if the meat is lean. Home-grown meats tend to be leaner than commercially fattened meats, so to be on the safe side, bread them. Besides, the breading tastes delicious.

LAMB, MUTTON, CHEVON

There are a great many recipes for this kind of meat, changing the taste by use of strong herbs and spices, including curry, garlic, mint, tarragon, thyme, rosemary, or wines and marinades. This is because sheep or goat meat is strongly flavored to begin with, and, if you have it as often as herdsmen and wanderers of the Middle East and Mediterranean do, it gets to be a bit of a bore.

The tenderest cuts are from the loin, sirloin, and ribs of lamb. If you're using shoulder of lamb, or mutton or chevon (goat meat), cook the meat longer. Mutton or chevon over 1 year of age also tends to taste stronger, if you don't cut the fat off and substitute a milder tasting fat.

CHOPS IN SOUR CREAM

Trim off excess fat. If chops are very long (as chevon chops are) cut through the bone and fold the "tail" up around the meat. Coat chops lightly in flour, and shake off excess.

Rub a cast iron frying pan lightly with suet. Set over open flame, and heat it until the pan smokes a bit.

Sear:

3 to 6 chops

for a minute or two on each side. Remove meat. Melt:

2 Tb. lard

and add:

1 sliced onion
1 clove minced garlic

Sauté until limp. Add to them:

1 cup veal, chicken, or lamb broth

Return meat and simmer very slowly so the liquid barely bubbles, for 20 minutes, with a lid on the pot. Stir in:

1 cup sour cream

Serve with rice, green peas.

Variations

Using Yogurt: Use only very thick yogurt. After cooking the chops, remove them and boil down the liquid rapidly until it is as thick as you can make it. Then add **1 cup yogurt** and the meat. Serve at once.

Using Tomato Sauce: Instead of broth, cook chops in a light **Tomato Sauce** (pages 179-180). Do not add sour cream.

Curried: When you sauté the onions, stir in a little flour and let it cook for a minute before adding the broth. Add to the broth: **1 to 2 tsp. curry, 1 tsp. coriander** and **1 cup white raisins (optional)**. Cook until meat is tender. You could add sour cream to this, or not.

With Vegetables: Add sliced green peppers, mushrooms, or chunks of summer squash to any variation, 10 minutes before serving.

CHOPS IN WINE SAUCE

Trim meat, and marinate in White Wine Marinade (pages 183–184) for 24 hours:

3 to 6 pieces of lamb, mutton, or chevon

In a cast iron frying pan, heat 3 Tb. butter or lard. Sauté in it:

1 sliced onion
1 chopped carrot
1 clove minced garlic

Sprinkle over with:

3 Tb. fine flour

Simmer a few minutes, then add:

1 cup broth
1 cup white wine

Add marinated meat and simmer over very low heat, covered, for 20 minutes or until tender. If the sauce is not thick at the end, remove meat and boil rapidly until it is.

PORK

There are many cuts of pork that can be used in 1-inch slices, ranging from shoulder and rib cuts to loin chops and, tenderest of all, the tenderloin. Pork is delicious pan-fried, since it has so much fat; but it can also be simmered or baked after a quick sear, with equally good results.

The tenderloin may also be sliced quite thin and pounded thinner, as veal is, between layers of waxed paper. Care must be taken not to shred it, though.

When the cuts of pork are under 1 inch, you don't need to worry about getting trichinosis from inadequately cooked meat. It'll cook enough to be safe within 10 minutes. It's roasts, not chops, you want to watch.

PAN-FRIED PORK CHOPS AND VARIATIONS

Heat a heavy iron skillet over direct flame until it almost smokes. Dust chops with flour or breadcrumbs.
Sear:

3 to 6 pork chops

a couple of minutes on each side. Remove chops; render a bit of the fat, if necessary, and sauté 5 min.:

1 chopped onion

dust it with flour; cook a couple of minutes, then add:

1 cup beef or venison stock (or vegetable cooking water)

Cover and cook at 300° or simmer very slowly 30 minutes, or longer.

Variations

Sour Cream: Add:

1 cup sour cream

just before serving; stir into the sauce well and season with:

1 tsp. marjoram or summer savory

Sweet-sour With Apples: Add to the cooking broth, 10 minutes before serving:

3 sliced sautéed apples (firm ones, with flavor)

Mix and stir into the sauce:

juice of 1 orange, or ¼ cup cider
2 to 3 Tb. cornstarch

Stir and cook slowly as sauce thickens.

Creole: Sauté along with onions:

2 stalks chopped celery

Instead of broth, use:

1 to 2 cups canned tomatoes

and season with:

½ tsp. basil, ½ tsp. red or black pepper, ¼ tsp. paprika

SPARERIBS

Spareribs are most often pork, but any meat may be used. We found venison spareribs delicious. You don't have to serve a lot of them, either; the sauce is very rich.

Dust meat lightly with flour (it can be in large or single-rib pieces). Rub a heavy iron skillet with a little suet and brown meat on both sides, 2 or 3 minutes. Remove meat and make up:

Barbecue Sauce (page 181)

Along with the onion you may sauté other vegetables, such as:

½ cup carrot, eggplant, summer squash

Cover and simmer meat in sauce or bake at 300° for about 2 to 3 hours, until meat is tender. If pork is used and the sauce tastes and looks too fat, remove it and skim off fat; return to pan and reheat. Serve spareribs with **noodles or rice.**

VEAL

Veal has curious properties. It's very tender and white, and cooks almost as fast as fish; but if it isn't handled right, it will seem dry and tasteless and tough, because it has neither fat nor flavor. For this reason the best veal recipes all combine the meat with some sort of fat: ham, bacon, butter, and marrow fat, among them.

The tenderest cuts of veal—tenderloin and round—may be sliced, very thin, and then pounded even thinner. This process not only tenderizes the meat, but also changes the texture. The professional way is to lay the meat on the edge of a damp counter and give it glancing blows with the flat of a damp cleaver. If the meat sticks to your cleaver despite your best efforts, try sandwiching it in waxed paper.

Kid meat under a month old may also be used in these recipes.

WIENER SCHNITZEL

I'll never forget the German waitresses in a restaurant where a friend used to work hollering to the kitchen as they came in: "Vun SCHNIT-zel!" Schnitzel was popular because of its speed of delivery: the gourmet version of a hamburger.

Pound flat and douse in flour:

veal scallops

Heat in a heavy iron skillet:

¼ cup butter and 2 Tb. oil

Over fairly high heat, brown on both sides. How long you cook it varies from 2 to 5 minutes per side, depending on how thin you pounded it. Prick with a paring knife; when yellow juice runs out, it's done.

Braised Scallop Recipes
To braise scallops, pound, flour, and sauté them first, as above, but only use:

1 Tb. butter and 1 Tb. oil

Braised in White Wine: Remove scallops and sauté in the butter:

3 sliced green onions
1 cup sliced mushrooms (optional)

Sprinkle lightly with:

1 Tb. flour

and cook for a couple of minutes to take up the fat. Then add:

1 cup chicken or veal broth
½ cup dry white wine or ¼ cup Vermouth
2 tsp. tarragon or chervil (optional)

Boil this sauce down to about ⅔ cup liquid, which should be thick. You may add, if you like:

½ cup sour cream

Return scallops to sauce and just heat them, over mild heat, about 2 minutes.

Braised in Tomato Sauce: Remove sautéed scallops from the pan and, using the fat there, make a Fresh **Tomato Sauce** (pages 179–180). Lay the scallops in it, ladling some sauce over them; cover and set the pan on the side of the stove to stay just-warm for 30 minutes.

If the scallops are thick or if other cuts of veal are used instead, bake at 250° for 30 minutes or until the meat is tender.

COOKING HOME-CURED MEATS

Ah, the moment of truth is at hand. You have butchered it, salted it, pickled it, smoked it, and successfully protected it from vermin, varmits, molds, and ham boogies. Now what do you do with it?

First off, let me remind you that you still have, before you, a piece of uncooked meat. Unless it has been hot-smoked until fully cooked, the meat has not reached internal temperatures high enough to kill off any possibility of trichinosis. No matter how pink and tempting it may look inside, you must never, never, eat uncooked pork. If I sound overemphatic it is mainly because, according to the U.S. Department of Health, most people who get trichinosis get it from eating improperly cooked pork or nibbling uncooked homecured pork. The best method of determining when a large piece of meat is cooked in the middle is to use a meat thermometer. Trichinae are certainly all killed at temperatures above 150°, but it is best to cook the meat to an internal temperature of 170°, just to be sure—and because the meat is fully cooked at 170°, anyway.

In general, home-cured meat is saltier, smokier, drier, and more flavorful than the bland products one finds in supermarkets. So don't expect to be eating it in great whacking slabs. It is more along the lines of a sausage; you use bits of ham to cook with other foods, chopped into potatoes, eggs, along with bland meats such as fish or veal, or chopped into white sauce and tomato sauce, or added to jazz up a grain dish. But, first, cook it.

If your meat is brine-cured and smoked the shorter length of time (see page 262) for winter keeping, you may roast or braise it, as you see fit. If it's brine-cured only, it should be braised, especially if you kept it in the brine longer than the time necessary to just cure it; it'll be salty, and braising will help get some of the salt out. If it's a dry-cured, long-smoked Smithfield type ham, cook it in cider or beer.

SCHNITZ UND KNEPP

The **schnitz** is dried apples; the **knepp**, hot dumplings. Unmentioned in the descriptive title is the 3-pound ham that forms the basis of this old German dish.

Soak overnight in water to cover:

4 cups dried apples

In the morning, put water in a suitable pot together with:

1 3-pound ham

Add water so the ham is covered and simmer for 3 hours, just under a boil. Add the apples and:

2 Tb. brown sugar

Cook for another hour. Meanwhile mix up:

2 cups flour
1 tsp. salt
¼ tsp. pepper
4 tsp. baking powder
3 Tb. oil or melted butter
1 beaten egg
milk

Drop the stiff batter by teaspoonfuls into the hot liquid and cover; cook 15 minutes at a boil. Serve piping hot.

BAKED HOME-CURED HAM

Wash ham and scrub with a stiff brush in cold water; rinse. Remove all but ½ inch of fat over the thick end; leave the skin intact over the shank end, but cut in a diamond-shaped grid. Brush the entire ham with:

molasses.

Set a whole clove in each diamond. Set meat thermometer in the thickest part of the meat, not touching a bone.

Set ham on a rack in a lightly oiled roasting pan, fat side up. Bake it about 30 minutes to the pound, which, for a 15-pound ham, is a pretty long time—all day, in fact.

Take it out when the temperature of the meat thermometer reaches 150°, or, if you like a more "baked" texture, 170°.

BRAISED HAM

Wash ham and scrub with a stiff brush in cold water; rinse. Remove all but ½ inch of fat over the thick end; leave the skin intact over the shank end, but cut in a diamond-shaped grid.

Place in a kettle of simmering water and cook it about 10 minutes to the pound, or until the internal temperature (taken with a meat thermometer) reaches 125°. Remove ham and set it on a rack in a clean pot, immediately, with:

4 cups apple cider, beer, or half beer and half water, simmering
1 bay leaf
¼ cup molasses
5 whole cloves
½ whole nutmeg

Cover and let it simmer another 10 minutes to the pound, or until the internal temperature reaches 150°. If you would now like to make your cherished ham look halfway decent, carve it all over with a diamond pattern and coat it with molasses or brown sugar. For finishing a Smithfield, it is traditional to use a mixture of:

brown sugar
cornmeal
black pepper

Set this in a good hot oven for about 10 minutes, or until the sugar melts into the ham. Cool somewhat before slicing.

COOKING HOME-CURED BACON

It is never possible to slice your bacon as thin as store-bought sliced bacon, so even more care must be taken to cook it as slowly as possible, or the lean will burn before the fat renders. If you find it really impossible to cook bacon on the top of the stove, bake it on a wire rack in a 350° oven for 30 minutes, then finish in a pan if necessary. Or, if you have a modern broiler, cook under low flame about 7 minutes on each side.

CANADIAN BACON

An exact replica of cooking a ham—in miniature. Scrub and clean a Canadian Bacon (whole) and cover with:

water
cider or beer
1 bay leaf

Simmer for 45 minutes (if it's 1 pound) or 1 hour (if 2 pounds); then remove, set on a serving plate, and coat with a mixture of:

brown sugar
cornmeal or breadcrumbs
dry mustard

It may be easier to coat on if you dampen the mixture with a little Cider. Bake until sugar melts in a moderate oven, about 15 minutes.

FRIED CANADIAN BACON

Simmer a Canadian Bacon in water to cover for 1 hour, or cook as above. Cool and pan-fry, in a pan rubbed with grease, until the fat is golden.

Another method is to pan-fry without simmering it first. This is a really nice way to cook Canadian Bacon but you must be careful to cook it through and through (see warning at the beginning of this section). Like pork chops, you sear it first on each side, then cook over gentle heat for about 10 minutes.

COOKING MORE HOME-CURED MEATS

CORNED BEEF AND CABBAGE

Whatever corned beef recipe you use, keep it in brine no longer than recommended, else it will become too salty. To cook it, wash the meat in cold water, then submerge in cold water and bring just to a boil. (If it's oversalted, discard that water and start again.) Move the pot to a simmering spot and cook about 3½ to 4 hours (this for a 4-pound piece). In the last 30 minutes add potatoes, turnips, parsnips, Jerusalem artichokes; in the last 15 minutes add wedges of cabbage.

A PLAIN BOILED DINNER

This is a popular Nova Scotia dinner. Simmer a ham in plain water—a quart or so. In the last 30 minutes of cooking add potatoes and turnips, parsnips and carrots, cut in quarters. Ten or 15 minutes before serving add 2 cups or so of green beans.

The ham should be cooked about 20 minutes to the pound, in all. Serve with hot biscuits and apple jelly, pickled beets, mustard pickles.

PICKLED PIG'S FEET

Scrub 4 trimmed feet in cold water and soak 15 minutes in:

water to cover
2 tsp. baking soda

Drain, rinse, and cover with boiling water. Bring to a boil and move to a simmering spot for 2 hours or so. Skim the broth if foam accumulates. Add:

1 sliced onion
1 stalk celery with leaves
3 bay leaves
1 cup cider vinegar
1 Tb. peppercorns
1 tsp. salt

Simmer for 2 hours longer. Remove feet; strain

broth and chill to remove fat. Heat it again and add:

1 egg white and the shell

to collect stray foam; strain broth again and it will be clear. Boil broth down until you have just enough to cover the feet in a jar or loaf pan. Pour it over them and chill.

ORGAN MEATS AND TONGUE

LIVER

This is the only way I like liver. But just in passing I will mention that liver is also baked, creamed, served in sauce, braised and so forth (in other cookbooks).

PAN-FRIED CALF, BABY BEEF, SHEEP, OR CHICKEN LIVER

Dredge liver in flour and shake off excess. Cut into serving-sized portions; separate joined chicken livers.
Meanwhile heat in a heavy iron skillet:

4 Tb. bacon fat, lard, or chicken fat

When the fat crackles, add the liver. Cook until brown on one side; turn and brown. To see if livers are done, slice into them with fork and paring knife. Thin cuts cook faster; remove as done and serve dinner *AT ONCE*.

LIVER PÂTÉ

There are zillions of recipes for liver loaf that maybe-you-like and maybe-you-don't. The only surefire way I know of to make a pâté that is so wonderful that everybody loves it is with Cognac. Simmer in a small pan for 5 minutes:

¾ cup water
1 chopped onion
3 stalks chopped celery
1 lb. chicken livers or ½ lb. chicken livers and ½ lb. other liver

When the livers are tender, put them, and vegetables, through a meat grinder. Beat together and add:

1 egg
3 Tb. Cognac or other brandy
a pinch each of ginger, allspice, pepper
1 tsp. salt

¼ cup evaporated milk or cream

Sprinkle over with:

¼ cup white flour

and work it in. Set all this in a small greased casserole and top with:

3 strips uncooked bacon or ham fat

Bake for about an hour. Chill well before serving.

KIDNEY

Kidney, like liver, is an organ meat that is quite tender and delicious from a young animal, but tough and bitter from an old one. If the only kidney you have had is from mature beef, you are in for a pleasant surprise if you can get lamb or veal kidneys.

All kidneys should be well trimmed before cooking or even washing. Remove all the white membranes from the bottom (it's much easier to do it with a small pair of curved nail scissors) and the membrane surrounding them.

VEAL OR LAMB KIDNEYS

Trim as above. Flour lightly with:

white or whole-wheat pastry flour

Sauté gently in:

2 Tb. butter and 1 Tb. oil

until tender and pink only in the middle: 5 minutes on each side for veal, 2 or 3 for lamb. Remove and serve. Or you may move them to the warming oven and quickly make a sauce in the pan. Add to the butter:

2 sliced green onions

Cook rapidly for a minute or two, then add:

½ cup liquid: broth or wine or a combination
1 Tb. prepared mustard
1 Tb. lemon juice
¼ tsp. salt, ¼ tsp. ground pepper

Cook this down for about 3 minutes over rapid heat, stirring continually; return kidneys to pan, whole or sliced, then coat and serve.

Variations

Garlic: Sauté:

1 clove minced garlic

along with green onions; instead of mustard you may use:

1 Tb. paprika

Mushrooms: Sauté:

1 cup sliced mushrooms

in the butter; omit the mustard. Add just a:

dash of paprika

KIDNEYS FROM OLDER ANIMALS: Kidneys of a mature beef, mutton, venison, etc., require more preparation and cooking. Trim, removing all white membrane and hard material from the bottom. Wash:

2 beef or other kidneys

Cover with:

cold water

and:

2 Tb. cider vinegar or lemon juice

You may leave them overnight to soak in this mixture. Bring to a simmer and cook them for 30 minutes, in any case. Then remove and cool. They are now ready to be used in other cooking.

HUNTER'S BREAKFAST

Slice cooked kidneys as thin as you can. Coat with flour. Heat in an iron skillet:

2 Tb. fat

Sauté kidney slices for a few minutes on each side (not long). Take them out and lay them on slices of toast. Into the pan pour and cook as you stir:

½ cup to 1 cup beer (it can be flat)

If you want to get fancy, toss in a spoonful or two of leftover spaghetti sauce. Sprinkle in a little salt and paprika, or pepper. When the sauce is good and thick, pour it over the kidneys.

STEAK AND KIDNEY PIE

Slice cooked kidneys as thin as you can. Coat with flour and sauté in:

2 Tb. fat

for a couple of minutes on each side. Add them to a Beef Stew (page 196) during the last 15 minutes of cooking, along with carrots, small onions, etc. If you want this to really look terrific, fire the oven up to 400° or so and make up **Biscuits** (page 75) or **Flaky Pie Crust** (pages 94–95) and cover top with crust or cutout biscuits. Bake until the top browns, about 15 minutes.

Steak and Kidney Pie is also, traditionally, flavored by the addition of about ½ cup beer to the gravy.

Other Uses for Liver and Kidney Bits
Slice sautéed leftover bits of liver and kidney and add them to Spanish Rice (pages 153-154) at the last minute. Make up a name for the dish—Risotta Rognons or Rrrrrrris-otta—and say it with great confidence.

BRAINS

Brains should be very fresh and soaked, to firm them, for 3 hours in acidic water. As they soak, pick and peel off bits of membrane.
Simmer brains for 25 to 30 minutes in:

4 cups water
3 Tb. lemon juice

After this you may refrigerate them until you use them, which should be soon. They will require very little cooking and, since they are rather bland, should be served with an interesting sauce.

BREADED BRAINS

Coat raw or cooked brains (see above) with:
fine breadcrumbs
You may mix pepper or herbs in with the breadcrumbs (depending on the sauce you plan to use). Heat:
3 Tb. butter, oil, or lard
in a heavy skillet. Sauté brains about 2 minutes on each side. Cover pan and move to a simmering spot. Cook for 10 minutes.

Variations
With Tomato Sauce: Make a light Tomato Sauce (pages 179-180) and simmer them in that for the 10 minutes. Serve with grated cheese.
Savory Brains: Sauté:
1 sliced onion and 1 clove minced or crushed garlic
along with brains; sprinkle over on both sides with paprika as it cooks. Use:
bacon fat
for oil, if possible.
With Hollandaise: Dredge brains in flour, sauté in butter. Top with Hollandaise (page 177) when done. If you slice this in strips, people generally assume it's fish fillets.

SWEETBREADS

Only the sweetbreads of young animals are, generally, served by themselves. Those from mature animals can be added to stews or sausages.
To prepare them, soak in cold water, changing the water as it becomes cloudy. Then set in a pan and cover with:

cold water
juice of ¼ lemon

Simmer over low heat for about 5 minutes, and as soon as they are firm, remove them from the water and cool them in cold water.
Firmed, this way, it is much easier to remove the tough membranes and bits with a paring knife.
Sometimes sweetbreads seem better if they are pressed a bit. You can do this in a cheese press, or between two plates, with a flatiron on top—3 pounds for 2 hours should suffice.
Sweetbreads may be breaded and sautéed and served as in any of the recipes for Brains, or you may try this:

BRAISED CALF'S SWEETBREADS

Melt in a casserole dish or frying pan:
3 Tb. butter or bacon fat
Add and sauté 10 minutes, very slowly:
1 diced carrot
2 stalks diced celery
1 chopped onion
Arrange cooked or uncooked sweetbreads over the vegetables, and add:
½ cup dry white wine
1 cup chicken or veal broth
a pinch each of thyme, marjoram
2 Tb. chopped parsley
Cover and set in a 300° oven for 45 minutes; serve with sauce and rice.

HEART

BEEF HEART: MOCK GOOSE

A thrifty English country recipe for Christmas dinner. Two days before, wash and trim valves off the heart. Set the heart to simmer over very low heat (right side of stove) in:
water to cover
with:
1 onion, 3 peppercorns, and 2 Tb. vinegar

Cook until tender over course of 2 days. On Christmas Eve, skim the fat off the liquid and take up the heart; stuff with:

Bread Stuffing (page 189)

Sew the heart shut. Flour thickly all over, and lay over the top:

3 or 4 strips of bacon or salt pork

Set on a rack and bake at 300° for 2 hours, basting with fat to keep the surface from drying out where not covered. Decorate around with roast potatoes and carrots and turnips and pickled crabapples. Serve with applesauce and biscuits.

SAUTÉED VENISON HEART

The age of an animal determines the texture of the meat; sautéed heart is only for the young. We had this from a four-year-old buck, and it tasted just like porterhouse steak, believe it or not. I imagine you could do the same thing with calf or baby beef.

Slice the heart about ½ inch thick, across the grain. Dust with flour. Oil a frying pan lightly and heat until crackling hot, but not smoking. Cook the pieces about 3 minutes on each side. Cut into the centers to see if they are done; they should be just pink in the middle. Serve at once.

Heart is a very much richer meat than steak. You will not find it necessary to serve very large portions, and it should be accompanied by light foods —steamed vegetables, and noodles or rice.

TONGUE

Tongue can be cooked fresh, pickled, and smoked. It's very good for curing because the muscle is firm and holds together well. Lamb, mutton, chevon, pork, veal, venison, and beef tongues are all used, but the smaller ones are better. To cure and smoke tongue, see page 256.

PLAIN COOKED TONGUE

Scrub tongue well. If it is not well trimmed, along the back and bottom, clean it up a bit. Soak fresh tongue or cured tongue in cold water for 2 or 3 hours, to remove blood or salt, as the case may be. Drain; place meat in a pot. Add:

2 onions, stuck with cloves
2 carrots
3 stalks celery, with leaves

water to cover tongue
3 sprigs parsley
a small bag containing: ¼ tsp. peppercorns, ½ tsp. whole mustard seeds

Set the pot over moderate heat and bring to a simmer. Skim off the gray foam that forms on the surface.

Beef tongue, 3½ to 5 pounds, takes about 3 hours to cook.

Smaller tongues, 1 to 2 pounds, take 1½ to 2 hours to cook.

After cooking, remove tongue and carefully skin it. This is easier to do if you chill the tongue, in cold water, for a minute or two. Make a cut around the edge and peel back the top skin, then the bottom, which is rather more difficult. Remove any bits of bone and gristle.

Tongue can be served hot or cold. Usually it is accompanied by such tracklements as horseradish and mustard, boiled potatoes, pickled beets, sour cream, and so forth.

FRESH TONGUE IN WINE SAUCE

Prepare and cook fresh tongue as above, but only partly cook it:

Cook 1- 2-pound tongue 1 hour
Cook 3- 4-pound tongue 1½ hours
Cook 5-pound tongue 2 hours

Remove and skin as above. Meanwhile make up a sauce in a heavy iron skillet. Melt:

2 Tb. butter

Sauté:

2 chopped onions
3 diced carrots
1 clove minced garlic
2 ribs sliced celery

When they are limp, add:

2 to 3 cups good brown stock
1 Tb. tomato paste or 3 chopped tomatoes
1 bay leaf
½ tsp. thyme
1 tsp. salt
½ tsp. black pepper
½ cup good red wine or ¼ cup sherry

Simmer, covered, for 30 minutes. Then take out a little of the liquid in a cup and cool it; add to it:

2 Tb. cornstarch

Mix this into a paste and stir it into the sauce; continue to stir until it thickens.

Slice the meat, arrange it in a casserole, pour the

sauce over, and bake at 250° for about 45 minutes. To slice it evenly, start with vertical cuts at the base and gradually slant them more and more so that the last cut is almost horizontal.

CURRIED TONGUE IN TOMATO SAUCE

Prepare and cook tongue as above in basic recipe, but only cook it until three-fourths done. Meanwhile make a fresh Tomato Sauce, and simmer it over low heat.

Remove and slice tongue. Place in a casserole or frying pan along with:

2 sliced green peppers

Season sauce with:

1 tsp. curry

and pour over the meat. Cook in a warm oven at 250° to 300° for 45 minutes. Serve with rice or noodles.

TONGUE IN ASPIC

If you have the knuckles of the animal in question, you may cook them to extract the gelatin. Otherwise use gelatin and water, as follows in this recipe for two sheep's tongues:

Soak salt tongue overnight, wash fresh tongue. Simmer in water to cover for 1½ hours along with:

1 large onion stuck with 1 clove
1 bay leaf, 3 peppercorns
1 tsp. marjoram, ½ tsp. thyme
2 tsp. salt if meat is fresh

Cool, skin, and trim tongue. Strain the liquid and cook it down to about 2 cups. Add:

1 cup tomato juice

mixed with:

1 pkg. plain gelatin

Season if necessary with salt; add tongue and set in mold.

ABOUT RABBIT

Rabbit is a lovely meat, lean and white and tender. It's very much like the white meat of chicken, in fact, or like milk-fed veal. A rabbit has surprisingly little fat in it; probably it is all concentrated in the skin, which is removed. The presence of fat in or around meats keeps the temperature of the meat low; so lean meats cook faster and hotter and, if you're not careful, the protein toughens. Therefore you must be extra careful when cooking any sort of rabbit to keep the temperature low.

YOUNG RABBIT: Some people we know butcher rabbit at 2 and 3 months. They cook their rabbit just like chicken, as in any of the recipes here, baked or braised (or fried). This size of rabbit is admittedly a gourmet feast fit for a king, but not a king, queen, and two or three hungry little members of the royal family.

MEDIUM-SIZED RABBIT: We generally butcher rabbit at 4 or 5 months, when they are almost full grown, but not quite. This size of rabbit is still tender, but requires a little special care. First of all, I never brown them in fat, dredged or any other way. I just pop the meat in simmering broth and move it to the coolest part of the stove for a couple hours. Then about half an hour before dinner time, I remove the meat to the warming oven, or 150° oven, and make the broth into gravy or sauce. Medium-sized rabbit can also be baked, whole and stuffed, or in pieces, but you must take great care to coat the meat with fat and keep the oven below 300°.

OLD RABBIT: Rabbit over 5 months should be simmered in broth for about 4 hours or until the bones turn in the meat. Then you can make sauce of the broth, or chop large pieces of meat up for a stew.

WILD RABBIT: Unless you're an experienced rabbit hunter, assume that all wild rabbit is old and proceed with caution. Marinate overnight in one of the marinades (pages 184–185). Simmer in broth for 4 hours and make a good beer gravy to serve with it (see Venison Gravy, page 191).

BAKED STUFFED RABBIT

Baked stuffed rabbit looks a little strange, the first time, but it sure is good. Make a Bread Stuffing, about 2 cups, and stuff the ribcage. Tie up the rabbit around the stuffing a bit, pulling the hind legs up around it.

There are various ways to grease a rabbit. You can coat with oil, then flour. I like better, though, to rub it all over with a mixture of lard and flour and thyme. If I could afford it, I'd use butter.

Bake at 300° for about 2 hours, or until the

bone of a leg turns in the meat. Baste every half hour with fat.

This roast is good with gravy, which you can make with the pan drippings after the rabbit is done. Use milk to thin out the gravy, unless you have chicken or rabbit broth around.

BRAISED RABBIT IN GRAVY

Cut up a rabbit into 5 portions: four legs and the back. Set the liver and ribcage to simmer, covered, with water to cover and:

1 bay leaf
1 carrot
½ tsp. salt
1 onion stuck with 3 cloves
1 stalk celery
3 peppercorns
½ tsp. thyme

Let that cook slowly 4 hours if it is a 5-month rabbit, or 1 hour if it is a 3-month rabbit. You may marinate rabbit if you like—see pages 184–185. A couple of hours before dinner time, strain the broth. If you have not marinated the meat, you may add to it:

½ cup wine or beer

Set the rabbit pieces in the simmering broth. Do not allow it to boil or cook fast. Simmer for 1 hour, turning occasionally. Remove pieces and set them in a warm serving dish in the warming oven. In a small pot, heat:

3 Tb. butter

and add:

3 Tb. flour

Cook and stir until flour turns golden brown. Add the pot likker from cooking the rabbit, stirring as it thickens. Adjust seasoning, add rabbit, and serve.

Variation
Cook rabbit in Fresh Tomato Sauce (pages 179–180).

COOKING HOMEGROWN POULTRY

Often, chickens raised on the farm are not quite as plump and tender as commercial ones; the legs, in particular, tend to be rubbery. On the other hand, they do have more flavor, and also more nutrition. If you pay close attention to cooking, they can also be quite tender. Don't let the pot get too hot —either during browning, or simmering. The older the chicken, the more slowly it should be cooked.

If the legs are obviously quite tough and the tendons inedible, use legs separately, for broth making. In the case of a very old chicken, you'd do well to marinate it (see pages 184–185 for marinades).

CUTTING UP CHICKENS: Many recipes call for chicken cut into "serving pieces." You can quarter it, but I prefer to cut it into 8 pieces: 2 wings, 2 halves of the breast, 2 thighs, and 2 drumsticks. The rest of the chicken—neck and back—has much flavor but the meat is in tiny slivers, so it's better to use them in a broth pot. Generally if I'm going to stew a chicken, I cut it up early in the day and set the back and neck in a broth, along with vegetables (see pages 192–193), to simmer on the side of the stove all day. Then it's ready when I need it, to cook the meatier parts of the chicken in.

COOKING THE CHICKEN, YOUNG OR OLD: In most recipes, the meat is first wiped, coated with flour, and sautéed until golden. If your chicken is quite old, though, you might bypass that step and simply stew it. Finally, add spices and herbs as you see fit, but never salt your chicken or broth until serving time—salt draws out moisture, and makes the meat tougher.

STRETCHING CHICKEN A LONG WAY: Another method is to stew firm chicken first, then cool and cut it into small, bite-sized pieces, and add them to stir-fried vegetables or stew. Cook only long enough to heat them, in the final step, or they will become tough.

TENDERIZING OLD CHICKENS: If you're sure it's an oldie, but you'd like to do something nice with it: Rub the bird lightly with oil and set on a rack over about 1 inch of water in a covered dish. Cook over very low heat or in a 240° oven for about 45 minutes. Then disjoint and treat as you would younger, uncooked chicken.

Another thing you can do for old chicken is choose recipes that incorporate wine, lemon, yogurt, or tomatoes in the cooking broth itself, to help tenderize the meat as it cooks (it's not the same if you toss in half a cup of something just as you serve it).

BONING, CHOPPING, THIN-SLICING RAW MEAT: All these delicate operations are accomplished very easily if your chicken is half frozen when you work with it, and you use very sharp knives.

SUBSTITUTING OTHER BIRDS: Duck, goose, and other birds may be cooked in the same way as chicken, but remember as you do so that they are much fatter birds and the gravy or sauce is likely to need skimming; so allow time for that before the meal. Duck and goose are, however, more often roasted, and served with fruit-flavored sauces such as the gravy for Duck á l'Orange (pages 193-194). Game birds are very good when marinated and cooked as in Coq au Vin (see below).

BARBECUE CHICKEN

Divide chicken into serving-sized pieces; dry and dredge in flour.
Heat in a skillet:

¼ cup light oil

Brown chicken on all sides, as best as you can. Remove and set it on a rack in a roasting pan and stick it in a 300° oven for 30 minutes.
Take it out and coat pieces with:

Barbecue Sauce (page 181)

Cook 15 or 20 minutes longer, until a drumstick joint will separate easily, or the bone turns in its socket.

PAPRIKA CHICKEN

Divide chicken into serving-sized pieces; dry and dredge in flour.
Heat:

¼ cup light oil

Sauté:

1 finely chopped onion
2 Tb. paprika
1 clove minced garlic (optional)

Scoop out onion and brown chicken on all sides, about 20 minutes. Return onions to the pot and add:

1½ cups chicken broth
1 bay leaf

Simmer slowly until done, about 1 hour. You may add:

1 cup sour cream or thick yogurt

Serve at once with: **flat noodles and poppy seeds; cabbage, or cauliflower.**

MEDITERRANEAN COUNTRY CHICKEN

A favorite dish in southern Europe—a gardener's special.

Divide chicken into serving-sized pieces; dry and dredge in flour.
Heat:

2 Tb. light oil (olive oil, if you have it)

Sauté lightly:

1 diced onion
2 sliced carrots
2 stalks sliced celery
1 clove crushed garlic
1 sliced green pepper

Remove vegetables; sauté chicken until golden, about 20 minutes, adding 1 or 2 Tb. oil if needed. Add vegetables and:

1 cup chicken broth
1 cup stewed tomatoes
1 bay leaf
½ tsp. ground pepper
2 tsp. basil
2 Tb. chopped parsley

Heat until the liquid just bubbles; then set a lid on it and cook slowly for 1 hour. Just 10 minutes before serving, add:

1 cup broccoli or cauliflower flowerets
1 sliced green pepper

And, if you like:

½ cup red or white wine
a pinch of oregano

Serve with: **noodles or freshly steamed rice.**

CURRIED CHICKEN

Cook chicken as above; add:

1 tsp. curry powder

to the sauce. You may, for a change, omit the last-minute vegetables and add, instead:

3 sliced apples
½ cup currants or small raisins

COQ AU VIN

You can make this with just about any kind of wine, sweet or dry, even a little sour . . . I used to make it with Amontillado, which was terrific, if a little rich.
Divide chicken into serving-sized pieces; dry and dredge in flour.
Heat:

3 Tb. light oil

Sauté for 5 minutes:

1 sliced carrot

1 sliced onion or 4 sliced green onions

1 clove crushed garlic (optional)

Remove vegetables; sauté chicken until golden, about 20 minutes. Add vegetables and:

1 cup chicken broth

½ cup sherry or 1 cup wine

bay leaf

½ cup mushrooms (optional)

¼ tsp. ground pepper

pinch thyme

Heat until liquid just bubbles; cover and simmer very slowly for 1 hour. You may add to the broth, if the chicken is freshly butchered:

¼ to ½ cup chicken blood

Don't allow the gravy to boil or cook long after that.

BRAISED GOOSE

While a roast goose is a glorious sight and certainly nothing to complain about, many claim that waterbirds (including, also, ducks and wild fowl) are tenderer if cooked with moist heat. This recipe is for a young goose, of about 10 pounds; cook an older one longer.

If it is frozen, see about defrosting poultry (page 243) and take your time. Trim loose fat off the goose, especially on the inside. Chop wing tips off. Rub interior lightly with salt and stuff with:

Apple Stuffing (page 189)

Sew or skewer the ends shut and truss the bird up with soft cotton string so it holds together as it cooks. Prick skin all over with fork or skewer along the legs, back, and sides of breast, where there is the most fat.

Set goose on its side in a very large, lidded roasting pan along with:

4 cups beef, chicken, or veal broth

2 cups red wine

1 sliced onion

1 clove garlic

½ tsp. ground pepper

2 sliced carrots

3 sprigs fresh parsley

1 tsp. sage

Bring this mixture to a simmer, then set, covered, in a very slow oven, 200° to 300°. Check the goose now and then to see that the broth is just simmering, not boiling. After 1 hour turn goose on the other side. After another hour set it on its back. After 3 hours, keep an eye on it, either with a meat thermometer set in the fleshiest part (not touching bone) or by testing: meat is done when a drumstick moves in its socket, or thermometer reaches 185°.

Remove goose; drain off liquid into a tall beaker or glass bowl. Let the fat rise to the top and remove all but 1 or 2 tablespoons (a thin layer). Use some fat and the considerable juice to make a good goose gravy (see Poultry Gravy, pages 192-193). You may need more flour to thicken that amount of it; about ¼ cup will be right.

If you wish to serve your goose browned (although it will not matter much once it is carved) you may return it to the oven and fire up the stove while making the gravy. In a wood stove, the heat will come from the top of the oven as the stove heats up and will brown your goose in 15 minutes. In a modern oven, turn it up to 450° and bake for about 20 minutes, or until brown.

FISH

Fish is excellent food: high in protein and low in fat. Many people are now eating more fish and less flesh for this reason.

The three cardinal rules of fish cookery are: cook it fresh, cook it little, and cook it over low heat.

HOW TO TELL IF A FISH IS FRESH

A fresh fish has bright eyes, is pink under the gills, and has a slick or slimy skin. It flops when you handle it. Press your finger against the side; it should bounce up again. A fish that has gone by has cloudy eyes, feels stiff and squishy, and smells. "Fat" fish such as mackerel, lake trout, herring, and salmon will not keep as well as "lean" fish. If the fish is frozen, fat fish must be used up sooner too (see page 245 about how long to keep frozen fish). The oils in "fat" fish become rancid; they are not only unappetizing, but, if kept too long, they're also bad for you.

COOKING IT LITTLE, AND LOW

A fish is done when the internal temperature reaches 140° to 150°, and it's amazing how fast that happens. This is partly because the flesh is so lean. Even salmon (the fattest fish) isn't half as fat as red meat; and, since fat slows down the cooking of flesh, the leaner flesh of fish naturally heats through faster.

The amount of time it takes to cook a fish depends not on the weight of the fish, but on how thick it is. If you cook it any longer than is necessary, the protein becomes tough, the fish falls apart, and the penetrating aroma of cooking fish fills the kitchen. This often happens with "lean" fish, which are therefore thought to be "dry." But it's not true—no fish is dry to begin with. They are all at least 60 percent water, and will stay that way if you cook them gently, until just done.

ABOUT SALT

Salt draws out moisture and makes fish dry and tough. Don't salt fish until it reaches the table. They have lots of salt in them anyway.

LEAN FISH	FAT FISH
Bass, except striped	Albacore
Cod	Alewife
Flounder	Bass, striped
Grouper	Bluefish
Haddock	Bonito
Halibut	Butterfish
Kingfish	Carp
Octopus	Croaker
Perch, yellow	Grayfish
Pike	Herring
Pollock	Mackerel
Porgie	Mullet
Sole	Perch, white
Squid	Pilchard
Trout, brown	Salmon, all types
or brook	Sardines
	Shad
	Smelt
	Sprat
	Trout, lake or rainbow
	Tuna

CLEANING FISH

As with all game, fish will keep better if they're cleaned soon after being caught. They are not difficult to clean and a good job can be done by the shore of the lake or stream. Slit the belly from just below the head to the vent and pull out the entrails. A stick cut in the brush can be used to string a number of fish for carrying, running it through the mouths and gills.

Wash the fish and let it dry and drain on a rack before storing. Fish may be frozen, brined, salted, pickled, or smoked.

CUTTING UP FISH

It's best to leave your fish as whole as possible. The more you slice it up, the more opportunity there is for juice to escape. The MicMac Indian method of cleaning small fish was to cut a tiny slit just under the gills and squeeze the innards out, from the tail up. They had the right idea. You may find it easier to clean them by opening them up (see above, about Cleaning Fish) but, when you can, leave the head and tail on, and, more important, the skin. You don't have to eat those parts, but what you do eat will be much tastier if they're left on during cooking.

If the fish has large fins and scales, as with carp, black bass, etc. and you wish to remove them, they will be easier to remove before the head is taken off. Cut slits on either side of each fin with a knife and then pull it out; this way you will get the bones beneath along with the fins. Scrape the scales off with a dull knife or the back of a sharp one, against the grain. You need not get all the scales, just the large ones.

Whole Fish: Wash quickly in cold water, clean, and wash insides. Small ones can be floured and pan-fried or broiled; large ones are good stuffed and baked.

Steaks: To cut fish "steaks," leave skin on. Cut vertical slices about 1½ to 2 inches from behind the gills to just above the tail. Make the last piece somewhat larger, 3 inches or so.

Fillets: To remove skin, make a shallow cut behind each gill and down the middle of the backbone. Hold the head in one hand, and tear flesh toward the tail with the other. If it sticks, you may have to do a little scissor work here and there to free it.

To remove fins, make a slit on each side of it, then pull it straight out.

To fillet, make a slit along one side of the backbone, close to it, from gills to tail. Then run your finger along inside the flesh to free it a little. Insert knife and work it along as you pull the fillet up and off, front to back. Some fish are easier to fillet than others and all fish are easier to fillet when freshly caught.

COOKING THE FISH

PAN-FRYING SMALL FISH

Pan-frying is one of the best ways to cook, on a

wood stove, such small fish as brook trout, mackerel, small salmon, smelt, and fillets. Always flour the fish before pan-frying. You may add seasoning to the flour, such as:

pepper, paprika, tarragon, chervil

but never add salt, as it draws out moisture and dries the fish.

Heat:

2 Tb. butter or oil

in a heavy iron skillet over direct flame. Add the fish when the fat bubbles, and sauté until just golden on each side. If the fish is rather large, 1 to 2 pounds, you should move the pan to a cooler spot on the stove to finish cooking it through for 5 or 10 more minutes.

To make an excellent quick sauce, use butter rather than oil, and as soon as the fish is done, take it out and pour:

½ cup white wine

in the pan; tilt it so the wine runs around, let it bubble for a minute, and pour it over the fish. Or you may use:

¼ cup water

and:

juice of ¼ lemon

Otherwise simply serve the fish as is or garnished with lemon slices.

BROILING FISH

Broiling is an excellent method of cooking fish, but if it is more than 1½ inches thick, cut it into steaks or fillets. Brush lightly with vegetable oil; you may season with pepper, paprika, or herbs, but do not salt. Or you may coat the fish (after oiling) with fine dried breadcrumbs.

Set the fish on an oiled rack. It is much easier to turn the fish if you use a flat rack perforated with holes than if you use a wire rack. Preheat the broiler 10 minutes.

Set the fish 1 inch from gas flame, or 5 inches from an electric unit. If your broiler has a door, leave it open. Turn fish in 5 to 10 minutes, when it is cooked halfway through. Whole fish will cook more slowly than steaks or fillets.

If you have a wood stove, see about broiling meats, page 197, on the coals of the wood stove firebox. This can be done only on particular makes of wood stoves. Really, it's more fun to build a little fire outside, let it burn down to coals, and cook fish on racks over the blue flame. Always use only hard wood when broiling fish on any fire.

FISH IN WINE

This is a lovely way to serve fillets, or whole 1- to 2-pound firm-fleshed fish.

Heat in a heavy pan:

2 to 3 Tb. butter or clarified butter

Sauté for a few minutes:

4 or 5 chopped green onions

Flour fillets or fish and sauté them lightly on each side, 1 or 2 minutes each. Then add:

½ to 1 cup white wine

2 Tb. chopped parsley

Pop a lid on the pan and cook the fish until just done; 140° by the meat thermometer, 10 or 15 minutes, in general, over very low heat. Remove fish to a warm place or warmed dinner plates. Move the pan over direct heat and reduce the sauce until it is almost thick. Pour over fish and serve at once.

BAKED STUFFED FISH

This is a very elegant thing to do with a large fish. To see whether it is done, you should really have a meat thermometer, otherwise you'll be poking it full of holes during the cooking, letting juice escape, not to mention appearance.

Clean and stuff (see stuffings, pages 188–189) a large fish; better to leave the head on. Set on a rock in a baking pan. (If you wish the pan to later not smell of fish, line it with aluminum foil.) Insert meat thermometer through a gill into the thickest part of the meat. Bake at 300°:

20 minutes if 1 inch thick

30 min. if 2 inches thick

35 min. if 3 inches thick

Remove fish when thermometer registers 145°, or at 135° if fish is to be kept warm in the warming oven for a while.

BAKED FISH STEAKS

Oil steaks lightly, or butter them. Set on a rack in a lined baking pan. You may, if you like, squeeze lemon juice on them, or shake on a little paprika, but don't salt them. Bake at 300° for 25 minutes or so. Serve with lemon wedges.

FISH BAKED IN MILK

Choose firm-fleshed fish steaks or fillets. Set them in a baking pan along with:

1 onion sliced in rings
1 cup milk
½ tsp. finely ground white pepper

Sprinkle over the fish:

2 Tb. flour

Bake about 25 minutes, or until the internal temperature of the fish is 145°.

SALT FISH

Salt fish is handy, but not as nutritious or tender as fresh or frozen fish. It should be soaked overnight in fresh water, and if very salty, you should change the water twice. They will still, after all that, be salty, and should be cooked with potatoes which will take up the salt. Lay pieces of herring or other salt fish in between layers of Scalloped Potatoes (page 27) and omit salt from recipe.

SWEET-SOUR FISH

This is an excellent way to serve haddock. For each person you will need:

a small piece of firm fish

and:

½ green pepper or a whole carrot

The sauce will do for 4 servings.

Cut the haddock in small pieces—strips, if possible —about the size of your thumb. Lay them together on a board and sprinkle them with:

white pepper

Grate over them:

a little ginger root

Turn and treat the other side.

Cut carrots or peppers in long strips. If using carrots, steam them until almost, but not quite, tender, about 15 minutes. Set aside.

Mix up:

1 egg and half an eggshell full of water
3 Tb. whole-wheat pastry or unbleached white flour
3 Tb. cornstarch

Dip each piece of fish in this mixture and lay it on a wire rack to drip for 15 minutes.

In a small heavy pan mix:

¼ cup water
¼ cup cider or wine vinegar
¼ cup brown sugar
juice of ½ orange
2 Tb. wine or sherry
1 Tb. cornstarch

Heat and stir until sauce thickens. Set on the right front burner of the stove (very low heat) to simmer; add water as needed to keep the sauce liquid until you are ready to serve.

Heat:

¼ cup vegetable oil

in a small heavy pan. Fry pieces of fish until golden brown on each side. Drain on brown paper and set on a plate in the warming oven, or at 100°, or in a covered dish.

If you are using peppers, fry them for half a minute in the same oil.

Arrange fish and vegetables on a plate in a star pattern; pour over sauce and serve at once.

PICKLED HERRING

Small, dense-fleshed herring, called milter of matje, are used in Europe for pickling as they are. Our local Bras d'Or herring are bigger and looser, so I always salt some of the moisture out of them to firm them up first. To do this, sprinkle coarse salt liberally over whole herrings, and let them sit 12 to 24 hours. If you salt them too long, though, they'll get red and tough. After salting, or without salting, here is the recipe I use:

Clean:

6 herring

and set to soak 24 hours in ice water. Meanwhile, combine, in an enameled saucepan:

¾ cup vinegar
1¼ cups water
1 Tb. pickling spices (bay leaf, whole mustard, pepper, and coriander)
⅔ cup white sugar

Bring to a boil, and cool overnight—not in the refrigerator.

The next day, cut the heads off the herring, and cut a slit down each back. Then cut a shallow slash across each side just above the tail to get started, and using the tail as a handle, peel the skin off each side, tail to front. Finally, fillet them, in the same direction, using your fingers to separate the meat from the long bones. (The small bones will dissolve in the pickle.) Rinse the pieces, and dry them.

Peel and slice very thinly:

3 large red or sweet onions

Grind or chop fine:

milch from the herring (optional step)

Tear the herring into small pieces as you layer it in a suitable container with onion slices in between. I use pint-sized wide-mouth jars, but you could use a stone crock or plastic container. Sieve out the spices, mix in the milch (if you're using it) and pour the brine, cold, over the herring. Refrigerate.

It is said that herring can be eaten in a week, but I consider a month best. After three months they begin to get unpalatably soft.

SLOW POKES

This is a Nova Scotia recipe for cooking any of the herring-type fish (including alewife, gaspereau), which have a terrific lot of thin but prickly bones. Long slow cooking in vinegar will dissolve most of the bones. One recipe advises that if you use "the vinegar off pickled beets," it will give the fish a "salmon color."

Fillet the herring, removing the backbone. Roll each fillet into a spiral and skewer it together with a toothpick. Set them in a greased baking dish. Pour over them:

1 cup pickle juice or ½ cup vinegar and ½ cup water
1 tsp. sugar
1 Tb. mixed pickling spices (pepper, mustard, bay leaf, coriander)

Bake in a 200° oven for 1½ hours. Serve with coleslaw, boiled potatoes, and hot fresh biscuits.

SHELLFISH

Common along the New England and Maritime coast are a dozen or so shellfish of various sorts, the largest in numbers being the mollusks oysters, clams, and mussels. Consult local advice as to whether they are safe to eat before setting out to gather some: ask the local Department of Agriculture or Marine Resources in your area each season. In the last 10 or 15 years many beds have become too polluted to be safe; mollusks pick up many diseases and pollutants, such as hepatitis. In the summer months, Red Tide may also be a problem in warm waters, particularly the Bay of Fundy. In many areas, however, mollusks are safe and free for the gathering, a wonderful source of good food that is almost as enjoyable to forage as it is to eat.

Once gathered, or purchased, keep them cool and moist. Set them in a bucket of clean salt water, overnight, to let them cleanse out sand, etc. (Oysters and clams are better at this than the smaller mussels; if you value your teeth, don't gather mussels from sandy mud flats.) Use only those that remain closed tight; discard any that open and stay open.

OPENING SHELLS WITH HEAT: Always scrub shells with a stiff brush before opening them, and trim off beards, seaweed, anything that might harbor sand.

Most people steam or bake the shells open. It's so much easier. To steam them open, use a pan with a good tight lid. Set shellfish with the most-curved side of the shell down (to hold in liquid when it opens) on a rack or handful of very well rinsed seaweed over boiling water. Boil rapidly until the shells open. With thin-shelled varieties, it'll take only a few minutes, but we've had some oysters around our house that resisted heat for half an hour. To bake them open, set them on a rack, curved side down, over a baking pan or dish. Bake at 450° or more until open.

As soon as the shells open, even a crack, you may remove them to drain out the juice and extract the meat. Don't rinse unless it's absolutely essential, and save the juice.

OPENING SHELLS RAW: Many shellfish, such as clams, mussels, cockles, and scallops, can be opened by running a thin-bladed knife between the shells. Quahogs are stubborn, but as children we learned that if you leave them in cold water, in a quiet place, for an hour or so, and then go to work alone, stealthily slipping them out and quickly inserting the knife, it's a lot easier to work your way through a bucketful. As you open, use 3 bowls: one for juice, one for clams, and one for tough neck trimmings or muscles.

Raw oyster opening is an art. It sounds simple: break the "bill" or thin edge with pliers, insert knife, open oyster. But only experience can tell you where the best place to break it is, and how to strike it so that bits of shell don't get inside. Work slowly, and watch your hands: oyster shells are awfully sharp. Once you get it open, inspect under good light for shards of shell. Rinse (alas) if you suspect. Drain juice into one container, set oysters in another.

After shucking your raw shellfish, strain the juice through a sieve lined with muslin. It can be used

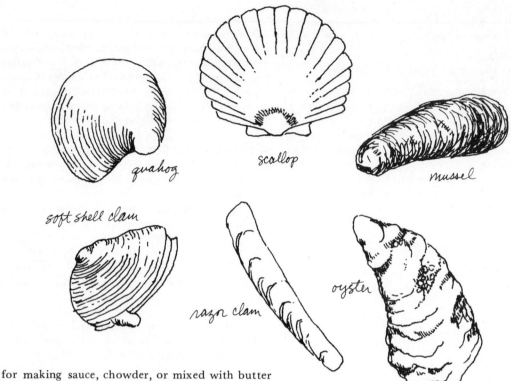

quahog

scallop

mussel

soft shell clam

razor clam

oyster

for making sauce, chowder, or mixed with butter or lemon juice to dip shellfish in as you eat them.

RAW SHELLFISH

Before serving, strain juice and cut shellfish free; return it to the shell and pour over the juice. If you like, mix juice with lemon juice or a little white wine. Or serve with a sauce such as the following: 3 or 4 hours before serving, mix and chill:

1 cup strained stewed tomatoes or tomato catsup
2 Tb. wine vinegar
1 Tb. freshly grated horseradish
1 Tb. onion, minced or crushed in garlic press
1 clove crushed garlic
½ tsp. salt
1 tsp. Tamari soy sauce
¼ tsp. ground white pepper

The best shellfish for serving raw are, of course, oysters; but cherrystone clams are a close second, and I've eaten lots of mussels and softshell clams raw and enjoyed them. I would say that large quahogs can be a little tough, though.

STEAMED SHELLFISH

When I was about sixteen I had a friend with a bicycle-built-for-two, and we used to pedal several miles to the nearest harbor and gather mussels. I remember one morning my parents arose to find us steaming a gallon or more of mussels for breakfast; to their absolute horror, we had melted every bit of butter in the house with garlic. They stayed inside muttering into their coffee while we ate mussels on the front porch. All of them.

Clams and mussels should be steamed over water until they just open; any longer and they will be overcooked and tough. Oysters are steamed until the edges just curl.

BAKED SHELLFISH

Bake shellfish in a very hot oven until they just open. Take them out and sprinkle with:

salt, pepper, grated onion, a dot of butter
Bake until the edges curl, about 10 minutes at 400°.

Variations
1. Cover with **a square of bacon**; bake as above.
2. Cover with a mixture of cooked minced **greens**

214

and onions; top with **breadcrumbs fried in bacon fat**. Bake as above.

SHELLFISH STEW

Really, this is just shellfish cooked in milk, but you'll find it very good and surprisingly filling. It should be served in wide soup dishes, with oyster crackers . . . a little white wine . . .
Melt:

4 Tb. butter

Add:

1 pint oysters or other shellfish

Cook over low heat until oyster edges curl. Add:

1 qt. milk, 1 tsp. salt, a pinch of pepper

Simmer for about 5 minutes until the milk is just hot. Garnish with:

paprika and chopped fresh parsley

Variations

Clam Chowder: Cook **1 chopped onion, 3 large diced potatoes, and 3 stalks chopped celery** in butter; add **1 cup water** and **clam trimmings and juice, and 1 bay leaf.** Simmer until potatoes are done. Some people put them through a food mill; this is optional. You can mash them a bit with a fork if you like, too. Add **2 cups milk, and 1 to 2 cups shellfish.** Simmer until milk heats. Season with **salt, pepper, paprika, fresh parsley.**

Cream-Tomato Shellfish Bisque: Cook as for Chowder, but omit potatoes and substitute **1 cup tomato juice** for water. If you want to be really fancy, hit it with a dash of wine or sherry at the last moment.

CREAMED SHELLFISH

Make up a cream or white sauce (see page 174). Add shellfish, up to 2 cups. You can use any kind or a mixture, which is even better. If you add sliced green peppers, you can safely call it "à la king." Serve on toast, with a side dish of spring greens.

SHELLFISH STUFFING

Shellfish of any kind (not just oysters) are wonderful additions to bread stuffings of any kind (not just turkey). Imagine, mussels in stuffed eggplant or summer squash . . . in Turkey they like mussel stuffing so much that a dish is made called Midye Dolmasi, in which large mussels are steamed open and then mixed with cooked rice and finely chopped sautéed onions, currants, and parsley (and pine nuts), the mussel meat chopped and added, and the mixture stuffed back into the mussel shells, which are then tied back up and poached in fish stock for half an hour. These are eaten cold. They have very much larger mussels than we do, however, which are easier to tie up with bits of string.

BOILED LOBSTER

Lobster should always be alive, when bought, and kept cool until you are ready to cook them. If one dies before that, throw it out.
Bring to a rapid boil:

3 or 4 gallons water

Grasp lobsters behind the head and plunge them in, one at a time. Return lid to the pot and allow water to boil again, but time the cooking of the lobster from the moment you popped it in: 15 minutes, 10 if it's small. Remove with tongs at once. Cool under cold water for 1 minute. Turn each lobster on its back and split down the middle, using a sharp knife; first through the bottom shell, to uncurl the tail, then through the top. If you wish to clean it, at all, discard the dark vein running the length of the back, the small sac back of the head, and the gray-green spongy tissue on either side of the back. Leave in the bright green liver and red roe if any; they are delicious. Serve with lots and lots of hot melted butter, nut crackers, lemon wedges, white wine, French bread, and salad. The lobster meal may also be started off with a soup course; but you shouldn't try to serve too many things with it —like rice, or potatoes, or cooked vegetables.

13
FOOD STORAGE METHODS

PLAIN KEEPING: ROOT CELLAR AND ATTIC STORAGE: Some foods, such as roots, seeds, nuts, and certain fruits and vegetables, naturally keep out the air, and they can be stored over most of a winter, just as they are, as long as the right temperature and humidity are maintained.

DRYING FRUITS AND VEGETABLES: Many fruits, all herbs, and some vegetables can be dried, in small quantities, to be later eaten as snacks, or revived in a soup or stew.

Drying outdoors can be a little tricky in a damp, northern climate; often the process is best done over a wood stove, on racks suspended from the ceiling.

CANNING: Hot water bath canning is suitable for canning fruits, pickles, jams, and tomatoes, all of which have a certain amount of acid in them. This is especially useful if you don't have electricity (and a freezer).

JELLIES, JAMS, AND PICKLES: Many fruits and vegetables may be used to make an astonishing array of bottled "condiments" to liven up the bored old winter-farmhouse supper table.

FREEZING: Almost anything can be stored in a freezer, and many foods (such as fresh meats, green vegetables) can be stored only in a freezer. It's easier than canning, and the food is better for you than if stored by any other method. As a practical device, it knows no equal; but it does require electricity.

Other methods of food preservation include smoking and salting meats and fish (pages 251-265) and cheesemaking (pages 115-136).

PLAIN KEEPING: ROOT CELLAR AND ATTIC STORAGE

Husks, skins, and shells on some foods keep air out, and they can be stored over most of the winter, just as they are, if you maintain the right temperature and humidity, and are careful not to let them freeze.

ROOT CELLAR (Cool and damp)

Beets
Carrots
Jerusalem artichokes
Parsnips and salsify
Turnips and rutabagas
Potatoes
*Cabbages
*Cauliflower
*Brussels sprouts
*Kohlrabi
*Chinese cabbage
*Celery
*Head lettuce
*Leeks

Apples
*Oranges, lemons, grapefruit
*Pears

ATTIC (Cool and dry)

Winter squash and pumpkins
Onions
Garlic
Beans, peas, seeds
Grains
Dried fruits and vegetables

*indicates food will only keep for a limited time, 1 to 3 months.

ROOT CELLAR STORAGE

To store roots for any length of time, you must have a damp, cool root cellar. The temperature should be constantly just above freezing, no lower than 32° and never much over 40°. The humidity should be from 90 to 95%, or the roots will shrivel after a few months.

There are various ways to make root cellars. The commonest is in the cellar of your house, where it will be handy. However, in that case, you should install rodent-proof bins or cans. You can make one big bin, if you'd rather, but be careful to keep the apples away from the vegetables as apples give off a gas which hastens the decay of most roots.

If your house or cabin doesn't have a cellar, you can build one outside. Choose a well-drained slope where snow will pile up (snow insulates). In southern New England, it need not be deep; two feet will do. Farther north you should go down below the frost line, but the storage area doesn't have to be

entirely below it; the packing material and snow will serve to insulate it. Remove any nearby rocks; stone transmits frost.

The food may be packed in boxes, or barrels, or 50-gallon oil drums (you can get these from highway departments). Some people don't use containers, but this seems risky to me; rodents might discover your cache. If the climate is mild, you can set the containers directly in the earth, but in Nova Scotia we pack sawdust around them. The food should be packed in some insulating material—sawdust, sand, leaves, or straw; this also helps keep rot from spreading. Build a close-fitting lid which will be easy to remove, with a wooden handle, and provide a ventilation pipe with a cap on top to keep out moisture. Bank over the root cellar with plenty of leaves, or straw, and top with earth. Finally, dig a v-shaped drainage ditch to divert the water in case of a rainy spell or January thaw.

KEEPING ROOTS: Don't try to store anything until cold weather insures that the cellar will be cool enough to keep them. As you bring in each box of vegetables, trim off the tops to within ½ to 1½ inches of the crowns. Gently wipe off excess dirt and check for damage or disease. Sort the roots into three categories:

1. Undersized or damaged roots to be used within a month; you need not pack these in sand, just store them loose in a cardboard or wooden box;

2. Medium-sized, blemished, or odd-shaped roots (such as multirooted carrots) to be used within three months; store in leaves or sand in wooden crates and label as such;

3. Large, perfect roots to be used in late winter; store in leaves or sand in wooden crates and label as such.

outside root cellaring in buried barrels

217

Beets: 32 to 40°; 90 to 95 percent humidity; store loose or pack in sand or leaves. Pull beets as the hard frosts commence. Trim tops to within 1 inch; you may freeze or dry beet tops. Large beets will keep very well all winter.

Carrots: 32 to 40°; 90 to 95 percent humidity; store packed in sand or leaves. Keep an eye on your carrots after the first light frosts; sometimes rodents chew the tops off ones that are sticking out of the ground, making them unfit for long storage. Otherwise pull as the hard frosts commence. Trim tops ½ to 1 inch. Sort carefully and pack into graded boxes with damp sand or leaves. Keep carrots in a rodent-proof bin. Carrots will begin to wither and sprout new greens as the cellar warms up. If you want to have carrots in the early spring, leave a row in the graden, well hilled and mulched with leaves or straw. Dig as needed, after the ground thaws; these carrots will not keep well.

Jerusalem Artichokes: 32 to 40°; 90 to 95 percent humidity; store well-packed in damp sand. It is better, to my mind, however, to leave them on the plant until spring (see Spring Vegetables, pages 5–6).

Parsnips and Salsify: 32 to 40°; 90 to 95 percent humidity; store packed in leaves or sand. These do not really keep well; a couple of months is the maximum. They keep very well in the garden, however; hill the tops slightly and mulch well with leaves or straw. Dig as needed in the spring; they will not keep more than a few days.

Turnips and Rutabagas: 32 to 40°; 90 to 95 percent humidity; store loose. Turnips keep very well into the late spring.

Potatoes: 32 to 40°; 85 to 90 percent humidity; store loose. Dig potatoes after the first light frosts and harden them for a few days by leaving the sacks or boxes in a warm dry place (about 70°; your kitchen is fine). Sort into three categories:

1. the largest, most perfect potatoes for seed next year;
2. very small, damaged, or imperfect potatoes, for immediate use;
3. just ordinary potatoes.

Store potatoes loose in a dark, rodent-proof bin. If possible, it is better to spread them out over a large area than to pile them up in barrels or cans as they will rot without ventilation. Nothing smells or looks as terrible as a rotten potato.

KEEPING VEGETABLES: Celery, leeks, and members of the cabbage family may be kept for several months, with care. In general they store better with a little less humidity than roots (85 to 90 percent is optimum) and about the same temperature (32 to 40°). Some people store them in dry leaves or straw; I find it easier to hang them up by their roots, or root them in a bin of sand on the cellar floor. They will not, however, keep all winter, so use them up. If they start to go bad, get out your salt and vinegar and make a mess of pickles; or you may freeze them.

Cabbage: 32 to 40°; 85 percent humidity; store loose or in dry leaves or straw. Pull cabbages after the first few light frosts, leaving on all leaves and roots. Pick out any worms or insects. If you have a lot of cabbage you may store it by hanging it on nails or ropes suspended from the rafters, upside down. The big danger in storing cabbages is rot from too much humidity, so keep an eye on them. The firmer, larger heads of winter cabbage variety will keep the longest. If you have too many to use up by January, and they are beginning to go, make sauerkraut (see page 236).

Cauliflower: 32 to 40°; 85 to 90 percent humidity; store rooted in sand. Pull cauliflower after the first light frosts, roots and all. I have kept cauliflower this way, rooted, until Christmas. They may also be frozen or pickled with very good results.

Brussels Sprouts: 32 to 40°; 85 percent humidity; store rooted in sand. Pull Brussels sprouts after the first light frosts, roots and all; pull off the leaves and root them in sand in a very dark spot. They may last as long as the end of December if your cellar is not too damp. Don't bother to do this if the sprouts are very small as the outer leaves will yellow and become tough. Brussels sprouts can also be frozen.

Kohlrabi: 32 to 40°; 85 to 90 percent humidity; store rooted in sand. Pull off the outer leaves and pull plant, roots and all, after the first frosts. Kohlrabi will keep for a couple of months this way; you may also freeze or pickle it.

Chinese Cabbage: 32 to 40°; 85 to 90 percent humidity; store rooted in sand. A moderately good keeper, lasting for several months.

Celery: 32 to 40°; 85 to 90 percent humidity; store rooted in sand. Will keep into January or about three months. You may also freeze or pickle it.

Head Lettuce: 32 to 40°; 85 to 90 percent humidity; store rooted in sand. Large, firm heads will last from one to two months.

Leeks: 32 to 40°; 85 to 90 percent humidity; store

rooted in sand. Leeks will last all winter, even if very small.

KEEPING FRUITS: Fruits and vegetables should not be stored close to one another. Fruits will absorb odors from turnips, cabbages, etc.; and apples give off a mild sort of gas that makes potatoes and carrots rot. If all you have is one dark hole, store apples in a sealed can of some kind.

Apples: Some apples will keep all winter. Some won't last three weeks. The names of good keepers are Winesap, Spy, Delicious, and some of the newer kinds of McIntoshes, Courtland, Jonathan: the crisp, dense apples with thick skins. Wrap perfect fruit in newspaper or get a stack of pressed paper fruit racks from your local supermarket. Store at 32°, 80 to 90 percent humidity.

Oranges, Lemons, Grapefruit: If you should happen to want to blow your Christmas money on something nice, go see your local bulk shipping dealer about getting a crate of citrus fruit. It will keep quite well in the root cellar for a couple of months. Optimum temperature: 32°, 80 to 90 percent humidity.

Pears: Pick pears when full grown but still hard and green. You never know. Sometimes they will take months and months and months to ripen, but mostly they're all gone long before Christmas. Pack as for apples, see above. Store at 32°, 85 to 95 percent humidity.

ATTIC STORAGE

Winter squash, pumpkins, onions, dried beans and peas, and dried vegetables should not be kept in a root cellar, as it is much too damp and they will develop rot. A ventilated attic or room in the house or barn which does not freeze is the best place for them. If you don't have a dry place, surround them with straw or hay to absorb the damp. The temperature should be around 40 to 50°, and there should be plenty of ventilation or room for the air to circulate.

Winter Squash and Pumpkins: After the first light frost, cut squash from the vine and leave outside on a bed of straw or hay to cure the shells as they harden in the sun. Handle very carefully to avoid bruising. Store them on dry shelves, separated from one another, and check them every week or two for moldy spots. You may stop the mold by wiping it off but, if dark spots develop, use the squash or

pumpkin immediately. Mature squashes will keep longer than unripe ones.

Onions: Onions with thick stalks won't keep well. In short growing seasons, you may hasten the decay of the stalk by trampling over it at the end of the summer, a few weeks before harvest. At the first good frosts, pull the onions and let them sit for a week in a barn or dry shed; turn them over now and then to let all sides dry and paper over. If you wish to braid them, they may be kept in the attic or in any dry, cool room of the house; or you may trim the tops and keep them in a mesh bag. Use those with thick tops first; save the largest and best-formed for longest storage. Onions will keep until the weather gets warm and damp; usually they start to sprout in May. The green tops make very good salad material.

Garlic: Treat as for onions. They may be hung in the kitchen or, for longer storage, in the attic or an upstairs room.

Beans, Peas, and Other Seeds: All such things should be kept in clean, dry glass jars. If you are drying and storing your own seeds, you should first store them in a very warm place and after 12 hours see if any condensation has formed inside the jar; this will warn you that they are not completely dried and will rot in long storage.

Besides the moisture problem, there is also the rodent problem. It's no use saying, "But we *never* have mice"; if you keep seeds and peas and stuff around, you will soon.

An excellent source of good wide-mouthed jars is the dump. If the lids are rusty, you can repaint them.

Grains: Grains should be kept at any temperature under 65°. It doesn't matter if they freeze; the only problem is rodents. One solution is to keep them in galvanized garbage pails; they have nice tight lids and are just the right size for 50 or 100 pounds of grain. However, they cost. You might make bins of your own, out of wood, and line them with sheet metal; or just line around cracks and corners, where rodents usually chew holes. Grains kept in such a bin should be in burlap sacks. For short storage, you can use plastic garbage pails with tight lids, but they aren't proof against a determined rodent.

DRYING FRUITS AND VEGETABLES

Drying is a wonderfully compact way to store certain fruits and vegetables. Dried fruits are good for snacks, especially when you're hiking. They can also be soaked and cooked easily. Dried vegetables are useful in soups and stews, and some are good as snacks.

Fruits and vegetables that are easy to dry and that grow in New England and the Maritimes include:

apples
blueberries
huckleberries
cranberries
cherries
peaches
pears
plums
beans (green)
beans (seed beans and peas)
corn (flint, popcorn, and sweet)
greens, daylilies
mushrooms
peppers (green and hot)
pumpkin, and both summer and winter squash

If you are interested in keeping some nutritional value in the foods, you must take steps before exposing the fruits or vegetables to the air. These include: steam-blanching, ascorbic-acid coating, sulphuring, drying, and pasteurizing. See notes on each kind of food for the processes best suited to it.

STEAM-BLANCHING

With all vegetables, and some fruits, it is best to steam-blanch them before drying, to destroy the enzymes that eradicate the vitamins and toughen the food. Steam-blanched foods are also less likely to mold and decay during drying and storage. To steam-blanch, the cut food is set, 2 or 3 layers at a time, in a perforated steamer or rack over boiling water for a few minutes, with a tight lid on. The water must be boiling well; do not confuse water vapor, which is cloudy-looking, with steam, which is hot enough to burn your hand. Cool steam-blanched food at once, laying it on a damp cloth over a layer of ice, or submerging it in ice water.

USING ASCORBIC ACID

To prevent the loss of vitamin C in fruits such as apples, pears, and peaches, and to prevent discoloration when the vitamin C in them oxidizes and turns to tannin, coat the pieces as you cut them with an ascorbic acid solution made of 1 tsp. ascorbic acid to 1 cup water. Ascorbic acid can be bought at most drugstores.

USING SULPHUR

Sulphur is a mineral, which, like phosphorus or potassium, is necessary in small amounts. The reason for using it is partly to prevent discoloration; more important, it prevents loss of vitamins A and C as food is cut into and exposed to air. (It does not, however, prevent loss of vitamin B_1.)

Sulphur is available in a powder form called "sublimed sulphur," from some drugstores and country hardware stores.

To use sulphur, cut and lay out the food on non-metal trays (see below, "Trays"), which are set on bricks and separated so the fumes can circulate. Measure 1 tsp. sublimed sulphur per pound of food and heap it in a ceramic dish to one side of the trays. Cover everything with a great big cardboard box in which you've cut a little flap by the sulphur dish and poked a tiny hole on top on the side opposite the dish. Lift the box, light the sulphur, and let it burn with the flap up until it goes out. Then close the flap and time the treatment from then on. Exposure may be from ½ to 2 hours, depending on the food (see individual notes, below).

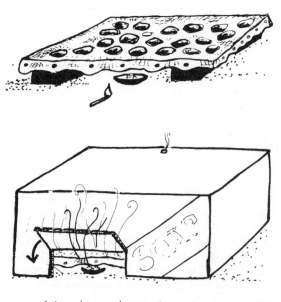

sulphuring dried fruits and vegetables

SUN DRYING AND INDOOR DRYING

To dry in the sun (or shade) choose a clear, dry, breezy day. Slice the food and spread it evenly on a clean cloth or non-metal racks. If there are bugs about, cover with cheesecloth.

Turn the food several times during the day, and bring it in before the dew falls. Continue drying for several days, until it reaches the right degree of dryness.

Some foods can be strung on knotted string; much easier to carry around. Others do well with one day on the rack, and then a few days on string. If it becomes rainy, or if you prefer to do it indoors, hang racks from the kitchen ceiling over the stove or in the attic; the attic must be ventilated, however, so that air can circulate. Let all foods cool before testing for dryness.

PASTEURIZATION AND STORAGE

Some foods (especially vegetables and blueberries) have a tendency to mold after drying. You can prevent this by pasteurizing them. After the food is fully dry, lay it on cookie sheets and set for 10 to 15 minutes in a closed oven at 175°. Remove, cool, and store in sealed jars at once. In damp climates it is particularly important to store dried food in jars.

TRAYS

Trays and drying racks should never be made of metal. Whatever you use is going to get dusty, spotted, and mucky, so the best thing is muslin, cheesecloth, or old sheets, tacked or hooked over nails on an old window frame. If the cloth sags, you can string some cord or baling twine under it to hold it up. When it gets dirty, take it off and wash it.

INDIVIDUAL NOTES ON DRIED FRUITS

APPLES: Use large, firm, sweet apples with good keeping qualities, such as Baldwin, Northern Spy, Winesap, Jonathan, Delicious, Russet. Some people peel them; I don't, but I do like to core them. Then slice them about ⅛ inch thick or so and dip them in ascorbic acid solution. Steam-blanch them 15 minutes or treat with sulphur for an hour.

Dry apples on racks or string on knotted cord and hang the cord looped over nails from the attic

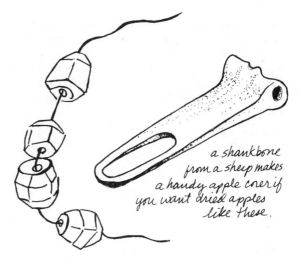

a shankbone from a sheep makes a handy apple corer if you want dried apples like these.

or kitchen rafters. Store when leathery (like suede).

To use, pour boiling water over them, just to cover. Let sit 1 hour or until soft; use in pies or baking as you would fresh apples. Our favorite use of dried apples is on long car trips; a pile of them on the dashboard has sustained many a weary mile.

BLUEBERRIES, HUCKLEBERRIES, CRANBERRIES: Set a cup or two at a time in a wire strainer and dip them into boiling water for 15 seconds to crack the skins; then dip in cold water to cool them. Spread on a cloth rack or non-metal screen and dry in the sun, or overhead in the kitchen or attic, 2 or 3 days, until quite hard. Pasteurize them by spreading them on a cookie sheet and setting them in a 175° oven for 10 minutes. To use, pour over boiling water to just cover, and soak 1 hour. Use in muffins, cakes, or cooked with other fruits.

CHERRIES: Painstakingly pit them; it's easier when they're fresh. Spread on cloth racks and sulphur them for 20 minutes. Set racks in the sun or overhead in the kitchen or attic; dry until leathery and sticky. To use, pour over boiling water to just cover and soak 1 hour or until soft; use in baking cakes, cookies, or mixed fruits.

PEACHES, PEARS: Choose just-ripe, sweet fruits. Cut in half and remove pits, cores. Dip in ascorbic acid. Steam-blanch 20 minutes, then place cut side up on cloth racks and treat them with sulphur for 1½ hours. If you are transferring them to another rack for drying, be careful not to spill them. Dry inside or out; be careful to cover them against flies.

They will take up to a week to dry out completely, until leathery. Turn several times a day during drying. To use, pour over boiling water to just cover, and soak 2 hours or until soft; cook with other fruits for compote, or chop into small pieces for use in cakes, cookies, etc. These are also very good eaten dried.

PLUMS: Cut them in half and stone them. Steam-blanch 15 minutes; spread, cut side up, on cloth racks and sulphur 1 hour. Dry indoors or in the sun until leathery; turn several times while drying, and be careful to cover them against flies. Set on cookie trays and pasteurize 15 minutes; cool and store. To use, pour over boiling water to cover and let sit ½ hour or until soft. Cook in mixed fruits or use as you would raisins or store-bought prunes.

FRUIT LEATHER: See page 39.

INDIVIDUAL NOTES ON DRIED VEGETABLES

Since vegetables do not have the quantity of acids and sugars which act as natural preservatives in fruits, it is much more important to steam-blanch before drying and to pasteurize after drying; otherwise they may develop mold in storage.

LEATHER BRITCHES GREEN BEANS: Use small, tender beans. Nip off the ends and steam-blanch them 15 minutes; cool over ice. Lay on cloth racks or string on knotted cord; dry indoors overhead in the kitchen or attic, or outside on a clear windy day. When they are leathery, stick them in the oven at 175° for 10 minutes. To use, soak in cold water 2 or 3 hours and then cook them in that water (it may take 1 hour or longer to tenderize them enough to eat).

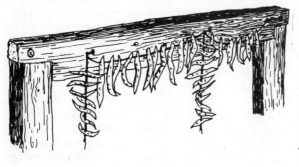

SHELL BEANS, LIMAS, PEAS: When pods are fully ripe but not yet brown, pick and shell them; spread to dry in the sun on cloth racks until hard; or dry in a wood stove warming oven. Another method, not so foolproof but easier, is to pull whole plants when the pods are ripe and hang them in the barn for a week or two; then bring them in and stuff them in a barrel in the kitchen or attic. Then, shell the pods as beans are needed. To use, spread beans out and pick over them, discarding any that have mold on them. Soak in twice as much water as you have beans, overnight; next day, cook in the same water (you may have to add more) until tender. Small beans take about 2 hours; large ones 4 hours; soybeans 6 hours or more. Peas and limas take about 2 hours. Home-dried peas are quite sweet and more like fresh peas than like split peas.

CORN: Popcorn and "flint" or "cow" corn (of which multicolored "Indian Corn" is a variety) is dried on the cob, either with the husks on, or peeled back. When dry, rub from the cob; to use, see pages 47–48 on corn in the Grains chapter. "Sweet" corn has a much softer skin and sweeter pulp. Turn back the husk an inch or two and pull out the silk. Pull off husks; steam-blanch the corn on the cob for 15 minutes. Cool in ice water. With a good knife, cut whole kernels from the cob and spread them on cloth racks to dry, 2 or 3 days, turning them over every so often, until hard. Another method is as follows:
In a large enamel or stainless-steel pot, mix:

10 cups freshly cut corn
½ cup brown sugar
½ cup milk
a pinch of salt

Cook and stir over low heat until it dries out. Spread on a cookie sheet and dry in a 150° oven or in the sun (cover with cheesecloth against insects). To use, soak in cold water until tender; cook in the same water, 1 hour or more, until tender.

GREENS, DAYLILIES: Choose young, tender leaves, daylily buds, or withered flowers. Set a handful (no more) loosely in a steamer and steam 5 minutes or until wilted. Spread on cloth racks, singly, to dry outside, or in the house; greens will take 2 to 3 days, daylilies up to a week. To use, just add dried greens to whatever soup, stew, etc. you are cooking, or boil directly in water. To use daylilies, soak first for 1 hour in cold water, then use as you would fresh daylilies. They are best in soups and stews.

MUSHROOMS: Use only fresh, young mushrooms, for the best flavor; at any rate, don't use any that have begun to rot. Wipe or wash and separate the caps from the stems. Spread on cloth racks and dry until leathery, almost crisp. Pasteurize 10 minutes in a 175° oven to prevent mold. To use, soak in cold water 1 hour; use in stews, soups, Chinese foods.

PEPPERS, HOT OR GREEN: Thread hot peppers, whole, on knotted cord; hang in the sun until crisp, or store in the attic. Green peppers should be split, cored, cut into strips or quarters. Spread on cloth racks and treat with sulphur ½ hour. Dry in the sun or indoors, on racks or knotted string, until quite crisp. To use, soak in cold water for ½ hour, then cook for use in rice or other grain dishes, stews, tomato sauces, etc. These are also quite good dried, as snacks.

PUMPKIN, WINTER SQUASH, AND SUMMER SQUASH: Use squash fresh from the garden. Slice quite thin; spread on cloth racks and sulphur for 1 hour. Dry on racks outdoors or in, or on knotted cord. The denser the squash, the longer it will take to dry; zucchini takes a few days, others take longer. Dry until quite crisp. Pasteurize 10 minutes in a 175° oven. To use, eat zucchini chips like potato chips; or soak all squashes in cold water to cover until soft, then cook in the water you soaked them in.

DRIED ROOTS

Some roots are dried and ground, such as chicory, comfrey, ginseng, sassafras. To get the most out of roots, dig them up in the late fall, when the strength of such a plant goes to the roots. To dry them completely, scrub them well and trim off any root hairs. Slice them into strips or diagonals, about ¼ inch thick, trying to keep the pieces more or less the same size and thickness. Dry them in a 100° to 150° oven for 2 or 3 hours; when you see some edges go brown, keep a close eye on them. They should be bottled or ground and bottled at once, or they will absorb moisture again.

DRIED HERBS

One of the easiest things to put by in the fall is the herbs. Herbs can be the very devil to get going in the garden, but they are a delight to harvest and dry and store. The house takes on a rich, spicy smell, as various crops come through . . .

The best time to cut herbs is just before the plant flowers, since that is when their oil content is highest. Cut them just after the dew dries off on what you can tell will be a clear hot day. Tie them up or spread on a screen, if they're small, and let them dry over the stove or in the attic, upside down (to make the oils flow into the leaves, they say).

Don't leave them hanging for weeks, but cut them down as soon as they dry; usually three days is enough.

Small herbs, such as parsley, celery leaves, thyme, chervil, oregano, rosemary, and basil, should be stored whole in tight bottles.

Larger herbs, such as dill, savory, mint, raspberry leaves, and seeds, such as caraway or anise, I find easier to deal with on a sheet. Spread the sheet out on the kitchen floor, wrap the dried stalks in it, roll them up, and twist with your hands. Then unwrap and pick out the stalks. The seeds and leaves can be separated through a large strainer. It's not a tidy job, but one you'll thank yourself for all winter.

As you bottle and store each batch of herbs, let the jar rest first in a warm spot, and then have a look at it. If the inside of the bottle is wet with condensed moisture, take the leaves out and dry them some more—or you'll have moldy herbs sooner or later.

BOUQUET GARNI

A Bouquet Garni is a little bunch of fresh or dried herbs tied together in a cluster (like a bouquet) or in a bag and suspended in a soup or stew pot—the idea being that people like the herb flavors but sometimes prefer not to be picking little twigs of thyme or soggy heads of dill out of their gourmet dinners.

Fish

1 head dill
3 leaves basil
1 sprig thyme

Chicken

1 sprig tarragon
1 leaf basil
1 sprig thyme

Beans

1 sprig savory
1 bay leaf

1 sprig oregano
1 whole clove
1 stick cinnamon

Red Meat

1 sprig thyme
2 sprigs rosemary
2 sprigs savory
1 sprig sage
2 sprigs marjoram

TARRAGON VINEGAR

Tarragon is a lovely herb, when fresh, but it gets tough and tasteless as it dries. It is much better to submerge tarragon leaves in vinegar. Use the vinegar in salads and the tarragon in cooking.
Mix:

1 qt. vinegar (any kind)
3 Tb. tarragon leaves

Store in a pretty bottle for 3 weeks before using.

FINES HERBES

This is a mixture of very finely crumbled herb leaves, to be served as a garnish for an omelet, soup, or in a sauce. Mix any or all:

basil chervil celery chopped chives marjoram savory parsley sage (not too much) tarragon thyme

CANNING

There are two basic processes used in canning:

1. Hot pack, cold pack, and hot water bath, used for "acid" foods such as fruits, pickles, and tomatoes;

2. Pressure canning, used for "nonacid" foods such as vegetables, meats, beans, soups, and stews.

I have not included any pressure canning in this book because of my inexperience; it is incredibly difficult to do on a wood stove.

HOT PACK: This is used for very acid foods, such as pickles and jams. The canning jar is filled with boiling hot food and syrup, and covered with a canning lid. As it cools, the lid is pulled down and seals itself.

HOT WATER BATH: This is used for slightly less acid foods, such as bottled fruits and tomatoes. The canning jar is filled with hot food, the seal adjusted, and then the bottle is submerged in boiling water for a period of time. Afterwards, as it cools, the lid is pulled down and seals itself.

COLD PACK: In "cold pack" or "raw pack" canning, the jar is filled with raw fruit, then filled with boiling liquid and submerged in boiling water for 10 to 30 minutes. Thus the food is cooked just as much as it would be if you were to pack it hot; moreover, it shrinks, anywhere from one third to half its volume (you wind up with half a jar of juice). For which reason, I prefer hot water bath, or hot pack.

PRESSURE CANNING: This type of canning requires the use of a pressure cooker large enough to hold the bottles; it is partly filled with water, sealed, and brought up to 15 or 20 pounds pressure. The pressure must be maintained, then, from 20 minutes to 2 hours, depending on the type of food you are canning. This is very difficult to maintain on a wood stove. The reason for all this hassle is to eliminate the possibility of botulism, a rare but extremely dangerous type of food poisoning that, once in a while, develops after eating from a jar or can of nonacid food that has not been pressure-canned long enough, or hot enough. Botulin toxin cannot be seen, smelled, or tasted, but it is so toxic that a tiny amount can kill you; and there isn't any antidote for it. It doesn't happen often, it's true. If you live in the country you probably know lots of people who have canned green beans in hot water baths all their lives and are doing fine at eighty-seven years old. But it's not worth the risk, if only for the sake of your own peace of mind.

If you have a wood stove and would like to get into pressure canning, you can do it on a Coleman stove, or a small propane stove. I canned 30 quarts of vegetables on a Coleman stove one year. They were pretty insipid tasting, I thought, for the trouble. And doubtless, after all that heat, they didn't have too many vitamins left.

PREPARATIONS FOR CANNING

Canning, more than any other kitchen endeavor, requires preparation and forethought; this is particularly true of canning on a wood stove. You have to lay in supplies, get organized, and set aside a day for it. If you plunge in, willy-nilly, you'll soon find yourself amid more chaos than you ever believed possible; but a properly planned and executed canning day can be a great delight. And, while freezing may be more practical, and dried foods cheaper, you can't beat that row of shining jars, cooling on the pantry shelf, for aesthetic glory.

CANNING EQUIPMENT

Jars and Tops: There are any number of old-fashioned types of jars. If you are buying some, check rims and lids for nicks and cracks.

Jars with dome-shaped glass lids and wire holders. These require a rubber ring between lid and bottle. The wires have three positions: off, on, and sealed or clamped. The bottles are processed with lids on but not sealed; the longer loop of wire is clamped down after the bottle has cooled.

Jars with flat glass lids and metal rings. They require a rubber ring between the lid and bottle. To process, you adjust the rubber ring and glass lid on the bottle, screw down the metal ring, and then unscrew it about ¼ inch—just a slight twist. After processing and cooling, tighten the band.

Jars with entire metal tops are not recommended because the lids are made of zinc, compounded with cadmium, a poison. The porcelain liner is not safe after many years.

The canning jars available today, in hardware stores, supermarkets, and direct from Ball Mason Jar (see address, page 237) have a two-part lid: a flat metal lid with a soft, rubbery underneath, and a metal ring to hold it in place. You adjust the lid and screw the band on. After processing the band is removed to test the lid. You can replace the band or leave it off for storage. New lids have to be bought every year; they cannot be re-used, but the bands can. You can buy lids separately, or in a package together with bands. These new jars are not as heavy as the old ones and once in a while they crack in processing; we have found that if

jar with wire holder

you send a jar that cracked *in processing* back to the Ball Mason Jar Company, they will replace it.

Jars are most common in two sizes: quarts and pints which take the same size lid. Sometimes you find two-quart jars, or half-pint jars, which take different sized lids.

Pots for Heating Fruits and Pickles: All containers used in processing these "acid" foods must be plastic, stainless steel, or enamel. Iron pots are out of the question, they darken the food and spoil the flavor; and aluminum is not a digestible alloy.

A Canning Kettle: This can be of any material but should be deep enough so you can set a quart bottle in it and cover with boiling water, with a few inches to spare at the top so the water won't boil over the top.

Miscellaneous Tools: You will need a paring knife, wooden spoons, tea towels, a bottle scrubber, and a gismo for lifting bottles out of the water.

If you have a wood stove, think about wood ahead of time, and split a good pile of beech, ash, or hard maple. If it isn't dry, pile it indoors by the stove for a few days. You are going to have to keep a hot fire (hard wood on top of hard wood coals) going for several hours, without too much hassle. Another possibility is an open outdoor fire. A campfire will boil huge pots of water in no time flat, compared with wood, gas, or electric stoves.

The food you're canning should be as fresh as possible. If canning applesauce, however, I usually try to make up several gallons in the days before canning it, and keep it cool (refrigerated). You can also make up fruit juices ahead and store them in pitchers.

THE STEPS IN HOT WATER BATH CANNING

1. Stoke up the fire, and set the canning kettle, half full of water, on to boil.

2. Meanwhile, wash out the jars in plenty of hot water and a little soap. Rinse in hot water and set upside down on a clean tea towel. Always wash out one pint bottle more than you think you'll need—you never know. If there's any serious question about there being bad germs in the bottles, sterilize them by submerging 15 minutes in the boiling water in the canning kettle.

3. Set your rubber rings or lids to boil in a small pot on the stove.

4. Prepare and heat the food to be canned—see individual instructions.

5. When the food is ready, turn each jar right side up, and fill it up to within ½ to ¼ inch of the top. You must always leave this air space.

6. Wipe the top rim and down a tiny bit around with a very clean, damp cloth. Fish a ring and lid out of the boiling water and adjust on top (see individual instructions on different kinds of tops on page 225). Set the bottle in the canning kettle.

7. When the last bottle is filled and set in the water (to fully cover the jars), start timing. Be sure to keep your fire going and your kettle boiling, not just simmering.

8. When the time's up, take out each bottle and set it in a draft-free spot. Don't mess with the lids until the bottles are cool; they will be loose until the air in the little airspace cools and contracts, pulling the lid down. Sometimes lids pop as they do this; sometimes not.

9. When the jars are cool, in 2 or 3 hours, you should remove each ring and carefully, gently, push up on each lid to make sure it is sealed on.
   If one lid isn't sealed on, just use the contents. If a number of them are loose, probably your hot water bath wasn't hot enough, or you didn't have the food good and hot before it went in the bottles. Empty out all the jars that didn't

seal, rewash the bottles, use fresh lids, and re-bottle the whole works, being sure, this time, that they get enough heat.

How many bottles can you can in a day? Usually two batches is all I can handle; that's about 14 jars, quarts or pints.

BOTTLED APPLESAUCE

Generally the best apples are very sweet ones; they can be a little on the soft side, or a little overripe. Throw in one or two tart apples now and then to keep up the flavor.

Generally I like to put up about 30 quarts of applesauce. It's very easy, people like it a lot, and it's versatile. You can serve it as dessert, or on pancakes, or with dinner (very nice with cornbread, or beans, or pork, or all three). Kids like it. It's instant food, of a kind in big demand and short supply in the winter.

Halve into a large enameled or stainless-steel pot:

a quantity of apples

Add half a cup of water or so, cover, and stew until apples are soft. Put them through a food mill. Add sugar or honey as needed. Don't add any spices. Store in the refrigerator up to 1 week.

When you have stewed up and accumulated around 2 gallons of applesauce, it's time to can them. Heat the applesauce very slowly, adding water if necessary to keep it liquid enough so it doesn't stick in the pans.

Fill bottles to within ½ inch of top, poking down each side with a knife to make sure there aren't any air bubbles. Wipe rims of jars with extra care, and adjust lids.

Process pints and quarts 20 minutes under boiling water; let cool 3 to 4 hours, and test lids.

BOTTLED BLUEBERRIES

No need to add sugar—blueberries (or huckleberries) make their own fine thick sweet syrup without any assistance. For every 2 quarts of blueberries, figure on 1 quart bottled.

Measure blueberries into stainless-steel or enameled pots; cover, and bring to a boil.

Wash an appropriate number of bottles; set lids and canning kettle of water to boil.

Fill bottles with boiling blueberries. Wipe rims and adjust lids. Set bottles in boiling water bath.

Time from the moment you put the last bottle in; boil the bottles for 20 minutes. Cool for 2 to 3 hours. Remove rings (if using modern lids) or tighten clamp or screw top (with older type bottles).

BOTTLED PEACHES OR PEARS

Pick Bartlett, or sweet pears, when ripe, but not soft, and store in a cool dark place until tender.

Choose peaches which are ripe but still firm and a little tart. If you wish to remove the skins, dip for a minute in boiling water; then halve, pit, and peel them.

As you cut up pears or peaches, dip in a solution of:

1 cup water
½ tsp. ascorbic acid, 1 tsp. citric acid, or 2 Tb. lemon juice

For every 4 qts. peaches or pears (sliced) heat together:

4 cups water
1 cup sugar or ½ cup honey

When liquid is hot, add fruit, and boil 5 minutes. Pack fruit in pint or quart jars; cover with boiling syrup, to within ½ inch of tops. Adjust lids, and process under boiling water in a canning kettle for 25 minutes. Cool 2 to 3 hours; check lids.

BOTTLED PIE APPLES

While I am a staunch advocate of leaving peels on things, I must admit that apple peels don't make it in canning. Certainly they shouldn't be thrown away, though. Use them to make jelly or throw in with the applesauce brewing. Or just eat them, as they are.

Peel, core, and slice into acid solution (as Pears, above):

20 or 30 firm tart apples
Brew up a solution of:

4 cups water
2 cups sugar

Boil the apple slices, a jarful at a time, in the hot syrup, taking them out after a few minutes, before they fall apart. Pack each batch in its jar and fill to within ½ inch of top of jar in the syrup. Adjust lids.

Process under boiling water in a canning kettle for 20 minutes. Cool 2 to 3 hours; check lids.

SPICED FRUITS

To spice and flavor pears, peaches, or pie apples, add a small bag of whole spices to the syrup as you cook it. (Don't add ground spices.) Ginger is nice with pears; cinnamon and cloves are good with apples and either of these is good with peaches.

BOTTLED RHUBARB

Toss together and let stand 4 hours in an enameled or stainless-steel pot:

a quantity of fresh, chopped rhubarb
½ cup sugar per quart

Bring slowly to the boil and cook for a few minutes, until hot through. Taste and add more sugar if needed. Pack, hot, into canning jars, leaving ½ inch head room. Adjust lids, submerge in boiling water, and process 10 minutes. Cool 3 hours or until cold; test lids.

BOTTLED PIE CHERRIES

Soak cherries in ice water to firm them before removing pits.
Mix:

6 cups cherries
Add:

1 cup sugar (or more, to taste)

Let sit 3 to 4 hours; then bring slowly to a boil, and pack into 2 pint jars leaving ½ inch head room. Adjust lids; process under boiling water 20 minutes (25 minutes for quarts).

BOTTLED CRANBERRY SAUCE

Sort and stem:

8 cups wild cranberries

Boil together:

4 cups water

3 cups sugar

in a stainless-steel or enameled pot; add cranberries and boil until the skins pop. Pour into 6 pint canning jars, leaving ¼ inch head room. Adjust caps and let cool 3 hours. Test lids.

BOTTLED TOMATOES

If you can grow them, or buy them cut rate in season, tomatoes are pretty easy to can, and very rewarding. If you eat a lot of dried beans, you need a lot of tomatoes, to make beans tasty).

Most tomatoes are acid enough to rule out the possibility of botulism, so they can be hot water canned. (The exceptions are yellow tomatoes, or those big, bland, overripe beefsteak tomatoes we all love to eat raw.) Always be sure to cut any bad or soft spots out of tomatoes before cooking them for canning. You may remove skins, or not, as you choose; to do so, scald them in hot water, then dip in cold and rub off the skins.

You should not can other vegetables with tomatoes (such as onions, peppers, etc.) by hot water bath; the sweetness of them will reduce the acidity of the tomatoes too much for safety.

TOMATO JUICE

Use the good parts of imperfect, half-rotten, or spotty tomatoes. Simmer until soft in an enameled or stainless-steel pot; stir often. Put through the fine sieve of a food mill. For every quart of juice add 1 tsp. salt. Store in a cool place up to 2 weeks. When you have accumulated enough juice, use for canning whole tomatoes, or:

Pour boiling hot tomato juice to within ¼ inch of the tops of canning jars. Adjust caps; process pints 10 minutes and quarts 15 minutes, under boiling water. Cool 2 hours; test lids.

TOMATOES IN JUICE

This is my favorite way to can tomatoes; you can even serve them, quartered, in salads. I use small whole tomatoes. If you use large ones, you should either quarter, halve, or core them. Peel if you like:

7 to 10 perfect tomatoes per quart

Pack them into canning jars; pour over, leaving ½ inch head room:

boiling tomato juice

Adjust caps; process pints 35 minutes, quarts 45 minutes, under boiling water. Cool 2 hours; test lids.

BOTTLED TOMATOES, HOT PACK

Skin, if you like, and core, if large:

7 to 10 tomatoes per quart

Put them in an enameled or stainless-steel pot along with:

1 cup boiling water

Cook them for 5 to 10 minutes, stirring and turning them so they heat through. Lift them into the jars, pack tight, to within ½ inch of top. Adjust lids; process pints 10 minutes, quarts 15 minutes. Cool 2 hours; test lids.

CATSUP

Chunk up:

2 or 3 dozen ripe tomatoes

6 onions

Put them in an enameled or stainless-steel pot. Boil until soft. Put through a food mill. Return to heat, adding to the mixture:

2 Tb. salt

1 cup sugar

Tie in a little cloth bag with a long string:

3 bay leaves

1 Tb. fresh ground pepper

1 Tb. mace

1 Tb. whole cloves

1 Tb. celery seeds

1 Tb. mustard seeds

1 tsp. allspice

2 sticks cinnamon

Set the cloth bag of spices in the catsup with the string trailing over one side of the pot. Simmer the mixture very slowly for 5 hours, stirring now and again to make sure it's not sticking. If it's easier, stew it in a low oven (200°). Remove the string bag and add to the catsup:

2 cups white vinegar

1 Tb. ground paprika

Boil rapidly for 5 minutes, stirring vigorously. Pour into 3 or 4 pint-size jars to within ½ inch of lid. Adjust lids. Cool 3 or 4 hours, test lids.

FRUIT JUICES

While I have never gotten my life so organized that I could bottle rows and rows of fruit juices, sufficient to have some every morning for breakfast, I do usually manage to put up a few pints of juice in case somebody comes down with an awful cold. My juices are very thick and bitter; they are really unsweetened concentrates, meant to be mixed with honey and water and drunk very hot. Besides doing wonders for a sore throat or stuffed sinus, they're very high in vitamin C. If you like, these juices may be spiced with cinnamon sticks, cloves, allspice berries, and whole nutmeg tied in a bag while they simmer.

BOTTLED BLACKBERRY CORDIAL

In an enameled or stainless-steel container, mash and heat:

a quantity of blackberries

When the berries lose color, hang them to drip overnight in a cloth bag. In the morning, wring out the bag, and return juice to the pan; for every quart, add:

½ cup honey

Boil until thick, and pour into pint-size canning jars, leaving ⅛ inch head room. Adjust lids. Cool 2 hours; test lids.

ELDERBERRY ROB OR CRANBERRY JUICE

Boil together in an enameled or stainless-steel pot:
equal amounts of berries and water

When the elderberries lose their color, or the cranberries burst, strain through cloth bag overnight; wring out bag in the morning. To each quart juice, add:

1 cup sugar

Boil and pour into pint canning jars, leaving ⅛ inch head room.

If you can get both at once, you should try mixing these two; they go together really well.

JELLIES AND JAMS

The canning of fruits and making of jams, jellies, and such are, to me, a rather special art; a jewel-like link between summer and winter. We seldom eat our jellies in the summer, but space them out over the long cold months. I like to label them with care, as:

RASPBERRY JAM
FROM THE RYAN'S PASTURE

or:

STRAWBERRY JELLY
MADE THE DAY CHRIS CAME TO TEA

That way, the taste remembers summer, in more ways than one.

After discovering that crabapple peels contain enough pectin to jell almost anything, I just use crabapple jelly, half and half with syrup or stewed berries or fruit pulp, to make jellies and jams of all kinds. (You have to save a little jelly for the spring and early summer berries—not always easy to do.) Later in the season I just stew the apples and whatever else is around (rose hips, plums, blackberries) together in the same pot, strain it, and make jelly out of it.

WHAT YOU NEED FOR JAMS AND JELLIES

1. One or two heavy enameled or stainless-steel medium-sized pots.

2. Cheesecloth (a couple of yards per season will do) and a place—you may have to devise something—where you can hang a bag of fruit to drip without it getting in anybody's way for 3 or 4 hours.

3. An old tin can half full of paraffin wax (for sealing jelly).

4. Lots and lots of sugar—at least 10 pounds per season . . . you can use honey if you don't mind everything tasting a little like honey.

5. Bottles. Jelly makers collect all sizes and shapes, even colors, of bottles; anything will do as long as it has a wide-mouth top and a decent lid (to keep the mice out). You especially need some very small bottles . . . keep an eye peeled for good ones at the dump.

CRABAPPLE SYRUP (HOMEMADE PECTIN): All apples, and many other fruits, contain pectin, an enzyme that causes the juice of the fruit to gel, after it has been cooked for a while and cooled. Crabapples have a great deal of pectin, and although they are quite tart and make a good jelly by themselves, theirs is a flavor that is easy to alter by the addition of juices and syrups made from other fruits that have little pectin of their own. By using an equal amount of crabapple juice, you may make jellies of juice from:

strawberries raspberries blackberries peaches elderberries cherries hawthorn berries rosehips mint

Or you may use crabapple syrup in combination with fruit pulp, to make a slightly jelled jam. Add 1 part crabapple syrup to 3 parts:

strawberries raspberries peaches cherries plums blueberries oranges pumpkin

SWEETENING: All jams, jellies, conserves, and the like take quite a bit of sweetening. You can use honey, if you like, but honey does have a slightly acid tang that flavors all jams and jellies made with it. Certainly if you use honey it should be very mild, light clover, wildflower, or orange blossom honey—something without too much taste of its own. The *Ball Blue Book* recommends using no more than half honey, the other half white sugar. I have always used only sugar, but I use less than most recipes call for; my system is to cut their amount of sugar in half, then add more as needed, to taste.

SPICES: If you wish to flavor jelly with spices, such as cinnamon, cloves, allspice, and ginger, don't add powdered spices; they taste weird after long storage. Instead, buy whole spices, tie them in a cloth bag (with a string trailing over one side of the pot) and simmer along with the fruit or syrup. Remove bag and dry out the spices; you can reuse them a couple of times.

MAKING APPLE SYRUP

Apples: use crabapples when possible; for apple jelly, red crabs make the brightest color jelly.

Chop apples in half (skins, cores, and all) into a large enameled or stainless-steel container with:

1 cup water for every 3 cups apples (roughly)

Stew over moderate heat until apples disintegrate, 1 to 2 hours. Stir the mixture; it should be liquid, like a cream soup; add water if necessary and cook a little longer to mix it in.

Line a number of ceramic or plastic containers with coarsely woven cloth, a handiwipe or 3 layers of cheesecloth. Ladel 2 cups apple glop into each and tie up the bag with strong cord; hang to drip over the bowl. Do not press or squeeze, but allow to drip 3 to 4 hours, or overnight.

This is "Apple Syrup," unsweetened. To sweeten it, add 1 cup white sugar or 3/4 cup honey for every

2 cups syrup and simmer until mixed. You may then use it on desserts or pancakes, can or freeze it, use it to make apple jelly, or mix with other fruit syrups to gel them.

It will keep up to 2 months in the refrigerator; store in a lidded jar.

The mush left over in the bag may be made into a passable applesauce to which you should add some tastier applesauce and plenty of spices to pick up the flavor.

THE STEPS IN MAKING JELLY

1. Never try to work with more than 4 cups of fruit syrup at a time when making jelly. For some reason, more than 4 cups just won't gel. So mix up your syrup, out of whatever, in an enameled or stainless-steel pot, and add:

2. Sweetening—for every 4 cups syrup:
   2 cups sugar or:
   1 cup sugar and 1 cup honey or:
   1½ cups honey

3. Bring to a rapid boil. Continue boiling rapidly for the entire time you cook the jelly (if possible, given the vagaries of wood stoves). Meanwhile set your can of paraffin in a pot of water to heat.

4. As "scum" forms on top, skim it off with a slotted spoon or ladle. (It's perfectly good stuff to smear on bread but it makes cloudy jelly.)

5. When the syrup has been boiling for about 20 to 30 minutes and has reduced by about a third, it is probably jelly. There is much glib talk about syrup "sheeting off a spoon" when it's ready. I have made gallons of jelly and I have yet to see it sheet off a spoon. (I keep trying: maybe it's a wet spoon? A cold spoon?) What I do is this: take a spoonful of hot syrup out and pour it on one side of a cool dish and set it on the windowsill for a few minutes. If it forms a thick skin within 2 or 3 minutes, it's likely jelly. After you have made a few batches of jelly, successfully, you will come to recognize the thickness of syrup ready to gel.

6. Pour the syrup into clean jars, recently rinsed. (Pour a little into a small glass for breakfast—and to find out if it really was jelly. Wait until you find out to label the jars. If it wasn't, and you really want jelly, pour it back in the pot, reheat, and cook some more.) Pour paraffin immediately over hot syrup in the jars, forming a very

thin seal. Allow paraffin and jelly to cool for an hour or so; then pour on a second, thicker layer of paraffin.

7. Next morning, label jar, screw on lid, and store in a cool, dark place.

APPLE JELLY

Homemade apple jelly has a wonderfully tart and fragrant flavor, quite a bit like currant jelly. If you use bright apples, it's quite red. You can make it of any sort of apples, but crabapples are best.
In an enameled pot, heat:

4 cups apple syrup
2 cups sugar

Boil 20 minutes, skimming off scum that forms on top. Test every 5 minutes after that. Bottle and seal.

Variations

SPICED APPLE JELLY

Put:

2 whole cloves, 1 stick cinnamon, a piece of ginger root, or 3 whole allspice berries

in a cloth bag; tie and cook in with the syrup for the first 20 minutes. Remove before bottling.

STRAWBERRY JELLY

Mash in a ceramic or enamel container:

2 cups wild strawberries
1 cup sugar

Hang in a bag to drip for 12 hours. Add an equal amount of apple syrup and sugar to taste (about a cup, but it varies; usually I have already sweetened the syrup, since it's canned or frozen). Bring to a rolling boil, skim, and boil until thick. Bottle and seal.

RASPBERRY JELLY

Bring to a boil in an enameled or stainless-steel pot:

4 cups crushed raspberries

When the berries are soft, hang them in a cloth bag for 4 hours; squeeze out the remaining liquid. Mix:

2 cups raspberry juice
2 cups apple syrup
1 cup sugar, if needed

Bring to a rolling boil, skim, and boil until thick. Bottle and seal.

BLACKBERRY JELLY

Bring to a boil in an enameled or stainless-steel pot:

4 cups crushed blackberries
2 cups water

When the berries are soft, hang them in a cloth bag for 5 hours; squeeze out remaining liquid. Mix:

2 cups blackberry juice
2 cups apple syrup
1 to 2 cups sugar, as needed

Bring to a rolling boil, skim, and boil until thick. Bottle and seal.

PEACH OR CHERRY JELLY

Mix in an enameled or stainless-steel pot:

4 cups sliced peaches or 4 cups whole pie cherries
1 cup water

Simmer until soft. Hang in a cloth bag 4 to 6 hours. Take:

2 cups juice
2 cups apple syrup
1 cup sugar, if needed

Boil rapidly, skimming as needed, until thick. Bottle and seal.

ELDERBERRY JELLY

Mix in an enameled or stainless-steel pot:

a quantity of elderberries (some stems are okay)
1 cup water

Stew until elderberries lose their color. Strain through a sieve. To:

2 cups elderberry juice

add:

2 cups apple syrup
2 cups sugar

Boil rapidly, skimming as needed, until thick. Bottle and seal.

HAWTHORN JELLY

Simmer together in an enameled or stainless-steel pot:

4 cups hawthorn berries
1 cup water
4 to 6 crabapple peels

When the hawthorns are soft, hang in a bag 4 to 6 hours. To 2 cups juice add:

2 cups sugar

Boil rapidly until thick, skimming as necessary. Bottle and seal.

MINT JELLY

Pour:

1 cup boiling water

over:

1 cup mint leaves (firmly packed in measuring)

Let stand for an hour or two; empty into a cloth and wring them out to extract juice. Mix and bring to a rapid boil:

4 cups apple juice
½ cup mint juice
1 cup sugar

Skim as necessary; boil until thick. Bottle and seal.

ROSE HIP EXTRACT: Gather wild rose hips after the first few frosts, as soon as they turn soft and bright red. Set them in a stainless-steel or enameled pot with a little water (½ cup) and cook slowly for a few hours until they become soft and fall apart.

Put the berries through a food mill with fine enough holes to sieve out the seeds. This is a plain, unflavored extract, very high in vitamin C, but without much taste. It may be stored up to 3 weeks in a closed jar in a cool place; it may be frozen, canned, or used in cooking.

ROSE HIP JELLY

Pour:

2 cups rose hip extract

through 2 or 3 layers of cheesecloth.
Add:

2 cups apple syrup
2 cups white sugar or 1 cup honey

Set this in an enameled or stainless-steel pot and boil it for about 30 minutes, until a spoonful, set on a dish, becomes thick and turns to soft jelly within 3 minutes. (It will be reduced about one third.) Pour into jars; seal with paraffin or canning lids.

JELLIES MADE FROM FRUITS WITH NATURAL PECTIN

RED CURRANT JELLY

Put in a stainless-steel or enameled pot:

a quantity of currants (it's okay if stems are on them)

Crush the bottom layer and cook until soft and colorless. Pack in a bag or two and drain for a few hours. Bring to a boil:

2 cups currant juice
1 cup sugar

Skim as needed, and boil until thick. Bottle and seal.

GRAPE JELLY

Sometimes Concord grapes will gel by themselves (usually when underripe) and sometimes you have to add a couple of apples.
Mash:

a quantity of Concord grapes

Cook until soft, and strain through a cloth bag. Bring to a boil:

4 cups grape juice
2 to 3 cups sugar
2 Tb. apple syrup, if needed

Skim as needed, boiling until thick. Bottle and seal.

JAM MAKING

Jams, in a way, are easier to make than jellies; if they don't gel, it's no big deal, you can still spread them on bread. On the other hand, jams should be bottled in canning jars, with properly sealed lids. Otherwise they are likely to get moldy if the paraffin seal isn't perfect (and it never is).

As far as I am concerned, jams, preserves, conserves, and marmalade are all variations on the same thing.

WILD STRAWBERRY PRESERVES

You may leave the hulls on, if you like. If using cultivated strawberries, add a little lemon juice and cut the berries in half; then hull them.

Combine in an enameled or stainless-steel pot:

4 cups wild strawberries
2 cups sugar

Allow them to sit for about 3 hours, to draw the juice. Heat slowly, stirring, and add:

1 cup apple jelly

Heat and stir until boiling. Boil for 15 minutes. Let them cool and sit in a cool place, covered, overnight.

Next day, pack in 2 pint jars. Adjust lids, and process underneath simmering water (185°) for 20 minutes. Cool the jars and after 2 hours, test lids.

PLUM JAM

Pit and chop into an enameled or stainless-steel pot:

2 quarts ripe plums

Add:

1 cup apple syrup

Heat slowly and simmer until soft. Taste and add by half cups, tasting after each addition:

1 to 3 cups sugar

As the mixture thickens, stir to prevent sticking. Pour, boiling hot, into 4 pint-size canning jars. Wipe rims of jars, adjust lids, and allow to cool for 2 hours before testing lids.

RASPBERRY JAM

You can use this recipe for any sort of berry, from gooseberry to blueberry, but adjust sugar as needed. Some berries (such as Eastern blackberries) are too seedy to make good jam.

Crush in an enameled or stainless-steel pot:

1 gal. berries
2 cups sugar
2 cups apple syrup

Simmer for several hours, until thick. It will cook down quite a lot. Add sugar as needed, to taste; stir often, as it gets thick. Bring it to a good rapid boil and pour it into 4 or 5 pint-size canning jars. Adjust lids and let cool 3 hours. Test lids.

ORANGE MARMALADE

Most commercial oranges are dyed, and allergists warn that the skins of such oranges should not be used for making marmalade. Uncolored oranges may be ordered from: Mixon Fruit Farms, P.O. Box 2918, Bradenton, Fla. 33505. They are much fresher, sweeter, and tastier than ordinary oranges. The best marmalade is made with either slightly unripe, sour oranges, or else a mixture of sweet oranges and lemon juice.

Halve the oranges (and lemons) and remove the seeds.

The easiest way to chop oranges and lemons is to stuff them, skins and all, through the coarse blade of a meat chopper. If you haven't got one, then remove the skins in quarters, pile them together, and slice into thin slivers with a sharp knife. Chop inner fruit coarsely.

Place in a ceramic or plastic crock:

3 or 4 chopped oranges
1 chopped lemon
2 quarts water
4 cups sugar or 2 cups honey

Cover and let sit overnight. Next day, dump them into an enameled or stainless-steel pot and bring to a boil; simmer for a couple of hours as they thicken. Taste and see if more sweetening is needed. When a test spoonful, cooled on a plate, is thick enough for you, pour the boiling hot marmalade into 5 pint jars. Adjust lids, allow to cool 3 hours, and test lids.

Variations

Jelled Marmalade: Substitute for 2 cups water:

2 cups apple syrup

Pumpkin Marmalade: This makes three times as much marmalade, but tastes about the same as ordinary marmalade. Cut **a small pumpkin** in half and remove pulp and seeds. Cut into chunks, and slice the chunks into small slabs about 1 inch by 1 inch and ⅛ inch thick. Let them sit overnight with the oranges and lemons, along with:

twice as much sweetening

Proceed then as in marmalade, simmering until pumpkin is translucent and syrup thick. Pack in 12 to 15 pint jars, cool 2 to 3 hours, and test lids.

Carrot Marmalade: A variation on pumpkin. Substitute for the pumpkin, **4 cups cooked sliced carrots**. Use in all, only **6 cups sugar** (or **3 cups honey**).

Rhubarb Marmalade: Add to any of the above recipes:

3 cups diced raw rhubarb
1 cup sugar or ½ cup honey (or more, as needed)

PEACH PRESERVES

If the peaches are fuzzy and you wish to remove the skins, dip them for 15 seconds in boiling water for easier peeling. Combine in a ceramic or enamel container:

12 sliced peaches
3 cups sugar

Let them stand overnight in a cool place. Next day set them in a heavy enameled or stainless-steel pot and heat slowly to a boil; boil for 30 minutes, or until fruit becomes translucent. Stir gently as syrup becomes thick. Pour, boiling hot, into 4 pint-sized canning jars; adjust lids, and seal. Let cool 2 to 3 hours before checking lids.

PICKLING FOODS

There must be about ten million pickle recipes in North America. Everybody has their favorites; these are mine.

There are a couple of things I'd like to say about pickles. One is that you don't really need to seal the jars, as long as the stuff stays submerged in good strong "pickle" (that's professional pickler's talk for the vinegar–sugar–spice mixture). Nor do you need to cook or slice the vegetables, really. You can use cider vinegar if you don't mind the taste and a little brown color.

My husband's grandfather used to take any cider that went to vinegar and set it in crocks in the cellar, maybe throw in a little olive oil, salt, a few pinches of seeds. Then, as fall progressed, he'd toss in any ripe vegetables from the garden that weren't getting eaten. Maybe he chopped them up; who knows. Probably they were a little brown and sour and appley and just what you want on a cold day in January. Now that's what I call real pickling.

Pickles can be served, as they are, with meats, fish, or as hors d'oeuvres. They can be chopped fine as relish, or added to sauces; some pickles (such as the mild Vegetable Pickles) are most excellent in salads.

ABOUT CUCUMBERS: The cucumbers you ordinarily see in the supermarket aren't suited to making most types of pickles. Pickling cucumbers are, by comparison, much smaller; their skins are lumpy, but much more tender; their flesh is firm, and, when raw, slightly bitter; they have little of the pulpy center and very small seeds. Be sure your cucumbers are the right kind or they will wind up

as pickle slush garnished with bits of thin green leathery skin. (Exception: see recipe for Sweet Pickles.)

ABOUT FRESHNESS: The only way to get a crisp pickle is to start with a crisp vegetable; therefore, all vegetables must be absolutely fresh (in other words, picked the day you pickle them).

DILL PICKLES OR DILLY BEANS

For pickles: Use ripe, but not overblown, pickling cucumbers. Slice lengthwise into 4 or 6 pieces.

For beans: The best beans I've used yet are the mammoth, leathery beans of the Scarlet Runner pole bean.

This recipe makes about 4 quarts. Choose jars that are just the size of the cucumbers or beans. Pick a dill flower for each jar and set it in, upside down, so the flower makes a star pattern. Then pack each jar. You will need about:

4 quarts beans or 24 cucumbers

Don't leave any beans or cukes sticking up above liquid level in the jar. Boil together in an enameled or stainless-steel pot:

5 cups water
5 cups white or cider vinegar
2 Tb. mustard seed or mixed pickling spices
½ cup salt
1 clove garlic for each jar, if you like garlic

Pour the boiling pickle to within ¼ inch of the top of each jar. Distribute garlics; add a few fronds of dill to each jar if you like. Wipe rims of jars, and adjust lids and rings.

Set the jars in boiling water to cover, and boil 10 minutes. Lift them out and set to cool, 2 to 3 hours, out of any drafts. Remove the rings and test lids by pushing up lightly on the edge with your thumb to make sure they are sealed.

Dill pickles and dilly beans are at their best the following summer, with very cold beer, on a sweltering day during haying.

VEGETABLE PICKLES

When the garden is at its height, everything coming in at once, I generally make a huge batch of mixed vegetable pickles. You may use any one of these vegetables alone in this pickle; but I find the contrast of a good mixture makes all of them much more interesting. Even after a year they will all be crisp and tart, but not too sour or strong flavored. The mixture looks glorious and makes a good present for a friend. This makes 8 pints.

In a large crock, bowl, or plastic bucket, dissolve:

1 cup pickling salt (pure, not iodized)
1 gallon water

Chop into it:

1 cup small red or white radishes
2 cups small carrots cut into 1-inch sticks of ½-inch diameter
2 cups tiny gherkin cucumbers or larger cukes cut in slices or sticks
2 cups celery cut in 1½-inch sticks
2 cups small fresh green beans
2 green peppers, cut in small strips or diamonds
1 medium-sized cauliflower, cut in flowerets
2 cups pickling onions or onions cut in chunks
2 cups small green tomatoes, quartered

Set a plate over these and weight with a quart jar of water. Leave in brine overnight. Next day, drain off the brine. Heat in a big enameled or stainless-steel pot:

2 cups water
3 cups white vinegar
¼ cup mustard seed
2 Tb. whole coriander seeds
2 cups white sugar or 1 cup honey

Add the vegetables and simmer until they are hot, about 20 minutes; distribute in jars and pour over the pickle, leaving ½-inch head room; do not allow vegetables to protrude over the liquid. Adjust lids and screw down tops. Set in a draft-free place and do not disturb lids until jars have cooled completely—2 or 3 hours. Remove rings and cautiously try the lids with your thumb to make sure they are tight. If not, wipe lid and rim of jar, return lid and ring to bottle, and boil it, submerged in water, for 30 minutes, remove, cool, and try again. Or use a new lid, if you'd rather.

SWEET PICKLES

If you make these with pickling cucumbers, they will be tart-sweet and dense, like relish. But if you make them with ordinary table cukes, they will be light and tender and translucent, almost like watermelon pickles, beloved of children . . . makes 4 pints.

In a large crock or plastic pail, mix:

½ cup pickling salt
⅓ cup vinegar
15 moderate-sized cucumbers

water to cover

Place a dish over the cucumbers and weight it down with a quart jar full of water. This should stand for 10 days in a cool place; but you should check it every couple of days, removing any scum and pushing down pickles that bob up.

At the end of this time empty out the cucumbers and wash them in cold water. Now make up the pickle; in an enameled or stainless-steel pot mix:

4 cups white or cider vinegar
6 cups white sugar or 3 cups honey

Tie in a bit of cloth and suspend in this mixture:

3 sticks cinnamon
1 Tb. mixed pickling spices, without hot pepper
2 tsp. cloves

Bring the pickle to a boil and simmer it for a bit while you chop the cucumbers into 1-inch chunks and return them to the crock. When they're all in, pour over the boiling hot pickle. Cover and weight; let stand for 24 hours.

Every day for 4 or 5 days drain off the pickle, heat to boiling, and pour it over the cucumbers. When you are ready to bottle them, clean out your jars and pack them with cucumbers. Heat the pickle; pour it over, leaving ¼ inch head room. Wipe rims and adjust lids; screw on rings. Set the jars in boiling water to cover and boil for 10 minutes. Remove jars; let cool 2 or 3 hours in a draft-free place until jars are cool to touch. Remove rings and test lids with your thumb, lightly. These pickles will keep up to 2 years.

SECKEL PEAR OR CRABAPPLE PICKLES

These are to be served with a fatty meat, such as goose, duck, pork, or lamb. Choose very small fruit that is unblemished, and run a large needle through each piece to prevent it from bursting. This recipe is for 4 pints; you will need:

2 quarts crabapples or seckel pears (about 30 fruits)

In an enameled or stainless-steel pot, combine and cook:

3 cups water
1½ cups vinegar
3 cups sugar (for pears)
5 cups sugar (for crabapples)

Tie in a bit of cloth and cook along with the pickle:

1 piece ginger root, about 1 inch square
2 sticks cinnamon
1 tsp. whole cloves or allspice

When the sugar is dissolved, submerge 3 or 4 fruits in it and boil them until tender: 5 minutes for crab-apples, 15 for seckel pears. Remove them carefully with a slotted spoon and pack in jars. When all the fruit is cooked and packed, pour the boiling syrup over them in the jars, leaving ¼ inch head space. Wipe rims and adjust lids and rings. Set jars in boiling water to cover and boil 10 minutes. Remove jars and allow to cool—2 or 3 hours, or until cool to touch. Remove rings and test lids with light pressure. Store until needed in a cool dark cellar.

SAUERKRAUT

Sauerkraut is shredded, fermented cabbage. The only ingredients are cabbage and salt; the rest is up to the lactic acid, which sours it. If you have a storage place that stays at around 38° you can keep it in a crock; otherwise, can it.

Quarter, shred fine, and weigh: Measure into a bowl:

CABBAGE	2½ PERCENT PICKLING SALT
5 lbs.	3 Tb.
10 lbs.	6 Tb.
20 lbs.	½ cup

Pack some cabbage in the bottom of a large crock or plastic bucket and follow with a sprinkle of salt; continue to layer cabbage and salt up to the top, stopping now and then to press down the mixture with your hand. Cover with a plate and weight with a quart jar of water; lay a cloth over the top to keep out dirt and bugs. Set it some place that will stay at around 65°. Every day skim the scum off the top of the brine and wash the plate. If the brine does not cover the cabbage, add a little more made of 2 tsp. pickling salt to 1 pint cold water.

For about 2 weeks, bubbles will rise to the top as it ferments. When they stop, wash the plate again, set it back on top, and cover the crock with a tight lid. Store at 38°, or bottle it.

If the cabbage should turn dark or slimy, it is probably being kept at too high a temperature; this can happen either during fermentation or storage. Throw it out and start over.

OTHER SOURED VEGETABLES

You can use turnips, radishes, Chinese cabbage. Shred or grate them, weigh, and proceed as above.

SPICING SAUERKRAUT

To 5 pounds of vegetables you could add 1 tablespoon caraway or dill seeds, a couple of bay leaves, mustard or pepper or coriander seeds, a couple of sliced onions, or some blanched garlic cloves.

CANNING SAUERKRAUT

Pack hot sauerkraut into canning jars, leaving ½ inch head room. Cover to top of sauerkraut with juice or brine made of: 2 Tb. salt to 1 qt. water.
Adjust caps. Process in boiling water 30 minutes.

USING SAUERKRAUT

Sauerkraut may be served cold, in salad, mixed with sprouts, and other vegetables; but you should first bring it to a boil and cook it with the lid off for 20 minutes, then cool.

Traditionally, however, it is served hot, with a buttery sausage such as boiled knockwurst, or with fat meats such as pork, ham, goose, or duck. It can be cooked alone or garnished with dill, caraway, bay leaf, onions, or garlic. An old Pennsylvania way of serving it is to drain off the liquid and replace it with beer; cook 20 minutes.

TUTTI FRUTTI

Ever since my father started growing Dwarf peach trees, my mother has been faced, every few years, with a couple of bushels of peaches to be dealt with (at once). She discovered, and I heartily recommend to anyone who can afford the brandy, this amazing stuff:
Mix equal parts:
brandy and sweet, ginger-flavored dandelion wine
sugar, if you like
Submerge sliced peaches as they ripen, holding them down with a dinner plate in a stone crock in a cool place (weight the plate with a jar of cold water and cover the crock). Add fruit as it comes along and liquor as needed. You may use, in addition to,'or instead of, peaches:
raspberries
strawberries
cherries
halved sweet pears

KEEPING BIBLIOGRAPHY

Freezing
For a more detailed look at all aspects of freezing,

The Complete Book of Home Freezing, by Hazel Meyer (Philadelphia: Lippincott). Hazel's very thorough; she's tried everything (twice); and she tells you what worked and what failed.

Canning
The best and most thorough book on canning is a 50¢ pamphlet called the *Ball Blue Book*, published by the Ball Brothers Co. of Muncie, Indiana. This pamphlet is packed with advice, photos, and quite a lot of really interesting recipes as well as the standard ones.

Root Cellaring, Drying
The best advice I've read so far on root cellaring and drying is an all-purpose book about the keeping of foods called *Putting Food By*, by Ruth Hertzberg, Beatrice Vaughan, and Janet Greene (Brattleboro, Vt.: Stephen Green Press). This book has sections on freezing, canning, and smoking foods as well, and is a pretty good reference guide for any farmhouse.

FREEZING

A freezer is a very useful tool. You can freeze almost any kind of food, and, if it is properly packaged, to keep air out and moisture in, freezing virtually eliminates the possibility of spoilage. The sections on freezing that follow are:

Grains and Nuts	Vegetables
Fruits	Cooked Foods
Meats and Poultry	Baked Goods
Fish and Shellfish	Eggs and Dairy Foods

POWER: Freezers require electricity. Consequently, many people who would actually rather live without being plugged in to the Great American Power Scene find themselves living with wires and poles and nuclear reactors and All the Modern Conveniences. Or, sometimes, they decide not to buy that nice old farm back in the hills, because they could never install a freezer.

Our solution has been to keep the freezer at a friend's house and kick in something for the electric bill. When I want a bunch of broccoli or a pound of venison, I go visiting instead of trek to the Superama. Another possibility in some towns is the commercial freezer locker, in which you can rent space by the month or the year.

FREEZERS: There all kinds of freezers. Look around before you buy one. First of all, make sure it's large enough. You just look in there and figure out for yourself how much will fit; don't take anybody's word for it. Think ahead. Are you planting a garden? How about buying a side of meat? Or, say, a case of broccoli in season, to last all year?

You may be able to get a freezer secondhand. The world is filled with people who bought the wrong size, or are moving next month, or are getting on in the years and can't take the freezer to that condominium flat in town. Ask around for a month or two, maybe tune in to your local radio's early morning Swap Shop. There are stand-up freezers and chest-type freezers. Both are good.

A freezer, any freezer, works best if it is kept in a room where the temperature is between 50 and 60°. For some inscrutable reason known only to manufacturers, they do not work as efficiently in

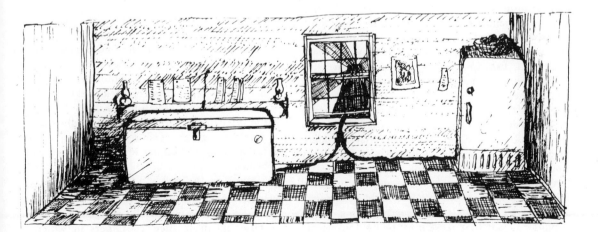

very cold places (like outdoors, or in a subzero out-building). They should not be subjected to damp-ness (they will rust); and they should be placed well away from the wall so you can clean away lint, which is a fire hazard, around the motor.

Maintaining a Freezer: Periodically, a freezer has to be defrosted and cleaned. Most people do it once a year, in June, when the freezer is at its emptiest.

Unplug the freezer, first of all, and move all the food into the fridge, which you can set at the low-est setting. You can hasten the defrosting with pans of hot water, but these must not come into direct contact with the freezer walls or sides, so use racks or inverted pans to put the hot water containers on. You may scrape away at the ice with a dull knife, being careful not to chip the surface which, in some models, is surprisingly fragile.

When all the ice and water is cleaned out, wipe the entire inner surface with a solution of baking soda and warm water (*don't* use soaps—imagine, briefly, bleach-flavored peas). Be sure the entire freezer is bone dry before you start it up again. Run it empty for a couple of hours before returning the goods.

Power Failures: If the power goes off, *don't open the freezer*. The temperature will stay constant for at least 24 hours. After that it varies; the larger (and fuller) your freezer is, the colder it will stay.

When the power is restored, check the contents at once. Partly thawed and then refrozen foods will be tougher and less flavorful, even if they aren't a total loss. Completely thawed foods must be used at once, except for high-acid fruits (for ex-ample, applesauce) or baked goods, such as bread, cake, biscuits. You should be particularly fussy about the things which have a short lifespan in the freezer anyway, such as fish, shellfish, and organ meats; use them right up. As long as they stay hard, meats will probably be okay, but you must not, on any account, refreeze completely thawed meats, poultry, or fish. The bacteria which were arrested in freezing commence their activities at a terrific rate as they thaw; in 24 hours at 70°, a thawed steak was found to have over a million bacteria in it. You might, I suppose, control the population explosion by cooking and refreezing thawed meats. They won't be gourmet items, but at least they would be safe to eat.

After a power failure in which some of your stored foods were partly thawed, you should go through and mark all the labels with a red marking pen to remind yourself that these must be used up within the month. (A curt and furious slash will do.)

The Freezing of Food: The most important thing about keeping frozen foods is the maintenance of a constant temperature of 0 to 5° F.

The second most important thing is the freshness (and youth) of the food you put in the freezer. Fish, shellfish, and vegetables must be absolutely fresh. Fruits are less perishable. For meats, see the particular type, below.

The third factor is the packaging, if you are planning to keep the food longer than a few weeks. Special freezer wrap is necessary to exclude air and keep in moisture, and the food must be wrapped tightly and sealed carefully.

Freezer Wraps and Materials: Over the years you will accumulate a lot of freezing materials, but if you are starting from scratch, be prepared to shell out a few bucks. Freezing materials aren't cheap. However there is some consolation in the fact that you can reuse plastic bags and containers, year after year.

What to Use

1. For evenly shaped meats, such as roasts and steaks, for butter, cheese, and so forth, you may use coated or laminated freezer paper. These are marked as such and available in hard-ware stores, grain stores, and sometimes super-markets or discount stores.

   Freezer paper is only good for foods with a firm, geometric shape, which you can package tightly with a stiff wrap. Freezing paper should be sealed with freezer tape, a special tape which will adhere even at very low temperatures.

2. For odd-shaped meats, poultry, fish, and so forth, you should use a flexible freezer wrap such as thermoplastic or heavy freezer-weight aluminum foil.

3. For almost anything, particularly fruits and vegetables, plastic freezing bags are the greatest. Because they are so strong, moreover, you can use them year after year. They come in all sizes, even big enough for a 15-pound turkey. Some fruits and vegetables (or meats, such as liver) are of a nature that will freeze in a solid brick if the filled bag is placed in a small cardboard box; then the bag can be removed and the box reused for packing something looser, such as peas or beans.

4. For liquids, purées, and foods packed in liquid (such as shellfish) the best thing is plastic con-tainers. As long as the lid fits tightly, you can reuse all those nice containers in which ice

cream, yogurt, etc., are packed; but be careful not to use any with cracked or split lids. The best ones, of course, are specially made for freezing; they last longest and are square, saving space and stacking neatly.

You can also use glass jars, but be careful to use only jars which have a wide mouth. If you are being professional, Ball Mason Jar Company makes a special freezer jar. Be particularly careful when freezing in glass to leave ½ inch per pint and 1 inch per quart head room as frozen liquid expands.

You can use old coffee cans, but they should be lined with plastic bags, partly because the lids don't really seal out air and partly because the flavor of coffee somehow stays in those cans forever.

FREEZING GRAINS AND NUTS

As long as the protective husk or shell of a grain or nut is left intact, there is no need to freeze grains, seeds, or nuts. Once you crack the shells or grind them, however, you are faced with a storage problem. After two weeks at 60 or 70°, such foods as wheat germ, nuts, seeds and whole grain cereals and flours lose their flavor. After a month they may begin to go rancid.

Fortunately for those who prefer to buy flour preground and nuts without shells, they may be kept very easily in the freezer. Just be sure you pack them tightly in air-proof freezer bags, with an outer plastic or paper bag to prevent breakage of the inner bag. Just open the bag and take out what you need as you need it; no defrosting is necessary. They will keep for a year, perhaps more.

FREEZING FRUITS

Fruits are very easy to freeze, and keep very well in the freezer. Fruits that have been frozen are very good in all kinds of cooking and baking. To eat them raw, do not allow them to completely thaw; eat frozen or half-frozen.

You will find that in general I try to use as little sugar of any kind as possible, and much less than in other freezing instructions, which, for some unknown reason, will have you using mountains of it. We eat raw fruit without sugar; why add so much to frozen fruits? If you always add only as much as your taste dictates, you will soon find yourself using much less. And some fruits (such as blueberries or peaches) just don't need any at all.

If you are going to add sugar or honey anyway

when you thaw and cook the fruit, then you might as well add it before freezing, because sugars do help to preserve things. Just don't add any more than you need to. Don't overlook the possibilities of combining sweet and tart fruits, too, such as cranberry-orange relish, or blueberry-apple pie.

PREPARATIONS FOR FREEZING FRUITS

1. Washing: If your fruit comes from commercial growers, chances are it has been sprayed for various diseases, fungi, or insects; better wash it under cold running water. If you grew it or picked it wild, though, there's no need to wash it unless it's dirty.

2. Slicing and Ascorbic Acid: As soon as you slice into most fruits, the vitamin C in them begins to oxidize and turn into tannin. There's nothing "bad" about brown fruit, but it does have less vitamin C, and it doesn't look as pretty. The best way to prevent this is to slice it directly into a mixture of:

1 tsp. ascorbic acid to 1 cup cold water

Ascorbic acid is just pure vitamin C. As far as I know there's nothing wrong with it, nutritionally speaking, but if you prefer you can use:

2 tsp. citric acid to 1 cup cold water

Or if you really prefer to be very organic and don't mind the lemon flavor you can use:

1 Tb. lemon juice to 1 cup cold water

APPLES: Apples turn brown when sliced into, so if you wish to retain the light color and vitamin C in them, slice them into ascorbic acid, citric acid, or lemon juice solution (see above).

1. Unsweetened Dry Pack: For use in pies, cobblers, other baking. Choose firm, tart apples. Slice around the core, leaving skins on, into acid-water solution. Dry with paper or a towel; pack in plastic bags.

2. Syrup Pack: For use in pies, cobblers, other baking, dessert topping. Choose firm, tart apples. Make up a syrup by heating together until well mixed:

4 cups water

2 cups sugar or 1 cup honey

Cool and add:

4 tsp. ascorbic acid, 2½ Tb. citric acid, or juice of 1 lemon

Slice apples directly into this mixture, tossing after each apple. When you have enough to fill a plastic container, pack apples in and cover with syrup. To keep apples submerged, wad cellophane or plastic under the lid. Leave 1 inch per quart air space to allow for expansion of liquid when frozen.

239

3. *Applesauce*: Choose sweet apples; if bland, add a tart one for every 10 sweet apples to insure flavor. Quarter or slice whole apples (peel, core, and all) into:

2 cups water
2 tsp. ascorbic acid, 1 Tb. citric acid, or 2 Tb. lemon juice (optional)

Toss apples as you add them to coat them with liquid, and remove them into a large enamel or stainless steel pot from time to time. When you have a potful, set on a tight lid and add 1 cup of the liquid; bring rapidly to a boil and cook apples until quite soft, ½ to 1 hour. Put through a food mill. Add water if needed; add sugar or honey if needed, but leave out spices. Cool and pack in plastic or coated cardboard containers (you can use milk cartons); leave 1 inch per quart to allow for expansion. If you're short on stiff containers, line them with plastic bags; fill them, freeze until solid, remove bag of applesauce, and reuse containers.

4. *Cider*: Homemade, or unpasteurized, unpreserved cider may be frozen as any juice, but commercial ciders usually have preservative chemicals in them that sour in freezing.

BANANAS: Bananas discolor and lose much flavor when frozen, but they can be kept, mashed, for use in banana bread (who cares what color they turn). Mash and freeze in small containers, or, if pints are the smallest containers you have, mash and pack in small plastic bags in pint containers (two bananas are enough for a banana bread).

SOFT BERRIES: By which is meant, blackberries, boysenberries, raspberries, and the like. Any berries such as this, which are seedy when raw, are going to be twice as seedy after freezing. Moreover, the texture of the berry is utterly destroyed when it thaws. Pick over berries before freezing.

1. For use in syrups, sauce, ice cream, baking, heat together:

   1 cup water or berry juice
   ½ cup sugar or ¼ cup honey

   Submerge fruit in cooled syrup in pint-sized plastic containers.

2. For use as separate fruit—as a garnish in whipped frozen desserts, ice creams, or Bavarian Yogurt Cream. Scatter berries on a cookie sheet and freeze; when hard, pack together in plastic bags or plastic containers.

HARD BERRIES: By which is meant blueberries, huckleberries, elderberries, Saskatoon, or serviceberries. These can be bagged just as they are; you don't even have to pick over them if you don't have time. Frozen raw blueberries are an exceptionally wonderful thing to have on hand; they are excellent on cold or hot cereal, yogurt, or custard-type desserts; you can throw a handful in a cake or muffin or pancake batter, or just hand them out to instantly quiet even the most aggravated child . . .

BERRIES, TART: Such as gooseberries, cranberries, currants. More than likely, you are going to be mixing these with sugar or some other sweetening, so you might as well mix them before freezing, 1 cup to the quart. Or you may pack them in a sweet syrup of 2 cups sugar cooked with 4 cups water (and cooled). In the case of cranberries, though, you should try packing some chopped together with an equal quantity of chopped oranges (skin, pits, and all). This makes a very excellent relish for fatty meats such as pork, moose, duck, or goose—as well as the traditional turkey.

Never use coated cardboard containers for packing these berries in wet form, as their extreme acidity sometimes prevents them from completely freezing and the container won't last forever.

CHERRIES, TART: Pie cherries come ripe but once a year, and they are among the most rewarding things to have in the freezer. Before setting down to the laborious business of pitting them, you may firm them up by soaking them for an hour in ice water.

For Pies, Baking: Pack raw, dry, and pitted, or rolled in ½ cup sugar to 2 cups cherries.

For Dessert Toppings: Mix and heat 1 cup sugar to 4 cups water until sugar dissolves; cool. Pack cherries in plastic (never coated cardboard) containers; cover with syrup, leaving ½ inch head room per pint for expansion.

GRAPEFRUITS, ORANGES, AND LEMONS: Use half the fruit to make juice. Cut the other half in sections, removing rind but leaving on the white which is an important nutritional part of citrus fruits. Pack fruits in juice, leaving ½ inch head space per pint for expansion. Use plastic containers only. To use in fruit cocktails or served raw, these are best if they are eaten half-thawed, with ice crystals still in them.

PEACHES: Peaches are among the fruits which

oxidize, or turn brown, most rapidly. There are two separate and distinct methods for dealing with peaches, depending on whether you like peaches (yellow) or peaches (brown). Needless to say, it takes at least twice as long to freeze peaches (yellow). I am a personal fan of peaches (brown), but I will take them (any way I can get them) in Nova Scotia.

Peaches (Brown): If you want to skin them, immerse them in boiling water for 1 minute (using a wire basket for speed and convenience). Peel quickly, slice and pit, and pop into a light syrup or plain water to cover. Freeze packed in liquid in waterproof plastic containers.

Peaches (Yellow): Before cutting into the peaches, fill a large container with two quarts of ice water and add 1 Tb. ascorbic-citric acid. Also prepare sugar or honey syrup: 2 cups honey or 3 cups sugar to 4 cups hot water; stir and cook until mixed, then cool. Have ready your pint- or quart-sized plastic freezing containers, each about a third full of syrup. Ready? Peel a peach, under cold running water. Slice or halve it directly into the water-acid bath. Before starting on your next peach, put a plate on top of the water bath to keep the peaches from floating. When you have enough peaches to fill a container sliced up, pack them in, cover with syrup, and crumple a piece of plastic or cellophane in the top to completely submerge them. Seal, and freeze. On to the next.

Defrost peaches (yellow) in the refrigerator until almost, but not quite, completely thawed. Serve still frosty, or use in cooking immediately, to prevent browning.

Whew.

PEARS: The oxidation or browning which in other fruits is mostly a matter of looks is, in pears, a more vital matter, affecting the delicate flavor and texture as well as the color. You should pack them as you would Peaches (yellow) above.

PLUMS: Soak plums in ice water to firm them before gently pitting them. Pack whole, in plastic bags. If you wish to serve them peeled, drop whole frozen plums in ice water and they will peel easily within a few seconds.

For mashed plums, run them through the food mill and add ½ tsp. ascorbic acid per quart; stir well and pack in rigid containers, leaving ½ inch per pint head room.

RHUBARB: Imagine my delight to discover that the freezing process somehow changes the chemistry of rhubarb so that it requires less sugar to sweeten a pie than one ordinarily needs!

For Pies: Pack raw, sliced in 2-inch chunks, and bagged.

For Desserts: Cook and sweeten with sugar or honey as you would for the table. Pack in pint or quart containers (plastic only) leaving ½ to 1 inch head room.

STRAWBERRIES: I have never met anybody who wouldn't rather eat strawberries as strawberries than as mush or syrupy sauce or whatever. So I think the best way to freeze them is whole and unadulterated. To avoid having them freeze all in a mess, spread them thinly on a baking tin and quick-freeze until solid; then package them together. To serve, do not allow them to thaw completely! For use in ice cream, of course, they thaw somewhat before freezing again.

FREEZING MEATS AND POULTRY

HANGING, CHILLING, AND SUBDIVIDING: Before freezing, freshly butchered beef is ordinarily hung, to age, refrigerated, for 12 or more days. If you buy your beef ready cut, you may assume that it has been hung and is ready to freeze, after 24 hours of chilling.

Pork, lamb, venison, moose, bear, and veal, however, are usually frozen within 1 to 3 days after killing, and need only be chilled for 24 hours before freezing.

Rabbit, squirrel, and other small game are chilled 24 hours.

Poultry is frozen after 24 hours of chilling; but game birds, such as partridge, are hung for 3 days, in a cool place.

If you are planning to buy sides of meat, ready butchered but cut up to your specifications, you will do well to sit down for an hour with a diagram and figure out just how you want the meat cut up; make a few notes, or take the diagram with you. Some cuts have different names in different localities. In any case, butchers are notoriously fast with the knife, and in seconds your Christmas roast will lie in slices if you don't know when to speak up. Have your meat cut (or cut it yourself) to the size you need, and no larger; you have no idea, unless you've tried to cut it, how hard frozen meat really is.

PACKAGING: Meat must be wrapped up very carefully to keep it from drying out or going rancid in the freezer. These are two separate and distinct problems that should be taken very seriously.

Drying Out or Dehydration: Sometimes referred to as "freezer burns," occurs fairly quickly if the meat is unwrapped; if wrapped in plain butcher paper, it will take up to three weeks. The result is a dry, gray, tasteless flesh that even your dog won't want, unless he's a teething puppy with a taste for old leather. To prevent this, you must surround the meat as closely as possible with a moisture-proof material, and seal it.

Rancidity: Caused by oxygen in your freezer combining with fat cells in your meat, causing the fat to change to highly unpalatable fatty acids. The more fatty the meat (such as pork, salmon, duck, etc.) the more likely this is to happen; hence fatty meats have a shorter maximum storage length in the freezer. You must be sure to seal the meat in a kind of wrap that does not let air through. Ordinary sandwich wrap, aluminum foil, and butcher paper are too porous.

To wrap ordinary, geometric-shaped cuts of meat (such as roasts), fold freezer paper closely around it as illustrated:

Odd-Shaped Pieces: Such as poultry or standing rib roast, which have bones protruding, must be packaged with extra care to keep the wrap from tearing when they are moved around by somebody hastily hunting for the ice cream. You can ball up plastic or waxed paper around the sharp bone ends within the package. Wrap them in something flexible, freezerweight pliofilm or aluminum foil. Birds go well in big freezer bags; to seal them closely, dip them in a bath of cold water and twist the end before sealing with a wire twisty. To be absolutely proofed against breakage, encase the bird or rib section in a net bag, stockinet, or an old sock.

Hamburgers, Steaks, Chops, Etc.: May be packaged accordian style between two layers of freezer wrap so that you can take out just what you need, when you need it.

Bones: If you are short on freezer space, you should consider boning your meats, tying the roasts into rounds. These and other bones may be used to make soup stocks, which you can freeze in pint- or quart-sized plastic containers. This stuff is very useful for gravies and sauces as well as soups. Be sure to leave an inch or so of expansion space at the top of the containers.

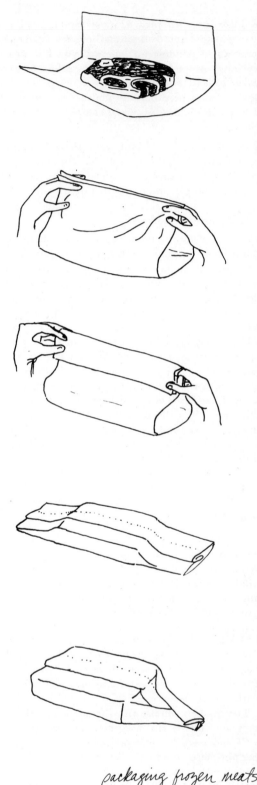

packaging frozen meats

COOKING FROZEN MEATS AND POULTRY: There is no question that it's best to thaw meat slowly and completely before cooking it. It takes hours and hours; large roasts even take days, but it is still best, for maximum tenderness, flavor, and nutrition. Nevertheless, there are times when even the most foresighted and conscientious of cooks may suddenly be faced with the necessity of cooking frozen meats.

You can cook beef, pork, veal, and lamb frozen. (You can't, really, cook poultry, or variety meats; they must be thawed.) To cook solidly frozen meat, use low temperatures and cook it longer than usual. How much longer depends on the size, thickness, and type of meat. For example, a frozen beef pot roast should be cooked twice as long; this means 50 minutes to the pound instead of 25. A frozen beef steak, rare, would be cooked 1¼ times as long as if it were fresh or completely thawed. The tenderer, thinner, and smaller the piece, the quicker it will thaw and cook through. The following list may help you estimate how much longer to cook frozen meats:

FROZEN BEEF:	TIME	TEMP.
Rare roasts:	x 1¾	300°
Medium roasts:	x almost 2	300°
Well-done roasts:	x 2	300°
Pot roast:	x 2	300°
Stew:	x 1½	300°
Rare steak:	x 1¼	slow broil
Medium steak:	x 1½	slow broil
Hamburgers:	x 1¼ to 1½	slow broil

FROZEN VEAL:	TIME	TEMP.
Roast leg:	x 2	300°
Roast loin:	x almost 2	300°
Roast shoulder:	x 1¼ to 1½	300°
Breast:	x 1¼	300°
Chops:	x 1½	slow broil

FROZEN LAMB:		
Roast leg:	x 1¼	300°
Roast shoulder:	x 1¼	300°
Chops:	x 1¼	slow broil
Stew:	x 1½	slow simmer
Patties:	x 1¼	slow broil

FROZEN PORK:		
Fresh ham:	x 1¾	300°
Fresh butt:	x 1¼	300°
Fresh shoulder:	x 1¼	300°
Loin roast, tender:	x 1¼	300°
End loin:	x 1½	300°
Chops:	x 1¼	slow broil
Spareribs:	x 1¼	slow broil or 300°
Smoked ham:	x 1¾	300°
Smoked shoulder:	x 1¼	300°
Smoked ham steaks:	x 1¼	slow panbroil

These statistics are more or less gleaned from the recommendations of the National Live Stock and Meat Board, so they don't give any lists for game. I should imagine that venison and moose would be about the same as beef, and that rabbit and other small game should, like poultry, be thawed first.

If by chance your reason for cooking unthawed meat is that you are returning to a cold house and cold wood stove, you can put that frozen meat in the cold oven as you light the stove. The slow rise in temperature will help thaw it a bit and you'll be that much ahead of the game and closer to your meal.

THAWING FROZEN MEATS: The more slowly meat defrosts, the tenderer and juicier it will be. Thus, the best way to defrost it is in a refrigerator, wrapped in its freezer wrapping. The larger (and tougher) the piece, the longer it will take to defrost. Plan ahead, when you decide to use meat from the freezer, basing your calculations on the following guide:

Large roasts (beef rib or rump, leg of lamb or
   pork): 7-10 hrs. per lb.
Small roasts (veal, lamb shoulder, etc.): 6-9 hrs.
   per lb.
Steaks, chops, sliced liver, kidneys: 6-8 hrs.
Stewing meat: 10-12 hrs.
1 lb. packet of ground meat: 10 hrs.
Hamburger or sausage patties: 4-6 hrs.
½ lb. of fatback or bacon: 1-2 hrs.

If you feel confident about the tenderness of your meat, you may defrost it (in its original wrap) at room temperature, and cut the time in half.

Poultry have such a tendency to dry out when thawed at room temperature that I really cannot recommend it. They should always be thawed in their wrappings, in the refrigerator, for the following periods of time:

Whole birds (depending on size): 6-8 hrs. per lb.
Split broilers: 3 hrs. per lb.
Pieces: 2 hrs. per lb.

All thawed meats, poultry, and fish should be cooked within a few hours of becoming thawed, since otherwise the enzymes, bacteria, and yeasts that were arrested by freezing will suddenly start to multiply like mad (as in a spring thaw) and the meat will spoil rapidly. This is particularly true of fish and shellfish; but you should also keep an eye on poultry and ground meat.

FREEZING COOKED MEAT: You can freeze all types of cooked meat and poultry, but only certain ones come out well. (It's crazy to freeze cooked fish, I think, since fish takes so little time to cook anyway.) The dishes that freeze best, and make the most sense to freeze, are stews and casseroles. You can also freeze cooked roasts; it is best to put them in whole, and slice after they thaw, so that less flesh is exposed to the air. You may also freeze whole cooked birds, unstuffed, or in large pieces. Be sure to wrap these tightly in clingy type freezer wrap or foil, and again in paper.

FREEZING FISH AND SHELLFISH

All seafood is extremely perishable—before, during, and after freezing. It freezes well, but you must take special care to keep it from going bad.

First of all, be sure your fish (or shellfish) is fresh (see page 209, about fish). If you are dealing with a bought fish, make sure it hasn't been frozen already: see if it'll float. A thawed one won't.

Behead the fish just above the shoulder bones around the gills, leaving those large bones in to give it structure. Leave the tails on, for the same reason.

SMALL FISH: Very small fish, such as smelt or 9-inch trout, are best frozen whole, uncleaned, in liquid—either water or fish broth. Pack them in a suitable plastic container or a bag-lined coffee can; chill overnight, making sure they are completely covered by liquid, and freeze the next day.

MEDIUM-SIZED FISH: Ordinary sized fish, around 9 to 15 inches, may be frozen whole, cleaned, well wrapped in foil or clingy freezer wrap, and again in butcher paper. Be very careful to seal fish packages by folding the edges of the inner wrap together. The outer wrap is important, as it keeps the inner wrap from breaking (frozen fish tails are sharp!). Or a medium-sized fish may be filleted (see page 210).

LARGE FISH: It is easiest, in the long run, to cut large fish into fish steaks and wrap them stacked, as you would hamburgers (see next page). However, once in a long while you might want to go to the trouble to save a large fish whole, for a mob feast. The best way to do that is to put the whole fish in the freezer, unwrapped, and freeze it solid for 24 hours. If you have a special quick-freeze compartment, do it in there; if not, lay it up against the coldest wall of the freezer. When it is hard through, take it out and dip it in water; refreeze until the glaze is hard, redip, refreeze, and so on, until you have built up about ¼ inch of ice on the fish. No other wrapping is needed; but you should renew the dip every 3 weeks or so.

LOBSTER AND CRAB: Lobster and crab are best cooked whole, chilled 24 hours, wrapped double and frozen. In addition to conserving the internal moisture the double wrap will help keep your freezer from smelling like a fish market.

SHRIMP: Behead shrimp, but leave in the vein (which is small, and inoffensive); chill, wrap well, and overwrap, or freeze in liquid.

MOLLUSKS (CLAMS, OYSTERS, MUSSELS): The only mollusk you can be sure of being fresh is a live mollusk, which means it is tightly closed. You can steam them open and freeze them in the steaming liquid, to keep for only 2 or 3 months; or pry them open (see page 213) and freeze in their own liquid, for up to 10 months.

FAT FISH FREEZING WITH ASCORBIC ACID: Those fish that have a high percentage of fat are more perishable, even in the freezer, than lean fish. You must be extra careful to seal air out of their packages in order to keep the fat from becoming rancid. Even so, they sometimes spoil; but you can combat this tendency by treating them first with a solution of 1 teaspoon ascorbic acid to 1 pint cold water. Just dip in the fish, for 30 seconds, then drain, wrap, seal and overwrap.

THAWING: Fish and shellfish become dry and tough when cooked frozen. They should be thawed in their wrappers, in a refrigerator or at about 350°.
Large whole fish: 8–10 hrs. per lb.
Fillets, halves, steaks, or small fish: 4–6 hrs. per lb.
Fish or shellfish in pints of liquid: 12 hrs.
Fish or shellfish in quarts of liquid: 18 hrs.

1.

2.

3.

4. HAMBURGERS

FISH STEAKS

MAXIMUM STORAGE TIMES FOR MEATS, POULTRY, AND FISH: The amount of time you may keep a given piece of meat in your freezer varies, according to the type of meat, how large it is, and how cold your freezer is. Lean meats keep longer than fatty meats because there is less fat to oxidize. Large pieces keep longer than small pieces because less surface is exposed.

Here is a list of the maximum storage times for certain cuts of meat. Remember, too, that many states have maximum legal storage times for game meats, and some require licenses for you to keep them frozen.

MONTHS AT 0°

Beef and Venison:	
Roasts, steaks	14
Stewing size pieces	12
Ground meat, oxtails	8
Liver, heart, tongue, kidneys	4
Brains, tripe	1
Veal:	
Roasts, chops, steaks	12
Thin cutlets, cubes	10
Ground meat	6
Liver, heart	3
Tongue	4
Sweetbreads	1
Pork (fresh), Moose, Elk:	
Roasts, chops, steaks	12
Cubes	6
Ground	4
Ground and seasoned	2
Liver, heart	2
Tongue	4
Sweetbreads	1
Pork (cured):	
Ham and shoulder	6
Bacon, small pieces	3
Lamb:	
Roasts, chops	14
Cubes, thin cuts	12
Ground meat	8
Liver, heart, tongue	4
Kidneys	3
Sweetbreads	1
Chicken, Turkey, Duck, Goose, Game Birds:	
Whole	12
Halved or cut up	10
Sliced or boned	6
Livers	4
Fish, Shellfish:	
Lean whole fish*	12
Lean fillets*	8
Fat whole fish*	8
Fat fillets*	6
Cooked shrimp, lobster	3
Shellfish in liquid	10

*For list of lean and fat fish, see page 210.

FREEZING VEGETABLES

Freezing vegetables is not quite as simple as freezing meats, fruits, and grains, because you don't freeze them raw. They must be blanched first, to destroy enzymes which will otherwise wipe out most of their vitamin content and toughen them slightly. Vegetables frozen raw look the same, and some of them taste the same; but their food value and texture are radically different.

There are two ways to blanch: in boiling water or in steam. Since the vitamin you are most commonly trying to preserve is vitamin C, and since vitamin C is water-soluble, I usually stick to steam. The one exception is with greens (such as chard, spinach, pigweed, kale, collard, mustard and turnip greens). The nature of the leaves makes it hard for the steam to surround each leaf.

Boiling is easier than steaming. If you'd rather boil everything, subtract one minute from the time given below for steaming each type of vegetable.

After blanching, the vegetables must immediately be chilled, to halt the cooking. This is done in very cold water or ice water. Then they are quickly dried and packaged.

WHAT YOU WILL NEED:

A Steamer: Mail order houses, and sometimes supermarkets, sell something called a "spaghetti cooker" which is inexpensive and ideal: a deep, enameled pot with an inner enameled fitting which is full of holes, like a sieve—and a lid. Or, you can use an expandable steamer in a pressure cooker or cast iron pot; or a wire mesh basket in a pot tall enough to accommodate it with a lid on. Whatever your arrangement, you should allow for plenty of water to get very hot: 6 quarts or more, at 212°. Do not be deceived by great clouds of water vapor arising out of the depths of your pot. Steam is not water vapor, nor is it visible. Make sure the water is boiling rapidly and steadily.

Cold Water: Cold well water will do, but you have to keep changing it. Better is ice water; best of all is ice water in an insulated picnic bucket large enough to hold a wire mesh basket. Of course, if you have a freezer, you can freeze lots of ice, in bread tins, pots, whatever. Add about 1 Tb. salt per gallon to the water.

Towels: You'll need a good supply of clean absorbent dishtowels, or a roll of towel paper, or just newspaper, to dry the vegetables thoroughly before freezing.

Bags: Oh go on, splurge, freezer bags are good for a couple of years and, unlike the ones you've been hoarding, they aren't full of holes. You'll also need some twisty wire things, or rubber bands.

THE PROCESS: All set? Put the vegetables, chopped into uniform pieces, into the steamer (no more than a pound or two at a time); steam 2 to 5 minutes, depending on the type (see below); pull them out, dump into a wire basket, and immerse immediately in ice water. Move them around with your hands for 1 minute or until they feel cold. Then pull them out and spread on towels or paper. As soon as they are relatively dry, bag them. Immerse the bag in ice water up to the neck to expel all the air in there. Tie it up tight; (stick it in a box, if you're using boxes) and on to the next.

HOW LONG WILL THEY LAST? Blanched frozen vegetables will keep for a year, at the most. Unblanched, give them 2 months, maximum. Partly thawed and refrozen vegetables should be eaten within a month.

Note: to blanch in boiling water bath, add 1 minute to time given for steam.

Asparagus: Asparagus freezes well; short fat tips are the most tender. Chop into 2- to 4-inch lengths; sort tips and stalks for separate steaming. Save woody bases for soup stock. Steam tips: 3 minutes. Steam stems: 5 minutes. Cool in ice water 3 minutes.

Lima Beans: Green lima beans freeze well; white ones are starchy. Shell beans and pick over them. Steam baby limas: 2 minutes. Steam large limas: 3 minutes. Cool 1 minute.

Green or Yellow Beans: Pick fresh and freeze immediately; old beans will become tough. Nip off tops. Freeze small beans whole, chop or french-cut large ones with a diagonal cut. Label as such. Steam small new beans: 3 minutes. Steam chopped beans: 3 minutes. Steam frenched beans: 2 minutes. Chill in ice water 3 minutes, or until quite cold.

Beets: Beets store very well in a root cellar (see page 218) and become rubbery when frozen, hence I don't recommend freezing them.

Beet Greens: See Greens, below.

Broccoli: Use dark green parts only. Split large heads, use small flowerets whole. Check carefully

three ways to fill plastic bags easily

for worms if you suspect their presence. Steam flowerets: 3 minutes. Steam halved heads: 5 minutes. Steam sliced stalks: 7 minutes. Chill in ice water 2 minutes, or until cold. Excellent.

Brussels Sprouts: Use dark green parts only. Brussels sprouts freeze well. Sort and steam separately. Large heads: 6 minutes. Small heads: 3 minutes. Cool 5 minutes in ice water. Excellent.

Cabbage: Cabbage isn't terrific frozen, but it can be done. Chop fine, grate, or freeze in wedges. Steam shredded: 2½ minutes. Chopped: 3 minutes. Wedges: 4 minutes. Chill shredded or chopped cabbage 1 minute, wedges 3 minutes.

Carrots: Leave small carrots whole, chop larger ones or slice into fingers. Package some in small bags for use in soups, stews. They're okay, nothing special, but very good for you. Steam whole: 5½ minutes. Steam fingers: 5 minutes. Steam sliced or diced: 4 minutes. Chill whole carrots 3 minutes; fingers and sliced or diced, 1 minute.

Cauliflower: Divide into uniform-sized flowerets; inspect carefully for worms, to whom cauliflower is a sort of hotel. Steam flowerets: 5 minutes. Chill 3 or 4 minutes, or until cold. Excellent.

Celery: Not, alas, to be used raw; but celery may

be frozen for use in stir-fry, stews and soups, or as braised celery. String it if it needs it; cut into 1-inch lengths. Steam: 4 minutes. Chill 1 minute in ice water.

Chard: See Greens, below.

Corn on de Cob: Hoo boy. Now you know why you got the freezer. However, to get tender corn in January, you must either pick your own or buy it off the stalk; the sugar turns to starch within a few hours, and the sweetness to tastelessness. Pick only young ears with pale yellow kernels.

Corn really hasn't much in the way of vitamins, so I blanch by boiling, and soak it a good long time. It isn't vitamins I'm after. It's corn on the cob.

Pick and husk, and plunge into boiling water: Medium ears: 5 minutes. Small ears: 4 minutes. Cool 15 minutes in ice water. Wrap each ear in its own bag and freeze; when hard, collect ears and bag together.

Another way to freeze corn on the cob, I am told, is just to stick it in the coldest part of the freezer, with the husk on, and, when hard, bag the ears together. No blanching. I just heard about that one; haven't tried it. They say it's only good for 2 months.

To cook these gems, put them in a big pot of cold water and put it on the stove; they'll be done when the water is boiling.

Creamed Corn: This is a better method for dealing with slightly tougher corn. As usual, pick, husk, and prepare it as fast as possible. Blanch whole ears in boiling water and chill (see above). With a very sharp knife, rapidly slice half-kernels off around each ear into a bowl; then turn your knife around and, with the dull edge, go down the rows again, squeezing out the milky juice. Refrigerate until chilled through. This stuff is easier to pack in plastic containers than bags.

Whole Corn: Use young or old corn; pick, husk, and prepare it within a few hours. Blanch whole ears in boiling water and chill (see above, Corn on de Cob). With a very sharp knife or a corn cutter, carefully remove whole kernels without including pieces of cob.

Cucumbers: Cucumbers can't be frozen raw, but they can be frozen sort of half-pickled. Slice into plastic containers containing a mixture of half water, half vinegar, and 1 tsp. each salt and sugar. They make an interesting winter salad with canned or frozen whole tomatoes, onions, and a generous spoonful of dill.

Eggplant: Eggplant will change color as you blanch it, but who cares if it's going to wind up buried in a pot of tomato paste. Cut into ½-inch slices, blanch a few at a time. Steam slices: 4 minutes. Cool 2 minutes in ice water. Be careful to dry them enough. Package in plastic containers with sheets of paper between layers. Eggplant freezes moderately well, becoming slightly limp.

Greens: Pick only the greenest, freshest, youngest greens; wash well. Boil tender greens (spinach, young chard, kale, beet greens, pigweed, poke shoots, etc.) 1 or 2 minutes. Boil strong greens (mustard, turnip, collards) 3 minutes. Chill in ice water 1 minute. Package in bags within boxes or cans; remove later and stack. Be sure to label them! And freeze lots—they're good.

Kohlrabi: Kohlrabi freezes very well, but do be careful to choose only young ones in which there are no woody fibers—there's no way to cook those old ones so they're edible. Trim, slice ½ inch thick. Steam: 1 minute. Chill 1 minute or until cold.

Milkweed Pods: Gather milkweed pods when young and tender; cut off stems, but leave whole. Immerse in boiling water; boil one minute, drain. Repeat process twice more. Chill 2 minutes.

Mushrooms: Mushrooms may be frozen in a wide variety of ways, depending on how you want to use them. They may be broiled, brushed with butter, or sautéed in butter or olive oil until just-not-done, and so frozen (best in a plastic container.) They may be blanched in boiling water to cover, to which a little fresh lemon juice is added. Or they may be frozen raw, unblanched, uncooked, which is certainly the easiest way, if not the tenderest end a mushroom can come to. Whatever process you decide on, you probably won't want more than ½ to 1 cup at a time, so package them accordingly. Another nifty mushroom product that does well in the deep freeze is a sauce base stock, made by simmering mushroom stems, peelings, etc. all day with a stalk of celery and half an onion, a dash of salt, maybe some pepper. Strain and freeze in a labeled container, leaving an inch or so rising space.

Can you freeze wild mushrooms? Sure you can, same as store-bought. Puffballs, tender Oysters, Morels, Fairy Rings, Chanterelles, and Meadow Mushrooms all do well. I don't know about Inkies, they might be a little mushy.

Parsnips and Salsify: These freeze pretty well; chop or slice them. Steam slices: 3 minutes. Chill 3 minutes.

Peas: The prince of frozen vegetables, so long as you catch them young. Old peas are pretty disappointing. Two pounds in the pod equals 1 pint, alas, but if you have a lot of willing podders, go to it. Steam podded peas: 1 minute. Chill 1 minute and dry carefully.

Peppers: The best peppers for freezing are the thickest-shelled types, such as the California Wonders. Slice or halve; remove cores. Steam halves: 3 minutes. Steam slices: 2 minutes. Chill 2 minutes; dry well, package, and freeze. As every freezer owner soon discovers, you can freeze peppers raw; they taste just the same, but have very few of the zillions of vitamins left that they started out with. Unbeknownst to the best of us.

Potatoes: You can't freeze raw potatoes, and, believe me, everybody has tried. There are two ways you can freeze potatoes. (1) French-fried. Consult some other cookbook if you want to freeze french-fried potatoes; I am not having any truck with them in this book. (2) Baked-Stuffed potatoes, see page 26. Cool and wrap them in polyethylene wrap; freeze.

It's okay to freeze cooked stews and hashes with potatoes in them, although the defrosted end product will be a little rubbery.

Pumpkin: See Winter Squash, below.

Rutabagas: See Turnips, below.

Snow Peas: Edible podded peas freeze well. Nip off ends, slice diagonally, and steam in small quantities (a cup at a time) for 2 minutes. Chill 3 minutes, dry, and pack. I often package these together with other vegetables suitable for soup or stir-fry. To use them in Chinese cooking, steam rather than sauté them.

Spinach: See Greens, above.

Squash, Summer: Summer squash and zucchini aren't ace freezers, but they're okay. They get a little limp and watery. Use only very young and small ones; slice, and steam a few at a time. Steam slices: 4 minutes.

Squash, Winter: Winter squash and pumpkin may be frozen cooked and mashed, baked, or steamed in pieces. It doesn't work out blanched. Steam slices: 15 minutes. Chill well (24 hours) before freezing.

Tomatoes: Oh, tomatoes. There are lots of things you can do with tomatoes and they can all be frozen. First of all, sort them. Throw all the imperfect ones (minus their imperfections) in a juice pot, and simmer them for an hour or two; sieve or strain out seeds and skins.

Freeze juice as is or use it to pack whole tomatoes in.

To pack whole tomatoes, skin them by steaming or quickly immersing them in boiling water; then simmer 5 minutes in water or tomato juice. Cool them; chill them 24 hours in the refrigerator; pack in stiff containers. Leave an inch head space for expansion.

To pack raw tomatoes, you need a stand-up type freezer with a fast-freezing compartment. Use small, young, perfect specimens; put them directly in contact with one wall of the fast-freeze unit. After 24 hours remove the cracked skin and pack the tomatoes in small bags. To use, add to a salad at the last minute and serve before they are entirely thawed. With crossed fingers.

Turnips: Turnips and rutabagas keep fine in the root cellar, but if you want to freeze them, go ahead. Cut off tops and slice or cut in ½-inch cubes. Steam slices: 4 minutes. Chill in ice water 4 minutes.

FREEZING COOKED FOODS

The dishes that make the most sense to freeze are, of course, those that take the most amount of time and energy to prepare. Cook or bake them until just about done but a little on the light (or underdone) side; cool, wrap, and freeze. To revive them, bake in a 400° to 450° oven for half an hour, or longer, as needed.

CASSEROLES: Especially those involving 14 chopped ingredients and a number of cooking procedures. They may be held together with cream sauce, tomato sauce, cornstarch-type sauce, or simply gravy.

GROUND MEAT DISHES: Such as meatballs, stuffed vegetables, and meat pastries. They all freeze very well and are easy to make in quantity; my next-door neighbor freezes about 100 cabbage rolls at a time.

BEAN DISHES: Whole or mashed, cooked beans freeze well. I like to make up masses of soybean purée and freeze it in the winter for use in the summer, when I seldom run the stove for 6 to 8

hours at a time, and would rather be outside gardening than inside cooking anyway.

SOUPS: The ones that do best are thin soups with a broth base and a couple of vegetables, or cream soups. Mass-mixture soups may be frozen if you leave out the grain or noodles.

INSTANT LUNCHES: A good use for the freezer is stowing away food for people who lunch away from home, whether at school, job, in the woods, or on a town trip. A pile of really fine sandwiches, a stash of individually wrapped pastries, cookies, or cupcakes, and any leftovers like that chicken leg or a couple of egg rolls can all go into a box marked "Lunches Away," thus insuring that even if you run out of bread or cookies, they'll be able to grab something.

WHAT YOU CAN'T FREEZE: By now you must have guessed that you can really freeze any kind of cooked food, but there are a few exceptions:

1. Things that rely on eggs as the basis for their texture don't hold up in the freezer.

2. Cooked grains become watery and sort of sandy textured, even if frozen in a soup or casserole.

3. Raw potatoes and plain boiled or baked potatoes become rubbery and lose liquid, although they are fine if first mashed, as in baked stuffed potatoes or potato soup.

FREEZING BAKED GOODS

Yeasted and unyeasted breads, quickbreads, pies, cakes, and cookies all freeze very well, with few exceptions. They are best if used within 4 months, but you can keep them up to a year. Baked goods do have a tendency to dry out the longer they're kept, and you should plan to use them up within a few days of thawing.

YEASTED AND UNYEASTED BREADS: The best breads for freezing are those made with oil and honey or molasses, and not overbaked. Herb and cinnamon breads tend to lose their flavor, alas. Rolls are a good thing to freeze; you can always thaw a few in a hurry to pad out a skimpy meal or welcome some unexpected company.

QUICKBREADS, COFFEE CAKES, COOKIES: The richest and dampest do best; the dry ones get a little crumbly. Don't frost or fill cakes until after you thaw them. Spice cakes lose flavor, but fruity cakes are fine. To keep cookies from getting broken in storage, package them in plastic bag-lined coffee tins.

PIES: You can freeze fruit pies, meat pies, or vegetable pies, either baked or unbaked, very successfully. Don't, however, attempt to freeze custard pies, quiches, or anything else with eggs as a base.

The main problem in freezing pies is keeping the top crust from breaking in storage. Buy cheap aluminum pie plates; bake pies into half of them and invert the other half over the cooled pies. Wrap each in a plastic bag and stack them in one corner of your freezer.

To bake an unbaked frozen pie, set it unthawed in a 400° oven for 1 hour; to reheat a baked frozen pie, bake at 400° for 30 minutes.

Meat pastries and pies with potatoes in them should be baked before freezing.

COOKIE AND BISCUIT DOUGH: While any dough or batter may be frozen, the only ones that really make life easier, instead of more complicated, are cookie and biscuit doughs. You can freeze the dough in flat lumps, to roll out, or in bars, to slice.

FREEZING EGGS AND DAIRY FOODS

EGGS: Eggs frozen in their shells will expand and the shells will crack. You may freeze eggs as follows:

Whole Eggs: Mix with a fork and add (to keep yolks from congealing): ¼ tsp. salt or 1 tsp. sugar per 4 eggs. Pack in plastic containers or pour into divisions of ice cube tray (try to find egg-sized dividers) and later remove and package together in a plastic bag for individual use.

Egg Yolks: Mix together egg yolks and add: ½ tsp. salt or 1 tsp. sugar per 3 egg yolks. Be careful not to incorporate air into the egg yolks. Freeze in small ice cube containers; empty out cubes and wrap in plastic before packaging together in a plastic bag.

Egg Whites: Mix together egg whites, being careful not to beat in air, and package in ice trays or plastic containers.

Label all eggs well. Eggs will keep from 1 to 2 years. Defrost eggs in a cool place if possible, unopened; use at once.

MILK AND CREAM: Both of these should be pasteurized before freezing. Remember to allow 1 inch per quart for expansion. Cream will whip after freezing, and milk is all right, but both will have an odd texture due to the fat separating from milk solids as they thaw. Milk and cream may be kept up to 4 months. Allow 2 hours per quart to defrost them at room temperature.

BUTTER: Butters, lards, and all fats freeze easily, keep up to a year, and are unchanged. You should rewrap store-bought lard and butter, though, as the paper wrappers will not keep them from going rancid.

CHEESE: Until a cheese is cut into there is no need to freeze it, but if you have half a wheel, cut it into 1-lb. chunks and seal in freezer plastic. Keep for 6 months maximum (for best flavor). Soft cheeses don't freeze well.

COTTAGE CHEESE: Cottage and other fresh cheeses are said to freeze well, up to 4 months, but I find dry curds, frozen and thawed, have the texture of finely ground bubble gum. I used up quite a lot of this stuff in Spinach Pie, but I can't say as how I'd do it again. It probably would have been better if I had added cream or milk to the curds.

14

DRYING, CURING, AND SMOKING MEATS AND FISH

The process of treating meats by any of these methods is a race between your efforts and the commencement of decay. Much attention must be paid to the preparation of the meat, thorough chilling, and maintenance of low enough temperatures. Different methods are suitable in different climates, or even different seasons of the year.

The decision to cure and smoke meats is not one you take lightly. A good deal of time and effort goes into converting a piece of raw meat into cured meat; but the effort is worth it if you have no other method of keeping it longer than a few days. Moreover, the amount of trouble you go to, curing a whole pig, is not much greater than it would be to cure one small piece. The main thing is to locate suitable containers, cool places, and set up a smokehouse. After that it is simply a matter of keeping track of what you're doing, and making sure you do the next step when it's time to do it.

My proportions may seem huge. Thirty-three pounds is, in fact, about how much bacon there is on a pig. If you have a pound of bacon every ten days, that's about how much bacon you eat in a year, anyway.

Meat to be cured should be absolutely fresh, and *must not have been frozen*; nor should it be frozen after curing. Supermarket frozen hams and bacons aren't cured or smoked by these same methods; they use chemicals we'd rather avoid. Meat will keep, at cool temperatures, in the cure, until it has reached the limit of time specified in the recipe for

that kind of cure; after that it will gradually become too salty. If you wish to keep it longer, you should smoke it. In general, cures alone will keep meat (depending on size) up to a couple of months, thus stretching out your meat time. Wet-cured and smoked meat will keep up to 5 months, if the weather is cold (as, in the winter); and dry-cured, long-smoked meat will keep up to a couple of years, with luck.

DRYING MEATS AND FISH

In arid climates, meat dries easily; the Plains Indians cut buffalo into strips and hung it over sticks to dry. Eskimos in the Arctic dried caribou the same way. But in New England and the Maritimes, the air is much too humid 99 days out of 100. However, early travelers devised a method of making:

JERKED BEEF OR VENISON

Cut the meat of the hind leg into strips, along the grain, about 2 to 3 inches wide. Soak them for 1 hour in a mixture of: 1 cup salt and 1 qt. water.

Meanwhile build a good fire of hardwood and let it die down to glowing coals. Lay the meat over racks made of green hardwood twigs and sticks, and prop these racks near and above the fire. Don't let the fire blaze up or the meat will cook instead

251

of dry. Let the meat dry for 5 or 6 hours over the fire; then hang inside cloth or paper bags (to protect from flies, although they probably won't bother with smoked meat) in the sun until leathery.

PEMMICAN

Take several strips of jerked venison and pound to a fine powder. Mix with rendered fat to make a soft, thick dough. Then pound and work in berries or dried berries that have been soaked in water. Chokecherries and blueberries were most commonly used. I'm sorry I don't have the proportions for this dish. Indians in Nova Scotia used to travel great distances to gather and dry blueberries for this purpose, from the great headlands of Cape North. (There are still more blueberries growing there than I have seen anywhere else.)

DRIED FISH

Dried fish, like jerked meat, is best done over a bed of hot coals; but in very dry weather it may be done in the open air. Choose dense-fleshed fish, such as cod, halibut, flounder, pollack, or such. Take off the head just in front of the shoulderbone, and split the fish; remove the backbone. Very large fish are sometimes cut into strips, still joined at the collarbone. Wash and soak in brine (as for Jerked Beef, above); then hang over a bed of coals or in a shady place, with a good wind, on a hot day. Turn every couple of hours if fish is lying on a rack. Dry until leathery. Store separate from other foods—it smells pretty fishy.

CURING MEATS, POULTRY, AND FISH

There are two methods of "curing" flesh:
One is the dry-salt method, in which salt or a

combination of salt, sugar, and spices is rubbed into the flesh to extract moisture rapidly. This leaves the meat somewhat tougher than the wet method, but since it is very quick, it is useful in warm climates or hot weather.

The other method is by immersing the flesh in a brine of salt and water and, usually, sugar and spices. This process can be followed by smoking the meat, or the meat can just be left in the cure until used. Various combinations of these processes have been devised and there is a wide variety of possibilities open to you, depending on your resources, and how you want it to taste and how long you want the meat to keep.

TYPES OF MEAT

Almost anything can be cured, but the best-tasting cured meats are those with a high percentage of fat and a mild flavor. The most commonly cured meat is pork. Beef, however, if well fattened, is good, although not as tender as pork. Veal is too lean and tender to cure. Lamb and chevon are cured in parts of Russia, but they are said to have a somewhat strong flavor. Game is generally thought to taste too gamy but may be cured as sausage, with pork fat added. Turkey is very good smoked, and so is goose and duck, but in general birds don't keep too well; the meat tends to fall apart. Fish is wonderful, smoked or cured; lean fish take salt more quickly, but the fat ones taste better.

PREPARATIONS FOR CURING MEATS

When you decide to cure a piece of meat, or an entire carcass, make sure that the animal is bled properly and chilled quickly and thoroughly. There is no point in trying to cure a shoulder full of blood clots; the salt will not penetrate. To insure rapid chilling, take extra care not to kill an excited overheated animal; bleed it at once, and clean and split the carcass swiftly. And do it in cold weather. You can't cure meat until it is thoroughly chilled by overnight hanging at 35° to 40° F. (1° to 3° C.). Meat that has been frozen will not take the cure, either; some subtle change in cell structure takes place in freezing.

GENERAL EQUIPMENT USED FOR CURING:
A Thermometer: It's essential to keep track of the

temperature of your meat—before, during, and after curing. Any household thermometer will do, as long as it is marked in degrees of 1, not 5, and accurate to within 1 or 2 degrees.

Crocks: Ceramic crocks are perfect, but not essential. You can use containers made of enamel, pyrex, or (dare I admit?) plastic garbage pails. I guess stainless steel would be okay, but other metals are definitely out. Wooden barrels are great if you can get them. Scrub it well and pour in boiling water to clean out bacteria.

A Large Scale: Large enough to weigh accurately up to 25 pounds. Meat, salt, and other ingredients are measured by weight in curing. A bathroom scale is seldom accurate enough to weigh 1 pound of sugar or 15 pounds of ham.

A Salinometer: Helpful, but not absolutely necessary. A salinometer measures the salinity of the brine.

A Large Calendar: Marked off in boxes, so you can remind yourself when to overhaul the meat.

INGREDIENTS IN CURING:

Salt: The main ingredient is the salt, and it should be PURE salt, not iodized table salt. Pure salt is variously sold as pickling salt, kosher salt, even rock salt; or you may use sea salt (in old English recipes called bay salt).

1 cup salt = 12 oz. salt

1 lb. salt = 1⅓ cups salt

Sugar: Since salt used alone tends to harden the meat, sugar is often mixed in with it, in a ratio of 1 part sugar to 4 parts salt. Sugar also improves the flavor, partly because it feeds bacteria that change it to lactic acid, which (as in cheese) tastes good. Sugar helps the color, too. Brown sugar or honey are also used.

Saltpeter: Meat is naturally red due to hemoglobin, which quickly oxidizes and turns brown, and, eventually, gray. If you add saltpeter to your curing mixture, in a ratio of 1 ounce saltpeter per 4 pounds of salt, the color of the meat will stay pink. If you don't, it won't. Saltpeter (potassium nitrate) converts to sal prunella (potassium nitrite) faster if it is used in combination with sal prunella, in a ratio of 1 to 10 (about ¾ teaspoon to 1 ounce should do it). These chemicals help preserve the meat, but only very slightly, and if you don't mind gray hams, you don't have to add them. Recent studies in England indicate that these chemicals, in combination with coffee, may be carcinogenic. Or you can substitute citric or ascorbic acid, in the same proportion, although it will not hold the pink color as long as saltpeter will.

Herbs and Spices: Ground pepper, bay leaves, garlic, and juniper berries are often mentioned in old cures; sometimes allspice berries, marjoram, basil, tarragon, and thyme are used. Almost certainly the pepper and juniper berries, and probably the other spices as well, help to keep the meat. Certainly they do wonders for the taste. These spices are added to the dry cures, not the wet ones.

Commercial Cure Mixtures: The Morton Salt Company sells a number of products for curing meats, among them a dry-cure mixture called Sugar Cure (with or without smoke flavor), and a wet-cure mixture called Tender Quick. These mixtures contain salt, sugar, pepper, saltpeter, and sal prunella, all in the proper proportions. You can write for an order form and price list at:

MORTON SALT COMPANY

P.O. Box 355

Argo, Ill. 60501

Temperature: Temperatures between 33° and 38° F. (1° to 3° C.) are absolutely essential during the process of curing and storing. If it freezes, the salt won't penetrate. Over 38° F. (3° C.) the meat may spoil.

THE DRY-CURE METHOD

In the dry-cure method, salt and other ingredients are mixed very thoroughly and rubbed into the chilled meat. Since this method extracts a great deal of moisture from the meat, the product is very firm and dry, compared to wet-cured meats. It is best used for seasoning fancy meats, which are to be sliced very thin, as in sandwich meats: examples are Smithfield and Westphalian hams, which are then smoked and aged for a year. Dry-cure is rapid, and safer in warm weather, but care should be taken not to leave the meat in salt too long; small cuts (such as bacon) have a larger surface area than hams, and will easily become oversalted.

DRY-CURED HAMS AND SHOULDERS

Weigh the meat to be cured. For every 50 pounds of meat, mix:

3 to 4 lbs. pure salt

¾ to 1 lb. sugar or brown sugar or maple sugar

optional:

1 oz. saltpeter
¾ tsp. sal prunella
1 oz. crushed black pepper

Divide the mixture in half. Set the meat on a few hardwood sticks or a wooden rack in a container, providing some means of drainage so it will not sit in a pool of liquid as it cures. Rub half the mixture into the meat, allowing about 1 pound mixture for a 20-pound piece, but decreasing to about ⅓ pound for a 10-pound piece. Poke the mixture in along the bones and into the hocks. Rub it over other surfaces in a circular motion. If you are packing it in a barrel, set the larger pieces on the bottom, and don't pack it so tightly that it can't drain through. Don't pack deeper than three feet or so. Cover.

Allow 2 days per pound curing time for large hams and shoulders, but only 1½ days per pound for small or thin cuts. On the third day the meat should be removed and rubbed with the second application, using the other half of the cure mixture. Or you can divide the second half into two parts and rub half of it in the third day and the other half the tenth day. In any case it should be moved around, turned, and inspected, and you should keep an eye on the temperature so that it doesn't get above 45° F. (7° C.). Keep the meat covered.

You can omit the second application if you want a milder cure (for smaller pieces, or those which are to be used soon).

When it's cured, take it up and wipe it dry. To smoke it (it'll keep better if smoked) hang to dry first for 2 weeks in a cool dry place. See Smoking, pages 259-262. Otherwise refrigerate and use within 30 days.

DRY-CURE WITH MORTON'S MIXES

Along with their products, Sugar Cure and Tender Quick, the Morton Salt Company recommends, in their booklet *A Complete Guide To Home Meat Curing*, that you follow a particular process that includes pumping liquid curing mixture (Tender Quick) into the heavier pieces of meat. This, they say, helps eliminate the possibility of "bone taint," a sourness that can occur in large hams or other pieces if the salt doesn't completely penetrate before the meat begins to spoil. They sell, for this purpose, a "Meat Pump," a sort of large syringe and various replacement parts for it. As the liquid mixture strikes from within, a dry mix (Sugar Cure) is applied to the outside. If you want to cure by

their method, send off for a copy of their price list, and order some Sugar Cure, Tender Quick, a Morton Meat Pump, and a copy of their excellent booklet, which tells you how to cure meats by their method using their products. As of 1975, all that would cost about 10 dollars. See address, page 253.

DRY-CURING SMITHFIELD-TYPE HAM

It is said that the hogs for these special hams are fattened on peanuts; but others say that corn will do just as well. In any case, cut the hams long, with the shank on. Dry-cure, as above, for a week; then overhaul and change the salt; pack and hold 1½ days per pound. Then wash the hams, dry them, and coat in a mixture of 10 parts cornmeal and 1 part ground pepper. Smoke them (see pages 258-262) at 70° to 90° F. (21° to 32° C.) for 10 days to 2 weeks, depending on size. Then hang to dry in a cool, dry room. See page 263. Smithfield hams are ripe after they have been aged for an entire year.

DRY-CURED BACON

Some old salts cure their bacon along with their hams, but it really doesn't make much sense. Bacon cuts are so much smaller that they need different handling. You should start curing bacon within 24 hours of slaughtering the pig. The best method of making fancy bacon is the Box Cure, in which the bacon slabs are packed in a box with dry cure and allowed to soak in the moisture that comes out of them.

The Box
Should be about the size of your bacons, 10 by 20 inches or so, and just deep enough to hold the amount of meat you're curing (a 12-inch box will hold the bacon of 2 or 3 hogs). Make the box out of hardwood, something like maple or oak, such as you would use in smoking meats. A rack should be made out of the same material to fit inside it and hold the meat down under the brine it makes.

The Cure
Weigh the bacons. For every 33 lbs., mix:
1⅔ lbs. pure salt
1 lb. brown sugar or maple sugar
optional:
1 oz. saltpeter

¾ tsp. sal prunella

Or you can use, for 33 lbs. of bacon:

**1 lb. Morton's Tender Quick or 1¼ lbs. Morton's
Sugar Cure**

Rub the chilled and trimmed bacons very well
with the cure mixture, on all sides, using a circular
motion. Sprinkle some cure on the bottom of the
box and pack the bacons in, skin side down. Tamp
each one flat to eliminate air pockets, and sprinkle
cure over the top. Lay the rack on top of the meat
so that when you close the lid it will hold them
down firmly, but not gouge into the meat.

Rehaul and pack the meat in a different order in
7 to 10 days. If there was any cure left over, add it
at this point. Box bacon should be cured for 1½
days per pound (an 8-pound bacon for 12 days).
Then take it out, soak 30 minutes in tepid water,
and scrub clean. Hang to dry; they may be smoked
or not, as you choose (see pages 258-262).

CANADIAN BACON

A Canadian bacon is the loin cut of a pig, separated
from the bone. Cut the fatback off the loin, leaving
about ¼ inch fat on it. Then bone the meat, running the knife the length of it with the flat of the
blade pressed against the ribs and the tip touching
the backbone. Canadian bacon can be dry-cured or
wet-cured, using Morton mixes or your own. Weigh
the meat. For every 25 lbs. mix or measure:

Wet Cure

**2 lbs. Morton's Tender-Quick
1 gal. water (boiled and cooled)**

or:

**1½ lbs. pure salt
1 lb. brown sugar
1 gal. water (boiled and cooled)**

optional:

**1 oz. saltpeter
½ tsp. sal prunella**

Wet Cure Directions

Pack loins in a crock or wide container. Pour cure
mixture over them to cover; weight them with a
plate and clean rock or jar of water to keep them
submerged. Cover crock. Keep at 36° to 38° F. (2°
to 3° C.) for 5 days; then overhaul, changing positions of meat. Continue to cure 2 weeks in all.
Remove, soak in tepid water, and dry. Rub with a
mixture of 10 parts cornmeal and 1 part pepper.

Wrap each loin tightly in clean cloth and tie every
1½ inches. Keep at 36° to 38° for 2 to 3 weeks.
If you wish to keep them longer, smoke them
lightly (see pages 258-262).

Dry Cure

1½ lbs. Tender-Quick

or:

**1 lb. pure salt
½ lb. brown sugar**

optional:

**¾ oz. saltpeter
¼ tsp. sal prunella**

Dry Cure Directions

Divide cure into 3 portions. Rub the first into the
loins and let them rest for 2 or 3 hours. Rub in the
second portion and let them rest 24 hours (they
should be kept at 36° to 38° F., 2° to 3° C., all
this time). Rub in the third portion and pack them
closely together. Cover and leave for 5 days; then
overhaul, changing positions of loins. Continue to
cure until 10 to 14 days; remove, soak in tepid
water, and dry. Rub with a mixture of 10 parts
cornmeal and 1 part pepper. Wrap each loin lightly
in clean cloth and tie every 1½ inches. Keep at 36°
to 38° for 2 to 3 weeks maximum. If you wish to
keep them longer, smoke them lightly (see pages
258-262).

THE WET-CURE METHOD

In the wet-cure method, the salt, sugar, and whatever else you use are dissolved in water, and the
meat submerged. This method is favored by many
because of the tenderer, milder product. However,
it is only really safe in very cold weather and, even
then, once in a while a large ham will go sour in
the middle before the brine penetrates. To help
keep this from happening, run a thin-bladed knife
in along the bones of your big hams, or inject brine
into them with a Meat Pump (see under "Morton's
Mixes," page 254). Keep a thermometer on or in
your barrel at all times, and check it 2 or 3 times a
day if you suspect temperatures over 38° F. (3° C.).
If a thin white scum appears on top of the pickle,
that is all right; but if the brine becomes "ropey"
or slimy, haul the meat out at once, clean it with
tepid water and brushes, scald the container, and
make new brine. Continue with the cure schedule,
if you think there is a chance the meat wasn't

tainted; if it was, you'll be able to smell it well enough. Spoiled meat, thank heavens, isn't something you have to guess about. But there is the chance that only the brine was affected, if you were checking it every day.

USING A SALINOMETER: If you're mixing brine with a salinometer, add less salt than the recipe calls for, and then gradually add more until it registers the right degree. Brine for hams and shoulders should register 75°. If you're replacing brine after a week, make it up to 70°; if after two weeks, to 65°. Spareribs and loin or Canadian bacon are cured in a lighter, 65°, brine. Corned beef, tongue, and lamb can be cured in 75° brine, or lighter brine, if you prefer (but it will not keep as well); birds are cured in 70° brine.

PACKING THE MEAT: Set the chilled, trimmed meat in your container, skin side down, and close to one another but not squeezed out of shape. If you're packing the bacons in with the hams, lay them in first, flat on the bottom. After that arrange the heavier hams and shoulders, and then the lighter meats. Take your time arranging them. Cover with brine mixture until they just begin to loosen and float up a bit. Then weight them with a round of wood, clean plates, rocks, or bottles of water—anything to keep them under the surface without mashing them.

On the third day and the tenth day, take them all out and rearrange them. This is to make sure the brine gets at all sides of each piece.

Big pieces, of 15 pounds or over, are cured 4 days to the pound. Smaller hams, of 5 to 10 pounds, are cured 5 days to the pound. So a big ham would be in there about 2 months, and a smaller one would only take a month. Mark the date when you put in each piece, and perhaps (if you're as absent-minded as I am) make notes on the appropriate days to take out each piece (which you have weighed and calculated time for).

When the cure is complete, take out the pieces and wash them in tepid water. Allow them to dry, hanging free, at least overnight—or longer, up to 2 weeks, as weather permits. They should neither freeze nor go over 40° F. (4° C.). If the meat is not to be smoked, it should be used up within the month—but if smoked, it will keep for a year or more, maybe, with luck. To test the insides, run a skewer through the middle and smell it. See about keeping cured meats, on page 263.

BRINE RECIPES FOR PORK: Weigh the meat and measure out ingredients proportionate to it. Mix with water that has been boiled and cooled, in a scalded container. Submerge chilled meat; add more brine as needed to cover.

These recipes are all for 50 pounds of meat.

SWEET PICKLE BRINE

Mix:

4 lbs. pickling salt
1 lb. white or brown sugar
1 oz. saltpeter (optional)
1 tsp. sal prunella (optional)
3 gals. water

LIGHT SPICED PICKLE BRINE

Mix:

2½ lbs. salt
½ lb. sugar
½ oz. saltpeter (optional)
3 cloves crushed garlic
2 oz. whole pickling spices (mixture of pepper, mustard, coriander, and bay leaves)

HONEY CURE

Honey permeates meat more quickly than sugar and salt; it also adds a very special delicious flavor to the meat. To dissolve it thoroughly you should boil it with the water; might as well boil all the ingredients together.

Mix:

4 lbs. pickling salt
2 lbs. honey
2 lbs. blackstrap molasses
1 oz. allspice
4 oz. black pepper

optional:

¾ oz. saltpeter
1 tsp. sal prunella

CORNED BEEF

Corned or chipped beef, venison, moose, and tongue can be treated in the same way. The best cuts for corning are fatty pieces, a little tough but not too dense: brisket, plate, and chuck are usual. Cut the meat into slabs, with the grain, about 1½ to 2 inches thick, and then into 5- to 6-inch squares. Tongues may be left whole or cut up; sometimes they are "pumped" with a syringe, if large, to insure getting at the middle. Chill all meats before treating.

Weigh the meat. For every 20 lbs., use:

1½ lbs. pure salt

Rub some of the salt into the meat. Sprinkle some on the bottom of the container, and arrange the meat so it is close but not packed tight. Sprinkle salt over every 5-inch layer, more or less, and some on top. Leave it overnight in a cool place (the whole time it is curing it should be at 36° to 38° F. (2° to 3° C.) and no more than 40° F. (4° C.). At no time should it be allowed to freeze. The next day boil a couple of gallons of water. Add to 1 gallon:

½ lb. brown or white sugar

optional:

½ oz. baking soda

3 Tb. saltpeter

Cool the water to 38° F. and pour over the meat so it just covers, and add more water as needed to just cover it. When the pack loosens and begins to float, stop adding water and weight the top with a plate, clean rocks, bottles of water—anything to hold it down without squashing the meat. All meat must be submerged.

After 3 to 5 days, pour off the liquid and repack the meat, moving the pieces around so that those that were on top are now on the bottom and vice versa. Pour the pickle back on it and reweight it.

Small pieces will be ready in a week; larger pieces should be cured 2 days to the pound. If a piece is to be left in longer than this it will be okay, generally, for another two or three weeks, but when you use it, you should first soak it in cold water or perhaps even parboil it and discard the first water, then boil it again, since it will be very salty. That's why it's usually cooked with potatoes.

Corned beef may be smoked, but it still won't keep as hams do. If rubbed with pepper and smoked lightly, it will be (more or less) like pastrami. (See about smoking, pages 259-262.)

Corned beef may also be pickled in Morton's Tender Quick, using 2 pounds of Tender Quick per gallon of (boiled, cooled) water.

CORNED LAMB AND CHEVON

Lamb and chevon may be corned, but if you've never had it, you might find it wise to do a test run before you decide to do a whole lot. It's pretty funky. In the Middle East and eastern Europe it's even lightly smoked, but it's even wilder that way. Treat as for corned beef, but don't say I didn't warn you. If you want to try something really far out, take the corned lamb and cut it into stew-sized pieces, and marinate overnight in a mixture of:

1 qt. boiled cooled wine vinegar
1 qt. boiled cooled water
3 large cloves peeled garlic
3 heads dill

Skewer and cook as shish kebab, or eat it raw. (As hors d'oeuvres, before a rousing game of Buz Kashi?)

CURED BIRDS

The curing of fowl is mostly done as a preparation for smoking them, and while the meat will keep much longer than it would raw (a month or so) it isn't really done with keeping in mind so much as for the gourmet effect. You can cure whole birds, rapidly, in dry salt, or legs and breasts, for longer. Fat birds such as goose, duck, and specially fattened capons are best.

CURED WHOLE BIRDS

Butcher the bird with the neck long. Be very careful as you pluck the bird not to tear the skin. Clean it, and remove the feet. Cut through the neck skin down the back and peel it away; tuck the neck into the front body cavity or remove it; seal this cavity with the neck skin and run a skewer through both wings and this seal to hold it.

Heat a pound or so of salt in the oven. Meanwhile, boil a large pot of water and parboil the bird for 5 minutes; then remove it and carefully rub in the hot salt, for 10 or 15 minutes. Stuff the main body cavity with fresh herbs, parsley or chervil or thyme, what you will, and tie up the legs to hang. Wrap the bird in muslin and hang to smoke (see page 264).

Another method of curing whole birds is to immerse them in brine, made of:

1½ lbs. pure salt
4 oz. brown or white sugar
1 gal. boiled cooled water

optional:

1 Tb. saltpeter
1 pinch sal prunella

Weight them down, keep at low temperatures (see

other brine recipes) and cure for 3 or 4 days before smoking.

Many recipes recommend that you also pump the breasts and legs with a salt and water mixture, both in dry-curing and brine-curing. Use 10 percent of the brine for this.

CURED BREASTS AND LEGS

Legs can be cured as they are, but sew the two halves of the breast together by the skin, and use the recipe above for brine. You can leave them in the pickle up to 3 days before smoking.

CURING FISH

Any kind of fish can be cured: fresh or salt, lean or fat, big or small. All should be split, although you can leave the bones in small fish (they'll dissolve). Fillet large ones, but leave the "collarbones" on to hold the pieces together. Thick-skinned fish such as carp, black bass, etc., should be skinned, and the fins cut and pulled out. Weigh the fish after preparing it. Use only pure salt: pickling, kosher, or dairy salt.

For every 4 lbs. lean fish allow 1 lb. salt.
For every 3 lbs. fatty fish allow 1 lb. salt.
(See page 210 for lists of lean and fatty fishes.)

Fish can be dry-salted or brine-cured. The dry method is better in summer or in warm climates, since it works faster and the fish keeps longer; the brine method, however, gives a tenderer product and is better for fatty fish, which won't keep forever in any case.

DRY-SALTED FISH

After beheading and splitting or filleting the fish, soak it for an hour in clean brine (⅓ cup salt to 1 qt. water) and scrub it with a brush. Rinse again and dry for 15 minutes or so.

Dredge each fish in salt, thoroughly, using the proportions above, and stack them to drain, skin side down. This should be done on open slatted boards, outside. Leave them in the salt for two days, but move them around and scatter more salt between layers after the first day. In warm weather one day should do it.

When they're firm, scrub off the salt (use burlap or a brush, and rinse in clean brine). Then lay them out to dry. In Newfoundland and Nova Scotia this is done on open wharves, since the sun isn't

strong enough to "rust" them; farther south, they should be under cover. Turn them every 4 or 5 hours the first day, and bring them in every night, stacked out of the dew, skin side down except the top layer. Dry them 4 to 6 days, until leathery. Press the flesh with your finger; if no impression is left, they're done. Wrap in waxed paper, and store them in wooden boxes in a cool dry place.

Problems: If you have flies, build a smoke smudge out of hardwood. If it rains, keep them in stacks out of the rain, but repile them every day, and scatter salt in the layers. If they "rust" or mold, scrub off the spots with brine.

BRINE-CURED FISH

After beheading and splitting or filleting the fish, soak it for an hour in clean brine (⅓ cup salt to 1 qt. water) and scrub it with a brush.

Scatter salt on the bottom of the curing crock or barrel. Dredge each piece well in salt (see proportions, above) and build up fish in the barrel in even layers. Scatter more salt over each layer. Pile them skin side down, except the top layer.

Weight the fish down with a clean plate, clean rocks, or bottles filled with water. The fish will make its own brine.

Small fish will cure in 2 or 3 days. Thicker, larger, or fatter fish will take a week to 10 days.

When the cure is done, take out the fish and make a fresh brine. Use part of it to wash and scrub them in, the rest to repack them in. Reweight them and store in a cool, dark place.

Fish in brine will keep up to 9 months if the weather is cool. If it's warm, you should keep an eye on the brine, and change it if the barrel begins to smell or look scummy, or if the brine gets slimy. In the summer, figure 3 months maximum keeping time.

SMOKING

Smoking is generally done with two aims in mind: one, smoked meats generally keep better than unsmoked meats. Two, smoking changes and enhances the flavor (and texture) of the meat.

There are several reasons why smoked meats keep better. One is that the smoke contains a number of trace elements that help to preserve it. Another is that during smoking, moisture evaporates, leaving the meat 10 to 15 percent lighter. The outer skin, fat, and flesh is also hardened to form a protective seal against molds and insects; and, finally, the smell of smoke repels many insects (though not all). Of course, there are other factors that enter into the business of keeping meat—including the type of meat, the cut, the curing process, temperatures, and how long it is smoked at what temperatures. You will have to read this entire section to find them all.

Many people smoke meat just to change the flavor and texture. If you intend to eat the meat as soon as it is smoked, you might as well hot-smoke it, at temperatures between 200° and 225°, and thus cook it at the same time. See instructions for this method on pages 187–188.

ABOUT FAKE SMOKE: Most hams, bacons, and other cured meats available on the commercial market today aren't really smoked. They're cured in a smoke-flavored brine. A mixture of curing agents with smoke flavor in it may be purchased from the Morton Salt Company (see address, page 253). The Morton people claim that it consists of the curing agents of smoke, as well as the flavor, but who knows what that is (I asked, and they didn't tell me). In any case, it seems obvious that the other effects of smoking are bypassed and that the meat, however tasty, will not keep for long periods of time, as true smoked meat does.

THE SMOKEHOUSE

There are quite a number of ways to contrive, build, and concoct smokehouses or boxes, ranging all the way from sticks propped over smoking coals to elaborate concrete constructions designed to hold dozens of hams, turkeys, fish, and so forth. Certainly you should take into consideration the amount of meat you will be smoking, and for how long, and build according to your needs. Here are just a few of the many possibilities:

CAMP SMOKING: If you want to cold-smoke some fish or other meat for a short period of time—say, on a camping trip—almost anything will do for a smokehouse. You could build a small tipi or bend some green saplings into a low structure like a sweat lodge, and drape tarps over it, or raincoats (anything you use will smell smoky afterwards, however). Build a fire pit and trench as for a proper smokehouse (see below); cover the trench with green sticks, ferns, or rocks. Use wood ashes to bank the fire overnight.

BARRELS: A large hardwood barrel, or 50-barrel oil can, with top and bottom removed, is adequate for smoking the parts of one pig, two turkeys, or a dozen fish. If using a wooden barrel, make sure it's seasoned and tight; often the staves will dry out and separate. An oil drum is a better bet if you can get it clean (set fire to the oil, and burn it out, then scald it out and scrub well). A wooden box or crate will also do as well, but make sure it's all hard wood.

Set the barrel uphill from the fire pit, which should be about 10 feet away. Dig the fire pit into the side of the hill so that it can be completely covered, to damp the fire down, and keep it just simmering for days on end. (If you dig it at the bottom of the hill water may collect in it.) Dig a trench up from the pit to just under the barrel, and line with ceramic drainpipe or stovepipe. (You can just cover it with sheet metal and earth, if the soil is firm enough to hold.)

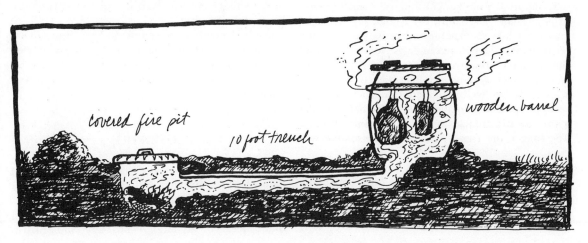

covered fire pit   10 foot trench   wooden barrel

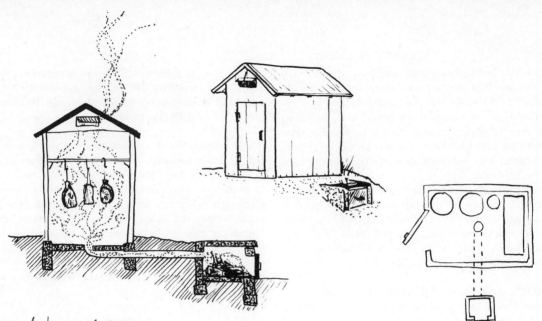

smokehouse design

The barrel will need a large lid and some poles to hold the lid up at various angles as you adjust the flow of smoke.

CONVERTED REFRIGERATOR OR COOK-STOVE: A trip to the dump may yield a good smokehouse. To convert a fridge, first of all, find one with a workable door. Strip out the compressor, wires, fixtures, plastic fittings, and galvanized metal parts. Drill an 8-inch hole in the bottom or lower side, and another in one upper corner, with a butterfly valve or pivoted metal flap, so it can be adjusted to keep a draft going. Sometimes you can use the original rack supports to hold up poles for hanging the meat—or you can drill holes of your own to insert poles into.

To supply the smoke, you can use a small brazier of hot "coals" and chips, off to one side and covered by a box so that the smoke will go into the refrigerator. (Maybe you can devise something using the vegetable drawer out of the fridge?) One problem with refrigerator smokehouses is that they tend to be so well insulated that they get hot, so if you're cold-smoking, it might be better to dig a fire pit and trench, as in a barrel smokehouse. The longer the trench, the more the smoke will cool.

A cookstove makes an awfully small smokehouse, only suitable for fish or sausage or for hot-smoking delicacies. On the other hand, it's pretty good for that—especially if the door still has a thermostat. Strip and convert it as you would a refrigerator.

A SMALL SHED: Sure, if it's reasonably small, and tight, and you have no other uses for it. Once a smokehouse, always a smokehouse, as they say. Proceed as below.

A PROPER SMOKEHOUSE: You can build a smokehouse out of just about any material: plywood, boards, logs, rocks, cement blocks. The only requirements are that you keep the smoke in, the rain out, and allow the smoke to travel through. For this purpose you do need to fit into the top an adjustable ventilator.

The firebox or fireplace has to be outside the building, with a pipe or trench running up to the floor of the building. If you're going to use the smokehouse a lot, it's best to arrange the smoke inlet so that you can clean it, some way. It has to have a lid, of course.

Don't depend on screening to keep flies out of the meat. During smoking, there isn't any problem; but if you plan to hang the meat there before or after smoking, in bug weather, wrap it in brown paper.

THE FIRE

The fire should be started and built up several hours before you start smoking. Then, when it dies down, there will be a good bed of coals.

Never use any kind of resinous soft wood to smoke meats of any kind. Almost any kind of hardwood can be used but some are said to have a better flavor than others. Southerners talk of hickory, ash, walnut; Vermonters use only maple, the English swear by oak sawdust, and in Nova Scotia alders are sometimes called "smokewood." The Morton Salt people say cherry and maple are best, and many others say apple is. If hardwood is in short supply, dried cobs from cow or flint corn are an old favorite. In any case, make sure you have a good supply, and that it's dry (bring it into the kitchen for a while if you're waiting out some rainy weather). If your special smoking wood is in short supply, make the fire out of any hardwood and cut the special stuff into small pieces to throw on the coals when you're smoking the meat. To keep a fire going all night, use a big piece of wood with a knot in it, well banked.

ABOUT COLD-SMOKING

Cold-smoking is done at low temperatures of 70° to 85° F. (21° to 29° C.), for long periods of time, ranging from 24 hours to several weeks. Meat finished this way will be very strongly smoke-flavored, rather firm and dry, and will keep over the winter, in New England; some cuts (such as hams) may be kept for a year or longer. Cold-smoking doesn't have to be done all at once, after the first day or two. If the fire dies out, you can start it up again and keep going. You should count only the time it is really being smoked, however. If the weather gets too cold (down to 0° F., or −17° C.) bring the meat in to a cool room or the cellar overnight, rather than risk letting it freeze.

PREPARING THE MEAT FOR SMOKING

PORK: Hams, bacons, shoulders, and loin or Canadian bacons may be cold-smoked, for keeping. To cure them first, see pages 252–257. After curing, run a sterile skewer through the larger cuts of meat, near the bones; draw it out and smell it, to make sure the meat isn't tainted in the middle.

Scrub the meat in tepid water to remove excess salt. Hams and shoulders should be strung through the shank end with strong cotton twine or baling twine, several inches in from the end. To hang bacons, run a skewer through the flank end and thread the cord below the skewer. Lay other cuts on a light rack, for the time being. Let them all dry and drain for a couple of days, making sure they stay cool.

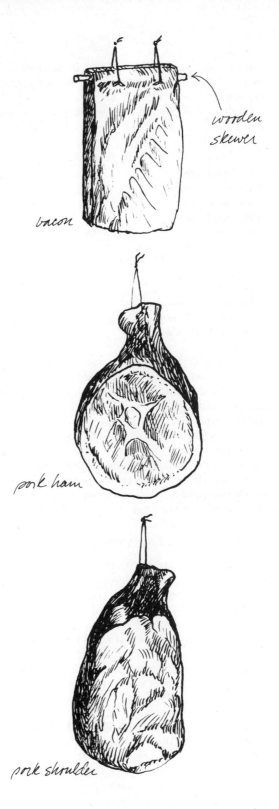

wooden skewer

bacon

pork ham

pork shoulder

how to hang meat for smoking

When you are ready to smoke them, you may first coat them with seasoning. Here are two possible mixtures:

Grind fine or pound together in a mortar and pestle:

1

4 Tb. black pepper
4 Tb. white pepper
1 Tb. dried garlic
3 Tb. dried onions
1 Tb. paprika

2

4 Tb. black pepper
1 Tb. red chili pepper
1 Tb. celery seeds
3 Tb. coriander seeds
2 Tb. mustard seeds

Or you could just pound up the contents of a 4-ounce box of Mixed Pickling Spices. It's better to grind or pound them fresh, though, than to use preground spices, which are usually hot but not flavorful.

To stretch the mixture out you could add cornmeal to it.

Before you smoke the loin, Canadian bacon, or other cuts, tie them up securely. Canadian bacon is usually wrapped in muslin and tied at 1½- to 2-inch intervals with string.

BEEF AND LAMB: If these were cured in a very strong brine, then it might be well to soak them overnight in cold water, and let them dry for another 24 hours before smoking. In any case, wash well in tepid water and scrub clean. These can be hung by stringing cord through and around them, or, if small, laid on racks covered with aluminum foil. Punch holes in the foil and lay the racks over trays lined with aluminum foil to prevent them from dripping juices on the floor. They may be coated with ground spices, as with pork (see above).

BIRDS: Birds taken from the cure should be rinsed thoroughly inside and out, and propped or hung to drain first one way for 6 hours, then the other way. You may rub seasoning (see pork) into the skin, or not, as you choose. Other dried herbs, such as sage, dill, marjoram, may be added to the mixture.

Hang the birds, neck end up, in double cheesecloth or cloth bags that fit closely. You may skewer the wings to the neck if you wish.

TEMPERATURES FOR COLD-SMOKING

Cold-smoking may be done in the most makeshift of smokehouses; but you do need a reliable oven thermometer. Start the fire well in advance, and when you have a good bed of coals, bank it well and adjust the smokehouse to the right temperature, and then start smoking.

MEAT AND CUT	F.	C.	TIME (In Smokehouse)
METHOD ONE: FAST COLD-SMOKING: This is used to smoke meats that are to be kept for a few months in a cool place (as, in the winter).			
Pork: bacon	75°–85°	24°–29°	24–36 hours
Ham and shoulders	100–120	38–49	48 hours
Canadian bacon	75–85	24–29	24 hours
Sausages	85–95	29–35	12–18 hours
Beef and lamb	100–120	38–49	24–36 hours
Turkey	110	43	20 hours
METHOD TWO: SLOW COLD-SMOKING: This is used to smoke dry-cured hams that are to be kept for longer periods, a year or more.			
10-lb. ham	70°–85°	21°–29°	10 days
15-lb. ham	70–85	21–29	12 days
20-lb. ham and over	70–85	21–29	15 days

KEEPING CURED MEATS

Keeping cured meats is sort of unpredictable. There are so many variable factors. No two pieces of meat are the same size, shape, and density; and nobody's storage room (unless it's a refrigerator) stays at exactly 35° F. (2° C.) all the time. All I can do here is give some general advice.

Cured meat, unsmoked, doesn't keep more than a month. It should be submerged in brine and you should check both brine and meat once a week, or more often. Sometimes you read that it can be taken out and hung. Well—I tried it once, and it didn't work. Maybe my cellar was too damp; it was certainly cold enough.

Keep most cured, smoked meat in cool, dry, well-ventilated storage. Allow each piece free circulation by hanging it separate from the other pieces.

If it gets warm in there (as in a January thaw) transfer the meat to a refrigerator or give up and eat it.

To protect against rodents, attach at least a foot of wire to the string and secure it well. Don't hang meat near a ledge. Set traps.

To protect against mold, coat the meat with cornmeal and ground pepper, mixed together. Check hams now and then; wipe off mold with a vinegar-soaked rag.

To protect against "ham beetles," "skippers," and other insects, wrap each piece of meat well in brown paper. Check now and then to make sure dripping fat doesn't make holes in the paper. This is really only a problem in warm weather, but it's a rough one; flies small enough to get through ordinary windowscreen can lay eggs on the meat, which hatch into maggots, who burrow into the meat.

Meat with skin around it (such as legs) keeps better, of course; so hams keep better than shoulders, and shoulders better than bacon, or corned beef.

Do not allow meat to freeze. If it does, use it at once.

To test meat for rancidity, run a sterile skewer through—and smell it.

SMOKING FISH

Fish is a pretty bland food, and those who traditionally live on it (Scandinavians, Chinese, and islanders the world over) soon discovered the fine art of smoking fish. To construct and use a smoke-house, see pages 259–260. Most smoked fish doesn't really keep very well; if your aim is long storage, use the dry-salt method under Bloaters for a lean type of fish, and cold-smoke it for about a week.

Some fish are called "lean" and others "fat." The lists seem kind of arbitrary; maybe the best thing to do is cook a sample and eat it and decide for yourself. Here's a list, anyway, of some smoke-able northern fish, also see page 210.

FAT

bass	mackerel
bluefish	salmon
herrings, etc.	trout (most of them)

LEAN

carp	pollack
cod	sea bass
flounder and other flatfish	sheefish
haddock	smelt
halibut	sturgeon
perch	sunfish
pickerel	whitefish

In general, fat fish need to be brine-soaked and smoked for longer periods than lean fish. Fat fish don't keep as well as lean fish.

CLEANING AND PREPARING THE FISH: Small fish, a pound and under, should not be cut more than necessary. Leave heads and tails on. To clean them, cut a small slit under the throat and pinch together the inner gills to pull out the innards; with the other hand, run your thumb up the belly from the anus to press the innards up and out. (This is called "gibbing.") Rinse well.

Larger fish may be either split or filleted. Some fish seem to do better if the head is left on and the belly cut to clean it; mackerel is often done this way, because the flesh tends to fall apart if it's cut too much. With others, particularly cod, haddock, halibut, and pollack, it's customary to split them up the backbone, leaving the belly intact, so you can remove the bones. You should, however, leave the "shoulder" bones, just below the gills, to hold the meat together. To fillet, see page 210. The skins and shoulder bones of most fish should be left on for smoking, even if they are filleted.

Always scrub out the inside of the fish very well, using brushes and tepid water to remove all traces of blood and innards.

Fish, unlike other meats, may be frozen before curing and smoking.

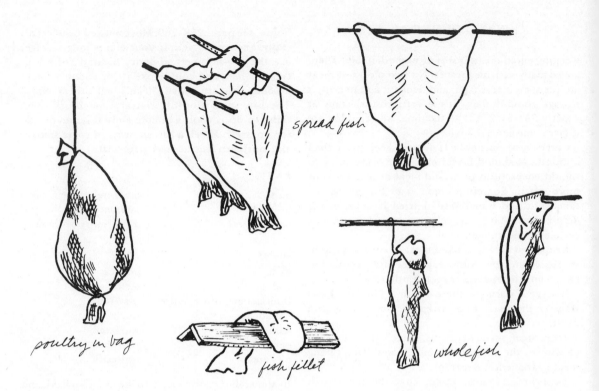

spread fish

poultry in bag

fish fillet

whole fish

THE BRINE: You can vary the flavoring ingredients in your brines, but it's a good idea to choose a ratio of salt-to-water and stick with it. As you go along, keep track of the lengths of time you kept your fish in brine; then, if it's too salty, next year (or next batch) you can just reduce the time. Everybody has different ideas about how much salt is enough.

MILD BRINE

4 gals. water
8 lbs. pure salt
1 lb. dark brown sugar or ¾ lb. honey
1 cup lemon juice
2 Tb. crushed white pepper
2 heads flowering dill

STRONG BRINE

4 gals. water
7 lbs. pure salt
2 cups blackstrap molasses
½ cup tamari soy sauce
½ cup lemon juice or vinegar
2 smashed onions
3 cloves crushed garlic

How long to soak the fish? Much depends on the thickness. Time a split 2-pound fish as two 1-pound fish.

WEIGHT	LEAN FISH	FAT FISH
under ¼ lb.	30 minutes	40 minutes
¼ to ½ lb.	45 minutes	1 hour
½ to 1 lb.	1 hour	1¼ hours
1–2 lbs.	2 hours	2½ hours
2–3 lbs.	2½ hours	3 hours
3–4 lbs.	3 hours	3½ hours

After soaking the fish in brine, rinse it well in cold water to clean off excess salt.

Next the fish must be hung for 2 or 3 hours to dry and form a "pellicle," a sort of shiny skin that will help it hold together during smoking. Wet fish most always fall apart.

HANGING: Pictured above, with methods of cutting fish, are the various ways of hanging. You should not hang fish by skin and flesh alone, but hook it under a bone. Nor is it wise to drape fillets over a pole; they tend to curl and break.

SMOKING: Fish can be hot-smoked or cold-smoked.

In hot-smoking, the fish is usually cold-smoked first; the longer it's cold-smoked, the smokier it will taste. In general, you can go by this chart; for specific recipes, see below.

COLD-SMOKING:	TEMP.	TIME
Whole small fish to be used within 2 weeks	70° F. (21°C.)	24 hours
Whole small fish to be kept	70° F. (21°C.)	100 hours

HOT-SMOKING:		
Large split fish, fillets	90° F. (32°C.) then 170° F. (77°C.)	3-4 hours 45 to 60 minutes

SPECIALTIES:

BLOATERS

Large herring are used. They are scaled, and washed, but not gutted, and the heads and tails are left on. Sometimes a light dry-cure is applied; they are dredged in salt or in a mixture such as:

2 lbs. pure salt
1 lb. brown sugar
4 oz. crushed or ground mixed pickling spices

Leave fish packed in cure for 12 hours, in a cool place. Or you may omit the cure; bloaters are often unsalted. Smoke 2 to 4 hours, depending on the size, at 70° to 85° F. (24° to 29° C.). Bloaters should be refrigerated and used within 2 days; clean, fillet, and fry or grill.

RED HERRING

This is heavily salted, and keeps quite well. Clean and wash the fish, and apply dry cure as above, for bloaters. Leave the herring in cure for a week, in a cool place; check and repack after 3 days, applying more cure as needed.

Rinse and hang to dry for 2 hours. Smoke at 70° to 85° F. (24° to 29° C.) for a week. To cook red herring, soak it overnight, then steam until tender; if it's still too salty for your taste, cook it with potatoes, as in a scalloped potato dish—something like that.

Red herring may be stored at cool temperatures for a year or more, but since it has a strong smell, wrap it well in plastic and keep it away from things like butter.

KIPPERED HERRING

Split herring down the back, and remove backbone and innards, cleaning thoroughly. Soak it for 30 minutes in Mild or Strong Brine (page 264). Rinse, hang 2 hours. Smoke for 12 hours at 85° F. (29°C.). Kippered herring will keep for about a week if refrigerated, but it should be very well packaged, since the smoke smell is very strong.

SALMON

This is really a West Coast specialty, since there are so few Atlantic salmon left. It may be called "Nova Scotia," but I ain't seen any around here.

Salmon are split, but skins should be left on. Clean well and soak in Strong Brine (page 264) for 30 minutes. If you like, you can add a shot of rum to the brine. Hang and dry for 2 to 3 hours. Smoke at 90° F. (32° C.) for 3 hours, then raise the temperature to 170° F. (77° C.) and hot-smoke for 45 minutes to 1 hour, until cooked and tender.

Smoked salmon is fully cooked and may be served in small slices, rolled around cream cheese, or as sandwich meat, or in egg dishes, or cream sauce. It must be kept refrigerated and used within 2 weeks.

SMOKED EELS

Soak in either Brine (page 264); rinse, then dip briefly in boiling water, open, and clean them. Smoke at 140° F. (60° C.) for 2 hours if small or 4 hours if large.

SMOKED OYSTERS AND OTHER SHELLFISH

Steam open, and soak in Mild Brine (page 264) for 30 minutes. Rinse. Cover in a rack with tin foil, oil it lightly, punch holes in the foil and set it over a metal tray. Set the oysters (or whatever) on it and smoke at 75° to 85° F. (24° to 29° C.) for 30 minutes, then raise the temperature to 150° F. (66° C.) and smoke until the gills dry, about 30 minutes. Test by taste. Pile them in a clean jar and toss with olive or sesame oil. Refrigerate for at least 1 hour, tossing in as much oil, every 10 minutes or so, as they will absorb. Eat within 24 hours for best flavor.

15

MAKING WINES, BEER, AND COLD DRINKS

WINE

I'm not really going into all this as deeply as the subject deserves. A few recipes will give you a basic idea of the methods of extracting juices, sweetening, and fermenting wines.

For more detailed information and for ordering equipment, write to Milan Laboratory, 57 Spring Street, New York, N.Y. 10012. They mail supplies all over the U.S. and Canada. A book they recommend is *Winemaking at Home*, by Homer Hardwick (available in hardback, Funk & Wagnalls, $6.95; and in paper, Pocket Books, $1.50).

Nor am I about to pretend that I've gotten so good at producing homemade wines that they all come out delicious, or even drinkable. But that's partly because I'm finicky and don't much care for sweet wines. I keep experimenting toward dry ones, and that means that some of them are too sour. Take apple wine, for example: the apples I've been using are some soft, sweet yellow ones, with a lot of juice, and I never make wine with them until they're spotted and almost rotten. Now, if, one year, I were to taste these apples and find that due to the dryness of August, or a blight, or something, they had come in a little more tart, I'd add a pound or so of sugar to the wine. If there had been too much rain, and they were tasteless, I might add some other sort of apples along with them. Or I might mix the apple wine, at some point, with some chokecherry that was a little on the dry side, or

some blackberry that had come out too sweet.

Perhaps it would help if I explain the process by which juice becomes wine. Initially, the fruit is pounded, sliced, mashed, or cooked with water; sometimes it's left to sit for a few days. Then you strain out the liquid, through cloth, and add sugar, if needed, and yeast. Some fruits are sweet enough so that they supply their own sugar to the yeast. In any case, the yeast must have sugar. Sometimes if you just leave fruit juice in a warm place, a "wild" yeast ferments it naturally. These wild yeasts are unpredictable; some are tasty, and some aren't. Wine-making suppliers and some delicatessens supply wine-making yeast, and it's good stuff. In some wines you can use baking yeast (the kind you use baking bread). It tends to taste "yeasty," though, unless the wine is very strong-flavored to begin with. One way to reduce this undesirable flavor is to use soft yeast, sold in blocks; smear it into rye toast and float it on the surface of the wine. That way it doesn't get so well mixed in with the wine (and you use rye because it hangs together better).

Whatever the yeast, it goes to work converting oxygen into carbon dioxide, and sugar into alcohol. You see the carbon dioxide—the little bubbles—coming up to the top. If the wine is capped or bottled too early, it's this rapid production of carbon dioxide that blows the lid. At first the action of the yeast will be very rapid. After 5 or 6 days, though, it slows down quite a lot, and other organisms can invade if the mixture is left exposed

to the air. So at this point, you want to seal off the air. But how can you do that without exploding your container?

Well, one method is to "cork lightly." Thus, bubbles are supposed to be able to escape—up the sides of the cork? Mine always come off, and the wine is left uncorked until I discover it. Another method, which really works only for very thick, sweet wines, is to just set it aside in a crock or glass jar, covered with cloth. This doesn't work for light, dry wines at all. They absorb all sorts of weird flavors, and become sour, or worse. So we come to the third, and best method, the "fermentation lock." They sell devices for this purpose, but you can make one, easily, especially if you have access to a chemistry lab, or know somebody who does their own plumbing. What you need is a tube, running out of the top of the bottle, with an underwater exit point. That's all. It's just a device that makes it possible for carbon dioxide to get out without air getting back in through the tube. Once you set it up, make sure, periodically, that the water container is full.

Finally, you need a siphon tube and bottles. Many wines accumulate sludge on the bottom, either particles of fruit or yeast, and it doesn't contribute anything to the flavor. That's why you siphon instead of pour. In the case of a really sludgy wine, siphon it into containers, letting it rest and settle again for 5 or 6 hours, until it's clear on the bottom. More or less. Then bottle it.

The bottles, like everything else you use in making wine, have to be spanking clean and may even be sterilized if you want to make sure there's no residue of Other Flavors in them, not to mention undesirable organisms. And corks, alas, have to be bought new each year—old corks are no good, for reasons you can guess at.

BLACKBERRY WINE

In a clean, scalded crock, crush:

2 qts. ripe blackberries

Pour over them:

3 qts. boiling water

Cool to lukewarm. Add:

1 tsp. wine yeast or ¼ cake baking yeast spread on rye toast

Cover lightly and let it sit in a warm spot (70°-80°) 3 or 4 days. Strain through cloth-lined sieve into a gallon jar and add:

2 cups sugar or 1¼ cups honey (heat honey to stir it in)

Set a fermentation lock in the lid and let it rest 3 months. After Christmas, siphon into bottles, and cork well. It will be good any time but best in the early summer.

BLUEBERRY WINE

Boil: **1½ gals. water**

Add: **3 qts. blueberries**; let them simmer for 30 minutes. Dump into a cloth-lined sieve, and tie up the ends of the cloth to hang overnight. Add:

4 to 6 cups sugar
3 cups raisins
1 Tb. wine yeast

Set in a crock for 5 days, or until bubbling stops, then strain it. Put in large glass jars fitted with fermentation locks and let them brew for 2 months. Then siphon off the juice and let it sit overnight. If more sediment has settled out, siphon again, into bottles; cork. This is a dry wine, a bit heavy, very good with meat or aged cheese or Italian food.

CHOKECHERRY WINE

Chokecherries are beautiful; but what on earth do you *do* with them? Boil together for 30 minutes:

3 lb. chokecherries
1 sliced lemon
1 lb. raisins
1 gal. water
6 cups sugar

Let it cool to lukewarm; then add: **1 Tb. wine yeast.**

Set it over the warming oven to brew for 5 days, or until bubbling stops; stir daily. Strain into a gallon jug, through cloth. Set a fermentation lock in the top and set in a cool place, 50° to 65°, for 3 months. Then siphon into another gallon jug and let it sit with a lid almost—but not quite—screwed on, for 3 months. Bottle, cork, and store until chokecherry season rolls around again. This is a very dry, fine wine.

ELDERBERRY WINE

Use only very ripe elderberries. You can pick them half ripe and they will ripen in a bucket. Strip from their stems and simmer:

4 qts. elderberries
1 gal. water
1 sliced lemon

When the berries lose their color, strain the liquid, and add:

4 cups sugar

Cool to lukewarm; add:

1 Tb. wine yeast or 1 cake yeast spread on rye toast

Set in a crock, covered, on top of the stove, for 4 or 5 days. When it stops working, strain it through cloth into a glass jar with a fermentation lock. Set it to work for 3 months; siphon into another container, let it settle overnight, and siphon into bottles. Cork and store in the cellar for 3 months longer.

PARSLEY WINE

Parsley wine is a local, Cape Breton specialty, and many people grow parsley just to make wine of. (Dolly MacKay warned me not to plant it too far from the house, though—the deer love it.)

Pack as you measure:

4 cups parsley heads

Set it in a crock, along with:

2 sliced lemons
2 sliced oranges
1 lb. raisins

Pour over all:

1 gal. boiling water

Let this sit for 3 days, covered; every day mash it up with your hands. On the fourth day, strain through a cloth; warm it up some and add:

4 to 6 cups sugar

1 Tb. wine yeast

Now set the crock on the top of the stove and let it work for a week or until the bubbling stops. Then strain it into a glass jar with a fermentation lock and let it work in the cellar for a couple of months, until clear and still. Siphon, let rest overnight, and siphon again, into bottles. Let it rest, corked and cool, 6 months. This is a delicate, white wine, with just a hint of sweetness.

APPLE WINE

Apple wine gets made, around our house, whenever we happen to have a whole bunch of apples going soft at once. I make batches now and then through the fall, as I sort through the crates of what we've gathered, for pies and sauce and this and that. I take a 5-gallon bucket, and half fill it with boiled water and about:

50 apples

I just leave the apples whole, brown spots and all, but cut out any mold. I set the bucket up on top of the stove and leave it there 5 days, with a lid on. Then I take off the lid and taste the liquid. If it isn't sweet, I add about:

1 to 2 lbs. sugar

Then I stir it up, maybe mash it a bit, and let it sit for 5 days longer. The apples always ferment; some people add yeast, but I don't. Then I take it down, and strain it through a cloth-lined sieve, and fill clean bottles, and lightly cork them. I set them in the cellar, and check every day for a week or two; sometimes the corks blow. After 2 weeks, if there's sediment in the bottles, I pour the wine off into other bottles; in any case, push the corks down tight. It's good for about 3 months, after which it generally goes sour.

APPLE CIDER

To make real cider, you can use any kind of apple, the sweeter (and riper) the better. You need a chopper and a press. The chopper chops the raw apples up into what's called a "cheese." Then with the press you extract juice. People I know have experimented with all kinds of jacks, levers, and so forth; one couple succeeded in raising their barn a couple of feet with a homemade device that was meant to press down the apples, but nobody seems to have had any luck making cider without a screw-type apple press.

a. apples
b. chopper
c. engine
d. apple press
e. cider

Cider will keep, in a cool place, for a couple of months at the most. After that it starts going hard, and the released carbon dioxide blows corks, or breaks bottles, or turns to cider vinegar, if unsealed. You can fit it with a fermentation lock (see above) and have hard cider, though. When bubbles stop rising, it'll keep for years if sealed.

BEER

If you can get the equipment and the ingredients, it isn't very hard to make beer. It doesn't taste exactly like store beer, but it's damned good, if aged properly. The secret to aging it is to always make a new batch well ahead of running out of the old stash. We find it best to make beer either in the dead of winter or the dead heat of summer, because it has to be kept at about 75° for about a week. If the brewing vat is under 70° it takes too long to brew and tastes heavy. Also you must have a storage place under 50° for capped bottles. I remember one time I set two full cases under the front window of a third floor apartment in July. At about 4 a.m. I awoke to what I was sure was somebody shooting at the house. So did the neighbors, until the unmistakable fragrance of hops filtered down through the house, and the truth of the matter dawned on us all.

EQUIPMENT:

1. A lot of beer bottles. The reusable kind, made out of solid glass, such as you get in Canada, is better than no-deposit no-return, which cannot take as much pressure. Measure bottles; many "pints" really hold 12 ounces and a "quart" bottle really holds 22 ounces. Always rinse out bottles as soon as they are emptied, or the yeast film on the bottom will glue down in. Before using, soak bottles for 15 minutes in very hot water with a little Ivory liquid or some such mild dish soap. Rinse thoroughly and invert to drain for 10 minutes.

2. A 5-gallon crock. We use plastic—it works fine. Don't use metal.

3. A bottle capper. Available from some hardware stores.

4. Bottle caps, ditto. Sometimes these are hard to come by; if you find a source, stock up (they're cheap).

INGREDIENTS:

1. A can of hop-flavored malt extract. There are many brands: our favorite is John Bull.

2. Beer yeast: You can use bread-making yeast, but the beer doesn't taste as good, and more yeast sediment is left in it.

3. 2½ pounds white sugar. Haven't tried anything else, but maybe . . . remember, molasses is half as sweet and honey is twice as sweet.

BEER RECIPE

This recipe is for a 2-pound 3-ounce can of Hop Flavored Malt Extract, but I've used it for 2-pound cans as well. If your can is radically lighter or heavier, alter the recipe to suit it.

1. Clean and scald a 5-pound crock or plastic garbage pail. Boil a kettle of water. Open the can of **Malt Extract** on both ends and press the syrup into the crock. Dissolve it with **1 qt. hot water** (or less—but measure whatever you put in). Add **4⅓ cups sugar**, or 1 pound for every pound of malt syrup. Stir until syrup dissolves. Then add 3 gals. plus 3 qts. water, or water to make 4 gallons in all. Add cold water at first, then tepid, to make it the right temperature to start yeast working—around 75 degrees.

2. Dissolve **1 pkg. beer yeast** or **1 Tb. baking yeast** in a half cup of the liquid. In a few minutes, when it's mixed in, add it to the crock.

3. Cover the crock and set to brew for 4 or 5 days. We generally set our crock at the top of the stairs, where it's sure to be warm. During the time of fermentation, scum rises to the top, about which there is some disagreement in our family. I say, skim it off. My husband says, stir it down.

4. On the fourth or fifth day, if the brew has been bubbling right along, fermentation will slow down considerably. Lift the crock gently and carry it downstairs. Let it rest a few hours to settle again. Siphon into another container and let it rest a few hours or overnight. This business of siphoning makes a big difference in the quality of your beer. Do not siphon the last couple of inches of sediment out of the bottom of the bottle. It may be good for you but it tastes awful in beer. We also clarify beer by adding a couple of egg whites to pick up impurities and floating particles of yeast.

5. Bottling: Wash all the bottles immediately before filling them. Using a dry funnel, add:

   ½ tsp. sugar to each "quart" bottle or
   ¼ tsp. sugar to each "pint" bottle

   Be organized about it—too much sugar can blow your lids. Dip some beer and strain through cheesecloth into a pitcher. Fill bottles to within 1 inch of the top. Cap with bottle capper.

6. Set bottles upright in the root cellar or cool room. Hold off for 2 weeks. This is another area in which there is a good deal of room for discussion around our house, and the only way to settle the question is, of course, a trip to the cellar.

THE FINE ART OF POURING HOME BREW: Keep bottle upright for several hours before opening. Uncap; tilt gently over pitcher or large mug, and pour at a slight angle until bottle is nearly empty. Leave the last half inch in the bottle. Never stop pouring once you start, until you reach this last bit.

ABOUT FOAMY BEER: Foamy beer happens when the beer goes on fermenting rapidly in the bottle. You want it to ferment a little, to be lively; that's why you put sugar in the bottles. But you don't really want it to come out looking like bubble bath. Besides, foamy beer is a close relative of exploding beer bottles.

Foamy beer is often the result of too much sugar in the bottles. But it can also happen if the beer hasn't stopped working before it's bottled. Which, in turn, happens if it isn't kept warm enough while brewing.

To pour foamy beer, open it over the sink and shoot it into a very large pitcher. Let settle 5 or 10 minutes.

COLD DRINKS

In the hot and sticky afternoons of making hay, your parched throat begs for something—but it's a thirst that can't be quenched with water, and if you try, you'll get too bloated to work. Instead, try a glass of one of these:

RASPBERRY SWITCHEL

Cover: 1 qt. raspberries
with: 1 qt. white vinegar
Let stand overnight. Strain through cloth and

squeeze out the juice. Add:

2 cups white sugar

Bring to a boil; if you like, you can pour into bottles and seal them until needed. To make Switchel of it, mix:

2 Tb. mixture
1 glass ice-cold well water

MOLASSES SWITCHEL

Boil together:

1 qt. water
1 cup apple cider vinegar
½ cup molasses
½ cup brown sugar

1 inch ginger root

Let it simmer 30 minutes. Cool. Add water as needed, to bring it up to 2 quarts in all.

ROSE HIP JUICE

Mix:

2 cups rose hip extract
1 cup apple syrup
1 cup white sugar or ½ cup honey
juice of ½ lemon

Stir together in a pitcher until sugar or honey dissolves. Serve cold, garnished with mint leaves or crushed lemon balm; or serve hot, perhaps steeped with a bit of stick cinnamon and a couple of cloves. Water may be added if you like a thinner drink.

16

KITCHEN TALK AND PANTRY RECIPES

KITCHENS, COUNTER SPACE, AND TOOLS

There is a trend, these days, toward the small and compact kitchen, with everything hidden in handy cupboards, and very limited counter space. Such kitchens are fine for people who use mostly "convenience" foods. But you will go crazy in a small kitchen if you are trying to process raw materials into a year's food supply. To make cheese, jelly, pickles; to can, freeze, or process grains and meats; to bake bread and cookies and brew wines or beers; and, at the same time prepare three meals a day and keep the sink clear, you need lots of space, lots of counters, open shelves, cool storage places, warm shelves, and a nice big double sink. Your tools, pots and pans, and foodstuffs should be so arranged that you can find what you need when you need it. Many people who move into old farmhouses find that part of the old, spacious kitchen has been partitioned off for a cubbyhole kitchen; before long, they're tearing down the walls to open it up again. Usually they find, to their delight, that the kitchen was designed for farmhouse cooking. But if you're building from scratch, keep in mind that you will probably want:

A cool pantry or summer kitchen for storing the vegetable overflow in summer, brewing crocks of pickled meats and vegetables in the fall, and storing all sorts of odd things in the winter;

Two counters, one for projects, and one for cooking meals;

Space around a large sink for piles of clean and dirty dishes, pots, cheeses, vegetables, fish, whatever; not to mention enough space by the sink so that one person can wash while the other works at food preparation;

And, if you're planning to install a wood stove:

A good draft, over the stove, to cool the place off in the summer heat when you're running the stove in spite of the temperature;

A warm place to store wood, not too far from the door, and not too far from the firebox, either.

TOOLS

It certainly helps to have a good collection of kitchen tools. They aren't, really, expensive, but sometimes they look expensive because cheap versions are available at the local chain stores. For half the price, you can get a garlic crusher which the garlic comes out the back of; enamelware which chips the first time you burn the rice in it; bowls that crack, and all sorts of spoons and spatulas and things with plastic handles that come off.

Where do you get good tools? One place is a restaurant supplier. Another is the more expensive French cookery pot-and-pan stores in New York, which have catalogues and do business by mail. For some items, though, you just have to hunt around, advertise, look through country-type magazines, and check out "Country Stores" geared to the tourist trade—sometimes they carry some item

like a cider press or a meat grinder to give their less expensive items atmosphere.

There are a few items I find essential. Among them:

A food mill: There are two I know of, both under 10 dollars. The best is the one put out by Mouli (a French company) which has 3 plates.

A large ceramic mixing bowl: for making bread, nothing can beat it. Ceramic ware holds heat and distributes it evenly.

A grain mill: These come in a variety of sizes and styles, ranging from 20 to 200 dollars. Grinding your own grain by hand with a small mill can be a tedious chore; larger stone mills do it faster and better. Or you can hook a little mill up to the wringer attachment of an old wringer type washer, if there's a mechanic in the family with a lot of patience.

A good collection of plastic buckets, and plastic garbage pails. Endless uses for these, from gathering apples to corning beef.

A good set of kitchen knives: at least two paring knives, a thin-bladed boning knife, a pocket knife, a serrated bread knife, and a long heavy French or Japanese vegetable chopping knife.

A stainless-steel or enamel pressure cooker, for steaming and for cooking grain. I seldom pressure-cook with mine, but find the tight lid endlessly useful. It should have a steaming rack to fit in it.

Muslin cheesecloth: buy a packet of Curity muslin baby diapers. Tear in half and separate the two layers. For making cheese, jelly, straining broth, etc.

A mortar and pestle, for mashing and grinding small amounts of spices, breadcrumbs, nuts, etc.

A cast-iron frying pan: almost essential with a wood stove.

Some enamel pots with tight lids: you need enamel any time you cook an acidic food, such as jelly, or any fruit, tomatoes, or pickles.

A large enamel canning kettle, not only for canning; this will have many uses. Be very careful of them. The only brand I know of chips very easily, and then rusts through.

And, of course, an endless assortment of bowls, pots, spoons, egg beaters, and so forth. For very specific items relating to particular jobs (like making cheese, or canning) see those sections in the book.

MEASURING

It's good to have a measuring cup and spoons. But you don't need to use them all the time. They're not always around; the cup's in the sink, baby's got the spoons. Learn how to cook without them, because you can save a lot of time. Here's how you do it:

Pour a teaspoon of salt in your hand. Look at it. Now dump it back into the box and, guessing, pour about a teaspoon into your hand. Measure it. Pretty close, weren't you?

Set the teaspoon in a cake pan so it's level. Using the cap of the vanilla bottle, see how many capfuls equal one teaspoon. Now you know.

Take down your measuring cup and one each of

whatever cups you keep around (ours are all different). Pour a cup full of water into each one. See how far up on the cup it comes; then pour half, and a quarter cup in each. You begin to get a pretty clear idea of what each one contains after a while.

Cut a pound of butter into quarters; then with a wet sharp knife cut one quarter into eight equal pieces. Each of these is a tablespoon; save them for cooking.

MEMORIZE:

3 tsp. = 1 Tb.

4 Tb. = ¼ cup

½ lb. shortening = 1 cup shortening

¼ lb. cheese = 1 cup grated cheese

And: When you cook grain, the eventual volume will be the same as the amount of water you put in. For example, 1 cup rice plus 2 cups water equals 2 cups rice; 1 cup rice plus 3 cups water equals 3 cups (mushy) rice.

PANTRY SUPPLIES

If you live a long way away from any city, it makes sense to order your basic supplies once a year, from a wholesaler. Shipping costs are expensive, but not nearly as expensive as buying foods retail, or making a yearly trek to a large city, only to discover the store is out of half the things you wanted; not to mention hassles like the car breaking down, the kids getting sick, parking, etc. After a year or so in the country you can pretty much tell what you'll need for a year, or, anyway, what you can afford this year. Most large cities now have wholesale health food or macrobiotic supply houses that deal in grains, dried fruits and nuts, dried milk, and an assortment of things like molasses, tamari soy sauce, miso, noodles, beans, teas, and so forth.

Other things you can buy in bulk include:

Coffee: Buy coffee beans, which keep better than ground coffee, and are often cheaper anyway. Grind it in the grain grinder.

Tea, beer and wine yeast: large city stores, I'm afraid.

Yogurt and cheese cultures: see Cheesemaking.

Citrus fruits, fresh vegetables in the winter: These can often be bought by the crate from the same distributors who sell them to the supermarkets. Oranges and lemons and grapefruits will keep for a month or more if you buy them fresh (that is, unexposed to heat in the store) and put them in a 35° F. root cellar. Many vegetables bought this way keep well too: celery, cabbage, broccoli, cauliflower.

COOKING WINE

Even if you are a firm teetotaler, you can safely cook with wines; during cooking, the alcohol all evaporates, leaving only the pleasant aroma and flavor that only wine can give. Wine also has a tenderizing effect on meats, fish, and poultry, since it's a little acid.

If you're not a teetotaler, you may have discovered that it is almost impossible to keep a bottle each of white and red on tap for cooking use only. Ah, but you can. Add a level teaspoon of salt to each bottle. Undrinkable—but perfectly cookable.

SOME HOMEMADE SPECIALTIES

HOMEMADE MUSTARD

To shell homegrown mustard seeds, gather stalks and pods before the pods burst open, and wrap them in a sheet. Stamp on it, unwrap and sift the contents through a coarse colander.

Grind or pound the seeds to a fine powder, for Dried Mustard.

HOT MUSTARD

Mix:

2 Tb. flat beer

1 Tb. olive oil

¼ cup mustard powder

MODERATE MUSTARD

Pour: 1 cup boiling vinegar or water over ¼ cup dried mustard.

Let stand 15 minutes; stir as it cools. Drain off vinegar and reheat to the boil, repeating the process in all 3 times.

Then add to the drained paste:

1 tsp. sugar

½ tsp. salt

1 Tb. olive oil

HOMEMADE VINEGAR

Vinegar is not, as everybody supposes, an Act of God that happens to wine or cider if you don't watch it; it's the byproduct of a yeast that is able to endure a more acid environment than most. You can make it by letting your wine ferment too long; but you should eventually siphon it off and bottle it, just as you would wine, or cider. These vinegars will be milder than white vinegar; they are better for things like salads and pickled herring, but for long-term storage, they're a little too chancy. Sometimes they become bitter, or cloudy, due to the sediment that you can never quite get out of them.

Another way to make a fruit vinegar is to add the fruit or juice or wine directly to white vinegar, in whatever proportions please you.

HERB VINEGARS

Everybody knows about tarragon vinegar: stick a sprig of tarragon in a vinegar bottle, and 3 weeks later, behold! Tarragon vinegar. You can also use chervil, rosemary, thyme, savory, parsley—in fact, any herbs, alone, or in combination. You can also add spices like peppercorns, coriander, mustard, mace, celery seeds. If you want to add garlic, slice it in and boil it with the vinegar, and strain it out after 24 hours.

Add in all: 3 Tb. herbs

To: 1 qt. any kind of vinegar

Let it sit, tightly capped, for a month. Then strain it and rebottle. Keep up to 1 year.

ROOT CHICORY

Leaf chicory, wild chicory, or dandelion roots may all be used for making substitute coffee, but specially developed root chicory seeds, available from large seed houses, have much thicker and mellower roots. Whatever your source, pull them in the fall, after the first few light frosts, and chop off the greens completely, at the top of the roots. (If any greens are left on, they will wither; and if you have a lot of roots to roast, it will take some days.)

Scrub off the dirt and small rootlets; rinse. Store clean roots in a dry place up to 3 weeks, during which time you should roast them whenever you have an opportunity.

To roast them, slice them ¼ inch thick and arrange on a rack or cookie sheet. Put them in a very slow oven, 150° to 250° (no higher), and after an hour take them out and cool them, and remove any roots or parts that have dried—they're done. Return the sheet to the oven; check again in 30 minutes. If any are still damp, roast them some more, but check in 15 minutes. It is easy to burn them if they get too hot, so watch the oven.

Smash them up in a mortar or wooden bowl; grind as you would coffee. Store in a screw top jar, out of light and heat.

To mix chicory with coffee, add 1 part chicory to 3 parts coffee. Or you may use it together with roasted ground barley; or invent your own mixture.

ABOUT MISO, AND TAMARI SOY SAUCE

These are both products of fermented soybeans. They are made by soaking and steaming a grain—either barley, rice, or wheat—and adding a fermenting mold called, in Japanese, a "tane koji." The mash is kept quite warm for several days, and then added to cooked soybeans, along with quite a lot of salt. After which it is set aside to age for periods ranging from 6 months to 3 years.

Tamari soy sauce: after aging, the residue in the bottom of the vat is squeezed or pressed to obtain "tamari."

Kome miso: made from rice and soybeans, this is a soft miso, mild in flavor, and often used after only 6 months aging. Recommended for small children and nursing mothers. It tastes a lot like Muenster cheese.

Mugi miso: this is made from barley and soybeans, and aged longer.

Hacho miso: made from soybeans alone, this is the darkest, strongest product, and keeps the best. It tastes more like aged Vermont Cheddar.

FOOD VALUE: Tamari and miso are delicious flavorings and make good bases for soups and sauces. They keep practically forever without special storage, and have no harmful or even questionable side effects. They are high in protein, and, particularly, those amino acids notably lacking in grains. Therefore, a dish of brown rice and tamari is much higher in protein than a dish of brown rice.

SOURCES: The only good source for either product in this continent is Erewhon, a distributor of natural and organic foods, based in Boston, at 33 Farnsworth Street. They also have a distribution center in California. In Canada bulk Erewhon foods can be ordered from Manna, 29 Leslie St., Toronto. I have sampled tamaris from other sources and found them oversalted and underflavored.

ABOUT COMMERCIAL SOY SAUCE: Commercial soy sauces are an entirely different product. They are made in a few weeks with a chemical process using sugar, soy mash, and chemical preservatives. They taste entirely different from tamari soy sauce and have been linked in recent research to the rise of stomach cancer in Japan since World War II.

ABOUT MAKING YOUR OWN MISO AND SOY SAUCE: Recipes for mugi miso and tamari soy sauce are given in Cornelia Aihara's *Chico-San Cookbook*. Koji-Kin, the starter, is available from Erewhon (see above) in Boston or California. Ordinary soybeans and grains from North America are used in making the Japanese products—so there's no reason why you couldn't try making your own.

BABY FOODS

No two babies start eating at the same time, or eat the same foods. But some general principles may be applied: for example, most babies are started out on grains and fruits, and other foods added one at a time, and gradually. You need not worry too much about a "well-balanced diet," especially at first. It is more important to give foods that the baby likes, so as to work up some enthusiasm about the whole idea of food—which, to a little baby, is kind of weird in the first place. There is a very good section on introducing foods in *Baby and Child Care*, by Dr. Benjamin Spock, which you should have, anyway, if you live way out in the country, because it covers so many aspects of caring for babies (like how to tell measles from scarlet fever, and so forth).

FIRST CEREAL

This is what I always feed my kids for the first 2 or 3 months of their eating adventure. Put: **1 cup rolled oats** into a pot with: **3 cups boiling water.** Cook over very low heat for about 1 hour. Then put it through a food mill using the smallest size holes. Store in a covered plastic container in the refrigerator; it will keep for 1 week.

To serve, mix a little cereal in a small enamel pot with:

a little pasteurized milk (or reconstituted dry milk)

heat until it's just your skin temperature. When you have them, you can add some:

fresh mashed banana or applesauce

However, any cereal mixed with banana should not be put back in the refrigerator.

PURÉED FRUITS

Slice and cook in a little water: **apples, plums, ber-**ries, peaches, apricots—whatever you have. When they become soft, put them through a food mill. You should not use a blender for this, because berry seeds and fruit skins should be sieved out. If you think the fruit needs it, you can cook into the purée: **a little honey.**

If it isn't thick enough, mix into cold purée: **a little cornstarch** (1 Tb. per cup) and heat and stir until thick and clear. Keep 1 week if refrigerated, or you can freeze baby-sized portions in an ice cube tray, dumping them out into a communal bag or container when hard.

PURÉED VEGETABLES AND MEATS

Generally I find babies aren't overenthusiastic about plain puréed vegetables, with the possible exception of carrots and winter squash or pumpkin. I wouldn't argue about it. As soon as they get teeth, they'll be only too happy to sink them into all sorts of raw vegetables, so don't worry.

This is even more true about meats—babies and even small children very often will not eat meat at all, no matter how much you grind it up. So, why bother. There's lots of other stuff to feed them.

PURÉED SOUPS

On the other hand, if you cook together a whole mess of vitamin-rich vegetables and a few chicken bones and some rice, and put it through the mill, they'll probably love it. By the time you get around to introducing such sophisticated fare, your baby will probably appreciate a little texture in the food. So put it through the coarse plate of the mill, and maybe throw in a little whole cooked rice grains, too.

Instead of (or along with) chicken flavoring, you may add a little miso or tamari soy sauce just before serving. Babies love them.

Other Foods

Cottage Cheese: For a very little baby, mash with a fork. Otherwise serve plain. A meal my children always used to enjoy was cottage cheese, raw slices of summer squash (to pick up and chew and throw around) and a small cup of tomato juice. (Baby Lasagne?)

Baby Custard: Mix an egg yolk and ¼ cup milk or fruit juice, a touch of honey if needed. Bake at 300° for 20 minutes in a heat-proof cup. Cool before serving. Note: it is unwise to serve any food with a high concentration of egg whites to a small child. They may develop an allergy to egg white if it is eaten too soon.

Egg Yolk: Hardboil an egg, and mash the yolk with a fork. Add a sprinkling of ground toasted sesame seeds and a tiny touch of salt, and about 1 tsp. milk to soften it.

BREAKFASTS

If you're going to do any work in the day, breakfast is your most important meal. That doesn't mean you have to mound your plate with six kinds of food; but it does mean that you need a good stash of complete protein under your belt. It could be oatmeal and milk; or it could be last night's leftover beef stew. Some good breakfast ideas can be found in Nikki and David Goldbeck's *The Good Breakfast Book*.

What we eat, ordinarily, in the winter, is hot cereal; in the summer, we eat homemade Familia or Granola, with lots of fresh berries. When guests come, or we have an egg surplus (or we get sick of cereal), we have egg-on-toast. Here are some good breakfasts:

Hot cereal with milk and dried fruit or bananas or frozen fruit

Hot cereal with tamari soy sauce and butter (and gomasio)

Egg on toast (soft-boiled or poached)

French toast

Pancakes with fruit syrup

Hot biscuits, scrambled eggs, home-fried potatoes

Toast and cheese (goat cheese in brine is very good for breakfast)

Blintzes (they take forever; it'll be brunch, really), applesauce, and sour cream

Some people hate breakfasts. For them, something special should be provided; whether or not they like it, they still need it. Perhaps they might like:

Yogurt with fruit

A toasted cheese sandwich, or a ham sandwich

A milkshake of milk, yogurt, honey, and fruit— and a couple of hot bran muffins

Leftover rice pudding, bread pudding, oat pudding

Cup custard and oatmeal cookies

TRAVELING FOOD

Once you get used to eating Real Food, it's hard to swallow the glue they pass off as food in most eateries. Not to mention the incredible cash output they demand for their plastic-packaged morsels of synthetic, stale, tasteless junk. So, whether you're off to town for the day, or en route to visit your sister in New Mexico, it's a good idea to pack up some traveling food.

GRAINS: Bread was probably invented for traveling purposes. Dense, compact, slightly damp bread keeps longer than light, well-risen breads. If the weather is very dry, store in plastic; otherwise, don't—it'll just mold after a few days. (You can slice mold off, though—it doesn't mean the bread is bad to eat; it just isn't as tasty.) Other ways to pack traveling grain: take along plastic containers of sprouts and grains to soak. Crackers keep well, stored in airproof containers. Quickbreads don't keep well at all; they become dry and crumble easily. Make up some Familia and Granola, and carry dried milk.

PROTEIN: Cheese, of course, is the best traveling source of protein. Take along several kinds if you can: variety helps a lot in limited circumstances. If you're out in the wilds, you can hunt, snare, and fish; if you're on the road, you can stop at a supermarket for a bit of ham, sausage, or milk products such as yogurt and cottage cheese. They will keep for a couple of days, anyway, without refrigeration. Sprouts and nuts are also good protein sources. And peanut butter!

VEGETABLES: If you're in the woods, equip yourself with a good forage book, such as *Stalking the Wild Asparagus*, by Euell Gibbons. There's no point in backpacking turnips when you're surrounded by good stuff to eat. Even if traveling by superhighway, a true forage fanatic can spot wild edibles alongside the road, or find them near a campsite. It's sort of fun to find out what grows in different places, anyway. If you're in just too much of a hurry, though, take things that keep: roots, mostly, and things that can be sliced and munched on raw.

FRUITS: Dry them. Buy them. Eat lots, especially if you're going short on vegetables; they have just as many of the same vitamins.

OTHER: If you're going out camping and cooking, always take some oil and a little flour. Oil is about the hardest thing to supply to the foraged diet;

about the only wild thing that has it in large supply is nuts.

COOKING FOR A MOB

You were just planning supper, having on hand for the purpose two flounder fillets and a handful of fresh greens, when in walks Jack and Penny and their two kids, over to visit from their farm 30 miles away, bringing to meet you their old buddies Low and Allie from West Virginia. Low, it turns out, went to school with your sister, and is interested in goats, so you go on down to the barn and after you get through rapping about Toggenburgers vs. Nubians and showing them the weird chickens that lay blue eggs (when they lay) they remember a sixpack of warm beer in the car and you, suddenly, remember that you have a dinner to cook and the stove must be nearly out. And what on earth are you going to make, anyway?

Having been faced with this situation several hundred times in the last 10 years, I would like to make a few astute observations:

1. Forget about fancy cooking. Make something easy, which you can cook with your eyes closed and one hand tied behind your back, which is, more or less, the general effect of having visitors in the house.

2. Don't try anything that requires you to get the oven up to 400°, unless your stove is a real eager beaver, and it's 30 below out, and your kitchen is not too well insulated . . . more likely it's summer, and you're all going to sit around the kitchen, so keep the stove at a comfortable minimum.

3. Don't worry about quantity too much. People will eat less because they're talking so much. Better to provide a continual stream of munchies and one basic dish than an entire well-balanced meal of the sort you usually serve, multiplied by however many people you have.

MUNCHIES: One friend I have always pours a cup or two of sunflower seeds into a frying pan and stir-roasts them as soon as guests show up. That's a pretty good start. And you can always slice up a bowlful of raw vegetables: carrots, Jerusalem artichokes, turnips, celeriac, celery, and, in season, green peppers, tomatoes, peas in the pod, green beans, cauliflower and broccoli flowerets, etc. Cheese is always good, and, of course (if you have them) bread or crackers. Pickles are terrific.

THE MAIN DISH: Ah. This depends so much on what you have lots of. Skim rapidly through the "Hasty Suppers." There are a few good ones under "Works of Art"—such as Moussaka, Quiches (if you're good at pie crust), and Meatloaf. In season, you can rely on the garden for endless variety: Stir-Fried Vegetables and rice, complemented by cheese or beans, sunflower seeds, or an omelet, for protein. When the big summer squashes are ripe, you can serve great boats of stuffed squash (see page 12). And don't forget soups, many of which are quick.

Since what you serve depends on what's in stock, it's well to think ahead and keep a little extra food on hand when you know that people are likely to be coming by. A can of tomatoes, a packet of noodles, and a "company cheese" can save a lot of hassle. Or, if you have a freezer, it's possible to freeze small packets of fish, ground meat, or even a whole casserole.

And before you start cooking, make a quiet inquiry or two. Even if you aren't vegetarian, some of your guests may be.

DESSERT: You don't have to serve dessert, of course. But if you want to—well, fruit is the easiest, best, and usually the most liked. In the summer, that's easy; in the winter, you might have canned applesauce, or frozen blueberries (great for kids—they all get blue faces). If you'd rather bake something, choose an easy cake rather than a pie or cookies. Or, for a supper slim on protein, a simple baked custard is good.

DISHES: Keep in mind as you figure out your meal that somebody (not you) is going to have to do one hell of a lot of dishes; go easy on the mixing bowls and serving plates! If you can, serve dessert (and anything else) in a communal dish, or on the dinner plates.

RECOVERY FOOD

When somebody in the house is sick, they usually can't (or don't want to) eat the same food as when they're well. Particularly, they aren't too interested in foods that are difficult to digest. That's sensible. The energy the body normally puts into working, thinking, and digesting should be all going into getting better. Which is why, as you recover, you feel stupid, lethargic, and not too hungry.

The body still needs some things, though. It needs a minimum level of protein. It needs quite a lot of liquid, and it needs vitamins.

For the protein, the best thing is clear soup. It could be meat stock soup or miso or tamari soup. Both are easy to digest and both are adequate to the minimum protein needs of average invalid recovery. You might add noodles or brown rice to the soup—it's good to have a little roughage, keep the system working in there. A piece of toast or crackers, maybe. But go easy on the butter; substitute jam, or honey. Have lots of juice, cold or hot, on hand. You can make the juices into gelatins, for a solid version of the same thing.

Extra vitamin needs depend on the nature of the illness. If there's any kind of infection, vitamin C will help. You can't get too much vitamin C; if you do, by any chance, your system can easily eliminate it (this is a medical fact, not a wild guess). Some people like to take it by pills; I like to make up a lemonade or fruit juice, heavily spiked with powdered or granular ascorbic acid, such as they sell in supermarkets for canning. We keep a lot of that around in the early spring, when vegetable supplies run low and cold bugs seem to be on the rampage. A stash of canned blackberry, rhubarb, or other juice helps add variety to the juice pitcher. Or throw in a few canned or frozen berries.

If you wind up having to take antibiotics, make sure to get enough B vitamins, since many will be destroyed by the antibiotics. Have wheatgerm in your bread or cereal, or sprinkled on yogurt.

For other special vitamin needs, consult Adele Davis's *Let's Get Well*. And ask the doctor when you get a chance. Many doctors simply forget to give dietary advice, until you ask or even mention that you heard such and such was helpful for your problem.

INDEX

288